瑷珲海关
历史档案辑要

章程协议
（第二卷）

黑龙江省档案馆　编译

社会科学文献出版社
SOCIAL SCIENCES ACADEMIC PRESS (CHINA)

目 录

1. 1909 年《瑷珲分关暂行试办章程》

No 325 . Commrs.   INSPECTORATE GENERAL OF CUSTOMS,
Harbin. No.27,931.
                                        Peking, 16th June, 1909.

            Sir,

            1.   I send you, herein enclosed, two

                despatches from the Shui-wu Ch'u regarding

                        the Regulations for the opening of

                        Trade at Aigun, and on the Sungari

                        River:

                and I also enclose the English and Chinese

                versions of the Regulations themselves.

            2.   You will observe that these Regulations

                follow pretty closely the lines of those proposed

                by you, though certain modifications - none, in

                principle, of any great importance - have been

                introduced, as the result of consultations between

                the Board and myself.

            3.   You are to notify these Regulations

                to the public and officials and that Trade will

                be conducted under them, from the 1st of July,

                in the case of the Sungari Trade, and from the

                1st August in the case of the trade of Aigun.

N. A. Konovaloff, Esquire,   4.

        Commissioner of Customs,

                Harbin.

            4.   You are to have the Regulations

                carefully translated into Russian, and the whole set,

                in the three languages, English, Chinese, and Russian

                is to be published as was done in the case of the

                Harbin Regulations.

            5.   You will observe that the Protocol, and

                not the 1858 Tariff, is now to be applied at Aigun

                This arrangement has been made on the inference (i)

                that there is no reason why trade on the River

                Amur and at the land frontier should be conducted

                on different principles; and, (ii) because all up

                river import cargo is largely sea-borne cargo from

                Vladivostock, originally imported there from various

                provenances abroad.

            6.   You will also observe that certain duty

                leviable at Sansing has been reduced, as a

                provisional measure, to one half of that proposed

                in your original draft.

            7.   It is assumed that the Staff already

                                                        at

at your disposal is almost sufficient for your

present needs, and that it will be quite

sufficient, with Mr. Steinacher as Acting

Tide-surveyor at Harbin and Mr. Strehlneek as

Examiner at Aigun. If one or more additional

Tidewaiters are required they had better be

taken on locally.

    I am,

      Sir,

     Your obedient Servant,

    (Signed) R. E. Bredon

     Acting Inspector General.

True Copy:

  2nd Assistant, A.

Copy

No. 358. Commr.   Inspectorate General of Customs.

Harbin. No. 28,572.   Peking, 18th August, 1909.

  Sir,

No 895 I have to send you, enclosed, for
your information and guidance, copy
of a Shui-wu chu despatch informing
me that the Russian Minister has
instructed the Russian Authorities at
Harbin to accept the Provisional
Sungari Trade and Harbin River,
Sansing and Lahasusu Customs,
Regulations in their present form, pending
the termination of the negotiations
regarding changes therein, to be promptly
commenced between the latter and yourself,
on the condition, however, that any
changes that may be agreed upon
will be retrospective, and will take
effect from the date on which the rules
in their present form came into
operation. The result of these
negotiations and the changes
proposed are to be submitted by
you by despatch, accompanied by
a Chinese version, for the approval
of the Shui-wu chu. In the meantime
you are to report the local developments
in this affair resulting from the
        Russian

N. Konovaloff, Esquire,
Commissioner of Customs,
 Harbin.

Russian Minister's action.

I am,
    Sir,
      Your obedient Servant,
(Signed) R. E. Bredon
      Acting Inspector General.

True copy:

2 nd Assistant, A.

税務處刻行署總稅務司

為劄行事查茲奉派等處添設閣下俄頒事及公司皆不承認

一事奉據東三省總督及濱江道通先後電當本處特派

外務部速興俄使商定見邀去澹差非滋称再四磋磨脉抄俄

廓使來茲於何擬將法堅不承認任李郡再四磋磨肱行議

官諮法商具草略函送去後現難該使回滋称已特飭本司

宜籍將該章程先認惟將來竹有會商将改乃何之應處有

應為之能力印伈由該章程頒布之日起資行益布約飭該處

稅務司印將該章程會自李國官員商約等因俄使既將該

稅務司印將該章程會自李國官員商約等因俄使既將該

章程先認應由貴處特飭署總稅務司運飭該處稅務司

會同俄員妥商辦理除公電東三省督撫外兹抄錄原送節略

兹行查丠聲後等因合來除公咨外相應鈔錄原件劄行

署總稅務司查四電飭濱江關稅務司連四羅照並申複等

庶可足須此劄者 附件 宣後元年六月二十九日

處字第捌百玖拾伍號

縣錄外務部坂撫廓使節略

瑷珲公函三批指啥蘇蘇同通商口岸分設閣下並訂

試辦章程一手送任李大庄興

貴大庄面商談信

貴大庄先印將以上各閣下及所擬松花江行船章程究大誤

惟擬與咸豐八年及光緒七年和約條款於俄商窑礵之處提議商

酌是以鄙意大臣特飭該廠稅務日桁該章程回查有於城內

窑礵之處管詳商酌擬容候核改以期妥協至黑龍江係中樹云

界其竹期章程廣揚四以上兩引兩條酌由中俄兩國商訂本大

臣先即時提議示尺

Copy

No. 364. Comms.

Harbin No 28,709.

Inspectorate General of Customs.

Peking, 30th August, 1909.

Sir,

  In continuation of my despatch No. 358/28,572 of the 18th instant: Sungari Trade, and Harbin River, Sansing and Lahasusu Customs Regulations provisionally accepted by Russian Minister, pending termination of the negotiations regarding changes therein to be commenced between the Russian Authorities at Harbin and yourself:

  I have to send you enclosed, for your information and guidance, copy of a letter from the Shui-wu Chu forwarding a Memorandum prepared by the Wai-wu Pu, which describes in detail the negotiations with the Russian Minister preceding his provisional acceptance of the above rules.

      I am,

       Sir,

     Your obedient Servant,

     (Signed) R. E. Bredon

     Acting Inspector General.

N. A. Konovaloff, Esquire,

Commissioner of Customs,

  Harbin.

True copy:

  CAO

2nd Assistant, A.

From J.G. no. 364

税務處呈批署總稅務司

迺查哈尔濱等處設立關卡及松花江黑龍江行船章程俄使
業已允諾一事有准外務部咨送與俄使節略當經本處俟
錄呈核查並函行署總稅務司詳飭遵辦在案茲復准外務
部將前項此事情形詳細節略函送前來相應抄錄原件咨送
鈞察查其事前飭飾濱江關稅務司遵照可也須至咨者

日祉
附件
宣統元年七月卄日   信字第壹百叁拾叁號

抄錄外務部節略

愛琿哈尔濱三姓拉哈蘇蘇各設關卡及議訂松花江黑龍江行船

章程等事本年四月二十二日業將本部節略及俄使來咨鈔咨貴署此
事前後辯論情形咨未及詳叙諸再言其崖略查愛琿等處
開關日期送任本部興會俄使俟東將於所訂松花江行船章
程監不詳誌且引咸豐六年愛琿和約第一條及光緒七年改訂
條約第十八條來相詰責本部當駁以中國並未全廳愛琿條約
惟日俄所立泊司木斯條約已將中俄在松花江獨得行船之權
利讓出現時俄國在洒洲西廠地位較之一千九百三年以前實不
能相提並論蘇中國在各滨愛琿通商華條實行中日會議條
約之三事與兩約之章行未指明何國船隻交
吾准在松花江行駛惟凡行駛该四之船均須遵守此章盖

锡装署总税务司议具洋文论与阅看该使以谓洵司不肯
之约日使出口曾强词辩解我国未肯先认中国以约能章涉此
约而置号而约於不顾断辩论相持不决李都以为该约论卡
业已次芽阅嗣彼表遲延不识势必阻礙全局擬一节略
草擬面與礤商令其先譲阅章新舊约增置不論该使
姓先後朝多方支展争划盡阅必欲增引咸豐八年及光緒七
年而约力诸洲玉坚不肯承李都公同詳约中俄而约於我尚看
利益之慶新不能金康该芽明中難引及和约董未楢室松花江
只准俄国獨占利權不准他国行船贸易语句尚属动五黑
龍江係中俄玉界與松花江之左右皆境因名昕有不同芽昕内阅

卜而筆聲敘则俄亦已默認而江有別其好船章程亦由中俄擬
境棋議當令该使典原福芳儀英文妥奪都涵稜虽送修裝畢
總稅務司庄浚推勤尚祈流弊是以汉正芽略並送该使現該
使院将该章光識而有以浚觇此高约之廉務奇随時錯備
哈尔溪阅道及稅務司等篝约機宜安為同虑而玉等

　　　　　　　　　　　　　随信字芽壹百叁拾叄號

致哈尔滨关第 325/27931 号令　　　　海关总税务司署（北京）1909 年 6 月 16 日

尊敬的哈尔滨关税务司：

　　1. 兹附上税务处关于瑷珲及松花江沿岸关卡所拟章程的令文两份及章程的汉英文本抄件。

　　2. 从中可知，章程内容与贵署所提各项建议基本一致，虽有略微改动之处，但所涉事项皆非十分紧要。改动之处皆为本署与税务处商议之结果。

　　3. 请向公众及地方官员公布章程内容并说明对于松花江上的往来贸易，相关章程将自 7 月 1 日起施行，对于瑷珲地区的往来贸易，相关章程将自 8 月 1 日起施行。

　　4. 请谨慎完成章程的俄文译本，此等章程与哈尔滨关海关章程一样，须以汉、英、俄三种语言颁布。

　　5. 令文中指示，瑷珲分关将遵循中俄协约行事，而非 1858 年税则。如此安排之依据为：（1）黑龙江上游及陆路边境往来之贸易所依准则不应有异；（2）黑龙江下游而来的进口货物主要为自符拉迪沃斯托克（Vladivostok，即海参崴）而来的海运货物，而此等货物最初亦是自其他各国出口至符拉迪沃斯托克。

　　6. 此外，贵署所提交之章程草案中的三姓分关应征关税税率已经减半。

　　7. 哈尔滨关当前的人员配置应当可以满足现阶段的工作需要，待戴纳格（J. Steinacher）先生至哈尔滨关担任署理头等总巡，史德匿（E. A. Strehlneek）先生至瑷珲分关担任二等验货后，人员方面将会更加充足。如还需铃子手，最好于当地雇用。

您忠诚的仆人

（签字）裴式楷（R. E. Bredon）

署总税务司

该抄件内容真实有效，特此证明。

录事：周骊（C. H. B. Joly）二等帮办前班

致哈尔滨关第 <u>358/28572</u> 号令　　　海关总税务司署（北京）1909 年 8 月 18 日

尊敬的哈尔滨关税务司：

　　兹附上税务处第 895 号令抄件，以供参考。内称俄使已命俄国驻哈尔滨官员将哈尔滨江关、三姓分关、拉哈苏苏分卡及所拟松花江行船试办章程允认，唯将来所有会商酌改之处，应有反为之能力，并由该章程颁布之日起实行。请呈文汇报与俄国官员会商之结果及拟议更改之内容，并附中文译本，以供税务处审批。另请汇报俄使下达此命令后，此事于当地有何进展。

您忠诚的仆人

（签字）裴式楷

署总税务司

该抄件内容真实有效，特此证明。
录事：周骊　二等帮办前班

致哈尔滨关第 364/28709 号令　　　　　海关总税务司署（北京）1909 年 8 月 30 日

尊敬的哈尔滨关税务司：

续 8 月 18 日海关总税务司署致哈尔滨关第 358/28572 号令：

俄使已暂时允认哈尔滨江关、三姓分关、拉哈苏苏分关及所拟松花江行船试办章程，待哈尔滨关税务司与当地俄国官员会商后，再行酌改。

兹附上税务处来函抄件一份，内附外务部为说明俄使将上述试办章程允认之过程的节略一份。

您忠诚的仆人

（签字）裴式楷

署总税务司

该抄件内容真实有效，特此证明。

录事：周骊　二等帮办前班

2. 1911年《瑷珲分关临时章程》

No. 623. Commrs.

Harbin. No. 34,972.

INSPECTORATE GENERAL OF CUSTOMS,

Peking, 6th February, 1911.

Sir,

1.   I have to send you, enclosed, for careful perusal, copy of Shui-wu Ch'u Despatch No.1,698 summarising a report from the Aigun Taotai to the Heilungchiang Governor and Manchurian Viceroy on a Petition of the Provincial Assembly praying amongst other requests for the abolition of the Liangchiat'un Barrier of the Aigun Custom House. You will see that the Taotai proposes

(a) failing the abolition of the Liangchiat'un Barrier - which he considers superfluous seeing that it can be circumvented by goods going to Russia and that the Taheiho Barrier on the river, which it is said to be impossible to evade, suffices for controlling purposes - to define clearly the collection powers of the Aigun Custom House and its Barriers vis à vis those of the local Tax Offices on the prerogatives of which the Liangchiat'un Barrier is alleged particularly to encroach by collecting duty on the trade of the (Chinese) 100 li Frontier Zone on provisions of the inhabitants, etc.;

(b) to grant the privilege of duty exemption equally to Chinese and Russian merchants upon the banks of the Amur;

(c) to put a stop to the over-valuation of goods and to accept the values given on the original delivery bills (發票) presented by merchants;

and (d) by introducing improved procedure to prevent the delay

The Commissioner of Customs,

H A R B I N.

delay to which Russian ships are said to be subjected at the Taheiho Barrier, as this leads vessels to avoid the place and hinders trade.

With regard to (c) and (d) the Board directs an enquiry to be made and the alleged abuses to be remedied by you if they really exist. As to the first point raised, it wishes the questions of the abolition of the Liangchiat'un Barrier, or of the delimitation of jurisdiction between the Maritime Customs and the Local Tax Offices to be thoroughly gone into and reported on by you promptly, as the revision of the Aigun Customs Rules, now under consideration, presents a suitable opportunity for dealing with these questions. You are accordingly instructed to supply the Report required, accompanied by a Chinese version in duplicate.

2.   While the abolition of the Liangchiat'un Barrier would appear to be out of the question as, in the absence of control there, all imports could be declared at the Taheiho Barrier as going into the Chinese 100 li Frontier Zone, a clear definition of the respective jurisdiction of the Maritime Customs and of the Local Tax Offices is necessary. Your predecessor has alluded to this subject several times semi-officially and Part II, Article 9 of the draft of the revised Aigun Customs Rules, copy of which I enclose, is worded so as to facilitate such a delimitation. In this connection it would interest me to know whether the Taotai's statement that the Liangchiat'un Barrier is only 40 odd li distant from Aigun city is correct, and also what its distance is from the bank of the Amoor.

The second point raised by the Taotai would seem to be covered by paragraphs 2 and 3 respectively of Part II, Rules 3 and 4 of the draft of the new Aigun Customs Rules.

Your reply should be accompanied, for convenience of reference, by a pen and ink sketch plan showing position of Aigun

Aigun and the Barriers referred to.

    I am,

     Sir,

    Your obedient Servant,

    (signed) F. A. Aglen,

  Officiating Inspector General. ad interim.

True copy:

  2nd Assistant, A.

AIGUN CUSTOMS *Provisional* ~~PROVINCIAL~~ REGULATIONS.

1. Shipping.

1.

  Customs Officers will board vessels entering and inspect them after clearance outwards; they may claim access to any part of the vessel at any time during her stay in port.

2.

  All vessels in port must anchor at places assigned by the Customs upon their entry within its limits where all formalities of entry will be attended to with despatch.

3.

  Neither cargo nor passengers may be landed or shipped before permission has been given by the Customs. Cargo landed or shipped without such permission is liable to confiscation.

4.

  Manifests and Customs Covers must be presented, on arrival, to the Customs.

5.

  Manifests must contain a true and full account of all cargo on board, including duty-free goods, giving marks, numbers, and contents.

  Manifests must be signed by the Master or the responsible agent of the vessel concerned who will be held responsible for their correctness.

6.

  For presenting a false manifest the master or the responsible agent of a vessel will subject himself to a fine not exceeding Hk. Tls. 500.

  All unmanifested or contraband goods found on searching a vessel will be dealt with according to treaties or, in certain cases, also according to the practice of other ports in China.

  For all manifested inward items of cargo found short on

         board

board, their respective duties must be paid.

7.

Shut-out goods will be recognised as duty-paid goods only on the condition that they be presented immediately for re-examination.

8.

Vessels must produce their papers for inspection when called upon by any Imperial Chinese Maritime Customs or Inland Barrier Official acting on behalf of the Imperial Chinese Maritime Customs boarding them at the ports or en route.

9.

Customs employées may be put on board of vessels to search them or to accompany them for the purpose of surveillance.

10.

At the option of the Captain or the responsible agent of the vessel the Customs may seal the hatches of the vessels; such seals must not be broken until the vessel reaches a port where she has to work cargo and until the necessary permission has been obtained. The breaking of seals or opening of sealed hatches with fraudulent intentions will entail liability to a fine not exceeding Hk.Tls.500.

11.

For working cargo or passengers on Sundays or holidays as well as on week days out of the regular working hours - 6 a.m. to 6 p.m. - Special Permit Fees must be paid. These fees will be provisionally collected according to the Table appended hereto.

12.

Masters of vessels are expected to report to the Customs any changes in the channel, accidents to shipping, loss of guiding marks, wrecks, and other noteworthy events.

13.

Trade in the following articles, viz.; gunpowder and other explosives, shot, cannon, fowling pieces, rifles, muskets, pistols, saltpetre, sulphur, spelter and all other munitions and

implements

implements of war and sport and salt is prohibited; arms found on board, not covered by certificates showing them to be for self-defence or ship's use, will be confiscated. The export abroad of rice, husked and unhusked, and Chinese copper cash and coins is also prohibited. The importation of foreign copper coin blanks, copper coins, and copper cash is likewise forbidden. The importation from Russian and exportation to Russia of Opium is prohibited.

14.

Infraction of Customs Rules and Regulations will render the merchant or vessel concerned liable to the infliction of fines not exceeding Hk.Tls.500.

The Russian merchant or vessel subjected to a fine has the right to pay the fine to the Customs under protest and petition against it to the Russian Consul.

In case of the non-payment by a merchant or vessel of a fine imposed by the Customs, as well as in cases of repetition of a breach of Customs Rules and Regulations by the same merchant or vessel, making the infliction of the maximum fine of Hk.Tls.500 necessary, or in the event of it being necessary to inflict a heavier penalty, the Chinese Customs addresses, whenever Russian subjects are concerned, the Russian Consul for further treatment of the case.

———————

The above regulations are to be considered as provisional and experimental and are subject to additions and modifications when, and if, necessary.

———————

PART II.

Dues and Duties.

1.

The Imperial Maritime Customs collect exclusively Customs levies and do not levy any Inland or other duties or taxes. They also collect Transit Dues, but for the present and until further notice do not collect either Tonnage Dues or River Dues.

All local taxes, when such are due, will be levied on cargoes before their loading into, or after their discharge from, vessels in order to avoid detention of the latter.

2.

Import Duties and Transit Inward Dues (collected at half Import duty rates) on Foreign goods are leviable according to the Revised Import Tariff of 1902.

Export duties on Native goods are leviable according to the General Tariff of 1858 as well as Transit Dues outwards and Coast Trade Duty, both collected at half Export duty rates.

Goods unenumerated in the Tariffs, whether Imports or Exports pay 5% ad valorem.

3.

Imports from Russian Ports.

On goods coming from Russian ports Import and Transit duties are leviable in accordance with Art. 2 of Part II when these goods are destined for places beyond the limits of the 100 li (50 versts) Zone.

Goods, however, imported into the limits of this Zone are not subject to any duty.

Transit Dues are leviable on duty-free goods at the rate of 2½% ad valorem, and on dutiable goods at one half of the rates of the existing tariffs.

4.

Native Goods.

Native goods imported from Chinese places not covered by

any

any certificate issued by a Maritime Custom House are liable to a full duty. When covered by a certificate issued by a Maritime Custom House, they will be treated in accordance with the rules in force at the Treaty Ports of China.

Native goods exported will pay the Tariff Export Duty, and will receive Duty Receipts.

Native goods exported to places within the limits of the Russian 100 li (50 versts) frontier Zone are exempt from payment of export duty.

5.

Documents in proof of payment of duties and dues are issued on the lines of the general rules in force at the Treaty Ports of China; cargo from one Trade Mart to another which is not covered by these documents is liable to confiscation.

6.

Dues and Duties are payable on Imports before goods are removed from Customs supervision, on Exports before shipment.

7.

Re-exports and goods under Transit Certificates are entitled to same Customs treatment as at the Treaty Ports of China.

Note. The fact of the actual re-exportation across the river will be certified by the Taheiho Controlling Barrier.

8.

Before goods can be shipped, application must be made to the Customs, who, after examination of them, will collect duty and issue Permit to Ship.

9.

The Controlling Barriers at the limits of the 100 li Zone (Liangchiat'un etc.) will levy a full duty on both foreign and Native goods passing the 100 li (50 versts) frontier Zone from Aigun which are not accompanied by Duty Proofs, as well as control native goods brought from the interior under Outward Transit Certificates (Art. 10).

Merchants upon giving bonds or depositing sufficient amounts

with

with the Customs, will have the option of paying such duties at
the Aigun Head Office.

10.

Transit Certificates, Outwards, for conveyance of native
produce from the interior for ultimate export abroad, will be
issued in accordance with the practice of the Treaty Ports in
China. A bond for six times the estimated Export Duty must be
handed in together with the application. On arrival of the
produce at the Controlling Barrier, three times the duty must be
deposited. If the goods are exported abroad within six months
from the time of arrival one and a half duty will be returned,
one duty will be brought to account as Export Duty, and one half
duty as Outward Transit Dues. If not exported abroad within
the specified time the deposited amount of three times the duty
will be retained by the Customs and brought to account.

The above Regulations are to be considered as provisional
and experimental and subject to additions and modifications when,
and if, necessary.

True copy:

2nd Assistant, A.

税务处剳行代理总税务司

为剳行事宣统二年十二月十四日准东三省总督黑龙江巡抚咨

称据爱珲道呈称照议局议员呈撤爱珲梁家屯海关税

卡英诸分别出入税则一案李刘查明梁家屯之卡存撤暨该

闰税等处改生议咨行税务处核议微等情咨该核震等因

查误通两陈各情约有四端一梁家屯距爱珲城只四十余华

里盖非百里界线俄国阿穆尔省一带益多由爱境运往各口岸之

货凡由轮船运往松花江者不向爱闰报税由哈运微界者松李

已减免口税爱闰亦不任收取即玉稽查有里内分卡已足控

制凡由陆贩运俄国货可以绕越梁家屯与爱城而不能绕越黑

河是梁家屯卡实属废痈弊病既切商艰且芽任费二

梁家屯之卡闰设於不产稽查出入之地夺出入口税可收道微收百

里闰货卖之货暨落城各境运运之货此里地方税局庶收之捐不

敛捐膏海闰进出之税必向设卡以来土人日用饮食零物一概

微收有未除票者有除票而重敛目务地方税为图海闰已好不

便重微一时不能分清权限在税局为失产收之税而误闰卡等

微者不过借教闰支殊为失策三梁家屯芽搜最甚者在多栖货

价譬如行商以百金价值贩货运玉梁家屯该卡税员验货

估价作百五十金商贩口此货价值有费票为凭税员曰货运玉

爱其价已值百五十金海闰税章如是商贩岂可知何黑河之卡

017

三船運商貨亦往往受此等擾四黑河以下於夏秋商貨船停
泊並不隨到隨驗以便稿不願束停華商貨物多卸
於俄岸華民食用均須購自俄埠愛城市面更形蕭索奇異
於為洞驅魚誤道因擬挽救之策四竊一愛珲関與地方局
税宜割分一官辦江水岸華商俄商宜同享免税利
益三愛関估價奇擾商民宜交通四原貨業亲傾月辭批四
愛関查驗貨船遲誤宜速偹改良東厦查愛珲関税章
俟厦試辦如果有佑價奇擾商民及查驗貨船遲延等弊亚
應查明汉民薪法玉梁岽屯亲否君戴関税亦卯朔與地方
税割公權孤之處現值俄国駐京大臣請議修汉愛関章程正

宜改時委等預理相応刋行於此總稅務司查照俗誌
閧税務月運四退引等議申覆以憑核辧可也須至劄者
右劄第壹千陸百玖拾捌號
宣統二年十二月二十五日

致哈尔滨关第 <u>623/34972</u> 号令　　　海关总税务司署（北京）1911 年 2 月 6 日

尊敬的哈尔滨关税务司：

　　1. 兹附税务处第 1698 号令文抄件，请详阅。从该令文可知，瑷珲道台此前向东三省总督及黑龙江巡抚汇报了咨议局请求裁撤梁家屯分卡等事，并提出：

　　（1）对于运往俄国之货物，必经之路并非梁家屯分卡，而是大黑河分卡，因此于管控而言，大黑河分卡一处足矣，梁家屯分卡并无留用之必要。此外，梁家屯分卡对黑龙江华岸 100 里边境区内贸易之土货所收之捐，本应由地方税局征收，因此即使裁撤一事无法实现，瑷珲关税与地方局税亦应划分界限；

　　（2）黑龙江两岸华商俄商应同享免税特权；

　　（3）瑷珲海关对货物估价过高，应以商人出具之发票原件所示金额为准；

　　（4）据报大黑河分卡查验俄国货船有延误之情况，以致轮船绕行，有碍贸易发展，应改之。

　　关于（3）（4）两项，税务处已下达指示予以调查，如确有不当之处，请改之。至于（1）项，望贵署可对梁家屯分卡裁撤与否及海关与税捐局的征税权限问题进行深入调查，尽快呈交报告，报告附中文版，一式两份。鉴于《瑷珲分关章程》修订草案仍在审议之中，因此目前正是处理上述问题之良机。

　　2. 既然凡进入黑龙江华岸 100 里免税区之货物均可于大黑河分卡报明查验，梁家屯分卡裁撤一事似乎便无须再议，但海关与税捐局的管辖权限确有界定之必要。哈尔滨关前任税务司曾多次于半官函中提及明确权限一事，本文随附之《瑷珲分关章程》修订草案抄件中亦有与此相关之条款（《章程》第二部分第 9 条）。另请说明，瑷珲道台所述之梁家屯分卡与瑷珲相距 40 余里一事是否属实，梁家屯分卡与黑龙江江岸之距离又是多少？

　　至于台所提之（2）项，《瑷珲分关临时章程》修订草案中亦有涉及。

　　为便于查阅，请于回函中附上瑷珲分关及各分卡位置草图。

您忠诚的仆人

（签字）安格联（F. A. Aglen）

代理总税务司

该抄件内容真实有效，特此证明。
录事：周骊（C. H. B. Joly）二等帮办前班

《瑷珲分关临时章程》

第一部分　船运

1. 凡船只进出口岸时，皆由关员上船查验；船只停泊港口期间，船上无论何处何时，关员均可前往检查。

2. 所有船只在口岸内均须按海关指定地点停泊，照章办理一切手续。

3. 凡船只载货搭客未经海关许可以前，均不准任意上下。如未经海关许可而装卸货物，将酌核罚办充公。

4. 凡船只进入口岸时，即应将舱口单及各关所签函件呈阅查验。

5. 舱口单须将该船所载货物切实开明，免税之货物亦应详列，标识、号数及货物内容亦须在单内注明。

舱口单须由该船主或委托负责代表人签名做证，如有差错，唯其是问。

6. 出入各船，如有呈递错误舱口单，该船主或负责代表人将被处以不超过 500 海关两之罚金。

凡在船上搜出的未登记货物或违禁物品，皆按条约规定处理，某些情况，也可按中国其他口岸惯例处理。

凡于舱口单上载明之货物，运入时如发现有短装之情况，必须补缴相应关税。

7. 凡船只装载货物因故退回，须立即赴海关呈验，否则将不予视为完税之货物。

8. 凡中国海关或内陆分卡关员代表中国海关在口岸或沿途各处上船检查并向船只索取执照时，该船须将执照交出。

9. 海关可派关员在船上搜查或与船同行以监视。

10. 船内舱口是否由海关加印铅饼，可由船长或船只负责代表人决定；待该船已抵下货口岸呈验准许后，方能撤毁铅饼。如有蓄意毁撤铅饼或私自开舱者，将被处以不超过 500 海关两之罚金。

11. 凡船只在礼拜日或放假日及非寻常办公日所定办公时刻（上午 6 时至下午 6 时），欲装卸货物、上下搭客，须先请领专单，呈缴单费。此项单费暂时按照后列之表缴纳。

12. 如遇航路改变、船运事故、航标丢失、船只失事等要事，船主应具呈海关。

13. 火药等爆炸物、弹丸、大炮、猎枪、步枪、滑膛枪、手枪、硝石、硫黄、锌块及其他战备军火武器、食盐，均禁止装运；以上军火武器，如在船上无执照为凭，证明为自卫或船只使用,概行充公。已去壳或未去壳之稻米、中国铜元制钱不得运输出口; 外国铜元饼、铜币、铜钱不得运输入口; 鸦片禁止出入口俄国。

14. 商人或船只,如有违反海关规章,将被处以不超过 500 海关两之罚金。

俄籍商人或船只,如被处以罚金,在向海关支付罚金前,有权向俄国领事提出抗议和申诉。

商人或船只,如未按海关要求支付罚金或屡次违反海关规章,将被处以 500 海关两的最高罚金,如有必要加重处罚时,凡涉及俄籍商人或船只者,中国海关将致函俄国领事商议后续处理办法。

以上为暂行试办章程,必要时,将另行增改,以期妥善。

第二部分 税钞

1. 中国海关专门负责征收关税,内陆及其他税捐不在征收之列; 另将征收子口半税,但船钞及江捐暂不征收,如有调整,另行通知。

船只如有应纳地方税,须于上下货物前后缴纳,以免被滞留。

2. 洋货进口正税及入内地子口半税(税率为进口正税之半)均按照 1902 年改订进口税则征收。

土货出口正税、出内地子口半税及复出口半税(后两项税率均为出口正税之半)均按照 1858 年税则征收。

凡税则未载之货物,不论进出口,均按值百抽五征收。

3. 自俄国口岸进口之货物:

自俄国口岸运来之货物,如欲运往 100 里(50 俄里)边界免税区以外各地,须按章程第二部分第 2 条所定征收进口正税及子口半税。

如欲运往 100 里(50 俄里)边界免税区以内各地,则无须征税。

对于子口半税,如为免税货物,则按 2.5% 征收,如为应税货物,则按现行税则所定税率之半征收。

4. 土货:

自内陆各地进口之土货,如未持海关凭证,须征收正税; 如有凭证,则按照中国通商口岸现行规定征税。

凡出口之土货,均征收出口正税,并发给完税收据。

土货如运往 100 里(50 俄里)边界免税区以内各地,则免征出口正税。

5. 税捐完纳凭证，须按照中国通商口岸通则签发；货物往来各商埠时，如未持完税凭证，概行充公。

6. 对于应纳之税捐，进口货物应于离开海关监管范围前完纳，出口货物应于装货前完纳。

7. 复出口及持有运照之货物，享有与中国其他通商口岸同样的海关待遇。

备注：货物实际复出口之情况将由大黑河稽查关卡核实。

8. 货物装船前，即应报运，海关查验后将予征税并签发装船准单。

9. 土洋各货自瑷珲通过100里（50俄里）边界免税区时，如未持已完正税凭单，须于此处稽查分卡（梁家屯等）完纳正税一次；对于自内地运来之土货，分卡还须负责相应三联报单事宜（参阅第10条）。

商人如能出示保单或于海关缴存足够之金额，亦可选择至瑷珲总关完纳此等税项。

10. 凡由内地运输土货到埠，并最终出境外国者，可按中国通商口岸办法发给三联报单。货物报运时，须呈交一份金额为六倍出口正税的保单；运抵稽查分卡时，还须缴存三倍税金；如于运抵后的六个月内出口至外国，海关将退还1.5倍税金，余下1.5倍税金则分别记作1倍的出口正税及0.5倍的出口货子口税；如未于规定时间内出口至外国，缴存之三倍税金将由海关扣留入账。

以上为暂行试办章程，必要时，将另行增改，以期妥善。

该抄件内容真实有效，特此证明。

录事：周骊二等帮办前班

3. 1912 年《哈尔滨关区税款征收与管理制度》

No. 802.
I.G.

REVENUE: Collection and Control of:
Assessment and Payment of Duties into
Bank; Memorandum on System of, by Mr
Actg.Deputy Commr. J.W.H.Ferguson (in
reply to I.G.Circ.No.1889); forwarding.

Harbin, 30th April, 1912.

Sir,

I have the honour to acknowledge the receipt of your
Circular No. 1889:

> calling for a report on the system followed by
> ports for checking the payment into banks of
> Duties assessed.

The system in vogue in this District, of assessing,
paying in, and recording, Duties, differs in some important
points from the principles followed and practice adopted at the
Treaty Ports in China Proper, chiefly owing to the absence of
banks at the inland places where Sub-offices function. I
have therefore called upon the Acting Deputy Commissioner, Mr
J. W. H. Ferguson, who is in special charge of the Revenue
Account of this District, to draw up an explanatory Memorandum,
which, besides furnishing the information called for in your
Circular, gives a general sketch of the special conditions under
which the Revenue is collected at the various Sub-offices in this
District. From his Memorandum, which I beg to submit herewith,
it will be seen that at the River Ports, (Harbin River Customs,
Sansing, Lahasusu, Aigun), no cargo is released under any circumstances until payment of the duties due has been made to us
direct. As all moneys are collected by the Assistants in Charge
at these Offices against Duty Receipts signed by themselves
without a bank intervening between Customs and applicant it is
simple to ensure this rule being duly carried out. It is also a
standing rule that no Receipt is signed unless and until it has
been entered in the Duty Sheets. It is however a different
matter at Manchuria and Suifenho where the fundamental principle,
of demanding payment of duty before releasing the cargo, had

perforce

To

The Inspector General of Customs.

PEKING.

perforce to be abandoned. As will be seen from the Memorandum
a thorough system of checks has been instituted and although the
cargo is allowed to proceed before the duties have been paid in,
the signature of the Railway Customs Agent on the Daily Duty
Lists turn these documents practically into a Promissary Note so
that the Revenue security is sufficiently covered. The main
objection to this mode of procedure is the time that must
necessarily elapse before Duties are paid into the Harbin Bank.
The system, however, although differing in so many points from
the usual Customs practice, has been well thought out and is the
outcome of many negotiations with the Railway Authorities.

I have the honour to be,

Sir,

Your obedient Servant,

(signed) W. C. Haines Watson,

Commissioner.

APPENDIX.

MEMORANDUM ON SYSTEM OF REVENUE COLLECTION IN HARBIN DISTRICT
(AIGUN, SANSING, HARBIN RIVER CUSTOMS, MANCHURIA AND SUIFENHO).

GENERAL REMARKS: Seeing the peculiar conditions under which Custom
Houses function and trade is carried on in this
District, it need cause no surprise that the System of Revenue
Collection differs considerably from that obtaining at Treaty
Ports in China. Special circumstances called for special
methods, and, since a start was made with the collection in
February, 1908, a system has gradually been evolved, which, while
adapting itself to local requirements, offers the necessary safe-
guards that duties are properly assessed, collected, and accounted

for

for,　In describing the practice in vogue, Manchuria and Suifenho may be grouped together as the same procedure applied to both of them.　The Harbin River, Sansing, Lahasusu and Aigun (Taheiho) Offices, which deal chiefly with riverine trade, follow a different system which is more like the one in force at the Treaty Ports.

MANCHURIA AND SUIFENHO:　The principal difficulty which confronted us from the outset at Manchuria and

Main difficulty confronting Customs.

Suifenho was the fact that the bulk of the cargo handled by these two Offices - Import and Export - was passing in transit unaccompanied by either agents or owners.　It was not feasible to detain the goods until Customs liabilities had been met, and no banks existed at either place which could represent the owners. This difficulty was overcome by arranging that the Chinese Eastern Railway Company should open offices at both the Eastern (Suifenho) and Western (Manchuria) termini which would act as representatives vis a vis the Customs of the cargo owners - that is, declare to the Customs, present the necessary documents, and pay the duties due.　The Offices - which are called "Customs

CUSTOMS AGENCIES:

Agencies" - have been duly established and, on the whole, function satisfactorily.

OFFICE PRACTICE:　If we follow the passage of documents for a certain lot of cargo through the Customs we

Bills of Lading.

see that the Bills of Lading (duplicates) are sent to our station office by the Railway Customs Agency.　They are translated and then passed on to the Goods Godown.　There the cargo is examined. After examination these duplicate bills of lading are stamped, dated and initialled by the Senior Examiner.　The cargo is now released and reloaded in railway cars drawn up for the purpose alongside the godown platform after which the cars are plumbed.　The duplicate bills of lading are then sent to the General Office where duty is assessed and duly recorded on the

Duty Memos.

bills of lading and usual Duty Sheets.　The Duty Memos., called "Billets" in Russian, are then made out in duplicate, separate forms being used for Imports (vide Appendix 1) and

Exports

Exports (vide Appendix 2) and are sent in to the Customs Agency by special chit book.　The duplicate Bills of Lading are filed in the General Office.　Just before a train leaves all the original Bills of Lading are handed in by the Agency to the General Office where they are checked with Duty Sheets and the duplicates handed in before and stamped with Commissioner seal if in order,

Clearance of train.

after which the Clearance Office issues a clearance for the train and the plumbs are removed from the cars.

The procedure just outlined applies more especially to

"Freight" cargo.

the cargo carried by freight trains, which passes Manchuria and Suifenho in transit to Harbin or other Chinese Stations along

"Local" cargo.

the line.　In the case of local cargo, i.e., cargo destined for either Manchuria or Suifenho, the owner applies personally to the General Office, handing in his Bill of Lading.　Duty is assessed and recorded and paid by applicant over the counter against a

Duty receipt for Cash Payment.

numbered Duty Receipt (vide Appendix 3) of which a carbon copy is kept for archives.　Bill of Lading is stamped and initialled and on presentation of this document, together with Duty Receipt, owner can take delivery of his consignment from Railway Godown.

In addition to the usual Customs Daily Sheets, separate

Daily Duty Lists.

Duty Lists, (vide Appendix 4) are compiled, in Russian, one for Import and one for Export, on which all the Duties are entered. At the end of each day these Duty Lists are totalled up, checked with duplicate Bills of Lading, signed by the Assistant in Charge of Office and sent to the Agency for countersignature in token of correctness.　One copy is handed to the Agency, one sent to the Harbin Head Office and one kept for record.　The

The Agency, similarly, keeps its own Lists of Duties assessed by the Customs - and for which, consequently, the Agency accepts liability - taken from the amounts on the Duty Memos., which are also sent daily to the Customs to be checked and countersigned, thus establishing a useful double check.

The Railway accepts full responsibility for the collection

"Through" cargo.

of all the Duties assessed by the Customs on "through" cargo as per original Bills of Lading and Duty Memos. sent to the two

Customs

Customs Agencies at Manchuria and Suifenho, and the following
checks are instituted to ensure that these amounts are in reality
paid into our bank account:-

Duty "Demands". For the Duties collectable through the Railway the Stations
Manchuria and Suifenho prepare for every five days a "Demand"
(vide Appendix 5), in duplicate, showing Import and Export Duties
for each day being furnished by the Daily Lists above referred to.
These Demands are signed by both the Assistant in Charge of the
Station and the Railway Customs Agent.   They are then sent to
the Harbin Head Office and there carefully checked with the
Daily Duty Lists sent to it direct by the Manchuria and Suifenho
Offices.   The date of despatch to the Railway Administration and
the date when the money is due, i.e., within 8 days (exclusive of
Sundays and Holidays) from date of despatch, are noted on it and
one copy is forwarded forthwith to the Railway Revenue Department,
the other being filed for record.   The moneys are paid fairly
punctually by the Railway direct into the "Chinese Customs Revenue
Account" with the Russo-Asiatic Bank at Harbin.   The Railway
Revenue Department always sends to the Commissioner a copy of its
letter to the Bank, and the Bank informs the Commissioner of the
amounts paid in and as these are checked with office copy of the
five - daily "Demands", which in their turn must agree with the
Checks applied. Daily Duty Lists, the chain of checks is complete and track is
kept of all duties from the time of their assessment at the
Station until paid into Revenue Account at Harbin.

Besides sending to the Harbin Head Office copies of the
"Daily Lists" and five-daily "Duty Demands", the Manchuria and
Suifenho Offices also send to Harbin ten-daily statements (vide
Appendix 6) made out in Roubles and Haikuan Taels of all Duties
received.   Monthly Lists, (vide Appendix 7) the totals on which
are checked with the three ten-daily Statements of corresponding
period, are also sent to Harbin and these furnish the material for
compiling the Monthly Statement of Collection (B.-8) forwarded to
the Inspectorate.

The Railway covers itself by handing over the goods to
consignees

consignees only after the duty - as per Customs Duty Memo. pinned
to Bill of Lading - has been paid, or failing which, by selling
the goods by auction.

The following two examples show the time that elapses
before Duties are paid into our Bank Account.

Manchuria Demands Nos. 203 and 204, for duties collected
during period 16th to 20th and 21st to 25th January,1912,
were received at Head Office on the 28th January and 4th
February, sent to the Railway on same dates, paid by the
latter into the Bank on the 10th and 13th February,
respectively, acknowledged by the Bank to Commissioner
on the 13th and 19th February and on the same dates entered
in the Head Office Revenue Account.

Several attempts have been made to accelerate the process, and
to diminish the time during which duties are "en route", but so
far without avail.

HARBIN RIVER CUSTOMS.   A special feature of Customs practice at the River
Customs is that, with the exception of a few amounts, due
from Railway steamers, which are paid direct into our Bank Account
by the Railway Administration, all duties are paid by applicants
Duties paid to "Cashier". over the counter to the "Cashier", usually a Tidewaiter specially
detailed for this duty under the direction of the Assistant in
Charge.   All applications - Russian and Chinese - are translated
numbered, and then sent to the Examiner who returns them to the
General Office when dealt with.   Duty is then assessed and a
Duty Receipt. numbered Duty Receipt (vide Appendix 8) made out (with a carbon
duplicate).   The application with Duty Receipt pinned on to it,
is then sent to the Cashier who enters it in his Cash Book and
collects duty from the applicant, handing him in return a number
which serves to identify later on the owner of the application.
The Cashier initials the Receipt in token of having received the
amount stated on it, and sends it on to the Assistant in Charge
of the General Office who signs it.   The duty is then entered on
the Duty Sheets, after which Receipt and Shipping O rder are
both sealed with Commissioner's seal and subsequently handed to
applicant.

applicant.   No cargo is allowed to be shipped without stamped
Shipping Order, to which must always be pinned the Duty Receipt
initialled by the Cashier and signed by Assistant in General
Office.   The same rule applies of course to Import cargo to
land which a stamped "Permit" and Import - Duty - paid Duty Receipt
must be presented.   At the end of each day the carbon copies of
the Duty Receipts are checked with entries on Duty Sheets and the
Cashier's collection.   The latter two are totalled up for the day
and the duty collected paid at once into a branch of the Russo-
Asiatic Bank by Assistant in Charge of General Office accompanied
by Cashier.

SANSING OFFICE.   The General Office practice, and checks applied, at
Sansing is much the same as at the Harbin River Customs
General Office Practice. the principal difference being that there is no special "Cashier"
to receive the duties which are here all paid over to, and received
by, the Assistant in Charge of the Office.

Imports.   IMPORT CARGO is allowed to be landed under Customs supervision as soon as the ship's documents have been checked.
Applications are then made out and duty assessed and collected by
the Assistant who issues a signed and sealed Duty Receipt, after
which the cargo is released.

Exports.   EXPORT CARGO is always examined, Examining Officer or one
of the Chinese Clerks makes out the application on which duty - if
any - is assessed, calculated and checked, everything being ready
for payment when applicant (having arranged about the shipment of
his cargo with a steamer) brings the Shipping Order to the Office.
Duty Receipts issued by Assistant. Duty is then paid to the Assistant, receipt issued, and Shipping
Orders sealed with Commissioner's seal.   The Assistant in Charge
collects all duties himself and personally checks Daily Sheets,
carbon copies of Duty Receipts and actual money collected, the
latter being at once entered in a "Cash-in-safe" Book.   As no
cargo is released inward or outward unless duties have been paid
Ten-daily Statement. there are never any outstanding accounts.   A Ten-daily Statement
of Collection (vide Appendix 9) is made out from the Duty Register
after having been carefully checked with Daily Sheets and "Cash-
in-

in-safe" Book, and then sent on to Harbin Head Office.

Monthly Revenue Account. A "Monthly Revenue Account" (vide Appendix 10), being a complete
record of all moneys passing through that account during the
month - including Lahasusu Barrier - is also sent to Harbin where
it is checked with the Ten-Daily Statement.   The Revenue
collected at Sansing is usually retained by the Assistant in Charge
to meet office expenditure.   The equivalent of the amount
so appropriated is accounted for as "Remitted to Harbin" and is
refunded to the Harbin General Revenue Account by the Accountant
at Harbin.

LAHASUSU: Lahasusu is a Barrier subordinated to the Sansing Office.
Method of collection. The method of collection is the same as at Sansing, to which
office it has to account for its collection.   Ten-Daily and
Monthly Statements of Collection (vide Appendix 11) are however
sent direct to Harbin as well as to Sansing.

AIGUN SUB - DISTRICT.   The Assistant in Charge of the Aigun Customs is
stationed at Ta-heiho, officially called a
Barrier (分卡) but more important than Aigun itself.   Another
Barrier is established at Liangchiat'un.   We have to deal here
with Overland trade and Steamer traffic.

Overland trade.   All goods from the interior must pass Liangchiat'un and
are there examined.   The applicant usually requests to pay
"Cargo Memo". duties at Taheiho in which case a Memo. descriptive of the cargo
is made out in triplicate (with pencil and carbon paper), one
copy being handed to applicant in a sealed cover for transmission
to Taheiho General Office; the second copy being sent later to
the Assistant in Charge for checking purposes, while the third is
kept for record.   All Chinese merchants must find a guarantor
at Liangchiat'un who undertakes to pay whatever duty is leviable
in case applicant fails to report to the General Office at Taheiho.
Russian merchants present a written and signed application on
which the Customs can base a claim for duties after the goods have
passed the Barrier and do not arrive at Taheiho.

"Steamer traffic"   Cargo carried by steamers consists mainly of goods having
paid full Export duty at Harbin - and which are therefore free on
importation

importation at Aigun - or of cargo re-exported by steamer or junk
to small places on the Amur which is duty free because remaining
in the Free Zone.

"Cargo to Free Zone".

As at Sansing, the Assistant in Charge himself collects
all duties and issues Receipts signed and sealed by himself entering the amounts so received in the Revenue Account "Cash - in -
safe" Book, which is totalled up at the end of each day and must
tally with Duty Sheets, office copies of Receipts issued and
actual collection.   Ten-Daily (vide Appendix 12) and Monthly
(vide Appendix 13) Statements of Revenue Collection, drawn up on
lines similar to those sent by the Sansing Office, and showing
the Revenue collected at the three Offices, are forwarded to
Harbin Head Office.

System of Collection.

Revenue Statements.

Unlike Sansing, where the Revenue collected is appropriated
for office expenditure, the collection of the three Aigun Offices
is wholly paid into the Russo-Asiatic Bank at Blagovestchensk.
An account called "Chinese Customs Duties Account" is opened there
in the name of the Commissioner of Customs, Harbin, and moneys
paid in cannot be taken out again by the Aigun Assistant.   The
funds necessary to meet current office expenditure are remitted to
Aigun by the Harbin Office through the Russo-Asiatic Bank.

HARBIN HEAD OFFICE REVENUE ACCOUNT: As already explained, the Sub-offices render their
Revenue Accounts to the Harbin Head Office.   At
Harbin these are under the special care of the Deputy Commissioner
It is his duty to watch that all Moneys collected are properly
accounted for, daily, five-daily, ten-daily and monthly.   He
keeps a General Revenue Account of the collection for the whole
District, and sees that all the moneys reported as received by the
various offices in the District find their way eventually, and
with the least delay possible, into the Russo-Asiatic Bank at
Harbin and Blagovestchensk, and are duly acknowledged.   He also
prepares a Quarterly Revenue Statement, showing Collection of
District for quarter, payments made from the Revenue, and Balance
in hand at end of Quarter, copy of which is submitted to the
Inspector General.

                    (signed) J. W. H. Ferguson,
                     Acting Deputy Commissioner.

                                        LIST

LIST OF DOCUMENTS IN USE IN THE HARBIN CUSTOMS DISTRICT FOR
COLLECTION, ASSESSMENT AND PAYMENT OF DUTIES.

Appendix 1 :   DUTY MEMO. (for duties payable through Railway)
                used at Manchuria and Suifenho.   (IMPORT)

"   2 :   "   "   "   "   "   (EXPORT)

"   3 :   DUTY RECEIPT for duties paid in cash at
                Manchuria and Suifenho.

"   4 :   DAILY DUTY LIST (Manchuria and Suifenho).

"   5 :   FIVE-DAILY "DEMAND" for duties payable
                through Railway.

"   6 :   TEN DAILY REVENUE STATEMENT
                (Manchuria and Suifenho).

"   7 :   MONTHLY REVENUE STATEMENT
                (Manchuria and Suifenho).

"   8 :   RIVER CUSTOMS DUTY RECEIPT

"   9 :   SANSING TEN DAILY REVENUE STATEMENT.

"   10 :   "   MONTHLY   "   "   .

"   11 :   LAHASUSU MONTHLY AND TENDAILY REVENUE STATEMENT.

"   12 :   AIGUN TEN DAILY REVENUE STATEMENT.

"   13 :   "   MONTHLY   "   "   .

N.B.   The above documents, together with a carbon copy of
        Memorandum, are on file in the Deputy Commissioner's
        Office.

              True copy:

              2nd Assistant A.

呈海关总税务司署 <u>802</u> 号文　　　　　　　　哈尔滨关 1912 年 4 月 30 日

尊敬的海关总税务司（北京）：

　　海关总税务司署第 1889 号通令收悉：

　　"为要求各口岸报告核查税款估定及交存银行所遵行之制度事。"

　　哈尔滨关区税款估定、交存及登记之现行制度与内地通商口岸所遵行之原则及惯例在某些重要方面确有不符之处，主要因各分关所设之地还未设有银行。因此已令主管本关区税收账目的署副税务司费克森（J. W. H. Ferguson）先生草拟报告一份，除提供通令要求之信息外，还将说明各分关征税之情况。特将此报告附上，从中可知，本关区沿江各口（哈尔滨江关、三姓分关、拉哈苏苏分卡及瑷珲分关）仅于货物直接在关完纳税款后允准放行。所有税款皆由分关管理帮办亲自征收并相应发给完税收据，海关与报关人之间并无银行干预，如此十分易于执行且无舞弊之可能。另外按照惯例，完税收据均须于记入税款登记表后再行签发。然而，满洲里和绥芬河两处分关，因受实际情况所迫，无法遵循先收税再放行的基本原则。但如报告所述，两处分关已建立了颇为完善的核查制度，而且虽允许货物于完税之前过关通行，但每日税收账目皆会由铁路报关行签字确认，此等凭证实与欠票无异，可保税收万全。唯如此一来，税款存入哈尔滨银行的时间会有延迟，略显不足。然无论如何，此制度虽与海关惯例有多处不合，但确已经过周密考虑，且为与铁路当局多番协商之结果。

您忠诚的仆人

花荪（W. C. H. Watson）

哈尔滨关税务司

附录

哈尔滨关区（瑷珲分关、三姓分关、哈尔滨江关、满洲里分关及绥芬河分关）

税款征收与管理制度报告

概述：哈尔滨关区之情况较为特殊，海关职能及地方贸易均受此影响，因此本关区的税款征收制度与中国其他通商口岸的现行制度存在较大差异，亦不足为奇。毕竟特殊情况需要特殊对待，且自 1908 年 2 月开始征税起，哈尔滨关区的征税制度便一直在不断调整，不仅要适应地方需求，还要切实保证税款之估定、征收、入账等手续不出差错。鉴于满洲里和绥芬河两处分关实行的手续相同，在下文汇报时，将并做一处；而哈尔滨江关、三姓分关、拉哈苏苏分卡及瑷珲（大黑河）分关因主要应对水运贸易，实行的则是另一套制度，与其他通商口岸的现行制度更为类似。

满洲里分关和绥芬河分关：

自于满洲里及绥芬河两地设关以来，海关面对的主要困难在于，经当地运输之货物，不论进出口，大多皆无代理人或者货主随行。因此如欲按海关正常手续办理，在税款缴清之前扣押货物，实不可行。但两地又皆无银行，无可为货主代理者。为克服此困难，最终商定由中东铁路公司分别于铁路东（绥芬河）西（满洲里）两端设立办事处，以代表货主办理海关手续，即代理报关、呈交必要凭证、支付应纳关税。此等办事处被称为"报关行"，自设立以来整体运行良好。

办公惯例：查阅货物通过海关后留下的凭证可知，首先由铁路报关行将提单（抄件）交至关署，翻译完成后再送至关栈，货物于关栈接受查验后，超等验货再于提单抄件上加盖印章、注明日期并签下姓名首字母。目前，货物放行后，均由关栈平台一侧停靠的铁路专车重新装载，装完后车辆会加盖铅封。随后提单抄件会被送至分关公事房，关员计税后会于提单抄件及税款登记表上记录载明，并开具一式两份的"税款缴纳证"（俄文中又称"Billets"）、进出口货物使用单独表单［分别参见"哈尔滨关区税款征收、估定及支付所用凭证清单"（下文省略）之附录 1 及附录 2］，最后通过专门的送信簿送至报关行。提单抄件留于公事房存档。报关行须于火车启动前将所有货物的提单原件呈交至公事房，经与税款登记表及先前递交之提单抄件核对无误后，将盖上税务司印章，并由结关处为该次列车签发结关单照一份，并撤毁上述车辆之铅封。

上述手续主要适用于由货运火车运输之货物，此等货物通常经满洲里或绥芬河转运至哈尔滨或铁路沿线的其他境内车站。至于当地货物，即目的地为满洲里或绥芬河之货物，皆由货主亲自至分关公事房递交提单。报关人于台前办理完计税、登记、交税手续后，关员会为之签发一份带有编号的"完税收据"（参见附录3），收据复联留关存档。提单由关员加盖印章并签下姓名首字母后，货主可凭此提单及完税收据至铁路仓库提领货物。

除海关日常税款登记表外，进出口货物还各有一份单独的俄文"每日税收账目"（参见附录4），以载明所有税收信息。每日工作结束后，税收账目须汇总累加，经与提单抄件核对无误后，由分关管理帮办签字，再送至报关行会签以证无误。每日税收账目之抄件，一份交与报关行，一份呈交至哈尔滨总关，还有一份留存记录。报关行亦有自己的税收账目，数据来源为税款缴纳证，每日皆会交与海关核对签字。由此，双方便建立起非常有效的双向核对机制。

海关为"通运"货物计税后，征收工作由铁路方面全权负责，征收依据为提单原件及海关发送至满洲里和绥芬河报关行的税款缴纳证，为确保税款如数汇入海关银行账户，特设立以下核查机制。

对于对铁路货物应征收之税款，满洲里及绥芬河两处分关每五日便会编制一份"五日税收执据"（参见附录5），一式两份，列明每日所收之进出口税款，数据均取于上述"每日税收账目"。"五日税收执据"由分关管理帮办及铁路报关行签字后，会发送至哈尔滨总关，再由总关关员将之与满洲里及绥芬河两处分关先前发送之"每日税收账目"进行仔细核对。"五日税收执据"上会载明发送给铁路管理部门的日期及税款应付日期（即自发送日期起的8日内，不含星期日及假日）。"五日税收执据"抄件，一份发送给铁路征税部门，一份留存归档。铁路方面会按时将税款直接汇至华俄道胜银行哈尔滨分行的"中国海关税收账户"。随后铁路征税部门会将发给银行的函文抄件发送给哈尔滨关税务司一份，银行方面亦会将税款到账金额告知税务司。最后此等信息还须与"五日税收执据"之底稿进行核对，而"五日税收执据"又须与"每日税收账目"所列相符，由此便形成了一套完整的核查链。而所有税款，自于分关计税起至汇入哈尔滨关税收账户止，均有记录，可以追踪。

除了向哈尔滨关税务司发送"每日税收账目"及"五日税收执据"外，满洲里及绥芬河两处分关还会发送"十日税收报表"（参见附录6），列明所收税款之卢布及海关两金额。此外还有"每月税收报表"（参见附录7），上面的总额将与三份相应日期内的"十日税收报表"进行核对。最后再根据以上各项数据编制每月征收报表（B.-8）并呈与总税务司。

铁路方面,为保险起见,仅会在收货人将"税款缴纳证"(钉于提单上)上规定的税款缴齐后,再移交货物;如不能及时缴齐税款,便会以拍卖的方式将货物卖掉。

通过以下两例可知税款存入海关银行账户之前的时间消耗情况。

满洲里分关为 1912 年 1 月 16 日至 20 日及 1 月 21 日至 25 日所收税款编制之"五日税收执据"第 203 号及 204 号,分别于 1 月 28 日及 2 月 4 日送达哈尔滨总关,并于相同日期发送给铁路部门;铁路方面分别于 2 月 10 日及 13 日将税款汇入相应银行;银行方面则分别于 2 月 13 日及 19 日向哈尔滨关税务司确认税款到账,税款于同日存入哈尔滨关税收账户。

尽管已多次尝试加速办事流程,缩短税款"在途中"的时间,但是尚未有成功之例。

哈尔滨江关:

按照哈尔滨江关之惯例,除铁路轮船应纳之税款由铁路管理部门直接汇入海关银行账户外,其他所有报关人均亲至江关结关台向"出纳"支付一应关税。"出纳"通常由特派之钤子手担任,在管理帮办的指导下完成此项工作。所有报单,无论是汉文还是俄文,经翻译并编号后,均交由二等验货带回公事房处理,包括计税及开具一式两份且带有编号的"哈尔滨江关完税收据"(参见附录 8)。完税收据随后钉到相应的报单上,一并交与"出纳",由其将此记入现金簿,并向报关人征收关税,发给号码(以作证实报单持有人身份之用),最后再于"哈尔滨江关完税收据"上签下姓名首字母以示确已收到收据所载金额,并将之交与公事房管理帮办签字。税款登记表完成登记后,"哈尔滨江关完税收据"及装货单上会加盖哈尔滨关税务司印章并交与报关人。装货单上如无税务司印章或未钉上带有"出纳"姓名首字母签字及公事房管理帮办签字之"哈尔滨江关完税收据",概不允许装货。进口货物亦是如此,即必须出示加盖印章之"准单"及进口税"哈尔滨江关完税收据"。每日工作结束后,"哈尔滨江关完税收据"复联皆须与税款登记表及出纳所征税款进行核对。当日税款登记表所载数据与"出纳"所征税款须汇总累加;并由公事房管理帮办在"出纳"的陪同下将当日所收税款存入华俄道胜银行哈尔滨分行。

三姓分关:

三姓分关的征收手续及核查办法与哈尔滨江关基本相同,唯此分关并未安排专门的"出纳"收税,而是由分关管理帮办直接征收。

进口货物:船舶证件检查完毕后,货物便允许在海关的监督下卸载,随后即可填具报单。分关管理帮办完成计税征税工作后会为之签发完税收据,并于上面签字盖章,之后货物便可放行。

出口货物：所有出口货物均须接受查验，并由验货关员或者华籍同文供事开具报单，并据此完成关税的估定、计算及核对工作。待报关人（已安排好轮船装载货物）携装货单至关时，除支付税款外，其他一切手续均已办理完毕。分关管理帮办收税后，会签发完税收据，并于装货单上加盖税务司印章。所有关税，均由管理帮办一人征收，每日税款登记表、完税收据抄件及实际征收税款亦由其亲自核对。其中，实际征收税款均直接记入"暂存本关银柜的现金"簿中。鉴于所有货物，不论进出口，均须于完纳税款后放行，因此三姓分关从无未结账目。此外，分关还会根据税收记录（须与每日税款登记表及"暂存本关银柜的现金"簿核对）编制"三姓分关十日税收报表"（参见附录9），并发送至哈尔滨总关。

三姓分关（包括拉哈苏苏分卡）当月所有税款记录均会载入"三姓分关每月税收报表"（参见附录10），并发送至哈尔滨总关，由总关将之与"十日税收报表"进行核对。三姓分关所征之税款通常会由管理帮办留存以应对办公支出。挪用之款再以等额记作"汇至哈尔滨总关"的款项，并由哈尔滨关司账退还至哈尔滨关税收总账户。

拉哈苏苏分卡：拉哈苏苏分卡隶属于三姓分关，征收手续基本相同，所收税款均须向三姓分关报账。但分卡的"拉哈苏苏分关每月及十日税收报表"（参见附录11）须同时直接发送给哈尔滨总关和三姓分关。

瑷珲分关：

瑷珲分关管理帮办现驻于大黑河，此处名义上虽为分关，但实际上的重要性已经超过瑷珲所设分关，此外梁家屯还设有一处分卡。此分关之贸易主要有陆路贸易及轮船运输两类。

陆路贸易：凡自内地运来之货物，均须经由梁家屯分卡，并接受查验。报关人通常会被要求至大黑河缴纳税款。若如此，则须开具一份货物信息备忘录，一式三份（使用铅笔及复写纸）。一份密封后交与报关人带至大黑河分卡公事房，一份稍后交给管理帮办以供审核，一份存档记录。报关人如为华商，则须于梁家屯寻得担保人，以在其未能至大黑河分卡公事房报明交税的情况下，支付应纳之关税；如为俄商，则须出具一份手写报单并签字，以便在货物通过梁家屯分卡但未运抵大黑河的情况下，海关可据此报单索要相应税款。

轮船运输：由轮船载运之货物，主要有两种情况。一为已于哈尔滨关完纳出口正税者，运入瑷珲关区时免征税；一为由轮船或民船复出口至黑龙江沿岸小镇者，因仍在边境免税区内，故亦免征税。

与三姓分关之情况相同，此分关亦由主管帮办亲自负责征收一应关税，签发完税收据并签字盖章,将所收税款记入"暂存本关银柜的现金"簿中。每日工作结束后须将"暂存本关银柜的现金"簿所载数据汇总累加,确保与税款登记表、完税收据底稿及实际所收税款相符。"瑷珲分关十日税收报表"(参见附录12)及"每月税收报表"(参见附录13)的编制办法与三姓分关类似,亦须包含下辖各分卡征收之税款,并发送至哈尔滨总关。

与三姓分关不同的是,三姓分关所征税款可由管理帮办留存以应对办公支出,而瑷珲分关所征税款须全部存入华俄道胜银行布拉戈维申斯克(Blagovestchensk)分行。海关已于该银行以哈尔滨关税务司之名开立账户,户名为"中国海关税收账户"。税款一经存入,瑷珲分关帮办便无法再支领。至于瑷珲分关所需办公经费,则一直由哈尔滨总关通过华俄道胜银行哈尔滨分行汇寄。

哈尔滨总关:

税收账目:如前文所述,各分关均将税收账目呈交至哈尔滨总关,由哈尔滨总关副税务司专门管理。副税务司负责每日、五日、十日及每月税收报表的审查工作,确保规范无误;为整个关区编制税收总账目,确保各分关呈报所收之税款皆有据可查,能够尽快存入华俄道胜银行哈尔滨分行及布拉戈维申斯克分行,能够及时到账;编制季度税收报表,以示整个关区的季度税收、税款支出及每季度末的税收盈余情况。季度税收报表抄件将呈送至海关总税务司署。

费克森

哈尔滨关署副税务司

哈尔滨关区税款征收、估定及支付所用凭证清单

附录 1： 税款缴纳证（针对铁路运输货物的应收税款）

于满洲里及绥芬河分关使用（进口货物）

附录 2： 税款缴纳证（针对铁路运输货物的应收税款）

于满洲里及绥芬河分关使用（出口货物）

附录 3： 完税收据（针对以现金支付之税款）

于满洲里及绥芬河分关使用

附录 4： 每日税收账目（满洲里及绥芬河分关）

附录 5： 五日税收执据（针对铁路运输货物的应收税款）

附录 6： 十日税收报表（满洲里及绥芬河分关）

附录 7： 每月税收报表（满洲里及绥芬河分关）

附录 8： 哈尔滨江关完税收据

附录 9： 三姓分关十日税收报表

附录 10： 三姓分关每月税收报表

附录 11： 拉哈苏苏分卡每月及十日税收报表

附录 12： 瑷珲分关十日税收报表

附录 13： 瑷珲分关每月税收报表

注：上述凭证及报告抄件均存档于哈尔滨关副税务司办公室。

4. 1913 年《呼玛河分卡稽查办法》

Copy
1.055
I.G.

Customs Barrier at Humaho:
Question of establishment of;
submitted. Report on Humaho
and Moho, by Mr. P. Barentzen,
3rd Assistant, a; forwarded.
Instructions requested.

27th November, 1913.

Sir,

The possible abolition of the Chinese
half of the Frontier Free Zone before the
Amur is again open to navigation in 1914
requiring consideration, my attention has
been directed to points on the Chinese side
of the Upper Amur at which a certain
amount of trade, so far uncontrolled by the
Customs, has developed. These are Humaho
(呼玛河) and Moho (漠河), the latter
sufficiently well-known in connection with
gold-washing, situated at 166 and 497 miles
respectively above Takeiho (vide Map of Harbin
District in Vol. 1, Decennial Report, 1902 –
1911 – Humating and Mohoting). Mr. Paul
Barentzen, Third Assistant, a, in charge of
the Aigun Office, has made enquiries and
studied the question of establishing a Customs
Barrier, under Aigun, at Humaho, and I
now beg to submit, enclosed herewith, copy
of his report – which does him credit and
shows he is taking an intelligent interest
in his work – for your perusal. From it you
will gather:

(See Aigun Despatch Report)
(10 Nov. 1913)

   1. That Humaho is the supplying centre
      of the gold-mining and washing
      district.

The Inspector General of Customs,
    Peking.
                                   2.

   2. That the annual value of the direct
      Russian trade to Humaho and Moho
      is estimated at Hk. Tls. 154,000.

   3. That the value of the trade from
      Takeiho to Humaho and Moho during
      the last sleigh and shipping seasons
      (1912-1913) is estimated at Hk. Tls.
      729,000.00.

   4. That by the establishment of a Barrier
      at Humaho the trade which now finds
      a convenient route via Blagovestchensk
      for evading the Chinese Customs, would
      remain on the Chinese side of the
      Amur, enter to be shipped to
      Humaho and Moho direct from Harbin
      or via Takeiho, paying duty at
      Harbin.

   5. That very little revenue probably
      would, therefore, be collected at
      Humaho.

   6. That there is practically no export
      from the two places mentioned.

   7. That the estimated expenditure amounts
      to some Roubles 4,100.00 per annum.

It would seem, therefore, that whether
or not the Free Zone is abolished, Customs
interests would be well served by extension
of control to Humaho, and as it would be
advantageous to know in good time whether
to make arrangements, I have the honour
to bring the matter thus early to your notice
and request your instructions in the matter.

I have the honour to be,
Sir,
Your obedient Servant,
(Signed) R. de Luca
Commissioner.

————————

Append.

Rules: Steamer Trade:

1. Steamers bound for Chinese places up river to hand in at Taheiho Customs two manifests, each in duplicate, to give correct description, weights and values of Blagovestchensk and Taheiho cargo respectively.

2. Taheiho Officers to examine on board as much Blagovestchensk cargo as quantity, time and space will allow and mark result on the manifest, one copy of which to be sent to Humaho in sealed cover.

3. Taheiho Office to issue cargo-certificate for all cargos from Taheiho to Humaho and Moho and to send it in sealed cover to Humaho.

4. Humaho Officer to examine all cargos from Blagovestchensk to Moho on board, charge duty (if not originating in Free Zone) and then release steamer. Humaho cargo to be examined afterwards on the beach and released, — if from Blagovestchensk (and

(and not originating in Free Zone) upon payment of duty.

5. Cargo-certificate for export cargo from Moho and Humaho to Taheiho to be sent by Humaho Officer in sealed cover to Taheiho, but no duty to be levied at Humaho.

Sleigh Trade:

6. Taheiho cargo to be examined and each sleigh and caravan of sleighs to be given a cargo-memo showing all details. Upon arrival at Humaho to be released after examination.

7. Cargoes from Russian side to be examined and duty charged at Humaho (if not originating in the Free Zone).

True Copy:

2nd Assistant A.

呈海关总税务司署 <u>1055</u> 号文　　　　　　　哈尔滨关 1913 年 11 月 27 日

尊敬的海关总税务司（北京）：

　　虽然 1914 年航运开通之前，中国境内的边境免税区应否撤销，尚在斟酌之中，但经查，黑龙江上游华岸部分地区之贸易已有发展之势，只是迄今一直未由海关稽查管控。所涉城镇主要是呼玛河和漠河，两地分别位于大黑河上游 166 英里及 497 英里（参阅 1902—1911 年《各口海关十年报告》第一卷"哈尔滨关区地图之呼玛廷及漠河廷"）。其中，漠河以淘金而广为人知。现负责瑷珲分关的三等帮办前班巴闰森（P. G. S. Barentzen）先生对在呼玛河设立海关分卡并由瑷珲分关管辖一事已展开调查研究，特此附上其报告抄件，呈请审阅。从中可以看出，巴闰森先生对其工作很有热忱，亦颇具能力，值得称赞。报告中指出：

　　1. 呼玛河为金矿及淘金区的物资供应中心。

　　2. 俄国每年直接对呼玛河及漠河的贸易额预计可达 154000.00 海关两。

　　3. 1912—1913 年大黑河对呼玛河及漠河的贸易额（雪橇贸易及船运贸易）约有 729000.00 海关两。

　　4. 于呼玛河设立分卡后，现经小路取道布拉戈维申斯克（Blagovestchensk，即海兰泡）以逃避中国海关稽查之贸易，只能选择自哈尔滨直接运至呼玛河或漠河，或者选择途经大黑河，且须于哈尔滨关完纳税款。

　　5. 因此海关于呼玛河所设分卡可征收之税将会极少。

　　6. 呼玛河及漠河几无货物出口。

　　7. 呼玛河分卡设立后的年支出约为 4100.00 卢布。

　　有鉴于此，似乎无论边境免税区撤销与否，如能将海关之稽查范围拓至呼玛河，于关而言，皆属有益。为能及时安排，以占先机，特此呈文汇报，望予指示。

您忠诚的仆人

（签名）卢力飞（R. de Luca）

哈尔滨关税务司

附件

呼玛河分卡稽查办法

船运贸易：

1. 凡驶往黑龙江上游华岸各地之轮船,均须于大黑河分卡递交两份货物舱单,均为一式两份,载明对货物的准确描述、重量及于布拉戈维申斯克和大黑河两地的价格。

2. 凡自布拉戈维申斯克运来之货物,均须先由大黑河分卡关员登船检查。关员在数量、时间及空间允许的情况下尽力查验,并将结果于货物舱单上注明,最后再将货物舱单抄件密封发送至呼玛河分卡。

3. 凡自大黑河运往呼玛河或漠河之货物,均由大黑河分卡签发货物证明书,密封后发送至呼玛河分卡。

4. 凡自布拉戈维申斯克运往漠河之货物,均由呼玛河分卡关员登船检查,原产地如非免税区,还须征税,之后方可放行轮船。凡运至呼玛河之货物,均由关员于前滩查验放行,但对于自布拉戈维申斯克运来且原产地不在免税界内之货物,须于征税后放行。

5. 凡自漠河或呼玛河运至大黑河之货物,均由呼玛河分卡签发货物证明书,密封发送至大黑河,但不征税。

雪橇贸易：

6. 凡自大黑河运往漠河或呼玛河之货物,均由大黑河分卡查验并为雪橇及雪橇拖车按车辆发给货物备忘录,载明货物详细信息；运抵呼玛河后,分卡关员须于查验后再予放行。

7. 凡自黑龙江俄岸运来之货物,均由呼玛河分卡查验,原产地如非免税区,还须征税。

该抄件内容真实有效,特此证明。

录事：周骊（C. H. B. Joly）二等帮办前班

5. 1919 年《临时理船章程》

Copy

1970

I. G.

*Proposed Provisional Harbour
Regulations for Taeiho: draft of,
forwarded.*

Harbin, 15th August, 1919.

Sir,

1.   With reference to your telegram of 7th June (in reply to my letter of 3rd June): instructing that Mr River Inspector Garden, in consultation with the Assistant-in-Charge at Aigun and the Taeiho Taoyin should occupy himself regarding all matters pertaining to Harbour control at Aigun/Taeiho and should suggest provisional Harbour limits and Harbour regulations adapted to local conditions based on treaty port traditions and practice;

I now have the honour to submit herewith enclosed, a draft of provisional regulations for the Port of Taeiho. In his despatch enclosing these Regulations the Assistant-in-Charge points out that they are based on the Hankow and Kiukiang Regulations copies of which were obtained by Mr River Inspector Garden, that the standard set of Regulations given in I. G. Circulars Nos. 2060, 2124 has been adhered to as closely as possible —

possible — the only alterations made being such as are necessitated by local conditions — and that they have been supplied to the Taeiho Taoyin.

A Russian translation is being made here and will be forwarded as soon as it is finished — which however may take some time.

2.   I take this opportunity to remark that there exist no Harbour Regulations for the Port of Harbin.

3.   A copy of this despatch and its enclosure is being sent to the Coast Inspector.

I have the honour to be,
Sir,
Your obedient Servant,
(Signed) P. Gowedon,
Commissioner.

The Inspector General of Customs,
Peking.

References:-
From I. G.
Telegram of 7/6/1919.

True copy:

2nd Assistant, A.

Copy

Coast Inspector's comments on Harbin No. 1970, J. G.

In the Provisional Harbour Regulations for the Port of Taikho, Article 24, lines 1 and 2 should read
"The blowing of steam whistles, sirens or _other sound signals_, except for the purpose......"
and on line 5 of the same article it is not clear whether Article 22 or 23 is referred to. It should be Article 22.

An inset plan of the harbour should be printed with the Regulations should the survey of the harbour have been completed in time.

It is recommended that Harbour Regulations be compiled for the Port of Harbin; they are badly needed. Conditions, however, at that port are so extraordinary that there may be found many difficulties that may be almost insurmountable.

(Signed) T. J. Eldridge,
Coast Inspector.

Coast Inspector's Office,
Shanghai, 22nd August, 1919.

True copy:

C. A. Jo
2nd Assistant, A.

Copy

Provisional Harbour Regulations for the Port of Taikho.

The following Provisional Regulations, which have been agreed to by the Authorities of the Powers concerned, are issued for the information and guidance of all concerned.

Commissioner of Customs.

Custom House,
Harbin,..........

1.- The term "vessel" in these Regulations refers to vessels of foreign type. Regulations concerning native-type craft are embodied herein only so far as is necessary for their due control when working in connexion with foreign-type vessels. They are regulated in other respects by special notifications.

Anchorages

2.- The Upper and Lower limits of the Harbour are respectively from Shih Shan T'ou Hill to below the Public Park.

The anchorages for foreign-type vessels are:-

(a)

2.

(a) For vessels other than those provided for in (b), for which special anchorages have been assigned, between the Upper and Lower limits of the Harbour as defined above.

(b) For vessels carrying mineral oil and explosives, and those subject to quarantine regulations, outside the Upper Limit of the Harbour.

3.- Vessels shall moor in accordance with instructions from the Harbour Master, and shall not ship their births without a special permit, except when outward bound after having obtained their clearance papers.

Vessels may not lie in the stream at single anchor.

4.- Vessels which have determined births are allowed to proceed to them without stopping except as provided in Clauses 6, 13, and 16 of these Regulations.

5.- Applications for births or for permission to shift must be made at the Custom House by the Shipmaster, the First Officer, or the Pilot in charge, or Agent of Steamship Company, when the necessary instructions concerning the birth will be given.

Munitions

3.

Munitions.

6.- Vessels having on board as cargo any high Explosives or the specially prepared constituents of such, any loaded shells or more than 100 pounds of gunpowder, any quantity of small-arm cartridges in excess of 50,000 rounds, or any other fixed ammunition of which the aggregate quantity of powder charges exceeds 100 pounds, shall anchor as provided for in Article 2.(b), and fly a Red flag at the fore; and in regard to the discharge of same, they shall abide by the instructions received from the Custom.

Vessels having to receive on board any such explosives shall observe similar precautions.

This rule shall not apply to small-arm cartridges when carried in a properly constructed magazine, so fitted as to admit of its being flooded by a sea-cock operated from the upper deck, in which case the number of cartridges allowed to be carried is not limited.

7.- Men of war and other Government vessels may take on board or tranship explosives within anchorage (a), provided that such explosives are handled only by their own crew under the command of an Officer.

8.-

4.

8.- Any transfer by boat of explosives, arms, or ammunition must be covered by a special permit, which will be issued at the Harbour Master's Office upon the owner's written application giving the registered numbers of the boats to be thus employed.

9.- No lighters or other boats, except those which have permanent decks or coverings, shall be allowed to receive any of the articles mentioned in Clause 6 of these Regulations; and all such articles when received on board any such lighter or boat must be stowed under deck within the permanently closed-in space.

10.- Every craft, except men of war, of whatever description, conveying explosives through any part of the waters of the port shall exhibit a Red flag, not less than 6 feet by 4 feet, at the fore-mast-head, or where it can best be seen; and in case of all boats or lighters thus employed which are not fitted with masts, the Red flag must be exhibited at a height of not less than 12 feet above the highest part of the deck or house.

11.-

5.

11.- The storage of explosives of any sort shall not be allowed anywhere on or near the shore of the river (within the Harbour Limits) or its affluents in the neighbourhood of Tahsia, except after due consideration and sanction of the Customs and Chinese Authorities.

12.- No fires, for cooking or any other purpose, and no smoking shall be allowed on board any lighter or other boat when going alongside a vessel which has explosives on board, nor while there are any explosives on board such lighter or boat.

Mineral Oil.

13.- Vessels arriving with mineral oil, or cargo of a highly inflammable nature, shall anchor as provided in Article 2, (b), and must remain there till all such cargo has been discharged. Vessels loading such cargo shall do so only where it is permitted to be discharged, and from there proceed out of the Harbour. Vessels in anchorage (a) are permitted to handle a quantity of kerosene not exceeding 50 cases.

14.-

6.

14.- No fires, for cooking or any
other purpose, and no smoking shall
be allowed on board any lighter or
other boat when going alongside a
vessel which has naphtha, benzine,
and other highly inflammable cargo
on board, nor while there are such
naphtha, benzine, and other highly
inflammable cargo on board such
lighter or boat.

15.- The storage of naphtha, benzine,
or other highly inflammable cargo
shall not be allowed on or near
the shore of the river (within the
Harbour Limits) except with the
permission of the Customs and
Chinese Authorities.

Infectious Diseases.

16.- Vessels having any infectious
disease on board, or any disease
suspected to be infectious, or the
body of a person who died, or is
suspected of having died, of an
infectious disease, shall, on
approaching the port, hoist the
Quarantine Flag, anchor as provided
for in Article 2, (6), and keep the
flag flying until pratique has been
granted.

No person shall be permitted
to leave or board such a vessel
without

7.

without a permit from the Harbour
Master or Port Health Officer.

Vessels arriving from any
port declared to be infected shall
abide by the instructions received
from the Customs Authorities.

Conservancy.

17.- No wharves, jetties, or landing
shall be built, pontoons, hulks,
or buoys moored, and no reclaiming
or other riparian work commenced,
without the permission of the Harbour
Master - applications for such permission to be endorsed by the
Chinese Authorities.

18.- All buoys shall be subject to
the control of the Harbour Master;
and when they are so placed as to
obstruct the passage of vessels or
are not moored in such a way as to
economise berthing space, the Harbour
Master shall be at liberty to order
them to be shifted. In case of
refusal or neglect on the part of
the owners of a buoy to shift its
position as directed by the Harbour
Master, the latter may cause it to
be removed at the cost of the
owners.

19.-

8

19.- Ballast, ashes, garbage, refuse, spoil obtained by dredging or otherwise, etc., must not be thrown either into the river in summer, or on to the ice in winter, or on the river bank. Vessels wishing to discharge ashes or other refuse must do so outside Harbour Limits.

The road along the foreshore, within Harbour Limits, is to be kept free of all obstructions, such as garbage, building materials, etc., in order to allow free loading and discharging of vessels. Neither is cargo to be stored on the fore-shore without special permission of the Customs Authorities.

20.- In the case of wrecks within the Harbour, which form a danger to navigation, if no active steps have been taken within reasonable time as specified by the Harbour Master, the wreck will be removed or destroyed by the Marine Department of the Customs, at the owner's expense, if claimed by the Customs.

21.- Pontoons and/or barges are to be moored in the positions assigned them by the Harbour Master. Their moorings will not be allowed to interfere with the free passage of vessels

9.

vessels proceeding to or from other pontoons or barges, or in any way impede the fairway of the river at any stage of the water. Anchors inshore must be buried sufficiently deep not to endanger cargo-boats, native craft or launches. Neither pontoons or barges nor steamers lying alongside thereof are allowed to make lines fast to the Bund in such a manner as to cause obstruction to craft plying inside.

Miscellaneous.

22.- Vessels are required to conform to the "Special Navigation Regulations" issued by the River Authorities, within Harbour Limits.

23.- Vessels under way within the Harbour are to proceed at no greater speed than is necessary to keep the vessel under control.

24.- The blowing of steam whistles or sirens, except for the purpose of signalling in accordance with the "Special Navigation Regulations", referred to in Article 22, or for the purpose of warning vessels of danger, is strictly forbidden.

25.-

10.

25.- All vessels shall keep on board a sufficient number of hands to clear and pay out chain. The hawse must always be kept clear.

26.- No vessels, except men of war, may use swinging booms. Swinging booms should be rigged in from sunset to sunrise.

27.- No merchant vessel shall fire cannon or small arms within the Harbour.

28.- Lighters and other boats are not to be made fast to vessels in such a manner or in such numbers as to interfere with the free passage of other boats or vessels through the Harbour.

29.- Sampans with runners are prohibited from boarding vessels until the Customs Boarding Officer has left the vessel or otherwise given permission for such craft to come alongside. Masters of vessels should assist to their utmost the Harbour Authorities in having this rule observed.

30.- In case of fire occurring on board a vessel in port, the fire bell must be rung immediately by that vessel, and by those above and below her, and the signal N.H. International

11.

International Code ("Fire: want immediate assistance"), hoisted by the burning vessel, if possible, and by those above and below her during the day, or the anchor light lowered and hoisted continually during the night. Notice should immediately be given to the Harbour Master.

31.- To provide for the safety of navigation on the Amur River, all vessels are to abide by the Special Regulations issued by the River Authorities.

32.- Any person infringing these Regulations may be prosecuted before his national Authority; and any vessel involved in such infringement shall be liable to have its entrance, working, and clearance stopped by the Customs until such infringement shall cease.

Notice

1.- Masters of vessels or Pilots

12.

Pilots are requested to report
to the Harbour Master any abnormal
shoal water they may have
discovered, also any vessel
that may be aground and
obstructing a channel, and if
any aid to navigation is in
distress or out of position.

2.- At the Harbour Master's
Office may be seen all local
Harbour Notifications and
Notices issued by the River
Authorities.

呈海关总税务司署 <u>1970</u> 号文   哈尔滨关 1919 年 8 月 15 日

尊敬的海关总税务司（北京）：

1. 根据海关总税务司署 6 月 7 日电报（为回复哈尔滨关 6 月 3 日信函）：

"应令巡工司贾登（H. G. Garden）先生与瑷珲分关代理税务司及道尹商议后着手处理瑷珲分关 / 大黑河的港口管理工作，并依据通商口岸之传统及惯例拟订适用于当地的临时港口界限及理船章程。"

兹附上大黑河口岸《临时理船章程》草案。瑷珲分关代理税务司呈送此章程草案时，于其呈文中指出，此章程乃参照巡工司贾登先生所得之江汉九江两关章程抄件所拟，起草时已尽量遵循海关总税务司署通令第 2060 号及第 2124 号所载之章程整套标准样本，改动之处皆因当地情形实有此必要，并称已将此草案发与大黑河道尹。

章程俄文译本已在翻译当中，一经完成，将立即呈交。但以当前情况来看，还需一段时日。

2. 另借此机会汇报，哈尔滨关尚无《理船章程》。

3. 此呈抄件及附件已发送至巡工司。

您忠诚的仆人

（签名）柯必达（P. J. Grevedon）

哈尔滨关税务司

关于哈尔滨关致海关总税务司署第 1970 号呈的意见

大黑河口岸《临时理船章程》第二十四条前两行应为：

"鸣放汽笛或其他声响信号……"

本条第五行参照之款系第二十二条还是第二十三条，并不明确，实际应为第二十二条。

港口测量如已完成，港口平面插图应与章程一并印行。

哈尔滨口岸对《理船章程》之需要十分迫切，建议草拟一份。唯该口岸情形颇为特殊，起草过程必将困难重重，有些问题甚至难寻应对之策。

（签字）额得志（T. J. Eldridge）

巡工司

江海关巡工事务局

1919 年 8 月 22 日

该抄件内容真实有效，特此证明。

录事： 周骊二等帮办前班

哈尔滨关致海关总税务司署第 1970 号呈附件

大黑河口岸《临时理船章程》

兹公布下述章程,希有关各方一体知照遵行。其中各条,业经有关当局同意照准。此布。

哈尔滨关税务司

一、本章程中"船舶"一词系指洋式船舶而言。章程中有关华式船只之规定仅以共与洋式船舶有关之作业为限。其他方面有关华式船只之管理,见各专项公告。

锚地

二、停泊界限上至西山头,下至公园后身。

洋式船舶锚地:

(一)除(二)款规定中之船舶另有专门停泊地点之外,余者皆应停泊于上述界限之间。

(二)凡各种船只装有煤油爆裂物料及归《防疫章程》所规定者,皆应停泊在本港口上流停泊界限以外。

三、凡船只停泊事宜均须听由理船厅指示,所有停泊的船只除已领有海关准放行之红单者可以任便开行外,其余未经领有特别准单各船只,均不得擅自移泊。

凡船只停泊时,不准只下一锚。

四、凡有固定泊位之船只,除照本章程第六、十三和十六之规定外,准其不必停驶,径直进入泊位。

五、凡船只欲停泊或欲移泊,须由船主或大副或引水员或轮船经理人报告海关,候其指示一切。

军火

六、凡船只载有爆裂之物或制造爆裂物之材料或开花炮弹或超过一百磅之火药或超过五万粒之枪弹或各式子弹内所装之火药总数超过一百磅之额者,均须遵照本章程第二条(二)款所载之地点停泊,并于前桅上悬挂红旗一面;卸载时亦应遵照海关指令办理。

凡船只欲在本港口内装载以上各项爆裂之物,亦须遵照上条办理。

凡船只装载小枪子弹(small-arm cartridges)者,如将该枪弹装入装载军火合适之货仓,其舱内应装有活水门机关,可由舱面灌水入内,以备不时之需,则其船装载此项小枪子弹时,不在上项取缔的办法之列,亦不限定数目。

七、凡军舰及官船等,可在本章程第二条(一)款内所列泊船地点装载爆裂物或将爆裂物搬运别船,只须该船官员指挥本船水手装载搬运之。

八、凡船只搬运爆裂物、武器或弹药,必须由货主现行以书面形式报告理船厅,领取特别执照,并须于报告内将欲用船只注册之号数声明。

九、除有固定甲板或耐用苫盖物之驳船或他项船艇外,任何驳船或船艇均不得收载本章程第六条所载各物,一旦收载物品时,必须载于甲板下或固定之封密处所。

十、无论何式船只,除军舰外,凡装载前项爆裂等物在本港口内行驶者,须备红旗一面,其旗长至少须在六尺,宽至少须在四尺,悬挂前桅之顶或最易瞭望之处; 如其船并无桅杆,亦应将红旗设法悬高,最低亦须距该船面或舱房顶最高处一丈二尺。

十一、凡未经海关及本埠地方官斟酌许可,不准将爆裂物品囤积在本港口沿岸一带。

十二、凡驳船或他种船只靠近装有爆裂物料之船,或其船上装载有此等爆炸物料者,均不准吸烟,不准生火煮饭或出于其他目的点火。

矿物油

十三、凡装载煤油或最易燃烧物品之船只进入本港口时,须在本章程第二条(二)款所指定地点抛锚。在此项货物未经卸载之前,该船不得移动。所有欲装此货物各船,只准在上列准卸此种货物之地点装载。事毕,即由该处直接驶出本港口。在本章程第二条(一)款所言停泊界限内抛锚的船只装卸煤油,均不准超过五十箱。

十四、凡驳船或他种船只驶过装载有石脑油、石油醚或其他易燃烧物品之船只,或本船上装载有此种最易燃烧等物者,均不准吸烟,不准生火煮饭或出于其他目的点火。

十五、未经海关关员及本埠地方官许可,不准将石脑油、石油醚或其他易燃烧物品囤积在本港口沿岸一带。

传染疫病

十六、凡船内有传染疾病或疑似传染疾病者,或船内停有死于传染疾病或疑似传染疾病之尸身者,该船必须于接近港口时,系挂有疫旗号,应在本章程第二条(乙)款内所定抛锚地点停泊。如未有卫生员验疫之执照,不准将旗放下。

且未经领有此项执照之前,如未领理船厅或口岸卫生员特许之执据,无论何人,在船上者不准下船,在船下者不准上船。

凡来自宣布有传染疾病口岸的船只,概须遵照海关关员指示。

河港管理

十七、未经理船厅批准,不准兴筑各式码头或驳岸,或设置浮码头、废船浮标,以及填筑江岸淤滩或兴修别项一切河岸之工程。如有以上各事,须先由本埠地方官签准。

十八、凡浮标概归理船厅管理。如其浮标所设地位有碍船只行驶,或占用驳船地位,理船厅可令该标主将浮标移开。若标主不遵行命令或怠忽职责,理船厅可直接代其移开,一切费用则仍归该标主人照付。

十九、凡船只压载重物、煤木炭灰、废料、垃圾等物,以及无论是否由疏浚而来之泥土,均不准抛弃江岸之上,夏日不准抛弃江中,冬日不准抛弃冰上。凡船只如欲抛弃煤木炭灰及垃圾等物,须抛弃在本港口界外。

在本港口界限内沿江马路一带,需整理清洁,不准储存一切妨碍物,如灰土及建筑材料,以便轮船上下货物。未经海关特许,商人之货物不准堆积江岸。

二十、凡船只在本港口内撞沉,有碍行驶之水道者,如该船东不遵理船厅斟酌情理所定之期限将该沉船动工移置,海关海政局即可代为移置或摧毁,一切费用仍归船东照缴。

二十一、凡设置浮码头或驳船等,均须在理船厅指定之处停泊,该船锚链不准与别家来往之轮船等船有所阻碍。无论江水涨落,均不得与水道有所妨碍。其傍岸之锚必须深埋泥内,以免损坏来往货船、民船或小轮。其浮码头或驳船或靠近浮码头之轮船及驳船,将锚链系紧于江岸时,不准有碍浮码头内来往之船只。

杂项规定

二十二、凡在本港口界限内来往之船只,均须遵照航路厅所订之《行驶章程》。

二十三、凡在本港口内来往之船只,均不准快速行驶,其行驶速率应以能够控制船身前行为宜,以防对他船造成危险。

二十四、凡船只在本港口内停泊或行驶时,除遵照本章程第二十二条提及之《行驶章程》所规定的应鸣放汽笛,以及为警示他船有危险而鸣放汽笛之情形外,均不准擅行放用。

二十五、凡船只均需配备足用之水手,以整理和收放锚链。其左右锚链不得互搭,也不得缠绕。

二十六、凡船只除军舰外,均不准于船边支用横杆。所有军舰支出之横杆,应自日落起至日出止概行收进。

二十七、凡商船在本港口内鸣炮放枪概行禁止。

二十八、凡驳船及其他小船靠拢大船,速度不得太快,数量不得太多,不得妨碍港口内其他船只的行驶。

二十九、凡接客之舢板,须待海关检查员离船后,始准登轮接客;如因他故,经海关检查员的特许,亦可登轮接客。各船主亦应当全力协助港口实行此项规则。

三十、凡船只在本港口内如遇火灾,必须立即鸣钟示警,在日间须悬各国通语旗中标记 N.H. 字样的信号旗(即"有船失火,速来救援"之意),其上下停泊之船,亦须同时鸣钟悬旗;如遇夜间,则将信号灯升起降下,不得稍有间断,并应立即呈报理船厅。

三十一、为航行安全起见,凡船只来往黑龙江上者,均须遵照航路厅所拟之《行驶章程》。

三十二、凡人员如违以上章程,可向其本国官吏控告。凡违反章程之船只,海关可以不准其报关装卸货物和结关。待该船遵守此章程后,始准照行。

布　告

一、凡船只发现礁石沙滩情况异常、船只搁浅阻碍航路或者航路标志受损或移位,均应由该船船主或引水员报知理船厅。

二、凡航路厅颁布之有关于本港口江面之各种警船布告,均存于本港口理船厅处,方便随时查阅。

6. 1920 年《黑龙江行船章程》

No. 2248

Harbin.   No. 78,057

Inspectorate General of Customs,

Peking, 27th April, 1920.

Sir,

    With reference to my despatch No.2189/76,660 and previous correspondence on the subject of:

    Amur River Navigation:

I append, for your information and guidance, copy of Shui-wu Ch'u despatch No. 523, from which you will see that, in view of the political changes that have since taken place in Siberia rendering it out of the question to open formal negotiations with the representatives of the Russian Government, it has been decided to conclude a temporary arrangement for the Navigation of the Amur by Chinese vessels by means of local negotiations between the Heilungchiang Tuchün and the de facto Russian authorities of the Amur Province in Siberia.

    I have accordingly to request you to render all possible assistance to the Tuchün in effecting these local arrangements.

            I am, etc.,

            (Sgd) F. A. Aglen,

            Inspector General.

The Commissioner of Customs,

      HARBIN.

税務處令

准外交部洛開案查商訂黑龍江行船章程一事准吉林省長督軍會咨
以據報俄員因政局關係一時不能與會通以變通以促進行之處請核
復等情正核辦間准黑龍江督軍來電主張以地方名義與阿省開
議本部以開江在即航事早定於我亦屬有利當經電照准轉飭達
辦理在案除分行外應抄送本部與黑龍江督軍往來各電咨達照
洽等因查開江在即航章以早定為宜現既主張以地方名義與阿省開議
自應照辦准咨前因相應抄錄原電令行總稅務司查照轉飭濱江關稅務
司遵照接洽可也此令附抄件　中華民國九年四月二十二日

第五二三號

照錄外交部收黑龍江督軍來電　九年四月七日

外交部交通部鑒統密據黑河巴司令張道尹冬電稱航行事原派濱江
關道及壽增在哈會議現俱俄政變遷哈埠舊黨恐難代表而新黨我又
難承認推想在哈開議甚難如能照原議在哈商訂固佳否則俄航權機關均
在阿省可與外部所擬大綱四條以地方協訂名義與阿省開議既與事寔
便利並為將來正式條約張本且名為地方協訂亦不為承認新黨也開江
在即請速催詢電示等情當經電據濱江董道尹復稱航行事俄領以政
局關係須呈請俄使示導為詞固之開議無期巴司令張道尹所稱擬大
綱以地方協訂名義與阿省開議似屬直接周妥等語除電巴司令張道尹
先如所擬預備仍候部示外請速查核電復以便飭遵孫烈臣魚印

照錄外交部致黑龍江督軍電九年四月十日

魚電悉此事俄新黨曾向駐黑河穡總領事提議本部以新黨未經我承

認仍令照原議辦理現在尊意既贊成速辦巴司令張道尹暨董道尹

均主張一致開江在即航章早定於我亦屬有利所擬以地方協訂名義與

彼開議事屬可行應請飭知照辦外交部

隨 第 五 二 三 號

致哈尔滨关第 <u>2248/78057</u> 号令　　　　海关总税务司署（北京）1920 年 4 月 27 日

尊敬的哈尔滨关税务司：

　　根据海关总税务司署第 2189/76660 号令及此前函文：

　　"为黑龙江航务事。"

　　兹附上税务处第 523 号令抄件，以供参考。内称鉴于俄政府代表因西伯利亚政局关系一时不能参与正式协商会议，故决定由黑龙江督军与西伯利亚阿穆尔省俄当局以地方名义商定中国船只于黑龙江上的行船暂行办法。

　　请尽力协助督军实现地方协议签订之事。

您忠诚的仆人

（签字）安格联（F. A. Aglen）

总税务司

7. 1921 年《哈尔滨关税务司与中国银行哈尔滨分行经理关于海关税款转代征协议》

15 Commrs.   Inspectorate General of Customs,

gun No. 87,200   PEKING, 17th December, 1921.

SIR,

I am directed by the Inspector General to acknowledge receipt of your Despatch No. 12 :

reporting that you had received a request from the newly opened Branch of the Eastern Provincial Bank that the notes of this Bank which were about to be circulated in the local market might be accepted by the Customs in payment of duties, and that you had replied to this request, in terms identical with those of the Harbin Commissioner's reply to a similar request which he had received, to the effect that such acceptance of the notes of the Eastern Provincial Bank must be a matter of private arrangement between that Bank and the Bank of China with which Bank the Customs had an official Agreement for the collection of duties;

and, in reply, to say that your action as reported is approved. The Harbin Customs Agreement with the Bank of China still covers the Aigun Customs

Revenue

The Commissioner of Customs,

A I G U N.

Revenue which the Bank of China undertakes, under the Agreement, to remit direct to Shanghai in dollars at par, charging a remittance fee of 6 %. The Bank of China therefore can only accept in payment of duties other currencies than those mentioned in the Agreement at its own risk.

In view of the fact that the separation of the Aigun Office from the Harbin Office will become complete in January next, you should take steps to enter into a separate Agreement for the collection and remittance of your Revenue either with the local branch of the Bank of China, if this is of sufficient standing, or, otherwise, with the Harbin Office of that Bank. The Agreement should be drawn up on the lines of the Harbin Customs Agreement, a copy of which is appended for your guidance, and a copy of the proposed Agreement should be sent to the Inspectorate

for

for approval before signature.

       I am,

          Sir,

    Your obedient Servant,

                    Chief Secretary.

APPENDIX

Agreement between the Harbin Commissioner of Customs and the Manager of the Harbin Branch of the Bank of China for the collection of Customs Revenue.

Agreement made this 29th day of March in the year one thousand nine hundred and twenty-one to take effect from the 1st day of April in the year one thousand nine hundred and twenty-one between the Harbin Commissioner of Customs R. C. L. d'Anjou (hereafter called the Commissioner), acting under the authority and on behalf of the Inspector General of Customs, on the one part, and the Agent of the Branch Office of the Bank of China at Harbin (hereafter referred to as the Bank), acting under the authority and on behalf of the Bank of China, on the other part.

1. The Bank undertakes to receive the Customs revenue as directed by the Commissioner and admits full responsibility for the funds collected so long as they are lodged in the Bank.

2. The Bank shall lodge all Customs revenues in accounts to be opened in the name of Commissioner as

合同

此合同於中華民國十年三月二十九日立定即於十年四月一日實行哈爾濱關稅務司章書五稅務司

授以代其辦理之精者中國銀行哈爾濱分行總理銀文涯

條款四俚銀行由中國銀行授以代其辦理之精者

二銀行由中國銀行授以代其辦理之精者

雙方議定條款如左

一銀行先照稅務司指定辦法辦理收稅其收存之稅於法立具稅務司名下之帳簿稅務司有

二銀行所收各稅款須照稅務司指定辦法辦稅其收存之稅於法立具稅務司名下之帳簿稅務司有

銀行時銀行擔有完全之責成

as may be directed by him, and the Commissioner has authority from the Inspector General to draw on these accounts.

3. The Bank shall remit the collection at such times and in such manner as may be directed by the Commissioner. All remittances from Harbin to Shanghai shall be in dollars at par. The Bank is not to receive any remittance fee.

For local remittances from Out-stations to Harbin or vice versa the Bank will be entitled to the following remittance fees:
(a) Sansing ......4‰
(b) Lahasusu......5‰
(c) Aigun ....6‰
(d) Manchouli....3.50‰
(e) Suifenho.....3.50‰
For direct remittance from Aigun to Shanghai 6‰ remittance fee will be due to the Bank.

Interest on Revenue Collection Balances at the rate of 2½ per mille and per month will be paid by the Bank.

4

4. The Bank shall provide offices for the receipts of duties at a convenient distance from the Custom House. But under present circumstances in order to facilitate the collection of revenue, all the Bank's offices for the collection of Customs revenue shall be established in the Custom House. The Bank's Staff there employed shall make their own arrangements as regards quarters. The revenue moneys may be kept in the Custom House, but the Customs will not be responsible for their safe custody in any case. Branch offices for receipt of duty and Service disbursements are to be opened at Harbin, Taheiho, Manchouli, Suifenho, Sansing and Lahasusu and at Sub-Offices of Harbin and Taheiho and Sansing where required.

5. The Bank undertakes to provide a collecting staff of such capacity and in such numbers as will ensure, in the opinion

of

總稅務司核以隨時由各該帳內提取款項之權

三銀行所存說款其匯解之期及手續均聽稅務司指令辦理其由哈爾濱滬之款以到大津計算無折無扣銀行免取收匯費至各關匯兌及由哈濱往各分關之款銀行應收匯費如左

甲 三姓四厘
乙 拉蘇蘇五厘
丙 璦琿六厘
丁 滿洲里三厘五毫
戊 綏芬河三厘五毫

由璦琿匯滬匯費係六厘

其存款利息定為月息二厘五毫

四銀行辦理收稅事宜須於海關近便之地設備有辦公處蓋為便利收稅起見凡收稅辦公處可以附設於關內而住室由行員自擇款項可存關內惟過嘉外之數海關不負責任其應設收稅辦公處之處如哈爾濱璦琿滿洲里綏芬河三姓拉哈蘇蘇等分關八處其所設分關於綏芬三姓璦琿始蘇蘇等分關八處

五銀行允辦理收稅貨其人員須有其熟諳辦稅兩有技能

of the Commissioner, the prompt transaction of business with the merchants in order to avoid errors and delay.

6. The Bank undertakes to record the collection under different headings as fixed by the Commissioner, and to submit daily - and/or other periodical - statements that he may wish to be supplied with.

7. The Bank undertakes to receive the duties, which are payable in Haikuan Taels, in big Silver Dollars (Pei-yang, Yuan Shih K'ai and Hongkong) or in Bank of China and/or Bank of Communications big dollar notes (new issue of the branches of the two said Banks) at their face value as long as such notes are at par with silver dollars (notes shall be issued to meet duty payers requirements). The rate for Haikuan Taels vis-a-vis Silver Dollars and/or notes issued by the Bank of China and the Bank of Communications is fixed at Hk.Tls.100.00=$156.65.

The

The Bank is responsible to the Commissioner for the actual amount of dollars collected at the above rate(i.e. in clean Silver Dollars or in Bank notes, that are redeemable at par).

8. For collection of revenue the Bank shall receive a commission of dollars 10 on every dollars 1,000 collected. River dues are excluded from revenue on which commission is chargeable. This commission is to be paid at the end of each month.

9. This agreement is provisional and subject to modification if necessary after trial on condition that before any changes are made they must first be submitted to the Inspector General and Head Office of the Bank,Peking, by Commissioner and Bank, Harbin, respectively, and the modifications approved in Peking before they come into force. In the event of the Bank desiring to cancel this agreement, one month's notice must be given to the Commissioner. Similarly, the Commissioner will give

one

one month's notice of his desire to terminate this agreement. The Commissioner, however, reserves full right at any time to make whatever special arrangements for the receipt of duties the safety of the revenue may demand, and in lieu of one month's notice, to terminate this agreement the Bank shall be entitled to receive remuneration in the terms of Article 8 to the end of the month following the date on which it ceased to receive the duty collection.

10. The Bank undertakes to open such Service Accounts at the Head Office and at the sub-offices as the Commissioner may direct. It is optional to the Commissioner whether these accounts be kept in Haikuan Taels or Dollar currencies, but the relation between the two currencies will be the same as the collection rate(Hk.Tls.100.00 = $156.65). These accounts will be fed by transfer from revenue accounts and will have the same treatment as regards interest as revenue accounts.

In

有立即撤銷合同之權如照此辦理

該銀行仍須自截止代收稅項之日

起展至次月底止照第八條所載辦

法得其酬勞之費

十 銀行允照稅務司指定辦法在哈爾濱總關及

各分關立其海關名下各項經費帳簿此項帳

得內應分關平銀帳簿即照微稅行平銀關平關

大洋銀關照領上項帳簿內各款係由稅款項下

撥過其月息仍按稅款辦法辦理

In witness whereof the Parties to this Agreement have hereunto set their hands and seals the day and the year first above written, in triplicate, one copy being retained by each of the signatories as under and one copy being forwarded to the Inspector General of Customs at Peking.

(Signed) R. C. L. d'Anjou,
　　　　　　Commissioner of Customs.

(Customs Seal)

Manager of Harbin Branch of
the Bank of China.

(Signed) 張文澍 (Seal)

True copy :

A. H. Forbes.

Acting Assistant Secretary.

致瑷珲关第 <u>15/87200</u> 号令　　　　海关总税务司署（北京）1921 年 12 月 17 日

尊敬的瑷珲关税务司：

　　第 12 号呈收悉：

　　　　"致函汇报：瑷珲关收到东省银行新开分行的请求，询问海关是否有可能接受该行拟在本地市场流通的纸币作为关税支付货币。并且哈尔滨关税务司也收到类似请求，瑷珲关对该请求的回复与哈尔滨关税务司相似，回函大意是说海关与中国银行已签订关于税款代征方面的正式协议，能否接受东省银行纸币作为征纳货币取决于该行与中国银行的私下协定。"

奉总税务司命令，现批复如下：兹告知，对汇报中采取的行动予以批准。哈尔滨关与中国银行签订的协议也涵盖瑷珲关税收，根据协议规定，中国银行负责将其税款按面值直接汇寄至上海，并收取 6‰ 汇款手续费。因此，除协议中提到的征纳货币外，中国银行倘若接受其他货币需自担风险。

　　鉴于哈尔滨关下级机关瑷珲关的独立进程将于次年一月完成，贵署应采取行动，与当地的中国银行分行单独签订瑷珲关税款代征与汇寄协议，倘若该分行不能长期维持经营，可与该行哈尔滨办事处签订相关协议。该协议的订立应以哈尔滨关协议为基础，随函附上该协议副本，供您参照执行。此外，拟定协议应先给海关总税务司发送一份副本进行审核，批准后方可签字。

您忠诚的仆人

包罗（C. A. Bowra）

总务科税务司

附件

哈尔滨关税务司与中国银行哈尔滨分行经理关于海关税款代征的协议

本协议于 1921 年 3 月 29 日由总税务司授权代表哈尔滨关税务司覃书（R. C. L. d'Anjou）（以下简称为"税务司"）与中国银行授权代表中国银行哈尔滨分行经理张文湛（以下简称为"银行"）签订。协议于 1921 年 4 月 1 日生效。

一、银行按照税务司指定办法代征关税，并对已存入银行的代征税款负全部责任。

二、银行应按照税务司指定办法将全部税款存入税务司名下账户，税务司有总税务司授予其随时从该账户提取款项的权限。

三、银行应按照税务司命令在指定期限以指定方式汇寄税款。由哈尔滨至上海的所有汇款按面值（现大洋）计算。银行不得收取汇费。

凡由各分关汇寄至哈尔滨关及由哈尔滨关汇寄至各分关的税款，银行应收的汇费如下：

1. 三姓…………4‰

2. 拉哈苏苏……5‰

3. 瑷珲…………6‰

4. 满洲里………3.5‰

5. 绥芬河………3.5‰

由瑷珲直接汇寄至上海的汇费为 6‰。

银行税款余额利息定为月息 2.5‰。

四、银行应在税关近便之地设立收税办事处。兹为便利收款起见，凡收税办事处都应设在税关内。办事处银行职员的住宿自行安排。所收税款可在税关内保存，但若发生意外，税关对其安全概不负责。必要时，银行应在哈尔滨关、大黑河关、满洲里关、绥芬河关、三姓关和拉哈苏苏关以及在哈尔滨关、大黑河关和三姓关的分关设立税款代收和公署费用支领的分支机构。

五、银行需派出足够的合格代征税办理人员，依税务司之见，他们应能确保快速处理商贾业务，避免出错和延误。

六、银行需按照税务司确定的名目将经手税款分别注明，并且依照税务司之意每日或按期出具指定报表送交给税务司处进行核对。

七、海关所征各项税款原按海关两核计，现在银行代征税款也可以收取大洋（即银圆，如北洋袁世凯像银圆及香港银圆）或与银圆等值的中国银行和交通银行大洋票（即哈尔滨中交两行新发行的纸币，用以满足纳税人缴税需求）。海关两与银圆/大洋票的固定兑换比率为：100 海关两折合大洋票 156.65 元。银行向税务司交付的代征税款为按上述汇率折算后的实收总额（即按纯银圆或等值兑换的两行大洋票交付）。

八、鉴于银行负责代征税款，除江捐外，应由海关给予银行佣金，即照所收数额每 1000 银圆提 10 银圆。佣金需在每月月底全数照付。

九、本协议作为暂行办法，如有修改必要，须先将修改内容分别经税务司转呈总税务司、经哈尔滨分行转呈中国银行北京总行，双方核准修改后方可生效。银行如欲撤销协议，须提前一个月通知税务司，同样税务司如欲撤销协议，须提前一个月通知银行。但是，为税款安全起见，税务司随时有对税款做出任何特别安排以及立即撤销协议的权利，该银行有权自停止代征税款之日起至次月底按照第八条规定办法收取代征佣金。

十、银行按照税务司指定办法在总行及哈尔滨分行开立相关海关账户。税务司可选择海关两账户或大洋票账户，但这两种货币的兑换比率仍与代征时的兑换比率相同（即 100 海关两 = 大洋票 156.65 元）。将税收账户内的资金通过转账转入这些账户，其月息仍按税收账户办法办理。

本协议一式三份，双方需在本协议所载日期签字盖章，各执一份，第三份转发北京海关总税务司署留存，特此证明。

（签字）覃书

哈尔滨关税务司（海关签章）

中国银行哈尔滨分行经理

（签字）张文湛（签章）

8. 1921 年《瑷珲关署理税务司与中国银行大黑河支行行长为收税事所签合同》

Aigun/Taheiho 19th December, 1921.

Sir,

Following upon your instructions for the financial separation of the Aigun Customs from the Harbin Customs from 1st January, 1922, I have the honour to submit an Agreement for the collection, custody and remittance of Revenue Moneys and for the keeping of Service Moneys, drafted in consultation with the Bank of China, the most reliable of the local Chinese Banks.

The Agreement follows closely on the lines of the one signed on 29th March 1921 between the Commissioner of the Harbin Customs and the Bank of China, with the following modifications :

1. The percentage paid to the Bank for collecting the Revenue is increased from 1 per cent to two per cent; the difference is explained by the comparatively

Inspector General of Customs,

PEKING.

comparatively smaller collection of this Office.

2. The remittance fee is provisionally fixed at twelve per mille on Shanghai, and 6 per mille on Harbin, while the Agreement with the Harbin Customs provided for remittances at par from Harbin, and for a fee of 6 per thousand for remittances from Aigun.

As far as the first point is concerned, it would be probably cheaper for the Customs to hire shroffs on their own account. Three shroffs (two for Taheiho, one for Aigun) would cost little over 200 dollars a month, while 2 % of the collection for this year (some Hk. Tls. 110,000, not including Famine Surtax which is collected free of charge) would amount to Hk. Tls. 2,200. On the other hand the Bank is responsible for the shroffs and the moneys; we are given a more favourable rate of interest on current accounts than other depositors (5 % against 2 %), and exceptionally favourable remittance rates.

As for the second point, you know that this is a very bad time for negotiating a fixed rate of remittance, and I think that it is an advantage to have one, although subject to revision

at

at 15 days' notice, and the rate granted the Customs is remarkably low, when compared with the rate of 5 %, applied to the general public and merchants. I hope, besides, that conditions will improve shortly, when I shall do my best to obtain cheaper rates. — I am of opinion that for the present it would be difficult to get more favourable terms from any Bank, considering the state of the markets, the distance from Shanghai and the defective and somewhat dangerous communications, and the Bank of China is the best suited for the Customs : I therefore recommend that this Agreement be approved.

The drafting of this Contract has been much delayed because the Acting Manager of the local Branch of the Bank was unwilling to commit himself during the absence of Mr. Ma, Manager "in partibus", who, for the last two months, has announced several times his intention to come, and has never attempted the "crossing" from Tsitsihar to Taheiho for fear of the Hunghutze. Only five days ago he definitely gave up the attempt, and went to Liaoyang, when I hastily negotiated with the Acting Manager, who had

to

to wire to Changchun for instructions. — In view of the unavoidable delay in submitting the draft for approval, and considering the convenience of starting the new Agreement from January next, I would be glad to receive your approval by telegram.

It was my intention to insert a clause re the eventual opening up a new stations, but the Bank did not agree, as the amount of collection there could not even be guessed now. However, the Manager promised that he would provide suitable Shroffs, whenever required, the Customs paying their salary and providing accomodation.

I have the honour to be,

Sir,

Your obedient servant,

Acting Commissioner.

Agreement between the Aigun Acting Commissioner of
Customs and the Manager of the Taheiho Sub-branch
of the Bank of China for the collection of
Customs Revenue.

Agreement made this   day
of   in the year one
thousand nine hundred and twenty-
to take effect from the 1st day
of January in the year one
thousand nine hundred and twenty-
two between the Aigun Acting
Commissioner of Customs G. Boezi
(hereafter called the Commissioner),
acting under the authority and on
behalf of the Inspector General of
Customs, on the one part, and the
Manager of the Sub-branch of the
Bank of China at Taheiho (hereafter
referred to as the Bank), acting
under the authority and on behalf
of the Bank of China, on the other
part.

1. The Bank undertakes to
receive the Customs revenue as
directed by the Commissioner and
admits full responsibility for the
funds collected so long as they
are lodged in the Bank.

2. The Bank shall lodge all
Customs revenues in accounts to be
opened in the name of Commissioner
as

ge may be directed by him, and the
commissioner has authority from the
Inspector General to draw on these
accounts.

3. The Bank shall remit the collection at such times and in such
manner as may be directed by the
Commissioner. All remittances from
Aigun-Taheiho to Shanghai shall be in
Dollars (the remittance fee shall be
1½ per mille). This rate is, however,
subject to change on fifteen days'
notice being given by either party.

In case money is to be remitted
to Harbin, the remittance fee shall
be 8 per mille.

Interest on Revenue Collection
Balances at the rate of 2½ per mille
and per month will be paid by the
Bank.

4. The Bank shall provide
offices for the receipt of duties at
a convenient distance from the Custom
House. But under present circumstances in order to facilitate the
collection of revenue, all the Bank's
offices for the collection of Customs
revenue shall be established in
the Custom House. The Bank's
staff there employed shall make
their

合同

此合同於中華民國　年　月　日立定即於十一年一
月一日實行愛琿關署稅務司包安濟六條款內但由黑
稅務司授以代其辦理之權者中國銀行黑河支行行
長　雙方議定條款如左

除款內但中國銀行授以代其辦理之權
一銀行允照稅務司指定辦法辦理收
稅其收存之稅款在銀行時銀行機
司名下之帳簿稅務司有
負完全之責任

二銀行所收各稅款須由稅
務司指定辦法具稅
務司指定辦

三銀行所存稅款其滙解之期及手續均
由稅務司指令辦理其與愛琿天黑
河滙滬之稅款以現大洋計算滙費每千
元十三滬費行市如有更改須事前聲明
由愛琿火車河滙至哈爾濱每千元六元
至存款利息定為月息二厘五毫

總稅務司　授以隨時
由各該帳　內提取款
項之權

四銀行辦理收稅事宜須於海關
近便之地點備有辦公處為
便利收款起見凡收稅辦公處
可以附於關內而住室由行員
自擇款項可存關內惟遇一意外

their own arrangements as regards quarters. The revenue moneys may be kept in the Custom House, but the Customs will not be responsible for their safe custody in any case. Branch offices for receipt of duty and service disbursements are to be opened at Aigun and Paheiho.

5. The Bank undertakes to provide a collecting staff of such capacity and in such numbers as will ensure, in the opinion of the Commissioner, the prompt transaction of business with the merchants in order to avoid errors and delay.

6. The Bank undertakes to record the collection under different headings as fixed by the Commissioner, and to submit daily - and/or other periodical - statements that he may wish to be supplied with.

7. The Bank undertakes to receive the duties, which are payable in Haikwan Taels, in big Silver Dollars (Pei-yang, Yuan Shih

shih K'ai and Hongkong) or in Bank of China and/or Bank of Communications big dollar notes (new issue of the branches of the two said Banks) at their face value as long as such notes are at par with silver dollars (notes shall be issued to meet ready payers' requirements). The rate for Haikwan Taels vis-a-vis silver Dollars and/or notes issued by the Bank of China and the Bank of Communications is fixed at Hk. Tls. 100.00 = $156.33. The Bank is responsible to the Commissioner for the actual amount of dollars collected at the above rate (i.e. in clean Silver Dollars or in Bank notes, that are redeemable at par).

8. For collection of revenue the Bank shall receive a commission of dollars 16 on every dollars 1,000 collected. This commission is to be paid at the end of each month.

9. This agreement is provisional and subject to modification if necessary after trial on condition that before any changes are made they must

之璦海關不負責
任其應設收稅辦
公處之處如愛理
與大黑河兩處

五銀行允辦理收稅
人員其人數才識須足
資接待客商敏提能
副稅務司之意者俾免
監誤貽延等弊

六銀行允按驗稅務司
所定名目將經收稅
款分別註明逐日並
按期像臨稅務司之
意開具清冊送由
稅務司核對

七按關所徵各
項稅款本按
閻平銀計
數銀行允即
按大洋銀行允現

如北洋袁世凱像及站人三種或兌現銀圓之中交國幣
新發行之（允許納現與現大洋同抵收）大洋票按折算其折算之定數
即像按閻平銀一百兩折合大洋鈔元現或中交國幣
新發行之大洋票一百五十六元六角五分所有徵收之款銀行允
近按徵稅行市一每閻平一百兩核大洋鈔現
一百五十六元六角五分交付現大洋鈔現銀之

八銀行代收稅項
九此合同係
者行試辦如
有修改之必
吳將項隨所
修改經稅務
司呈日繳稅

應向海關驗手斟
若費即與所收稅
款每大洋一千元提
給二千元係每月
底令敷照付

中交兩行
閻鈔券
哈爾濱

must first be submitted to the
Inspector General and Post Office of
the Bank, Aigun, by Commissioner, Aigun,
and Bank, Heiho, respectively, and
the modifications approved in Peking
before they come into force. In the
event of the Bank desiring to cancel
this agreement, one month's notice
must be given to the Commissioner.
Similarly, the Commissioner will give
one month's notice of his desire to
terminate this agreement. The Commissioner, however, reserves full right
at any time to make whatever
arrangements for the receipt of
duties the safety of the revenue
may demand, and in lieu of one
month's notice, to terminate this
agreement the Bank shall be entitled
to receive remuneration in the terms
of Article 8 to the end of the
month following the date on which it
ceased to receive the duty collection.

10. The Bank undertakes to open
such Service Accounts at Aigun/Taheiho
as the Commissioner may direct. It
is optional to the Commissioner
whether these accounts be kept in
Haikwan Taels or Dollar currencies,
but the relation between the two
currencies

currencies will be the same as
the collection rate (Hk. Tls. 100.00
= $166.66). These accounts will
be fed by transfer from revenue
accounts and will have the same
treatment as regards interest as
revenue accounts.

In witness whereof the Parties to this Agreement have
hereunto set their hands and seals the day and the year
first above written, in triplicate, one copy being retained
by each of the signatories as under and one copy being
forwarded to the Inspector General of Customs at Peking.

Acting Commissioner of Customs.

Manager of Taheiho Sub-branch
of the Bank of China.

稅司銀行辦報總行進方稅准後定期實行銀行如放將此合同撤銷須
在一個月以前達知稅務司如稅務司欲撤銷此合同赤須一個月以前達知
銀行惟若因維持稅項起見應另定徵收稅項特別辦法稅務司仍守有
立部撤銷合同之權如照此辦理該銀行仍須自截止代收稅項之日起
辰至次月辰止照第八條所載辦法得其酬勞之費

十銀行免與稅務司指定
辦法在愛琿天黑河立
其海關名下各項經費
帳簿此項帳簿內應分關平銀
帳簿鄉銀平銀稅銀洋市兩合大
洋一百五十六元大洋鄉
六角五分計算

銀帳簿第上項帳簿
內各款係由稅款
項下撥過其月息
仍按稅款辦法辦
理

呈海关总税务司署 <u>16</u> 号文　　　瑷珲关／大黑河署理税务司 1921 年 12 月 19 日

尊敬的海关总税务司（北京）：

　　按照贵署指示，瑷珲关将于 1922 年 1 月 1 日起与哈尔滨关财务分离。现呈交一份与中国银行协商后所达成之合同（关于税款之代征、保管及汇寄等事项）。

　　该合同谨照哈尔滨关于 1921 年 3 月 29 日与中国银行所签协议拟订，但有以下修改：

　　（1）支付银行之酬劳费由 1% 升至 2%；因相较于哈尔滨关，瑷珲关税款较少，故有此改动。

　　（2）汇费暂定办法：由瑷珲（大黑河）汇至上海之税款，汇费每千元十二元，汇至哈尔滨之税款，汇费每千元六元；哈尔滨关与中国银行所签协议之规定为，由哈尔滨汇至上海之税款，以面值汇兑，由瑷珲（大黑河）汇至哈尔滨之税款，汇费每千元六元。

　　就第一点而言，若由海关自行雇用管账员，似乎更为经济，毕竟三名管账员足矣（大黑河两名，瑷珲一名），每月预计仅须 200 余银圆，而向银行支付酬劳费用，即全年税收（约 110000 海关两，不含免佣金代征之附征赈捐）的 2%，一年则需 2200 海关两。不过，若由银行管账员管理税款，海关账户可享 3% 的利率，而其他储户仅享 2%，汇费方面亦可享受特殊优待。

　　至于第二点，如贵署所知，当前时机不宜协商固定汇费，目前所定汇费虽可于提前十五日彼此通知之情况下做出修改，但于海关而言，已是十分有利，与普通百姓及商人高达每百元五元之汇费相比，银行应允海关之汇费已是极低。不过，待形势转好后，本署会继续争取与之协商更低的汇费。然目前市场情况既是如此，而本地与上海又相距遥遥，交通往来又有种种艰难险阻，海关恐怕很难从其他银行获得更优惠的条款，中国银行乃最适合海关之选，遂特请批准此合同。

　　此前，中国银行大黑河支行"名义"行长马先生一直未在本地，而代理行长又一度不愿承办签署合同之事，故此合同之起草一事被耽搁良久。马先生于过去两月间，曾数次声称要自齐齐哈尔来至大黑河，但因忌惮土匪"红胡子"，并未付诸行动，并于五日前，明确表示不会过来，随后便前往辽阳。鉴于此，本署已与代理行长协商合同之事，其已向长春发送电报寻求指示。此合同若可于明年一月开始实行，可谓最为适当之安排，然于目前而言，向贵署呈交合同草本请示批准之事势必会有所延误，故望贵署以电报批示，对此不胜感激。

　　本署原计划于合同中增加有关新设分卡之条款，但银行以税收金额尚无法预料为由予以回绝,不过代理行长已允诺,会根据海关需要提供合格的管账,唯须由海关为之支付薪俸,提供食宿。

您忠诚的仆人

包安济(G. Boezi)

瑷珲关署理税务司

瑷珲关致海关总税务司署第 16 号呈附件

瑷珲关署理税务司与中国银行大黑河支行行长

为收税事所签合同

　　此合同于 1922 年 1 月 1 日实行。瑷珲关署理税务司包安济（条款内但云"税务司"）由总税务司授以代其办理之权者，中国银行大黑河支行行长（条款内但云"银行"）由中国银行授以代其办理之权者，双方协定条款如下。

　　一、银行允照税务司指定办法办理收税，其收存之税款在银行时，银行担负完全之责任。

　　二、银行所收各税款须照税务司指定办法立具税务司名下之账簿，税务司有总税务司授以随时由各该账内提取款项之权。

　　三、银行所存税款，其汇解之期及手续均听税务司指令办理；其由瑷珲（大黑河）汇沪之税款以现大洋（银圆）计算（汇费每千元十二元）；汇费行事如有更改，均于十五日以前彼此通知；由瑷珲（大黑河）汇至哈尔滨之税款，汇费每千元六元；存款利息定为月息二厘五毫。

　　四、银行办理收税事宜，须于海关近便之地照备有办公处；兹为便利收款起见，凡收税办公处，可以附于关内，而住室由行员自择；款项可存关内，唯遇意外之变，海关不负责任；其应设收税办公处之处如瑷珲与大黑河两处。

　　五、银行允办理收税人员，其人数才识须足资接待客商，敏捷能副税务司之意者，避免怠误耽延等弊。

　　六、银行允按照税务司所定名目将经收税款分别注明，逐日并按期依照税务司之意开具清册送由税务司核对。

　　七、海关所征各项税款，本按关平纹银计数，银行允即按现大洋（即银圆），如北洋、袁世凯像及站人（香港银圆）三种，或兑现银圆之中交国币（即哈尔滨及大黑河中交两行新发行之国币券——此券纳税与现大洋同样收用，且其票额须符纳税之用）。大洋票折算征收，其折算之定数（即行市）系按海关两一百两折合现大洋（即银圆）或中交国币（即哈尔滨及大黑河中交两行新发行之国币券）大洋票一百五十六元六角五分。所有征收之款，银行允通按征税行市（即每关平一百两核大洋一百五十六元六角五分）交付现大洋（即银圆或兑现之中交两行国币券）。

八、银行代收税项应由海关给予酬劳费，即照所收税数每大洋一千元提给二十元，于每月底全数照付。

九、此合同作为暂行试办，如有修改之必要时，须随时修改，经税务司呈由总税务司，银行转报总行，双方核准后，定期实行。银行如欲将此合同撤销，须在一个月以前通知税务司；如税务司欲撤销此合同，亦须一个月以前通知银行。唯若因维持税项起见，应另定征收税项特别办法，税务司仍守有立即撤销合同之权，如照此办理，该银行仍须自截止代收税项之日起展至次月底止，照第八条所载办法得其酬劳之费。

十、银行允照税务司指定办法在瑷珲（大黑河）立具海关名下各项经费账簿，此项账簿内应分海关两账簿（即按照征税行市每海关两一百两合大洋一百五十六元六角五分计算）和大洋（即银圆）账簿，上项账簿内各款系由税款项下拨过，其月息仍按税款办法办理。

双方已于合同所载之日签字盖章，以资证明。此合同一式三份，双方各执一份，第三份抄件已呈至海关总税务司署（北京）留存。

> 瑷珲关署理税务司
> 中国银行大黑河支行行长

9. 1922 年《瑷珲海关与中国银行关于税款代征办法的草拟协议》

INSPECTORATE GENERAL OF CUSTOMS,

PEKING, 2 th January, 1922.

COMMRS.

No. 87,635

Sir,

I have to acknowledge receipt of your

despatch No. 16 :

submitting, for my approval, a draft Agreement
for the collection, custody and remittance of
Revenue moneys, etc., drawn up in consultation
with the local Manager of the Bank of
China; and explaining that this draft
Agreement follows closely on the lines of
the corresponding Agreement now in force
at Harbin with certain modifications as to
(1) the commission to be paid to the Bank
for cost of collection, and (2) the question
of a fixed charge to be made by the Bank
for remitting your Collection to Shanghai;

and of your telegram of 24th December last :

reporting that the Bank of China had
withdrawn its offer of a fixed rate for
remitting funds to Shanghai but was
prepared to make such remittances at the
best market rates ruling at the time.

In reply, I have to instruct you as

follows :

With

The Commissioner of Customs,

AIGUN.

With reference to the Bank's proposal
that it should receive for the cost of
collecting your Revenue a commission of $20.00
per $1,000.00 collected, I am of opinion, as
notified to you in my telegram of 28th December
last, that such a commission is too high,
especially in view of your estimate as to what
the cost of collection would be if you hired
shroffs for the purpose on your own account.
You should therefore discuss the matter further
with the Local Manager of the Bank of China,
bearing in mind the principle that the commission
paid to the Bank should be fixed at such a
figure, or at such a rate, as will secure that
the amount actually paid to the Bank will
correspond as nearly as possible to the actual
out-of-pocket expenses which the Bank is put to
in the collection of Revenue on our behalf. The
argument which you advance in favour of accepting

the

the Bank's proposal, _viz_: that we are given a more favourable rate of interest on our Current Account than other depositors, and especially favourable rates for the remittance of our funds to Shanghai, is not a sound one; for the questions of " interest on Current Account", "remittance rates on Shanghai" and " commission for cost of collection" are separate and distinct matters which should not be confused the one with the other, or in any way made inter-dependent if it can be avoided. Further, it is to be borne in mind that it is of great advantage to the Bank to handle our collection and to have the privilege of remitting these funds to Shanghai assured to it - advantages for which, _per se_, the Bank should be ready to offer favourable rates both for interest on current account and for remittances to Shanghai.

                With

With regard to the Bank's proposal to remit your Collection to Shanghai at the best market rates ruling, I consider that it would be advisable to secure a more definite arrangement, and to adopt, if possible, a method of procedure similar in principle to that recently proposed by the Harbin Commissioner. The details of this procedure are still under discussion, but the principle has been approved, and I therefore append for your guidance copy of Harbin despatch No. 2568 and of my reply thereto.

You should also communicate with the Harbin Commissioner with the object of securing, as far as possible, uniformity of procedure in the banking arrangements of your respective establishments.

A copy of this despatch is being sent to the Harbin Commissioner.

        I am, Sir,

        Your obedient Servant,

        Inspector General.

Appendix No.1.

The Harbin Commissioner to the Inspector General.
_____

No. 2568.   Custom House,

I. G.   Harbin, 29th December, 1921.

Sir,

1. With reference to the " Agreement between
the Harbin Commissioner of Customs and the Manager
of the Harbin Branch of the Bank of China for
the collection of Customs Revenue" in this District
submitted in Harbin despatches Nos.2328 and 2359
and approved of in Inspectorate General's despatch
No. 2509/83,153, I beg to report that the Manager
of the Bank of China, Harbin, has approached me
with a view to having certain clauses in the
Agreement amended. The Bank argues that the
expenses of collection at Harbin and especially
at the out-stations in this district are so heavy,
and that the cost of remitting to Shanghai has
increased to such a considerable extent during the
last months, while they are bound by Agreement to
remit at par, that the Bank is losing heavily.
The amendments desired concern Articles III and
VII of the present Agreement.

2. In Article III the first clause provides
as mentioned above, that the Bank shall remit the
Revenue to Shanghai at par. As transfer fees
on Shanghai have been fluctuating between 2½ per
cent

cent. and 8 per cent. during the last months,
the Bank's desire to have this clause amended
is quite reasonable. After an exchange of
correspondence and after personal interviews with
the Manager of the Bank, the following amendment
has been agreed upon subject to your approval:
"The Bank shall remit the collection at such
times and in such manner as directed by the
Commissioner. All remittances from Harbin to
Shanghai shall be made by the Bank at
remittance fees to be fixed at the
end of each quarter, between the Commissioner
and the Bank, the remittance fee agreed upon
to be as low as possible in relation to
market rates".

It should be explained that the Bank is
most anxious that all remittances of revenue to
Shanghai should be made through their agency, and
not through the Foreign Banks who now insist
upon cashing of notes, and refuse to accept
local bank notes when in large amounts. The
Bank is not anxious to make a profit on these
remittances so long as they handle all remittances
to Shanghai; they are prepared to fix the
quarterly remittance charge at a nominal figure.
The idea of the Bank is to retain as high a
silver reserve as possible, which is only possible
if remittances are not handled by Foreign banks
who would drain these reserves by cashing local
notes.

The

The Bank has consented to let the fees for local remittances from the outstations to Harbin and **vice-versa** remain as heretofore.

3. Another amendment to Article III of the Original Agreement is sought by the Bank, who wishes to cancel the clause whereby interest is payable by the Bank on Revenue Collection balances at the rate of 2½%. Taking into consideration the heavy expenses of collection at the out-stations, the great risks of transferring money from these out-stations to Harbin in these troublous times, and the very reasonable charges for local remittances I would beg to recommend the cancellation of the clause now objected to by the Bank.

4. The next amendment proposed by the Bank concerns the clause in Article VII whereby the Bank undertakes to receive the duties, which are payable in Haikuan Taels, in silver dollars of certain denominations and/or in banknotes of the Banks of China and Communications. The Bank desires to be at liberty, after consultation with the Commissioner, to receive, besides silver dollars all such local banknotes that are redeemable at their face value in an unrestricted manner. The idea is this: the bank is at present more or less bound to accept the notes of the Three Eastern Provinces Bank (Chang Tso-lin's Bank) and of other local Chinese Banks, with whom they exchange their local issue of notes; and the clause of our Agreement whereby only the notes of Banks of China and Communications are accepted in

in payment of duty is embarrassing to them. There is no objection on my part to the amendment of this clause, as our Agreement provides that the Bank shall be responsible to the Commissioner for the actual amount collected in silver dollars or in such notes that are redeemable at their face value in an unrestricted manner.

5. The last amendment sought by the Bank relates to Article VIII and the rate of commission to be paid by the Customs. The Bank suggests an increase of the commission to 15% on Revenue collected at Harbin and 20% on collection at the out-stations. I have succeeded in dissuading the Bank from pressing this point, in view of the cancellation of interest on Revenue collection balances (Article III).

6. A copy of the amended Articles III and VII in English and Chinese is appended hereto. All remaining Articles remain as heretofore. I beg to recommend the amendments as shown in the appendix, to come into force from 1st February, 1922.

I have the honour to be,

Sir,

Your obedient Servant,

(Signed) R.C.L. d'Anjou,
Commissioner

Appendix.

Proposed Amendments to Original Agreement of 29th March, 1921.

Article III. The Bank shall remit the collection at such times and in such manner as may be directed by the Commissioner. All remittances from Harbin to Shanghai shall be made by the Bank at remittance fees to be fixed at the end of each quarter between the Commissioner and the Bank, the remittance fee agreed upon to be as low as possible in relation to market rates.

  For local remittances from out-stations to Harbin or *vice-versa* the Bank shall be entitled to the following remittance fees:

(a) Sansing   4‰.
(b) Lahasusu   5‰.
(c) Manchouli 3.50‰.
    and Suifenho

No interest on Revenue collection balances will be paid by the Bank.

Article VII. The Bank undertakes to receive the duties, which are payable in Haikuan Taels, in big silver dollars(Peiyang,Yuan Shih-k'ai and Hongkong) or in such local big silver dollar Bank Notes that are redeemable at their face value without restriction and in

an

an unlimited amount. The rate for Haikuan Taels *vis-a-vis* silver dollars and/or local Bank notes as defined above is fixed at Haikuan Taels 100.00=$156.65. The Bank is responsible to the Commissioner for the actual amount of dollars collected at the above rate(*i.e.* in clean silver dollars or in local Bank notes that are redeemable at their face value without restriction and in an unlimited amount).

Appendix No.2.

The Inspector General to the Harbin Commissioner.

87,833

5th January, 1912.

Sir,

I have to acknowledge receipt of your despatch No. 2568 :

reporting, with regard to the Agreement with the Bank of China for the collection of Customs Revenue, that the local Manager of that Bank had approached you with a view to obtaining the amendment of certain clauses in the Agreement, as follows :

(1) that the Bank should be allowed to charge a fee for remitting the collection to Shanghai;

(2) that the Bank should not be required to pay interest on Revenue Account balances;

(3) that the rate of the Commission paid to the Bank for cost of collection should be increased; and

(4) that the Bank should be at liberty, after consultation with the Commissioner, to receive all such local banknotes, without discrimination as to the issuing Bank, as are redeemable at their face value in an unrestricted manner;

and submitting for my approval the draft of the

Commissioner of Customs,

HARBIN.

the amendments to the original Agreement which you propose to make.

In reply, I have to instruct you as follows :

With reference to the Bank's request that it should be allowed to charge a remittance fee, for the reason that the cost of remitting dollars to Shanghai has of late increased to such an extent that the Bank is unable to remit at par, as required by the Agreement, without considerable loss, I am quite prepared to allow such a remittance fee to be charged as will enable the Bank to remit the Collection without loss. But the proposed amendment to Article 3 as drafted by you is too vague in its terms. It is not clear, for example, whether the procedure is to be (1) that the fee " fixed at the end of the quarter " is to be in force during the ensuing quarter, or (2) that the Bank will remit as usual during the Quarter, the fee

to

to be charged for these remittances being
decided upon by the Bank and Commissioner at the
end of that Quarter.   Further, you state that
the Bank is prepared to fix the quarterly
remittance charge at a " nominal figure ": what is
exactly meant by this is again not quite clear;
moreover if the fee is, in fact, to be a nominal
one, it would be better to decide once for all
what this fee should be, or, at least, to arrange
definitely how it is to be arrived at.   You
are requested, therefore, to elucidate this point,
giving a concrete example of how the procedure
you propose to adopt will work in actual
practice.

        With regard to the Bank's request to be
absolved from the payment of interest on Revenue
Account balances, I have to say that as the
Bank holds for the greater part of a month a
considerable sum of Revenue moneys in your Revenue

                                        Account

Account, it is only reasonable, and in accordance
with existing practice elsewhere, that it should
be required to pay a fair rate of interest on
daily balances.   That it should not be required
to do so in consideration for waiving certain
other claims is a compromise of which I do not
approve.   The clause in Article 3 which deals
with this point should therefore be allowed to
stand.

        With regard to the Bank's claim for an
increase in the commission paid by the Customs
for cost of collection - a claim which you state
the Bank would be prepared to waive in
consideration of the proposed cancellation of the
clause requiring the payment of interest on
Revenue Account balances - I have to point out
that " interest on Revenue Account " and " commission
for cost of collection" are two quite separate
questions which should not be confused or made
inter-dependent.   The commission paid to the Bank

                                        for

for cost of collection should be fixed at such
a figure, or at such a rate, as will make the
amount actually paid to the Bank correspond as
nearly as possible to the actual out-of-pocket
expenses which the Bank is put to in the
collection of Revenue on our behalf. You should
therefore ascertain what the Bank's actual
expenses really are, so that, if necessary, the
commission may be increased. But in this
connection your attention is particularly called
to the fact that the Harbin Revenue Collection
for the year 1921 (excluding Aigun showed an
increase of over Hk.Tls.550,000 as compared with
that of 1920, and that the Bank therefore
received as commission for cost of collection in
1921 some Hk.Tls.5,500.00, or, say, $8,000.00, more
than in 1920. The matter of the cost of
collection should therefore be carefully
investigated before any claim for an increase

in

in the commission is admitted.

With reference to your statement that the
Bank has consented to allow the fees for local
remittances to and from the out-stations to
remain as heretofore - in consideration, as it
would seem to be implied, for being allowed
to charge a fee on remittances to Shanghai -
here, again, the two questions at issue, viz:
that of local remittances and that of remittances
to Shanghai - should be kept distinct. If the
local remittance charges as at present in
force were originally based on the actual cost
of making these remittances and are not purely
"nominal fees", they should be revised if
necessary, rather than be allowed to remain at
a lower figure than the actual cost of
remittance would justify in consideration of some
other concession granted.

With reference to the Bank's request that it
should be at liberty, " after consultation with

the

the Commissioner" to accept all such banknotes,
without discrimination as to the issuing bank,
as are redeemable at their face value in an
unrestricted manner, I do not approve of any
alteration in the terms of the Agreement which
would authorise the Bank to accept in payment
of duties other notes than those of the
two Government Banks which at present they are
authorised to accept under certain conditions.
It is true that the Bank would still, under
the terms of the Agreement as you propose
to amend it, be responsible to the Commissioner
for the actual amount of dollars collected in
silver or in such notes as are redeemable at
their face value in an unrestricted manner
but the Bank proposes that it should be
authorised to accept the notes of other than
the Government Banks only "after consultation
with the Commissioner", and if, after consultation
                                               with

with the Commissioner, the Bank were authorised
to accept such banknotes and, later, these notes
became depreciated while still in the Bank's
hands as part of the Collection, the Bank would
probably refer to the Commissioner's authority
given, and might endeavour in this way to
evade its responsibility under the Agreement.

Article 7 of the Agreement should therefore
remain unchanged, and any arrangement which the
Bank of China may make with other Banks with
regard to the acceptance of their notes must
be a matter of private arrangement between
the Banks concerned made entirely at the Bank
of China's own risk.   So long as the
remittance of the Collection remains, as in
accordance with present arrangements, in the
hands of the Bank of China, the Bank should
have no difficulty in fulfilling the terms
of Article 7 of the Agreement as it now
stands.   You

You are requested to report further
on the matter after further discussion with the
local Manager of the Bank of China.

I am,

Sir,

Your obedient Servant,

(Signed) F.A. Aglen,

Inspector General.

True copies:

Acting Assistant Secretary.

致瑷珲关第 <u>25/87635</u> 号令　　　　海关总税务司署（北京）1922 年 1 月 20 日

尊敬的瑷珲关税务司：

第 16 号呈收悉：

"呈交一份与当地中国银行分行经理协商后达成的税款代征、保管和汇寄协议草案，请予批准；本协议草案严格遵循现行有效的哈尔滨关相关协议，并提请注意以下两点：（1）支付给银行的税款代征佣金问题和（2）银行汇寄税款至上海的固定手续费问题。"

另外，贵署去年 12 月 24 日发送的电报已收悉：

"汇报中国银行已取消按固定费率汇寄税款至上海的服务，但同意以一定时期内的最优市价办理上述汇寄业务。"

现批复如下，请遵照执行。

关于"瑷珲关税款代征佣金应照所收数额每 1000.00 银圆提 20.00 银圆"的银行提议，正如去年 12 月 28 日我发送的电报所述，我认为此佣金费用过高，尤其是考虑到您给出的代征成本估值（在贵署雇用管账员管理本关账户的情形下）。因此，您应与当地的中国银行分行经理再次协商此事，协商应秉承以下原则：支付给银行的固定代征佣金数目或费率应能确保实际支付给银行的金额尽可能相当于银行代表我们征税所花费的实际费用。关于您接受银行提议的理由，即：我们的往来账户享受比其他存户更优惠的利率，尤其是汇款至上海的费率比较实惠，这一理由并不充分；"往来账户利率""上海汇款费率"和"代征佣金"是三个互不相关的问题，切勿混淆，避免因任何方式将三者纠缠在一起。此外，还需谨记银行帮助我们代征税款有利可图，并且其汇款至上海享受特惠，鉴于此情况，银行给我们提供的往来账户利率和汇寄至上海的汇费本应是优惠价格。

关于银行希望以最优市价收取汇寄至上海的手续费的提议，我建议制订一份更加明确的协定，必要时采取类似哈尔滨关税务司最近提议的操作规程和方法。该操作规程仍在商榷之中，但其原则已予以批准。为了便于您参照执行，随函附上哈尔滨关第 2568 号呈及我对该呈的批复。

您也应当与哈尔滨关税务司沟通，尽可能确保各自关区银行业务协定方面的操作规程一致。

同时,此令副本已抄送给哈尔滨关税务司。

您忠诚的仆人

安格联(F. A. Aglen)

海关总税务司

附件 1

哈尔滨关税务司致总税务司函

呈海关总税务司署 2568 号文　　　　　哈尔滨关税务司 1921 年 12 月 29 日

尊敬的海关总税务司：

1. 关于提交哈尔滨关第 2328 号和第 2359 号呈，并经海关总税务司署第 2509/83153 号令批准的本关《哈尔滨关税务司与中国银行哈尔滨分行经理关于海关税款代征的协议》，中国银行哈尔滨分行经理与我协商修正了几条协议条款，现将有关情况报告如下。银行认为代征哈尔滨关及其分关税款投入巨大，而且上一个月汇寄上海的汇费成本大幅增长，但他们受协议约束，仍然按照平价汇寄，导致银行损失惨重。其欲要做出的修正涉及当前协议的第三条和第七条。

2. 如前文所述，第三条第一项要求银行按平价将税款汇寄至上海。考虑到上个月上海的转账费用在 2.5% 与 8% 之间波动，因此银行希望修正此项的请求非常合理。与银行经理进行书信沟通和面谈之后，达成以下修正条款，等待您的批准。

"银行应按照税务司命令在指定期限以指定方式汇寄税款。凡由哈尔滨至上海的所有汇款，其汇费按税务司与银行的协定优惠价格收取。在每个季度末对此价格按市价重新商改一次。"

需要指出的一点是，银行十分渴望通过其分支机构而不是外国银行办理所有转账至上海的税款汇寄业务，因为款项数目较大时，外国银行坚持要求兑现纸币，拒绝接受本地银行纸币。银行只需能够办理所有转账至上海的税款汇寄业务即可，他们并不担心能否从中盈利。银行预备为每个季度的汇费确定一个数目。银行的想法是尽可能多地保持银圆储备，而外国银行办理汇寄业务时要求将本地纸币兑换为银圆，因此只有在此业务不需要用外国银行办理的情况下，才有可能实现银圆储备的保持。

银行已同意由各分关汇寄至哈尔滨或由哈尔滨汇寄至各分关的本地汇款手续费仍按照原来费率保持不变。

3. 关于原始协议的第三条，银行请求的另一项修正是希望解除"银行税款余额利息定为月息 2.5‰"这一条款。考虑到在各分关代征税款投入巨大，在动荡不安的年代将资金从各分关转运至哈尔滨的风险较高，再加上给予我们的本地汇费极为优惠，我恳求并建议解除该项银行有异议的条款。

4. 银行提出的下一项修正与第七条的条款有关,依据该条款,海关所征各项税款原按海关两核计,现在银行代征税款也可以收取一些指定银圆或中国银行和交通银行发行的纸币。银行希望在与税务司协商之后,自行决定收取除银圆之外所有本地可以按面值无限制兑换的纸币。提出此修正的原因如下。按照目前协议规定,银行虽然可以与东三省银行(张作霖的银行)和中国其他本地银行互兑各自发行的纸币,但基本上不能接受其他银行的纸币;我们协议里的关税征纳仅接受中国银行和交通银行纸币的规定令他们的处境十分尴尬。我对此条款的修正没有异议,因为我们的协议规定,银行采用银圆或本地可按面值无限制兑现的纸币将实收税款总额交付给税务司。

5. 银行提出的最后一条修正与第八条海关支付的代征佣金有关。银行建议将哈尔滨关税款代征佣金增加至15‰,将其分关税款代征佣金增加至20‰。鉴于已取消代征税款余额利息(第三条),我已退回银行佣金上涨的要求。

6. 随函附上中英对照版第三条和第七条修正条款。余下其他条款均保持不变。我恳求并建议上述修正条款(如附件1所示)于1922年2月1日生效。

十分荣幸成为

您忠诚的仆人

(签字)覃书(R. C. L. d'Anjou)

哈尔滨关税务司

附件1

1921年3月29日原始协议的建议修正条款

三、银行应按照税务司命令在指定期限以指定方式汇寄税款。凡由哈尔滨至上海的所有汇款,其汇费按税务司与银行的协定优惠价格收取。在每个季度末对此价格按市价重新商改一次。

由以下各处汇寄至哈尔滨或由哈尔滨汇寄至各处的汇费如下。

（1）三姓　　　　　　　　　　4‰

（2）拉哈苏苏　　　　　　　　5‰

（3）满洲里和绥芬河　　　　　3.50‰

所存税款余额概不计息。

七、海关所征各项税款原按海关两核计,银行代征关税现也可以收取现大洋（即银圆,如北洋袁世凯像银圆及香港银圆）或本地可按面值无限制兑现的大洋纸币。海关两与上述银圆/本地纸币的固定兑换比率为：100海关两折合156.65银圆。银行向税务司交付的代征税款为按上述汇率折算后的实际总额（即按纯银圆或本地可按面值无限制兑现的纸币交付）。

附件 2

总税务司致哈尔滨关税务司函

致哈尔滨关第 2784/87633 号令　　　　海关总税务司署（北京）1922 年 1 月 20 日

尊敬的哈尔滨关税务司：

第 2568 号呈收悉：

"情况汇报如下：关于与中国银行签署的关税代征协议,该银行的当地分行经理前来找我协商,请求更改一些协议条款,修正如下。

（1）凡将代征税款汇寄至上海,允许银行收取汇款手续费；

（2）免收税收账户余额利息；

（3）提高银行代征佣金；

（4）在与税务司协商之后,银行可自行决定接收当地银行纸币,只要纸币能以面值无限制兑换,就可以一视同仁地对待所有纸币。

并且根据您的建议,呈交原始协议的修正条款草案,请予以审批。"

现批复如下,请遵照以下指示执行。

关于银行希望收取汇费的请求,鉴于最近汇款至上海的成本确有大幅增长,银行若按照协议以平价汇寄,必会遭受巨大损失,因此我准许银行收取此类汇费,确保银行不会因汇寄代征税款遭受损失。但您起草的第三条建议修正条款描述过于含糊。举例来说,汇费收取程序不清晰：是（1）"每个季度末协定"的汇费在下一季度执行,还是（2）银行在本季度内先照常汇寄,然后再按照本季度末银行与税务司商定的费率收取此等汇款的手续费。再者,据您所述,银行愿意将季度汇费固定在一个"象征性数目"：其确切含义仍然不清楚；此外,如果说该收费实际上是象征性收费,那么最好一劳永逸地确定该费用的数目,或者最起码明确安排费用商定方式。因此,您需要对这几点详细阐明,并针对您所提出的操作程序,给出能在实际工作中起作用的具体示例。

关于银行希望免除支付税收账户余额利息的请求,我的意见是：因为在每月的大部分时间内,银行都会保管贵关税收账户的巨额税款,并且参照其他海关的现行做法,银行应当合理支付每日余额的利息。其因为放弃某些权利要求而想要免除利息支付,这样的折中选择是我所不赞成的。因此,第三条中关于此问题的条款仍按原来规定,不予修改。

关于银行希望提高税款代征佣金的请求，据您所述，考虑到已经建议解除支付税收账户余额利息的条款，银行愿意放弃此请求。对此，我必须指出的一点是，"税收账户利息"和"代征佣金"是明显不同的两码事，二者不得混淆或纠缠在一起。支付给银行的固定代征佣金数目或费率应能确保实际支付给银行的金额尽可能相当于银行代表我们征税所花费的实际费用。因此，您应查明银行的实付费用，如果相差太大，可以考虑提高佣金。但在这一点上，您需特别注意，相比 1920 年，1921 年的哈尔滨关税款上涨了 530000 余海关两，因此 1921 年银行收到的代征佣金约为 5300 海关两，相比 1920 年增长了 8000 银圆。因此，应当在仔细调查代征成本后再决定是否提高佣金。

关于"银行已同意由各分关汇寄至哈尔滨或由哈尔滨汇寄至各分关的本地汇款手续费仍按照原来费率保持不变"这一点，这似乎暗示允许银行对汇寄至上海的业务收取更高的手续费，此处仍有两个问题应区分对待，即：本地汇款汇费和汇寄至上海的汇费。如果目前现行的本地汇款汇费最初不是单纯的"象征性费用"，而是基于实际汇款成本确立的费用，那么必要时应当加以修订。因得到一些其他特惠而保留比实际汇款成本低的数目，这是不合理的。

关于银行希望"在与税务司协商之后，可自行决定接收当地银行纸币，只要纸币能以面值无限制兑换，就可以一视同仁地对待所有纸币"的请求，我并不赞同对此协议条款进行任何修改，因为这会授权银行除接收两家公办银行的纸币（在特定条件下授权银行接收的纸币）之外，还可以接收其他银行的纸币。的确，根据您建议修正的协议条款内容，银行仍然需要用银圆或可按面值无限制兑现的纸币将实收税款总额交付给税务司，但银行提议授权其"在与税务司协商之后"方可接收除公办银行以外的银行纸币，倘若在税务司协商之后，银行获得接收此类纸币的授权，而之后这些纸币若有贬值，且银行的代征税款仍然包含这些纸币，那么银行可能借口已得到税务司的授权，试图以此逃避本协议规定的责任。

因此，本协议第七条应保持不变，凡中国银行与其他银行关于接收其他银行纸币的协定，均为相关银行之间的私下协定，完全由中国银行自行承担风险。只要税款汇寄仍然处于中国银行控制之下，那么根据当前约定，银行履行本协议第七条的规定应无困难。

请与当地的中国银行分行经理进一步讨论，然后向我汇报讨论结果。

您忠诚的仆人

（签字）安格联

海关总税务司

10. 1922 年《稽查黑龙江往来船只进出口货物之各项章程》

Aigun Taheiho 31st March, 1922.

Sir,

1.　　　One year ago the Harbin Commissioner, in his despatch No. 2348, reported that, after the abolition of the duty free zone in August 1914, goods brought by water to Aigun and Taheiho from places on the Chinese side of the Amur, and *vice versa*, were, for some unknown reason, continued to be passed free of duty, while the Lahasusu Barrier promptly started taxing this traffic; pointed out that goods moved along the Sungari, passing a Customs station even *en route*, were taxed one full duty, and proposed that the anomaly of one station (Aigun - Taheiho passing free of duty the same traffic which was fully controlled and taxed by another station (Lahasusu) be removed as soon as possible,

　　　requesting

Inspector General of Customs,

　　P. I P G.

requesting your authority to start levy of duty at Aigun - Taheiho from the beginning of the Navigation season, 1921.

　　　You sanctioned the proposal (despatch No. 2528/83,594) not without foreseeing the difficulties of applying in practice this right principle.

　　　The Harbin Commissioner made all necessary arrangements with the Superintendent and the Heilungchiang Authorities (despatch No. 2379) and the public was notified accordingly.

　　　But soon an agitation against the new Taxation was raised in Aigun and Taheiho, the Chambers of Commerce appealed to the Shui Wu Ch'u, and the Harbin Commissioner in his despatch No. 2394 recommended the temporary postponement of the taxation.

　　　You approved the postponement (despatch No. 2570/84,176) and in your despatch No. 2595/84,551 you conveyed the Shui Wu Ch'u's opinion that the merchants' protest was due to vague uneasiness regarding the results of the new taxation, and that the opposition would probably subside if the rules of the new taxation were clearly laid down in the

Aigun

Aigun Customs Regulations.

2.　　　　In paragraph 13 of my despatch No. 32 concerning the Liangchiat'un Barrier, I had the honour to point out that it would be advisable to force the local merchants to withdraw their opposition to the levy of Duty on Amur Traffic and Coast Trade Duty, as a condition *sine qua non* for granting relief in the matter of overland taxation. - It is my opinion that we could find no better opportunity for settling definitely the question of taxation in this District, and for re-shaping the whole system of control.

3.　　　　In accordance therefore with your instructions and the wishes of the Shui Wu Ch'u conveyed in your despatch No. 2595/84,531, I have prepared a draft of New Regulations, which embody the changes suggested by the abolition of the duty-free zone, the repudiation of the Russian Treaties and the bringing in line of this Port, as far as possible, with general practice at Treaty Ports in China.

　　　　The draft has been submitted to the Superintendent, who has found no objection, and I have the

the honour to enclose :

Enclosure No. 1.　　　three copies of the English Version

Enclosure No. 2.　　　three copies of the Chinese Version

Enclosure No. 3.　　　one Memorandum commenting on the proposed New Regulations

Enclosure No. 4.　　　one copy of the Provisional Aigun Regulations of 1909 (the only one in stock)

　　　　No Russian Version could be prepared here, for lack of a capable translator; I approached the Harbin Office some time ago, but they were too busy. I would suggest that the translation be either made at the Inspectorate, or by the Harbin Russian Secretary after approval of the English and Chinese Versions. - The printing of the New Regulations should anyhow be made in Harbin, there being no facilities here.

4.　　　　In his despatch No. 2346, the Harbin Commissioner estimated the additional Revenue to be derived from levy of Duty on Amur Traffic at Hk. Tls. 30,000 ; I agree with him that this figure, and also my estimate given in Aigun despatch No. 32, is well on the side of moderation.

　　　　　　　　In

In 1921, the total value of Native Goods imported by River was Hk. Tls. 1,846,326, out of which about 70 % came from Harbin or the Sungari; the remaining 30 % would be subject to Amur Taxation for a value of   Hk. Tls.   554,000

The Native Exports by River to Chinese Ports amounted to Hk.Tls. 540,000, of which about 400,000 went to Amur places; half the amount however may be proved to be re-exports, once we tax this traffic; there remain   Hk. Tls.   200,000

To these should be added the rafts, both for here and for Blagovestchensk (other than those originating from, and sent to, Siberia), the value of which can be conservatively estimated at   Hk. Tls.   400,000 paying mostly ad val rem duty.

          Total value   Hk. Tls. 1,154,000

If the value of Foreign Goods imported from Siberia through some Chinese Place on the Amur, or moved without our knowledge now (e.g. from Blagovestchensk to Humaho direct) be added, the total volume of Trade will amount to Hk. Tls. 1,200,000 - on which more

more than Hk. Tls. 30,000 would be almost certainly collected.

5.   The levy of Duty on Amur Traffic and the enforcement of the proposed Regulations raise the question of the opening of new Stations on the River and of Barriers Inland, at important places where Trade may be best controlled. - I have accordingly written a short Memorandum on Trade Routes and Trade Centres in this District; the information I got from various sources, captains of steamers and merchants. Most of it needs confirmation, and I propose to investigate further before making definite suggestions, and if necessary - with your consant - to proceed myself (or to delegate a Member of the Staff to proceed) up river as far as Humaho and down river at least as far as Chik'ot's, in order to form a judgment on the spot.

However, you will see that a Barrier above Tahsiho, about nine verst away, is an absolute necessity if we are to tax Amur Traffic, especially rafts. I hereby have the honour to ask your sanction to the opening of this Barrier, which may be closed later, if it is proved that a Station at

          Humaho

Numaho can control practically all of the Timber Trade from up-river.

6.   If the Customs are to control the Trade along the Amur in summer, what about the same Trade in Winter, by sleigh ? As it is, merchants now almost always come and declare cargo shipped by sledge, as far as Numaho, on one side, to Chik'ot's and Taip'ingkou and other places, down river. - They do not pay duty, but seek protection from the Likin by having their applications stamped by the Customs; they would for the most part willingly pay duty, I am sure. - I believe that we should contend that Traffic along the River is controlled by us in Winter as well as in Summer - and merchants, if well informed, would support this point of view, especially if we open up other Stations (Numaho, Chik'ot's), where we can protect goods at destination. I have the honour to ask your instructions on this point; should you decide not to enforce levy of duty on the Winter Traffic along the River for the present, I would suggest that we go on as heretofore stamping the applications, so that our present position may not be weakened.

7.

7. ...   Under separate despatch I have the honour to forward draft of Harbour Regulations, to supplement the General Regulations now submitted.

Another despatch will deal with the levy of Coast Trade Duty on Goods moved between this Port and the Sungari, and another one with the craft necessitated by the enforcement of the General and Harbour Regulations, and for the proper control of Trade and suppression of Smuggling.

- I have the honour to be,

Sir,

Your obedient Servant,

Acting Commissioner.

Enclosure No. 1 to Aigun Despatch No. 37 to I. G.

PROPOSED NEW CUSTOMS REGULATIONS FOR THE CONTROL OF
VESSELS' MOVEMENT, IMPORT AND EXPORT OF CARGO
ON THE RIVER AMUR.

I.—SHIPPING.

1. Vessels navigating and trading on the Chinese side of the Amur must stop at all the Offices of the Chinese Maritime Customs en route and pay duty there according to Regulations. The Offices of the C. M. Customs at present opened are Aigun and Tabeiho, but more may be established in future.

All vessels loading cargo on the Chinese side of the Amur at places below the lowest Customs station for Russian places below Lahasusu, are to report and pay duty at the Lahasusu Office of the Harbin Customs; similarly all vessels loading cargo at Russian Ports below Lahasusu for places on the Chinese side of the Amur below the lowest Customs station, are to report at Lahasusu and pay duty there.

2. Customs Officers will board and inspect vessels entering into or clearing from Port; they are to be given free access to any part of the vessel at any time during the execution of their duty.

3. All vessels must anchor at places assigned by the Customs, and must in every respect conform to the Harbour Regulations.

4. Neither cargo nor passengers may be landed, shipped or transhipped before permission has been given by the Customs. Cargo or passengers' luggage landed, shipped or transhipped without such permission is liable to confiscation, and if passengers are thus landed or shipped the vessel is liable to a fine.

5. Manifests, ship's papers, baggage lists and sealed Customs covers must be presented to the Customs on arrival at a Port, as well as a Memorandum stating places visited en route, passengers and/or cargo discharged and/or shipped at those places. Outward bound vessels, when wishing to clear, must present a Manifest and baggage list; if there are in order, and all duties and dues have been paid, the vessel will be allowed to clear. - Covers, packages, etc., when entrusted to a ship's Officer for delivery to the Customs at Port of destination or any port en route, must be kept in a safe place, untampered with, until handed over to the Boarding Officer.

Manifests and baggage lists must contain a true and full account of all cargo on board, including duty-free goods, giving separate statements for each place of shipment and destination, marks, numbers and contents. Manifests must be signed by the Master of the vessel or other responsible Agent, who will be held responsible for their correctness.

6. Shut-out goods will be recognised as duty-paid goods only on the condition that they be presented immediately for re-examination.

7. Vessels must produce their papers for inspection when called upon by any Chinese Maritime Customs Official acting on behalf of the C. M. Customs who may board them at the Ports or en route.

8. Customs Employés may be put on board of vessels to search them or to accompany them for the purpose of surveillance. Customs Officers have the right to search cargo, luggage, passengers and crew, and to muster passengers for the control of Passports, in accordance with Special Regulations; all facilities must be given them in the discharge of their duty.

9. Vessels having on board cargo covered by Customs Documents must not call at Russian Ports en route; should any

any vessel disobey this Regulation, the Customs will ignore
the documents covering the goods. Vessels however have the
option of having their cargo sealed up as per clause 10
of these Regulations; and cargo arriving with seals intact,
even if the vessel has called en route to a Russian Port,
will be considered as covered by Customs Documents.

10. The Customs are at liberty to seal the hatches
of vessels, or part of the cargo, or horses; such seals
must not be broken until the vessel reaches a Port where
she has to work cargo, and until the necessary permission
has been obtained.

11. For working cargo or passengers on Sundays or
Holidays as well as on week days out of the regular
working hours, Special Permit Fees must be paid. These
fees will be collected according to the Table appended
hereto.

12. Trade in Opium and Poppy seeds is absolutely
forbidden. Export abroad of rice, husked and unhusked,
and Chinese copper coins and cash, importation of foreign
copper coins blanks is likewise forbidden. - Trade in the
following articles is prohibited except under Bond by
qualified Medical Practitioners, Druggists and Chemists (in
accordance with Special Regulations): morphia and cocaine
and hypodermic syringes, and all derivatives of opium and
cocaine, or anti-opium remedies containing opium or any
derivative of opium and cocaine. - Trade in arms and
ammunition, implements of war and salt is prohibited,
except under Special Permits.

Any such article, or any other article the trade in
which may at any time be prohibited or restricted by the
Chinese Government, if found on board not covered by proper
documents, will be confiscated.

13. Presentation of false Manifest, unauthorised
breaking of seals, or any other infraction of the above
rules

rules will render the vessel, or in case of Overland Trade
the merchant, liable to a fine not exceeding Hk. Tls. 500,
or to the infliction of other penalties in force at the
Treaty Ports in China.

II. DUTIES AND DUES.

14. All vessels and their tows have to pay Tonnage
Dues once in every four months, at the rate of four mace
per ton, if of more than 150 tons burden, and of one
mace per ton, if of 150 tons or under.

> Note. No Tonnage Dues will be collected until fur-
> ther Notice. A System of River Dues, as now in
> force on the Sungari, may be substituted for
> the Tonnage Dues.

15. Duties will be levied in accordance with the
Tariffs in force at the Open Ports in China. (Goods unenumerated in the Tariffs, whether Foreign or Native, shall
pay at the rate of 5% ad valorem.)

16. Foreign Goods arriving at a Port unprotected by
proper Customs Documents must pay one full Import Duty,
and will receive a Duty Receipt.

17. Import Duty-paid Foreign Goods reshipped in China
within three years of payment of duty in the original
conditions, will be passed duty-free and will receive
Documents to cover them as long as they remain under
Customs jurisdiction.

Foreign Goods presented for shipment uncovered by proof
of former payment
a) if for another place in China, must pay one
full Import Duty and will receive, in addition to a Duty
Receipt, Documents to cover them as long as they remain
under Customs jurisdiction;
b) if for abroad, and of unquestionably foreign
origin, will be passed free.

18. Foreign Goods sent to a Manchurian Trade Mart will,
on

on payment of one full Import Duty, receive a Manchurian Special Exemption Certificate in accordance with Special Regulations, and be exempt from further taxation en route and at destination.

Sent to the Interior

19. Import Duty-paid Foreign Goods sent to places in the Interior must pay

a) either Inland Taxes at the Barriers met with en route;

b) or Transit Dues calculated at half the Import Tariff (or 2½ % ad valorem in case of articles free by Tariff) in which case they will receive Transit Certificates, and be exempt from Inland Taxation en route to the place of destination.

Re-exported abroad

20. Foreign Goods, covered by Duty Receipts, re-exported abroad within three years in the original conditions, will receive Drawback for the original Import Duty, in accordance with the Regulations in force at other Treaty Ports in China.

Note 1. The fact of the actual re-exportation must be certified by one of the Controlling Barriers.

Note 2. Goods covered by Manchurian Special Exemption Certificate are not entitled to drawback privileges, with the temporary exemption of goods imported at Manchuuli brought overland to Tahsiho, and re-exported to Blagovestchensk.

NATIVE GOODS Imported by River

21. River-borne Native Goods arriving at one of the Customs Stations

a) if accompanied by proof of payment of Export and Coast Trade Duty at another Office of the C. M. Customs, will be admitted free;

b) if accompanied by proof of payment of Export Duty only at another Office of the C. M. Customs, must pay Coast Trade Duty calculated at half the Export Tariff;

c) if not emanating from a Port must pay a full Export Duty, and will receive a Duty Receipt.

Note.

Note. Until further Notice, no Coast Trade Duty will be levied on goods moved along the Amur.

22. Native Goods declared for Export must pay a full Export Duty and will receive a Duty Receipt; if destined for another Port they must pay Coast Trade Duty at destination.

Note. Until further Notice, no Coast Trade Duty will be levied on goods moved along the Amur.

23. Native Goods covered by proof of former payment of Export Duty, or of Export and Coast Trade Duties, if re-exported to another place in China within one year in the original conditions, will be passed free and will receive documents exempting them from further levy of Export Duty, or Export and Coast Trade Duty, as the case may be, as long as they remain under Customs jurisdiction.

24. Export and Coast Trade Duty-paid Native Goods sent to a Manchurian Trade Mart within one year of payment of duty, will receive a Manchurian Special Exemption Certificate in accordance with Special Regulations, and be exempted from further taxation en route and at destination.

25. Duty-paid Native goods, re-exported abroad within 12 months in the original conditions

a) if they have paid Export Duty only, will be passed free;

b) if they have paid Export and Coast Trade Duty, will receive Drawbacks for the original Coast Trade Duty.

Note 1. The time limit for re-exportation of Cattle is six months.

Note 2. The fact of the actual re-exportation must be certified by one of the controlling Barriers.

Note 3. Goods under Manchurian Special Exemption Certificates are not entitled to Drawback privileges.

26.

26. Transit Certificates, for the conveyance of Native Produce from the Interior for ultimate export Abroad within a fixed time limit, will be issued in accordance with the Regulations in force at other Treaty Ports in China. The goods, in addition to Export Duty, must pay Outward Transit Dues at the rate of half the Export Tariff (or 2½% _ad valorem_ in the case of articles free by Tariff), and will be exempted from Inland Taxation _en route_.

27. The controlling Barrier at Liangchiat'un (or any Barrier that may be established in future) will levy a full duty on both Foreign and Native Goods arriving from - or going into - the Interior, which are not accompanied by Duty Proofs.

Merchants, upon giving adequate guarantees, or depositing a sufficient sum of money, will have the option of paying such duties at the Customs Stations to which the goods are destined.

————————

The present Regulations are subject to additions and alterations when, and if, necessary.

N. B. the term "Port" for the purpose of these Regulations means a place when an office of the C. M. Customs is established

The term "Vessel" applies to Steamers and Junks, and also Rafts (except as regards Tonnage Dues). The Raft traffic is regulated by Special Notifications.

<u>ALTERNATIVE ARTICLE 27 (OVERLAND TRAFFIC).</u>

27. All goods, Native and Foreign, imported overland, must report at the Liangchiat'un Barrier (or any other Barrier that may be established in future) where they will be examined; merchants must produce a guarantee

that

that the goods will be presented within 15 days to the Aigun or Taheiho Customs (or any other Customs River Station on the Amur Which may be established in future) where goods of unquestionably native origin will be released duty-free, and foreign goods will pay full Import Duty unless covered by proof of former payment.

All goods, Native and Foreign, intended for export by overland route, must previously be declared to the Custom House at Aigun or Taheiho (or any other Customs River Station on the Amur that may be established in future), where they will pay full Export or Import Duty unless covered by proof of former payment, and will receive appropriate documents to cover them. - All goods must subsequently report at the Liangchiat'un Barrier (or any other Barrier that may be established in future), where goods and documents will be inspected and checked

————————

呈海关总税务司署 <u>37</u> 号文　　　　　瑷珲关 / 大黑河 1922 年 3 月 31 日

尊敬的海关总税务司 (北京)：

　　1. 1921 年哈尔滨关税务司在哈尔滨关第 2348 号呈中汇报："1914 年 8 月免税区废除后，经水运往来于黑龙江华岸各地与瑷珲及大黑河之间的货物，不知因何原因，仍然可以免税通过，鉴于此，拉哈苏苏分关即刻对往来于该段航道之货物开始征税；同时，沿松花江航道运输之货物，途经各海关分卡时均须缴纳正税；如此一来，同一航道运输之货物经瑷珲 / 大黑河分关之时，可免税通过，但经拉哈苏苏分关之时，却须缴纳正税，实属乱象，兹提议尽快整治；请求批准瑷珲 / 大黑河分关于 1921 年航运季伊始之际开始征税。"

　　海关总税务司署第 2528/83594 号令批准了该提议，同时指出实施该提议之难处。

　　哈尔滨关税务司与海关监督将一切安排妥当后，于哈尔滨关第 2379 号呈中将此事呈报黑龙江省政府，同时向公众布告此事。

　　但不久，瑷珲及大黑河出现了反对新征税项的声音，商会亦向税务处提出撤销该征税一事之申请，鉴于此，哈尔滨关税务司于哈尔滨关第 1394 号呈文中建议暂缓执行征税事宜。

　　海关总税务司署第 2570/84176 号令批准了暂缓执行征税之建议。此外，海关总税务司署第 2579/84531 号令中传达了税务处之意见："商人之所以如此反对，主要因为新征税项之结果尚不明朗，令人感到不安。若《瑷珲关章程》可以对新征税项做出明确规定，或可平息反对之声。"

　　2. 本署于瑷珲关第 32 号呈 (第 13 段) 中提及梁家屯分卡时指出，以对黑龙江航道上的货物运输征税作为减免陆运征税之必要条件，迫使商人同意该新征税项，应属明智之举。兹认为，此乃解决瑷珲关 / 大黑河地区征税问题的最佳时机，亦可借机重新整顿海关管理系统。

　　3. 因此，根据海关总税务司署之指示以及第 2595/84531 号令中传达的税务处之意见，本署草拟了一份新章程，内容上涵盖了废除免税区所带来的影响以及对俄国条约之否定，同时尽量做到与中国通商口岸之惯例保持一致。

　　新章程草案已呈交海关监督审阅，海关监督对此并无异议，遂特此附上：

　　三份新章程英文版抄件 (附件 1)

　　三份新章程中文版抄件 (附件 2)

　　一份关于新章程草案的意见通函 (附件 3)

　　一份 1909 年《瑷珲关临时章程》抄件 (现存唯一的一份)(附件 4)

但由于没有合适的俄文翻译员，新章程目前没有俄文版；本署曾向哈尔滨关提及此事，但它们因公务繁忙而无暇处理此事。兹提议，待新章程的中文、英文版本通过后，由海关总税务公署或者哈尔滨关俄文文案来译制俄文版。此外，鉴于本口岸无印刷设备，新章程须于哈尔滨关印制。

4. 哈尔滨关税务司于哈尔滨关第 2348 号呈中预计，黑龙江航道开始征税后，税收将增加 30000 海关两；本署对此表示赞同，此外，瑷珲关第 32 号呈提交之预算亦非常适度。

1921 年，经水运进口的土货总价值为 1846326 海关两，其中 70% 由哈尔滨关或松花江航道征税；剩余 30% 由黑龙江航道征税，价值 554000 海关两。

经水运由中国口岸出口之土货，总价值为 554000 海关两，其中价值 400000 海关两的货物皆运至黑龙江沿岸地区；然而，对黑龙江航道征税时发现，其中半数为复出口之货物，因此实际可征收之货物价值仅为 200000 海关两。

除此之外，由木筏运至大黑河地区以及布拉戈维申斯克（Blagovestchensk，即海兰泡）地区之货物（源自或运往西伯利亚之货物除外）亦应计算在内，保守估计为 400000 海关两，大多按实际价值征税。

鉴于此，由黑龙江航道征税之货物总价值为 1154000 海关两。

若将从西伯利亚经由黑龙江华岸各地进口之洋货，或经由目前海关尚不知晓的路线（如自布拉戈维申斯克至呼玛河地区）进口之洋货计算在内，贸易总额将达 1200000 海关两，由此所征之税收额或将超过 30000 海关两。

5. 鉴于目前不仅需要对黑龙江航道的运输货物进行征税，还需实施拟议的新章程，因此或需考虑于航道沿岸或于内陆地区适宜管控贸易之地设新分卡。鉴于此，本署已就黑龙江地区的贸易路线及贸易中心撰写了一份简要报告；但因收集信息之渠道较多，包括船长和商人等，故大部分信息仍需要确认。兹认为，在做出明确建议前仍然需要深入调查；如有必要，若贵署同意，可派遣本人（或者其他海关职员）前往呼玛河至奇克特河段实地巡查，以作判断。（附件 5）

若海关要对黑龙江航道之运输货物（尤其是通过木筏运输之货物）进行征税，则须于大黑河上游 9 俄里处设一处分卡。因此，特呈文申请批准开设此分卡，但若今后实际情况证明，呼玛河分卡完全可以管控黑龙江上游而来之木料贸易，则可撤销该分卡。

6. 海关既已将管控黑龙江航道的夏季贸易一事列入计划之中，是否亦需要考虑于冬季对使用雪橇进行的贸易进行管控。目前，商人在呼玛河至下游地区奇克特、太平沟等地之间使用雪橇运送货物时，大多会前往海关申报，但并不交税，而是缴纳厘金，以便得到海关签印凭证,使其货物受到保护;本署确信商人大抵还是愿意交税的。兹认为,海关应于冬季继续管控黑龙江沿岸的贸易,不仅如此,甚至还可于呼玛河、奇克特等地设立分卡,以便在运输目的地为货物提供保护,至于商人方面,若可向其说明其中之利害,亦会得到支持,遂请贵署予以指示;若贵署决定对黑龙江沿岸的冬季贸易进行征税一事需要暂缓,则本署建议,继续如此前一样为商人签印申报文件,以维护海关之地位。

7. 另函附寄《理船章程》草案,作为《总章程》之补充文件。

本署另呈送两份呈文,其中一份呈文是关于对大黑河口岸与松花江之间运输之货物征收土货复进口半税之事,另一份呈文是关于《理船章程》的实施问题以及贸易的合理管控和对走私活动的抑制问题。

您忠诚的仆人

包安济（G. Boezi）

瑷珲关署理税务司

瑷珲关致海关总税务司署第 37 号呈附件 1

稽查黑龙江往来船只进出口货物之各项章程

一、船只

1. 凡于黑龙江航道华岸航行贸易的船只路经沿途各中国海关须停靠完纳税项。现已设立瑷珲与大黑河二关,未来会添设分关分卡。

船只在黑龙江下游华岸最下游分关各处装货至拉哈苏苏下游俄国各地方,须在哈尔滨关的拉哈苏苏分关报明完纳税项;在拉哈苏苏下游俄国各地方装货至黑龙江华岸最下游分关各地方,亦须在拉哈苏苏海关报明完纳税项。

2. 凡船只进出口岸时,皆由关员上船查验,关员执行职务时,船上无论何处何时,关员均可前往检查。

3. 所有船只在口岸内均须按海关指定地点停泊,并遵守《理船章程》。

4. 凡船只载货搭客未经海关许可以前,均不准任意上下,亦不准倒载。凡未经海关许可而装卸倒载货物或行李,酌核罚办充公; 私自上下搭客亦应由海关议罚。

5. 凡船只进口岸时,即应将舱口单、牌照、行李单及各关所签函件呈阅查验,并须将沿途所停各地及在各地所装卸货物、上下搭客开单列明呈报海关。凡船只欲结关开行时,须将舱口单与行李单呈递,若单据符合规程,支付所有应纳税钞后,方能允许结关。委托船员将海关各函件等物送至所达口岸及沿途口岸,须慎重存放,不得损坏,至交与验船员为止。舱口单与行李单须将该船所载货物切实开明,免税之货亦应详列,载货与卸货地点须分别开列标识、号数,货物内容亦须在单内分别详细注明。舱口单须由该船主或委托负责代表人签名做证,如有差错,唯其是问。

6. 凡船只装载货物因故退回,须立即赴海关呈验,否则将不予视为完税之货物。

7. 凡关员代表中国海关向船只索取执照时,该船须将执照交出,关员又可在口岸或沿途各处上船检查。

8. 海关可派关员在船上搜查或与船同行以监视,关员有搜查货物、行李、搭客与水手之权,并可按照《专章》齐集搭客以便检查护照,船员应竭力协助以便关员执行职务。

9. 凡船只载有海关执照为凭之货,沿途不得停泊俄岸,如不遵此章程,则该执照不生效力,但可照本章第十条规定由海关将货物封固,到口岸时,铅饼不动,该船虽沿途停泊俄岸,该货亦按照有执照为凭办理。

10. 船内舱口或所载货物之一部分或马匹均可由海关随意加印铅饼,待该船已抵下货口岸呈验准许后,方能撤毁铅饼。

11. 凡船只除礼拜日或放假日及寻常办公日所定办公时刻外,欲装卸货物、上下搭客,须先请领专单,呈缴单费。此项单费应按照后列之表交纳。

12. 鸦片及罂粟子一概禁止装运。已去壳或未去壳之稻米、中国铜圆制钱不得运输出口;未铸之外国铜圆饼不得运输入口;吗啡、高根注射器及存有鸦片及高根之制造品,或戒烟药品含有鸦片或鸦片与高根所制造之品,除有《专章》规定之医生、药商及化学家按照专章在开具保呈准外,一概禁止装运;军火、军械、食盐,除有专照,均禁止装运。

以上所开各种违禁品或中国政府随时禁止运输或限制运输之物,如在船上无执照为凭,概行充公。

13. 出入各船,如有呈递错误舱口单或私自毁撤铅饼,或有违犯以上各章,即由海关处罚,不超过 500 海关两之罚金或照中国通商口岸现行之办法处罚;如系陆路运输之货物违犯以上各条,此则货主由海关照以上条例处罚。

二、税钞

14. 船钞

凡船只及拖带之船只每四个月须缴纳船钞一次;凡载重 150 吨以上,则每吨每次应纳船钞海关两 4 钱,150 吨及 150 吨以下,则每吨每次应纳船钞海关两 1 钱。

注意:此项船钞待发布通知后,再行征收;但可按照松花江航行办法征收江捐代之。

15. 税率

关税按照中国通商口岸现行之税则征收,凡税则未载之洋土各货均按值百抽五征收。

16. 洋货进口

凡洋货如无海关执照为凭,一经口岸,须完纳进口正税一次,海关即发给收税凭单。

17. 洋货出口

凡已完进口税之洋货,如自完税之日起三年以内原包复出口至中国各地,此除免纳关税外,在海关范围以内则由海关另行发给执照为凭。

洋货无海关证明纳税凭照,则办法如下。

(1)如报出口至中国他处,应完进口正税一次,海关除发给收税单外,如在海关范围以内,则另行发给执照为凭;

(2)如报出口至外国而原货确认洋原产地,则免征税。

18. 洋货进入东三省已开商埠

洋货进入东三省已开商埠,完纳进口正税一次后,按照《专章》由海关发给东三省洋货免重征专照,运至指定地点及沿途,一概免重征。

19. 洋货进入内地

凡已完进口税之洋货进入内地之办法如下。

（1）或逢关纳税,过卡抽厘;

（2）或请领入内地子口单,完纳子口税,该税照进口税率之半征收（免税货物按2.5%征收）,沿途概免重征。

20. 洋货复出口到外国

洋货之有收税单为凭,于三年以内原包转运至外国,按照中国通商口岸现行办法准领取已完进口正税之存票。

注1：此等复出口货物应由分卡证明

注2：凡有东三省免重征专照为凭之货不得领取进口税之存票,唯由外国进入满洲里陆路运至大黑河,再由大黑河转运俄境布拉戈维申斯克（即海兰泡）之货暂时不在此列。

21. 土货由水路进口

由水路运输之土货至海关所在地方

（1）如有他处中国海关所发之执照证明已完出口正税及复进口半税者,则免征税款;

（2）如有他处中国海关所发执照证明已完出口正税者,应按照出口税之半完纳复进口半税;

（3）如非来自口岸者,应完纳出口正税一次,由海关发给收税凭单。

注：凡往来黑龙江沿岸之货,此项复进口半税待发布通知后,再行征收。

22. 土货由水路出口

凡报出口之土货,应完纳出口正税一次,由海关发给税单,如运至他处口岸,应在指定地点完纳复进口半税。

注：凡往来黑龙江沿岸之货,此项复进口半税待发布通知后,再行征收。

23. 土货复出口至国内各地

凡土货有已完出口正税执照为凭,如一年以内原包复出口至国内各地,且在海关范围以内,除免纳出口税外,应领免再纳出口正税之执照,如有已完出口正税与复进口半税之执照,则领免再纳出口正税与复进口半税之凭照。

24. 土货转运至东三省已开商埠

凡已完出口正税与复进口半税之土货，如自完税日起一年以内运至东三省已开商埠，应按照《专章》领取东三省土货免重征专照，运至指定地点及沿途概免重征。

25. 土货复出口至外国

凡已完税之土货一年以内原包复出口至外国

（1）如已完纳出口税，则免征税；

（2）如已完纳出口正税与复进口半税，则准予领取复进口半税之存票。

注1：牛类复出口之期限为六个月；

注2：此等复出口货物应由分卡证明确系出境；

注3：凡有东三省免重征专照为凭之货，不得领取复进口半税之存票。

26. 土货由内地运输到埠

凡由内地运输土货到埠，并于所定期限内出境外国者，可按各通商口岸办法发给三联报单，此项货物除完纳出口正税外，按出口正税之半完纳子口税（免税之货则应纳2.5%），沿途分卡概免重征。

27. 陆路运输货物

凡无完税凭证之土洋各货或入内地或出内地，经过梁家屯分卡（或以后添设他处之分卡），须在该处分卡完纳正税一次。

商人如具殷实之保证或交充足之押款，可于指定地方之海关完纳关税。

以上各章程如有必要时，即可酌量添改完善。

注：本章程所载"口岸"字样是指中国海关设立之地点，所载"船只"字样是指轮船、民船、木筏（木筏不在船钞条例规定之内），木筏贸易另行规定。

又拟27一条请核对示范

27. 陆路运输进口

凡进口由陆路运输进口之土洋各货，应在梁家屯分卡（或以后添设海关分卡）报明查验；商人须担保所运货物必于15日以内在大黑河或瑷珲（或以后瑷珲关添设黑龙江沿江之分关）二处海关呈验；凡确定土产之货免税放行，洋货若无完税凭单，应纳进口正税。

凡出口由陆路运输出口之土洋各货，应先在瑷珲或大黑河（或以后瑷珲关添设黑龙江沿江之分关）二处海关呈报，如无完税凭单，应纳出口或进口正税一次，由海关发给执照，凡此种货物须在梁家屯分卡（或以后添设分卡）报明，以便查核货物与执照是否相符。

11. 1922 年《陆路来往货物拟议章程》

Aigun/Taheiho 31st July. 2

Sir,

1. I have the honour to acknowledge the receipt of your despatch No. 42/89,154 :

transmitting the Board's approval and yours of the suggested scheme for the taxation of goods passing the Liang-chiat'un Barrier, requesting particulars of the procedure, and asking explanations on the proposed patrol system,

and, in reply, to report that I have come to an understanding with the Aigun and Taheiho Chambers of Commerce, and that they agree to guarantee all the inward cargo passing the Barrier, belonging to Members of the Chambers. Copy of the proposed Regulations is appended (Append No. 1) together with an English translation (Append No. 2).

2. I have the honour to solicit your approval of

Inspector General of Customs,

PEKING.

of these Regulations, which represent a progress over existing practice: the Chambers of Commerce substitute themselves as guarantors to the Liangchiat'un Inns for the bulk of the cargo, and they agree to appoint a representative at the Barrier for the busy season. We will have the advantage of handling and examining cargo in the presence of a responsible agent; while the time limit for presentation of cargo and payment of duty at Aigun or Taheiho is reduced from thirty to fifteen days.

From the correspondence exchanged - copy of which is appended (Append No. 3) - you will see that the Chambers of Commerce accept the proposed Regulations "subject to revision if necessary"; but I believe there will be very little friction in the future, and that the essential part of the Regulation will not be repudiated. Should any time the Chambers of Commerce refuse to continue guaranteeing cargo, we can always fall back on the Liangchiat'un Inns, or on a system of cash deposits; what is most important is to see that goods passing Liangchiat'un report (and pay duty) at Aigun or Taheiho.

3. I regret that the Superintendent did not

support

support my contention that goods destined for export overland should be taxed, unless covered by Duty proof; my opinion was based on the difficulty of distinguishing at times between goods of the same kind which may originate as well in Manchuria as in Siberia (e.g. certain furs). The procedure has however been modified to suit the decision of the Board; but in all cases, goods, foreign or native, passing the Barrier outward bound, are to be covered by documents from the Aigun or Taheiho Customs, as it would be too difficult to settle at the Barrier any doubt about the foreign or native origin of the goods.

4.   In accordance with your instructions, I have clearly explained to the Merchants' representatives the mechanism of "Special Exemption Certificates for small lots re-exported from mart of original destination" (Circular No. 1784). - I must add that all the negotiations have been conducted with the help, and in the presence of, the Superintendent, who is therefore fully informed and has already reported to the Shui Wu Ch'u.

5.   The system of patrols is in my opinion an absolute necessity. Goods are smuggled across to or from

from Siberia, right under our nose, three, four, five miles from the Custom House, especially at points where the Russian Customs have a Station, e.g. Upper Blagovestchensk; there are nowadays good roads leading from Taheiho to these places, whence flour, spirit, rice and other commodities are shipped in large amounts. This state of things is harmful enough now; but if we allow it to exist after goods imported overland will be passed free, it will mean that all Native Goods can be safely exported abroad without paying duty, even after having been presented to the Custom House. - Besides, the moral effect of this state of affairs is deplorable : people wonder why a serious organisation like the C. M. Customs let contraband go unchecked in the immediate neighbourhood of their Stations ; I overheard Russians, who do not well understand our position, hint at the illicit benefits that Customs Employes must derive by allowing this traffic; I have even received a petition from the Ferry Company asking the Customs to stop the unfair competition of ferries below and above Harbour Limits.

6.   This traffic should be checked. Of course,

- while

- while in theory we may claim jurisdiction over
the whole Amur frontier,-in practice we cannot pretend
to forbid traffic across the River all along the
Amur at distant places; but we can rightly forbid
- and in fact stop almost entirely - international
exchange of goods in the neighbourhood of our Stations
extending the prohibition as we open more Stations.
For the present, traffic at points between Aigun and
Tsheiho, as also for some distance above Tsheiho and
below Aigun has no reason to be other than
smuggling, and we may solicit the Chinese Government
to forbid it, except at Aigun and Tsheiho.

7.   I append copy of correspondence with the
Superintendent (Append No. 4), in which he states
that the Defence Commissioner is ready to give us
the support of his soldiers. To the Military we
could therefore entrust the fiscal defence of the
frontier on the stretch between Aigun and Tsheiho,
and at the extreme wings of the forbidden area,
where smuggling is limited to commodities that cannot
be passed through either the Chinese or the Russian
Customs (Opium, Spirit, etc) ; but in the immediate
vicinity of the Ports, where even bulky commodities
                                                        can

can be smuggled with profit, it is essential that
we have our own guards, even if they be helped by
soldiers. For the sake of economy, we may for the
present leave to the soldiers exclusively the preventive work around Aigun, as long as traffic is
comparatively unimportant there.

        The duty of our Guards would mainly consist
in frequently patrolling the frontier up to a certain
distance from the Station, keeping a sharp lookout
for any suspicious movement of goods, getting as
much information as possible on smuggling, and
stopping themselves, under ordinary circumstances, cargo
trying to cross without permission. But for more
responsible expeditions, they should only act under
the leadership of a Foreign Out-Door Officer - if
necessary, with the collaboration of soldiers, so as
to minimise danger. - Serious resistance could only
be expected of the smugglers, if our men were
unarmed; this District is lawless, but not in the
immediate vicinity of this Port, or of Aigun; here
people are at times hard to deal with, because they
do not see a display of force on our part: we
will be much more respected, even in Tsheiho, when
we have a small Guard of our own.
                                                Besides

Besides, it is to be considered that, spirit, opium, and the like, which must always be passed as contraband, will carefully avoid our patrols, while other goods, trade in which is permitted on payment of duty, are worth smuggling only if the expense does not exceed the amount of duty payable - therefore they would not be carried too far from Taheiho once reported there - and the risk is minimum. So that we may reasonably expect that the simple presence of our patrols will drive contraband of opium, spirits, etc. farther away from our Ports, and stop, almost entirely, the smuggling of dutiable cargo.

However, we certainly require good men to fill the job, because the work is hard, and, after all, there is always an element of danger, however small, in checking contraband, even in Taheiho, as well as on any frontier. To me, it is essential that these men be armed; people here are not used to see Authority devoid of arms, while a military uniform accompanied by a rifle commands respect and is in itself a splendid protection. The Russian Customs, like frontier guards in practically any Country, have no hesitation in shooting at anyone caught while trying

to

to run across the border without permission: bullets have occasionally flown across to Taheiho, eliciting strong protests from the Chinese Authorities and the Customs; however, the position and traditions of the C. M. Customs are different, and I would be careful to give instructions not to use weapons unless in case of absolute necessity. That this is not difficult to obtain is shown by the example of our Liangohiat'un Guards, which, for years, have been patrolling the back roads duly armed, and never used their rifles yet.

9.   The proposals submitted in my despatch No. 32 are modified and complemented as follows, also with a view to economy :

    a) the Military should be asked to see that nothing crosses the River, in winter or summer, on a stretch extending from a point twenty miles above Taheiho to another twenty miles below Aigun - except such places as are directly controlled by the Customs;

    b) a reward equivalent to Informant's Fee should be issued by the Customs for all cargo seized by the soldiers on the above-mentioned frontier, and handed over to us; the Commissioner may at his discretion issue higher rewards (up to 50 % of the value of the goods) for seizures made under conditions of serious difficulty

or

or risk;

c) two barriers should be established, one above, one below Taheiho, as shown on the accompanying map :

1) one opposite Upper Blagovestchensk, at Ngoniuho (卧牛河) or Ngoniulatze (卧牛硌子), near the terminus of a good road from Taheiho, on a hill right on the edge of the water, affording an excellent view of the frontier for miles up and down river

2) one on an Island opposite to the mouth of the Zeia River - another vital point in the smuggling system - where a small detachment of soldiers is encamped;

d) the question of patrolling an area around Aigun by our own means may be left in abeyance for the present - to be brought up if the overland traffic with Aigun increases together with contraband movements near Aigun;

e) the summer patrolling may be reduced and partly substituted with frequent inspections by motor launch ; four guards for the Upper, three for the Lower Barrier would do, while in winter the boatmen should be transformed into guards, some being added to the barriers, others working in conjunction with the barriers from Taheiho Headquarters;

f) the guards at Liangchiat'un should be increased from two to four as already proposed ; they should be supplied with horses, which are now lent by the Messenger who has two;

g) the Guards should be paid an initial salary of Hk. Tls. 10 or 11 per month, according to ability; horses and harness should be bought

by

by the Customs; fodder to be supplied in fixed quantities per month;

h) horses with saddle and harness should be also provided for seven boatmen, to be transformed into guards for the winter ♯ fodder being supplied as above;

i) one extra junior Tidewaiter should be appointed for supervision duty at the Barriers; but, for economy's sake, we may detail one of the Foreign Officers from Taheiho to the Barriers replacing him with a good Chinese Tidewaiter for duty in Taheiho.

10.   As regards the location of our Barriers, the one up-river is over two verst from the nearest soldiers' camp, which is at Wutaoho (五道河); I would suggest that a batch of six or eight soldiers be detached for duty at our Barriers. The Defence Commissioner has expressed his willingness to do so as an exceptional favour, but we must supply one large room, and supply firewood for the winter; I would earnestly recommend a little extra expense; it will bring us so much added safety. - I have also considered the advisability of making the Upper Barrier a Duty-Collecting Office, but I have discarded the idea : the traffic crossing there is solely justified for the present by the non-payment of our Duties; once duty is to be paid, merchandise will find it

useless

useless to make a detour from the straight path, via Taheiho and Blagovestchensk.

11.   It would be very useful to supply each of the Barriers with a small two-oared gig, to be manned by the guards; at the Lower Barrier it would also serve the purpose of maintaining communications opened with the mainland. One old gig, very much out of shape, can be repaired tant bien que mal; now it has been laying for years with the refuse, but it can be made use of for a Barrier; another should be built.

12.   The expenses of the Patrol System could be summed up as follows (maximum per year):

Initial Outlay:	Hk. Tls.
One log Cabin for the Upper Barrier, with accomodation for guards and soldiers	700.00
One log Cabin for Lower Barrier	500.00
One small gig	165.00
Horses : 14 for Taheiho, 4 for Liangchia-t'un @ $ 40.00 = $ 720 =	480.00
Harness and saddles : 18 sets @ $ 30.00 = $ 540 =	360.00
Total Initial Outlay Hk. Tls.	**2,205.00**

Recurring Expenses (annual)	Hk. Tls.
Guards : 7 for New Barriers, 2 for Liangchist'un @ 11 per month	1,188.00
One Foreign Tidewaiter : @ 100 p.m.	1,200.00
Forward	2,388.00

	Forward Hk.Tls.	2,388.00
Food for 18 horses @ $ 100 per year per horse, = $ 1,800 =		1,200.00
Firewood for 7 months: 2/3rds to Guards, full to soldiers		150.00
Petty Cash (kerosene Oil, etc)		120.00
Total Recurring Expenses Hk.Tls.		3,858.00

which could be reduced to 3,438, if, instead of a Foreign Tidewaiter, there be appointed a Chinese Tidewaiter, say, at Hk. Tls. 65 per month.

13.   The merchants have asked, if possible, to introduce the new procedure from 1st September; if you are agreeable I would have no objections, even if the patrol system is not yet established : heavy overland traffic does not start until the beginning or middle of October.

I have the honour to be,

Sir,

Your obedient Servant,

Acting Commissioner.

Aigun Despatch No. 64 to I.G.

Append No. 2.
_____

VERSION OF PROPOSED REGULATIONS FOR THE CONTROL AND
TAXATION OF CARGO MOVED ON THE OVERLAND ROUTE
(TSITSIHAR - AIGUN - TAHEIHO)

1. All cargo incoming and outgoing by the Overland Route must be declared to the Liangchiat'un Barrier; cargo passing by the back roads will be confiscated, if found out by the Customs.

Cargo Inward.

2. All cargo coming overland must be declared to, and presented for examination at the Aigun or Taheiho Custom House within 15 days after passing the Liangchiat'un Barrier.

3. The Aigun and Taheiho Chambers of Commerce shall hand in to the Customs a general guarantee for the cargo consigned to the firms affiliated to the Chambers, engaging themselves to pay duty on goods free by Regulations - and to pay duty and a fine on dutiable goods - in case of failure to report to, and present for examination at, the Aigun or Taheiho Custom House within the fixed time limit.

4. Firms expecting cargo by the overland route shall make out a bond, in duplicate, giving in full the description of the goods, quantity and destination (Aigun or Taheiho), and declaring that the goods will be presented for examination (or payment of duty) at the Aigun or Taheiho Custom House - the original is to be stamped with the firm's seal and to be vised by the Chamber of Commerce. Both copies shall be presented to the Liangchiat'un Barrier, where the cargo will be checked with the Bond. The original Bond shall then be sent to the Custom House at the place of
destination

destination, and the duplicate shall be handed back to the merchant to accompany the goods to the Aigun or Taheiho Custom House for examination there. (Specimen of Bond attached). Firms not guaranteed by the Chamber of Commerce, wishing to import cargo overland shall, as heretofore, be guaranteed by the Liangchiat'un Inns or deposit a sufficient amount as security.

5. Cargo coming overland shall be examined by the Aigun or Taheiho Customs, and passed free if native - charged duty if foreign, unless covered by duty proof. The original copy of the Bond shall then be returned to the merchants.

Cargo Outward.

6. All cargo going overland must be declared to, and presented for examination at, the Aigun or Taheiho Custom House.

7. Cargo going overland shall, after examination, be passed free if native and pay duty if foreign - unless covered by duty proof.

8. Applications for foreign and native goods going overland shall be presented in duplicate - one copy to be stamped by the Customs and handed to the applicant to accompany the goods, which must be declared at the Liangchiat'un Barrier and shall be released if found in order.

9. Cargo going overland not covered by stamped permits issued by the Aigun or Taheiho Customs shall be detained.

10. Horses and vehicles of undoubtedly native origin for the private use of local merchants and inhabitants shall, if not carrying cargo, be free to pass the Barrier both ways and shall not be unnecessarily delayed. Foreign horses and vehicles not covered by duty proof shall, as heretofore, be guaranteed or be secured by deposit according to Regulations.
11. Goods

11.   Goods manufactured and produced in China and coming from Chinese places shall be considered as Native Goods.

12.   The Aigun and Tsheiho Chambers of Commerce shall appoint a representative who will reside permanently in Liangshint'un during the winter season, and be present whenever packages are opened for examination by the Customs Office.

呈海关总税务司署 <u>64</u> 号文　　　　　　　瑷珲关 / 大黑河 1922 年 7 月 31 日

尊敬的海关总税务司（北京）：

1. 根据海关总税务司署第 42/89154 号令：

"对于经由梁家屯分卡来往之货物的拟议征税办法，税务处及海关总税务司均已批准，请提交详细章程，并对拟议巡缉办法做出进一步解释。"

兹汇报，本署已与瑷黑两地商会达成协定，由商会为入会各商号经梁家屯分卡之货物提供担保。随呈附上拟议章程抄件（附件 1）及其英文译本（附件 2）。

2. 该拟议章程较现行惯例改进之处良多，此前凡经由梁家屯分卡之货物，若须担保皆由店户出具，而今商会将代以开具，并同意于运输旺季指派代表至梁家屯分卡常驻，协助分卡关员检验货物，此外，过卡后至瑷珲口岸或大黑河口岸报验纳税之时限亦从 30 日减至 15 日。有鉴于此，特此申请批准该拟议章程。

兹附与商会往来信函抄件（附件 3——商来字第八号及商去字第八号），从中可知，商会同意拟议章程"如有必要，可随时修订"。然兹认为，该拟议章程于今后实际操作中应不会有何冲突之处，条款主旨亦不会遭到驳斥。如遇商会拒绝继续担保之情况，货物仍可照梁家屯店户担保办法办理或交以押款，唯确保货物过卡后可至瑷珲和大黑河两处海关报验（纳税）即可。

3. 因产自满洲及西伯利亚之同类货物（如皮货）极易混淆，故本署此前提出，经陆路出口之货物除持有已经完税之凭照外，即应征税，但遗憾的是，海关监督未予认同，最终只得照税务处指示做出修改；但考虑梁家屯分卡难以对货物为洋产或是土产做出分辨，拟议章程已有规定，凡货物经由梁家屯分卡出口者，无论洋土，均须持有瑷珲或大黑河两处海关签发之凭照。

4. 本署已奉贵署指令，向商人代表就海关总税务司署第 1784 号通令所规定之"小宗货物自初始目的地贸易市场复出口时的特别免重征执照"发放办法做出解释说明。此外，海关监督亦参与了整个协商过程，并提供帮助，因此了解所有情况，业已向税务处报告。

5. 关于巡缉之事，本署认为实有必要。目前，货物往来西伯利亚走私者甚多，走私之地距海关不过三四五英里之遥，甚至有自俄国海关所设分卡之处［如布拉戈维申斯克（Blagovestchensk，即海兰泡）上游］走私者；而且，如今自大黑河通往此等去处之路颇多，面粉、酒、大米及其他货物皆可大宗运输。走私之害已是十分严重，海关若继续纵容,一旦经陆路进口之土货获准免税通行,也就意味着,所有土货即便送交海关报验,随后亦可免税安全出口至国外。而且,走私之事已为海关带来诸多负面影响,人们疑虑,为何中国海关这一庄严的组织机构会允许货物在其管辖范围附近免受查验走私至国外,甚至有传言称,俄国人(对海关处境不甚了解)暗讽海关职员从中获取非法利益,本署业已收到渡船公司请求海关制止其他渡船于港口界限上下游所行不当竞争之举的请愿书。

6. 当然,于理而论,整个黑龙江边境均可纳入海关的管辖范围,但于实际而言,对于黑龙江沿岸偏远一带的跨江运输,海关亦是鞭长莫及;不过,对于海关附近的跨江运输,若增设分卡,扩大防范界限,倒是可以遏制甚至杜绝走私之事。目前,瑷珲与大黑河两地之间,大黑河上游以及瑷珲下游各地走私猖獗,或可请求中国政府于瑷珲及大黑河以外各地打击走私。

7. 兹附与海关监督往来信函件抄件(附件4——监去字第三十六号及监来字一百九十八号),从中可知,镇守使(Defence Commissioner)已同意随时为海关提供兵力支持。如此一来,瑷珲与大黑河两地之间以及黑龙江沿岸边缘区域的防护工作便可委托军方接管,在此等区域走私之货物仅限于中俄两国海关禁运一类(鸦片、酒等);然于港口附近,大宗货物仍可走私并从中获利,因此海关应配备为己所属之卫兵,此外,恐怕还需要士兵襄助,不过为节约经费,目前仅需士兵负责瑷珲周边的防护工作,毕竟瑷珲口岸往来货物运输相对无甚紧要。

8. 而卫兵则主要负责于海关关卡附近的边境区域定期巡缉,留心一切有可疑行迹之货物,尽量搜集走私相关信息,一般还需拦截未经许可擅自过江之货物,但远途巡缉须有洋籍外班关员的领导,如有必要,还可请士兵协助,以降低危险。此外,若卫兵未配备武器,走私者极有可能会做出强烈反抗;瑷珲关区整体法纪松散,但大黑河和瑷珲两处口岸及邻近之地尚可,唯民众有时难以应对,皆因瑷珲关未向其动用过武力,因此若可有自己的卫兵队,海关必会更受重视,在大黑河的威望亦会有所提高。

诚然,酒、鸦片等公认之违禁品势必会于过江时设法逃避海关巡查,但其他缴税后便可出口交易之货物,如欲走私,必会考虑走私价值和风险,只有在走私费用低于应纳税金时,走私才会有价值,因此此等货物于大黑河口岸报验后,不会运至太远的地方走私出口。有鉴于此,相信只要在口岸附近安排卫兵巡缉,鸦片、酒等违禁品便不会再出现于海关管辖范围之内,应税货物的走私之事亦会就此杜绝。

巡缉工作颇为艰苦,须择良人担此重任,而且于大黑河此等边境之地搜查违禁品,或多或少都具有一定的危险性,鉴于此,兹认为,应为负责巡缉之卫兵配备武器; 而且,此地政府从未以无配备武器之态示人,军服加步枪威慑更甚,于其自身亦为绝佳之保护。 俄国海关如他国边境卫兵一样,遇有未经许可试图过境之人,一概射杀,有时子弹甚至会飞入大黑河,中国政府及海关对此已表示强烈抗议。不过,本署深知中国海关的情况和惯例与之不同,届时必会命卫兵小心谨慎,如无绝对必要,不得动用武器。梁家屯分卡卫兵巡缉后路时素来配有武器,但迄今未有开火之例,由此可见此命令之实施并无难处。

9. 秉持经济原则,现对瑷珲关第 32 号呈中所提建议做出如下修改及补充。

（1）请军方负责于冬夏两季对黑龙江自大黑河上游 20 英里至瑷珲下游 20 英里之间的沿岸各地（海关直接管理之地除外）进行监管,确保无未经允许过江之情况。

（2）凡士兵有于上述边境缉获物资并上交海关者,可由海关发给举报费; 若缉获物资时情况较为艰难或风险过大,税务司可自行决定为之增加赏金（至多为缉获物资价值的 50%）。

（3）于大黑河上下游各增设一处分卡:

① 一处设于布拉戈维申斯克上游对岸,在与大黑河相通的一条大路终端附近（卧牛河）,此处位于水域边缘山坡之上,视野绝佳,河流上、下游数英里之边境状况皆可尽收眼底;

② 一处设于结雅河河口对岸的岛屿处,此处亦为走私要地,现已驻有一支士兵队伍。

（4）派遣海关卫兵于瑷珲周边地区巡缉之事或可暂行搁置,待瑷珲陆路运输及附近的走私活动增多之时再行商议。

（5）巡缉工作至夏日时便可相应减少,还可使用摩托艇; 至冬日,水手可担任卫兵之职,一部分派驻分卡,一部分负责分卡与大黑河总关之间的巡缉工作,其中 4 人负责上游分卡,3 人负责下游分卡。

（6）驻守梁家屯分卡之卫兵仍依此前提议由两名增至四名,并为之配备马匹; 当前马匹均为信差所借,而信差亦仅有两匹马。

（7）卫兵的初始薪俸可定为每月 10 海关两或 11 海关两,依个人能力而定; 马匹及马具均由海关购置; 饲料按月定量发放。

（8）为 7 名于冬季担任卫兵之水手配备马匹,附带马鞍等一应马具,并如上所述发放饲料。

（9）需另指派一名初等钤子手负责监督分卡工作; 但为节省经费,可自大黑河选派一名洋籍钤子手至分卡,另择一名合格的华籍钤子手分担其于大黑河之事务。

10. 此外,鉴于上游拟设分卡之地与士兵营地(五道河)仅相距两俄里,建议届时由6名或8名士兵驻扎该分卡,对此镇守使已表示愿意支持,但提出须由海关提供相应房间及冬季所需木桦。特此申请批准小笔额外经费,此举将为海关更添一层安全保障。本署曾考虑于此分卡征税,但商人绕路至此,皆因可免税通过,若开始征税,便不会再有过往者,毕竟经由大黑河及布拉戈维申斯克过境才为最近之路,故此作罢。

11. 为便于两处分卡卫兵工作,应为各卡配备一艘双桨小船,下游分卡还可借此与陆地保持通信。瑷珲关现有一艘旧船废弃多年,虽已残破不堪,但维修后仍可供分卡使用,因此仅需另外再造一艘船。

12. 上述巡缉办法费用预算如下(每年之上限)。

初期经费:	海关两(两)
于上游分卡修建木屋一处,供卫兵及士兵居住	700.00
于下游分卡修建木屋一处	500.00
建造一艘小船	165.00
马匹:大黑河 14 匹;梁家屯 4 匹 每匹 40.00 银圆,共 720 银圆	480.00
马鞍及马具:18 套,每套 30.00 银圆,共 540 银圆	360.00
初期经费总计:	2205.00
(年度)日常性支出	海关两(两)
卫兵:新分卡 7 人,梁家屯分卡新增 2 人 每人每月 11 海关两	1188.00
1 名洋籍钤子手:每月 100 海关两	1200.00
18 匹马饲料:每匹每年 100 银圆,共 1800 银圆	1200.00
7 个月所用木桦:卫兵木桦费用的 2/3;士兵木桦费用的全部	150.00
小额现金支出(煤油等)	120.00
(年度)日常性支出总计:	3858.00

若以一名华籍钤子手代替洋籍钤子手,每月薪俸仅为65海关两,则费用可缩减至3438海关两。

13. 商人询问此新规定可否于9月1日起实施;若海关总税务司署予以批准,本署则无反对意见。虽然巡缉队伍尚未成形,但于陆路运输并无影响,毕竟陆路运输至 10 月初或中旬方会开始增多。

您忠诚的仆人

包安济(G. Boezi)

瑷珲关署理税务司

瑷珲关致海关总税务司署第 64 号呈附件 2

陆路来往货物拟议章程

（经齐齐哈尔—瑷珲—大黑河路线运输之货物的管理及征税办法）

译 本

一、由陆路来往货物须在梁家屯分卡报验,如不报关由他路偷过被关查出者,即行充公。

运来货物

二、凡由陆路运来货物于梁家屯分卡经过,在十五日以内应到瑷珲或大黑河海关报验。

三、瑷珲及大黑河两商会开列入会各商号来货保单一纸,担保其免征货物在定期内不来黑瑷两关报验应负缴纳税款之责任,再应征货物在定期内不来黑瑷两关报验应负缴纳税款及罚金之责任。

四、各商号来货应开具正副担保之单各一纸,将货色及数量并指运地点(瑷珲或大黑河)详注,并声明过卡以后十五日内到黑瑷两关报验(或纳税),正张本号盖印戳记,并由商会验讫盖章,一并送往梁家屯分卡,该分卡与货单查核相符,送回指运地点海关,副张交给商人同货物来黑河瑷珲两关报验(保单程式另详);如并未由商会担保,各商号来货时仍照梁家屯店户担保办法办理或交足数押款。

五、由陆路运来货物由瑷珲或大黑河海关查验后,土货免税放行,洋货除持有已经完税之凭照外,应即征税。洋土各货查验应征应免后,将保单正张交还该商。

运往货物

六、凡由陆路运往货物应在瑷黑两关报验。

七、由陆路运往货物,若为土货,查验后免税放行,若为洋货,除持有已经完税之凭照外,即应征税。

八、凡由陆路运往洋土货物开具报单两纸送关查验,其一纸由关盖印交还该商,该商持此同货到梁家屯分卡报验，如货单相符，立即放行。

九、凡由陆路运往货物到梁家屯分卡，如无黑瑷两关放行凭证，即行扣留。

十、凡本地商民往来车马并不装货，且确是土产并自用者，均得自由来往分卡，不得无故为难；倘有洋车马无完关税之执照者，仍需具保或交以押款。

十一、凡中国制造品及出产来自中国各地方者，一概均认为土货。

十二、瑷黑两商会公举代表一人，每至冬令常驻梁家屯，遇有必须开箱或解包检验之货，该关员跟同商会代表检验。

12. 1922 年《中俄黑龙江航行地方临时协议》

47.

I. G.
6

Aigun / Taheiho 5th August, 2.

Sir,

1.   In continuation of my despatches Nos 44, 47 and 54, and in reply to your despatch No.5e/90,054: concerning the Aids to Navigation on the Amur,

I have the honour to report that collection of Dues and the measures taken to enforce it have met with no objection on the part of the Merchants or Steamer Agencies, which were consulted when the Agreement was being discussed. Only the military have claimed, as usual, certain exemptions; I have been able, however, to turn most of their claims down, and I hope to bring them in line altogether. Collection of Dues on passengers tickets is also satisfactory as far as it can be: we cannot control in toto the Companies' statements, and must rely on them to a certain extent. - At Lahasusu, collection was started on

The Inspector General of Customs,
PEKING.

on 17th June; the assistant in charge of that station has recently reported that he has been able to collect duty, also on cargo originating on the Sungari and destined for Russian Ports, without the need of additional staff.

2.   In compliance with your request, I am sending an English translation of the Agreement signed on 27th May (Append No. 1). I would like to point out to two gross mistakes which - inter alia - throw light on the poor and careless way in which the text was compiled. One concerns the half Tariff dues leviable on cargo carried by Junks and Rafts: the text seems to apply it only to general cargo, while it was meant to apply also to Timber, Cattle, Fowls, etc ; after consulting with the Taoyin, I have followed the spirit, not the letter, of the clause. Another mistake occurs in connection with the division of the River into two sections for duty-paying purposes : the text (Chinese and Russian) only mentions Taheiho (Sahalian), not Blagoveschensk, whereby the Russians claim that the division into two sections only applies to the Chinese side -: they accordingly collect full Dues for any distance travelled and half

half additional dues on cargo originating on the chinese side, which has only paid half Tariff dues. It is hard to make the Russians change their mind; as it is, the Chinese do not suffer, as they contribute less and get the same benefit as the Russians.

3.   On the 26th July I despatched Mr. G. R. Baukham, Senior Out-door Officer, on a tour of inspection of the Aids-to-Navigation as far as Habarovsk, in company with Engineers of the Russian Water Transports and with a Member of the Taheiho Chamber of Commerce, appointed by the Taoyin. Mr. Baukham absence is felt here, but I decided to rather go to some inconvenience than to be altogether in the dark concerning conditions on the River. - Of course, I would welcome an early arrival of the River Inspector, whoever he be; I expect that negotiations with Mr. Ignatieff are being carried through the Harbin Commissioner, who is much in a better position than I am for that ; but, should the appointment of Mr. Ignatieff meet with difficulties and be long delayed, I would suggest that Mr. Sweeting - or another capable man - be appointed as soon as possible, provided they be willing to take up seriously the study of the Russian language.

language. - I am afraid that the delays deprive us of a precious experience; and, should the projected Conference on the navigation of the Frontier Rivers and Aids to Navigation be held in Aigun, it would be of great value to the Customs to have first-hand knowledge of facts and competent technical advice.

4.   Concerning the suggestion put forward by the Harbin Commissioner, and taken up by me, to have one Section of the Amur directly administered by China, I am under the impression that Mr.Garden's objection against two Administrations was directed against the division according to territory, i.e., the Chinese side to be controlled by the Chinese, the Russian side by the Russian; which, of course, is very unsatisfactory. But, if we had one section (both sides of the River), I am persuaded that we may run it on the same lines as the Russian, with the same efficiency, and more or less at the same cost; the advantages would be many : check (direct) on expenditure on half of the River, increased prestige for China - and, for us, a better knowledge of at least half the Frontier, which may be turned to

use

use also for fiscal purposes. - I would therefore like to know whether I could suggest this plan, after having ascertained the probable expenditure, at the forthcoming Conference.

5.   I have also the honour to forward copy in Chinese (Append No. 2) and Russian (Append No. 3) of 16 Supplementary Rules drawn by the Joint Commission, defining the control over work and expenditure, and some points in connection with the collection of Dues. An english translation of the chinese text is also appended (No. 4). These rules were submitted to the Heilungchiang Provincial Authorities by the Taoyin, and approved in the present form. The Taoyin, on 22nd July signed them without my knowledge, and I have, naturally, reserved your approval - which I have the honour to solicit, notwithstanding the fact that the text could not be amended and perfected as much as would have been desirable, owing to the total incomprehension of the Taoyin's representative who conducted the negotiations for him.

I had proposed, and the Russians had accepted, another Article which ran as follows :

"Chinese

"Chinese Vessels when navigating the section "from Kasakevitch to the sea (海 口) will "pay River Dues on the same proportion as "Russian Vessels."

This Article, for vague reasons of a political nature, has been rejected by the Provincial Authorities.

Copy of this despatch is being sent to the Harbin Commissioner.

I have the honour to be,

Sir,

Your obedient Servant,

Acting Commissioner.

Aigun despatch No. 67 to I. G.

Append No. 1.

Translation of Chinese Text of "Provisional Local Agreement concerning Navigation on the Amur".

The Heiho Taoyin of the Republic of China and the Director of the Russian Amur Government Water Transport Office have discussed the question of the collection of Dues on cargo and passengers carried by Chinese and Russian Steamers, Junks and Rafts, and on Rafts, navigating the Amur for the upkeep of the Channel of the Frontier River, the maintenance of Aids to Navigation and the improvement of navigation therein. - The Heiho Taoyin of the Republic of China on one side and the Director of the Russian Amur Government Water Transport Office on the other, with a view to the improvement of navigation on the Amur (Heilungchiang) and considering the frontier relationship of both countries, have come to the present Agreement.

For this purpose, the Heiho Taoyin of the Republic of China has nominated as his representatives with full powers :

Mr. Wang Shu, Secretary for Foreign Affairs and

Mr. Ch's Hsi-chen, Adviser for Foreign Affairs,

and the Director of the Russian Amur Government Water Transport Office has nominated as his representative with full powers :

Mr. Engineer Lagutin, Chief of the Amur Navigation Office.

1. RULES FOR THE WORKING OF THE AGREEMENT.

Art. 1. This provisional local Agreement shall become operative from the date of signature by both parties, and shall be in force during the navigation season of 1922 (the 11th year of the Republic of China).

Art 2.

Art. 2. The interest of both parties being involved, the present Agreement will have the character of a mutual understanding. Owners of vessels and those in charge of Rafts navigating on the frontier waters of the Amur shall be responsible for (the payment of Dues for ?) the upkeep and navigation therein. The present Agreement, being of a local and mutual nature shall not effect the Navigation Rules and other Amur Regulations in force, nor shall it interfere with the freight rates in China and Russia.

II. RULES ON COLLECTION OF DUES AND EXPENDITURE.

Art. 3. The Tariff of Dues to be paid on cargo and passengers carried by steamers and Junks shall be fixed at a meeting of Chinese and Russian Shipping Companies, public bodies and those interested in shipping, to be called by the Heiho Taoyin of China (concurrently Commissioner for Foreign Affairs) and the Director of the Russian Amur Government Water Transport Office.

Art. 4. The procedure for collecting Dues on passengers and cargo shall be fixed jointly by representatives appointed by the Director of the Amur Government Water Transport Office and by the Heiho Taoyin of the Republic of China.

Art. 5. Questions concerning the collection of Dues on cargo and passengers carried by Chinese and Russian Steamers, Junks and Rafts, or on Rafts, as well as concerning the supervision of expenditure and other matters shall be fixed by additional rules to be agreed upon by a Sino-Russian Joint Commission, to be convened after the conclusion of this Agreement.

Art. 6. Chinese and Russian Steamers, Junks and rafts on the Chinese side shall pay Dues to the C. M. Customs; on the russian side, to the (Commission under the control of the) Amur Navigation Office.

III. RULES CONCERNING AIDS TO, AND IMPROVEMENTS OF NAVIGATION.

Art. 7. All works in connection with Aids-to-Navigation, the erection

erection of lights and signals, the removal of shoals and wrecks, and others of a similar nature, shall be undertaken by the Amur Navigation Office. The expenses for such works shall be defrayed from the total amount of Dues collected on both sides on cargo and passengers. Such undertaking shall, on the part of China, be temporarily entrusted to the Russians, in the name of the local authorities.

Art. 8. The above-mentioned works shall be undertaken in proportion to the amount of Dues collected. The Amur Navigation Office shall, according to Art. 5, submit beforehand the plans to the Sino-Russian Joint Commission for approval.

Art. 9. Misunderstandings arising from the working of this Agreement shall be settled by a Third Commission, whose decision shall be final; no other action will be taken.

TARIFF.

Dues on Cargo shall be calculated by the pood, according to the description of the goods. Building Materials, iron, cast iron, steel and leadware, cereals, hay and fodder, vegetables, salt, coal and charcoal, and agricultural machines other than wooden shall pay 1 cent per pood. All other cargo shall pay 2 cents per pood. Cargo carried by Junks and rafts shall pay half of the Tariff applied to those carried by steamers.

DUES ON TIMBER. Timber for firewood and building purpose shall pay ½ cent on a length of three sajens and on a thickness of 7 vershok. Firewood shall pay 10 cents per square sajen, on a thickness of ¾ to 1 arshine.

CATTLE. Large ones shall pay 30 cents per head; small ones 15 cents per head.

FOWLS. Fowls, irrespective of size, shall pay 1 cent each.

DUES

DUES ON PASSENGERS' TICKETS. Dues on passengers' tickets shall be at the rate of 5% ad valorem, irrespective of class.

REMARKS.

1. For the sake of justice, the Amur River shall be divided into two sections for the collection of Dues on cargo and Passengers' tickets - one from Taheiho to Kasakevitch, the other from Taheiho to Pokrovka. For each section, half of the Tariff shall be paid.

2. The amount of Dues collected on cargo and passengers' tickets by both sides shall be deposited by the collecting offices in Chinese and Russian Government Banks. Nothing shall be drawn except when duly sanctioned and endorsed by the two Presidents of the Commission.

3. The Sino-Russian Joint Commission shall be composed of eight members. The Presidents shall be the Heiho Taoyin (of China) and the Russian Amur Government Water Transport Office Director. The remainder of the Members, an equal number on each side, shall be nominated by the two Presidents.

4. Dues on cargo and passengers' tickets shall be collected on cargo and passengers carried by steamers, junks and rafts navigating on the Amur. The Ferry shall not be included in these Regulations.

True Translation

[signature]

Acting Commissioner.

兹根據本年五月二十七日所簽訂之中俄黑龍江航行地方臨時協議第五款之規定另擬

細則暨收捐辦法如左

一　所有收入一切捐款專為修理中俄兩國交界之黑龍江全部航路暨安設燈照之

用不得移作別項用途

二　一切測量修江工程安設燈照清理礁石或沉物及其他一切工程得由中俄兩委員長

各派專門委員一人預將計畫工程製造圖表編成預算各三分送呈兩委員長批准

後施行如兩委員長不同意時交合組委員會核議

三　中國委員長得隨時派員實地調查修江工程及各項開支賬簿過有疑義時中國

代表與俄水道局監督不能在當地解决者得提出合組委員會議决依行之如再

不能解决由第三委員會解决之第三委員會組織法中俄兩委員長指定合組會

外同等人數組織之

四　俄水道局每半月得將每段工程各項開支清單經俄總司賬暨黑河道尹之代

表簽字抄送中俄兩委員長查核

五　修江一切工程在此協約期間暫委託俄水道局兼辦一切人員不另支薪但中俄

雙方由所收捐款項下得各提百分之十成以資兩岸收捐機關辦公

六　凡航路調查員因公出外得由中俄兩國官憲發給長期護照妥為保護

七　凡航路調查員因公外出時乘中外兩國輪船不給票價俄國水道局得予以

相當協助並供給各項船隻及住房等項

八一切開支字據須經中俄兩委員長或中國委員長所派之代表批准後始准登
記賬簿

九所收捐歙無論數目多寡須發給票據並留存根

十每月底須將中俄兩岸收捐確數由經徵機關報告合組委員會

十一會此無一定地點如中國委員長召集開會時會議地點即在中國地方俄委員
長請召集開會時會議地點即在俄國地方中俄兩委員長輪流主席

收捐辦法

十二凡船隻照章完納江捐後艙口單由微收機關(即海關或水道局)加特別鈐記

十三過江貨物暨客票無論由華輪或俄輪運載應在輸出地方完納江捐孔入口
各貨登於艙口單內而該艙口單按本條第十二款所定業經微收機關加蓋特
別鈐記者不得重徵如無以上憑據者應在卸貨地點徵收

十四客票捐之徵收限於航行黑龍江全部依照臨時協議第六款之辦法中國方面

由海關代收俄國方面由水道局所屬之委員會收之但過江搭客票捐無論由
華輪或俄輪載運應在上船地方完納

十五凡貨物由此岸運往對岸者(如黑河運布卑)暨由黑河運至黃河或由黃河運至
黑河兩卑之貨物應按點捐額減半徵收

十六此細則於雙方簽字後發生效力其有效期間與地方臨特協議同

外交　顧　問　車席珍

黑河道尹兼愛琿交涉員宋文郁

Aigun despatch No. 67 to I. G.

Append No. 3.

Russian Text of Additional Regulations and collection
Procedure in accordance with Provisional Agreement of 27th
May 1922, re Aids to Navigation on the Amur.

ИНСТРКЦIЯ

Руссо-Китайской Коммиссiи, дѣйствующей въ порядкѣ
ст. 5-й Временнаго Мѣстнаго Соглашенiя отъ 27-го
Мая 1922 года объ обложенiи грузовъ на русскихъ
и китайскихъ паровыхъ и не паровыхъ судахъ,
плавающихъ по находящейся въ обоюдномъ пользованiи
рѣкѣ Амуру и объ обложенiи плотовъ и грузовъ
на нихъ особымъ грузо-пассажирскимъ сборомъ на
нужды поддержанiя исправности обстановки фарватера
на находящейся въ обоюдномъ пользованiи рѣкѣ Амурѣ
и для улучшенiя условiй плаванiя по ней.

1/ Всѣ средства полученные отъ грузо-пассажирскихъ
сборовъ по всей пограничной рѣкѣ Амуръ, предназна-
чаются только для установки судоходныхъ сигналовъ,
освѣщенiя ихъ, удаленiя подводныхъ камней и карчей
и вообще на работы по улучшенiю условiй плаванiя
по рѣкѣ Амуру. Расходованiе же выше означенныхъ
средствъ на какiя-либо другiя потребности ни въ ко-
емъ случаѣ не допускается.

2/ Проэкты, планы и смѣты предполагаемыхъ работъ
составляются спецiальными лицами, назначенными съ
каждой стороны по отдѣльности Предсѣдателями Руссо-
Китайской Коммиссiи. Составленные проэкты, планы и
смѣты изготовляются въ трехъ экземплярахъ и
подаются на утвержденiе Предсѣдателями Руссо-
Китайской Коммиссiи, если при утвержденiи представ-
ленныхъ проэктовъ, плановъ и смѣтъ возникнетъ
разногласiе, то таковые передаются для дополнитель-
наго обсужденiя въ Коммиссiю въ полномъ ея составѣ.

3/ Китайскiй Предсѣдатель Руссо-Китайской Коммиссiи
имѣетъ право въ любое время командировать своего
свѣдущаго

свѣдущаго человѣка для осмотра произведенныхъ и
производимыхъ работъ, провѣрки правильности ихъ и
правильности расходованiя денежныхъ суммъ и записей
ихъ въ приходо-расходныхъ книгахъ. Въ случаѣ возни-
кновенiя недоразумѣнiй по тѣмъ или инымъ вопросамъ,
если эти недоразумѣнiя не разрѣшатся совмѣстно съ
представителями Управленiя Водныхъ Путей Амурскаго
бассейна на мѣстѣ, вопросы передаются въ смѣшанную
Коммиссiю; если же и здѣсь не будетъ вынесено
рѣшенiя, удовлетворяющаго обѣ стороны, то спорные
вопросы передаются для окончательнаго рѣшенiя согласи
договора въ особую третейскую коммиссiю, назначаемую
Предсѣдателями Руссо-Китайской Коммиссiи поровну въ
каждой стороны изъ лицъ, лично не заинтересованныхъ
въ результатахъ рѣшенiя спорныхъ вопросовъ.

4/ По истеченiи каждыхъ 15 дней Амурское Водное
Управленiе должно представлять Предсѣдателямъ Руссо-
Китайской Коммиссiи выписи изъ отчетныхъ книгъ
каждаго участка по работамъ, произведеннымъ на нихъ
за это время, за подписью бухгалтера Амурскаго
Воднаго Управленiя и Китайскаго представителя отъ
Дао-инъ.

5/ Производство перечисленныхъ выше работъ, на время
дѣйствiя сего соглашенiя поручается русскому
Управленiю Водныхъ Путей Амурскаго Бассейна, служащiе
котораго за общее руководительство работами отъ
Руссо-Китайской Коммиссiи особаго назначенiя не
получаютъ. 10% суммы сборовъ на Китайской сторонѣ
отчисляются Китайской Таможнѣ и 10% суммы сборовъ
на Русской сторонѣ отчисляются Управленiю Водныхъ
Путей Амурскаго бассейна.

6/ Лица, отправляемые для контроля, должны имѣть
при себѣ на право свободнаго передвиженiя на
Русской и Китайской сторонѣ установленные охранные
листы

листы отъ русскихъ и китайскихъ властей пользуются особымъ содѣйствіемъ ихъ.

7/ Всѣ лица, командируемыя для осмотра произведенныхъ и производимыхъ работъ, пользуются правомъ безплатнаго проѣзда въ предѣлахъ командировки, какъ на русскихъ, такъ и на китайскихъ пароходахъ и, кромѣ этого, Дирекція Амурскаго Государственнаго Воднаго Транспорта обязана предоставлять командированнымъ лицамъ, при исполненіи возложенныхъ на нихъ обязанностей, всѣ необходимыя удобства, какъ-то: средства передвиженія и квартиру.

8/ Всѣ расходные документы могутъ записываться въ отчетныя конторскія книги только послѣ провѣрки ихъ и подписанія ихъ Предсѣдателями обѣихъ сторонъ Русско-Китайской Комиссіи или законными замѣстителями ихъ.

9/ Означенныя въ договорѣ учрежденія или законно уполномоченныя ими лица, по полученіи грузо-пассажирскаго сбора, обязаны выдавать плательщикамъ онаго установленнаго образца квитанціи съ написанными на нихъ и на корешкахъ прописью полученными суммами.

10/ По истеченіи каждаго мѣсяца Управленіе Водныхъ Путей Амурскаго бассейна и Китайская Таможня обязаны подавать Русско-Китайской Комиссіи подробный отчетъ о категоріи и суммѣ произведенныхъ сборовъ.

11/ Засѣданія Русско-Китайской Комиссіи происходятъ на территоріи той страны, Предсѣдатель которой является иниціаторомъ вопросовъ, подлежащихъ обсужденію на созываемомъ засѣданіи. Предсѣдатели Комиссіи руководятъ засѣданіями ея по очереди.

ПОРЯДОКЪ СБОРОВЪ.

12/ На манифестахъ, имѣющихся на судахъ, послѣ уплаты попуднаго сбора, учрежденіями, взимающими таковой /Управленіе Водныхъ Путей Амурскаго бассейна и Китайская Таможня/, ставится штемпельный грифъ о взысканіи сбора.

13/

13/ Всѣ товары, слѣдующіе съ одной стороны на другую, погруженные на русское или китайское судно, должны быть оплачены попуднымъ сборомъ на мѣстѣ отправленія. Всѣ грузо-пассажирскіе сборы взыскиваются по мѣсту отправленія судна. По прибытіи судна на мѣсто назначенія производится провѣрка объ уплатѣ всѣхъ грузо-пассажирскихъ сборовъ. Если при провѣркѣ будетъ обнаружено, что имѣются грузы, не оплаченные указаннымъ сборомъ или не исполненъ § 12-й настоящей инструкціи, то сборъ производится по мѣсту прибытія судна.

14/ Грузо-пассажирскіе сборы взимаются по всей пограничной рѣкѣ Амуръ, согласно § 8-го подписаннаго нами Временнаго Соглашенія грузо-пассажирскіе сборы взимаютъ: на Китайской сторонѣ - Китайская Таможня, а на Русской - агенты Амурскаго Воднаго Управленія. Всѣ грузо-пассажирскіе сборы, независимо отъ національности владѣльцевъ судна, въ случаѣ перехода его въ заграничное плаваніе, выплачиваются на мѣстѣ погрузки или высадки на пароходъ /судно/.

15/ Всѣ товары, перевозимые съ одной стороны на другую, противолежащую, а также изъ Сахаляна въ Благовѣщенскъ и въ рѣку Зею и обратно изъ рѣки Зеи и Благовѣщенска въ Сахалянъ на другихъ судахъ оплачиваются половинными сборомъ.

16/ Эта инструкція имѣетъ силу только на время заключеннаго Временнаго Мѣстнаго Соглашенія.

/Подписалъ/ Хэйхэскій Дао-инь: Сунъ

Совѣтникъ при Дао-инь по Дипломатическимъ Дѣламъ: Че

Главный Директоръ Амурскаго Государственнаго Воднаго Транспорта:Хилиновичъ

Директоръ по техническо-эксплоатаціонной части А.Г.В.Т. Инженеръ Путей Сообщенія:Лагутинъ

Aigun despatch No. 66 to I. G.

Append No. 4.

Translation from Chinese Text.

Additional Regulations and Collection Procedure in accordance with Article 5 of the Provisional Local Agreement concerning Navigation on the Russo-Chinese frontier section of the Amur, signed 27th May, 1912.

1. All the duties collected will be used for repairing the waterway on the Sino-Russian frontier section of the Amur as well as for the erection of Aids-to-Navigations (lights and signals) and shall not be used for any other purpose.

2. The Chinese and Russian Presidents of the Commission shall each appoint a technical man who shall make out plans and estimates in triplicate concerning surveying and improvement works, the establishing of Aids-to-Navigation, removal of shoals and wrecks and works of a similar nature. The plans and estimates will be submitted to both Presidents of the Commission for approval; in case the Presidents do not agree, they are to be submitted to the Joint Commission for discussion.

3. The Chinese President shall appoint a representative to investigate on the spot into the works and accounts; if if there is any doubtful point which cannot be settled between the Chinese representative and the Director of Water Transports, it must be referred to the Commission; if the Commission cannot agree, the question will be referred to a third Commission, to be composed of uninterested Members, appointed in equal number from each side.

4. The Water Transports Office will submit every fortnight a Statement of expenditure according to work done on each section, duly signed and certified correct by the Russian

Russian Chief Accountant and the Taojin's representative, to be submitted to the two Presidents for inspection.

5. The conservancy work is entrusted to the Russians Water Transports as long as the Agreement is in force; no extra salary is due to the Staff for this work, but one tenth of the Collection will be deducted as cost of collection by both collecting Offices.

6. All Officers (and Officials) proceeding on duty (on inspection) shall be given a long term passport from the Chinese and Russian Authorities and shall be given due protection.

7. All Members of the Staff or Officials proceeding on duty (inspection), shall enjoy free passage on both Chinese and Foreign (Russian?) Steamers; the Water Transports will give all facilities in the way of small boats, house accommodation, etc.

8. Payment bills must be approved by the two Chinese and Russian Presidents (or the Chinese President's representative) before they can be entered in the Accounts.

9. Receipts shall be given for all Dues collected irrespective of the amount and the butts will be kept.

10. The collecting Offices will report at the end of each month the actual amount of dues collected to the Joint Commission.

11. There is no fixed place for the meeting: if the Chinese President calls for a meeting, it will be held on the Chinese side; if the Russian President calls for a meeting, it will be held on the Russian side. The Chinese and Russian Presidents shall take turn as chairman.

REGULATIONS CONCERNING THE COLLECTION OF DUES.

12. The Manifests of Vessels are to be specially stamped by the collecting Offices (C. M. Customs or Water Transports) after payment of River Dues according to Regulations.

13. Dues on goods and passengers which go from one side to the

the other of the river will be collected at place of
origin irrespective of the nationality of the vessel. No
dues will be collected on arrival on goods covered by
manifests especially stamped by the collecting Offices
as per Article No. 12. Without this proof they are to
pay at place of destination.

14. Dues on passengers' tickets will be levied only for the
distance travelled on the Amur. In accordance with Art.
6 of the Provisional Agreement, Dues will be collected
by the M. M. Customs on the Chinese side and by the
(Commission under the control of the ?) Russian Water
Transports on the Russian side. Dues on passengers going
from one side to the other of the river will also be
collected at the place of origin, irrespective of whether
the vessel is Chinese or Russian.

15. Goods moved from one shore to the shore immediately
opposite (as from Tahaiho to Blagoveitchensk) and going
from Tahaiho to the Seia or from the Seia to Tahaiho
and Blagoveitchensk will pay half Tariff Dues.

16. These Regulations will become operative from the date
of signature by both sides and will last as long as
the Provisional Agreement is valid.

              (Signed) Sung Wên-yü,
       Heiho Taoyin and Commissioner for Foreign
                  Affairs.

              (Signed) Ch'e Hsi-chên
       Adviser on Foreign Affairs to the Heiho
                  Taoyin Office.

True Translation

Y. Jochi

Acting Commissioner.

呈海关总税务司署 <u>67</u> 号文　　　　　瑷珲关／大黑河 1922 年 8 月 5 日

尊敬的海关总税务司（北京）：

1. 根据瑷珲关第 44 号呈、47 号呈及 54 号呈，及海关总税务司署第 58/90054 号令："关于黑龙江航务。"

兹报告，讨论协议时商议的征收江捐事宜及征收办法，均未受到商人和轮船代理的反对；只有军方如往常一样要求免除一定税额，但大多已被本署驳回，希望可保持各方征税标准一致。目前，向乘客征收船票税一事进展顺利；但海关在一定程度上须依靠船运公司，因此无法完全管控其征税标准。拉哈苏苏分关于 6 月 17 日开始征税；负责的帮办近期汇报称，其目前人员能够应对征税事宜，包括向自松花江运至俄国口岸之货物征税，无须增加人员。

2. 按照要求，兹附 5 月 27 日所签协议之英文译本（附件 1）。需指出两处严重错误，尤能体现协议文本编制手法之粗劣。一处错误涉及按照半价税率向民船及木筏所运货物征税；协议文本似乎仅说明按半价税率向普通货物征税，由此便意味着半价税率亦适用于木料、牛、家禽等；与道尹商议之后，本署已抛开协议字面所示之意，仅按照条款原意进行征税。另一处错误涉及将航道分成两段来征税：协议文本（华方协议及俄方协议）仅提到大黑河（库页岛 Sahalian），并未提及布拉戈维申斯克（Blagovestchensk，即海兰泡），俄方借此声称将黑龙江航道分成两段征税仅适用于黑龙江航道华岸各地；而俄方则无论里程长短，均相应按全价税率征税，同时向源自黑龙江航道华岸各地之货物（已于瑷珲关支付一半关税）额外征收一半关税。目前已很难让俄方改变主意；尽管如此，华方亦并无损失，毕竟如此一来为航路标志维护工作摊付之款项便会少于俄方，但却可以与俄方同样受益。

3. 本署已于 7 月 26 日派遣超等外班关员博韩（G. E. Baukham）先生前往黑龙江航道巡查航路标志之状况，随行人员包括俄阿穆尔国家水运局数名工程师及道尹委派的一名大黑河商会成员，此次巡查将远至哈巴罗夫斯克（Habarovsk，即伯力）。博韩先生出行后，海关各项事宜多有不便之处，但本署宁愿如此，亦不愿对航道之状况一无所知。当然若巡工司可以早些上任，无论任命何人，本署定当欢迎；此外，本署希望与易保罗（P. I. Ignatieff）先生协商之事可以由哈尔滨关税务司出面，其身份比本署更为适合；但若易保罗先生任命之事遇到困难，甚至要延迟很久，则建议尽快任命崔邓（H. S. Sweeting）先生或其他可胜任之人，只要其愿意认真学习俄语即可。若与边界河道航务工作及航路标志相关的会议最终于瑷珲关召开，海关将受益匪浅，不但可以直接了解航道的实际情况，亦可得到有价值的技术建议,然而若任命巡工司之事延迟太久,恐怕其会错过此良机。

4.哈尔滨关税务司曾建议由中国直接管理一段黑龙江航道,本署对此表示赞同。贾登(H. G. Garden)先生也曾提出反对由两个组织来管理黑龙江航道,但其反对的是按照中俄领土将黑龙江航道划分后,由华方管理航道华岸一侧,由俄方管理航道俄岸一侧;对于贾登先生之见解,兹表示赞同,毕竟若由中俄双方分开管理黑龙江航道华俄两岸,效果必不会理想,但若由华方管理包括航道两岸在内之一段航道,并按照俄方之工作方式、工作效率甚至相似之费用来管理,必会受益良多。一则,中国可以(直接)核查航道的一半支出,有助于提高威望;二则,海关可以对至少一半的边境更加了解;再则,财政方面或许亦会得益于此。因此兹请示,可否在确认大概支出后,于即将召开的会议上提出此项计划。

5.兹附由中俄联合委员会起草的《补充细则》(共计16项)之中文版抄件(附件2)及俄文版抄件(附件3),《补充细则》列明与航路标志工事和支出相关的各项管理事宜,以及与征税相关的一些重要事项。兹附中文版《补充细则》的英文译本(附件4)。道尹已将《补充细则》呈交黑龙江省政府,并获得批准。7月22日,道尹未告知本署便直接签署了《补充细则》。尽管由于当时代道尹出面协商的代表因不了解状况,而导致最终细则之版本令人不甚满意,而且现在已经无法按照预想予以修改完善,但仍呈请贵署批准。

此外,俄方已经接受本署提议的另项一条款,如下。

"中国船只航行于嘎杂克维池(Kasakevitch)至海口河段时,按照与俄国船只相同之比例支付江捐。"

然而,省政府以此条款之政治性质为由已予以否决。

此抄件发送至哈尔滨关税务司。

您忠诚的仆人

包安济(G. Boezi)

瑗珲关署理税务司

瑷珲关致海关总税务司署第 67 号呈附件 1

《中俄黑龙江航行地方临时协议》（华方）译本

中华民国黑河道尹与俄阿穆尔国家水运局督办共同商议向航行于黑龙江内之中俄两国轮船、民船及木筏运货载客收捐之事宜，以筹款维护边界河道之航道及航路标志，整顿各江段航运之状况。大中华民国黑河道尹与俄阿穆尔国家水运局督办双方为整顿黑龙江航运状况，改善中俄两国关系，特于此订立协议。

中华民国黑河道尹特派外交科长王杼，外交顾问车席珍为全权代表；

俄阿穆尔国家水运局督办特派俄阿穆尔水道局局长工程师拉古丁（Lagutin）先生为全权代表。

第一条、办事规则

第一款、此临时协议自双方议决签字之日起生效，有效期间以 1922 年（中华民国十一年）航运季期间为限。

第二款、此协议涉及中俄双方之利益，中俄双方已就此达成共识。凡于黑龙江边界河道行驶者，无论船只之主人或木筏之负责人，均对航道有应负之责任。此协议属地方协议之性质，并不牵动或变更现行航务条例或其他以往黑龙江章程，亦不影响中俄两国运费之规定。

第二条、收捐与开支之规则

第三款、凡轮船与民船所载之货物与搭客应交之捐额，均由双方规定之；中华民国黑河道尹（兼任交涉员）与俄阿穆尔国家水运局督办召集中俄两国船运公司和各团体以及与航务有关系者共同议决实行。

第四款、收货票捐之手续由中华民国黑河道尹与俄阿穆尔国家水运局督办双方所派之代表共同规定之。

第五款、凡关于中俄两国轮船、民船及木筏运货载客之收捐问题及监督各项开支等事，待本协议签订后，由中俄联合委员会另定细则行之。

第六款、收捐办法中国方面无论中俄两国轮船、民船或木筏均由中国海关一律收捐；俄国方面无论中俄两国轮船、民船或木筏均由俄阿穆尔水道局所属之委员会一律收之。

第三条、维护航路标志及整顿航运之办法

第七款、关于航路标志维护之工事,包括安设灯照标桩,清理江底礁石或沉物及其他一切工作,均由俄阿穆尔水道局承办,所需费用应由中俄两国货票捐全数收入开支。但上述修江安设灯照标桩各项工程,凡在中国方面者,将以地方政府之名义暂时委托俄岸承办。

第八款、关于前项工程之限度及手续,应以双方所收捐款数目为比例。俄阿穆尔水道局照第五款之规定预拟办法送呈中俄联合委员会批准。

第九款、履行此协议时如遇疑难发生,此项问题应由中俄双方合组之第三特别委员会裁决之,该委员会之裁决即为最后之解决,不得再行提起诉讼。

税率(捐额)

货捐: 按普特计算,依货物之种类定收捐之额。如一切建筑材料、铁、生铁、钢、铅制品、谷物、草料、蔬菜、盐、煤炭以及农具机器非木类者,每普特均收捐一分;余者每普特均收捐二分。但由民船或木筏运来者,轮船一律减半。

木料捐: 燃料及材料,三俄丈长,一俄寸厚之大木收捐半分;再长者以此类算;木样,俄尺四分之三长者至一俄尺长者,每平方俄丈收捐一毛。

牲畜: 牲畜大者,每头收捐三毛,小者每头收捐一毛五分。

飞禽: 飞禽无论大小收捐一分。

票捐: 票捐不分等级按票价收百分之五。

附言

一、为收货票捐公允起见,黑龙江航道分为两段征收,一为由大黑河至嘎杂克维池,一为由大黑河至波克罗夫卡(Pokrovka),每段按捐额全数收二分之一。

二、中俄双方于货票捐收入后由收捐机关交中俄国家银行保存,支出时,须经中俄联合委员会两位委员长签字方得支用。

三、中俄联合委员会拟订八人,以中华民国黑河道尹与俄阿穆尔国家水运局督办为委员长,其余委员六名由委员长各指定中俄三人充之。

四、征收货票捐乃对黑龙江上下游驶来之轮船、民船及木筏所运之货客而言,横江渡船不在此限。

瑷珲关致海关总税务司署第 67 号呈附件 4

《补充细则》（华方）之英文译本

兹根据 1928 年 5 月 27 日所签订之《中俄黑龙江航行地方临时协议》第五款之规定，另拟细则及收捐办法如下。

一、所有收入一切捐款专为修理中俄两国交界之黑龙江全部航道以及安设灯照标桩之用，不得移作别项用途。

二、一切测量修江工程，安设灯照标桩，清理礁石或沉物及其他一切工程得由中俄联合委员会两位委员长各派专门委员一人将计划工程制造图表编成预算各三份，送呈两位委员长批准后施行；如两位委员长不同意时，交中俄联合委员会核议。

三、中国委员长得随时派员实地调查修江工程及各项开支账簿；遇有疑议时，中国代表与俄阿穆尔水道局监督不能在当地解决者，须提交中俄联合委员会议决后行之；如再不能解决，则由第三委员会解决之，第三委员会由中俄双方委员长指定中俄联合委员会以外之人按同等人数组之。

四、俄阿穆尔水道局每半月得将每段工程各项开支清单经俄总司账及黑河道尹之代表证实准确无误，并正式签字后，呈送中俄两位委员长查核。

五、修江一切工程在此协议有效期间，暂委托俄阿穆尔水道局兼办；一切人员不另支薪，但中俄双方由所收捐款项下各提百分之十成以资两岸征收机关办公。

六、凡调查员因公务（检查）外出，得由中俄两国政府发给长期护照，并妥善保护。

七、凡调查员因公务（检查）外出时，乘中外（俄国）两国轮船不给票价；俄阿穆尔水道局得予以相当协助，并供给各项船只及住房等项。

八、一切开支字据须经中俄两位委员长或中国委员长所派之代表批准后开始登记账簿。

九、所收捐款无论数目多寡，须发给票据并留存根。

十、每月底须将中俄两岸收捐确数由征收机关报告中俄联合委员会。

十一、会址无一定地点；如中国委员长召集开会时，会议地点即在中国地方；如俄国委员长召集开会时，会议地点即在俄国地方。中俄两位委员长轮流任主席。

收捐办法

十二、凡船只照章完纳江捐后,舱口单由征收机关(即中国海关或俄阿穆尔水道局)加特别印花。

十三、过江货物及客票,无论由华轮或俄轮运载,应在输出地方完纳江捐。凡入口各货登于舱口单内,而该舱口单按本条第十二款所定业经征收机关加盖特别印花者,不得重征。如无以上凭据者,则应在卸货地点征收。

十四、客票捐之征收限于航行黑龙江,全部依照《临时协议》第六款之办法,中国方面由中国海关代收,俄国方面由俄阿穆尔水道局所属之委员会收之。但过江搭客票捐,无论由华轮或俄轮载运,均应在上船地方完纳。

十五、凡货物由此岸运往对岸者(如大黑河运往布拉戈维申斯克),及由大黑河运往结雅河或由结雅河运往大黑河及布拉戈维申斯克者,应按照捐额减征收。

十六、此细则于双方签字后发生效力,其有效期与《地方临时协议》相同。

(签字)宋文郁

黑河道尹兼瑷珲关交涉员

(签字)车席珍

黑河道尹公署外交顾问

此译本内容真实有效,特此证明。

包安济　瑷珲关署理税务司

13. 1922 年《为与税捐局划清界限事之各项办法》

COMMRS.

No. 91,319

INSPECTORATE GENERAL OF CUSTOMS,

PEKING, 30th September, 1922.

Sir,

  With reference to my despatch No.68/90,437 (having reference to Aigun despatches Nos.23 and 55 and I.G. despatch No. 42/89,154):

  instructing you to inform the Superintendent that the Shui-wu Ch'u had not communicated to me any approval of the Working Agreement which had been arranged with the Local Tax Office, that I did not approve of this Agreement, and that pending instructions from myself you were not authorised to give effect to it;

  I now append copy of correspondence which has passed between the Shui-wu Ch'u and myself on this subject from which you will see that at the request of the Ch'u I set forth my views concerning the proposed Agreement explaining for what reasons I found myself unable to approve of it, and that the Ch'u

Commissioner of Customs,

AIGUN.

  Ch'u has replied concurring with these views and informing me that the Superintendent has been instructed to confer with yourself and the Local Tax Office with the object of coming to a more suitable arrangement whereby the Customs and the Local Tax Office may be enabled each to function within its own properly defined limits.

  The principles on which you should endeavour to arrive at an agreement are set forth in § 7 of my despatch No. 42 to Aigun and in my despatch No.298 to Shui-wu Ch'u cited above, and you are now authorised to discuss the matter further with the Superintendent and the Local Tax Office with the object of coming to an Agreement on these lines.

  You should be careful in these discussions to refrain from giving your definite consent to any arrangement that may be proposed in order that my approval may be obtained before the

Superintendent

Superintendent submits them to the Ch'u as a
definite Agreement locally made.

   I am,

    Sir,

   Your obedient Servant,

    Inspector General.

I.G.despatch No. 81 to Aigun,

   Appendix No.1.

税務處令第一一九六號　中華民國十一年九月四日

案據愛琿關監督呈稱前奉鈞令勸將愛琿關與黑河徵收局權限劃清以免衝突等因遵

經邀集愛琿關包稅務司包安濟黑河徵收局綱局長保將到著會函結果關局雙方合議

擬具辦法六條呈奉鈞處指令准予備案并經咨准黑龍江財政廳咨復意見相同會銜印

發佈告辦法六條呈奉總稅湯司令開戒關與徵收局所應劃清辦法六條凝辦施行等因查

此案自春准并佈告實行後關局毫無窒碍商民稱便似未便作為無效應請鈞處飭行

等情而來本處查愛琿關與黑河徵收局應劃清權限一事前准黑龍江省長咨來有所衡

處以此事應由愛琿關監督會同該關稅務司與黑河徵收局和衷商辦以免將來容疑本

突令行愛琿關監督遵辦及於上年第一九八三號令行知總稅務司轉令該關稅務司遵

照辦理文內并聲明俟辦結後呈復本處備案等語去訖旋據愛琿關監督將會同該關

稅務司暨黑河征收局長擬具辦法六條呈送到處復經本處以所擬辦法六條既保由關

局雙方合議妥揚應即准予備案指令議區遵照在案復據該區督呈稱前情究竟再

項辦法因何得雖施行之處相應鈔錄原辦法六條令行總稅務司查照過即查明具復以

憑核辦可也令附鈔件

照錄愛琿海關副分權限辦法六條

計開

一由水路越路運到黑河貨物須先由海關查驗完畢再問征收局查驗經雙方查驗後始
准入棧

二運輸過江貨物凡向應由征收局征收稅捐者無論客貨自貨概由商號於同一日完納
稅捐領有票照始准運貨至江沿先經征收局驗處查驗貨票相符再赴海關報驗一
經海關查驗放行征收局放出不再干預

三如運貨出境之商號或客人遍反周條之規定經征收局查出以漏起漏驗責令存實棧

店補前正稅外加十倍處罰（火烈民提犯者始少）貨准檢查件數不開驗扣留仍准
出境存貨商號不得以客貨諉卸

四出口貨經海關驗華放行征收局在橫江口有必須起驗時征收局長會同海關稅務司
視臨啟驗如征收局長與海關稅務司因要公不能親到雙方派同等高級員代行視
驗客驗華放行出口征收局稅行其他職務海關不加干涉

五商民偷漏海關稅海關自行查辦征收局稅捐征收局自行查辦
征收局不負責任偷漏征收局稅捐征收局自行查辦
海關不負責任

六以上辦法係海關征收局會議意見相同如蒙核准施行遵辦

黑河道尹容會

財政廳公佈周知並行知的會飭勤各商一體遵守

黑河征收局局長劉保培

總稅務司呈復　稅務處來字第二九八號　中華民國十一年九月十九日

呈為遵令查明瑷琿海關與黑河徵收局副分權限原擬辦法碍難情形復請

鑒查飭辦事奉到第一一九六號

令以全抄等因奉此竊查此案於未奉

鈞令以前瑷琿關稅務司榮將該關與徵收局所擬劃清權限辦法六條呈請核准施行當

由總稅務司令復以原擬辦法實與海關向來辦事之宗旨不無

牴觸茲就其原辦法有所抵觸各條陳明於下　第一條所載由水路陸路運到黑河貨物

須先由海關查驗完畢再同征收局查驗經雙方查驗後始准入棧云　查海關對於運到

黑河之進口商貨此經查驗征收稅捐在海關方面即無再行干涉其貨之權　第二條

所載運輸過江貨物凡問應由征收局徵稅捐著無論客貨自貨破由商號於前一日完

納稅捐領有票廠始准運貨至江沿先經征收局驗票處查驗貨票相符再赴海關報驗一

經海關查驗放行徵收局不再干預云　查海關向不能勒令商人於赴關報驗以前將其

所運各貨報於他項機關且海關亦不能勒令商人將其出口貨物於運出口前一日先完

稅項亦不准於查驗貨物之先徵納稅項　第四條所載出口貨經海關驗畢放行徵收局

在橫江口有必須復驗時徵收局長會同海關稅務司親赴查驗如徵收局長與海關稅務

司因要公不能親到等安派員代行高級員復驗出口貨如出口徵收局長與海關執行其他

職務海關不加干涉　云　查此條所擬親臨視驗已經驗畢之貨物似欠妥協其他機關對

於會同視驗貨物亦屬未合蓋是之故總稅務司飭令該稅務司設法定明惟海關能在江

沿行使職權所有徵收局在江沿上設立之公事房豐派委之官員均應允予撤廢方屬正

當辦法令遵照會商辦理去後伏思海關辦事向有明確之宗旨為保守此項宗旨起見

已遂奉本年第五六九號

令准辦法將梁家屯分卡爭的大加整頓是以謀總稅務司意見該徵收局亦應將在大黑

河徵捐事宜加以改革俾責歸清權限綠海關與徵收局同處立殊無理由海關祗能於

關放中外通商之地域內施行其職務則鹽金機關不應在海關管轄地方之內施行其權況

鈞處第一二三六號函附擬訂松黑等江中俄行船章程草案之第四條載明中俄兩國各

項商船往來貿易應各照所在沿海關章程交納關稅船鈔等語有案備或海關與徵收局

按所具辦法會同施行職務未免將兩機關範圍混在商人即不能分辨何爲海關所徵

之稅何爲徵收局所徵之捐且恐俄人恩及中國政府對於松黑行船章程第四條載明辦

法相背以致中國欲徵收關稅以外之捐必致俄政府亦收同等待遇方法在俄方面

亦欲徵收關稅以外之捐將來恐難免發生交涉凶以上各等情形反復籌思似應一面由

政府劃定海關權限之區地不准徵收局在海關範圍以內施行一面將此次愛琿關與徵

收局所商擬辦法由該關監督鈔請總稅務司深寬

核准之谷辦法母庸實議總稅務司深寬

鈞處飭令該監督悉知此次商擬辦法業經再行考核殊欠妥協尤宜鑒於現在中政府正

與俄政府商擬松黑兩江杭行江則此次商擬之辦法自應暫爲緩行並冀中國政府從

速權定海關在大黑河地方之範圍以清權限而雖關務是否有當理合備文復請

税務處令第一三一三號　中華民國十一年九月二十三日

案交愛琿關與黑河徵收局劃分權限一事前據愛琿關監督來呈以准該關稅司來

函此案奉總稅務司令該關與徵收局所擬劃清權限辦法六條礙難施行等因查此案自

奉准并佈告實行後關局彼此稱的民稱似未便作爲無效應請對處轉行總稅務司

轉飭愛琿關遵照辦理以免突而待原案等情本處應當以所擬辦法六條既係由關局雙

方台議突協凶凶何復有礙施行之處令行總稅務司呈復前凶是前項劃清權限辦法有未

稱全抄等凶前來本處復查此案既據總稅務司呈復前項辦法確有未

臻妥治之處仍由愛琿關監督會同該關稅司與黑河徵收局將前項辦法改訂

務使關局權限分明於徵稅抽捐不致侵越牽混以臻妥治而免衝突除分令外相應令行

總稅務司查照轉令愛琿關稅務司遵照辦理一俟辦安即呈復本處備核可也此令

袁振華
趙學謙　同校

English draft of I.G. despatch No. 298 to Shui-wu Ch'u
(in reply to Shui-wu Ch'u despatch No. 1196).
———————

The Inspector General states that before
receipt of Ch'u despatch under reply the Aigun
Commissioner submitted the proposed agreement to him
and he replied that it could not be sanctioned
because it was contrary to Customs principles for
the following reasons:

1. The Customs cannot agree to have any jurisdiction
    over imports once they have paid duty and passed
    out of Customs control.

2. The Customs cannot insist on merchants storing
    their goods in any particular place before they
    are reported to the Customs for export; nor
    can they insist on export duty being paid a day
    before the goods are exported; nor should they
    allow duty to be paid before examination.

3. It is not right that any other institution
    should interfere with, or take part in, the Customs
    examination of goods; or that the Commissioner
    himself should supervise such examination in the
    manner the agreement requires.

The Inspector General therefore instructed the
Commissioner to endeavour to arrange that the Customs
only should function on the Bund and on the foreshore,
and that the Tax Office should remove their Ferry
Office from the foreshore and their officers from
the Bund. This would be the correct procedure. The
Customs follow certain well-defined principles, and in
order to maintain those principles they have
regularised their position at the Liangohiat'un Barrier

in

in accordance with the instructions of Ch'u
despatch No. 569. I. G. therefore thinks that
it is the duty of the Tax Office also to
regularise their position at Tahsiho; for it is
wrong in principle that the Customs and Likin
offices should function on the same spot. The
Customs can only function at places open to foreign
trade and likin offices should not function within
the area over which the Customs have jurisdiction.

Another and a very important argument is
as follows :

In the proposed draft of rules for
navigation on the Sungari and Amur rivers (enclosed
with Ch'u letter No. 1236) Article 4 reads :
" Chinese and Russian shipping trade shall pay
  whatever Customs duties and Tonnage dues are
  leviable according to the Customs Regulations of
  the locality ".

If the Customs and the local Tax Office
work together in the manner suggested by the agreement
or if their spheres of jurisdiction are confused as
at present, importers and exporters will easily
make mistakes as to what taxes are charged by the
Customs and what are charged by the Tax Office, and
the Russians may think that Article 4 of the
above Regulations is being infringed and that the
Customs are collecting, or helping to collect, other
than Customs duties; and they may retaliate on their

side:

side and charge other than Customs duties also,
thus leading to complications and international
disagreement.

For all these reasons the Inspector General
is strongly of opinion that (1) the sphere of the
Customs' jurisdiction should be definitely laid down
and that the Tax Office should not function within
that sphere; and (2) that the proposed arrangement
between the Aigun Customs and the Tax Office
reported to the Ch'u by the Superintendent should
not be put into force.

He hopes therefore that the Board will
inform the Superintendent that on further
consideration the arrangement is unsuitable at present
especially in view of the negotiations which are
going on between the Chinese Government and the
Russian Authorities with regard to the navigation
of the Amur River, and for the same reason he also
hopes that steps may be taken at an early date
to define the sphere of Customs jurisdiction.

致瑷珲关第 81/91319 号令　　　　　　海关总税务司署（北京）1922 年 9 月 30 日

尊敬的瑷珲关税务司：

根据第 68/90437 号令（参照瑷珲关第 23 号和第 55 号呈以及海关总税务司署第 42/89154 号令）：

"指示贵署告知海关监督：关于与税捐局（即黑河征收局）合议拟订办法六条的报请核准，税务处并未与本署沟通；本署也未批准该办法；贵署须等待我的进一步指示，不得执行该办法。"

兹附税务处与本署之间有关此事的往来通信副本。据此所示，应税务处要求，本署就拟订办法给出意见，阐明不予批准的理由。而税务处复函同意了本署的意见，并告知，已命令海关监督与贵署及税捐局会谈，以拟订处更为稳妥的办法，借此厘清海关与税捐局的权限。

关于贵署应遵循的办法拟订原则，参见海关总税务司署致瑷珲关第 42 号令第 7 条及本令文引用的海关总税务司署致税务处第 298 号呈。兹授权贵署与海关监督和税捐局进一步讨论此事宜，以上述内容为准则，拟订最终办法。

贵署应当注意，在会谈中请勿针对任何提议的办法表示明确赞成，从而赶在海关监督将相关内容呈送至税务处作为地方已确立的办法之前，首先征得本署批准。

您忠诚的仆人

安格联（Francis Arthur Aglen）

海关总税务司

海关总税务司署致税务处第 298 号呈（税务处第 1196 号令复函）

海关总税务司呈复,在收到税务处第 1196 号令前,瑷珲关税务司已将该关与税捐局所拟的划清权限办法呈请核准实行,当时海关总税务司署致瑷珲关令回复说,办法有悖于海关一向恪守的原则,不予批准,主要原因如下。

1. 海关不赞同对于已完税和放行过关的进口货物在海关方面具有再行干涉的权限。

2. 海关一向不能勒令商人在报关出口前将货物先行报于其他机关,且海关也不能勒令商人将其出口货物于运出口前一天完纳出口税,更不准在查验货物之前就先征纳关税。

3. 其他任何机构干涉或参与海关验货的做法都欠妥,瑷珲关税务司按照办法所要求的方式协助其他机关亲自监督验货也不合职责要求。

故,总税务司指示瑷珲关税务司设法定明,唯海关能在江边道路和前滩行使职权,而税捐局应当将其在江边道路和前滩上设立的公事房及委派官员均予以裁撤,方属正确的解决办法。海关办事一向有明确的原则,为恪守这些原则起见,已遵照税务处第 569 号令指示,对梁家屯分卡事务大加整顿,以明确职责权限。于是,海关总税务司认为,税捐局也应在大黑河征捐事宜上加以改革,划清权限;原因是,海关与税捐局同处并立,从征税原则上来讲欠妥。海关只能在开放中外通商贸易的地区履行职务,而厘局不应在海关管辖地方之内越权征税。

况且还有另外一个重要原因:

税务处第 1236 号函附件松花江和黑龙江行船章程第 4 条规定:"中俄两国贸易船只均应遵照当地海关章程缴纳关税和船钞。"

倘若海关与税捐局按照所拟办法联合征税,两家机关的管辖范围必会像现在一样混在一起,进口商和出口商很难分辨哪些税种为海关所征收,哪些税种为税捐局征收,而且恐怕俄国会认为这违反了上述章程第 4 条规定,并质疑海关欲要征收或者帮助其他机关征收关税以外的税捐,进而俄国政府可能要求同等待遇,在俄方面也欲征收关税以外的税捐,将来难免会发生国际纠纷和分歧。

鉴于以上理由,总税务司强烈认为:（1）中国政府应当明确划定海关的管辖权限范围,并命令税捐局不得在海关权限范围内行事;（2）瑷珲关与税捐局之间所商,并由该关海关监督报请税务处核准的各项办法应当无效。

故,总税务司希望税务处告知海关监督,经过再三考虑,在当前情形下,特别是鉴于现在中国政府与俄国政府正在商议黑龙江航行办法,此次商拟办法非常欠妥。并且总税务司还希望中国政府尽早采取措施,以确定海关的管辖权限范围。

14. 1923 年《为松花江和黑龙江船只检查工作之各项章程》

No. 35. Service.

Aigun.   No. 831.

CUSTOM HOUSE,

Harbin , 23rd March, 1923.

Sir,

    With reference to Aigun Despatch No.96 to I. G. and my comments thereon dated 9th instant, copy of which was sent to your address, I am forwarding, enclosed herewith, a Memorandum prepared by Mr H. Abrahamsen, Chief Tidesurveyor, on our methods of inspection of steamers, for the guidance of your Inspecting Officer. For the sake of uniformity at Sungari and Amur ports it would be highly desirable that these methods be followed as closely as possible. I am also supplying you with a copy of the Russian Technical Rules regarding fire prevention and appliances and life-saving apparatus which this office has found very useful as a guide. I am also enclosing copy of my remarks to the Tidesurveyor concerning the application of these rules, etc.

    A copy of this Despatch is being sent to the Coast Inspector.

        I am,

          Sir,

        Your obedient Servant,

                Commissioner.

To

    The Commissioner of Customs,

      AIGUN.

MEMORANDUM.

Harbour Master's Office,	To
Harbin, 21st March, 1923.	The Commissioner of Customs,
	HARBIN.

Re – uniformity of inspection of ships on the Sungari and Amur Rivers.

    I append herewith a free translation of the rules of construction and equipment of vessels as were required by the Board of Navigation (old regime) on the Amur also a copy of my letter to you commenting on same, as well as copy of your decision in the matter as to what extent these rules should obtain.

    At your request I submit the following, which may be of interest to the Taheiho Office.

    Inspection is principally based on safety to passengers and accordingly I consider the following the most important points.

Machinery. Boiler must be safe from explosion.

Equipment. <u>Lights and their positions</u> should be scrupulously correct.

    <u>Steering gear</u> should in all respects be beyond reproach.

    <u>Life saving appliances</u> should be of the best and placed in readily accessible place, and not stowed away in boxes, or worse still, in store rooms.

    <u>Fire appliances</u> should be such as to meet emergency requirements, and these appliances, buckets, hoses, etc., should not be used for any

                 other

other purposes - always in place, and ready at hand.

All main entrance doors to passenger and crew Quarters must **without exception** open Outward, doors in cabins may open inwards if the windows are large enough for a person to pass through without difficulty, and providing there is a deck landing outside, in cabins with windows facing directly over the side doors must open outward even to corridors.

Anchors and Chains of proper size and lengths, and fitted in such a manner that they can easily be "let go" and that there a proper means of "checking" the cable.

Hull. From a safety to passenger point of view is of less importance, but a ship should not be permitted even so, to go too far - as if for no other reason she should be fit for her voyages and not sink and possibly block a narrow fairway.

Where to look for defects.

Boiler and engine. I leave this to a qualified marine engineer.

Lights. See that they are of a reasonable regulation pattern, that if lit by electricity that all outside contacts are in order, and above all see that there are actually a set of oil lamps which fit the light to be used if the dynamo fails. See that the lights are fitted as quoted in Regulations for Prevention of Collisions at Sea (Rules concerning lights, etc.) and issued by I.G. 1912, a copy of which ought to be at Taheiho Office.   See

See that the glass of the side lights are properly coloured and not painted, or both white, and fitted with a red and/or green globe, as if dynamo breaks down these lights cannot be used by putting in oil lamps - or in alternative demand a double set of lights for oil lamps. See that a regular mast head light is carried and not merely a megaphone shaped tube on the mast fitted with electric light, as it does not show at the angle required.

See that they do not substitute a mast head light for a stern one, this done frequently.

Steering Gear. See that the wheel is properly fitted, and that chain or wire is securely fitted to the barrel and not merely connected with a couple of turns.

If steam steering gear let the inspecting engineer examine the engine and see that the steam valves work properly.

When examining the chain pay particular attention to chains in covered up places and where they work over sheaves and pullies, slack up the links and examine where they join up.

See that there are no hooks or as connections on rods, no patent connecting links are allowed - rods should be welded - see there is a thimble in the wire connection as it is often the case that the wire is good while the shackle is worn out the "bieght" in the eyesplice.

See that the segment or tiller is securely fitted on rudder shaft.

See that all bolts in sheave leads are entirely removed, demand new pins if worn especially where

leads

leads are at right angles as the pressure here is immense.

Steam steering gear must have heavier fittings than hand.

Life saving appliances. Examine the buoys, if found heavy, throw them overboard, if they float with about 70% above water they are all right.

See that you pick the most hidden life belts for examination, preferably examine all - you will generally find that neck and breast straps are missing on many - also canvas or drill covering rotten.

See that they are stowed in light boxes, they must be open or only covered by glass doors - the boxes should be so light that if necessary they could be broken without difficulty.

Fire Hoses should be fitted in same manner.

See that the hose is securely fitted on to the couplings they can often be pulled off by hand, see that the couplings to nozzle is of same gauge, it often happens that they are of different size, also see if they fit on the various pipe connections.

Doors to cabins have been dealt with.

Anchors and Chains. See that the anchor and chains are of proper size and length and that the end s of chains are securely fastened - accept no patent links on large steamers, on smaller vessels only if the patent link is twice the diameter of the chain itself.

Hull, Iron. Outside inspection while ship is lifted in winter berth is really the most effective - a sounding

sounding hammer is used for testing - there is really no fixed limit for thickness of plates as a lot depends on "Build" in a ship where frames are closer the plates are of less consequence than on a ship where frames are further apart etc.

Inside inspection is not much good without knowing the outside condition of the plates below water line, a good inspection of frames should however be made, especially in closed up spaces, peaks under boilers are generally the worst places - if any cement has been used it must be left to the discretion of the inspecting officer whether to pass it or not.

Hull, Wood. Inspect bilges and if good the rest of the ship is generally in order, bilges always deteriorate first - if one frame is bad but the next one on either side is good, there is little danger, but it should be pointed out to those concerned that the frame should be replaced the next season, if two or more frames next to each other are bad they must be removed or strengthened in some manner and a remark made on the inspection certificate "permitted to sail on condition that owners promise to repair next season" this does not help the weak spot but serves as an agreement, that if an attempt is made to back out the following year, the owners themselves are to blame if refused permission to sail.

As an **Average Rule**, if the vessel below water line is 50% good and frames and various keelsons reasonably good she passes, special attention should be

be paid to the condition of the hull under the
boiler.

There have been instances where a hull has been
bad, but still permitted to sail as tug only, i.e.
carry no cargo or passengers.

The superstructure concerns more the question of
comfort rather than safety, and hence is of less
consequence.

General Remarks.

As there are no hard and fast rules, the
regulations as laid in the appended translation is
used as a guide only - discretion must be exercised,
to take a stand which cannot be maintained must be
avoided - in fact "make the best of a bad job" as
the saying goes.

When the vessel eventually clears, make a rough
check of lights, buoys, belts and fire appliances as
it has occurred that these articles have been borrowed
from another vessel during the inspection.

(signed) H. Abrahamsen,

Harbour Master.

APPENDIX.

Masters, Officers, Engineers and Crew.

On Russian ships plying in Russian waters all
are certificated men, and ships are run under such
supervision that the control leaves nothing to be
desired.

On Chinese ships about 25% of Masters are
certificated, officers seldom, and more rarely still
engineers - but as far as the latter are concerned
most of the ships running on the Sungari are engined
in the most simple manner, so that besides blowing
up a boiler little harm can be done, even though
engines are controlled by less competent people.

The non-certificated Master if Russian is often
an old Pilot and fills his billet well - there are
others however who must be excluded.

Chinese often ask to be registered, and here
comes the more difficult problem - he may have sailed
mate for some years which has mainly consisted of
selling tickets, keep track on cargo and make up
manifests, etc., but has never been in charge of a
watch, and hopelessly incompetent.

As there are no laws governing examination or
laws demanding a certificate we are again back to the
rule of "Making the best of a bad job".

The following may be a guide. (Chinese vessels only).

Certificated men.   Never questioned.

Ex-Pilots, Russian.   By showing proofs of Service, i.e.
    testimonials from known firms and other
    reliable masters, they are granted
    permission to sail.

Ex-Pilots, Chinese.   Ditto, even if having sailed as
    assistant

assistant pilot.

Other Chinese.   Whom I may personally know from the coast, there are several whom I have known in sea going tugs at Tientsin and Taku as Laodahs or Quarter Masters - in fact they are brought up in tugs, also sailed on the Sungari in various capacities these are granted permission to sail.

     A few questions are asked as to the Rule of the Road, lights, etc., what would they do in case of fire with wind so-and-so, etc., any one which to the best of my knowledge is unfit to sail can be excluded on the strength of the answers to such various questions whether he is Chinese or Foreign.

     A register is kept of those who have a certificate or given permission to sail (I append three samples herewith) their certificates or testimonials are stamped and signed by the Harbour Master as a token of permission to sail - but this does in no way constitute a certificate as this control is merely a temporary measure pending the issue of proper navigation laws by the Chinese Government.

         (signed) H. Abrahamsen,

         Harbour Master.

True copies:

Unclassed Assistant.

To,

    The Commissioner of Customs,

        Harbin.

Sir:

    Herewith translation of official rules governing the principal safety precautions imposed by the Russian authorities upon vessels trading on the Sungari and the Amur.

    About 90% of the existing vessels were built while these rules were still in force, they are very reasonably effective and just, and if not adapted as _a whole_ could be used as a fundamental ruling for the inspection of vessels this spring.

    The Commissioner is respectfully requested to make his remarks on the appended copy for my guidance, i.e. what may be and/or not be accepted as official ruling for next inspection.

            (signed) H. Abrahamsen.

            Harbour Master.

Harbour Master's Office,

    Harbin, 25th February, 1922.

致瑷珲关第 <u>35/831</u> 号函　　　　　　　　哈尔滨关 1923 年 3 月 23 日

尊敬的瑷珲关税务司：

　　根据瑷珲关致海关总税务司署第 98 号呈及本署 3 月 9 日意见通函（抄件已发送至贵署），兹附超等总巡阿布兰森（H. Abrahamsen）先生关于船只检查办法的通函抄件，以指导瑷珲关检查关员之工作，望尽量采纳，以使松花江和黑龙江沿岸各口之检查办法保持一致。

　　兹附俄国关于防火、消防设备及救生设备之技术条例抄件一份，该条例于本关颇有助益；另附本署致头等总巡关于该条例的应用意见抄件。

　　此抄件发送至巡工司。

您忠诚的仆人

（签字）覃书（R. C. L. d'Anjou）

哈尔滨关税务司

哈尔滨关致瑷珲关第 35/831 号函附件

通函

由：	致：
哈尔滨关理船厅	哈尔滨关税务司
1923 年 3 月 21 日	

为松花江和黑龙江船只检查工作的统一事

兹附阿穆尔航政局（Board of Navigation on the Amur）（旧政权）所要求之船只建造及设备条例之译本、本人相关意见信函抄件及贵署关于条例应用办法之意见抄件。

另照贵署要求将于大黑河海关有益之信息列下，各项均以船只检查工作之基础——保障乘客安全——为主要考虑。

机器：锅炉须安全防爆。

设备：灯及位置：应准确无误。

操舵装置：应符合各项要求。

救生设备：应选用质量上乘者，并置于易取之处，不得置于箱内，更不得置于储藏室内。

消防设备：应满足应急需求；消防设备及水桶和软管等不得另作他用，不得移位，应置于易取之处。

出入主门：凡通向乘客和船员宿舍之门，均须向外开；船舱窗户若足够大可容一人轻易通过，则可将舱门设为向内开，然若船舱外为甲板，且窗户正对两侧，舱门则须向外开，即使通向走廊，亦须如此。

锚和锚链：长度和尺寸均应适当，并便于收放检查。

船体：于保障乘客安全而言，船体的重要性相对较低，但仍须满足航程要求，不应有下沉或无法通过狭窄航道之危险。

检查事项

锅炉及发动机：该项检查工作应交由合格的验船工程师。

灯：检查事项包括：能否合理调控；若为电灯,外部接触点是否一切正常；船上有无备用油灯,以备发电机停止工作时使用；所有灯是否均照海关总税务司署1912年颁布之《航海避碰章程》(与灯等设施有关之条例)(抄件应已发送至大黑河海关)安装；舷灯玻璃罩颜色是否正确且未涂漆,或者是否皆为白色且装有红色及/或绿色灯泡,是否备有相应油灯以备发电机停止工作时使用；有无标准头桅灯,而非仅于桅杆上安装喇叭筒状灯罩,再将灯泡安置于内,若如此,光照角度将无法满足要求；不得以头桅灯代替船尾灯(时有发生)。

操舵装置：检查舵轮是否安装妥当,链条或钢索是否牢固安装于圆筒之上(绝非仅仅缠绕数圈)；若为蒸汽操舵装置,则须检查发动机,确保蒸汽阀正常工作。

检查链条或钢索时,应着重检查被遮住处,遇有堆叠或过紧之处,应予以疏松并检查连接点；确保无挂钩,无明显连接；凡有需要连接之处,均须焊接牢固；确保连接处安有套环,因常有链条或钢索完好而接环处却已损坏之情况。

确保舵柄或舵叶牢固安装于舵轮之上。

确保导索槽轮中的螺栓已悉数拆除；销子如有磨损,尤其是在导线直角处(此处压力很大),必须换新。

蒸汽操舵装置的配件须重于手动操舵装置的配件。

救生设备：检查救生圈是否过重,将之掷入水中,若有70%浮于水面,则属合格。

择最隐蔽的救生衣进行检查,最好无遗漏之处；多数救生衣的颈部和胸部安全带容易缺失,甚至有帆布腐烂之情况。

确保救生设备置于轻薄的箱子内,便于打开或仅以透明玻璃盖之,以便需要时可以毫不费力地将之打破。

消防软管：安装方式须保持一致。

确保软管与接头安装牢固(常有徒手即可拔出之情况)；确保管口接头尺寸一致(常有尺寸不同之情况)；检查管口与管子是否匹配。

舱门相关要求已于上文提及。

锚和锚链：确保锚和锚链尺寸及长短适当,锚链末端安装牢固；大型轮船的锚链上不得有明显连接,小型轮船的锚链上亦仅可有锚链直径两倍大小的明显连接。

铁制船体：外部检查最宜于冬季轮船停泊时进行；应使用测深锤进行测试，但船板厚度并无严格限制，主要依轮船肋骨结构紧凑与否而定。

在进行内部检查之前，最好先检查船体外部的水下部分；船体肋骨亦须仔细检查，尤其是密闭空间内及锅炉下方；遇有使用水泥之处，须由检查关员自行决定是否合格。

木制船体：底舱最易损坏，应首先检查；若底舱完好，则轮船他处通常不会出现问题。若仅有一处肋骨损坏，而相邻肋骨完好，则几无危险，但应告知船主于下一航运季将之更换；若相邻两处或多处肋骨损坏，则须立即拆除，或以相同方式加固，并于查验证明书上注明"船主承诺于下一航运季开始前修理底舱，故准许航行"，此亦可作为一项协定，若船主次年未履行修理底舱之承诺，轮船将无法获准出航。

一般而言，若船只水下部分有 50% 状况良好，且肋骨和各处龙骨完好，则属合格。另须注意检查锅炉下方船体是否合格。

有时，船体受损亦可获准出航，但仅可作为拖船，即不得载货搭客。

轮船上层建筑主要涉及舒适问题，于安全影响甚微。

概论

轮船检查工作并无硬性规定，随附译本所载章程仅作参考指导之用，使用时须多加斟酌，避免出现无法控制之局面，尽力而为即可。

待船只最终结关时，再大致检查一次灯、救生圈、救生衣和消防设备，因此前有船只于检查期间互借此等物品之情况。

（签字）阿布兰森

哈尔滨关理船厅

哈尔滨关致瑷珲关第 35/831 号函附件

船长、船上职员、管轮及船员

凡往来于俄国水域之俄国船只，所配人员均有执业资格，行船亦受到严格监管。

然中国船只的船长中，有执业资格者仅占四分之一，职员中尚无有执业资格者，管轮中更是如此。不过松花江上往来的中国船只大多以最简单之方式安装发动机，因此虽然管理之人能力欠佳，但除有锅炉爆炸之危险外，几乎不会造成严重之损害。

至于无执业资格之船长，若为俄国人，则通常为老引水员且完全有能力应付船长之工作。其他无执业资格者，皆不应再任此职。

中国人通常会申请登记为船长，但其此前可能仅任大副一职数年，且工作内容亦不过是售票、追踪货物、制作舱口单等，并未有监管之经验，胜任之希望寥寥。

然因目前中国法律并未有相关考试及必须取得资格证之规定，故于海关而言，只能尽力而为。

在审核船长资格一事上，或可参考下列办法（仅针对中国船只）。

有执业资格者：从未质疑。

前引水员（俄籍）：出示工作证明（即由知名商行及其他可靠船长提供之证明信）后，准许出航。

前引水员（华籍）：同上，若此前担任过副引水员，亦照此办理。

其他中国人：本人熟识者中有曾于天津大沽一带的拖船上任老大或舵手之职者，还有于松花江上航行者（任各职者皆有），皆准许出航。

此外，还可询问与航行规则、信号灯等相关之问题，询问其如何于有风之日应对火灾，等等。依本人之经验，无论船长为华籍或洋籍，根据其对此类问题之回答，均可判断出其有无出航之资格。

对于有执业资格或准许出航者，皆应予以登记（随附三份样表），并由理船厅于其资格证或证明信上签字盖章，证明其已获准出航，然此仅为中国政府出台相关法律之前的临时办法，不可作为资格证书使用。

（签字）阿布兰森

哈尔滨关理船厅

哈尔滨关致瑷珲关第 35/831 号函附件

索引

轮船	页码
理船厅至税务司函	1
理船厅致税务司函——俄国（消防与救生）条例概略	2
锅炉；外部（第十四条）	7
水桶（第二十三条）	11
舱壁（第一至二条）	3
货舱及货物（第八条）	5
货舱；防火（第二十四条）	12
发动机及锅炉房（第十二及十三条）	7
消防设备（第十八、十九、二十、二十一及二十四条）	8/10/11/12
可拆地板等（第九及十条）	5
烟囱；材料及位置（第十一条）	6
舱口；栏杆（第六条）	4
短柄小斧（第二十三条）	11
软管（第二十二条）	11
救生艇（第二十五条）	12
梯子及手栏杆（第十五条）	7
灯、灯笼及蜡烛的用油安全（第十七条）	7
救生设备,安全带（第二十六条）	12
救生设备的分布（第二十六条）	12
张贴防火救生布告（第二十七条）	13
排水管及楼梯（第七条）	4
乘客安全（第四、五、十八及十九条）	4
茶壶外壳（第十六条）	7
舷侧舱口（第三条）	4
拖索；防火（第二十三条）	11

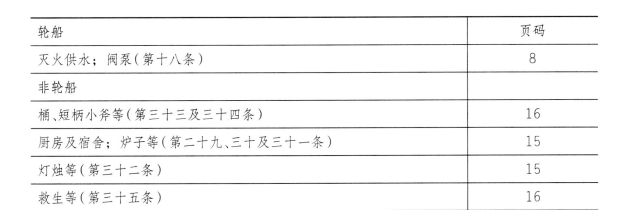

轮船	页码
灭火供水；阀泵（第十八条）	8
非轮船	
桶、短柄小斧等（第三十三及三十四条）	16
厨房及宿舍；炉子等（第二十九、三十及三十一条）	15
灯烛等（第三十二条）	15
救生等（第三十五条）	16

哈尔滨关致瑷珲关第 35/831 号函附件

理船厅致税务司函

尊敬的哈尔滨关税务司：

兹附俄政府为于松花江和黑龙江上贸易之船只所定之基本安全防范措施官方条例之译本。

现有船只中约有90%皆为条例施行期间所建造；此等条例颇有成效,且十分公正,即使无法全盘接受,亦可作为今春船只检查工作之基本标准。

望税务司对随附抄件给定意见,告知此等条例中是否有可作为今年船只检查工作的官方规定者。

（签字）阿布兰森

哈尔滨关理船厅

1922 年 2 月 25 日

15. 1923 年《黑龙江航路标志协议》

No. 119
L. G.

CUSTOM HOUSE,
Aigun/Taheiho, 22nd May, 1923.

Sir,

1.   In continuation of my despatch No. 110 :

     reporting negotiations, between the Taopin and the Russian Authorities, for the conclusion of an Agreement on Aids to Navigation on the Amur for 1923 ;

I have the honour to report that the Taopin says he has received instructions from the Heilungchiang Tuchün to insist on the inclusion into the Agreement of at least two clauses of a non-technical nature, viz :

    (a) that Chinese vessels be allowed to navigate to the Amur to the sea, against permission for Russian steamers (flying the red flag) to navigate the Sungari ; and

    (b) that the Russian gunboat at the mouth of the Sungari be withdrawn and that Chinese steamers navigating in Chinese waters be no longer searched by that gunboat.

2.   With the second demand, I believe, the Russians

Inspector General of Customs,
    P E K I N G.

Russians may be willing to comply : so far steamers arrived from Harbin have reported that they have not been searched. But Chinese competition in the river traffic with Habarovsk and Nikolaievsk is not likely to be allowed : new Regulations concerning complements of crew and certain formalities for Russian steamers, make it much more expensive to run vessels for Russians than for Chinese ; Russian local authorities consequently want to reserve the monopoly of transportation on the lower part of the Amur. — Negotiations seem to have reached a deadlock, and I am informed, through the Russian Unofficial Representative in Taheiho, that the Russians will soon give a definite reply in the negative.

3.   While negotiations were still progressing, at the eleventh hour, the Taopin has consented to my proposal to start collection of River Dues irrespective of the conclusion of an Agreement ; the Taheiho and Aigun Offices started collection on 16th May, and the Lahasusu Office began collecting on their own initiative since the opening of navigation, evidently believing that last year's Agreement was

      still

still valid.

4.   I have asked the Taoyin what he proposes to do if the Russians, as probable, definitely refuse to comply with his requests. His evident intentions were to use the collection in the upkeep of Aids <u>on the Chinese side</u> : However, I demonstrated, once more, that this is impossible, and then he suggested that the Customs come to an arrangement of their own with the Amur Navigation Office.

5.   This suggestion should, in my opinion, be taken up without hesitation. It is evident that the Taoyin does not want, as a matter of "face", to go back on his demands, and that he does not feel inclined to discuss the point with the Provincial Authorities. On the other hand, something must be done in the way of maintaining the Aids, for the benefit of navigation, and also of the Chinese position in these waters. The exclusive control by the Customs on matters pertaining to Aids to Navigation would undoubtedly make things much easier, avoid loss of time and squandering of money. - The objection that we, as an organ of the Central Government, could not conclude an Agreement with representatives of a Government not recognised by China may be easily overcome, by making the arrangement a local, temporary <u>modus operandi</u> : and it is to be remarked that the Taoyin was ready to conclude an Agreement as Commissioner for Foreign Affairs, on subjects not within his jurisdiction as Taoyin. - Should therefore the Taoyin definitely refuse to come to an arrangement which would exclude the clauses insisted upon by the Tuchün , and ask the Customs to take the question entirely into their hands, I have the honour to solicit your authority for the eventual conclusion, by the Commissioner with the Amur Navigation Office, of a local temporary convention of a purely technical character.

6.   The draft of the agreement, as proposed, is appended : it is more or less the same as proposed by the Commissioner to the Russian Navigation Office, and the principles underlying it have been approved by that Office, so that an understanding would be easy to reach. - Matters have dragged along for so many months, and work should have already been started

started on the Amur: a prompt conclusion is a
necessity, and I beg to solicit your approval of
my proposals by wire.

Copies of this despatch are being forwarded
to the Coast Inspector and to the Harbin Commissioner.

I have the honour to be,

Sir,

Your obedient Servant,

(Signed) G. Bozzi,
Acting Commissioner.

True copy
Wang yun ...
3rd Clerk, C.

A. 116

Append to Aigun despatch No. 116 to I.G.

MODUS OPERANDI

between the C.M. Customs, Aigun, and the Russian Amur
Navigation Office, Blagovestchensk, for the upkeep of
Aids to Navigation on the frontier stretch of the
Amur, for the year 1923.

1. The present modus operandi shall become
operative from the date of signature by both parties,
and shall be in force for the year 1923; but, if not
denounced by any of the parties at the end of
december, 1923, it will automatically continue in force
for another year.

2. The application of the present modus operandi
is entrusted to the Commissioner of Customs on the
Chinese side, and to the Director General of the
Amur Navigation Office on the Russian side.

3. All works in connection with Aids to Navigation,
the erection of lights and signals, and other work of
a similar nature, on the frontier waters from Pokrovka
to Kasakevich, shall be undertaken by the Amur Navigation Office. The Amur Navigation Office shall submit
for approval to the C.M. Customs a complete programme
of works, and estimates, within the limits specified
in annex 2. - The C. M. Customs will supervise the works
and expenditure.

4. In order to meet the expenses for ordinary
upkeep of the Aids, River Dues shall be collected on
both sides, according to the Tariff specified in
Annex 2.

5. Chinese and Russian Steamers, Junks and Rafts,
on the Chinese side shall pay River Dues to the C.M.
Customs; on the Russian side, to the Amur Navigation
Office.

Office.

6. Out of River Dues collected on the Chinese
side, the C.M. Customs will contribute a share of
the expenses incurred by the Amur Navigation Office
in accordance with Article 3.

7. Rules defining the procedure for the collection
of Dues and for the supervision of works and expenditure
as well as the share to be contributed by the
C.M. Customs towards expenses incurred by the Amur
Navigation Office, are laid down in Annex 3.

ANNEX 2 : TARIFF.

The same as last year.

ANNEX 1

General plan of works and expenditure on Aids to
Navigation on the Amur (frontier stretch) by the
Amur Navigation Office, 1st January to 31st December,
1 9 2 3.

The stretch from Pokrovka to Kasakevitch will be
divided into 5 sections.

In accordance with 1922, there will be opened :

```
           Signal Stations        7
           Traffic Stations       2
           Water Gauge Stations   11
           Lighted Shallows       4
```

Works for erecting new beacons and repairing old
ones will be on the same scale as last year, (and
the expenditure proportional to that incurred in 1922.)

The list of Personnel of the Technical Section
and of the local Organisations will not exceed that
for the year 1922.

Only half the expenses of the Technical section
(which works as well for the Inland Rivers of Russia
as for the frontier stretch of the Amur) will be
debited to the estimates for the upkeep of Aids

to

to Navigation on the frontier waters.

(There will be one steam launch for the use of
the Technical Section and the inspecting Officials)

N.B. conditional upon perspective collection.
The total amount of expenses must not exceed
Gold Roubles . . . . -

N.B. to be fixed according to expected collection.

ANNEX 3 : REGULATIONS.

1. After payment of River Dues, the collecting
Office (C.M. Customs or Amur Navigation Office) shall
stamp the Manifests of vessels with a special stamp
showing that all Dues have been paid.

2. Dues on goods and passengers' tickets for
vessels which proceed from one side of the River to
the other, will be collected at the place of origin
irrespective of the nationality of the vessels. Dues
on passengers' tickets will be levied only for the
distance travelled on the frontier waters of the
Amur.

3. No River Dues whatever shall be collected
(on the Amur between Pokrovka and Kasakevitch) on
arrival of goods or vessels covered by manifests
specially stamped by the collecting Office as per
article 1. Without this proof of payment, vessels shall
pay River Dues at place of destination.

4. Goods moved from one shore to the other
immediately opposite (as between Taheiho and Blagovestchensk) and proceeding from Taheiho to the Zeya
and vice-versa, shall pay only 25% of the Tariff Dues.

5. Receipts shall be given for all Dues

collected,

collected, and the butts will be kept for inspection
by the parties concerned.

6. The plans and estimates called for by Article
3. of the *modus operandi*, and specified in Annex 1,
must be approved by the C.M. Customs before becoming
operative.

7. The C.M. Customs have the right to appoint
one or more representatives for the purpose of
investigating on the spot into the works and accounts
of the Amur Navigation Office : such representatives
must be given every facility by the Amur Navigation
Office, in the accomplishment of their duties, and,
as far as possible, also in the way of transportation,
house accommodation, etc., as required.

8. Officers and Officials of the C.M. Customs and
Amur Navigation Office proceeding on duty in connection
with the upkeep of the Aids, will be provided with
a long term passport from the Chinese and Russian
Authorities, and shall be given due protection. They
will also enjoy free passage on board Chinese and
Russian vessels.

9. The C.M. Customs will inform the Amur Navigation
Office each month of the amount of River Dues
collected.

10. The C.M. Customs will deduct 1/10th of the
Dues as cost of collection.

11. Out of the net amount of collection, the
C.M. Customs will first defray, each month, the expenses
of the Technical Adviser's Office, which will not
exceed $ 6,000.0. for the year 1923.

12. The balance of River Dues collection, and
no other sums whatever, will be available for
contributing towards the expenses incurred by the
Amur

Amur Navigation Office in accordance with plans and
estimates approved by the C.M. Customs. However, should
the balance of funds collected in 1923 prove
insufficient, the surplus of River Dues collection for
the previous year is to be used for the same purpose.

13. The C.M. Customs will contribute (funds
permitting) 50 % of the total expenditure incurred by
the Amur Navigation Office, in accordance with the
plans and estimates previously approved.

14. 75 % of the Customs share of estimated
expenditure will be advanced to the Amur Navigation
Office at the beginning of each month. The balance,
in accordance with actual expenditure, will be paid
as soon as proper accounts have been presented by
the Amur Navigation Office, or as soon as the C.M.
Customs are satisfied that the expenditure has been
actually incurred in accordance with plans and estimates.

15. No dredging operations, removal of stones, or
other work of an important nature are within the
scope of this *modus operandi* : no large conservancy
work should be undertaken by one side without the
consent of the other, on the Frontier waters.

16. Full accounts shall be presented by the
Amur Navigation Office for the whole year 1923, not
later than 28 February, 1924.

17. These Regulations shall be valid as long
as the *modus operandi*.

呈海关总税务司署 <u>119</u> 号文　　　　　瑷珲关／大黑河 1923 年 5 月 22 日

尊敬的海关总税务司（北京）：

　　1. 根据瑷珲关致海关总税务司署第 110 号呈：

　　"汇报道尹与俄方关于签订 1923 年黑龙江航路标志协议的协商情况。"

　　兹汇报，道尹称黑龙江督军已下达指示，要求于协议中添加以下两项非工程类条款。

　　（1）俄方应允许中国轮船由黑龙江出海，同时，华方亦将允许悬挂红旗的俄国轮船在松花江上航行；

　　（2）俄方须将停泊于松花江口的俄国炮艇撤回，停止在中国水域对中国轮船进行搜查。

　　2. 兹认为，第二项条款或许更容易让俄方接受，毕竟迄今为止，自哈尔滨关而来的轮船中尚未有遭遇俄国炮艇搜查者。但俄方可能不会同意中国轮船在哈巴罗夫斯克（Habarovsk，即伯力）及尼古拉耶夫斯克（Nickolaevsk，即庙街）地区进行航运和贸易；主要因俄国轮船及船员的相关新规定出台后，俄国轮船的运行成本大大增加，已远远高于中国轮船的运行成本，因此对于黑龙江下游的航运和贸易，俄国当地政府必已有垄断之意。至此，协商似乎已陷入僵局，且据驻大黑河俄国非官方代表称，俄方不日将正式拒绝道尹之要求。

　　3. 然协商仍在继续，道尹最后终于同意本署之提议，决定在签订协议之前，开始征收江捐；大黑河口岸与瑷珲口岸已于 5 月 16 日开始征收江捐，而拉哈苏苏口岸则早于航运开通后便开始自行征收江捐，显然，拉哈苏苏分关已默认去年的协议依然有效。

　　4. 本署已询问道尹，若俄方坚持拒绝其提议，其将如何应对。道尹表示可用江捐税收来维持中国一侧航路标志的维护工作。本署再次向其说明此法不可行后，其提出可由海关出面与俄阿穆尔水道局另行协商新的协议。

　　5. 兹认为，道尹之建议十分可取。显然，道尹不愿撤回要求，失去颜面，亦不愿与省政府进行协商。但为了维护中国航运之利益，为了保护中国在边界河道上的权力，海关实应在航路标志维护之事上采取有效的措施。而且，航路标志相关事宜若可由海关全权管理，事情便会更加简单，亦可避免浪费时间，浪费资金。当然，海关既为中央政府所辖，若与中国不承认的政府代表签订协议，必会有反对之声，但相信只要海关与之签订的协议仅为"临时办法"，便会无碍。此外，因协议中有超出道尹职权范围之事，道尹已同意以"交涉员"之身份签署协议。鉴于此，若道尹拒绝与俄方签署不含黑龙江督军所提两项条款之协

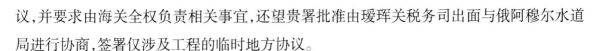

议,并要求由海关全权负责相关事宜,还望贵署批准由瑷珲关税务司出面与俄阿穆尔水道局进行协商,签署仅涉及工程的临时地方协议。

6. 随呈附上协议草案,与提供给俄阿穆尔水道局的协议草案内容大致相同;鉴于俄阿穆尔水道局已基本通过该草案,因此达成协议应非难事。协议一事已拖延数月,考虑黑龙江上的航路标志维护工作亟待开展,故恳请贵署使用电令发送批准公文。

此抄件发送至巡工司及哈尔滨关税务司。

您忠诚的仆人

(签字)包安济(G. Boezi)

瑷珲关署理税务司

该抄件内容真实有效,特此证明。

录事: 王友燮　三等同文供事后班

瑷珲关致海关总税务司署第119号呈附件

《临时协议》

中国海关瑷珲关与俄阿穆尔水道局为完成1923年黑龙江边界河道航路标志维护工作共同签署该协议。

1. 该《临时协议》自双方共同签署之日起生效，1923年开始执行；如1923年12月末之前双方均未提出废止该协议，协议有效期将顺延一年。

2. 该《临时协议》的双方责任人分别为中国海关（瑷珲关）税务司和俄阿穆尔水道局督办。

3. 凡涉及黑龙江边界河道自波克罗夫卡（Pokrovka）至嘎杂克维池（Kasakevich）河段的灯塔、标杆及其他航路标志的安设工作，均由俄阿穆尔水道局负责。俄阿穆尔水道局须向中国海关提交完整的工作计划和预算（具体限额见附录1），请示批准；中国海关须对俄阿穆尔水道局的工作进度和费用支出进行监督。

4. 中俄双方将分别于黑龙江边界河道的华俄两岸征收江捐（税率见附录2），以满足航路标志维护工作的费用支出。

5. 凡中俄两国的轮船、民船以及木筏，若航行于黑龙江航道的华岸一侧，则须向中国海关缴纳江捐，若航行于黑龙江航道的俄岸一侧，则须向俄阿穆尔水道局缴纳江捐。

6. 中国海关应照上述第三项条款所规定之支出，使用其于黑龙江航道华岸一侧所征收之江捐向俄阿穆尔水道局支付相应摊款。

7. 江捐征收细则、工作进度和经费支出监督规定以及中国海关应向俄阿穆尔水道局支付的摊款数额均见于附录3。

附录 1

俄阿穆尔水道局关于 1923 年 1 月 1 日至 12 月 31 日期间黑龙江航路标志维护的主要工作计划与支出计划如下。

黑龙江边界河道自波克罗夫卡至嘎杂克维池河段将划分为五个部分。

参考 1922 年的情况,将开放:

水深信号站	7 处
通行信号站	2 处
水位观测站	11 处
安设灯塔的浅滩	4 处

标桩的新建与修理数量以及相应支出比例均与 1922 年相同。

1923 年布拉戈维申斯克(Blagovestchensk,即海兰泡)技术部及各处的职员总人数不得超过 1922 年之数。

因布拉戈维申斯克技术部的工作范围包括俄国内陆水域和黑龙江边界河道两部分,故其支出仅有半数可记入黑龙江边界河道航路标志维护工作的预算之中。

(布拉戈维申斯克技术部及巡查专员可配备汽艇一艘。)

注:视实际税收情况而定。

支出总额不得超出_____金卢布。

注:最终支出限额根据预期税收金额而定。

附录 2 税率

江捐税率与去年相同。

附录 3 细则

1. 征税部门(中国海关或俄阿穆尔水道局)应在完税轮船的舱口单上加盖特殊印花,以示该轮船已如数完纳江捐。

2. 凡轮船由黑龙江过境者,无论国别,均应于出发地为其所载客货支付江捐。乘客船票所需缴纳的江捐数额应由轮船在黑龙江边界河道上航行的里程数而定。

3. 凡货物或轮船往来黑龙江自波克罗夫卡至嘎杂克维池河段者，若持有由征税部门加盖特殊印花的舱口单（参见条款1），则无须再次缴纳江捐；若无法于抵达后出示完纳江捐证明，则须于目的地缴纳江捐。

4. 凡货物直接往来黑龙江航道华俄对岸（如往返于大黑河与布拉戈维申斯克之间），或大黑河与结雅河之间者，均照税率的25%支付江捐。

5. 征税部门须向纳捐者发放收据，纳捐者须予以妥善保存，以便接受相关各方的查验。

6.《临时协议》第三项条款所涉之工作计划和支出预算，应提前提交中国海关审批。

7. 中国海关有权委派一名或多名代表对俄阿穆尔水道局的工作进度和费用支出进行实地查验；俄阿穆尔水道局须积极配合华方代表的工作，尽量为其提供交通、膳宿等方面的便利。

8. 凡中国海关和俄阿穆尔水道局人员有需要为航路标志维护工作外出执行公务者，均可由中俄双方政府签发长期护照，享受应有的保护，同时享有免费搭乘中俄两国轮船的待遇。

9. 中国海关应将所征江捐之数按月告知俄阿穆尔水道局。

10. 中国海关应从所征江捐中扣除10%的海关征税佣金。

11. 中国海关每月的净税收应首先用于支付航务专门顾问的办公经费，但1923年该项经费总额不得超过8000银圆。

12. 中国海关所征江捐的结余应用于向俄阿穆尔水道局支付摊款；若1923年江捐税收结余不足，则应使用1922年江捐税收结余以做填补。

13. 若资金允许，中国海关应照先前批准的工作计划和预算承担俄阿穆尔水道局全年支出的半数。

14. 中国海关应于每月月初向俄阿穆尔水道局支付其应付摊款的75%；实际支出的尾款，则须待俄阿穆尔水道局提交合理账簿后，或其根据工作计划和预算所产生的实际支出得到中国海关认可后，再行支付。

15. 该《临时协议》并不涉及疏浚河道、清理石块或其他重要工作：任何一方，若未经另一方同意，均不得于边界河道开展大型疏浚工作。

16. 俄阿穆尔水道局应于1924年2月28日前提交1923年账簿。

17. 细则有效期同《临时协议》。

16. 1923年《瑷珲关理船章程》

[J-28]

No. 150　　Commrs.

Aigun　　No. 96,349

INSPECTORATE GENERAL OF CUSTOMS,

PEKING. 22nd October 1923.

Sir,

　　With reference to I. G. despatch No. 113/ 93,787:

　　　　informing you that upon the approval and promulgation of the Aigun Harbour Regulations Mr. Baukham would be appointed Harbour Master:

and to I. G. despatch No.149/96,343 :

　　　　notifying the final approval of the Regulations:

I am directed by the Inspector General to inform you that Mr. G.g.Baukham, Acting Tidesurveyor (Examiner A), is appointed in addition Acting Harbour Master from the date on which the Regulations come into force, which date is to be reported in due course in your Return of Service Movements.

　　　　　　I am,

　　　　　　　　Sir,

　　　　　　　　　E.   Co-a-Inder.

　　Your obedient Servant,

The Commissioner of Customs,

　AIGUN.　　　　Chief Secretary Officiating.

HARBOUR REGULATIONS FOR THE PORT OF TAHEIHO

瑷珲關理船章程

1. The term "vessel" in these Regulations refers to vessels of foreign type. Regulations concerning native-type craft and rafts are embodied herein only so far as is necessary for their due control when working in connection with foreign-type vessels and for purposes of keeping the fairway clear of obstruction. Native-type craft and rafts are regulated in other respects by "Special Notifications."

一凡本章程所載船隻字樣係指洋式船隻及本身

管理排所有他項事宜則另有專章不在本章

通章倘有妨礙航路等事以便于管理及維持航

物所有限制之內其蒹葭木船起卸貨路與洋式船隻

ANCHORAGES.

2. The upper and the lower limits of the Harbour are respectively from Hsi Shan T'ou Hill to below the Public Park. The anchorages are as follows:-

停泊界限

許用界限左

停泊界限

二本口界限上至西山嘴下至公園

(a) For foreign-type vessels other than those provided for in (c), for which special anchorages have been assigned, between the Wu Tung Co.'s Wharf and the Custom House Winter Road Office (Kuantulu).

甲凡洋船隻除局於為指所指者外均應停泊於大通公司碼頭與海關戊路卽官茂戊路稽查處之間

(b) For junks and rafts, between the Upper Limits of the Harbour and the Wu Tung Co.'s Wharf and between the Custom House Winter Road Office (Kuantulu) and the Lower Limits of the Harbour.

乙凡民船筏木排均應停泊於本口上界與大通公司碼頭之間與海關戊路卽官茂戊路稽查處與本口下界之間

-2-

(c) For vessels of any type carrying mineral oil or explosives, and those subject to Quarantine Regulations, outside the Lower Limits of the Harbour, alongside the "Island".

3. Vessels shall moor in accordance with instructions from the Harbour Master and shall not shift their berths without a special permit, except when outward bound after having obtained their clearance papers.

Vessels may not lie in the stream at single anchor, nor drag anchors.

Rafts on arrival shall anchor or make fast outside the Upper Limits of the Harbour, and shall not proceed to their assigned moorings in the Harbour without having obtained permission from the Harbour Master.

4. Vessels which have determined berths are allowed to proceed direct to a point in the stream opposite their berth, except as provided for in Articles 6, 13 and 16 of these Regulations. Steam and motor-launches are allowed provisionally to enter and clear both at the Ferry Office and at the Winter Road Office (Kuantulu). The ferry from Taheiho to Blagovestchensk is worked under a special agreement.

-3-

5. Applications for berths or for permission to shift berth must be made at the Harbour Master's Office by the Ship Master, the First Officer, or the Pilot in charge, when the necessary instructions concerning the berth will be given. If a vessel be instructed by the Harbour Master to shift her berth, she shall do so.

MUNITIONS

6. Vessels having on board as cargo any high explosives or the specially prepared constituents of such, any loaded shells, or more than 100 pounds of gunpowder, any quantity of small-arm cartridges in excess of 50,000 rounds, or any other fixed ammunition of which the aggregate quantity of powder-charges exceeds 100 pounds, shall anchor as provided for in Article 2, (c), and fly a RED flag at the fore by day and exhibit a RED light by night; and in regard to the discharge of the same, they shall abide by the instructions received from the Customs.

Vessels having to receive on board any such explosives shall observe similar precautions.

This rule shall not apply to small-arm cartridges when carried in a properly constructed magazine, so fitted as to admit of its being flooded by a seacock operated from the upper deck, in which case the num-

-4-

ber of cartridges allowed to be carried is
not limited.

7.　　Men-of-war and other Government
vessels may, on application to the Harbour
Master, be permitted to take on board or
tranship explosives within anchorage (a),
provided that such explosives are handled
only by their own crew under the command
of an Officer.

8.　　Any transfer by boat of explosives,
arms or ammunition must be covered by a special permit, which will be issued at the Harbour Master's Office upon the owner's written
application giving the registered numbers of
the boats to be thus employed.

9.　　Lighters or other boats, before
being allowed to receive on board any of the
articles mentioned in Article 6 of these Regulations, shall be inspected by the Harbour
Master and, if suitable, shall receive a permit; all such articles are to be stored on
board as directed by the Harbour Master.

10.　　Every craft, except men-of-war,
of whatever description, conveying explosive through any part of the waters of the
port shall exhibit a RED flag, not less than
six feet by four feet, by day, and exhibit a
RED light by night, at the foremast head or
where it can best be seen; and in case of all

-5-

boats or lighters thus employed which are not
fitted with masts, the RED flag or RED
light must be exhibited at a height of not
less than 12 feet above the highest part of
the deck or house.

11.　　The storage of explosives of any
description shall not be allowed anywhere on
or near the shore of the river within the
Harbour Limits except after due consideration and sanction of the Customs and local
Authorities.

12.　　No fires, for cooking or any other
purpose, and no smoking shall be allowed on
board any lighter or other boat when going
alongside a vessel which has explosives on
board, nor while there are any explosives on
board such lighter or boat.

MINERAL OIL

13.　　Vessels arriving with mineral oil
or cargo of a highly inflammable nature,
shall anchor as provided in Article 2, (c),
and must remain there until all such cargo
been discharged and fly a RED flag at
fore by day and exhibit a RED light by
it. Vessels loading such cargo shall
do only where it is permitted to be dis-
ged, and from there proceed out of the
rbour. Vessels in anchorages (a) and
are permitted to handle a quantity of

即不在
與所
此領所定
列取之
表限

七凡英艦及官船等如經
理船廳允准在本章第
條甲船所得停泊界限内
其餘搬移爆裂物或軍
火等物須由貨主先行
搬運別船之料取具特
别執照並須於報呈呈
内將現用船隻注號註
明最為穩當

八凡轉運軍火品類或裝載物
除兵艦及官船外所有
大等物必項由貨主先行
行報告理船廳領取特
别執照並須於報呈呈
内將現用船隻注號註
明

九凡駁船或他項船隻如領受
載本章第六條所載各物
應由理船廳驗駁如屬安
當即由理船廳發給許可
領在該四英尺問應裝搬前
須照裝船特應遵照理船
廳指示

十無論何式船隻除兵艦外凡
裝載爆裂物在内行駛時
該船應備紅旗一面其
長五英尺寬四英尺最多
在問則代以紅燈如其船

連無桅杆之駁船將
該旗或燈設法裝
高至低甲板頂設
或船面高樓房頂
最高之處高出
十二英尺

十一凡未經安藏及未安藏
方官特許不准將
爆裂物在本口各
岸一帶擅自
七條

十二凡駁船或他項駁船
艇靠近裝有爆裂物
之船或未附有此
等爆裂物者均不准
為煮飯或因他事生
火亦不准吸烟等事

裝油船類

十三凡船隻裝載煤油或最易燃燒之物
進口時應停泊依本章第二條丙款所指
定之地點在此項貨物未經卸盡前懸該
船不論晝夜問則代以紅旗一面問應懸
紅燈各船只准在允准卸貨裝貨地點
卸貨各物並准在上列卸貨裝貨地點
地點裝載其物事即由該廳處其駛出口
在本章第二條甲乙款内停泊之船隻

173

-6-

kerosene oil not exceeding 50 cases. Bulk
oil steamers are required to take all such
precautions as are customary in their trade.

14.   No fires, for cooking or any
other purpose, and no smoking shall be allowed on board any lighter or other boat
when going alongside a vessel which has
naphtha, benzine, or other highly inflammable cargo on board, nor while there is
naphtha, benzine, or other highly inflammable cargo on board such lighter or boat.

15.   The storage of naphtha, benzine,
or other highly inflammable cargo shall not
be allowed on or near the shore of the
river (within the Harbour Limits) except
with the permission of the Customs.

INFECTIOUS DISEASES.

16.   Vessels having any infectious
disease on board or any disease suspected
to be infectious, or the body of a person
who died, or is suspected of having died,
of an infectious disease, shall, on approaching the Port, hoist the Quarantine Flag,
anchor as provided for in Article 2, (c),
and keep the Quarantine flag flying until
pratique has been granted. No person shall
be permitted to leave or board such a vessel without a permit from the Harbour Master
or Port Health Officer.

-7-

Vessels arriving from any Port
declared to be infected shall abide by the
instructions received from the Customs Authorities.

CONSERVANCY.

17.   No wharves, jetties, or bunding
shall be built, pontoons, hulks or buoys
moored, and no reclaiming or other riparian
work commenced, without the permission of
the Harbour Master, nor continued unless according to his directions. Applications
for such permission are to be endorsed by
the local Authorities.

18.   All buoys shall be subject to the
control of the Harbour Master; and if they
are so placed as to obstruct the passage of
vessels or are not moored in such a way as
to economize berthing space, the Harbour
Master shall be at liberty to order them to
be shifted. In case of refusal or neglect
on the part of the owners of a buoy to shift
its position as directed by the Harbour
Master, the latter may cause it to be removed at the cost of the owners.

19.   Ballast, ashes, garbage, refuse,
spoil obtained by dredging or otherwise,
etc., must not be thrown either into the
river in summer, or on to the ice in winter,
or on the river bank. Vessels wishing to

險方以資預防

船隻駛特許起卸經油准駛度所有之油船或近所用之船隻應遵照易燃品易品等物若均不准為煮飯或他事生火及吃煙等事

十四取船並他種船艦靠近裝有石腦油汽油苯等物之別種易燃煙之船或有此等物品者

燃燒品物自已儲

十五凡未經海關特許不准將石腦油苯油及別種最易燃品物在本埠岸一帶儲

傳染疾病類

允三起駛無論何人在船上者不准

此項執照無論何人不頒此章第二條丙款所指定之近到口時懸掛疾病章船必須遵依有傳染疾病或疑似傳染疾病奇或死病有病之尸身或疑似

十六凡船內有傳染疾病或疑似傳染疾病

下者不准上船其來自己經宣布有傳染疾病口岸之船隻概應遵照海關指示

保護水道事務類

遵之指示本不准其繼續工作往等事或未經核准依水道河岸工式碼頭或駁岸或設置浮碼頭船地位浮船復行敷或多估泊

十七凡未報經理船廳批准並本埠地方官簽准不准興築各

標主人繳

十八凡浮標概歸理船廳管理如其浮標所設之地位有導船復行敷或移若不遵行或有防設標船地位理船廳可令改移或延行代其處移一切費用則份歸該

拋棄水上凡船隻如

十九凡船隻糞垃圾等物江岸之上不及且無論冬夏拋棄水中凡船隻知兩岸之上冬夏是否敷上無論是否拋棄

—8—

discharge ashes or other refuse must do so outside Harbour Limits.

The road along the foreshore, within Harbour Limits, is to be kept free of all obstructions, such as garbage, building materials, etc., in order to allow free loading and discharging of vessels. Neither is cargo to be stored on the foreshore or bund, nor is any building of a permanent or temporary nature to be erected without special permission of the Customs Authorities.

20. In the case of wrecks within the Harbour, which form a danger to navigation, if no active steps for removal have been taken within reasonable time as specified by the Harbour Master, the wreck will be removed or destroyed by the Marine Department of the Customs.

In case anchors are lost in the Harbour, the place must be buoyed and the Harbour Master notified.

21. Pontoons and/or barges are to be moored in the positions assigned them by the Harbour Master. Their moorings will not be allowed to interfere with the free passage of vessels proceeding to or from other pontoons or barges, or in any way impede the fairway of the river at any stage of the water. Inshore anchors must be buried sufficiently deep not to endanger cargo-boats, native craft or launches. Neither

—9—

pontoons nor barges, nor steamers lying alongside thereof, are allowed to make lines fast to the Bund in such a manner as to cause obstructions to craft plying inside.

MISCELLANEOUS

22. To provide for the safety of navigation, vessels both when navigating on the Amur, and within Harbour Limits, are required to conform to the "Special Navigation Regulations" issued by the River Authorities.

Towboats and other craft towing within Harbour Limits must be of sufficient power to maintain perfect control over their tows. Rafts moving within the Harbour must have a sufficient complement of crew and equipment to maintain a perfect control of their movements; and must keep at a fair distance from steamers and other craft at anchor, so as to avoid all possibilities of collision.

23. Vessels under way within the Harbour are to proceed at no greater speed than is necessary to keep the vessel under control.

24. The blowing of steam whistles or sirens, or other sound signals except for the purpose of signalling in accordance with the "Special Navigation Regu-

lations", referred to in Article 22, or for the purpose of warning vessels of dangers is strictly forbidden.

25.   All vessels shall keep on board a sufficient number of hands to clear and pay out chain. The hawse must always be kept clear.

26.   No vessels, except men-of-war, may use swinging booms.

Swinging booms should be rigged in from sunset to sunrise.

27.   No merchant vessel shall fire cannon or small arms within the Harbour.

28.   Lighters and other boats are not to be made fast to vessels in such a manner or in such numbers as to interfere with the free passage of other boats or vessels through the Harbour.

29.   Sampans with runners are prohibited from boarding vessels until the Customs Boarding Officer has left the vessel or otherwise given permission for such craft to come alongside. Masters of vessels should assist to their utmost the Harbour Authorities in having this rule observed.

30.   In case of fire occurring on board a vessel in port, the fire bell must be rung immediately by that vessel, and by those above and below her, and the signal N.H. International Code ("Fire, want immediate assistance") hoisted by the burning vessel, if possible, and by those above and below her during the day, or the head light lowered and hoisted continually during the night; notice should immediately be given to the Harbour Master.

31.   Any person infringing these Regulations may be prosecuted before the competent Authorities, and any vessel involved in such infringement shall be liable to have its entrance, working and clearance stopped by the Customs until such infringement shall cease.

32.   These Regulations are subject to addition and alteration when, and if, necessary.

NOTICE.

1.   Masters of vessels or Pilots are requested to report to the Harbour Master any changes in the channels, accidents to shipping, wrecks, or other noteworthy events, any abnormal shoal

通 告

water they may have discovered, and if
any Aid to Navigation is in distress or
out of position.

2.   At the Harbour Master's Office
may be seen all local Harbour Notifications and Notices issued by the River
Authorities.

失去等事
應即由該
船主或引
水人報知
本口理
船廳

一凡航路
應所出之警廳
理船示及本
船廳所出口
開於本江
之各橙口
船而 稽
應布於 存
廳本口理船
時變以使
開有隨船

致瑷珲关第 <u>150/96349</u> 号令　　　　　海关总税务司署（北京）1923 年 10 月 22 日

尊敬的瑷珲关税务司：

　　根据海关总税务司署第 113/93787 号令：

　　　　"通知自《瑷珲关理船章程》批准及颁布之时起，即刻委任博韩（G. E. Baukham）先生为理船厅。"

　　并且根据海关总税务司署第 149/96348 号令：

　　"通知《章程》已获最终批准。"

　　奉总税务司命令，兹告知，自章程生效之日起，委任代理头等总巡前班博韩先生兼任代理理船厅，并将此生效日期及时填写至"海关职员任调统计表"。

您忠诚的仆人

威厚澜（R. H. R. Wade）

代理总务科税务司

瑷珲关理船章程

1. 凡本章程中提及的"船只"术语均指洋式船只。华式船只及木排如有襄助洋式船只起卸货物或如有阻碍航路等情况亦归本章程管辖,以保证水上交通得以畅通无阻。其余华式船只及木排的所有其他事宜则另有专门章程管理。

停泊界限

2. 本港口界限上至西山头,下至公园后身。停泊界限如下:

(1)除了属于(丙)条内所指的船只另有专门停泊地点之外,其他洋式船只均应停泊在戊通公司码头与海关冬令过江检查处(即官渡路口)之间。

(2)凡民船及木排均应停泊在本港口上界与戊通公司码头之间或海关冬令过江检查处(即官渡路口)与本港口下界之间。

(3)凡装载矿物油或爆炸物料并根据《海港检疫章程》等候查验的船只,均应停泊在本港口下界之外,"岛上"沙滩之旁。

3. 凡船只停泊事宜均应听从理船厅指示,除领有结关单照的船只可以往外行驶,其他停泊船只如未领取特别准单,停泊地点不得擅自移动。

船只在江中停泊时,既不能只下单锚,也不能抛浮锚。

木排进入港口时,应当在本港口上界之外抛锚泊船或快速靠拢,未经理船厅许可,不得驶入港口内停泊。

4. 凡已有指定停泊地点的船只,进入本港口时如查无本章程第6条、第13条和第16条所述各事项,准予直接驶入指定停泊地点对面的江中。汽船及摩托艇均暂准进入本港口,在横江码头检查处或在海关冬令过江检查处(即官渡路口)报关。由大黑河至俄属布拉戈维申斯克(Blagovestchensk,即海兰泡)的渡江轮船另有专章规定。

5. 凡船只欲要停泊或移位,应由船主、大副或引水员报告理船厅,听候其指导。如有船只已经停泊,理船厅命令其移到他处,该船亦应遵照。

军火类

6. 凡船只载有高性能炸药或制造高性能炸药的材料、开花炮弹、超过一百磅的火药、超过5万粒子弹的轻武器弹药筒,或内装火药总重超过一百磅的整装式弹药,均应停泊在本章程第 2 条（丙）款的指定地点,并应在日间系挂一面红旗,夜间系挂一盏红灯;卸货之时,也应遵照海关指令办理。

凡船只欲在本港口内装载以上各项易爆炸物料,也应遵照上述办法办理。

凡船只装载轻武器弹药筒,应将该弹药筒装入结构合理的船舱弹药库内,且船舱内应装有船底阀,从上甲板操作该阀即可灌水入内,以免火灾,则装载此类枪弹的船只不在上项取缔办法之列。

7. 凡军舰及其他官船,经理船厅允准,可在本章第 2 条（甲）款所述停泊界限内装载爆炸物料或将爆炸物料搬运到其他船只,并且船只装载搬运时必须完全由该船官员指挥本船水手执行。

8. 凡转运爆炸物料或军火的船只（除军船及官船外）,必须由船主先行报告理船厅,申请领取特别执照,并在执照内注明欲要使用的船只的注册号码。

9. 凡驳船或其他船艇欲装载本章程第 6 条所载各物,应由理船厅检验,如属妥当,则发放装船许可;所有上述各物装船应遵照理船厅指示。

10. 除军舰外,无论何式船只,凡装载爆炸物料在本港口内行驶,均应在白日准备一面红旗,至少六英尺长,四英尺宽,系挂在前桅顶部或最易瞭望之处,夜间则代以红灯;如果使用的船艇没有安装桅杆,也应将红旗或红灯设法系挂到高处,至少比该船甲板或舱房顶高出 12 英尺。

11. 凡未经海关及本埠地方官特许,不得将爆炸物料擅自存储在本港口沿岸一带。

12. 凡驳船或其他船艇靠近装载有爆炸物料的船只,或其船上装载有此等爆炸物料,均不得吸烟,不准生火煮饭或出于其他目的点火。

油船类

13. 凡船只装载矿油或易燃的货物进入本港口时,应停泊在本章程第 2 条（丙）款内的指定地点。在上述货物未经卸下之前,该船不得移动,并且必须准备一面红旗,日间系挂前桅顶部,夜间则代以红灯。凡装载上述货物的船只,只准在上述此种货物准卸地点卸下,事毕,即由该处直接驶出本港口。在本章程第 2 条（甲）款和（乙）款内停泊地点停泊的船只,虽持有特许煤油起卸执照,但不得超过五十箱。所有散装油汽船应恪守此类贸易船只执行的预防方法。

14. 凡驳船或其他船艇靠近装载有石脑油、石油醚或其他易燃的货物的船只,或其船上装载有石脑油、石油醚或其他易燃的货物,均不得吸烟,不准生火煮饭或出于其他目的点火。

15. 凡未经海关特许,不得将石脑油、石油醚或其他易燃的货物擅自存储在(本港口)沿岸一带。

传染病类

16. 凡船内有传染病或疑似传染病者,或船内停有死于传染病或疑似传染病的尸身,该船必须在接近口岸时,系挂有疫旗号,并停泊在本章程第2条(丙)款内的指定地点。如未获得船只无疫通行证,不得将旗帜放下。如未领有理船厅或口岸卫生员签发的许可证,船上任何人都不得下船,船下任何人都不得上船。

凡来自已宣布有传染病口岸的船只,概应遵照海关指示。

水道保护事务类

17. 未报经理船厅批准,不得修建各式码头或堤岸,不得系泊各式浮筒、浮标或废船,不得填筑江河或开始其他河岸工程。除非遵照理船厅指示,否则不得继续开工。上述许可申请需经本埠当局签准。

18. 一切浮标均归理船厅管理。倘若浮标所设位置有碍船只行驶,或占用驳船位,理船厅可命令该浮标主将浮标移开。若浮标主不遵行命令或怠忽职责,理船厅可直接代其移开,一切费用则仍归该浮标主人照付。

19. 凡各种压舱物、灰烬、废料、垃圾,无论是否从港口疏浚而来,均不得随意丢弃,夏季不得丢弃江中,冬季不得丢弃冰上。凡船只如欲丢弃各种灰烬及垃圾,必须丢弃在本港口界外。

在本港口界内沿前滩马路一带,需整理干净,不得存放垃圾及建筑材料,保证道路不会阻塞,便于轮船起卸货物。未经海关特许,所有货物不得存放在前滩或堤岸上,也不得在该处建造永久或暂时性房屋。

20. 凡在本港口内撞沉的破船残骸对航行船只来讲有危险,倘若该船东未在理船厅规定的期限内将该沉船移走,海关海政局即可代为移置或摧毁。

倘若船只的锚在本港口内丢失,应于丢失位置设立一个浮标,并报告理船厅。

21. 浮筒和驳船均应在理船厅指定之处系留。其锚链不得对其余往来其他浮筒或驳船的船只有所阻碍。无论江水涨落,均不得妨碍水道交通。近滨船锚必须深埋在土中,以免损坏往来货船、华式船只或汽艇。无论浮筒或驳船,还是靠近浮筒或驳船的汽船,在将缆绳系紧到堤岸时,都不得有碍往来船只。

杂项类

22. 为航行安全起见,凡船只在黑龙江上及在本港口界内行驶,均应遵照航路厅另行颁布的"航行专门章程"办理。

凡拖船或其他种类船只在本港口内拖带船只,必须具有充足动力,能保持对被拖曳船只的完全控制。凡在本港口内往来行驶的木排,必须具有充足的船员和装备,以保持对木排移动的完全控制;并且必须与停泊的汽船和其他种类船只保持适当距离,以防相撞。

23. 凡在本港口内行驶的船只,其行驶速率应以能够控制船身前行为宜,不得速行,以防危险。

24. 凡位于本港口内的船只,除遵照本章程第22条所述的"航行专门章程"应鸣放汽笛或其他声音信号给予警示信号的情形,或者警示船只有危险的情形之外,其余所有情形,均不得擅自鸣笛或发出其他声音信号。

25. 凡船只均需配备数量充足的船员,以便整理和收放锚链。其左右锚链不得互搭,也不得缠绕。

26. 除军舰外,其余船只均不得于船旁支用横杆。

所有军舰支出的横杆,也应在日落至日出期间收回。

27. 凡商船均不得在本港口内鸣放火炮或使用轻武器。

28. 凡驳船及其他小船靠拢大船时,速度不得太快,数量不得太多,不得妨碍港口内其他船只的行驶。

29. 凡接客的舢板,应等待海关轮船检查员离船后,方可登船接客;如因他故,经海关轮船检查员的特许,也可以登船接客。各船主也应当全力协助港口实行此条规则。

30. 凡船只在本港口内如遇火灾,必须立即鸣钟示警,在白天须升起标有"N. H."字样的信号旗(此国际代码表示"有船失火,速来救援"),其上下停泊之船,也必须同时鸣钟系旗;如遇夜间,则将信号灯升起降下,不得间断。此外,应当立即将灾情报告理船厅。

31. 凡有人员违反以上章程,可向主管当局告发。凡违反章程的船只,海关有权阻止船只进港、装卸货物和结关。等到该船遵守此章程后,始准照行。

32. 本章程如有未尽事宜,将来会根据需要另行增改。

通告

1. 如果船只遇有航道变动或船只事故、沉没或其他紧要事项,比如在航行中发现异常浅滩,或航路标志受损或不在正确位置,该船船主或引水员应报知本港口理船厅。

2. 凡航路厅颁布的各种港口通知通告,均存于本港口理船厅处,方便随时查阅。

17. 1924 年《黑龙江航路标志协议》

2 Enclosures.

144.
I.G.

AIDS TO NAVIGATION ON THE AMUR: Agreement for 1923 & 1924 signed;
discourtesy of Russian officials; Taoyin suspicious & annoyed;
original estimates considerably scaled down; customs control over
expenditure adequate; appreciation of services of Technical
Adviser.

Aigun   29th. December, 1923.

Replied to in No. 163.

Sir,

1.   I beg leave to refer to Aigun

Despatch No. 119 :

AIDS TO NAVIGATION ON AMUR: Local
Agreement for 1923: probable failure
of negotiations between Taoyin and
Russian Authority, reported;
authority for the C. M. Customs
to discuss temporary local modus
operandi in accordance with
Taoyin's suggestion, solicited;
draft of proposed arrangement,
submitted;

and to report that an Agreement for 1923 and
1924, on the lines of the 1922 Agreement, was
signed at Blagovestchensk on the 28th. of October,
1923.   The Additional Rules were signed at
Taheiho on the 30th. November, 1923, but there
has been delay in supplying me with official
copies of the Chinese and Russian texts.   So
far as the new Agreement is concerned, present

conditions

The Inspector General of Customs,

Peking.

Entered in Corr. Index.

conditions continue in force until next December.
There are certain minor verbal alterations and a
few changes in the order of paragraphs but to
these, I venture the opinion, no objection can
be taken.   The Taoyin tells me that he has
signed the new Agreement under authority received
from the Shui-wu Ch'u and the Heilungchiang Sheng
Kung Shu and that it is from these same sources
that he has received permission to provide for
its continuance until the 1st. of December, 1924.

2.   Part 4 takes the form of an Appendix
in which reference is made to the claim of
Chinese shipping to be allowed to navigate the
Amur via Habarovsk to the sea (Nikolaevsk) and
back.   It does not come into operation and
forms no part of the Agreement but is placed on
record in order to prevent future misunderstanding
and so that China's case on the subject may not
go by default.   The Taoyin recognises that
this claim is one which is likely to arouse
acute division of political opinion, but he

maintains

maintains that permission to navigate the Amur to
the sea has been granted to Chinese vessels by
previous treaties and argues that he can no more
surrender such right, which he says he would be
doing if he were to omit to re-state it, than
the local Russian authorities can be expected to
admit it.

3.   The collection of River Dues this year
commenced on the 16th. of May, i.e. prior to the
receipt of permission from the Shui-wu Ch'u to
enter into a new Agreement, and the Officiating
Inspector General's telegram of the 10th. of June
instructed my predecessor that collection should
not have commenced without definite authority of
the Shui-wu Ch'u and directed him to request the
Taoyin to submit the arrangements made for the
collection of dues during 1923 to the Ch'u for
approval.   This was duly done and in June the
Taoyin wrote to the Director of the Russian Amur
Government Water Transport Office at Blagovestchensk
to

to propose an Agreement for 1923 on the lines of
the previous one.   The Director in his reply
insinuated that he favoured the suggestion, but
did not give any definite undertaking.   The
Taoyin thereupon wrote again in July and asked
for an answer one way or the other, but his
request passed unheeded and it was not until
September that this letter was acknowledged.   The
Russians have thus shown themselves unexpectedly
troublesome and the initial cause of their unfair
and unreasonable behaviour was undoubtedly the
quarrel over the issue by the Heiho Taoyin of
Frontier Passes which both sides considered substantial ground for breaking off commercial
relations and which continues to bar the way to
the restoration of normal conditions.   Their
reticence caused great offence and the Taoyin
complained to me at the time that he had not
been treated with the decencies of civilisation.
He said that the only possible deduction was
that the Russians were unwilling to come to any

Agreement

agreement for 1923 and proceeded to observe that he would not have any further dealings with them. There was no doubt about his personal feelings in the matter and at one time there appeared to be not the slightest probability of any advance towards the ending of the deadlock.   Eventually I was able to induce the representatives of the Amur Government Water Transport Office to ask me to arrange a meeting for them with the Taoyin and in passing on the request I submitted that it was our business to deal amicably with them and suggested that they should be courteously heard. The whole deadweight of those around the Taoyin was mobilised to persuade him not to accept my proposal and it was only after his adviser on foreign affairs had at last been successfully coaxed into no longer actively obstructing my suggestion that he gave way and consented, though with extreme reluctance, to grant the Russians an interview.

4.

4.   The representatives of the Amur Government Water Transport Office visited the Taoyin on the 15th. of October and the Director tendered forthwith an apology for not having replied earlier to his letters, but represented that his attitude in this matter had been twisted out of its meaning.   He explained that the Taoyin's *last* letter had been received at a time when, owing to the absence from Blagovestchensk of himself and his colleagues, the Water Transport Office had to all intents and purposes no effective existence as it was then temporarily under the control of subordinates who were unable to act with authority and consequently not in a position to take important decisions. The Taoyin, whose demeanour throughout was one of frank hostility, replied that it was an essential part of any Agreement that it should be concluded not at the end of the year, but at the beginning and he made no attempt to hide his impatience with what he rightly regarded as deliberate suppression of the truth.   He said that he could not listen

to

to any discussion about an Agreement for 1923 but
expressed willingness to sign during 1923 an
Agreement for 1924.   The Russians thereupon
allowed the question of an Agreement for 1923 to
drop but requested permission to send two vessels
with technical staffs on a tour of inspection of
Aids on the Chinese side of the Amur, pointing
out that during the months that had elapsed since
the establishment in July of a commercial blockade
no work had been attempted on the Chinese side.
They asked for an assurance that their staffs
would not be molested when landing on Chinese
soil for the purpose of inspection and observation.
The Taoyin replied that an inspection of the river
so late in the year could serve no useful purpose
and treated the suggestion as a joke, but the more
the matter was discussed the more difficult it was
for him to turn down so reasonable a request and
after I had submitted that the steps proposed were
manifestly necessary from our point of view unless
the whole business of supervision was to be a sham

his

his attitude gradually changed to at least a formal
courtesy and he granted the permission applied for.

5.   The Taoyin probably regarded his attitude
towards the Russians at this meeting both as the
discharge of a patriotic duty and as a means of
gratifying revenge upon those who had offended him,
but it seemed to me that the question of an
Agreement on Aids to Navigation of the Amur was
not so much his own private affair that he could
take it upon himself to decide upon its summary
rejection without giving close consideration to the
views expressed by the officer in charge of this
Custom House who, if I understand this question
correctly, may claim a direct and practical voice
on all matters affecting the welfare of shipping
which is so closely concerned with the proper
maintenance of the river.   I therefore remained
on after the Russians had left and discussed the
matter further with the Taoyin to whom I suggested
that our main concern should be the continued existence of the Agreement and our objective one of

equity

equity.   I pointed out that the trade on which
the livelihood of this district depended was made
possible solely by the existence of Aids to
Navigation which belonged to the Russian Government
and submitted that a certain sum of money was due
to the owner for the use of his property.   The
Taoyin seemed adamant in his opposition to my
proposal and said that he preferred to leave the
difficulty to settle itself and not to attempt any
sort of reconciliation.   He protested that any
estimate of work done by the Russians during 1923
would be sheer conjecture and that an Agreement
for 1923 was in consequence out of the question.
He talked a great deal about the dubious methods
and wilful discourtesy of the Russians, but his
objections were entirely frivolous and such as to
prove that he was swayed almost wholly by personal
considerations.   He proposed that the river dues
collected during 1923 should be used for carrying
out repairs to the Bund but dropped the idea when
I represented that these dues had been collected
for a specified purpose to be executed at a

specified

specified date and that we could not apply them
to other purposes without breaking our promise to
the people from whom they had been received.   A
few days later the Taoyin allowed his own persuasions
to be overborne and told me that he thought that
my view was the right one.   He said that after
considering the matter further he had come to the
conclusion that it would be advisable to sign an
Agreement and requested me to make the necessary
arrangements with the responsible authorities at
Blagovestchensk.   I did as he asked and the
Agreement followed.

6.   The Estimates submitted by the Russian
Amur Government Water Transport Office for the year
1923 proposed an expenditure of Gold Roubles 60,800
for the upkeep of Aids to Navigation on the
frontier stretches of the Amur, but an examination
of the various items demonstrated fully that in
their original form these estimates were undeserving
of credence and that those who were responsible
for framing them had no qualms of conscience about

the

the expediency of a little audacity. An attempt
was made to saddle us with a share of responsibility
for the upkeep of the section from Kazakevich to
Habarovsk, but such expenditure from our point of
view is unproductive because navigation via this
particular stretch to the sea is reserved for
Russian vessels and this section of the river can
therefore have no interest for Chinese shipping
which finds itself debarred from making any profit
out of the economic conditions of the time. We
have refused to allow this burden to be imposed on
us and have accepted a share of responsibility for
the upkeep of the five sections Pokrovka to Beketova;
Beketova to Kumara; Kumara to Poyarkovo; Poyarkovo
to Soyusnaya; and Soyusnaya to Kazakevich. The
inability of the Russian Water Transport Authorities,
owing to the commercial blockade, to accomplish any
work of importance on the Chinese side of the Amur
made it necessary for the Technical Adviser to amend
in detail and with great care the original estimate
of Gold Roubles 60,800 and after a great deal of
                                        argument

argument the Russians agreed to our counter-proposal
of Gold Roubles 19,000. The Technical Adviser's
estimate for a full year's work was Gold Roubles
40,000 as compared with the Russian estimate of
Gold Roubles 60,800.

It is well known that the authorities at
Blagovestchensk have got their domestic affairs into
such a terrible mess that under pressure of financial
necessities they have been obliged to dismiss many
of their employees, and the Technical Adviser, who
has naturally fuller and more accurate knowledge of
such that is going on there than I can readily
attain, tells me that there is basis for the belief
that in order to give work to a large number of
people who, without it, would have been destitute
of employment, a number of workmen usually employed
on sections of inland rivers were drafted to various
sections of the Amur. This attempt made by the
Russian authorities to ameliorate the lot of destitute
Russian citizens by economising upon their own expenditure at the expense of China was a breach of
                                        faith

faith and a misuse of official authority, but it has been successfully challenged and the estimates have been correspondingly diminished. The Russians further represented with varying degrees of positiveness that a Pyramid could not be erected for less than $35.30; that the minimum cost of a Beacon was $27.90; and that to keep these in a proper state of repair an expenditure of at least $20 and $10 would be necessary. But on a matter such as this common sense judges by practical experience and we have had no difficulty in showing that a Pyramid can be erected for from $15 to $20 and a Beacon for from $8 to $10, and that annual repairs should not exceed on an average $5 for the former and $3 for the latter.

8.   To the Taoyin the question seems to have been constantly presenting itself, What really becomes of the money that China pays out towards the upkeep of Aids to Navigation and he has suggested that unless we exercise very great care a good deal of it may be squandered on bogus claims to compensation

                for

for work done. He has heard from the Chinese Consul-General at Blagovestchensk of the financial embarrassment which has overtaken the authorities there and the idea that China's contribution may provide means for tiding over an awkward position evidently worries him very much. The suspicious mind may well hesitate to feel absolute conviction about the trustworthiness of the estimates with which we have to deal, considering the quarter from which they come, but with the help of a Technical Adviser, who knows all the ins and outs of this business, we are not likely to experience any difficulty in protecting ourselves against travesties of reality. I dissent utterly from the Taoyin's view that an Agreement is pretty certain to be strained to our disadvantage and hold, on the contrary, that the present arrangement whereby the actual work in connexion with river conservancy is done by the Russians is justified upon practical grounds of business and that in a given position like the present the proportions of give and take may be said to strike a fair balance. The

                common

common commodity of honesty is naturally the corner-
stone of any claim by the Russians upon moneys
collected by this office and it would be foolish
to cheat ourselves with the hope that people who,
according to my information, are chosen with two
exceptions from the most unexpected circles of
society without special aptitude for the duties
they are supposed to perform, will be able to
resist the temptation to go just a little further
than will bear examination when submitting statements
of expenditure. But this does not in the least
affect my view that our present system of insurance
against attempts to saddle us with estimates
artificially inflated above the amount really needed
to erect and maintain Aids to Navigation may be
considered both adequate and effective and that we
shall never have any difficulty in scaling down
estimates to a figure which it is right and proper
for us to pay. A dissatisfied customer can always
be depended upon to question his accounts and in
genuine cases mistakes are invariably rectified.
This year an attempt was undoubtedly made by the

                                    Russians

9.

Russians to manoeuvre an Agreement agreeable to
themselves and unfavourable to us but our control
has been very effective in practical result and
the Water Transport Officials have agreed to accept
a sum which in comparison with their expectations
must seem somewhat small.

A tribute is due to Mr. Ignatieff,
Technical Adviser, who has opposed himself honestly
and whole-heartedly to the attempts which have been
made to press inadmissible and vexatious demands,
and whose help has immensely facilitated the
settlement of all matters in dispute. The preparation of the estimates for 1923 afforded an
opening for misrepresentation concerning general costs
of which the Russians were not slow to avail
themselves and it is due to Mr. Ignatieff's ability
to acquire inside information and bring expert
knowledge to bear upon the examination of the
various details that we have been able to reduce
expenses and, to quote a case in point, prevent
the employment of swollen staffs which the Russian
delegates professed at the outset to regard as

                                    essential

essential, but which we know, and they have since
admitted, are unjustified.   Mr. Ignatieff has
that special knowledge of the situation that comes
from long acquaintance with conditions at Blagovestchensk
where for nearly fourteen years he held the
appointment of Assistant Director of the Amur Water
Transport Office and in whatever form he has been
consulted his advice has been invaluable.

I have the honour to be,

Sir,

Your obedient Servant,

R. F. Chingleawk

Commissioner.

REFERENCES.

Despatches.	
From I.G.	To I.G.
Comrs. No.	Port No.
58/90,054	44
74/90,942	47
85/91,680	54
93/92,051	67
107/93,376	77
108/93,388	91
(Telegram of	101
10th.June,	110
1923)	119

Aigun No. 144 of 1923.

Enclosure No. 1.

PROVISIONAL LOCAL AGREEMENT CONCERNING NAVIGATION ON THE AMUR.

(1923 - 1924)

The Heiho Taoyin of the Republic of China (concurrently
Commissioner for Foreign Affairs, Aigun District) and the
Director of the Russian Amur Government Water Transport Office
have discussed the question of the collection of dues on
cargo and passengers carried by Chinese and Russian steamers,
junks and rafts, and on rafts navigating the frontier section
of the Amur, Argun, the Ussuri and other rivers, for the
upkeep of the channel of the frontier river , the maintenance
of Aids to Navigation, and the improvement of navigation
therein.

The Heiho Taoyin of the Republic of China (concurrently
Commissioner for Foreign Affairs, Aigun District) on one side,
and the Director of the Russian Amur Government Water
Transport Office on the other, with a view to the improvement
of navigation on the frontier River and considering the
frontier relationship of both countries, have come to the
present Agreement.

The signatories to the present Agreement are as follows:-

SUNG WÊN-YU , Heiho Taoyin of the Republic of China
(concurrently Commissioner for Foreign
Affairs, Aigun District);

CH'Ê HSI-CHÊN, Adviser on Foreign Affairs to the Heiho
Taoyin Office;

A. N. LAGUTIN, Acting Director of the Russian Amur
Government Water Transport Office;

V. A. DEDUHIN, Secretary;

V. J. FEDOROFF, Chief of the Amur Navigation Office.

I.

I - RULES FOR THE WORKING OF THE AGREEMENT.

ARTICLE 1. - This Provisional Agreement shall become operative from the date of signature by both parties and shall be in force until the 1st day of the 12th moon of the 13th year of the Republic of China (1st December 1924). The consent of both parties is necessary before any change can be made in this Provisional Agreement.

ARTICLE 2. - The interest of both parties being involved, the present Agreement will have the character of a mutual understanding. Owners of vessels, irrespective of their nationality, and those in charge of rafts, navigating the frontier waters, shall be responsible for the payment of dues for the proper maintenance of the fairway. The present Agreement, being of a local and mutual nature, shall not affect the Navigational Rules and other Amur regulations at present in force, nor shall it interfere with the freight rates in China and Russia.

II - RULES ON COLLECTION OF DUES AND EXPENDITURE.

ARTICLE 3. - The tariff of dues to be paid on cargo and passengers carried by steamers, junks and rafts shall be fixed by the Heiho Taoyin of China (concurrently Commissioner for Foreign Affairs, Aigun District) and the Director of the Russian Amur Government Water Transport Office. The fixed tariff for collection of dues is laid down in Annex I.

ARTICLE 4. - The procedure for collecting dues on passengers and cargo shall be fixed jointly by Representatives, appointed by the Heiho Taoyin of the Republic of China (concurrently Commissioner for Foreign Affairs, Aigun District) and by the Director of the Amur Government Water Transport Office as provided for in Annex 2.

ARTICLE 5. - Questions concerning the collection of dues

on

on cargo and passengers, carried by Chinese and Russian steamers, junks and rafts, as well as concerning the supervision of expenditure and other matters, shall be fixed by additional rules as provided for in Annex 2.

ARTICLE 6. - Chinese and Russian steamers, junks and rafts on the Chinese side shall pay River Dues to the C.M. Customs; on the Russian side to the Russian Amur Navigation Office or departments under its control.

III - RULES CONCERNING AIDS TO AND IMPROVEMENTS OF NAVIGATION.

ARTICLE 7. - Expenditure on all works in connection with Aids to Navigation, the erection of lights and signals and others of a similar nature, on the frontier section of the Amur from Pokrovka (Lo Ku Po) to Kazakevich shall be defrayed from River Dues collected by both sides. The aforesaid works should really be carried out by both sides. to this Agreement, but for the sake of convenience work which properly speaking it should fall to the lot of China to undertake will be entrusted to the Russian Amur Navigation Office by China in the name of the local Chinese Authorities. Dredging operations and conservancy works requiring the expenditure of large sums of money, may be undertaken only with the mutual consent of both sides, and after plans and estimates have been submitted for approval to the Sino-Russian Joint Commission.

The Sino-Russian Joint Commission shall be composed of eight members, four being chosen from each side. The Presidents shall be the Heiho Taoyin (of China) and the Russian Amur Government Water Transport Office Director. The remainder of the members, three for each side, shall be appointed by the two Presidents.

ARTICLE 8. - The above-mentioned works shall be undertaken in proportion to the amount of dues collected.

The

The Amur Navigation Office shall, according to Annex 3, submit
plans and estimates to the Joint Commission before the
opening of the navigation season. No work can be undertaken
before these plans and estimates have been duly approved by
the members of the Joint Commission.

ARTICLE 9. - Misunderstandings arising from the working
of this Agreement shall be settled by a third Commission,
whose decision shall be final; no other action will be taken.
(The composition of this third Commission shall be settled
by the Chinese and Russian Presidents.)

Separate Note.

....

Section 4 which follows was introduced by the Chinese
side but it does not form part of the present Agreement
because it raises questions of a political nature which the
Russian local authorities have not the authority to deal
with. This is recognised by the Taoyin who, taking into
consideration the fact that a Sino-Russian conference for
the discussion of questions pending between the two countries
is shortly to be held at Peking, and recognising the
desirability of concluding an Agreement on Aids to Navigation
before the close of the present navigation season, has
therefore decided to accede to the repeatedly expressed
wishes of the Russian Commission and hereby agrees that this
4th. Section (Articles 10 -21) shall not come into operation,
but that it shall be appended merely for the sake of record
(so that China's case may not go by default).

(signed) SUNG WĚN-YÜ   (signed) A. N. LAGUTIN,
(Heiho Taoyin, concurrently   (Acting Director of
Commissioner for Foreign   the Russian Amur
Affairs, Aigun District.)   Government Water
                                Transport Office.)
(signed) CH'Ě HSI-CHĚN,   (signed) V. A. DEDUHIN,
(Adviser on Foreign   (Secretary.)
Affairs to the Heiho
Taoyin Office.)   (signed) V. J. FEDOROFF,
                                (Chief of the Amur
                                Navigation Office.)

APPENDIX.

APPENDIX.

10. Chinese and Russian vessels of every description shall have
the right to navigate freely the frontier waters of China
and Russia such as the Amur, etc., over which the two
countries jointly exercise sovereignty, but the vessels of
other powers shall not enjoy this privilege.

11. Chinese vessels of every description shall be allowed to
navigate the lower section of the Amur to and from the sea
and the Ussuri from Habarovsk to Kazakevich. Russian
vessels of every description shall be permitted to navigate
the lower section of the Sungari as far as Harbin. The
vessels of the two countries shall enjoy equal rights.

12. Chinese and Russian merchant vessels of every description
shall be allowed to clear for any port of the one country
from any port of the other country, and between the
various ports of either country, and on arrival to stop
and work cargo and passengers. All such vessels shall
observe local Customs, Navigational and other Regulations.

13. Chinese and Russian merchant vessels of every description
plying for the purpose of trade on the(frontier) rivers
shall pay Customs duties and Tonnage Dues according to the
Customs Regulations in force at the places visited. (Customs
Duties and Tonnage Dues paid by Chinese merchant vessels of
every description calling at Russian ports shall be equal in
amount to those paid by Russian merchant vessels of every
description. Similarly, Customs duties and Tonnage Dues
paid by Russian merchant vessels of every description calling
at Chinese ports shall be equal in amount to those paid by
Chinese merchant vessels of every description) Through
cargo, irrespective of ultimate destination, shall be passed
duty-free in accordance with the Customs Regulations of the
two countries.

14. Chinese and Russian vessels of every description shall be

allowed

allowed to ply from one port to another on the above-mentioned rivers and shall be granted suitable facilities for procuring provisions, fuel, or other supplies, for making necessary repairs, and for wintering and engaging pilots. If the erection of warehouses and wharves, as permitted by the local Regulations in force, should be found necessary for carrying on the trade engaged in by a merchant vessel of either country, application to lease the land required for these purposes, shall be submitted to the Chief Authority of the place concerned.

15. The fairways of the rivers on the frontiers between China and Russia shall be under the joint control of the two countries and separate Agreements shall be drawn up dealing in detail with the nature of the control to be exercised; the measures to be taken for the maintenance of Aids to Navigation; and conservancy matters in general. The disbursement of dues levied on merchant vessels of every description, and on cargoes carried by these, shall be strictly limited to the amount actually required to carry out the above-mentioned works.

16. China and Russia shall select officials within their respective territories to arrange for the control and inspection of vessels with a view to deciding as to their seaworthiness; to examine the crews and pilots of vessels; to maintain in effective condition the river banks; to supervise the erection of Lights and Beacons; to provide means for the prevention of plague; and generally to give all any information that may be required on matters affecting navigation. (The expressions "to maintain in effective condition the river banks", and "to supervise the erection of Lights and Beacons" are to be taken as applying to works beyond the scope of Article 15.)

17. Chinese and Russian merchant vessels of every description which call at a port when trading on the above-mentioned

rivers

rivers shall be required to submit to examination in accordance with the local Customs Regulations, but shall be free from vexatious restrictions.

18. Should one party to this Agreement find it necessary to adopt special measures for the examination of vessels belonging to the other party, intimation of the necessity, accompanied by statement and proofs, shall be communicated beforehand, and when the one party is apprised of the other party's approval the two sides shall take steps to institute a joint investigation into the matter. (e. g. Russia, without the consent of China, has stationed a gunboat at the mouth of the Sungari for the purpose of examining vessels. Such action on her part is arbitrary and contrary to the spirit of a mutual agreement and the gunboat should be withdrawn on the opening of steamer navigation.) The examination shall be carried out with as little friction and delay as possible and vessels shall not be unnecessarily detained.

19. The Chinese and Russian Authorities shall give due protection to (Chinese and Russian) merchant vessels of every description which are engaged in trade, and shall grant them all the necessary facilities.

20. It is agreed that the privilege of navigating the frontier rivers accorded to Chinese and Russian merchant vessels of every description is one which cannot be made over to the subjects of any other country and that it shall be permissable to engage as officers and crews(of these Chinese and Russian merchant vessels) people of Chinese and Russian nationality only.

21. Chinese and Russian merchant vessels of every description shall observe the laws of the country whose ports they visit.

Signed at Blagovestchensk on the 28th day of the 10th moon of the 12th year of the Republic of China (28th October, 1923).

ANNEX I.

1. Tariff. - Dues on cargo carried by steamers, barges, rafts, sampans and junks shall be calculated by the pood, according to the description of the goods. Building materials, iron, castiron, steel, and leadware, cereals, hay and fodder, vegetables, salt, coal and charcoal, and agricultural machines other than wooden shall pay 1 cent per pood. All other cargo shall pay 2 cents per pood.

2. Timber shall pay ½ cent on a length of three sajens and on a thickness of 1 vershok.

3. Firewood shall pay 20 cents per square sajen, on a thickness of 1 arshine and 15 cents per square sajen on a thickness of ½ arshine.

4. Fowls, fowls, irrespective of side, shall pay 1 cent each.

5. Cattle, large (Cattle and Horses) shall pay 30 cents per head; small (Pigs and Sheep) 15 cents per head.

6. Dues on passengers' tickets shall be at the rate of 5 per cent. ad valorem, irrespective of class.

7. Cargo carried by (Rafts) sampans and junks not in tow of steamers shall pay half of the Tariff applied to those carried on steamers.

8. The Amur River shall be divided into two Sections for the collection of River Dues - one from Taheiho to Kasakevich, the other from Taheiho to Pokrovka (Lo Ku Ho). For each section, half of the Tariff shall be paid. No dues will be collected on the Amur River between Pokrovka (Lo Ku Ho) and Kasakevich on arrival on goods which have already paid according to the fixed tariff.

ANNEX II.

ANNEX II.

1. One tenth of the collection will be deducted cost of collection by both collecting offices. This one-tenth goes to the Chinese Maritime Customs on the one side and to the Amur Navigation Office on the other side.

2. The manifests of vessels are to be specially stamped by the collecting offices (Chinese Maritime Customs or Water Transport Office) after payment of river dues according to Regulations.

3. Dues on goods and passengers' tickets which go from one side of the River to the other will be collected at place of origin, irrespective of the nationality of the vessel. No River Dues whatever shall be collected on the Amur between Pokrovka (Lo Ku Ho) and Kasakevich on arrival on goods covered by manifests specially stamped by the collecting Office, as per Article No.2. Without this proof of payment, vessels shall pay River Dues at place of destination.

4. Dues on passengers' tickets will be levied only for the distance travelled on the frontier waters of the Amur. In accordance with Article 6 of this Provisional Agreement dues will be collected on the Chinese side by the C.M.Customs, and on the Russian side by the Amur Navigation Office or departments controlled by said Office. Dues on passengers going from one side of the River to the other will also be collected at the place of origin irrespective of whether the vessel is Chinese or Russian.

5. Goods moved from a place on one shore to a place immediately opposite on the other shore (as from Taheiho to Blagovestchensk or going from Taheiho to the Zeia, or from the Zeia to Taheiho and Blagovestchensk)will pay one quarter Tariff dues.

6. Receipts shall be given for all dues collected, irrespective of the amount, and the butts will be kept.

7.

7. The plan for works and estimates as provided for in Annex 3 shall not be valid unless it is approved by the Sino-Russian Commission.

8. The Chinese President shall from time to time depute an officer to inspect the works and accounts. All facilities will be afforded this officer by the Russian Navigation Office when on inspection duty.

9. All Officers and inspection Officials proceeding on duty, shall be given a longterm passport from the Chinese and Russian Authorities and shall be given due protection.

10. All members of the staff or inspecting officials proceeding on duty, shall enjoy free passage on both Chinese and Foreign steamers; the Water Transport Office will provide all facilities in the way of small boats, house accommodation etc.

11. The collecting Office will report to the Joint Commission at the end of each month the actual amount of Dues collected.

12. A meeting of the Sino-Russian Joint Commission may be held whenever necessary. There is no fixed place for meeting; if the Chinese President calls for a meeting, it will be held on the Chinese side; if the Russian President calls for a meeting, it will be held on the Russian side. The Russian and Chinese Presidents shall take turn as chairman.

13. The Chinese side will not be responsible for expenditure exceeding the actual amount of Dues collected, and before meeting any claims will first deduct 10 % as cost of collection. (i.e. expenditure for Technical Adviser's Office; office allowance to Chinese President; Amur Navigation Office estimates).

14. Out of the net collection, the Chinese Commission will first defray each month the expenses of the Technical Adviser's Office and the Chinese President's office allowance, which are estimated at $8,000 and $2,000 a year respectively.

15. After payments have been made as outlined above the balance remaining

remaining will be available to meet the estimates submitted by the Amur Navigation Office, but the amount to be paid by the Chinese Commission shall not exceed 50% of the amount of the total estimates. The expenditure incurred by the Amur Navigation Office must be approved by the Sino-Russian Joint Commission as laid down in Article 7 of this Annex and shall be governed by the provisions of Annex 3.

16. 75 % of the Chinese Commission's share of the estimated expenditure will be advanced to the Amur Navigation Office at the beginning of each month. The balance of 25 %, in accordance with a statement of expenditure on account of work actually done, will be paid as soon as properly prepared accounts have been submitted by the Amur Navigation Office.

17. Money contributed by the Chinese Commission under the terms of this Agreement shall be used exclusively for the upkeep of Aids to Navigation on the Amur from Pokrovka (Lo Ku Ho) to Kazakevich.

18. Full accounts for the year shall be submitted to the Chinese President of the Sino-Russian Commission by the Amur Navigation Office not later than 1st March (of succeeding year).

19. These Regulations will remain in force for so long as the Provisional Agreement for the year 1923 is valid (i.e. till 1st. December, 1924)

ANNEX III.

ANNEX III.

GENERAL SCHEME OF WORKS AND EXPENDITURE ON AIDS TO
NAVIGATION (ON THE AMUR) FOR THE PERIOD FROM 1st JANUARY,1923
TO 30th NOVEMBER, 1924.

The frontier section from Pokrovka (Lo Ku Ho) to
Kazakevich will be divided, if possible, into 3 Districts
and in accordance with last year's procedure there will be
opened:

Signal Stations	7
Traffic Stations	2
Water Gauge Stations	11
Lighted Shallows	4

Expenditure in connection with the erection of new beacons
and repairs to old beacons will be on the same scale as last
year.

The personnel of the Technical Section and of the Local
Organisations will not exceed that of last year.   One half
only of the expenses of the Russian Technical Section (which
is responsible for the upkeep of Aids to Navigation not only
on the frontier stretch of Amur, but also on the rivers in
the interior) shall be included in the estimates of the
Sino-Russian Joint Commission.

There will be one steam-launch available for the personnel
of the Technical Section and the members of the Joint
Commission.

The total expenditure for the 2 years (1923 and 1924) shall
not exceed Gold Roubles 55,000.   It is agreed that the use
of dredgers (for the improvement of the waterway) is to be
subject to regulations which are to be drawn up (as occasion
requires) and included in a separate Agreement.

(signed)

(signed) SUNG WĒN-YU.   (signed) A. N. LAGUTIN,
(Heiho Taoyin(concurrently   (Acting Director of the
Commissioner for Foreign   Russian Amur Government
Affairs,Aigun District.)   Water Transport Office.)

(signed) CH'Ê HSI-CHÊN.   (signed) V. A. DEMCHIN,
(Adviser on Foreign   (Secretary.)
Affairs to the Heiho
Taoyin Office.)   (signed) V. J. FEDOROFF,
                                 (Chief of the Amur
                                 Navigation Office.)

Signed at Tsaiho on the 30th day of the 11th moon of the
12th year of the Republic of China (30th November, 1923).

True Translation:- _yehn an chang_
                   4th. Assistant A

Checked:- _R. J. Abegchenko_
Commissioner.

JAN 1924

COAST INSPECTOR'S COMMENTS ON AIGUN NO.144, I. G.,

DATED 29TH DECEMBER, 1924.

Docketed: Aids to Navigation on the Amur:
Agreement for 1923 & 1924 signed;
discourtesy of Russian officials;
Taoyin suspicious & annoyed; original
estimates considerably scaled down;
Customs control over expenditure
adequate; appreciation of services of
Technical Adviser.

It is satisfactory to know that the Aigun
Commissioner's efforts have met with success and
have resulted in a satisfactory agreement being
arrived at.

There is no doubt that Mr. Ignatieff has
proved himself to be a most valuable employee of
the Customs as Technical Adviser on Amur Aids to
Navigation matters.

(Signed) T. J. Eldridge,

Coast Inspector.

Coast Inspector's Office,   True Copy,

Shanghai, 18th January, 1924.
Supervisor.

呈海关总税务司署 <u>144</u> 号文　　　　　　　　　瑷珲关 1923 年 12 月 29 日

尊敬的海关总税务司（北京）：

1. 根据瑷珲关致海关总税务司署第 119 号呈：

"黑龙江航务：汇报 1923 年黑龙江航路标志协议的协商进展；道尹与俄方之协商或将以失败告终；申请按照道尹之建议，批准由海关出面与俄方协商并签订临时地方协议；呈送协议草案。"

兹汇报，中俄双方代表依照 1922 年协议所制定的 1923 年及 1924 年协议已于 1923 年 10 月 28 日在布拉戈维申斯克（Blagovestchensk，即海兰泡）地区签署，附加条款业已于 1923 年 11 月 30 日在大黑河签署，然本署尚未收到正式文本的中文及俄文抄件。新协议有效期至 1924 年 12 月；该协议文本的措辞和段落顺序略有改动，但相信俄方应不会有何异议。道尹告知本署，其已在税务处和黑龙江省公署的授权下签署了新协议，亦获准为新协议延续至 1924 年 12 月 1 日做好准备工作。

2. 新协议的第四部分为附录，华方于该部分提出应准许中国轮船经由黑龙江自哈巴罗夫斯克（Habarovsk，即伯力）至尼古拉耶夫斯克（Nickolaevsk，即庙街）河段出海。然该部分内容既未生效，亦未列入新协议之中，仅作记录之用，一则为防止将来中俄双发会对此事产生误解，二则为避免华方之诉求就此不了了之。道尹承认该项诉求或将引起政治性的争议，但坚称先前中俄条约中确有规定允许中国轮船经由黑龙江航行入海，因此即使俄国地方政府极有可能不予承认，其亦不会放弃该项权利，并称其意已决，如无更改，将不再重申。

3. 今年，瑷珲关于 5 月 16 日开始征收江捐，但当时税务处尚未下达批准签署新协议之指令；随后，海关代理总税务司于 6 月 10 日电令中向瑷珲关前任税务司说明，不应在得到税务处明确指示前开展江捐征收工作，请道尹将 1923 年江捐征收工作的安排上报税务处请求批准。皆已遵照办理。

同时，道尹于 6 月向布拉戈维申斯克的俄阿穆尔国家水运局督办致函，提议依照 1922 年协议制定 1923 年新协议。督办虽于回函中透露赞成之意，但却并未给出明确答复。道尹遂于 7 月再次致函，请其无论同意与否务必给出明确答复，但督办至 9 月方告知道尹该函已收悉。俄方此举虽令人有些始料未及，但显然与黑河道尹和俄国政府曾因过境小票一事而引发的矛盾有关，当时双方甚至因此而断绝了贸易往来，至今仍未能恢复如常。道尹认为俄方忽视其信件之行为十分无礼，有损其颜面，亦可说明俄方根本无意签署 1923

年新协议,遂称其日后亦不愿再与俄方有何往来。道尹有此情绪无可厚非,然中俄双方之协商亦因此而陷入僵局。最后,经本署协调,俄阿穆尔国家水运局代表终于答应与道尹会面,并由本署来负责安排。为妥善解决此事,本署劝说道尹以友善之态与俄阿穆尔国家水运局代表进行协商,然道尹身边众人皆劝说其不要采纳本署之提议,直到道尹的外交顾问应允不再阻拦之后,道尹才勉强同意与俄方会面协商。

4. 俄阿穆尔国家水运局代表于 10 月 15 日前来拜访道尹,其督办在与道尹会面后便立即就之前未能尽早回复道尹函件一事致歉,称其绝无故意怠慢之意,只因当时自己与同事恰好外出公干,未在布拉戈维申斯克,一应事宜均暂由其属下负责,但其属下职权有限,无法就重要事项做出决定,故未能及时回复道尹之函。然而,道尹认为此乃掩盖事实之托词,因此在话语间未掩饰其厌烦之意,甚至一度表现出完全敌视的态度,并称既是签订官方协议,则应于年初签订,而非年末,因此不愿再议签署 1923 年协议之事,希望可于 1923 年协商 1924 年之协议。俄方代表对此表示赞同,但指出,自 7 月贸易封锁后,黑龙江中国一侧的航路标志维护工作便已停滞,希望道尹可准许俄方派遣技术人员搭乘两艘轮船前去检查黑龙江航道中国一侧的航路标志现状,并确保技术人员在中国不受阻扰。但道尹认为,时至年末,检查黑龙江上的航路标志毫无意义,该建议实为无稽之谈。然而,随着讨论的进一步深入,道尹发现该建议甚是合理,难以拒绝,本署随后又向其说明,俄方此次巡查若无其他企图,于海关而言,确实很有必要,至此,道尹终于开始转变态度,表现出应有的礼节,并应允了俄方之要求。

5. 道尹在会见俄方代表时的态度可能是出于两方面的考虑,一是体现其爱国立场,二是震慑曾对其有过冒犯行为之人。然兹认为,凡涉及航运利益之事,本署,作为瑷珲关的负责人,均应有直接话语权,而航道维护工作更是与航运息息相关,黑龙江航路标志协议的签订事宜绝非道尹的私事,其不应对本署之意见置若罔闻,自行草率否决。因此本署在俄方代表离开后,建议道尹公正对待此事,并指出目前最重要的应是确保该协议得以续签,毕竟大黑河地区以贸易为主,若无航路标志,贸易则无法进行,而黑龙江航道现有的航路标志均属于俄国政府,因此华方向其支付一定的费用亦属合理。但道尹的态度依然十分强硬,表示宁愿让事态自然发展下去,亦不愿再同俄方进行和解,并坚持认为,俄方不可能再于 1923 年间完成任何工作,因此绝不会签署 1923 年协议,同时还反复强调俄方的办事方法不可靠,态度又傲慢无礼。但道尹的反对理由太过轻率,显然掺杂了过多的个人情绪。此外,道尹还提议使用 1923 年所征江捐修筑堤岸,但本署指出,江捐的征收目的早已确定,若将江捐税收挪用他处,则违背了最初对纳捐民众的承诺,道尹听罢便放弃了这一想法。数日后，道尹告知本署，经过深思熟虑后，其已认同本署之观点，决定签署协议，希望本署可同布拉戈维申斯克方面安排协商之事。本署已照办。

6. 俄阿穆尔国家水运局最初为 1923 年联合维护黑龙江边界河道航路标志工事所提交之预算为 60800 金卢布，但经核实后发现，各项预算皆不合理。俄方将黑龙江自嘎杂克维池（Kasakevich）至哈巴罗夫斯克河段的航路标志维护工事列入该预算之中，但实际上，该河段仅供俄国轮船航行入海，中国航运业无从受益，因此该河段的维护工事于华方而言毫无意义。华方已据此驳回该项预算，同时表示仅愿意为以下五段河道的航路标志维护工事承担费用，即：自波克罗夫卡（Pokrovka）至贝克托瓦（Beketova）河段；自贝克托瓦至库马拉（Kumara）河段；自库马拉至波亚尔科沃（Poyarkovo）河段；自波亚尔科沃至索伊斯纳亚（Soyusnaya）河段；自索伊斯纳亚至嘎杂克维池河段。

鉴于在中俄贸易封锁期间，俄阿穆尔国家水运局无法于黑龙江航道中国一侧开展大型工事，航务专门顾问已对俄方初始预算进行详细的审核与修改，最终得出之预算为 40000 金卢布，而非俄方所提之 60800 金卢布；经过一番协商后，俄方终于同意华方仅承担 19000 金卢布的摊款。

7. 众所周知，布拉戈维申斯克的政府因政务管理不善，导致财务压力较大，不得不解雇大批职员。对于此等情况，航务专门顾问远比本署了解得更全面、更准确。其指出，目前，俄国政府若无法提供工作，大批俄国工人都将陷入失业的困境，因此有理由相信，为了维持俄国工人的生计，俄国政府已将一些原本在俄国内陆水域工作的工人分散到黑龙江流域的各段河道上去。俄国政府实际上是企图让中国来承担其失业公民的安置费用，以节约本国的财政支出，此等行为实属滥用政府职权，有违诚信。所幸华方已成功瓦解俄国政府的企图，并将预算削减至合理额度。俄方随后又提出，每处角锥形标桩的安设费用至少需要 35.30 银圆，年维修费用至少需要 20 银圆；每处普通标桩的安设费用至少需要 27.90 银圆，年维修费用至少需要 10 银圆。但根据海关以往的经验，每处角锥形标桩的安设费用仅需 15 银圆到 20 银圆，年维修费用仅需 5 银圆；每处普通标桩的安设费用仅需 8 银圆到 10 银圆，年维修费用仅需 3 银圆。

8. 在道尹看来，中国摊付黑龙江航路标志维护费用一事的问题已愈发明显，其认为稍有不慎，该笔维护费用便很有可能遭到俄方的挥霍。道尹从中国驻布拉戈维申斯克总领事那里得知，当地俄国政府正面临财政危机，因此非常担忧俄方会挪用华方摊款来应对此次危机，同时对于俄方提交的预算是否切合实际提出质疑。但在本署看来，俄方其实很难在预算问题上动手脚，毕竟航务专门顾问几乎了解预算所涉事项的全部情况。

此外,道尹还认为协议内容必然会存在对华方不利的圈套,本署对此无法苟同。兹认为,该协议于中俄双方而言均十分公平,俄方负责河道维护的实际工作,华方摊付相应的费用,双方的付出与获得比例均衡,符合基本的交易原则。当然,虽说按照交易原则,俄方既向华方索要摊款,自应保证所提预算切实可靠,但华方若指望制定预算之人不会抬高报价,未免亦有些自欺欺人。尽管如此,本署依然相信,按照现行的审核制度,华方完全可以有效阻止俄方故意提高航路标志安设与维护费用预算之行为,完全有能力将预算消减至合理数额,如发现俄方账目有问题,亦可随时提出质疑,做出更正。今年,俄方的确试图签订对其有利,对华方不利之协议,但所幸华方最后很好地控制了局面,并取得了可喜的结果,俄阿穆尔国家水运局业已同意对协议所提出的预算金额予以大幅削减。

9. 在此特向航务专门顾问易保罗(P. I. Ignatieff)先生致以衷心的感谢。易保罗先生对那些无理要求的极力反对以及对工作的全身心投入,使得各种存在争议的问题都得以尽快解决。俄方在制定 1923 年预算时,故意抬高预算金额,幸得易保罗先生了解俄方的真实情况,熟知相关事务,能够从专业的角度对预算进行详细审查,以助华方成功削减预算,免于雇用不必要的俄国职员。俄方最初宣称,这些职员不可或缺,但后来经易保罗先生提醒,华方发现事实并非如此,俄方随后亦已承认。易保罗先生曾于布拉戈维申斯克的俄阿穆尔国家水运局担任副督办十四年之久,对当地情况十分了解,因此凡涉及航务之事,其给出的意见和建议均极有价值。

您忠诚的仆人

包安济(G. Boezi)

瑷珲关署理税务司

瑷珲关致海关总税务司署第 144 号呈附件 1

黑龙江航路标志临时地方协议

（1923—1924 年）

　　中华民国黑河道尹（兼瑷珲关交涉员）与俄阿穆尔国家水运局已就黑龙江、额尔古纳河、乌苏里江及其他边界河道上的中俄两国轮船、民船及木筏所载客货的征税问题，边界河道及航路标志的维护问题以及各段河道上的航运改善问题进行了协商。

　　中华民国黑河道尹（兼瑷珲关交涉员）与俄阿穆尔国家水运局督办，为改善边界河道的航路状况，促进中俄两国友好关系，现正式缔结协议。

华方：

中华民国黑河道尹兼瑷珲关交涉员　　　　宋文郁

黑河道尹公署外交顾问　　　　　　　　　车席珍

俄方：

俄阿穆尔国家水运局代理督办　　　　　　拉古丁（A. N. Lagutin）

文案　　　　　　　　　　　　　　　　　德杜新（V. A. Deduhin）

俄阿穆尔国家水道局局长　　　　　　　　费多罗夫（V. J. Fedoroff）

一、协议执行规章

1. 该协议自双方联合签署之日起生效,有效期至中华民国十三年十二月一日(1924年12月1日)止。凡对协议内容有任何改动者,均须征得双方同意。

2. 该协议与中俄双方利益密切相关,双方应互相予以理解。凡航行于边界河道上的轮船及木筏负责人,无论国别,均有义务为航路的维护支付一定费用。该协议仅于地方有效,不应影响现行《航务条例》或黑龙江上施行的其他章程之效力,亦不应影响中俄两国内陆水域的航运税率。

二、江捐征收及支出规章

3. 轮船、民船及木筏所载客货的江捐税率由中华民国黑河道尹(兼瑷珲关交涉员)与俄阿穆尔国家水运局督办共同决定。(税率见附录1)

4. 客货具体征税办法由中华民国黑河道尹(兼瑷珲关交涉员)与俄阿穆尔国家水运局督办各自委派的代表共同决定。(具体征税办法见附录2)

5. 关于轮船、民船及木筏所载客货的征税问题、税收使用监督问题以及其他各事,均由附加规则决定。(附加规则见附录2)

6. 凡中俄两国轮船、民船及木筏,若航行于黑龙江航道中国一侧,则须向中国海关缴纳江捐,若航行于黑龙江航道俄国一侧,则须向俄阿穆尔水道局缴纳江捐。

三、航路标志的安设与维护规章

7. 凡涉及黑龙江边界河道自波克罗夫卡(洛古河)至嘎杂克维池河段的航路标志相关工事,如安设灯桩、信标等,一应开销均由中俄双方江捐税收共同承担。上述工事本应由中俄双方共同完成,但为便于开展工作,一些本应由华方承担的工作将以中国地方政府之名义委托给俄阿穆尔水道局。凡涉及疏浚河道等需花费大量资金之工事,均须于双方同意,且相关疏浚计划和预算得到中俄黑龙江水道委员会批准后,再行开展。

中俄黑龙江水道委员会由八名委员组成,中俄双方各四名委员。委员长由中华民国黑河道尹与俄阿穆尔国家水运局督办共同担任。其他委员会委员由两位委员长指派。

8. 上述工作应依据双方江捐税收比例进行分配。俄阿穆尔水道局应于航运季开始之前将工作计划与相应预算上报至中俄黑龙江水道委员会,在工作计划与相应预算获得中俄黑龙江水道委员会批准之前,不得开展工作(参阅附录3)。

9. 工作进程中,若中俄双方在对协议条款的解释上存在分歧,应由第三方委员会予以裁决,第三方委员会所做裁决即为最终裁决,双方必须遵照执行(第三方委员会委员由中俄双方委员长共同指定)。

独立注释

以下内容(第四部分)由华方提出,但并未列入此协议之中,因该部分内容涉及政治性问题,俄国地方政府无权处理。道尹表示,鉴于中俄两国政府不日将于北京召开会议,商讨一应待定问题,且中俄地方政府均希望于今年航运季结束前签署一份航路标志协议,因此决定同意俄国航政委员会之提议,暂不施行第四部分内容,仅将之附于此协议之后,以为存照(以防止华方诉求就此不了了之)。

华方:

中华民国黑河道尹兼瑷珲关交涉员	宋文郁
黑河道尹公署外交顾问	车席珍

俄方:

俄阿穆尔国家水运局代理督办	拉古丁
文案	德杜新
俄阿穆尔国家水道局局长	费多罗夫

附录

10. 中俄两国各类船只均有权自由航行于中俄两国界河（如黑龙江等）之上，中俄两国对此等界河共同行使主权，其他国家船只不享有此等特权。

11. 中国各类船只应有权往来于黑龙江下游至公海河段，以及乌苏里江自哈巴罗夫斯克至嘎杂克维池河段。俄国各类船只应有权于松花江下游航行，最远至哈尔滨。在此等河段上，两国船只应享有同等权利。

12. 中俄两国各类商船均应有权在一国任一口岸办理结关前往另一国任一口岸或该国内其他口岸，并有权于各口岸停靠装卸客货。但所有此类船只均须遵守地方海关的《海关章程》及其他管理规定。

13. 出于贸易目的而往来于边界河道上的中俄两国各类商船均应根据当地《海关章程》缴纳关税或船钞。即，中国各类商船在俄国口岸所缴纳的关税或船钞数额应与同类俄国商船相同；俄国各类商船在中国口岸所缴纳的关税或船钞数额亦应与同类中国商船相同。凡通运货物，无论目的地为何处，均应照两国《海关章程》规定，予以免税放行。

14. 中俄双方各类船只均应有权于上述边界河道各口岸之间往来，各口岸均应为船只提供食物、燃料及其他补给品，如有必要，还应提供维修服务、过冬泊地，并协助雇用引水员。凡中俄两国商船在贸易时有修建货栈或码头需求者，只要当地现行章程允许，均可向当地主管机关提交租赁相关土地之申请。

15. 中俄两国边界河道应由两国共同管理，至于具体的管理细则、为维护航路标志而需进行的测量工事以及河道疏浚等工事等重要问题，应另行起草一份协议。须严格限制从各类商船及货物所征税款之支出，不得使支出超过上述管理工作的实际需要。

16. 中俄双方应各自委派国内官员负责以下各项工作：检查管理船只以决定其是否适宜出航；检查船只的船员与引水员以确定其是否符合资格；保证堤岸状态良好；监督灯标与立标的安设工作；提供防疫措施；提供一切航行所需之信息。（注："保证堤岸状态良好"与"监督灯标与立标的安设工作"均为第 15 项条款范围以外之工作。）

17. 凡中俄两国各类商船临时停靠上述边界河道各口岸进行贸易时，均应遵照当地《海关章程》接受检查，但无须接受不必要的限制。

18. 中俄双方若有一方认为有必要对另一方船只进行特殊检查，则须提前与对方进行沟通，说明检查的必要性，并附以充分的理据。检查之事，应待得到另一方准许后，由双方共同进行。（据此，俄方未经华方批准，便于松花江口岸停放炮艇以检查往来船只之行为乃独断专行,违反协议精神之行为,俄方应于航运季开始前将有关炮艇撤回。)此外,此等检查工作应尽量避免争执,尽快完成,不得无故扣押船只。

19. 中俄两国政府应尽可能对中俄两国各类贸易商船施以保护并提供所需设施。

20. 中俄两国各类商船所享有的在边界河道上自由航行之权利,不得转让给其他国家之公民,中俄两国商船仅可雇用中俄两国公民作为船员和驾驶员。

21. 中俄两国各类商船均应遵守口岸所属国之法律。

中华民国十二年十月二十八日（1923 年 10 月 28 日）签订于布拉戈维申斯克。

附录 1

1. 税率：轮船、驳船、木筏、舢板及民船,应根据所载货物的种类和重量(普特)决定; 建筑材料、铁、生铁、钢及铅制品、谷物、干草及饲料、蔬菜、盐、煤炭以及非木制农具,均为每普特 1 分; 其他货物均为每普特 2 分。

2. 长度 3 俄丈、厚度 1 俄寸的木料税率为 0.5 分。

3. 厚度 1 俄尺的薪柴税率为每平方俄丈 20 分,厚度 0.75 俄尺的薪柴税率为每平方俄丈 15 分。

4. 家禽税率：每只 1 分,无论大小。

5. 家畜税率：大型家畜(牛、马)每头 30 分; 小型家畜(猪、羊)每头 15 分。

6. 乘客船票税率：按面值的百分之五收取,无论舱级。

7. 未由轮船牵引的木筏、舢板及民船所载货物均按轮船所载货物税率的一半收取。

8. 黑龙江将分为两段征收江捐。一段自大黑河至嘎杂克维池,另一段自大黑河至波克罗夫卡(洛古河),每段均收取半数江捐。凡往来于黑龙江自波克罗夫卡(洛古河)至嘎杂克维池河段之货物,若于抵达口岸时已如数完纳江捐,则无须再次缴纳。

附录 2

1. 双方征税部门均须扣除所征税收的 10% 作为征税佣金,付与中国海关以及俄阿穆尔水道局。

2. 征税部门(中国海关或俄阿穆尔水道局)应在完税轮船的舱口单上加盖特殊印花,以示该轮船已如数完纳江捐。

3. 凡轮船由黑龙江过境者,无论国别,均应于出发地为其所载客货支付江捐。凡货物或轮船往来黑龙江自波克罗夫卡至嘎杂克维池河段者,若持有由征税部门加盖特殊印花的舱口单(参见条款 2),则无须再次缴纳江捐;若无法于抵达后出示完纳江捐证明,则须于目的地缴纳江捐。

4. 乘客船票所需缴纳的江捐数额应由轮船在黑龙江边界河道上航行的里程数而定。根据临时协议第 6 项条款之规定,黑龙江航道中国一侧的江捐由中国海关负责征收,俄国一侧的江捐由俄阿穆尔水道局或其下属单位负责征收。

5. 凡货物直接往来黑龙江航道华俄对岸(如往返于大黑河与布拉戈维申斯克之间),或大黑河与结雅河之间,或结雅河与布拉戈维申斯克之间者,均照税率的 25% 支付江捐。

6. 无论捐额多寡,征税部门均须向纳捐者发放收据,纳捐者须予以妥善保存。

7. 附录 3 所列之工作计划和支出预算,须经中俄黑龙江水道委员会批准后方可生效。

8. 华方委员长应时常派遣关员检查工作进度与费用支出情况,其间关员所需一应设施均由俄阿穆尔水道局负责提供。

9. 凡中俄双方人员有需要外出执行公务者,均可由中俄双方政府签发长期护照,并享受应有的保护。

10. 凡海关关员或负责检查工作的官员外出执行公务时,均可免费搭乘中俄两国轮船;小船、食宿等方面由俄阿穆尔国家水运局负责提供。

11. 征税部门应于每月月底向中俄黑龙江水道委员会报告当月实际征收捐额。

12. 如有必要,中俄黑龙江水道委员会可随时召开会议。会议举行地点据情况而定;华方委员长要求举行会议时,会议则在中国领土召开;俄方委员长要求举行会议时,会议则在俄国领土召开。中俄黑龙江水道委员会委员长由中俄双方委员长轮流担任。

13. 若最终费用支出超出华方实际所征税款金额,则超出部分华方概不负责;在摊付费用支出前,华方所征税款须预先扣除 10% 征税佣金(注:费用支出包括航务专门顾问办公经费、华方委员长办公经费、俄阿穆尔水道局支出预算)。

14. 中国航政委员会每月应从华方净税收中预先扣除航务专门顾问办公经费（每年8000银圆）以及华方委员长办公经费（每年2000银圆）。

15. 扣除上述经费后，华方剩余税款应当用于摊付俄阿穆尔水道局的支出预算，中国航政委员会的摊付数额不得超过预算总额之半数。如本附录第7项条款所示，俄阿穆尔水道局的一应支出均须经中俄黑龙江水道委员会批准，并按照附录3之规定执行。

16. 中国航政委员会应于每月月初向俄阿穆尔水道局支付其应付摊款的75%；剩余25%尾款，应根据实际支出情况，待俄阿穆尔水道局提交合理账簿后，再行支付。

17. 该临时协议所规定之中国航政委员会摊款仅可用于黑龙江自波克罗夫卡（洛古河）至嘎杂克维池河段的航路标志维护工作。

18. 俄阿穆尔水道局应于次年3月1日前向中俄黑龙江水道委员会华方委员长提交全年账簿。

19. 本附录所载细则有效期同《临时协议》，即至1924年12月1日。

附录 3

1923 年 1 月 1 日至 1924 年 11 月 30 日期间黑龙江航路标志维护工作计划与支出计划如下。

若条件允许,黑龙江边界河道自波克罗夫卡（洛古河）至嘎杂克维池河段将划分为五个部分；参考 1922 年的情况,将开放：

水深信号站	7 处
通行信号站	2 处
水位观测站	11 处
安设灯塔的浅滩	4 处

标桩的新建与修理数量以及相应支出比例均与 1922 年相同。

1923 年布拉戈维申斯克技术部及各处的职员总人数不得超过 1922 年之数。因布拉戈维申斯克技术部的工作范围包括黑龙江边界河道和俄国内陆水域两部分,故中俄黑龙江水道委员会仅承担布拉戈维申斯克技术部支出预算之半数。

布拉戈维申斯克技术部职员和中俄黑龙江水道委员会委员将配有汽艇一艘。

1923 年及 1924 年的总支出不得超过 55000 金卢布。中俄双方已协定,如需开展疏浚工作以改善河道,则将另行起草一份协议,重新列明各项细则。

本协议于中华民国十二年十一月三十日（1923 年 11 月 30 日）签订于大黑河。

华方：

中华民国黑河道尹兼瑷珲关交涉员　　　宋文郁

黑河道尹公署外交顾问　　　车席珍

俄方：

俄阿穆尔国家水运局代理督办　　　拉古丁

文案　　　德杜新

俄阿穆尔国家水道局局长　　　费多罗夫

该译本内容真实有效,特此证明。

录事：叶元章　四等一级帮办

审核人：贺智兰（R. F. C. Hedgeland）瑷珲关税务司

关于瑷珲关致海关总税务司署第 144 号呈的意见

1923 年 12 月 29 日瑷珲关致海关总税务司署第 144 号呈收悉：

"黑龙江航务：汇报签署 1923 年及 1924 年协议事；协商过程中俄方代表甚是无礼，道尹对俄方表示怀疑且心中不悦；初始预算得以大幅削减；海关对支出有充分管理权；对航务专门顾问表示赞赏与感谢。"

得知瑷珲关税务司的付出终得回报，成功签署了一份令双方皆满意之协议，吾心甚慰。

毫无疑问，黑龙江航务专门顾问易保罗先生在黑龙江航务相关事宜上经验丰富，于海关而言切实有益。

（签字）额得志（T. J. Eldridge）

上海巡工事务局巡工司

1924 年 1 月 18 日

该抄件容真实有效，特此证明。

录事：劳德迩（H. G. Lowder）监事员

18. 1925 年《黑龙江航路标志协议》

AMUR AIDS TO NAVIGATION:River Dues A/c.1924;Summary of Receipts & Payments (Chinese Commission)1924;Summary of Expenditure Technical Adviser's Office,1924;& Estimates for 1925,submitting:proceedings leading up to Agreement for 1925;Civil Governor's criticism of Technical
230.   Adviser's appointment & Taoyin's request;collection of River Dues
          at full tariff rate;difficulty caused by lack of funds;Bank of
          China's rate for loan;Amur
I.G.   Navigation Office's argument for Aigun   4th. August, 1925.
          erection of Aids on Sungacha & Ussuri;and claim for larger   230.
                                      Estimates, reporting.   I.G.

          Sir,   Replied to in No. 253   COPY

1.   I have the honour to refer to your

        despatch No. 235/103,576 (with reference to Aigun despatch

        No. 218 and your despatch No. 230/103,232):

                        Amur Aids to Navigation: Agreement for
                        period 1st. December 1924 to 30th. November
                        1925, signed by Authorities concerned:
                        Copy of Shui-wu Ch'u despatch to O.I.G.
                        in re forwarding;

        and to hand you herewith:

Appendix 1.   Copy of the Amur River Dues Account for 1924;
Appendix 2.   Copy of the Chinese Commission's Summary of
                Receipts and Payments for 1924;
Appendix 3.   Summary of Expenditure for Technical Adviser's
                Office for 1924;
Appendix 4.   Copy of the Declaration concerning the extension
                of the 1923/24 Agreement to 1925 (for
                the period from 1st. December 1924 to
                30th. November 1925;
Appendix 5.   Copy of the Detailed Estimates for 1925; and
Appendix 6.   Copy of letters received by the Heiho Taoyin
Appendix 7.   from the Russian Amur Navigation Office
                to which reference is made in the concluding paragraph of my despatch No. 218:

2.   The original Estimates for 1925, submitted by

        the Russian Amur Navigation Office in March of this

                                                        year

The Officiating Inspector General of Customs,

                        Peking.

                        Entered in Card-Index.

year, allowed for a total expenditure of Gold Roubles 65,000, i.e. 55,000 roubles for the Amur and 10,000 roubles for the Ussuri, but they were returned for revision by the Technical Adviser who suggested an expenditure of 37,000 Roubles for work on the Amur and 4,000 Roubles for the Ussuri. Subsequently amended Estimates were received for Gold Roubles 50,000 and Mr. Chebisheff, Director of the Amur Navigation Office, explained that these Estimates included a sum of 5,732 Roubles which it was intended should be spent on the Ussuri. The Taoyin declined to sanction any funds for work on the Ussuri and the Technical Adviser, who in the meantime had revised his former figures, informed Mr. Chebisheff that expenditure on the Amur should not exceed from 39,600 to 40,000 Roubles. Estimates for Gold Roubles 50,000 were again submitted by the Russian Amur Navigation Office in May and on this occasion Mr. Sidoroff, Director of the Amur Water Transport and the highest Soviet official with whom we have any dealings, insisted that we should not expect the necessary work on the Amur to be done for less than G.R.44,268 and that a sum of at least G.R. 5,732 would have to be spent

spent on reconstructing Aids to Navigation on the
Ussuri. The proposal to provide money for work on
the Ussuri, which had already been turned down, was
again negatived and Mr. Sidoroff's attention was further
invited to the fact that before leaving for Moukden
Mr. Ignatieff had expressed the view that if still
greater economy were exercised the Estimates for the
Amur could be reduced from G.R. 44,268 to G.R. 40,000.
Mr. Sidoroff pretended to be astonished that the
Technical Adviser before he committed himself to such
an opinion had not thought fit to discuss the question
with him. He insisted that in a matter of this kind
the Russian point of view must be allowed expression
and after referring to the increase in the price of
all materials and the high-growing cost of the
necessaries of life which made it necessary to raise
salaries, he said that he was certainly not going to
be content to say " ditto " on every occasion to
whatever opinion Mr. Ignatieff might choose to express.
I objected that the proposal to reduce the Estimates
to G.R.40,000 had been communicated in good time to
Mr. Chebisheff by the Technical Adviser, but the former,

knowing

knowing full well that his only course, if he wished
to retain his appointment as Director of the Navigation
Office, was to identify himself thoroughly with the
views expressed by his immediate chief, had not the
courage to agree that this was the case. The point
provoked a considerable amount of discussion and when
it was seen that I was not going to withdraw my
statement Mr. Sidoroff changed his tone and proceeded
to argue that the present system, if it was to
justify its continuance, ought to be a steadily improving system, yielding a service more and more near
the standard existing in pre-revolution days. He said
that the interests of both sides must always be
opposed to any measure calculated to restrict the
safety of shipping and that we should be led by our
own interests to accept his point of view and agree
to the figure (G.R.44,268) he had named for work to
be done on the Amur. Mr. Sidoroff added that it
would be impossible for him to concur in an arrangement upon the lines suggested by us and said that
unless we agreed to a sum that would enable him to
do the work as he considered it should be done he

would

would be forced to relinquish the Agreement altogether.
Mr. Chebisheff said the same thing in slightly
different words.

3.   It was not possible for me to say whether
the men employed by the Russian Amur Navigation Office
were being paid too little, just enough, or too much,
or whether the service to be expected at a cost of
G.R.40,000 would be as good as it should reasonably
be made.   These are questions which clearly required
consideration by some one possessing the necessary
technical and administrative knowledge and owing to the
absence at Moukden of the Technical Adviser, who alone
of those who represent China's interests is qualified
by training and experience to decide matters of
technical importance, the members of the Chinese
Commission were greatly handicapped by the lack of such
knowledge.   Having failed to reach agreement - I did
not consider myself justified in overruling the Technical
Adviser's opinion that with care a sum of G.R.40,000
might be made to suffice - the meeting adjourned and
the point at issue was referred by Telegram to the
Technical Adviser.   The latter replied that he would
be

Appendix.8.

Appendix 8.

be willing to sign Estimates for G.R.44,268 but said
that an effort should be made to persuade Mr. Sidoroff
to agree to a sum of G.R.42,000.   Previous to the
receipt of the Technical Adviser's Telegram I had informed the Taoyin that the proposal to reduce the
Estimates to G.R.40,000 had been rejected and that in
my opinion the rejection would have to be treated as
definite.   The Taoyin assented and said that poor
though we were it would be well to accept Mr.Sidoroff's
proposal and that further discussion should immediately
cease.   A sum of G.R.44,268 has therefore been agreed
to for 1925 and Detailed Estimates for this amount
were handed to me by the Technical Adviser on the 12th
of August.   There was, of course, no need whatsoever
for heat in discussing this matter, but Mr. Sidoroff,
the ex-sailor and political agitator, who as Director of
the Amur Water Transport is one of the highest officials
at Blagovestchensk, is often inclined to express his own
opinion without the usual civility and I think that the
scarcely veiled impertinence of the tone he is wont at
times to adopt is intended to create a sense of his
power and importance.

4.

4.   Mr. Chebisheff called at my office on the 6th. of July to say that he had been instructed by Mr. Sidoroff to submit anew to me the Russian Amur Navigation Office's views concerning work that should be undertaken on the Amur and also to ask me if I could not persuade the Taoyin to sanction work on the Ussuri during the present navigation season. Mr. Chebisheff referred to the efficient administration of the old imperial days when work in connection with the upkeep of Russia's frontier waterways was carried out at an annual expenditure of some 3,000,000 Roubles and represented that the Soviet's new programme aimed at nothing short of the complete restoration of Aids to Navigation on the Amur and elsewhere to their former prosperous condition. He said that the Soviet Government was so convinced of the urgency of this measure that it had sanctioned a grant of 400,000 Roubles for 1925 and that the subsidy for 1926 would be a still larger one. Mr. Chebisheff made reference to the fact that the local technical agreement had completed the third term of its existence on the 30th. of November 1924 and gave me to understand that though

his

his Department had worked it loyally, which he submitted was proved by the fact that cuts made by the Technical Adviser had been agreed to without demur, the Soviet Authorities had always hoped to secure a more satisfactory one and had only accepted it in the first instance because they knew that they could not do better at the time. He admitted that the various Agreements had not been altogether unsuccessful but insisted that the results obtainable when working within the narrow limits of the sums hitherto granted by the Joint Commission were inadequate. He gave it as his opinion that expenditure had been cut down to such an extent that a great deal of the equipment in use on both sides of the Amur was in a bad condition and expressed the view that we were erecting Beacons and Signals of a kind which would rapidly degenerate and call within a few years for excessive expenditure on maintenance and renewals. Mr. Chebisheff went on to say that China should recognise that a great increase in expenditure on her part could not be long delayed, not so much from the rise in wages and in costs of materials, as from the necessity of coming into line

with

with a partner which had decided on a policy of
thorough re-organisation as opposed to a policy of
" messing about " and suggested that the Taoyin, when
next determining the maximum amount which China could
pay during any one year should have regard to the
future and leave out of account what she could actually
afford to pay at the moment.   He added that purely
temporary construction was not building for the future
and pressed the inadvisability of reducing quality below
what he termed a reasonable minimum standard.   Mr.
Chebisheff also complained that nothing had been done
to develop the facilities for shipping on the *Seergacha*
and the Ussuri, two rivers belonging jointly to the two
countries.   He said that his government was anxious to
spend money on both of these rivers and that refusal
on China's part to be responsible for her share of
joint ownership would be in the nature of wilful discouragement.   He informed me that the Soviet's decision
to adapt all work in connection with river conservancy
to the ideal standard of quality would necessitate the
presentation of still higher Estimates during 1926 and
concluded by remarking that in an undertaking belonging

Jointly

jointly to two countries if one party completed his
obligations the other must find means to meet his
share of the bill.

5.   I venture to submit a few comments on the
views held by the Russian Amur Navigation Office.   The
case for the " cheap and nasty " type of signal and
beacon is, of course, that in face of the decline in
revenue we cannot afford anything better,   From an
ideal standpoint, half the aids to navigation on the
Amur would be better pulled down and replaced, but as
we have to reduce expenditure to a figure which can
be afforded we base our standard solely on the present
ability to pay.   The Technical Adviser fully recognises
the necessity of doing this and proceeding on the basis
of plans originally drawn up with a view to the
strictest economy he has steadily set his face against
raising quality above what is really necessary.   Mr.
Ignatieff tells me that we should be quite satisfied
with the beacons, pyramids, etc., of the present rather
small and cheap type which he says will last hot for
one year but for a few years if well constructed and
properly looked after.   He accepts as true the statement

that

that the Soviet Government has decided to take steps to improve the lot of their functionaries by increasing their salaries and tells me that a great number of these people are grossly under-paid and that some do not even receive their meagre normal salary at all punctually.   As regards the promise of G.R.400,000 which the Russian Amur Navigation Office is said to have received from Moscow - partly as payment for arrears of maintenance for which Moscow is responsible, but partly as a free grant to help the Navigation Office over its difficulties during the period of reconstruction - I have since been given to understand by Mr. Chebisheff:(1) that the grant has been reduced to G.R.300,000 on the ground that it should be possible to collect 100,000 roubles from river dues; and (2) that of the 300,000 roubles actually paid over, and the whole of which has already been spent, a portion was lent to certain other needy government departments, and his statement is therefore so vague that it is impossible to say at present what value it actually possesses.   I submit that the same criticism may be said to apply to his general remarks concerning the

state

state of the Upper Amur, the Ussuri, the Sungacha, the Argun and Lake Hanka, and that it would be contrary to reason for us to swallow blindfold his verbal assurance that practically the whole of the beacons, etc., on both sides of the Ussuri will have to be replaced.   The proposal to erect Aids on the Ussuri - work which the Russians had expected to be allowed to take in hand during 1925 - is a new one which ought to have been definitely announced to us in 1924 when Mr. Chebisheff submitted his Estimates to Moscow for work of this kind may fairly be considered just as important as dredging operations which are held to be " subject to regulations which are to be drawn " " up (as occasion requires) and included in a " " separate Agreement."   Any large scheme such as is now contemplated by the Russians would require close supervision by some qualified person employed by the Chinese Government and I have told the Taoyin that if our technical authority is to remain an obvious first step is to send the Technical Adviser to the Ussuri on a tour of inspection and that until this step has been taken it will not be possible for us to make

any

Aigun No.144
Enclosure 1.
Annex 111.

any reasoned or reasonable comment upon the scheme.
Hitherto we have had, as it were, to contest every
inch of our way and if we agree to Mr. Chebisheff's
proposal to let the Navigation Office do what it
considers is required first and discuss costs afterwards
we shall leave a wide field open for the uncontrolled
activities of a department which in the past has made
a persistent effort to let us in for excessive expenditure.

6.   In my despatch No. 218 I submitted that as
the collection of river dues at a half tariff rate
no longer provided sufficient funds to meet current
expenditure the proper course was to collect at the
full rate. When the proposal to do so was first
made the Chamber of Commerce and the representatives
of the Shipping Companies objected that owing to the
depressed state of trade moderate taxation was essential
and said that they were absolutely determined to resist
any increase in the present scale. They pleaded heavy
financial burdens and the pressure constantly exerted
on them for contributions by the provincial government,

           and

and the Taoyin fearing that the people's sympathies
might be estranged rejected the idea of an increase
in taxation as being unthinkable in the actual circumstances. Shortly after my despatch had gone forward
the Taoyin referred the question to the Civil Governor
and in due course he told me that he had come to
the conclusion that the collection of dues at a full
tariff rate would be a wise measure. He said that
on this point he was now thoroughly at one with me
and told me that he was armed with special authority
sufficient to overcome any opposition. When this
question was raised a second time the Chamber of
Commerce protested that the financial responsibility to
be assumed by this district in the matter of payments
to be made to the Russians should be limited to the
sum actually available after deduction of all expenses
and submitted that if any further money was needed it
should be obtained from the Chinese Authorities who
were not in areas of severe distress. The Taoyin
replied that responsibility for meeting expenditure in
connection with the upkeep of the Amur had been thrust
upon the Aigun District by the Civil Governor under

           orders

orders from Moukden, and when it became clear that he was no longer willing to view this matter from the standpoint of local interests the Chamber of Commerce

Appendix 9.

gave way and agreed to accept responsibility for the payment by merchants of river dues at a full tariff rate. They suggested, however, that during the navigation season river dues should continue to be collected at a half tariff rate only and that the further amounts due should be surrendered by them to the Customs at the end of the season and submitted a scheme which they considered would safeguard the various interests involved. I pointed out the objections to

Appendix 9.

this clumsy procedure and submitted that payment should be made to the Customs at the full tariff rate when cargo was applied for. The Chamber of Commerce accepted my proposal and the collection of river dues at a full tariff rate commenced on the 9th. of June 1925.

7.   The River Dues Collection during 1924 amounted to $17,291 as against $23,769 in 1923 and $31,137 in 1922.   The collection for the period from 1st. January to 31st. July, 1925, amounts to $9,381.97 - of

which

which, as can be seen by reference to Appendix 1, a sum of $5,917.85 has been used to settle claims which actually fell due in 1924 - and a large measure of optimism as to the recovery of trade will be necessary if we are to anticipate a river dues collection this year much in excess of $20,000. I have stated facts concerning the decline in the revenue of this port so often that there is some danger of wearying you by their repitition, but I beg leave to take this opportunity to emphasise the fact that with these figures before us as a visible proof of the pass to which things have come it is obvious that we are quite un-able to look calmy ahead and frame plans with the hope of carrying them out. I venture the opinion that if it is decided to accept the Soviet's point of view and go in for a policy of thorough reorganisation and sweeping reform a fundamental change in existing arrangements will have to be made because our present capacity for paying the Russians rests on a revenue earning basis, and if we take into account the history of the past few years it is safe to assume that in no circumstances can this district become self-supporting

in

in regard to Estimates totalling $100,000, of which
China's share would be 50%.   It seems to me that
our only chance of making ends meet is to exchange
the present variable annual sum at our disposal with
its uncertainty for a regular sum and that there are
two tolerable courses open to us and no more - a
loan from the Bank of China or a Grant-in-aid punctually
paid over by the Central Government.   I have told the
Taoyin that in my opinion steps should be taken without
delay to make it clear both to the Civil Governor and
to the Shui-wu Ch'u that this district is being asked
to find a sum of money which every one knows it is
utterly incapable of finding, and that if permission to
contract a loan is not forthcoming a formal request
should be made for an annual subsidy from Peking to
run for a period of years on the ground that national
resources should bear some proportion of the cost of
an international agreement.   The Manager of the local
branch of the Bank of China tells me that in return
for a loan he would require interest @ 12 per mille
per month on the security of the River Dues Account
guaranteed by the Customs.

8.

8.   It may be that my argument that the outlay
on the upkeep of the Amur is national in character
will not be upheld and that in hoping for money from
Peking I am asking for a miracle.   At the same
time it does not seem unreasonable to suppose that
new conditions must call for new policies and I submit
that as the fundamental difficulty underlying this
question is one we cannot solve ourselves it is
logical that we should look to others to find a means
of solving it for us.   As things stand at present
the position of the Chinese Commission is clear only
in the negative sense that it knows what it cannot
do.   Last month when the Russian Amur Navigation
Office asked for an advance of Gold Roubles 11,000
on account of work done during 1925 I was able to
pay them 5,000 Roubles ($5,100) only.

9.   There is another matter in connection with
the working of the local technical agreement to which
reference must be made here.   The position held by
Mr. Ignatieff as Technical Adviser is one which has
excited a certain amount of comment recently and the
feelings of many Chinese here appear to be crystallised
                                                    into

into the complaint that the Customs is doing too well out of the Agreement with the Russians. Mr. Ch'e Hai-chen, Adviser on Foreign Affairs to the Taoyin, holds the view that however much we may insist that the appointment of a foreign expert @ Hk.Tls. 400 a month is reasonably suitable to our needs, we cannot possibly pretend that it is reasonably suitable to our means , and that if a foreigner is engaged he should be paid a wage dependent on our actual financial position. The idea that the employment of a comparatively highly-paid foreign expert may become a continuing process never to end evidently worries Mr. Ch'e and if my information is correct he seeks to detach the control of the work on the Amur from the Customs and place it in the hands of a Chinese Bureau of Navigation. He maintains that a number of Chinese could be found sufficiently advanced in intelligence and education to undertake the necessary work and nags incessantly in his effort to persuade the Taoyin to the point of view that in this way economies could be affected.

10.   The Taoyin now tells me that the Civil

                        Governor

Governor has criticized Mr. Ignatieff's appointment adversely on the ground that his salary entails too great an addition to the ordinary charges on the river dues account. He has instructed the Taoyin that he considers the time inopportune for payment of a salary of Hk.Tls. 400 a month and has suggested that either Mr. Ignatieff's salary should be reduced to a sum within the compass of the river dues collection, or that a portion only should be paid at the present time and arrears made good as funds accumulate. The Taoyin tells me that he has informed the Civil Governor that the Technical Adviser's appointment was made by the Inspector General and that for this reason it would not be possible to take any such steps as suggested. I have explained to the Taoyin: (1) that salaries paid by the Inspector General are so fixed as to ensure a reasonable standard of living and that they cannot be based from month to month on the changing profitableness of trade; (2) that one result of entrusting the collection of river dues to the Customs has been to cheapen the cost of collection at a time when trade is not merely depressed but critical; (3)

                        that

that efficiency, without which there can be no real
economy, entered into the sphere of the Inspector
General's policy when selecting Mr. Ignatieff for the
position of Technical Adviser and that regarded from
that point of view the money devoted to the payment
of his salary should be considered as an insurance
premium against the risk of fraud which experience
has shown is not by any means a remote contingency;
and (4) that the essential point to keep in mind is
that the inescapable sequel to the weakening of the
control at present exercised by the Customs would be
to make it easy for the Russians to enjoy money to
which they have no claim and thereby to expose the
Chinese community to a form of blackmail. I have
submitted that we cannot afford not to continue the
employment of Mr. Ignatieff as Technical Adviser.

11.   On many occasions I have found the Taoyin
somewhat inclined to follow the lead of Mr. Ch'ê Hsi-
chen in matters concerning Aids to Navigation but during
the course of conversation a few days ago he admitted
to me that he disliked our contract with the Technical
Adviser, not on principle, but solely because of the

                                                      financial

financial difficulties it had brought in its train
and told me that he sought to amend it by the introduction of the principle that payment from river
dues account of the Technical Adviser's salary, the
Inspector General's 1/10th., and his own annual allowance of $2,000, should be made only after all claims
from the Russians had been satisfied. He assured me
that he accepted the view that it was safest and best
that the Customs should have the control of the work
done by the Russian Amur Navigation Office but went
on to say that it was his intention to represent both
to the Civil Governor and to the Shui-wu Ch'u that
the Customs should take a full share in the effects
of the trade slump by agreeing to the principle that
the recovery of Customs expenditure from the river
dues collection should depend upon ability to pay from
these funds, and that until it is known that these
funds suffice the Technical Adviser's salary, etc., shall
be advanced from Service moneys. The Taoyin requested
me to convey to the Inspector General his complaint
that the present practice whereby the Technical Adviser's
salary is secured as a first charge on the river dues

                                                      collection

collection thrusts upon him an altogether undue share of the burden of trade fluctuation and leaves him in an impossible position. His contention, reduced to its simplest elements, is that we are better off than he is. It will be seen from the above that our contract with the Technical Adviser, as it stands, does not suit the Taoyin, and I now await your instructions as to whether it would suit you if amended as he proposes. I should add that Mr. Ignatieff's salary this year has been issued all along from my Suspense Account, which has now lent the River Dues Account a sum of (Hk.Tls. 400 x 7 = Hk.Tls. 2,800 @ 156.65 =) $4,386.20, and that no money has been taken from the 1925 River Dues Account for Customs purposes beyond the Inspector General's one-tenth and a few sums required for the payment of certain minor expenses. There is precedent for drawing thus on Service funds, the Technical Adviser's salary throughout the whole of 1923 having been first advanced from Account D and afterwards recovered during the first quarter of 1924. (Vide 254/ March Quarter's A/c.D: Schedule 6:Voucher 4 and Schedule L: Vr.c.).

12.

12.   Granting the accuracy of my prediction that the River Dues Collection this year will amount to not more than $20,000, we shall require to meet our expenditure during 1925 a sum of roughly $36,334. Or to put it in another way, we are likely to be faced with a deficit of $16,334. Thus-

Estimates 1925 :	Gold Roubles 44,268 :	
China's Contribution -50%	G.R.	22,134
Allowance for Loss By Exchange	$	1,700
Allowance for Taoyin's Office	$	2,000
Allowance for Technical Adviser's Office	$	8,500
I.G.'s 1/10th. of Collection	$	2,000
Estimated Sum Required 1925.............	$	36,334
Estimated River Dues Collection 1925....$		20,000
Estimated Deficit 1925.................	$	16,334

13.   I regret the delay in submitting the Detailed Estimates for 1925. These were promised by the 3rd. of August at the latest but actually they were sent to the Technical Adviser by Mr. Chebisheff on the 12th. of this month only. I should add that Mr. Ignatieff, who left the port on the 25th. of March for Moukden, returned to duty here on the 25th. of July.

I

Aigun No. 230 of 1925.

Appendix. I.

Amur River Dues Account

Statement of Receipts and Payments for the year 1924

Prepared by: Certified Correct:

[signature]   [signature]
3rd Assistant, B   Commissioner

Custom House,
Aigun/Taheiho, 4th August, 1925.
13th

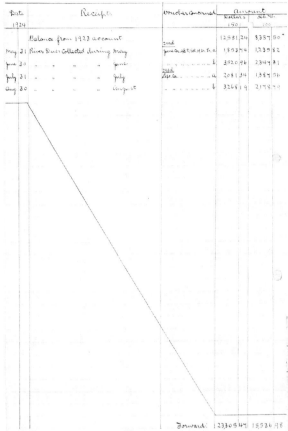

Date 1924	Receipts	Voucher Concerned	Amount Dollars 100	Amount 的 30 100
	Balance from 1923 account	2561	12,581.24	8387.50
May 31	River Dues collected during May	June 30. 经. Col. H.H. Tr. a	1853.74	1235.82
June 30	" " " " June	" " " " b	352.046	234.31
July 31	" " " " July	Sept. 30. " " b	208.34	138.56
Aug 30	" " " " August	" " " " b	3268.19	2178.70
		Forward:	12330547	15,536.98

Date 1924	Payments	Voucher Concerned	Amount Dollars 100	Amount 的 30 100
Jan. 25	Technical Adviser's Salary for January	2561 March 31. 经 Col. H.H. Tr. a	562.50	375.00
"	Loss by exchange on payment of Tech Adviser's Jan salary	" " " " 10	24.94	16.63
Feb.	Technical Adviser's Salary for February	" " " " 16	562.50	375.00
"	Loss by exchange on payment of Tech Adviser's Feb salary	" " " " 15	24.94	16.62
Mar. 4	Advance to Amur Navigation Office	" " " " 21	2,000.00	1333.34
" 25	Technical Adviser's Salary for March	" " " " 22	562.50	375.00
"	Loss by exchange on payment of Tech Adviser's Mar salary	" " " " 23	24.93	16.62
" 29	Tech Cost of firewood for Tech Adviser for March Qr.	" " " " 24	50.40	33.60
Apr. 25	Technical Adviser's Salary for April	2561 June 30. 1	562.50	375.00
"	Loss by exchange on payment of Tech Adviser's Apr salary	" " " " 2	24.94	16.62
" 29	Tech Cost of firewood for Tech Adviser for April	" " " " 3	9.80	6.54
May 26	Technical Adviser's Salary for May	" " " " 4	562.50	375.00
"	Loss by exchange on payment of Tech Adviser's May salary	" " " " 5	24.94	16.63
" 30	Removal of stones in Talaiho Harbour	" " " " 6	4.60	3.06
" 31	Tech of River Dues Collection for May	" " " " 7	185.37	123.58
June 14	Papers for Technical Adviser's Office	" " " " 8	17.10	11.40
" 19	Advance to Amur Navigation Office	" " " " 9	3500.00	2333.33
" 25	Technical Adviser's Salary for June	" " " " 11	562.50	375.00
"	Loss by exchange on payment of Tech Adviser's June salary	" " " " 12	24.94	16.63
" 30	Telegrams concerning depth of Tansing Shallows	" " " " 13	1.53	1.02
"	Ferry and carriage hires on service	" " " " 14	18.00	12.00
July 15	Tech of River Dues Collection for June	2561 Sept. 30. 1	352.10	234.73
" 26	Travelling expenses on inspection of aids	" " " " 3	104.50	69.66
"	" " " for 1st investigation re accident to S.S. Chiyang	" " " " 4	7.80	5.20
"	" " " ... 2nd	" " " "	15.00	10.00
" 28	Technical Adviser's Salary for July	" " " "	562.50	375.00
"	Loss by exchange on payment of Tech Adviser's July salary	" " " "	24.93	16.62
" 31	Tech of River Dues Collection for July	" " " " 8	208.13	138.76
Aug. 2	Advance to Amur Navigation Office	" " " " 9	3,498.00	2332.00
" 27	Technical Adviser's Salary for August	" " " " 12	562.50	375.00
"	Loss by exchange on payment of Tech Adviser's Aug salary	" " " " 13	24.94	16.63
		Forward:	14671.83	9781.22

227

Date 1924	Payments	Voucher concerned	Amount Dollars 100s	Hk Tls 100
	Forward		14671 83	9781 22
Aug. 30	Bunding of Takuho Foreshore	23rd Exp. a/c & Vrs	244 20	162 80
" "	Cost of River Dues Collection for August	" " " 14	326 82	217 88
Sept. 27	Technical Adviser's Salary for September	" " " 15	581 25	387 50
" "	Loss by exchange on payment of Tech. Adviser's Sep. Salary	" " " 18	26 77	17 18
" 30	Travelling expenses on inspection of Aids	" " " 19	131 30	87 54
" "	Petty Cash Expenditure for Tech. Adviser's Office during Sept. a/c	" " " 20	16 00	10 66
Oct. 13	Cost of River Dues Collection for September	29th Due a/c 1	371 43	247 82
" 17	Advance to Amur Navigation Office	" " " 2	3165 00	2110 00
" 25	Technical Adviser's Salary for October	" " " 3	600 00	400 00
" "	Loss by exchange on payment of Tech. Adviser's Oct. Salary	" " " 4	26 60	17 74
" 31	Travelling expenses for inspecting S.S. "Argun"	" " " 5	7 00	4 67
" "	Pay to a Chorpanoff for assisting Tech Adviser during Oct.	" " " 6	14 00	9 33
Nov. 7	Cost of River Dues Collection for October	" " " 7	258 55	172 37
" 14	Advance to Amur Navigation Office	" " " 8	2329 00	1550 00
" 22	Manifolding paper for Technical Adviser's Office	" " " 9	18 00	12 00
" 25	Technical Adviser's Salary for November	" " " 10	600 00	400 00
" "	Loss by exchange on payment of Tech. Adviser's Nov. Salary	" " " 11	26 60	17 73
" 29	Pay to a Chorpanoff for assisting Tech adviser during Nov.	" " " 12	29 00	19 69
" "	Cost of River Dues Collection for November	" " " 13	26 73	17 82
Dec. 24	Technical Adviser's Salary for December	" " " 14	600 00	400 00
" "	Loss by exchange on payment of Tech. Adviser's Dec. Salary	" " " 15	26 60	17 18
" 27	Cost of firewood for Tech. Adviser for Dec. a/c	" " " 16	36 00	24 00
" 30	Pay to a Chorpanoff for assisting Tech Adviser during Dec.	" " " 17	27 00	18 00
" "	Petty Cash expenditure for Tech. Adviser's Office during Dec. a/c	" " " 18	32 39	21 58
1925				
Jan. 17	Expenditure for Taojui Office in connection with Aids, 1924	miscel. 1	2000 00	1333 33
Mar. 20	Sending Shallow depth telegrams	" 2	26 66	17 77
" "	Kerosene oil for floating beacon during 1924	" 3	10 38	6 91
Aug. 19	Final payment to Amur Navigation Office	29th June a/c 1	388 83	258 92
			30097 90	20065 27

Appendix 2.

Date 1924	Receipts	Voucher concerned	Amount Dollars 100s	Hk Tls 100
	Forward		23305 49	15536 18
Sept. 30	River Dues Collected during September	29th Due a/c, a, b, & c	3714 27	2476 18
Oct. 31	" " " " October	29th Due a/c a	2589 50	1723 67
Nov. 29	" " " " November	" " " b	267 25	178 17
			29876 49	19915 00
	Balance due and accounted for in 1925 Account		225 41	150 27
			30097 90	20065 27

AIGUN NO. 230 OF 1925.

APPENDIX 2.

AMUR RIVER DUES ACCOUNT.

(CHINESE COMMISSION)

SUMMARY OF RECEIPTS AND PAYMENTS FOR THE YEAR 1924.

	Dollars.	Hk.Tls.
RECEIPTS:		
A.Balance from 1923 Account	12,581.24	8,387.50
B.Amur River Dues collected during 1924	17,291.25	11,527.50
C.Balance due and accounted for in 1925 Account	225.41	150.27
	30,097.90	20,065.27
PAYMENTS:		
1. 1/10th of River Dues Collection deducted by Aigun Customs as cost of collection	1,729.13	1,152.76
2. Expenditure incurred by Chinese Commission:-		
(a) Technical Adviser's Office	7,999.94	5,333.29
(b) Taoyin's Office	2,000.00	1,333.33
Total for Chinese Commission:	9,999.94	6,666.62
3. Expenditure for upkeep of Aids to Navigation on frontier section of Amur	18,368.83	12,245.89
Total: 2 and 3:	28,368.77	18,912.51
	30,097.90	20,065.27

According

AIGUN NO. 230 OF 1925.

APPENDIX 2.

According to Article 15 of Annex II of the Provisional Local Agreement for 1923-1924, the Chinese Commission is to pay 50 per cent. of the expenditure incurred by the Amur Navigation Office on the upkeep of Aids to Navigation on the frontier section of the Amur. The total expenditure of the above office for the year 1924 is Gold Roubles 35,334.87, the Chinese Commission's share being Gold Roubles 17,667.43. Payments made by the Chinese Commission are as follows:-

Date. 1924.		Dollars.		Gold Roubles.
March	7	2,000.00	=	1,800.00
June	19	3,500.00	=	3,281.25
August	2	3,498.00	=	3,300.00
October	17	3,165.00	=	3,000.00
November	14	2,325.00	=	2,500.00
1925.				
May	15	3,880.83	=	3,786.18
		18,368.83	=	17,667.43

China's obligation for the upkeep of Aids to Navigation on the frontier section of the Amur for the year 1924 has been fully met.

Prepared by:

3rd Assistant, B.

Certified Correct:

R.J.e Alemgelumle

Commissioner.

CUSTOM HOUSE,

Aigun/Taheiho, 4th.August, 1925.
13th.

APPENDIX 3.

AIGUN NO. 230 OF 1925.

APPENDIX 3.

SUMMARY OF EXPENDITURE FOR TECHNICAL ADVISER'S OFFICE

FOR THE YEAR 1924.

(a) Current Expenditure:	Dollars.	Hk.Tls.
Technical Adviser's Salary for 1924	6,881.25	4,587.50
Loss by Exchange on payment of Technical Adviser's Salary	305.07	203.38
2/3rds Cost of Firewood for Technical Adviser for 1924	96.20	64.14
Travelling Expenses	265.60	177.07
Pay to extra employee for assisting Technical Adviser	66.00	44.00
Stationery and Sundries	98.47	65.64
Total Current Expenditure:	7,712.59	5,141.73
(b) Local Aids to Navigation:		
Removal of Stones in Taheiho Harbour	4.60	3.06
Kerosene Oil for Floating Beacon	10.36	6.91
Sensing Shallows Depth Telegrams	28.19	18.79
Bunding of Taheiho Foreshore	244.20	162.80
Total Local Aids to Nav.:	287.35	191.56
	7,999.94	5,333.29

Prepared by:

3rd Assistant, B.

Certified Correct:

Commissioner.

CUSTOM HOUSE,
Aigun/Taheiho, 4th August 1925.
13th.

APPENDIX 4.

AIGUN NO. 230 OF 1925.

APPENDIX 4.

(TRANSLATION)

Declaration concerning the extension of the 1923/24 Agreement to 1925 (for the period from 1st December, 1924, to 30th November, 1925).

The Heiho Taoyin (concurrently Commissioner for Foreign Affairs, Aigun District) of the Republic of China, "SUNG WEI-YU; and the Director of the Amur Government Navigation Office of the Union of Soviet Socialist Republics, CHEBISHEFF, hereby declare that the Provisional Local Agreement concerning Navigation on the Frontier waters of the Amur concluded in the 12th year of the Chinese Republic (i.e. 1923) together with its Annexes will continue to be in force, with the exception of Annex III which will be regulated seperately; that the Regulations of the aforesaid Agreement and its Annexes shall be followed and not deviated from; that the above-mentioned Agreement with its Annexes shall be valid for not more than one year, and shall cease to be operative in the event of an understanding on matters concerning navigation being reached at the forthcoming Sino-Russian Conference before the 1st day of the 12th month of the present year (1st December 1925); that a provisional local arrangement will be discussed by both parties if by that date no settlement be reached at the Sino-Russian Conference; and finally that the toatl expenditure for the upkeep of Aids to Navigation for the present year shall not exceed the estimate of Gold Roubles 44,268.

In witness whereof SUNG and CHEBISHEFF have

hereto

hereto affixed their signatures and seals to the present Declaration made in the Chinese and Russian languages, in duplicate.

Done at Tsheiho this eighteenth day of the fifth month of the fourteenth year of the Republic of China, corresponding to the eighteenth day of May, in the year one thousand nine hundred and twenty-five.

(Signed and sealed) SUNG WEN-YÜ.
Taoyin.

(Signed and sealed) CHEBISHEFF.
Director.

Custom House,
Aigun, 4th. August, 1925.
13th.

APPENDIX 5.

ESTIMATES FOR THE YEAR 1925.

Estimates for the upkeep of Aids to Navigation on the frontier section of the Amur from Pokrovka to Kasakevicheva, a distance of 1842 kilometres divided into 5 Districts, for the period from the 1st December 1924 to the 30th November 1925, (i.e. for the year 1925) prepared by the Amur Navigation Office, and checked by Mr. P. I. Ignatieff, Technical Adviser.

I. Expenses of the Russian Amur Navigation Office.

Gold Roubles.

1/ 1 Director (Engineer) 12 months	200.00	2,400.00
2/ Director of Financial Department	140.00	1,680.00
3/ Accountant	42.00	504.00
4/ Clerk	29.80	357.60
5/ Director of Roads & Buildings	130.00	1,560.00
6/ Typist	33.00	396.00
7/ Surveyor, Aids Department	85.70	1,028.40
8/ 2nd Class Surveyor	51.00	612.00
9/ Surveyor for Water-measure tables	51.00	612.00
Total Salaries		9,150.00

II. Expenses for the Districts.

From Pokrovka to Kasakevicheva 1842 kilometres - 5 Districts.

1/ District of Djalinda: 323 kilometres, 2 Depth-signal Stations: Beitonovo and Permikino; 5 Lighted Shallows.

2/ District of Chernayeva: 345 kilometres: 1 Depth-signal Station: Upper Chernayeva; 1 Traffic Station Tsagayan; 9 Lighted Shallows.

3/

3/ **District of Blagovestchensk**: 395 kilometres, 2 Depth-signal
Stations: Markova, Konstantinova; 13 Lighted Shallows.

4/ **District of Innokentieva**: 399 kilometres, 1 Depth-signal
Station: Poyarkova; 6 Lighted Shallows.

5/ **District of Ekaterino-Nickolsk**: 380 kilometres, 1 Depth-
signal Station Boyus; 6 Lighted Shallows.

N.B. The figures between brackets indicate the number of
Depth-Signal or Traffic-Stations in each District.

Gold Roubles.	Distr.I.		Distr.II.		Distr.III.		Distr.IV.		Distr.V.	
	R.	K.	R.	K.	R.	K.	R.	K.	R.	K.
Salaries to District employees:										
4 District Surveyors 58.95x6 & 73.69x6	795	84	795	84	-	-	795	84	795	84
1 District Surveyor 65.70x6 & 82.13x6	-	-	-	-	886	98	-	-	-	-
5 Clerks 33.45x9	267	60	267	60	267	60	267	60	267	60
5 Foremen 37.50x6 & 43.75x6	517	50	517	50	517	50	517	50	517	50
4 Boys 25.20x12	302	40	302	40	-	-	302	40	302	40
Depth-signal Stations:	(2)		(1)		(2)		(1)		(1)	
Boatmen:2 each station, 2x26:19x5	563	80	281	90	563	80	281	90	281	90
Boatmen:each station, 25.25x5	-	-	302	50	-	-	-	-	-	-
Opening & operating Depth-signal Stations	71	72	35	86	71	72	35	86	35	86
Opening & operating Traffic stations	-	-	41	50	-	-	-	-	-	-
Replacing, repairing & maintenance in repair of Beacons as per detailed statement appended;	2,059	74	1,824	78	1,952	45	1,628	99	1,579	04
Repairs to buildings	150	00	150	00	150	00	175	00	175	00
Postage, telegrams, stationery, sundries	150	00	150	00	150	00	150	00	150	00
Heating	70	00	70	00	70	00	70	00	70	00
Light	20	00	20	00	20	00	20	00	20	00
Lighting Shallows: 39 Watchmen, 23.44 from 2 @ 11 5 months	(5)		(9)		(13)		(6)		(6)	
	351	50	539	12	879	00	375	04	431	98
Materials	129	62	189	67	316	79	125	86	157	19
TOTAL	5,429	82	5,488	87	5,745	84	4,745	99	4,774	25

Summary

Summary.	Gold Roubles.
District I	5,429.82
District II	5,488.87
District III	5,745.84
District IV	4,745.99
District V	4,774.25
5% for Medical Attendance	709.76
Stone work	400.00
Depreciation	2,073.47
Travelling expenses & Allowances	350.00
Grand total for 5 Districts	29,718.00

GENERAL ESTIMATE. Gold Roubles.

1.	Expenses for the frontier Districts (5)	29,718.00
2.	Expenses for the Amur Navigation Office	9,150.00
3.	Steam-launch for inspection & repairing Aids to Navigation	5,400.00
	Grand total 1925:	44,268.00
	Chinese share 1925: 50% Gold Roubles	22,134.00

Maintenance in Repair of Beacons & Boats at 5 Districts:
Detailed Statement.

Number of Beacons on the 1st November, 1924.	Number	Price Roubles	Total Sum Roubles
River type: Signals	1288		
" Shields	1726		
Sea type Pyramids	183		
" Shields	218		
Erection of New Beacons.			
River type: Signals	113	10.00	1130.00
River type: Shields			

	Number	Price	Total Sum.
		Roubles	Roubles
River type: Shields ...	197	2.52	516.69
		3.27	
Sea type : Pyramids ..	14	14.00	196.00
" Shields ..	18	5.95	107.10
Masts with Signals	2	- -	51.59
Posts with warning"Whistle"	1	- -	7.21
Total			2008.59
Repairs to Beacons.			
River type Signals ...	1194	1.12	1337.28
" " Shields ...	1555	-.10	155.50
Painting Signals	598	2.06	1231.88
" Shields	1555	-.37	575.35
Props erected	433	1.10	476.30
Sea type: Pyramids ...	172	1.55	266.05
Painting Shields	179	2.17	388.43
Small repairs			279.94
Total			4709.73
Repairs to Rowing Boats.			
Gigs	5	100.00	500.00
Yawls	5	30.00	150.00
Surveying boats	5	12.50	62.50
Watchers boats	5	7.00	35.00
Total			747.50
Repairs to the equipment of Boatmen (3 months)	10	33.58	1007.40
Total			8925.00$
Expenses for Lighting of Beacons.			
Kerosine ....pood	159.05	2.60	413.53
Wick 14 m/m ....arshine	59 -	-.15	8.85
Lamp glasses	273 -	-.30	81.90
Brushes	39 ½	-.25	9.75
Lamp burners.........	45 -	1.00	45.00
Matches ....packets	1482 -	-.15	22.23
White stuff ...arshines	117 -	-.45	52.65
Soap ....pounds	35 -	-.21	7.35
Repairs of boats	39 -	7.13	278.07
Total			919.33*

Expenses for the C.M.Customs,Aigun.

Expenses for the C. M. Customs, Aigun.

Salary for Technical Adviser: 12 months @ Hk.Tls. 400.00
Hk.Tls. 6,266.00 156.65 (local rate for salary).. $7,519.20

Travelling Allowances 500.00

Stationery 50.00

Postage & Telegrams 100.00

Firewood 75.60

Sundries & unforeseen 255.80

Total for C. M. Customs $8,500.00

Expenses for the Taoyin's Office $2,000.00

Grand Total $10,500.00

P. Ignatieff.

Technical Adviser on Amur
Aids to Navigation.

Custom House,
Aigun, 4th./13th. August, 1925.

APPENDIX 6.

AIGUN NO. 230 OF 1925.

APPENDIX 6.

(Translation).

Mr. Chebisheff, Director of the Russian Amur Navigation Office, Blagovestchensk, to the Heiho Taoyin.

Amur Navigation Office,

No. 1996.

Blagovestchensk, 24th. March, 1925.

All necessary work and repairs in connection with the maintenance of Aids to Navigation on the frontier section of the Amur (from Pokrovka to Kazakevicheva) during last year (1924) have been completed, as provided for by the Agreement which was concluded between the Russian Amur Government Water Transport and the Heiho Taoyin of the Chinese Republic, and the expenditure incurred has been kept within the Estimates for 1923 and 1924 which amounted to Gold Roubles 55,000, being 19,250 roubles for 1923 and 35,750 roubles for 1924.

Recognising that the safety of shipping renders necessary the further development of work, and having in view the restoration of Aids to Navigation to the condition in which they existed before the revolution, the Amur Navigation Office will undertake work during 1925 on repairs to Aids in the frontier waterways of the Amur from Pokrovka to Kazakevicheva and also on the Ussuri from Iman to the mouth (Habarovsk), and it is proposed to spend during 1925 a sum of 50,000 Gold Roubles, being 44,268 for the Amur and 5,732 for the Ussuri.

As the above mentioned Agreement of the 1st.

December

December (the Agreement for 1923 and 1924 which was signed on 28th. October 1923 and lapsed on the 30th. November, 1924) is no longer in force, and since Chinese shipping, as in previous years will continue to profit by the Aids to Navigation on the frontier waterways, it follows that work must be undertaken at the same time on both the Chinese and Russian sides. For the above reasons the Amur Navigation Office finds it necessary to propose to the Taoyin the renewal of the Agreement which has been in force during the past two years, the usual arrangement allowing for a mutual expenditure of 50% for the upkeep of the frontier waterways on the Amur and the Ussuri, to hold good.

The Amur Navigation Office is obliged to point out that expenditure for the dredging of the channels has not been included in the Estimates for the present year (1925) because this is work which depends on the nature of the general operations undertaken in the Amur basin, and cannot therefore be decided on now. For this reason an allowance to cover the cost of dredging work does not enter into the Agreement for the mutual maintenance of the frontier sections of the Amur and the Ussuri (during 1925).

But next year, 1926, it is the intention of the Amur Navigation Office to carry out dredging work both on the Upper Amur and on the Ussuri and it is expected that expenditure on the upkeep and lighting of the Amur, the Ussuri, the Sungacha and Lake Hanka will amount next year to a sum of 100,000 Gold Roubles.

In View of the approaching commencement of the

navigation

navigation season, the Amur Navigation Office would
request the Taoyin not to delay his decision regarding
the conclusion of an Agreement for 1925.

The Director of the Amur Navigatio Office,

(Signed) Engineer Chebisheff.

Translation made by:

2nd Clerk, B.

APPENDIX 7.

**Mr. Chebisheff, Director of the Russian Amur Navigation
Office, Blagovestchensk, to the Heiho Taoyin.**

Amur Navigation Office for
Inland Waterways,
Secretary's Memo. No. 2778.
Blagovestchensk, 18th. April, 1925.

In continuation of our letter No. 1996 sent to you
on the 24th. March, 1925, the Amur Navigation Office for
Inland Waterways declares that, while it is willing to
extend last year's local provisional agreement for the
maintenance of the frontier section of the Amur from
Pokrovka to Kasakevitch, it reserves the right to enlarge
the scale of operations and expenditure in accordance with
the sum named in the Estimates enclosed in the above
letter (NO. 1996).

Taking into consideration the fact that there will
not be enough money collected (as river dues) from
Chinese vessels to cover China's share of expenditure
incurred if work is undertaken on a larger scale than
is now the case, the Navigation Office suggests that the
Chinese Commission make payments in the same manner and
on the same scale as was done last year, and that payment of whatever further sum may be due be arranged for
prior to the conclusion of the Sino-Russian Conference
(by the Sino-Russian delegates).

Again, the Amur Navigation Office, with a view to
improving navigation, considers it necessary to carry out

work

work on the Ussuri. You are requested to note that
work in connection with Aids to Navigation on the
Ussuri was not allowed for in the 1924 Agreement, but
it is work of great importance and with the navigation
season about to commence consideration of this question
should not be postponed until the conclusion of the
Sino-Russian Conference. The Navigation Office therefore
asks you to allow Russian workmen to cross the frontier
for the purpose of undertaking repairs to Aids to Navigation on the Chinese side of the Ussuri, and to issue
the necessary passports. It could be left to the Sino-
Russian Conference to determine in what proportion the
expenditure incurred should be borne by the two sides.

This office would like to know when the Sino-
Russian Local Technical Commission will hold a meeting
to settle last year's accounts and decide the question
about the extension of the Agreement to the present
year (1925).

(Signed) Engineer Chebisheff,
Director of Russian Amur Navigation
Office.

(Signed) Illegible,
Secretary of Navigation Office.

Translation made by:

2nd. Clerk. B.

APPENDIX 8.

AIGUN NO. 230 OF 1925.

APPENDIX 8.
TRANSLATION.

Commissioner's Letter No. 144 of 15th. May, 1925.
to Heiho Taoyin.

The Russian Amur Navigation Office is claiming
an additional 4,268 Gold Roubles and the Technical
Adviser has telegraphed suggesting another 2,000 but
agreeing to allow them another 4,000 odd provided
that the Taoyin consents. The Commissioner thinks
that it would not be worth while to have unpleasant-
ness over such a comparatively small sum as (Gold
Roubles 4,268 - ½ =) Gold Roubles 2,134 and would like
to have the Taoyin's views on the point.

Heiho Taoyin's Letter No. 196 of 16th. May to
Commissioner.

The Taoyin quite agrees with the Commissioner and
requests him to arrange for Estimates for 1925 amounting to Gold Roubles 44,268.

Vide Summary of Non-Urgent Chinese Correspondence for May, 1925: Subject No. 4.

Translated by:

Commissioner.

APPENDIX 9.

AIGUN NO. 230 OF 1925.

APPENDIX 9.

TRANSLATION.

Taoyin's Letter No. 200 of 28th. May, 1925. to Commissioner.

The Heiho Chamber of Commerce have written to me as follows:

You have told us during the course of conversation that the insufficiency of the river dues collection to meet estimat -ed expenditure has formed the subject of correspondence between yourself and the Civil Governor and that it has been decided to obtain the extra money requir- ed by increasing the tariff rate. With the welfare of the district in view you have endeavoured, though without success, to discover other means of raising money, and are now bound to give effect to your instructions. The matter at issue had been discussed by the Chamber on many occasions but hitherto without arriving at any decision, but now in oredr to meet a difficult situation it has been proposed:

(1) That for the present the Chamber accept responsibility for the payment of the extra half rate it has been decided to collect;

(2) That the Taoyin inform the Customs that in future all merchants, foreign and Chinese, who import and export cargo, shall obtain from the Chamber, before before they apply at the Custom House, a Certificate which shall be handed in at the Custom House when cargo is examined and dues at the ordinary rate are paid, and serve as proof of the sum still due; and that on the basis of these Certificates the Chamber will collect from merchants the amounts owing, for surrender to the Customs, thereby evenly distributing the amount to be paid and minimising risk of disputes;

(3) That the Chamber will consult with the Customs as to the nature of the Certificate to be adopted in the event of the proposal meeting with the Taoyin's approval:

The above suggestions have been agreed to and preparations will be made to carry them out as soon as the Taoyin's reply is received.

The commissioner is requested to let the Taoyin know whether the above proposals are practicable or not so that the necessary instructions may be given.

Vide Summary of Non-Urgent Chinese Corres- pondence for May 10 1925: Subject No.6.

Commissioner's Letter No. 147 of 2nd. June 1925 to Heiho Taoyin.

With a steadily falling trade and cargo arriving in

in ever-diminishing quantities the River Dues Collection
is now no longer sufficient for the upkeep of the
river. The Chamber of Commerce Propose to make themselves responsible for the collection of the additional
amount required and in coming to the help of the district at a time of great difficulty they give evidence
of a commendably fine spirit.

The Commissioner fears, however, that for various
reasons the proposals made by the Chamber of Commerce
would be a difficult one to carry out. For instance,
the Chamber could not possibly make itself responsible
for the collection of river dues on cargo worked at
places below Aigun which at present pays at Lahasusu
(Harbin), and if these dues are not collected some
merchants will be getting better treatment than others.

Again, River Dues are paid both by foreigners
and by Chinese, and though the Chamber may be in a
position to deal with the latter it would not be
able to exercise any control over the former and the
result would be that Chinese merchants alone would
carry the burden of extra taxation.

Moreover, the suggestion that special certificates
should be applied for in the case of cargo imported
and exported would be a highly inconvenient arrangement
and one which could not possibly be made to work.

River Dues being used solely for the upkeep of
the channel, and collection at the present half-rate
having been shown to be in insufficient, the simplest
method would be to collect at a full rate on the
understanding that former practice be reverted to when
trade revives and payment at the half-rate again
suffices to meet requirements. If this simple method
be

be adopted merchants will have the assurance that
collection at the increased rate is a temporary measure
only.

It is known by everyone how greatly merchants
have the welfare of this district at heart, and now
that it has been decided that the maintenance of the
river channels is a local question the Commissioner
thinks that they will be willing to come forward and
help.

<u>Heiho Taoyin's Letter No. 202 of 8th. June 1925 to</u>
<u>Commissioner.</u>

The Commissioner's proposal to collect river dues
at a full tariff rate instead of, as is done at
present, at a half-rate only, on the understanding
that the collection of the additional half-rate will
be cancelled directly the state of trade makes such
a step possible, has been communicated to the Chamber
of Commerce who have replied that after giving the
matter further consideration they have decided to accept
the proposal.

<u>Vide</u> Summary of Non-Urgent Chinese Correspon-
dence for June, 1925: Subject No. 1.

Translated by:

Commissioner.

5 - SEP 1925

COAST INSPECTOR'S COMMENTS ON AIGUN NO.230, I.G..

DATED 4TH AUGUST, 1925, AND DOCKETED:
13TH

AMUR AIDS TO NAVIGATION: River Dues
A/c. 1924; Summary of Receipts &
Payments (Chinese Commission) 1924;
Summary of Expenditure Technical
Adviser's Office, 1924; & Estimates
for 1925, submitting: proceedings
leading up to Agreement for 1925;
Civil Governor's criticism of
Technical Adviser's appointment &
Taoyin's request; collection of river
dues at full tariff rate; difficulty
caused by lack of funds; Bank of
China's rate for loan; Amur Navigation
Office's argument for erection of
Aids on Sungacha & Ussuri; and claim
for larger Estimates, reporting.

N I L.

(Signed)   H. E. Hillman.
            Coast Inspector.

Coast Inspector's Office,
                            True Copy:
Shanghai, 26th August 1925.
                            Supervisor.

呈海关总税务司署 <u>230</u> 号文　　　　　　　　瑷珲关 1925 年 8 月 4 日

尊敬的代理海关总税务司（北京）：

1. 根据海关总税务司署第 235/103576 号令（参阅瑷珲关第 218 号呈及海关总税务司署第 230/103232 号令）：

"黑龙江航务：汇报中俄地方政府已签订 1925 年（即 1924 年 12 月 1 日至 1925 年 11 月 30 日）协议事；随附税务处致代理海关总税务司公文抄件。"

特此呈交：

黑龙江江捐账户 1924 年年度收支报表（见附录 1）

中国黑龙江航政委员会 1924 年年度收支报表（见附录 2）

1924 年航务专门顾问办事处支出报表（见附录 3）

关于将《1923/1924 年临时地方工程协议》展期至 1925 年（自 1924 年 12 月 1 日至 1925 年 11 月 30 日）的声明译本抄件（见附录 4）

1925 年预算报表（见附录 5）

俄阿穆尔水道局督办切比索夫（chebisheff）致黑河道尹信函译本（附录 6 及附录 7）（参阅瑷珲关第 218 号呈）

2. 今年 3 月，俄阿穆尔水道局提交了 1925 年初始预算，支出预算总计 65000 金卢布，其中 55000 金卢布计划用于黑龙江航路标志工程，10000 金卢布计划用于乌苏里江航路标志工程。但航务专门顾问核查后认为，对于黑龙江航路标志工程，37000 金卢布足矣，乌苏里江航路标志工程则仅需 4000 金卢布，遂将预算退回，请俄方重新修订。随后俄阿穆尔水道局将预算调整为 50000 金卢布，其督办且比索夫先生称该预算中包括乌苏里江航路标志工程所需之 5732 金卢布。然道尹拒绝为乌苏里江航路标志工程划拨任何资金，同时，航务专门顾问再一次调整了预算，并告知且比索夫先生，黑龙江航路标志工程的支出预算应控制在 39600 金卢布至 40000 金卢布以内。

5 月，俄阿穆尔水道局再次提交预算，金额依旧为 50000 金卢布。俄阿穆尔国家水运局局长西多霍夫（Sidoroff）先生以及曾与华方有过往来的苏维埃最高官员都坚持认为黑龙江航路标志工程的经费最低应不少于 44268 金卢布，而乌苏里江航路标志工程的经费最低应不少于 5732 金卢布。

但道尹再次驳回为乌苏里江航路标志工程划拨经费之提议。西多霍夫先生在知道易保罗（P. I. Ignatieff）先生在前往奉天之前曾提出可以更大程度地缩减开支以将黑龙江航路标志工程的预算由 44268 金卢布削减至 40000 金卢布后,佯装惊讶,认为航务专门顾问不应在未与其商量的情况下就擅自做出结论,坚称俄国对于此类问题有权提出意见,随后又谈到由于物价特别是生活必需品价格的暴涨,职员薪俸需要提高,并表示易保罗先生若对此有何异议,其亦不会妥协赞成。

本署对此抗辩称,航务专门顾问早已及时将降低黑龙江航路标志工程预算至 40000 金卢布的建议告知了且比索夫先生。但且比索夫先生深知,若想保住自己俄阿穆尔水道局督办之职位,唯一的办法就是无条件支持上级的一切主张,所以根本不会承认。对此双方争执不下,但当得知本署无意收回该言论之后,西多霍夫先生话锋一转,继续辩解道,若要证明继续沿用现行体制是正确合理的,就应对现行体制予以不断的改进,以使其服务标准无限接近于大革命之前;并称任何威胁航运安全的主张都是违背双方利益的,若同意该观点,就应该同意为黑龙江航路标志工程划拨总计 44268 金卢布的经费,因为这也是在维护华方的利益;最后又补充说道,其无法完全同意华方的安排,而且华方若不同意该笔预算金额,其将拒绝签订任何协议。且比索夫先生亦持此观点。

3. 本署无法判断受雇于俄阿穆尔水道局的工人之薪俸是偏少、恰好还是过多,亦无法判断 40000 金卢布之预算是否与黑龙江航路标志工程所需费用相称。此等问题均须由具备专业知识和管理能力之人来仔细考量,但由于唯一既可以代表中国利益又具备解决技术性难题经验的航务专门顾问当时尚在奉天,中国航政委员会中已无可解决此等难题之人。对于航务专门顾问认为若精打细算,40000 金卢布的预算或许足够之观点,本署不便擅自否决,遂未能与俄方达成协议,但随后便向航务专门顾问发送电报说明目前之情况,请其帮助解决。航务专门顾问认为 44268 金卢布的预算亦可予以同意,但还应尝试劝说西多霍夫先生同意将预算定为 42000 金卢布。在收到航务专门顾问电报回复之前,本署已告知道尹,俄方已驳回航务专门顾问关于将预算减至 40000 金卢布的建议,且态度十分坚决。道尹表示,虽然目前经济困难,但最好还是接受西多霍夫先生之提议,此事不必再议。最终,双方协定 1925 年预算为 44268 金卢布,航务专门顾问已于 8 月 12 日将预算明细交至本署。

其实对于这一问题,本无须进行任何激烈的讨论,只是西多霍夫先生——这位前水手、政治煽动者、俄阿穆尔国家水运局局长,总是冒昧地表达自己的观点,其惯用的口吻几乎毫不掩饰地表现出了傲慢无礼的态度,其用意不过是在夸显自己位高权重。

4. 7 月 6 日,且比索夫先生造访本署,称其奉西多霍夫先生之命前来说明俄阿穆尔水道局关于黑龙江航路标志工程具体事项的意见,并询问本署可否劝说道尹批准于今年航运季开展乌苏里江航路标志工程，随后又提到沙俄时期航路标志维护工作管理之高效，每年用于俄国边境水道的维护费用约达 3000000 卢布，并表示此次新工程，除了重建黑龙江及其他河道的航路标志以使之恢复到从前的繁荣景象之外，并无其他目的，还称苏维埃政府对此十分重视，已为 1925 年河道维护工程拨发 400000 卢布的经费，1926 年甚至还会更多。

且比索夫先生感叹，截至 1924 年 11 月 30 日，《地方工程协议》已走过三个年头，阿穆尔水道局一直坚守协议精神，对于航务专门顾问消减预算之提议，此前更是直接通过从未拖延，苏维埃政府对于此前的协议虽然都已接受，但只是因为了解当时形势所迫并无更好的选择，实际上一直希望可以签订一份更令人满意的协议。但且比索夫先生亦承认此前所签协议并非皆未如愿，只是认为中俄黑龙江航路标志联合委员会所拨金额十分有限，难以充分开展工作，比如黑龙江华俄两岸现有设备大多状况不佳，但因预算过低无法维修换新，而且目前所立的标桩和信标极易老化，几年内的维修换新费用只怕会更多，因此希望中国政府可以意识到，中国今后的支出势必会大幅增加，不仅仅是因为薪俸和材料方面的费用将会上涨，更是因为中俄双方若要继续合作，中国就必须与俄国保持步调一致，同意对航路状况进行彻底整改，不可拖沓。

且比索夫先生表示，希望道尹今后考虑中国摊款预算时，不要仅仅考虑当下的支付能力，要为将来做打算，临时性质的工程于将来而言毫无益处，消减预算只会降低工程的质量标准，绝非明智之举，并抱怨称松阿察河与乌苏里江本为中俄两国共同所有，迄今却仍未能开展任何的航路标志工程，还宣称苏维埃政府十分愿意为该两条河流上的航路标志工程投入资金，中国政府若拒绝支付摊款就是有意阻拦，而且苏维埃政府已经决定将航路维护工程的质量提高到理想标准，如此一来，1926 年的预算必然会更高，最后还指出，该项工事既是两国共同承担，若一方已履行义务，另一方则亦须尽力做到。

5. 对于俄阿穆尔水道局的观点，兹提出以下几点意见。

对于目前所立标桩和信标"廉价而品质低劣"之言论，本署必须强调，江捐税收减少后，华方确实无法负担起更高质量的标桩和信标。理想情况下，黑龙江上一半的航路标志都应予以重建，但因华方支付能力有限，只能消减预算。而且航务专门顾问易保罗先生对此完全赞同，坚决反对将质量提高至毫无必要的高水平，并认为目前的标桩十分合用，体积小，造价低，只要认真修建并精心维护，那么耐用期绝不只有一年，至少可以达到数年。

对于苏维埃政府已经决定采取措施提高职员薪俸以改善所有职员的生活水平一事，易保罗先生表示可信，并称目前俄国许多职员的薪俸都过低，有些甚至不能按时发放。

至于莫斯科 400000 金卢布的拨款,据说俄阿穆尔水道局已经收到,该笔款项一部分为政府本应结付的维修欠款,另一部分为帮助阿穆尔水道局渡过航路标志重建工作难关的无偿资助。但随后且比索夫先生又称:(1)该项拨款已减少至 300000 卢布,因江捐还可征得 100000 卢布;(2)300000 卢布的拨款确已拨发,但亦已用尽,其中一部分款项借予了某些需要资金援助的政府部门。对此,本署认为且比索夫先生之言论过于含糊,几乎不具有任何价值。

此外,对于且比索夫先生关于黑龙江上游、松阿察河以及兴凯湖(Lake Hanka)境况之言论,尤其是关于乌苏里江华俄两岸所有标桩皆须换新之观点,兹认为确有不实之处,不可尽信。俄方希望将乌苏里江航路标志工程列入 1925 年协议之中,但此既为新提议,且重要程度与河道疏浚工程相当,那么且比索夫先生就应于 1924 年在向莫斯科方面呈交预算之前提前正式通知华方,亦可照疏浚工程处理办法于协议中注明,关于乌苏里江航路标志工程,"如有需要,则将另行起草一份协议,重新列明各项细则"(参阅瑷珲关第 144 号呈附件 1 附录 3)。

对于俄方当下计划的任何大型工事,中国政府都应请专业人员进行监督审核。本署已向道尹说明,华方若欲在技术方面发表权威意见,首先就是需要派遣航务专门顾问前往乌苏里江进行巡查,否则将无法合理判断乌苏里江航路标志工程有无必要。迄今为止,华方一直未同意该项工事,因为一旦同意且比索夫先生之提议,允许先开展工作,后讨论费用,那么俄阿穆尔水道局势必会将工程范围扩大,并如从前一般迫使华方支付超额预算。

6. 本署已于瑷珲关第 218 号呈中说明,若继续按照半价税率征收江捐,实难以负担目前各项开支,应当按全价税率征收。然而,该建议一经提出,商会和航业公司代表即表示抗议,认为在贸易不景气的情况下,更应降低税率,反对海关加征关税,并称为维持税收,省政府已向他们施加了太多的经济负担和压力。起初道尹因害怕失去民心,反对提高税率,认为此举不切实际,但在本署将此事呈报贵署后不久,其便将此事呈报省长,并于数日后告知本署,其认为按全价税率征税应是明智之举,其在此事上与本署立场一致,且已获得特权可驳回任何的抗议。

当再次提及这个问题时,商会坚称,除所有必要开支外,该地区所承担的黑龙江航路标志维护费用不应超出其支付能力,若还需任何资金,应当向经济相对充裕的政府索取。道尹回复称,黑龙江省长受奉天当局的指令,已将承担黑龙江航路标志维护费用的重任强行施加给了瑷珲关区。商会在发现道尹不愿再从当地利益角度出发来看待此事之后,便做出了让步,同意以全价税率缴纳江捐,但建议,航运季期间仍按半价税率,另外一半在航运季结束之后再向海关缴纳，如此则可以保证多方的利益。本署认为该提议极不合理，认为商人应在申报货物时，向海关以全价税率完成对江捐的缴纳，商会最终予以接受。全价税率已于1925年6月9日开始实施。

7. 1924年江捐税收总计17291银圆，1923年为23769银圆，1922年为31137银圆。1925年1月1日至7月31日期间，共征得江捐9381.97银圆，其中5917.85银圆已用来支付1924年应付之款（参阅附录1）。今年若想征得20000银圆以上的江捐，就只能寄希望于贸易复苏了。

如本署此前所述，本口岸所征税收波动频率较大，已多次下跌，而且今后可能还会反复。通过上述数据，可以清楚地看到瑷珲关目前的财务状况，显然难以应对任何工事计划。有鉴于此，兹认为，如果决定接受苏维埃政府的意见，同意对边界河道航路标志进行全面彻底的整改，那么就必须对现行安排做出重大调整。目前，税收是向俄方支付摊款的唯一资金来源，但根据瑷珲关过去几年所征之数可以判定，对于俄方提出之100000卢布的预算（中国需承担50%），瑷珲关区绝无独立筹到足够资金的可能。本署认为，眼下唯一可行的办法就是以江捐账户作为担保向中国银行贷款或者向中央政府申请定期划拨财政补贴。

本署已向道尹建议，立即向省长和税务处说明，瑷珲关区无力筹集到全部所需经费，若向银行贷款之事无法获得批准，则应向北京方面正式申请年度补贴，毕竟中俄地方协议属于国际性质，政府应当承担部分费用。中国银行大黑河分行的经理已告知本署，海关若以江捐账户作为担保申请贷款，银行每月将收取12‰的贷款利息。

8. 然而，本署关于黑龙江航路标志维护费用属于国家支出的观点或许不会得到支持，对北京拨款的希望亦可能会落空。但目前情况特殊，仅靠地方之力，难以解脱困境，须有外力襄助，因此申请新政策亦合乎情理。面对当前之形势，中国航政委员会仅知晓其无能为力之处，毫无计策可施。俄国阿穆尔水道局于上月要求预付1925年航路标志工程部分摊款11000金卢布时，本署仅有5000金卢布（即5100银圆）可供支付。

9. 另外，关于易保罗先生担任航务专门顾问一事，最近争议不断，很多中国人开始抱怨，称海关从与俄方签订之协议中谋取利益。海关以每月400海关两的薪俸雇用一名洋籍航务专门顾问一事已然成为道尹公署外交顾问车席珍先生的困扰，其认为，即使该项需求确有必要，亦不应忽视实际情况而盲目做出决定，而且洋籍航务专门顾问的薪俸标准应当依海关的实际支付能力而定。若本署所得信息无误，车席珍先生已试图将黑龙江航路标志工作的管理权从海关分离出来并交由中国航政局；其坚持认为许多中国人无论从智力上还是受教育程度上来说,都足以担任航务专门顾问一职,而且亦会以经济角度为出发点,不遗余力地劝说道尹接受其意见。

10. 道尹告知,省长对聘用易保罗先生一事持批评态度,认为因此而支付的薪俸为江捐账户带来了额外的负担,而且每月 400 海关两的薪俸亦与时下经济状况不符,建议对易保罗先生的薪俸做出适当削减,或者目前仅支付其部分薪俸,余者待江捐资金积累起来后,再行结算。道尹表示已向省长说明,航务专门顾问一职乃由海关总税务司任命,其无法依照建议做出变动。

本署已向道尹解释:(1)海关总税务司所定薪俸乃以确保航务专门顾问合理的生活水平为基础,不应随每月收益变化而改变;(2)由海关征收江捐之益处之一是,当贸易萧条,形势危急之时,征收成本也会随之减少;(3)没有效率就谈不上真正意义的经济,海关总税务司在选择易保罗先生担任航务专门顾问时就已将效率问题纳入了考虑之内,从这个角度看,在航务专门顾问薪俸方面的投入,相当于一笔规避风险的保险金,因为从航务专门顾问的丰富经验来看,一切风险都将变成遥不可及的偶然事件;(4)削弱海关权力只会让俄方有机可乘,其若欲年取不当利益,甚至对中国航政委员会进行变相的敲诈勒索,也将变得轻而易举,不再继续任用易保罗先生为航务专门顾问将带来的损失不可小觑。

11. 本署发现,凡涉及黑龙江航务之事,道尹都比较倾向认同车席珍先生之观点,而且在数日前的谈话中,其坦言对任用航务专门顾问一事颇为反对,但并非针对此事本身,只是单纯出于对经费问题的考虑,并提出为挽救当前的局面,其打算引入一项新规定,即应由江捐账户来支付的航务专门顾问薪俸、10% 海关征税佣金及道尹公署 2000 银圆的年度经费,都需要等到将应向俄方支付的摊款结清之后再行支付。

道尹表示,其认同由海关负责监管俄阿穆尔水道局的工作是最为稳妥的,但亦打算向省长和税务处说明,海关应承担贸易萧条所带来的后果,以江捐账户的支付能力来决定海关各项支出的偿付事宜,比如航务专门顾问薪俸等支出就应于江捐资金充足时再行支付,并抱怨称,当前江捐税收已深受贸易波动的影响,为何还要首先保证航务专门顾问的薪俸,使其陷入不利之地,对此其希望本署向海关总税务司转达其不满。可以看出,道尹意在抱怨海关于江捐税收中获取了更大的利益,更不满意海关与航务专门顾问易保罗先生所订之合同。望贵署指示,是否需要照道尹之意对航务专门顾问的雇用合同做出修改。

航务专门顾问今年的薪俸一直由瑷珲关暂付款账支付,截至目前,共计支出 4386.20 银圆(即 400 海关两 ×7 个月 =2800 海关两,按 100 海关两 =156.65 银圆的汇率计算)。目前,除 10% 海关征税佣金和一些小额支出外,1925 年江捐账户中再无其他海关方面的支出。至于动用海关经费支付航务专门顾问薪俸一事，此前亦有先例，例如1923年航务专门顾问的全部薪俸便是由瑷珲关D账户预支，至1924年第一季度才予以偿付（参见第254笔/第一季度/D账户/费用项目6/传票字号4/和费用项目L/传票字号c）。

12. 若本署预测准确，今年江捐税收将不会超过20000银圆，但各项支出总计约达36334银圆，换言之，江捐账户可能面临16334银圆的赤字。

1925年总预算	金卢布	44268
中国摊款（预算的50%）	金卢布	22134
汇兑损失津贴	银圆	1700
道尹公署办公经费	银圆	2000
航务专门顾问办事处办公经费	银圆	8500
10% 海关征税佣金	银圆	2000
1925年支出预算总计	银圆	36334
1925年预计江捐税收	银圆	20000
1925年江捐账户预计赤字	银圆	16334

13. 对于延迟呈交1925年预算一事，本署深表歉意。原承诺最晚于8月3日呈交，但因且比索夫先生直到本月12日才将俄方的相关预算送交航务专门顾问审核，而易保罗先生之前又因事前往奉天（3月25日出发），至7月25日才返回，故而呈交1925年预算一事有所延迟，兹再次致以深深的歉意。

您忠诚的仆人

贺智兰（R. F. C. Hedgeland）

瑷珲关税务司

瑷珲关致海关总税务司署第 230 号呈附录 1

黑龙江江捐账户
1924 年年度收支报表

1924 年		收入	传票号	金额			
				150 银圆		100 海关两	
月	日	1923 年账户余额		12581	24	8387	50
5	31	5 月江捐税收	第 255 笔／第二季度,账户 D,费用项目 H,传票字号 a	1853	74	1235	82
6	30	6 月江捐税收	第 255 笔／第二季度,账户 D,费用项目 H,传票字号 b	3520	96	2347	31
7	31	7 月江捐税收	第 256 笔／第二季度,账户 D,费用项目 H,传票字号 a	2081	34	1387	56
8	30	8 月江捐税收	第 256 笔／第二季度,账户 D,费用项目 H,传票字 b	3268	19	2178	79
9	30	9 月江捐税收	第 256 笔／第二季度,账户 D,费用项目 H,传票字号 c	3714	27	2476	18
10	31	10 月江捐税收	第 257 笔／第四季度,账户 D,费用项目 H,传票字号 a	2585	50	1723	67
11	29	11 月江捐税收	第 257 笔／第四季度,账户 D,费用项目 H,传票字号 b	267	25	178	17
		1924 年江捐税收总计		29872	49	19915	00
		记入 1925 年江捐账户之金额		225	41	150	27
		总计		30097	90	20065	27

1924 年		支出	传票号	金额			
月	日			150 银圆		100 海关两	
1	25	1 月航务专门顾问薪俸	第 254 笔/第一季度,账户 D,费用项目 b,传票字号 9	562	50	375	00
1	25	1 月支付航务专门顾问薪俸汇兑损失	第 254 笔/第一季度,账户 D,费用项目 b,传票字号 10	24	94	16	63
2	25	2 月航务专门顾问薪俸	第 254 笔/第一季度,账户 D,费用项目 b,传票字号 16	562	50	375	00
2	25	2 月支付航务专门顾问薪俸汇兑损失	第 254 笔/第一季度,账户 D,费用项目 b,传票字号 17	24	94	16	62
3	7	预付俄阿穆尔水道局款项	第 254 笔/第一季度,账户 D,费用项目 b,传票字号 21	2000	00	1333	34
3	25	3 月航务专门顾问薪俸	第 254 笔/第一季度,账户 D,费用项目 b,传票字号 22	562	50	375	00
3	25	3 月支付航务专门顾问薪俸汇兑损失	第 254 笔/第一季度,账户 D,费用项目 b,传票字号 23	24	93	16	62
3	29	第一季度支付航务专门顾问薪柴费的 2/3	第 254 笔/第一季度,账户 D,费用项目 b,传票号 24	50	40	33	60
4	25	4 月航务专门顾问薪俸	第 255 笔/第二季度,账户 D,费用项目 b,传票字号 1	562	50	375	00
4	25	4 月支付航务专门顾问薪俸汇兑损失	第 255 笔/第二季度,账户 D,费用项目 b,传票字号 2	24	94	16	62
4	29	支付 1924 年 4 月航务专门顾问薪柴费的 2/3	第 255 笔/第二季度,账户 D,费用项目 b,传票字号 3	9	80	6	54
5	26	5 月航务专门顾问薪俸	第第 255 笔/二季度,账户 D,费用项目 b,传票字号 4	562	50	375	00
5	26	15 月支付航务专门顾问薪俸汇兑损失	第 255 笔/第二季度,账户 D,费用项目 b,传票字号 5	24	94	16	63
5	30	移除大黑河港口礁石	第 255 笔/第二季度,账户 D,费用项目 b,传票字号 6	4	60	3	06
5	31	5 月江捐税收扣除 10% 海关征税佣金	第 255 笔/第二季度,账户 D,费用项目 b,传票字号 7	185	37	123	58

续表

1924 年		支出	传票号	金额			
月	日			150 银圆		100 海关两	
6	14	航务专门顾问办事处信纸费用	第 255 笔/第二季度,账户 D,费用项目 b,传票字号 9	17	10	11	40
6	19	预付俄阿穆尔水道局款项	第 255 笔/第二季度,账户 D,费用项目 b,传票字号 10	3500	00	2333	33
6	25	6 月航务专门顾问薪俸	第 255 笔/第二季度,账户 D,费用项目 b,传票字号 11	562	50	375	00
6	25	6 月支付航务专门顾问薪俸汇兑损失	第 255 笔/第二季度,账户 D,费用项目 b,传票字号 12	24	94	16	63
6	30	三姓浅滩水深电报费	第 255 笔/第二季度,账户 D,费用项目 b,传票字号 13	1	53	1	02
6	30	渡船和马车租金	第 255 笔/第二季度,账户 D,费用项目 b,传票字号 14	18	00	12	00
7	15	6 月江捐税收扣除 10% 海关征税佣金	第 256 笔/第三季度,账户 D,费用项目 b,传票字号 1	352	10	234	73
7	26	巡查航路标志旅费	第 256 笔/第三季度,账户 D,费用项目 b,传票字号 3	104	50	69	66
7	26	第一次调查"吉阳"(Chi Yang)号轮船事故的旅费	第 256 笔/第三季度,账户 D,费用项目 b,传票字号 4	7	80	5	20
7	26	第二次调查"吉阳"号轮船事故的旅费	第 256 笔/第三季度,账户 D,费用项目 b,传票字号 5	15	00	10	00
7	28	7 月航务专门顾问薪俸	第 256 笔/第三季度,账户 D,费用项目 b,传票字号 6	562	50	375	00
7	28	7 月支付航务专门顾问薪俸汇兑损失	第 256 笔/第三季度,账户 D,费用项目 b,传票字号 7	24	93	16	62
7	31	7 月江捐税收扣除 10% 海关征税佣金	第 256 笔/第三季度,账户 D,费用项目 b,传票字号 8	208	13	138	76
8	2	预付俄阿穆尔水道局款项	第 256 笔/第三季度,账户 D,费用项目 b,传票字号 9	3498	00	2332	00

续表

1924 年		支出	传票号	金额			
月	日			150 银圆		100 海关两	
8	27	8月航务专门顾问薪俸	第256笔/第三季度,账户D,费用项目 b,传票字号 12	562	50	375	00
8	27	8月支付航务专门顾问薪俸汇兑损失	第256笔/第三季度,账户D,费用项目 b,传票字号 13	24	94	16	63
8	30	大黑河河滩筑堤	第256笔/第三季度,账户D,费用项目 b,传票字号 15	244	20	162	80
8	30	8月江捐税收扣除10%海关征税佣金	第256笔/第三季度,账户D,费用项目 b,传票字号 16	326	82	217	88
9	27	9月航务专门顾问薪俸	第256笔/第三季度,账户D,费用项目 b,传票字号 17	581	25	387	50
9	27	9月支付航务专门顾问薪俸汇兑损失	第256笔/第三季度,账户D,费用项目 b,传票字号 18	25	77	17	18
9	30	巡查航路标志旅费	第256笔/第三季度,账户D,费用项目 b,传票字号 19	131	30	87	54
9	30	航务专门顾问办事处第三季度办公经费	第256笔/第三季度,账户D,费用项目 b,传票字号 20	16	00	10	66
10	13	9月江捐税收扣除10%海关征税佣金	第257笔/第四季度,账户D,费用项目 b,传票字号 1	371	43	247	62
10	17	预付俄阿穆尔水道局款项	第257笔/第四季度,账户D,费用项目 b,传票字号 2	3165	00	2110	00
10	25	10月航务专门顾问薪俸	第257笔/第四季度,账户D,费用项目 b,传票字号 3	600	00	400	00
10	25	10月支付航务专门顾问份薪俸汇兑损失	第257笔/第四季度,账户D,费用项目 b,传票字号 4	26	60	17	74
10	31	检查"瑷珲"号轮船的旅费	第257笔/第四季度,账户D,费用项目 b,传票字号 5	7	00	4	67
10	31	支付10月协助航务专门顾问的酬金	第257笔/第四季度,账户D,费用项目 b,传票字号 6	14	00	9	33

续表

1924 年		支出	传票号	金额			
月	日			150 银圆		100 海关两	
11	7	10 月江捐税收扣除 10% 海关征税佣金	第 257 笔／第四季度，账户 D，费用项目 b，传票字号 7	258	55	172	37
11	14	预付俄阿穆尔水道局款项	第 257 笔／第四季度，账户 D，费用项目 b，传票字号 8	2325	00	1550	00
11	22	航务专门顾问办事处信纸费用	第 257 笔／第四季度，账户 D，费用项目 b，传票字号 9	15	00	10	00
11	25	11 月航务专门顾问薪俸	第 257 笔／第四季度，账户 D，费用项目 b，传票字号 10	600	00	400	00
11	25	11 月支付航务专门顾问薪俸汇兑损失	第 257 笔／第四季度，账户 D，费用项目 b，传票字号 11	26	60	17	73
11	29	支付 11 月协助航务专门顾问的酬金	第 257 笔／第四季度，账户 D，费用项目 b，传票字号 12	25	00	16	67
11	29	11 月江捐税收扣除 10% 海关征税佣金	第 257 笔／第四季度，账户 D，费用项目 b，传票字号 13	26	73	17	82
12	24	12 月航务专门顾问薪俸	第 257 笔／第四季度，账户 D，费用项目 b，传票字号 14	600	00	400	00
12	24	12 月支付航务专门顾问薪俸汇兑损失	第 257 笔／第四季度，账户 D，费用项目 b，传票字号 15	26	60	17	73
12	27	第四季度支付航务专门顾问薪柴费的 2/3	第 257 笔／第四季度，账户 D，费用项目 b，传票字号 16	36	00	24	00
12	30	支付 12 月协助航务专门顾问的酬金	第 257 笔／第四季度，账户 D，费用项目 b，传票字号 17	27	00	18	00
12	30	航务专门顾问办事处第四季度办公经费	第 257 笔／第四季度，账户 D，费用项目 b，传票字号 18	32	37	21	58
1925 年							
1	17	1924 年道尹公署办公经费	第 258 笔／第一季度，账户 D，费用项目 b，传票字号 1	2000	00	1333	33

续表

1924 年		支出	传票号	金额			
月	日			150 银圆		100 海关两	
3	20	三姓浅滩水深电报费	第258笔/第一季度,账户D,费用项目 b,传票字号 2	26	66	17	77
3	20	1924 年浮标所用煤油费	第258笔/第一季度,账户D,费用项目 b,传票字号 3	10	36	6	91
5	15	结付俄阿穆尔水道局尾款	第259笔/第二季度,账户D,费用项目 b,传票字号 1	3880	83	2587	22
		总计：		30097	90	20065	27

制表：叶元章　三等帮办后班

兹证明,报表正确无误。

贺智兰　瑷珲关税务司

1925 年 8 月 4—13 日,瑷珲关 / 大黑河

瑷珲关致海关总税务司署第 230 号呈附录 2

黑龙江江捐账户

（中国黑龙江航政委员会）

1924 年年度收支报表

收入：[150 银圆 = 100 海关两]

1. 1923 年江捐账户余额	12581.24	8387.50
2. 1924 年黑龙江江捐税收	17291.25	11527.50
3. 记入 1925 年江捐账户之金额	225.41	150.27
总计	30097.90	20065.27

支出

1. 江捐税收扣除 10% 瑷珲关海关征税佣金	1729.13	1152.76
2. 中国航政委员会支出		
（1）航务专门顾问办事处	7999.94	5333.29
（2）道尹公署	2000.00	1333.33
中国航政委员会支出总计	9999.94	6666.62
3. 黑龙江边界河道航路标志维护费用	18368.83	12245.89
2、3 项支出总计	28368.77	18912.51
总计	30097.90	20065.27

瑷珲关致海关总税务司署第 230 号呈附录 2

根据《1923/1924 年临时地方工程协议》（附录 2 第 15 条），俄阿穆尔水道局用于维护黑龙江边界河道航路标志支出的 50% 由中国黑龙江航政委员会承担。1924 年俄阿穆尔水道局支出共计 35334.87 金卢布，中国黑龙江航政委员会支付 17667.43 金卢布，明细如下。

日期	银圆	汇率	金卢布
1924 年			
3 月 7 日	2000.00	机动汇率	1800.00
6 月 19 日	3500.00	机动汇率	3281.25
8 月 2 日	3498.00	机动汇率	3300.00
10 月 17 日	3165.00	机动汇率	3000.00
11 月 14 日	2325.00	机动汇率	2500.00
1925 年			
5 月 15 日	3880.83	机动汇率	3786.18
	18368.83		17667.43

1924 年关于黑龙江边界河道航路标志的联合维护工程，中国航政委员会已向俄阿穆尔水道局履行应尽义务。

制表：叶元章　三等帮办后班
兹证明，报表正确无误。
贺智兰　瑷珲关税务司
1925 年 8 月 4 日，瑷珲关 / 大黑河

瑷珲关致海关总税务司署第 230 号呈附录 3

1924 年航务专门顾问办事处支出报表

（1）本年度支出	银圆	海关两
1924 年航务专门顾问薪俸	6881.25	4587.50
支付航务专门顾问薪俸汇兑损失	305.07	203.38
支付 1924 年航务专门顾问薪柴费的 2/3	96.20	64.14
旅费	265.60	177.07
航务专门顾问办事处其他职员薪俸	66.00	44.00
信纸费及杂费	98.47	65.64
总计	7712.59	5141.73
（2）维护当地航路标志支出		
移除大黑河港口礁石	4.60	3.06
用于浮标的煤油	10.36	6.91
三姓浅滩水深电报	28019	18.79
大黑河前滩的筑堤费用	244.20	162.80
总计	287.35	191.56
（1）（2）两项总计	7999.94	5333.29

制表：叶元章　三等帮办后班

兹证明,报表正确无误。

贺智兰　瑷珲关税务司

1925 年 8 月 4 日,瑷珲关 / 大黑河

瑷珲关致海关总税务司署第 230 号呈附录 4

关于将《1923/1924 年临时地方工程协议》展期至 1925 年（自 1924 年 12 月 1 日至 1925 年 11 月 30 日）的声明译本

中华民国黑河道尹兼任瑷珲关交涉司宋文郁先生与俄阿穆尔水道局督办且比索夫先生联合发表声明，签订于中华民国十二年（1923）的有关黑龙江边界河道航务的《临时地方工程协议》及其附件将持续有效，唯需要另议的附件 3 除外；双方务必谨守上述协议及其附件的规定，不得违背。上述协议及其附件的有效期不会超过一年，因中俄会议即将召开，如果双方能够就边界河道航务问题达成共识，则上述协议及其附件将于今年 12 月 1 日（1925 年 12 月 1 日）前废止；但即使双方未能在中俄会议上达成共识，也应讨论出一项临时的地方安排。今年用于维护航路标志的实际支出不得超出 44268 金卢布这一预算额。

宋文郁先生与且比索夫先生分别在声明书上用中文和俄文签字并予盖章。该声明书一式两份，双方各持一份，以昭信守。

中华民国十四年五月十八日（1925 年 5 月 18 日）订于大黑河。

（签字和盖章）宋文郁

（签字和盖章）且比索夫

1925 年 8 月 4 日，瑷珲关

瑷珲关致海关总税务司署第 230 号呈附录 5

1925 年预算报表

　　黑龙江边界河道自波克罗夫卡（Pokrovka）至嘎杂克维池（Kasakevich）河段，全长 1842 千米，共划分为五个地区（仅适用于 1924 年 12 月 1 日至 1925 年 11 月 30 日期间），该河段航路标志维护费用预算由俄阿穆尔水道局拟订，航务专门顾问易保罗先生负责核查。明细列下。

　　一、俄阿穆尔水道局支出预算：

职员薪俸（12 个月）	每月薪俸	总计
	金卢布	金卢布
督办（工程师）	200.00	2400.00
财务科科长	140.00	1680.00
财务科司账	42.00	504.00
财务科文员	29.80	357.60
路政建设科科长	130.00	1560.00
路政建设科打字员	33.00	396.00
航路标志股测量师	85.70	1028.40
航路标志股二等测量师	51.00	612.00
水文测量统计科测量师	51.00	612.00
总计		9150.00

　　二、黑龙江航道自波克罗夫卡至嘎杂克维池河段，共计 1842 千米，分为以下五个地区。

　　1. 加林达（Djalinda）地区：长 323 千米；设立两处水深信号站，贝托诺瓦（Beitonovo）站和派米津诺（Permikino）站；5 处设立灯塔浅滩。

　　2. 切尔纳耶瓦（Cherniaeva）地区：长 345 千米；设立一处水深信号站，切尔纳耶瓦上游站；一处通行信号站察尕岩（Tsagayan）站；9 处设立灯塔浅滩。

　　3. 布拉戈维申斯克（Blagovestchensk，即海兰泡）地区：长 395 千米；设立两处水深信号站马尔科沃（Markova）站和康斯坦丁诺瓦（Konstantinova）站；13 处设立灯塔浅滩。

　　4. 因诺肯季瓦（Innokentieva）地区：长 399 千米；设立一处水深信号站，波亚尔科沃（Poyarkova）站；6 处设立灯塔浅滩。

5.叶卡捷琳堡—尼科利斯克（Ekaterino-Nikolsk）地区：长 380 千米；设立一处水深信号站，索伊斯（Soyus）站；6 处设立灯塔的浅滩。

注：下表中括号内之数字表示各地区水深信号站或通行信号站之数量。

地区职员薪俸	地区 I		地区 II		地区 III		地区 IV		地区 V	
	卢布	戈比	卢布	戈比	卢布	戈比	卢布	戈比	卢布	戈比
地区测量师 4 名：（55.96×6+73.69×6）	795	84	795	84			795	84	795	84
地区测量师 1 名：（65.70×6+82.13×6）					886	98				
文员 5 名：（33.45×8）	267	60	267	60	267	60	267	60	267	60
工头 5 名：（37.50×6+48.75×6）	517	50	517	50	517	50	517	50	517	50
差童 4 名：（25.20×12）	302	40	302	40			302	40	302	40
水深信号站水手每站 2 名：（2×28/19×5）	（2）563	80	（1）281	90	（2）563	80	（1）281	90	（1）281	90
每站水手：（25/25×6）			302	50						
水深信号站的设立与运营	71	72	35	86	71	72	35	86	35	86
通行信号站的设立与运营			41	50						
标桩的更换、修理及维护（明细参见下表）	2039	74	1824	78	1852	45	1629	99	1579	04
房屋维修费	150	00	150	00	150	00	175	00	175	00
邮费、电报费、信纸费及杂项	150	00	150	00	150	00	150	00	150	00
供暖费	70	00	70	00	70	00	70	00	70	00
电费	20	00	20	00	20	00	20	00	20	00
于浅滩设立灯塔：需更夫 39 名，23.44 来自 2 ◎ 11（译者案：原文如此）需 5 个月 材料费用	（5）351 129	60 62	（9）539 189	12 87	（13）879 316	00 79	（6）375 125	04 86	（6）421 157	92 19
总计	5429	82	5488	87	5745	84	4745	99	4774	25

汇总

项　　目	金卢布
地区Ⅰ：加林达地区	5429.82
地区Ⅱ：切尔纳耶瓦（Chernayeva）地区	5488.87
地区Ⅲ：布拉戈维申斯克地区	5745.84
地区Ⅳ：因诺肯季瓦地区	4745.99
地区Ⅴ：叶卡捷琳堡—尼科利斯克地区	4774.25
5% 医疗护理费	709.76
移除礁石费	400.00
折旧费	2073.47
旅费/津贴	350.00
5个地区支出总计	29718.00

俄方总支出预算

项　　目	金卢布
1.边境各地区支出	29718.00
2.俄阿穆尔水道局支出	9150.00
3.汽艇（用于巡查及航路标志维护）	5400.00
总计	44268.00
1925年华方摊款（俄方总支出预算的50%）	22134.00

5个地区标桩与轮船维护明细表

1924年11月1日统计数量	数量	价格（卢布）	总计（卢布）
江式：信标	1288		
江式：盾形标桩	183		
海式：角锥形标桩	1726		
海式：盾形标桩	218		
新立标桩			
江式：信标	113	10.00	1130.00

1924 年 11 月 1 日统计数量	数量	价格（卢布）	总计（卢布）
江式：盾形标桩	197	2.52	516.69
海式：角锥形标桩	14	3.27	196.00
海式：盾形标桩	18	14.00	107.10
标杆	2	5.95	51.59
标杆（装置警笛）	1		7.21
总计			2008.59
维修标桩			
江式：信标	1194	1.12	1337.28
江式：盾形标桩	1555	0.10	155.50
信标涂漆	598	2.06	1231.88
盾形标桩涂漆	1555	0.37	575.35
立桩	433	1.10	476.30
海式：角锥性标桩	172	1.55	265.05
盾形标桩涂漆	179	2.17	388.43
轻度维修			279.94
总计			4709.73
维修划艇			
快艇	5	100.00	500.00
船载小艇	5	12.50	62.50
巡查艇	5	30.00	150.00
巡役艇	5	7.00	35.00
总计			747.50
维修水手设备（3 个月）			
设备	10	33.58	1007.40
总计			8925.00
点亮标桩			
煤油（普特）	159.05	2.60	413.53
灯芯 14mm（俄尺）	273.00	0.30	81.90
玻璃灯罩	59.00	0.15	8.85

1924 年 11 月 1 日统计数量	数量	价格（卢布）	总计（卢布）
刷子	39.00	0.25	9.75
煤油灯	45.00	1.00	45.00
火柴（盒）	1482.00	0.15	22.23
白布条（俄尺）	117.00	0.45	52.65
肥皂（磅）	35.00	0.21	7.35
小船维修	39.00	7.13	278.07
总计			919.33

中国海关（瑷珲关）支出

名目	银圆
航务专门顾问薪俸：1 年,每月 400.00 海关两 总计 6266.00 海关两 根据当地薪俸兑换汇率（100 海关两 =156.65 银圆）,即为	7519.20
旅费	500.00
信纸费	50.00
邮费与电报费	100.00
薪柴费	75.00
杂项与意外支出	255.80
中国海关支出总计	8500.00
道尹公署支出	2000.00
总计	10500.00

易保罗

黑龙江航务专门顾问

1925 年 8 月 4 日,瑷珲关

瑷珲关致海关总税务司署第 230 号呈附录 6

俄阿穆尔水道局督办且比索夫（Chebisheff）致黑河道尹函译本

俄阿穆尔水道局第 1996 号函

1925 年 3 月 24 日，布拉戈维申斯克

俄阿穆尔水道局已照俄阿穆尔国家水运局与中华民国黑河道尹所签协议规定，如期完成 1924 年黑龙江边界河道自波克罗夫卡至嘎杂克维池河段的航路标志维护工程，1923 年和 1924 年的维护费用共计 55000 金卢布，其中 1923 年为 19250 卢布，1924 年为 35750 卢布，均未超出预算额。

为保证航运安全，1925 年的航路标志维护工作还须继续，希望可将航路标志恢复到大革命之前的状态。因此，除黑龙江自波克罗夫卡至嘎杂克维池河段外，1925 年的航路标志维护工程还将扩至乌苏里江自伊曼至哈巴罗夫斯克（Habarovsk，即伯力）河段，两项工程预计支出 50000 金卢布，其中黑龙江河道为 44268 卢布，乌苏里江河道为 5732 卢布。

中俄双方于 1923 年 10 月 28 日所签署的《1923/1924 年临时地方工程协议》已于 1924 年 11 月 30 日失效。考虑到中国航运仍需依赖边界河道的航路标志，中俄双方仍须共同负责航路标志维护事宜，阿穆尔水道局认为有必要向道尹提出续签过去两年里中俄双方所签订的各项有关协议，双方各自承担一半的黑龙江与乌苏里江航路标志的维护费用。

须指出，1925 年预算中并未包括疏浚河道的费用，因该项工作有无必要需要取决于黑龙江流域的具体情况，目前尚无法确定，因此填补和疏浚河道的费用并未列入 1925 年黑龙江与乌苏里江航路标志工程的预算之中。

但俄阿穆尔水道局已计划于 1926 年开展黑龙江上游和乌苏里江的河道疏浚工作，预计明年用于黑龙江、乌苏里江、嘎杂克维池水道及兴凯湖的航路标志维护、照明等费用，共需 100000 金卢布。

鉴于航运季即将到来，请道尹尽快决定续签 1925 年相关协议之事。

（签字）且比索夫

俄阿穆尔水道局督办（工程师）

翻译人：王德懋　二等同文供事中班

瑷珲关致海关总税务司署第 230 号呈附录 7

俄阿穆尔水道局督办且比索夫致黑河道尹函译本

俄阿穆尔水道局

1925 年 4 月 18 日,布拉戈维申斯克

　　根据 1925 年 3 月 24 日俄阿穆尔水道局第 1996 号函,特此声明,为维护黑龙江边界河道自波克罗夫卡至嘎杂克维池河段的航路标志,俄阿穆尔水道局望续签《1923/1924 年临时地方工程协议》,同时保留对第 1996 号函随附预算的修订权利(扩大工程范围及增加相关预算)。

　　考虑到扩大的工程范围后,华方或将因江捐税收不足而难以支付相应摊款,俄阿穆尔水道局建议中国航政委员会仍照去年的付款办法来支付 1925 年摊款,具体付款事项应于中俄会议结束之前安排妥当。

　　为改善航运状况,实有必要于乌苏里江上开展航路标志维护工作,该项工作虽未能列入 1924 年协议之中,但其重要性不可忽视。如今航运季将至,该问题不可拖至中俄会议结束之后。请道尹批准俄国工人过境,以负责乌苏里江边界河道中国一侧的航路标志维护工作,并签发所需护照。至于双方各自需要承担的费用,可留待中俄会议上决定。

　　此外,望告知中俄黑龙江水道委员会何时可召开会议,以结算 1924 账目并讨论 1925 续签协议问题。

(签字)且比索夫

俄阿穆尔水道局督办(工程师)

(签字)(字迹模糊)

俄阿穆尔水道局文案

翻译:王德懋　二等同文供事中班

瑷珲关致海关总税务司署第 230 号呈附录 8

瑷珲关税务司致黑河道尹第 144 号信函

（1925 年 5 月 15 日）

译本

俄阿穆尔水道局最新提出的预算较航务专门顾问所定预算高出 4268 金卢布，航务专门顾问发来电报建议与俄方商议将预算定为 42000 金卢布，但道尹若同意，44268 金卢布的预算亦可应允。2000 多金卢布并非大数目，若因此而引发争端实在不值，望得知道尹对于此事之看法。

黑河道尹致瑷珲关税务司第 196 号信函

（1925 年 5 月 16 日）

译本

赞同瑷珲关税务司之观点，请开始筹备 1925 年预算，总计 44268 金卢布（参见 1925 年 5 月非紧急中文往来函摘由簿，第 4 号）。

翻译： 贺智兰　瑷珲关税务司

瑷珲关致海关总税务司署第 230 号呈附录 9

黑河道尹致瑷珲关税务司第 200 号信函

（1925 年 5 月 28 日）

译本

黑河商会近日来函称：

"关于江捐税收不足，难以应对支出，省长决定提高税率以增加收入一事，商会深知道尹已尽力寻找他法，奈何无果，只得如此。商会经多番讨论，虽仍未达成任何决定性意见，但为解当前困境，现提议：

（1）暂由商会负责征收另外半数税率之江捐；

（2）请道尹告知海关，今后凡商人欲进出口货物者，无论华籍或洋籍，均先向商会申请执照，再凭此执照至海关报明查验，并按照半价税率缴纳江捐；商会将凭此执照向商人征收另外半数税率之江捐，但征收时会平均分配纳税金额，力求减少纠纷；

（3）若道尹赞成上述提议，商会将与海关协商该执照的性质问题。

上述建议已由商会一致通过，待道尹回复后，便可即刻落实。"

请税务司就上述提议的可行性给出意见，以便道尹做出下一步指示。

参见 1925 年 5 月 10 日非紧急中文往来函摘由簿第 6 号。

瑷珲关税务司致黑河道尹第 147 号信函

（1925 年 6 月 2 日）

译本

随着贸易状况的不断下滑，货物交易数量也在前所未有地锐减，江捐税收已不足以支付维护航路标志的费用。商会主动提出负责尚缺的部分，以帮助本地区渡过难关，此举着实具有模范带头作用，但实际情况比较复杂，该提议恐怕难以付诸实践。

目前，瑷珲口岸下游运输之货物皆至（哈尔滨关）拉哈苏苏分关缴纳江捐，商会将无法实现对此类货物征收江捐，如此一来，商人所受待遇便不再均等。

此外，按照规定，华洋商人均须缴纳江捐，但商会方面仅能保证向华籍商人征收另外半数之江捐,对洋籍商人必然会束手无策,如此一来,则相当于华籍商人独自承受额外税款负担。

再者,关于让进出口货物之商人至商会申请特殊执照之建议,此举势必会为各方带来极大不便,难以执行。

征收江捐只是为了支付维护航路标志的费用,提高税率亦只是因以目前的半价税率征收江捐,难以应对支出需求,若日后贸易复苏,按照半价税率征收江捐便可满足支出需求,则会恢复以前的办法,按照全价税率征收江捐只是暂时之策。

瑷珲关区商人的实际利润有多么丰厚,尽人皆知;边界河道维护工作既为地方要事,相信商人必会愿意施以援手。

黑河道尹致税务司第 202 号信函

（1925 年 6 月 8 日）

译本

已将税务司关于暂以全价税率征收江捐,待贸易复苏后再恢复半价税率之提议告知商会,商会经过商议后决定接受。

参见 1925 年 6 月非紧急中文往来函摘由簿第 1 号。

翻译: 贺智兰　瑷珲关税务司

关于瑷珲关致海关总税务司署第 230 号呈的意见

1925 年 8 月 4 日瑷珲关致海关总税务司署第 230 号呈收悉：

"黑龙江航务：呈送黑龙江江捐账户 1924 年年度收支报表、中国航政委员会 1924 年年度收支报表、1924 年航务专门顾问办事处支出报表及 1925 年预算报表；汇报 1925 年协议进展；省长对航务专门顾问任用事持否定态度，道尹对此亦有相应意见；因缺少资金，提议按照全价税率征收江捐，或以黑龙江江捐账户为担保向中国银行贷款；汇报俄阿穆尔水道局关于松阿察河与乌苏里江航路标志工程的意见以及增加资金投入的要求。"

巡工司经研究无意见，特此函复。

（签字）奚理满（H. E. Hillman）

上海巡工事务局巡工司

1925 年 8 月 26 日

该抄件内容真实有效，特此证明。

录事：劳德迩（H. G. Lowder）监事员

19. 1926 年《黑龙江航路标志协议》

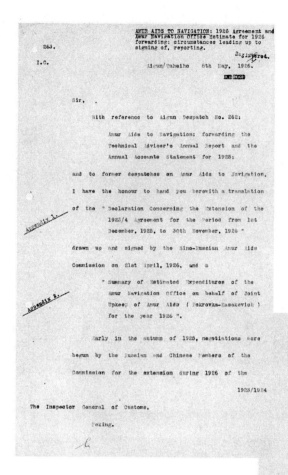

AMUR AIDS TO NAVIGATION: 1926 Agreement and Amur Navigation Office Estimate for 1926 forwarding; circumstances leading up to signing of, reporting.

263.

Registered.

I.G.

Aigun/Taheiho 8th May, 1926.

DESPATCH

Sir,

With reference to Aigun Despatch No. 262:

Amur Aids to Navigation: forwarding the Technical Adviser's Annual Report and the Annual Accounts Statement for 1925;

and to former despatches on Amur Aids to Navigation, I have the honour to hand you herewith a translation of the " Declaration Concerning the Extension of the 1923/4 Agreement for the Period from 1st December, 1925, to 30th November, 1926 " drawn up and signed by the Sino-Russian Amur Aids Commission on 21st April, 1926, and a

Appendix 1.

Appendix 2.

" Summary of Estimated Expenditures of the Amur Navigation Office on behalf of Joint Upkeep of Amur Aids (Pokrovka-Kasakevich) for the year 1926 ".

Early in the autumn of 1925, negotiations were begun by the Russian and Chinese Members of the Commission for the extension during 1926 of the 1923/1924

The Inspector General of Customs,

Peking.

1923/1924 Agreement, each side having notified the other that there were no objections to such extension. The Russian Amur Navigation Office in submitting its statement of plans of Aids work for the coming season placed before the Commission a very comprehensive and extensive programme. I beg to refer you to the Technical Adviser's Annual Report for 1925 (Aigun Despatch No. 262) for a detailed description of the proposals presented, which were:

(1) Aids on Kasakevich Waterway between Amur and Ussuri Rivers.
(2) Aids on the Ussuri as far as Hulin.
(3) Aids on the Ussuri beyond Hulin, on Sungacha River, and Lake Hanka.
(4) Dredgework on the Upper Amur above Taheiho.
(5) Rock removal on the Argun River.
(6) The usual Aids work on the Amur as per 1925 Agreement.

In considering the above proposals, the Chinese Members of the Commission found themselves faced with a situation presenting difficulties different from those of previous years. Beginning with 1925, the Russian Authorities ceased collecting River Dues from Russian ships, the Russian portion of the money needed for

joint

joint upkeep of Aids on the Frontier Rivers between Russia and China being provided by appropriations from Moscow, which, it was reported, had granted Roubles 780,000 to the Amur Navigation Office to meet its 1926 Aids programme for Frontier Waters and Russian Inland Waters in the Amur Basin. With large funds at their disposal, the Russian Members of the Commission were prepared and eager to carry on Aids work on the Frontier Waters much more extensive than the actual necessities of either Russian or Chinese shipping as now existing seemed to demand, and certainly - if the work was to be carried out jointly as in former years - far beyond the financial resources at the call of the Chinese Commission Members, who, due to the smallness of the River Dues Collection in 1925, were faced with a deficit, had been forced to negotiate a loan ($20,000) from the Sungari River Dues Account, and had drawn a first instalment of $10,000 to meet its 1925 obligations. As the prospect of the 1926 River Dues Collection being sufficient to meet expenditures was very slender and

as

as there were no signs of financial aid being extended from provincial or national authorities, it became more than ever necessary rigidly to confine the Aids programme for 1926 only to such work as was absolutely necessary.

The Technical Adviser's opinions on the various projects of the Amur Navigation Office have already been placed on record in his Annual Report for 1925 and his views were accepted in drawing up the final programme mutually agreed upon. Aids work on the Ussuri above Hulin, on River Sungacha, and on Lake Hanka was dropped; also rock removal on the River Argun; as for dredging on the Upper Amur above Tsheiho with its estimated expenditure of Roubles 80,000 - obviously financially impossible for the Chinese side to consider at this time - the Russian Navigation Office forwarded an official request, as this work could not be jointly undertaken in 1926, that the Office be allowed to carry on the work at Russia's entire expense. Such permission being outside the powers of the Commission to grant, the request was

forwarded

forwarded by the Heiho Taoyin to the higher Chinese
Authorities for consideration. The 1926 Aids programme
was therefore confined to the usual Aids work on the
Amur as carried out in previous years, the original
estimate - Roubles 75,296 - having been reduced to Roubles
60,031 which is Roubles 15,763 more than the 1925
estimate - the increase being largely due to Russian
national decrees increasing salaries to workmen -, and
to the restoration of Aids on the Kasakevich Waterway
and on the Ussuri River as far as Hulin, the original
estimate for this work - Roubles 14,875 - having been
reduced to Roubles 9,298. In view of the increase
in Chinese shipping between the Sungari and Ussuri,
and the urgent needs of Aids work on this section
of the frontier rivers as reported by the Technical
Adviser, the Commission decided favourably to consider
this project in spite of the low financial resources
of the Chinese side provided the Kirin provincial
authorities gave their approval and no difficulties
arose over boundary demarcations, the Waterway being
a long standing subject of controversy between Manchuria
and

and Russia. The Kirin authorities themselves had
been sufficiently impressed with the need for Ussuri
Aids to overlook provincial differences and authorise
the Heiho Taoyin to represent them in discussions,
and had agreed to send a representative to look after
their interests prior to the signing of a new
Agreement. The inconvenience caused the Customs and
the Russian Amur Navigation Office by dating yearly
agreements from 1st December instead of from the
beginning of each year was also discussed and it was
agreed to draw up the 1926 Agreement for thirteen
months from 1st December, 1925, to 31st December, 1926.
Having completed all the negotiations, it was decided
to hold a final meeting during the first week in
March, dependent on the arrival of the Kirin
representative, and sign the 1926 document.

In the meantime, the Heiho Taoyin had departed
for Fengtien on leave of absence and at the end of
February an official intimation was received that he
had been transferred to Suilantao, Heilungkiang, those
secretaries most conversant with Amur Aids questions
also

also departing to his new post. The non-arrival of his successor, the appointment of the Aigun Magistrate as Officiating Taoyin, the appointment of a Commissioner of Customs at Aigun, and also the non-arrival of the Kirin representative, caused unexpected delays and difficulties, and considering all the circumstances it was decided to draw up an agreement for 12 months similar to that of 1925 leaving the question of Aids on the Kasakevich Waterway and Ussuri for a later settlement. The new Agreement as per append was signed by the parties concerned on 21st April, 1926.

I have the honour to be,

Sir,

Your obedient Servant,.

Asst.-in-Charge, temporarily.

Appendix No.1

Annex No.1   Copy.

Official Record of the Meeting of the local Sino-Russian Technical Commission, held at Taneiho.

" 21 " April 1926.

Representatives:

Substitute of the Heiho Taoyin and Diplomatic

Official in Aigun . . . Mr. Chang-Lin

First Diplomatic Adviser . . . Mr.Ch's-Hsi-Chen

Commissioner of Customs at Taneiho . Mr. Petterson

Technical Adviser on Amur Aids . . Mr. Ignatieff

Consul of U.S.S.R. at Taneiho . . Mr. Toropoff

Director of Amur Navigation Office . Mr. Dianoff

Assistant of Director of A.N.O.,Engineer . Mr. Chevisheff

Manager of Way Department, Engineer . Mr.Mihailoff

Matter discussed:

1. The Agreement concluded on the 28th of October,1923, between the Amur Government Water Transport and the Heiho Taoyin of the Great Chinese Republic, will continue to be in force for the next 1926 year.

Decision:

1. Taking into consideration that the provisional Agreement of 28 October, 1923, renewed to the 1st December 1925, loses its force because of the end of the term, the Commission decided to continue the Agreement to be in force for one year, i.e. from the 1st Dec. 1925 to the 1st December 1926: with all Annexes, excepting Annex 3, which will be agreed separately.

If during the present year the Sino-Russian Conference takes place, and a new Agreement regarding the mutual use of frontier waterways should be decided upon, and signed before the 1st Decemb. 1926,the present Agreement ceases to be operative from the moment of signature of the new Agreement.

Matter discussed:

2. Estimate on repairs to and upkeep of Aids in the limites of the frontier section of the Amur, during the navigation season of the year 1926.

Decision:

Decision:

2. To sanction the Estimate on repairs to and upkeep of Aids in
    the frontier section of the Amur, during the navigation season
    of 1926, for the sum of Roubles 60,031. The sum of expenses
    must not exceed the sum estimated for the present year.

Matter discussed:

3. Account List of the expenses for the last 1925 year.

Decision:

3. To sanction the Account List for the last 1925 year, for a
    sum of Roubles 44,267.05, and make a final payment to the time
    of signement of this Record.

Matter discussed:

4. Records to be made.

Decision:

4. Records of meetings must be written in Russian and Chinese,
    and 2 copies, both Chinese and Russian should be handed to
    each party.

    (Signed) Chang-Lin, Officiating Heiho Taoyin

                Ch'e - Hsi-chen, Adviser on Foreign Affairs.

                Shen-Ting-yun Secretary, Taoyin's Office.

    (Signed) A.N.Dianoff, Director of the Amur Government

                                    Navigation Office

                G.D.Toropoff, Consul of U*S.S.R. at Taheiho.

                G.E.Mihailoff, Manager of Ways Department, Amur

                                Government Navigation Office

                        (signed) C.M.Petterson

                        Assistant -in-Charge, temporarily.

CUSTOM HOUSE,

Aigun/Taheiho,8th May,1926.

Appendix No. 2.

SUMMARY OF ESTIMATED EXPENDITURES OF THE AMUR
NAVIGATION OFFICE ON BEHALF OF JOINT UPKEEP OF
AMUR AIDS (POKROVKA-KASAKEVICH) FOR THE YEAR 1926.

		Gold Roubles.
1.	Salaries to District employees	13,959.00
2.	.. .. Depth-Signal Station employees	2,730.00
3.	.. .. Traffic Station employees	386.00
4.	Opening & operating Depth-Signal Stations	350.00
5.	.. .. .. Traffic Stations	51.00
6.	Reerecting, repairing, & maintenance of beacons	11,836.00
7.	Lighting beacons	4,565.00
8.	Repairs to buildings	800.00
9.	Postage, Telegrams, Stationery, Sundries	750.00
10.	Heating	350.00
11.	Light	100.00
12.	Travelling Expenses and Allowances	350.00
13.	5% for Medical Attendance	2,214.00
14.	Depreciation	2,238.00
15.	Upkeep s.l. "Yuni Pioneer"	8,600.00
16.	Maintenance of Technical Section (Amur Navigation Office)	9,150.00
17.	Removal of rocks	400.00
18.	Unforeseen	1,502.00
	Total	60,031.00

Signatures:
Mr.Chebisheff, Director of Amur Navigation Office
Mr.Pedoroff, Manager of Ways Department
Mr.Lapteff, Director of Financial Division

Blagovestchensk,15th January,1926.

Checked with detailed Accounts &
Statements on record in this Office
& certified Correct:

                        P.Ignatieff

                    Technical Adviser on Amur
                        Aids to Navigation.

Technical Adviser's Office,

            Custom House.

Aigun/Taheiho, 8th May ,1926.

呈海关总税务司署 <u>263</u> 号文　　　　　　　瑷珲关 / 大黑河 1926 年 5 月 8 日

尊敬的海关总税务司（北京）：

根据此前黑龙江航务相关信函及瑷珲关第 262 号呈：

"黑龙江航务：呈送航务专门顾问 1925 年黑龙江航务年度报告及 1925 年黑龙江航路标志年度财务报表。"

特此呈交由中俄黑龙江航政委员会草拟并于 1926 年 4 月 21 日签署之关于将《1923/1924 年临时地方工程协议》展期至 1926 年（自 1925 年 12 月 1 日至 1926 年 11 月 30 日）的声明译本（附录 1），以及俄阿穆尔水道局 1926 年联合维护黑龙江边界河道自波克罗夫卡（Pokrovka）至嘎杂克维池（Kasakevich）河段的航路标志支出预算报表（附录 2）。

1925 年初秋，中俄黑龙江航路标志联合委员会双方委员开始就 1926 年续签《1923/1924 年临时地方工程协议》一事进行协商，双方对此事均无异议。俄阿穆尔水道局于 1925 年初便向中俄黑龙江航路标志联合委员会递交了 1926 年航路标志维护工作计划，此次计划所涉工程范围较广，具体内容参见航务专门顾问 1925 年黑龙江航务年度报告（随附于瑷珲关第 262 号呈），计划主要内容如下。

（1）嘎杂克维池水道（连接黑龙江与乌苏里江）上的航路标志重建工作；

（2）乌苏里江至虎林河段的航路标志重建工作；

（3）乌苏里江至虎林以外河段、松阿察河及兴凯湖的航路标志维护工作；

（4）黑龙江上游（大黑河以上）的河道疏浚工作；

（5）额尔古纳河的石块清理工作；

（6）1925 年协议所规定的黑龙江航路标志维护工作。

上述提议使中俄黑龙江航路标志联合委员会华方委员陷入了前所未有的困境。自 1925 年起，俄国政府便已停止向俄国轮船征收江捐，俄方所需的共同维护中俄边界河道航路标志的费用均由苏维埃政府拨给。据悉，苏维埃政府近日已批准为阿穆尔水道局拨款 780000 卢布，用于资助 1926 年黑龙江边界河道与俄国内河的航路标志维护工程。由于资金充足，俄方迫切希望扩大边界河道航路标志维护工作的原有规模，但此等规模显然已超出航路标志维护工作的实际需要，如此一来，华方所需摊付的费用自然也将远远超出目前的实际支付能力。由于 1925 年的江捐税收不足，华方有关部门已然面临着财务赤字的危机，之前就已向松花江江捐账户暂借了 20000 银圆，现首期款 10000 银圆已经取出，用于结付 1925 年所欠债款。鉴于 1926 年的江捐税收在平衡收支方面尚且力有不逮，而且也无任何迹象表明省政府或者国家有增加财政补贴的打算，因此必须对 1926 年航路标志维护工作的规模加以严格限制。

航务专门顾问在 1925 年黑龙江航务年度报告中提出了对俄阿穆尔水道局各项提案的意见；中俄双方在商定最终协议时，也接纳了航务专门顾问的意见。目前，乌苏里江至虎林以外河段、松阿察河及兴凯湖的航路标志维护工作计划以及额尔古纳河的石块清理工作计划均已取消。至于黑龙江上游（大黑河以上）的河道疏浚工作，预计共需 80000 卢布，以华方目前的财务状况，显然无法予以考虑，俄阿穆尔水道局遂正式提出独立开展该项工作之请求，并说明全部费用将由其自行承担。然因此事已超出中俄黑龙江航路标志联合委员会的权限，黑河道尹已将之转呈上级部门，静候批示。

经协商，1926 年航路标志维护工程最终仍如往年一样仅限于在黑龙江上开展，预算业已由最初的 75296 卢布削减至 60031 卢布，但仍比 1925 年的预算多出 15763 卢布，多出的部分主要是因为俄国的国内法令要求增加工人薪俸。此外，嘎杂克维池水道以及乌苏里江至虎林河段的航路标志重建工作预算亦由 14875 卢布削减至 9298 卢布。

关于嘎杂克维池水道和乌苏里江至虎林河段的航路标志重建工作，中国航政委员会表示，鉴于中国轮船在松花江和乌苏里江之间的航运量日益增加，而且航务专门顾问报告中亦指出该两段河道的航路标志亟待重建，因此尽管目前华方的资金相当紧张，但仍然决定，只要吉林省政府予以批准，而且边界划分问题不会出现（长期以来，满洲与俄国之间一直存在河道归属之争），便会对该项工作予以考虑。吉林省政府方面也深刻意识到乌苏里江航路标志维护工作的必要性与迫切性，表示愿意抛开两省之间的差异，授权黑河道尹代表吉林省政府出席会谈，同意于 1926 年协议签署之前，派遣一名代表予以协助。

此外，以往海关与俄阿穆尔水道局之间所签订的协议都是自当年 12 月 1 日（而非次年年初）开始生效，由此带来诸多不便，此番中俄双方经过讨论，决定将 1926 年协议的有效期改为 13 个月，即自 1925 年 12 月 1 日起，至 1926 年 12 月 31 日止，同时商定待吉林省代表到来后，于 1926 年 3 月的第一周召开会议，正式签署 1926 年协议。

不料意外之事接踵而至，黑河道尹最初仅是休假前往奉天，但 2 月底便有官方通知称其已调任至黑龙江省绥兰道（Suilantao），一并调离的还有道尹公署熟悉黑龙江航路标志相关事宜的文案。在新任道尹到任之前，只能由瑷珲县长（知事）暂任护理道尹，又逢瑷珲关税务司重新任命，而吉林省代表又未到来，此番种种致使协议签订之事遭到搁置。随后，中俄双方协定仍照 1925 年协议办法为 1926 年拟订为期 12 个月的协议，嘎杂克维池水

道和乌苏里江至虎林河段的航路标志重建工作计划暂行搁置,稍后再议。中俄双方最终
于 1926 年 4 月 21 日签署了新协议。

您忠诚的仆人

裴德生（C. M. Petterson）

瑷珲关暂行代理税务司

附录 1

中俄临时地方工程委员会会议纪要

（1926 年 4 月 21 日于大黑河）

参会代表

黑河护理道尹兼瑷珲交涉员	章霖先生
第一外交顾问	车席珍先生
大黑河海关税务司	裴德生先生
黑龙江航务专门顾问	易保罗（P. I. Ignatieff）先生
驻大黑河苏俄领事	多罗波夫（Toropoff）先生
俄阿穆尔水道局督办	托阿诺夫（Dianoff）先生
俄阿穆尔水道局副督办（工程师）	且比索夫（Chebisheff）先生
俄阿穆尔水道局航路部经理（工程师）	米海依罗夫（Mihailoff）先生

提案

（一）为展期 1923 年 10 月 28 日俄阿穆尔水道局与大中华民国黑河道尹签订之协议至 1926 年事。

议决

（一）查 1923 年 10 月 28 日至 1925 年 12 月 1 日之临时协议现已期满不生效力，中俄黑龙江航路标志联合委员会决定续签该协议一年，即自 1925 年 12 月 1 日起至 1926 年 12 月 1 日止。除附录 3 需另议外，其余附件均同协议一并继续生效。

倘于本年内，中俄会议对于共用边界河道事宜达成新协议，并于 1926 年 12 月 1 日前成功签署，则本协议即行废止。

提案

（二）为 1926 年航运季期间黑龙江边界河道航路标志维护费用预算事。

议决

（二）批准 1926 年航运季期间黑龙江边界河道航路标志维护费用之预算，总计 60031 卢布，实际支出不得超出该预算额。

提案

（三）为 1925 年费用账目事。

议决

（三）批准总计为 44267.05 卢布的费用支出,确定中国航政委员会于本纪要签署之时支付尾款。

提案

（四）为会议纪要要求事。

议决

（四）会议纪要须分别以中文和俄文撰写,各一式两份,双方各执中、俄文本各一份,以昭信守。

华方：

黑河护理道尹	章霖
第一外交顾问	车席珍
道尹公署文案	沈廷荣

俄方：

俄阿穆尔水道局督办	托阿诺夫
驻大黑河苏俄领事	多罗波夫
俄阿穆尔水道局航路部经理（工程师）	米海依罗夫

（签字）裴德生

瑷珲关 / 大黑河暂行代理税务司

1926 年 5 月 8 日

附录2

1926年俄阿穆尔水道局支出报表

——用于维护黑龙江航道自波克罗夫卡至嘎杂克维池河段的航路标志

支出	金卢布
1. 各地区职员薪俸	13959.00
2. 水深信号站职员薪俸	2730.00
3. 通行信号站职员薪俸	386.00
4. 水深信号站的设立与运营	350.00
5. 通行信号站的设立与运营	51.00
6. 标桩的更换、修理及维护	11836.00
7. 标桩照明	500.00
8. 房屋维修	4565.00
9. 邮费、电报费、信纸费及杂项	750.00
10. 供暖费	100.00
11. 电费	350.00
12. 旅费及津贴	350.00
13. 5% 的医疗护理费	2214.00
14. 折旧费	2238.00
15. "先锋号（Pioneer）"汽艇的修理费	8600.00
16. 阿穆尔水道局技术部办公经费	9150.00
17. 移除礁石费	400.00
18. 意外支出	1502.00
总计	60031.00

签字：

阿穆尔水道局督办　　　　　　且比索夫

阿穆尔水道局航路部经理　　　费道罗夫（Fedoroff）

阿穆尔水道局财务科科长　　　兰坡特夫（Lapteff）

1926 年 1 月 15 日，布拉戈维申斯克（Blagovestchensk，即海兰泡）

20. 1926 年《无线电广播条例》与《运销无线广播电收听器规则》

325　COMMRS.

Aigun　No. 110,789.

INSPECTORATE GENERAL OF CUSTOMS,

PEKING, 30th December 1926.

Sir,

I append, for your information and guidance, copy of Shui-wu Ch'u despatch No. 1102 transmitting copies of the Radio Broadcasting Act and of the Regulations for Importation and Sale of Radio Broadcasting Receiving Sets promulgated by the Provincial Government of the Three Eastern Provinces on 13th October 1926.

You will see that the main features of the Act are that the North Eastern Radio and Long Distance Telephone Administration has been authorised to erect at suitable places in the Three Eastern Provinces and to operate Radio Broadcasting Stations; that firms are now allowed to import and sell, and people living in the Three Eastern Provinces are allowed to install receiving sets in accordance with the regulations promulgated by the North Eastern Radio and

The Commissioner of Customs,

AIGUN.

and Long Distance Telephone Administration; that when radio broadcasting receiving sets, accessories and spare parts are imported through any port in the Three Eastern Provinces, they must be examined by the inspector of the North Eastern Radio and Long Distance Telephone Administration, the firm concerned having previously obtained an import permit in accordance with the regulations; and finally that the smuggling of radio transmitters is to be punished by a fine of above two thousand and below ten thousand "Yuan" and by confiscation of the whole equipment.

The Regulations for the Importation and Sale of Radio Broadcasting Receiving Sets provide that the North Eastern Radio and Long Distance Telephone Administration will issue permits to Chinese and foreign firms applying for permission to import and sell receiving sets, accessories and spare parts; that Customs duty must be paid and that receiving sets must be examined by the inspector appointed by the North Eastern Radio and Long Distance Telephone Administration before they are permitted importation.

I

I have to request you, therefore, to allow importation of radio receiving sets, accessories and spare parts on payment of duty and on production of permits issued by the North Eastern Radio and Long Distance Telephone Administration.   You should request that Telephone Administration through the Superintendent to supply you with a specimen of the import permit issued by that Administration.   While it is laid down in Article 6 of the Act and Articles 12 and 14 of the Regulations, that smuggling of transmitters or receiving sets, accessories and spare parts is to be punished by a fine of over two thousand and under ten thousand "Yuan" and by confiscation of the apparatus, you are to note that standing instructions, both general and special, in the matter of disposal of confiscated wireless material, i.e. munitions of war (vide Circular No. 3056) seizure rewards and distribution of proceeds of fines and confiscations, are to be adhered to, and that fines on foreign importers or foreign firms can only be

be inflicted in accordance with the principles of the Joint Investigation Rules.

Finally, while inspection of receiving sets, etc., by the inspector appointed by the North Eastern Radio and Long Distance Telephone Administration before payment of duty is not to be allowed, facilities for such inspection may be given in consultation with the Superintendent and the inspector provided that it takes place after payment of duty and before release by the Customs.

I am,

Sir,

Your obedient Servant,

Inspector General.

Appendix.

税务处令第一一〇二号 中华民国十五年十二月十一日

案准镇威上将军公署咨开据东北无线电长途电话监督张宜呈称拟查广播无线电条例暨运销及装设广播无线电收听器各规则业经钧署通令各机关公布在案惟查运销规则第五条内载广播无线电收听器之商行应于机器进口以前请领护照方许输入义第七条内载东三省境内各口岸均须由职处派员检查等语现在奉饬注册请领护照之商行请领护照者已有数家职处应派员分往各海关实行检查所有东三省境内各海关似应于事前知照对於钧署所发之护照一律查照放行对於职处所派之检查员予以相当协助埋合检同华洋文条例各拾份备文呈请钧署鉴核容行税务处转饬东三省境内各海关监督税务司查照办理实为公便等情据此除指令外应检同附件行查照转令各海关监督税务司遵照并因各关道照外相应检同前案照既准前因应即照行除咨陆军交通等部查照遵照分令各关道照外相应检同前项华洋文条例规则各十分行应税务司查照此令附件

运销广播无线电收听器规则

第一条 东北无线电长途电话监督处为普及文化传播商品起见准许国内外各商行华人或西侨任何工厂或公司所制广播无线电收听器或附属品或著作等项须遵照本规则之规定

第二条 凡华人或西侨广播无线电收听器或附属品或著作之商行应遵照开请颁书式填送项项列商请领天东北无线电长途电话监督处注册请领给营业执照及标起该项标记安置於商行大门之上方准营业

凡华人广播无线电收听器或附属品或著作之商行家营业执照请领时对政营业执照所请

第三条 各商行如请领营业执照时应缴纳执照费现大洋二十四元此项执照

收用以一年为满此项应更换新照顾照应费

第四条 华人广播无线电收听器或附属品或著作之商行如请领营业执照时

　论缴纳税照费外悉缴保证金现大洋一千元

第五条　凡入广播无线电收听器或附属品或零件之商行於进口以前应
将发卖单机式说明书及详细材料项目单国应行於商行於进口以前应
报应电话监督处详开并领进口护照

第六条　凡入广播无线电收听器或附属品或零件之商行由中华民国现行
税则缴纳值外悉缴附进口护照时按值开目声明不实得由东北无线电
报应电话监督处派员按所估值估计其进口应照发部照所估值值缴纳百
分之十以昭公允

第七条　东三省现内各口岸均设有东北无线电长途电话监督处所派之食应
员凡进口之广播无线电收听器或附属品或零件等项须经检查员验明填具
发货单按箱所开数目容积及重量符合後方许进人

第八条　东北无线电长途电话监督处对於允许进口之收听器或附属品或零件
如认为有试验之必要时应随时应处请验

第九条　广播无线电收听器之发线方式内部装置不加误制谣须适合左列各项
一　祇能接收一百米达以上六百米达以下之无线电波者
二　不能任意更改作发报或发话用者

第十条　凡允许进口之广播无线电收听器或附属品或零件於发护照时按照发
货单及装箱单所开件数另给护照每於收听器上方可出售如係附
属品或零件除零屋小件不能粘贴护照者应就每一小包或每一小筒加贴护
照外其馀可以加钉者钉牢钉者粘贴或涂漆其未经粘钉涂漆之
收听器或附属品或零件一概不准出售

第十一条　凡各商行如将未贴钉护照或粘钉伪造护照之广播无线电收听器或附属
品或零件等项出售一经查出除将其货照没收其全部罚件外应处以
最大洋每具千元以下一千元以上之罚金

第十二條　凡在東三省境內之各商行如處本規則第二條之規定擅自僱人或
無線電播無線電收應器或附屬品或零件者一經查出除沒收其全部機件外
并照以退或以無線電機論處以現大洋一萬元以下二千元以上之罰金

第十三條　凡無線電播無線電收應器或附屬品或零件之商行對於購買此項收
應器或附屬品或零件之主顧應先繕造東北無線電合資會社之購機應單
方可發繕該項應單於購件之後即甫發送查主應於每月務令送還東北無線
電長處查照活該項應單如處本規則規定一經查出除收用此應棄就照外並
處以現大洋五千元以下一千元以上之罰金

第十四條　凡僱人無線電播無線電收應器或附屬品或零件之商行如不按照本規
則第五條辦理或收入收應器違反第九條所規定者一經查出除收附應棄就
照沒收保證金及其全部機件外並照以無線電機論處以現大洋一
萬元以下二千元以上之罰金

第十五條　凡運無線電播無線電收應器或附屬品或零件之商行於每月付收應器
或附屬品或零件出售時均應繕寫三聯單一種存提一種交購料者一種於月
務遵同時機處取封對照無天東北無線電長處電話監督處查悉又每周月務遵
將存貨應單論送付收應器或附屬品或零件均應詳細開列圖遵奉天東北無
線電長途電話監督處備查

凡繕寫貨三聯單及存貨應單將擴付進口日期並照號數所訂號率及購機處
軍減款詳細開明不得遺漏而寫各項如查有不符時被照本規則第十一條者
十三條或第十四條處以相當之罰金

第十六條　凡僱人無線電收應器或附屬品或零件之商行對於應徵各費者
不按時徵前卻於所存之保證金內扣除不足俾沒收其應付作抵

第十七條　凡無線電播無線電收應器或附屬品或零件之商行對於應徵各費者
不按時徵前卻其營業就照外並沒收其應付作抵

第十八條　各商行如須停止營業時應於十日以前通知奉天東北無線電長途

電話監督處註冊並將營業執照繳還其以前所存之保證金險將應繳各費扣除

外餘數一併退還

第十九條　本規則呈准

藏成上將某公署此准自公布之日施行如有未盡事宜切得隨時呈請修改之

遵前廣播無線電收聽器請領書

敬啟者敬為行現擬證人聲明電廣播無線電收聽器及附屬品及遵行對於

貴處所定遵前廣播無線電收聽器規則應恪遵守茲將應具請領書並開明各

項附繳本年營業執照費現大洋二十四元繳保證金現大洋一千元暨相應函請

貴處查照准予註冊並發給營業執照及課記為前此改

東北無線電長途電話監督處

一　收聽器之程式通籍

二　經理之姓名及閱籍

三　本行開辦及註冊機關

四　營業資本總數

中華民國　　年　　月　　日

現住

謹啟

领广播无线电收听器请领书

敬启者 敬禀公司现遵购领广播无线电收听器附属品及书件封发於
贵处所定运购广播无线电收听器规则 敬
贵处所藏本年营业或照费现大洋二十四元暨相应函请
於左並附缴本年营业或照费现大洋二十四元暨相应函请
贵处查照准予注册並发给营业执照及登记为荷此致
东北无线电长途电话监督处

一 本公司国籍及注册情册
二 营业资本几款
三 两营何项收应器
四 向何行购置
公司 批实

现住

中华民国 年 月 日
謹啓

运缴广播无线电收听器请领进口护照书

敬启者 敬禀公司向 国版（或敬总底订购）
附属品品 共壹千 共装
项货物杂货於 月 日由 运（或装）约於 月
旬抵 箱计值现大洋 元
目单共 份 並敬纳进口护照费 元相应函请
贵处查照接收並敬发进口护照一纸发给该粹
俟至所运发货单装箱单等项亦请於
俟候後发还送为荷此致
东北无线电长途电话监督处

附许

中华民国 年 月 日
謹啓

廣播無線電章程

第一條　東北無線電廣播電台應為普及文化傳佈商情起見於東三省境內擇相當地點設立廣播無線電台辦理廣播無線電業務

第二條　廣播無線電台應就每日規定時間內用無線電傳播新聞商情音樂歌曲演講等項以供公眾收聽其詳細辦法由該台另訂擬定至每日廣播節目擬登報款或印刷傳單宣佈之

第三條　廣播無線電台所發之新聞商情音樂歌曲演講等項凡居住東三省境內各省均得收領收聽之惟須超過送守東北無線電長途無線電廣播電長途電通

第四條　凡東三省境內所置之收聽卷聲附編軸以及零件等項住人東三省境內各口岸海關遇有由進舉運守東北無線電長途電新聞所擬定

第五條　廣播無線電收聽卷聲附編軸以及零件等住人東三省境內各口岸惟由此行進舉請領送日題冊外業須輪東北無線電該處電應派員檢查並詳細辦法另行擬定

第六條　無論何人或任何機關不得在東三省境內私運或私設任何廣播無線電業或應當廣播無線電乘運通限該其全部領卷外應廣播無線電務令遵照或有特殊情益以境大洋貳千元以上罰鍰惟本國機關單所設者不在此限

第七條　凡私人或團體有因事經東北廣播無線電台向公眾宣告或講演者須先將底稿商，請該台許可並繳相當之費用

章程协议

第八条　廣播無綫電台須用技達冠話線接通能導以便得當時候而敀合應時須治辨理

第九条　本規則呈奉核成上海市公會批准自公布之日施行如有未盡事宜均得隨時增訂增除改之

装設廣播無綫電收聽器規則

第一条　凡為收聽無綫電新聞演講商情音樂等項而裝設廣播無綫電收聽器者應遵照本規則之規定

第二条　凡欲裝設廣播無綫電收聽器者應遂照後開請領書式樣逐項開明先行函請當地或附近之東北廣播無綫電台成辦事處註冊并發給牌照單機者裝接後再請派員檢驗發給廣播無綫電收聽器執照及標記方可使用

第三条　凡欲裝設廣播無綫電收聽器者遂行呈領牌照單向釘有東北無綫電技達電話監督處特許營業標記之商行購件購妥並將該項悲單交經售之商行轉送東北無綫電長途電話監督處核其每付收聽器或所屬品或零件均須釘有東北無綫電長途電話監督處所發號牌万可聽買如用戶私機不釘號牌之機件一經查出除將該件沒收外並處以五十元以上一百元以下之罰金其釘有號牌之收聽器須適合左列各項之規定方可懸用

一 祇能收聽一百米遠以上六百米遠以下之無綫電波者

二 內部裝證不能任意變更爲發報或發話用者

第四條 裝設廣播無綫電收聽器之用戶如購用貼有號牌之零件自行裝配完成收聽器時應先送就近東北廣播無綫電台試驗繳納試驗費一元並請發給號牌標記及收聽器執照方可使用

第五條 廣播無綫電收聽器所用天綫不可接近電報電話電燈或其他電力用之綫路其接連地綫之處須不致有引火之虞又用戶調驗眞空管時不得故意發射電波致生擾亂

第六條 裝設廣播無綫電收聽器之原註册用戶住址或裝機地點變更時須通知原註册之東北廣播無綫電台聲明原委並記載新舊間裝設地點諸其派員檢查及更正原册又裝設收聽器之原註册用戶本人名號或機關名稱或商行字號如有變更時亦須函請原註册之東北廣播無綫電台更正

第七條 裝設收聽器之用戶應將所領執照置於裝設機器之處如攜帶該收聽器主他處時亦須帶執照同行以備檢查若執照遺失應立卽申請原執照之東北廣播無綫電台補發

第八條 裝設收聽器之用戶於請領註册時應繳納註册費現大洋一元裝設後請領執照時若用礦石式收聽器者應納執照費現大洋六元若用眞空管式收聽器者應納執照費現大洋十二元上項執照效用以一年爲限逾期應照章繳費更換新照

第九條 裝設收聽器之用戶如欲停止收聽廣播無綫電時應卽將機器及天綫拆卸並通知原註册之東北廣播無綫電台註册並繳還執照及標記該項機器欲重裝使用時應照本規則第二條重請執照及標記若用戶欲將該項機器移讓或轉售他人或他團證時應由新舊用戶聯名函請原註册之東北廣播無綫電台更名舊用戶須將執照及標記繳還新用戶應請另發執照及

標記

第十條　本規則第九條之重發執照標記及第七條之補發執照均須于申請時繳納手續費現大洋一元

第十一條　凡未經東北廣播無綫電台註冊發給執照標記私自設置廣播無綫電收聽器者一經覺察沒收其全副機器外並處以現大洋五百元以上二千元以下之罰金倘該項機器查與本規則第三條之規定不符時應按照廣播無綫電條例第六條處罰

第十二條　裝設廣播無綫電收聽器之用戶于機器裝安後不得將內部裝置變更或添置機件以收聽一百米達以上之電波或作發報或發話之用惟為增加廣播無綫電之收聽效用起見須添置附屬品或零件時應照本規則第二條先行函請廣播無綫電台發給聯機憑單方可購用如違本條規定即照第十一條處罰

第十三條　凡裝設廣播無綫電收聽器之用戶應將東北廣播無綫電台所發乙標記釘於大門上該項標記連同執照每年更換一次以顏色區別乙如遇無綫電檢查員檢查執照或試驗機器時應隨時任其查驗不得攔阻

第十四條　本規則施行前已裝廣播無綫電收聽器乙用戶尚未向東北廣播無綫電台註冊並領有執照者應于一個月內遵章補請註冊並領取執照及變牌標記逾期不報者按照本規則第十一條處罰

第十五條　凡由東三省境外各埠購買廣播無綫電收聽器攜入境內或住居東三省境內向境外各埠訂購收聽器使用者應於機器攜入境內以前先向東北無綫電監督處請領進口護照並照機器價值繳納百分之十進口護照費亦須照本規則第四條辦理該項機器價值由東北無綫電長途電話監督處按市價公平估計不得爭執如違本條所規定即照運銷廣播無綫電收聽器規則第十四條處罰

第十六條　本規則呈奉

督戎上將軍公署批准目公佈日施行如有未盡事宜仍得隨時呈請修改

乙

致瑷珲关第 <u>325/110769</u> 号令　　　　海关总税务司署（北京）1926 年 12 月 30 日

尊敬的瑷珲关税务司：

　　为了便于贵署顺利执行，兹附华方税务处第 1102 号令，以供参考。此令转发了东三省省政府于 1926 年 10 月 13 日发布的《无线电广播条例》及《运销无线广播电收听器规则》副本。

　　据此令可知，经授权在东三省适宜地区设立了东北无线电和长途电话监督处，运作无线电广播电台；根据东北无线电和长途电话监督处发布的条令，商行现可进口并出售接收设备，且东三省的居民可购买并安装接收设备；凡进口无线电广播接收设备、附件及零件在经过东三省口岸入境时，均需根据相关条例接受东北无线电和长途电话监督处稽查员及已取得进口许可的相关商行检验；最后，凡走私无线电发送机者将处以大洋两千"元"以上一万"元"以下的罚款，并没收全部设备。

　　《运销无线电广播收听器规则》规定，东北无线电长途电话监督处将向申请进口及售卖接收设备、附件及零件的中外商行发放许可；申请商行须支付海关税，且接收设备在许可入境前须经东北无线电长途电话监督处指定稽查员检验。

　　因此，经支付税款，且出示东北无线电长途电话监督处签发的许可后，敬请贵署允许无线电广播设备入境。贵署需要求东北无线电长途电话监督处通过海关监督向贵署提供该局签发的进口许可样本。《广播无线电条例》第 6 条及《运销广播无线电收听器规则》第 12 条及第 14 条规定，凡走私无线电发送机或接收设备、附件及零件者将处以大洋两千"元"以上一万"元"以下的罚款，并没收全部设备；在没收无线电物资〔即军需品（参见第 3056 号通令）〕、查封奖赏和分配处理方面，遵守常规及特殊标准指令；根据《会讯章程》仅对洋籍进口商或洋企进行罚款。

　　最后，在缴纳税款后，方可允许由东北无线电长途电话监督处指定人员对接收设备等进行检验，检验须在缴税后及海关放行前进行，可经咨询海关监督及检验员后提供检验所需设备。

您忠诚的仆人

安格联（F. A. Aglen）

海关总税务司

21. 1927 年《黑龙江航路标志协议》

Aigun   3rd May, 1927.

Sir,

with reference to Aigun despatch No. 144 of 29th December, 1923;

informing the Inspectorate of the signing of an Agreement for 1923/24 for continued maintenance of Aids on the Amur;

and to Aigun despatches Nos. 230 and 263;

communicating the renewal of the Amur Aids Agreement for the year 1925 and 1926 respectively, along the lines of the 1923/24 Agreement;

I now have the honour to report that the Agreement for the maintenance of Amur Aids for the period 1st December, 1926, to 30th November, 1927, was signed the 10th January, 1927, in the form of a protocol again renewing the Agreement of

Officiating Inspector General of Customs.

Peking.

of 1923/24.

Considerable delay has been encountered in getting authentic copies of the documents concerned. These are now enclosed as follows:

The Chinese version of the renewed Agreement.

The English translation of same.

The Russian version of the renewed Agreement.

The English translation of same.

It will be noted that there is considerable dissimilarity between the form and wording of the two versions. I had noticed the same discrepancies in comparing the documents concerning previous renewals and pointed them out to the Taoyin. The latter, however, said he wished to follow precedent as closely as possible and would continue to maintain the old form of Agreement to expedite its approval by the Provincial and Peking authorities. At the time of the signing of this Agreement the Russian delegates showed no interests in the wording of the Chinese version of the document and affixed

their

their names to it blindly. I should place on
record, however, that the Russian version was the
one used in the discussions and that it was
verbally approved at a joint meeting of the two
Commissions before the clean copies were drawn up
for signature.

The Russian Commission originally submitted
an entirely new agreement which, while retaining most
of the essential points of the old ones, omitted
many of their now obsolete provisions. It was a
much more business-like document than the previous
ones and met the approval of the Technical Adviser
and myself. The Taoyin, however, in respect to the
adoption of anything new was animated, as noted
above, by a desire to adhere to precedent as far
as possible. The Russian Commission, with a
conciliatoriness of spirit that has characterized
their attitude throughout the present negotiations,
recognised the Taoyin's position and withdrew their
proposal of a newly worded agreement.

During

During the negotiations leading up to the
renewal of the Aids Agreement the main difficulty
has been that of cutting down the estimate which
the Russian Commission, flush with funds, had fixed
at Gold Roubles 338,000. Of this amount we were
able to rule out at once, as being outside the
scope of the proposed Agreement, the following items:

Dredging of the Amur river	Gold Rbls.120,000
Aids to Navigation on the Ussuri	18,000
Aids and stone work on the Argun	20,000
Total:	Gold Rbls.158,000

This still left a balance of Rbls.180,000 to be
reduced to the limits of our slender purse.

The brunt of the negotiations which followed
fell largely on the shoulders of the Technical
Adviser. The latter, owing to his long experience
in the Amur Navigation Bureau, his five years with
the Chinese Aids Commission and to his good
relations with the members of Russian Commission (who
accept his advice and opinions to a marked extent),
was eventually able to bring the estimate down to

Rbls.60,000.

No.1.   Rbls.60,000. I append a summary prepared by the
Technical Adviser which shows in the first two
columns the estimates for different items as agreed
to in 1926 and for 1927 and in the third column
the estimates originally proposed by the Russian
Commission for 1927. When it is explained that
the Amur Navigation Bureau was extended a credit of
some Rbls.1,200,000 (afterwards reduced to Rbls.780,000
for 1927 by the Moscow Government it can be better
realized the sacrifices the Russian Commission made
in finally accepting estimates the Chinese share of
which is only Rbls.30,000, and it must be
attributed largely to the friendly feeling between
the personnel of the two Commissions, personified
in the Technical Adviser, that an Agreement so
satisfactory to the Chinese side was consummated.
At the same time I should add a warning that it
is doubtful if such a drastic pruning of estimates
will again be agreed to by the Russian Commission.

　　　　　Having pledged ourselves to an expenditure
of Rbls.30,000 as our half of the estimates for

　　　　　　　　　　　　　　　　the

the upkeep of Aids on the Amur during the coming
year, it is necessary to examine the sources of the
wherewithal to cover this expenditure and that of
the Office of the Chinese Commission. For 1927 the
budget for the Chinese Commission has been drawn up
as follows:

Chinese share of Amur Aids Upkeep	$30,000
Taoyin's Office expenses	2,000
Technical Adviser's Office	9,000
Customs - 1/10th River Dues Collection	4,500
Loss by exchange and unforeseen expenses	1,200
Total estimated expenditure	$46,700

　　　　　Receipts to meet this expenditure may be
estimated as follows:

River Dues Collection for 1927	$45,000
Advance from Sungari Aids	5,000
Balance carried forward from 1926	3,700
Total estimated income	$53,700

No.5.   I enclose a table showing the distribution
of the River Dues collection for 1926. It will be
seen that the total collection for Taheiho, Aigun
and Lahasusu for the year was $35,469. This

　　　　　　　　　　　　　　　　compares

compares favourably with the collection for 1925
which was $28,819. The increase is largely due
to the inauguration of the payment of Dues on
passenger tickets at Lahasusu on Ussuri traffic
toward the end of the year and to the increase
in the movement of cargo on that river. In
estimating the collection for 1927 at $45,000 I
have included the increase that will accrue from
raising the present tariff as mentioned in my
despatch No. 311. There was a credit of $20,000
still available in the Sungari Aids Account at
the end of 1925. Since then $5,000 has been
drawn (as shown just above in the Estimate of
Receipts for 1927) but it is believed that with
the increased tariff it will not be necessary to
again draw from those funds and that we may even
expect to repay some of the advance we have
received from Harbin.

The above budget shows a credit
balance of $7,000 at the end of 1927 but it is
expected,

expected, with the continuation of normal conditions,
that the surplus will be greater. The question of
joint restoration of Aids on the Ussuri, on the
other hand, has been the topic of lively discussions
between the two Commissions and it is probable that
an agreement will be entered into shortly along the
lines of the Amur Aids Agreement effecting the Aids
on the Ussuri. China's share in such a project
would amount to some $5,000 the first year (less
thereafter) and would reduce this surplus accordingly.
As the collection on the Ussuri traffic at Lahasusu
last year was some $10,272 we are morally
responsible for some improvement in the poor condition
of Aids to navigation on that river. The Taoyin
is strongly of this opinion too.

From Aigun despatches Nos. 230 and 263 it
will be seen that the question of Aids on the
Ussuri and Kasakevich waterways was brought forward
in both 1925 and 1926 when the necessity and
justice of assisting navigation on that river was
acknowledged

acknowledged by the Chinese Commission. However the dispute over the boundary in the vicinity of Harbarovsk has always proved a stumbling block, complicated by the fact that the above waterways lie in Kirin Province, and no agreement has yet been reached.

The present Taoyin, Chang Shou-tsen (張壽增), a far-seeing and energetic official, has given the question much attention and several conferences have been held to find a formula for drawing up an agreement that would satisfy both parties. He was loaths to enter into any, however, that would admit by implication or otherwise that Chinese steamers had not the right to proceed via the Amur to Harbarovsk and thence up the Ussuri, or vice versa. The Russian Commission, on the other hand, had not the power to discuss this question. I suggested as a solution of the difficulty that an understanding should be entered into by which the Chinese

Commission

Commission would look after the maintenance of the upper section on both sides of the Ussuri from Hulin (虎林) to Jaohohsien (饒河縣), a point about midway from Hulin to Harbarovsk, and that the Russian Commission maintain both sides of the lower section. This would allow the Russians a free hand in their section and the question of the boundary would not be raised. The Aids on the Kasakevich waterway would continue to be unattended for the time being. The Taoyin approved this idea and referred it to the Kirin authorities. At a later conference, on the question being brough up again, he definitely stated that no agreement could be entered into that did not admit the right of Chinese steamers to use the Amur and Ussuri as far as Harbarovsk. This created an impasse and at my suggestion it was mutually agreed that the question should be referred to the Sino-Russian Conference at Peking through the Moscow and Kirin authorities. On the 11th March of this year the

Taoyin

Taoyin formally wrote the Russian Commission that the Kirin authorities had notified him that the question had been duly referred to the Sino-Russian Conference at Peking on their part and that, pending a decision, nothing was to be done on the Ussuri by either Commission. The Russian Commission objected to these restrictions as they felt they were well within their rights if they wished to go ahead and place Aids on their side of the Ussuri (which was not in dispute) at their own expense - a perfectly natural view it seemed to me. Later on the Taoyin apparently saw that the position he had taken was likely to be ignored with good reason by the Russian Commission and he requested that his despatch be replied to in a manner that would permit the question being reopened. This has been done and the Taoyin informed me yesterday of his desire to resume the negotiations. It remains to be seen if he will drop political issues and allow the Chinese Commission to conclude a purely technical agreement.

Toward

Toward the end of 1926 the Russian Commission asked for permission to remove stones dangerous to navigation from the river bed of the Argun river, at their own expense. This request was granted by the Taoyin after he had referred it to Tsitsihar. Later on when that Commission proposed to erect Aids on both sides of the Argun he refused to give the necessary permission to work on the Chinese side. This refusal served somewhat to nullify the strength of the precedent created when consent was given to the Russian Commission to carry on work on both sides of a frontier river at their own expense, i. e. the case of removal of stones on the Argun just mentioned. It should be explained at the same time that there is no Chinese shipping on the Argun and practically no Russian traffic. For the Russian Commission to wish to undertake such projects as the maintenance of Aids on that river and the removal of stones from its bed at a cost of some $20,000 indicates a

superfluity

superfluity of funds that could only have been
obtained by exaggerating (to use a mild expression)
to Moscow the importance of part of the 1927
program of the Amur Navigation Bureau.

The project of the Russian Commission
to dredge the Upper Amur was renewed during the
year and has now become a "hardy annual". The
Taoyin at first flirted with the idea of jointly
undertaking some of the work suggested but eventually
adopted the Technical Adviser's opinion that, far
from jointly spending $120,000 in dredging that part
of the Amur, to facilitate the navigation of one
small Chinese and three small Russian steamers, no
dredging whatever was required at present. The
Russian Commission eventually came to the same
conclusion themselves and recently withdrew the
proposal entirely on the plea that the money could
be more expeditiously spent elsewhere.

The principal remaining subject under
discussion by the two Commissions during the past
year

year has been that of the formation of joint Rules
of Navigation for the control of Chinese and Russian
steamers on the frontier rivers. As far back as
April, 1920, I. G. despatch No. 2248/78,057 to Harbin
notified that office of the receipt of a despatch
from the Shui-wu Ch'u to the effect that on account
of the difficulty of opening "formal negotiations
"with the representatives of the Russian Government,
"it has been decided to conclude a temporary
"arrangement for the navigation of the Amur by
"Chinese vessels by means of local negotiations
"between the Heilungchiang Tuchün and the de facto
"Russian authorities of the Amur Province in Siberia".
This despatch concludes with the instructions that
the Harbin Commissioner is to render all possible
assistance to the Tuchün in affecting these local
arrangements. A copy of the Shui-wu Ch'u despatch
in question was not sent to this office so it is
not clearly understood to just what questions its
instructions referred.

In

In Aigun S/O No. 11 of the 5th April, 1922, the Acting Commissioner reports that the Amur Provincial authorities had submitted to the Taoyin the draft of a "Provisional Arrangement for the Navigation of the Amur and Sungari" and that he had also prepared for the assistance of the Taoyin a draft which would better protect the interests of the Chinese in conformity with the instructions of the above quoted despatch. In his S/O of the 24th May, 1922, in reply, the Inspector General informs this office that the question of the joint navigation of the Amur and Sungari had been taken up by various Boards in Peking and draft rules drawn up which would form the basis of discussion between the Chinese and Russian authorities concerned. In the meanwhile no steps were to be taken locally that would predjudice these negotiations. Nothing more is on record about the question until its mention in Aigun S/O No. 54 of the 15th February, 1926, where it is reported that the Russian Aids Commission (their letter of the 18th

18th December, 1925) is anxious for the adoption of joint regulations for the "Navigation of Frontier Rivers" and the "Inspection of Vessels" - a very ambitious program. It is further written that the Taoyin has refused to have anything to do with these questions as being outside of the sphere of interest of the Aids Commission. The Inspector General in his S/O of the 15th March, 1926, in reply, approves the stand taken by the Taoyin and says that "A shipping Law is quite extraneous to the Amur Aids. It is a national affair which cannot be localized".

The question was thereupon dropped until the 30th October, 1926, when the Russian Commission addressed the Taoyin, as President of the Chinese Aids Commission, pointing out that during the season just closed certain Chinese steamers had broken the rules of navigation as commonly accepted by all shipping on the Amur and again emphasizing the importance of an early

adoption

adoption of joint rules to secure the safety of both Russian and Chinese vessels.

It will be remembered that formerly all shipping on the Amur and Sungari was under the control of Russia and that suitable Rules of Navigation, Inspection, etc., were in force. Many Chinese were in the employ of the Russian steamers and received training on them. At the time of the break-up of Russia and the commencement of the running of Chinese owned steamers on the Amur and Sungari, the latter were manned largely by Russian Officers and Pilots and Russian trained seamen. As a result the traditions of the old Russian shipping was applied to the newly formed Chinese fleets and the Russian Rules of Navigation were adopted and have been followed. Recently the proportion of Russian Officers and Pilots on Chinese steamers has been steadily decreasing for various reasons and as they drop out they are replaced by badly trained and, in many cases, incompetent Chinese. On both

the

the Amur and Sungari, however, the Russian Rules of Navigation are still observed by the Chinese but on the Amur there is no Chinese authority for the use or enforcement of these Rules. The result has been that Chinese shipping on the latter river is answerable to no one in its manner of navigation and can break what are, to them, unwritten laws with impunity and to the great danger of life and property. That more accidents have not occurred is attributable to luck rather than seamanship but it is only a question of time, what with the steady decrease in the efficiency of Officers and Pilots on the Chinese steamers (Certificates not being required of them by the Customs), when they will occur with increasing regularity.

On the receipt by the present Taoyin from the Russian Commission of the above mentioned letter of the 30th October, 1926, he brought up the question of the adoption of suitable joint Rules of Navigation at a meeting of the Chinese Commission. I

related

related the history of previous negotiations, as
outlined above, and explained that the Inspector
General had taken the position that the matter was
one for discussion between the national authorities
of the two countries. The reasonableness of this
position was admitted by the meeting but at the
same time it was thought that, as the relations
between the national authorities of the two countries
were such as to prevent any early negotiations, it
would be well if simple rules of a non-controversial
nature - i. e. "rules of the road" - could be
adopted as desired by the Russian Commission, pending
the conclusion of a regular agreement between Moscow
and Peking. I could express no immediate opinion
as to the practicability of such a course in the
face of Inspectorate instructions and the matter
rested there.

No. 2.

On the 20th December, 1926, the Technical
Adviser received a letter from the Taoyin, copy
appended, informing him that he and the Manager of
the

the Tungpei Steamship Company had been appointed
as delegates to draw up joint Rules of Navigation,
that the Russian Commission was being requested to
appoint two delegates for the same purpose and that
the Provincial authorities were being informed of
his action. The Technical Adviser referred these
instructions to me whereupon I called at once on
the Taoyin and explained that Mr. Ignatieff was
detached as Adviser to the Aids only and that if
he wished to use him in any other capacity the
Inspector General's consent should first be applied
for through me, and quoting the precedent of the
former Taoyin applying for permission to appoint
the Technical Adviser as a delegate to the Moukden
Conference. At the same time I explained that the
Inspector General had taken the stand that Rules
of Navigation was not a question for arrangement
locally and to direct Mr. Ignatieff to proceed with
such negotiations would place him in a very
invidious position vis-a-vis the Inspector General.

The

The Taoyin soon saw the difficulties of the situation but having sent off his despatches he could not very well withdraw them and had no intention of doing so if he could. After a long discussion it was tentatively arranged that the two delegates appointed by the Taoyin should report the results of what would really be preliminary negotiations with the two Russian delegates to the Chinese Aids Commission which in turn could transmit them to the Shui-wu Ch'u, through the Taoyin and the Provincial Authorities, for approval. This _modus vivendi_ would solve the problem of instructions to the Technical Adviser outside the scope of his activities, and at the same time would place the conduct of the impending negotiations under the direction of the Aids Commission instead of the Taoyin.

I thereupon reported the forcing of the issue by the Taoyin to you in S/O No. 69 and was authorized in your S/O of the 22nd January, 1927.

to

to permit the Technical Adviser to cooperate in drawing up Rules within the scope of Article No. 30 of the international "Regulations for Preventing Collisions at Sea". This reads as follows:

Reservation of Rules for Harbours and Inland Navigation.

Art. 30.- Nothing in these Rules shall interfere with the operation of a special rule, duly made by local authority, relative to the navigation of any harbour, river, or inland waters.

On receipt of these instructions the Technical Adviser proceeded to draw up a draft of the proposed Rules of Navigation copies of which were submitted to you in S/O No. 72 and also to the Coast Inspector. A further copy was sent to the Harbin Commissioner as it is possible that the projected Rules may be adopted for the Sungari also as practically the same Regulations are followed there as on the Amur. The draft has since been submitted to the Russian Aids Commission who have returned it with certain

unimportant

unimportant modifications and additions to which the
Chinese Commission have no objections. I believe I
will have no difficulty in delaying further action
in the matter for a reasonable time until I have
received your instructions and the comments of the
Harbin Commissioner and the Coast Inspector.

It is now my idea that once the
Rules (satisfactory to the Customs) are approved by
the Joint Aids Commissions and forwarded by the
Taoyin to the Provincial authorities for transmission
to the Shui-wu Ch'u for its approval, that the
latter Board be requested to instruct you to put
them in force for the control of the Chinese
shipping on the frontier rivers. Where infringements
of Rules occur that involve both Chinese and
Russian vessels the local national authorities
concerned will take cognisance the Customs acting
in an advisory capacity.

This despatch, which covers fairly
fully the activities of the Aids Commission since
the

the reporting of the renewal of the Agreement in
1926, should be read in conjunction with the
Technical Adviser's Annual Report submitted in
Aigun despatch No. 313.

I have the honour to be,

Sir,

Your obedient Servant,

Acting Commissioner.

Appendixes.

Appendix No. 1.

SUMMARY OF ESTIMATES AGREED TO FOR UPKEEP OF
AIDS ON THE AMUR FOR 1926 AND 1927, AND OF ESTIMATES ORIGINALLY
SUBMITTED BY AMUR NAVIGATION BUREAU FOR 1927.

Particulars.	1926.	1927.	
	Estimate Agreed to.	Estimate Agreed to.	Original Estimate of Amur Navigation Bureau.
	Gold Rbls.	Gold Rbls.	Gold Rbls.
Salaries to District Employees	15,959	7,020	15,000
Salaries to Depth-Signal Station Employees	2,730	4,100	9,000
Salaries to Traffic Station Employees	386	427	1,000
Opening and operating Depth-Signal Stations	350	...	...
Opening & operating Traffic Stations	51	...	...
Erecting, repairing & maintenance of Beacons	11,036	11,900	30,000
Lighting Beacons	4,565	5,365	10,000
Repairs to buildings	500	500	1,000
Postage, telegrams, stationary, sundries	750	750	2,000
Printing	350	350	500
Freight	100	100	200
Travelling expenses & allowances	350	350	4,000
Cost for medical attendance	2,814	2,000	7,000
Depreciation	2,355	1,748	2,000
Motor-launch	6,600	18,500	60,000
Maintenance of District Office	9,150	6,000	36,000
Removal of rocks	400	600	1,000
Unforeseen	1,502	290	1,300
Total estimates agreed to	60,031	60,000	
Total of original 1927 estimate for Aids on Amur			180,000
Additional to Aids on Amur.			
Dredging work on the Amur			120,000
Placing Aids on the Ussuri			18,000
Removal of rocks on the Argun			6,000
Placing Aids on the Argun			12,000
Total of original estimate, 1927:			336,000

Technical Adviser's Office.
CUSTOM HOUSE.

Harbin, 3rd May, 1927.

Certified Correct:

P. Ignatieff

Technical Adviser on Amur
Aids to Navigation.

逕啟者業准駐黑俄領事函以華船海城大興不按航章

航行恐出危險請速雙方協定劃一航章以便兩國航業

家互相遵守等因准此查中俄交界河流航行遵碼章程

迄未協定此項章程關係輪船安危應各派專員協商

一俟商妥再由雙方簽字通行彼此航業機關遵守茲派

黑河航務分局局長陳廣起及

貴顧問擔任協商之職除分別報省並函復俄領暨分

行外相應函請

專門顧問易保羅

情形隨時詳告以憑核辦為要此致

查照會同陳局長進

黑河道尹兼璦琿交涉員張壽增

中華民國五年 十二 月 二 十 日

黑龍江璦琿交涉員公用箋

305

聲明書

大中華民國黑龍江省黑河道尹兼璦琿交涉員張壽增典大英帝亞社會聯邦共合國駐黑河領事人敝拉美德聲明中華民國十二年西曆一千九百二十二年度方所訂黑龍江等中俄地團定章河流航行地方協議暨附列之第二章第二節附件所定展期一年自中華民國十二年西曆一千九百二十二年十二月一日起至中華民國十二年西曆一千九百二十七年十二月一日止繼續有效似此專章加理在此期間內中蘇會議國際航行訂有辦法該項地方協議等件施行廢止本年修理黑龍江就此一切經費不降遇賴算全律之彰文隆執裝抏江及修理烏蘇里江鈉尔古納河等三項議外為此發雙方協訂聲明書一件計中俄文各如此互相簽字蓋印務執華文各一份以粘信字

大中華民國十二年一月十日
西曆一千九百二十七年一月十日

　　　　　訂於黑河

中國方面黑河道尹兼交涉員　張壽增

蘇聯方面駐黑河蘇俄領事　拉美德

航務東門會同易保羅

河樑弟國家水遈局局長尼河葵

河樑弟國家建局到局局長尼河葵

阿樑弟國家建局局長尼河葵

阿樑弟國字書處航務工程師客依羅夫

黑河道署外交科僉事卒庸珍

黑河道署外交科長次迓宋

璦琿關稅務司鋅傳費

航務東門會同易保羅

Jean Cocys
Tin-van-Chin
aux B.

Aigun despatch No. 315 to I. G.

Enclosure No.2.

Translation of the Chinese Version of the Protocol extending the 1923/1924 Agreement concerning Aids on the Amur for a further period of one year from the 1st December, 1926.

The Heiho Taoyin of the Heilungkiang Province (concurrently Commissioner of Foreign Affairs for the Aigun District) of the Republic of China, Chang Shou-tsen, and the Consul of the United Socialistic Soviet Republic at Taheiho, Melamed, hereby declare that the Provisional Local Agreement concerning Navigation on the Frontier Waters of the Amur River made for the twelfth year of the Chinese Republic (i.e.1923), together with Annexes numbers one and two, is to continue in force for another year from the first day of the twelfth month of the fifteenth year of the Republic of China (i.e.1926) to the first day of the twelfth month of the sixteenth year of the Republic of China (i.e.1927). If the Sino-Russian Conference be opened during the above mentioned period and an agreement be reached concerning the matters touched on herein, the present Agreement shall automatically cease to operate. The Total expenditure for the upkeep of Aids to Navigation on the Amur for the coming year shall not exceed the estimate of Gold Roubles 60,000. The dredging of the Amur, and works on the Argun and Ussuri are to be discussed separately.

To confirm the above Agreement this Protocol is made out, in the Chinese and Russian languages, in duplicate, and is signed and sealed by both parties.

Done

Done at Taheiho on the tenth day of the first month of the sixteenth year of the Republic of China corresponding to the tenth day of January, in the year one Thousand nine Hundred and twenty seven.

Representatives of the Chinese Aids Commission:

(signed) Chang Shou-tsen, Heiho Taoyin and Commissioner for Foreign Affairs, Aigun District.

" Ch'e Hsi-chen, Adviser to the Taoyin's Office.

" Shen Ting-jun, Chief of the Diplomatic Department of the Heiho Taoyin's Office.

" R. M. Talbot, Commissioner of Aigun Customs.

" P. I. Ignatieff, Technical Adviser to the Chinese Amur Aids Commission.

Representatives of the Soviet Aids Commission:

(signed) Melamed, Consul of U.S.S.R. at Taheiho.

" Dianoff, Director of the Amur Government Navigation Bureau.

" Chebisheff, Assistant Director of the Amur Government Navigation Bureau.

" Mihailoff, Engineer of the Amur Government Navigation Bureau.

True copy:

4th Assistant B.

Aigun despatch No. 315 to I. G.

Enclosure.No.3.

ПРОТОКОЛ

заседания Временной Местной Технической Комиссии в г.Сахаляне
Января " 10 " дня 1927 года.

ПРИСУТСТВОВАЛИ : Хейхэсский Дао-Инь и Дипломатический Чиновник в Айгуне .... Г. ЧЖАН-ШОУ-ДЗЕН

Комиссар Айгунской Таможни ...... Г. ТАЛБОТ

Старший Советник по Дипломатиче-
ской Части .... Г. ЧЕ-ПИН-ШАН

Технический Советник .... Г. ИГНАТЬЕВ

Консул СССР в г.Сахаляне .... Г. МАЛАМЕД

Начальник Управления Водных Путей
Амурского бассейна .... Г. ДИАНОВ

Помощник Начальника Управления
Водных Путей, Инженер .... Г. ЧЕБЫШОВ

Начальник Отдела Пути, Инженер ... Г. МИХАЙЛОВ

СЛУШАЛИ	ПОСТАНОВИЛИ
1/ Вопрос о продлении на 1927 год Соглашения между Правлением Амурского Государственного Водного Транспорта и Великой Китайской Республики Хэйхэсским Дао-Инем, заключенного 28 Октября 1923 года.	1/ Принимая во внимание, что временное соглашение от 28 Октября 1923 года, продленное до 1 Декабря 1926 года, потеряло свою силу за окончанием срока ПОСТАНОВИЛИ: 1/ Продлить это соглашение еще на один год, т.е. до 1-го Декабря 1927 года со всеми к нему приложениями, кроме приложения № 2,которое согласуется отдельно. 2/ Если в течение этого года состоится постановление, вырабатываемое ныне Советско-Китайской Конференции, в части ее касающейся совместного пользования пограничными путями, настоящее соглашение теряет свою силу.
2/ Смета на 1927 год по водному пути Амура в пределах общего пользования от Покровки до Казакевичевой протоки.	2/ Смету на 1927 год по обслуживанию водного пути общего пользования по Амуру УТВЕРДИТЬ в сумме 60.000 рублей.Сумма расхода не должна превышать исчисленную по смете сумму.
3/ Отчет по расходам, произведенным АВУ по ремонту и обслуживанию обстановкой р.Амура от Покровки до Казакевичева в навигацию 1926 года.	3/ Отчет за 1926 год в сумме 59.800рублей УТВЕРДИТЬ И расчет по этому отчету закончить.
4/ Производство других работ на реках общего пользования, как-то: камнеуборные и обстановочные работы на Аргуни, землечерпание на Амуре и обстановка на Уссури.	4/ Работы на прочих путях общего пользования подлежат особому согласованию в заседаниях Местной Технической Комиссии по каждому роду работ отдельно.
5/ О составлении протокола.	5/ Протокол должен быть составлен на русском и китайском языках по 2 экземпляра, из которых по одному экземпляру русского и китайского текста получает Комиссия с Китайской стороны и по одному экземпляру - Комиссия со стороны СССР.

ПОДПИСАЛИ :

Председатель Временной Местной Технической Комиссии со стороны СССР, Консул СССР в Сахаляне
Г.И. Меламед

Член Комиссии Начальник АВУ
Дианов
Чебышов
Михайлов

подлинным верно

Председатель Комиссии с Китайской стороны, Хэйхэсский Дао-Инь
Чжан-Шоу-Дзен

Член Талбот
Че-Пин-Шан
Игнатьев

True copy:
2nd Clerk B.

Aigun despatch No. 315 to I. G.

Enclosure No.4.

P R O T O C O L.

Minutes of a meeting of the Russian and Chinese Aids Commission at Taheiho on the 10th January, 1927.

Representatives:

The Heiho Taoyin and Commissioner of
    Foreign Affairs in Aigun   Chang Shou-tsen

Commissioner of Customs, Taheiho   Mr. Talbot

Diplomatic Adviser to Taoyin   Ch'e Hsi-chen

Technical Adviser on Amur Aids   Mr. Ignatieff

Consul of U.S.S.R. at Taheiho   Mr. Malamed

Director of Amur Navigation
    Office   Mr. Dianoff

Assistant Director of Amur
    Navigation Office   Mr. Chebisheff

Manager of Way Department of
    Amur Navigation Office   Mr. Mihailoff

Subject discussed:

1.   The continuation during 1927 of the Agreement concluded on the 28th October, 1923 between the Soviet Amur Government Water Transport and the Heiho Taoyin of the Great Chinese Republic.

Decision:

Taking into consideration the fact that the provisional Agreement of 28th October, 1923, extended to the 1st December, 1926, has now expired, the Commission decides:

a) To continue the existing Agreement for one year, i.e. to the 1st December, 1927, with all Annexes except Annex 3 which will be considered separately.

b) If during the present year the Sino-Soviet Conference

Conference should arrive at an agreement regarding the mutual use of frontier waterways, the present Agreement is automatically cancelled.

Subject discussed:

2.   Estimate of expenditure for the year 1927 on that part of the Amur in mutual use between Pokrovka and Kasakevich Waterway.

Decision:

To sanction the estimate of a sum of Rbls. 60,000 to be expended on that part of the Amur in mutual use. The expenditures for the year must not exceed this estimate.

Subject discussed:

3.   Detailed statement of expenditures made by the Amur Navigation Office on the upkeep of Aids on the Amur from Pokrovka to Kasakevich for the year 1926.

Decision:

To approve the statement of expenditure as made out at a total of Rbls. 59,000 and to arrange for the final payment due from the Chinese Commission.

Subject discussed:

4.   Other operations on the waterways of mutual use, i.e. removal of stones and establishment of Aids on the Argun, dredging of the Amur and the placing of Aids on the Ussuri.

Decision:

The above mentioned operations will be discussed and agreed to separately at special joint meetings of the two Commissions.

Subject

Subject discussed:

5.   Records to be made.

Decision:

     Minutes of meetings must be written out in Chinese and Russian and 2 copies of each handed to each party.

(signed)

President of the Russian Commission Mr. Malamed

Members of the Russian Commission Messrs.Dianoff

                                       Chebisheff

                                       Mihailoff

President of the Chinese Commission

     and Heiho Taoyin   Chang Shou-teen

Members of the Chinese Commission Messrs.Talbot

                                       Ch'e Hsi-chen

                                       Ignatieff

True copy:

2nd Clerk B

Aigun despatch No.315 to I.G.

Enclosure No.5.

SUMMARY OF AMUR RIVER DUES COLLECTION DURING THE YEAR 1926.

	Category I Poods	Category I $	Category II Poods	Category II $	Timber Units	Timber $	Firewood Sajens	Firewood $	Cattle Head	Cattle $	Fowls No.	Fowls $	Passenger Tickets $	Total $
May Taheiho	73,682	875.73	59,483	1,085.15	17,77?	127.43	1,03?	80.26	6	0.90	...	...	336.33	2,505.8?
Aigun	5,62?	8?.??	1,40?	2?.??							...	...		52.1?
June Taheiho	127,127	1,842.6?	68,515	1,197.86	19,95?	232.84	2,69?	329.87	14	1.95	25	0.25	606.61	4,112.0?
Aigun	24,944	134.1?	3,027	46.40	2??	0.63	1?	2.30			20	0.10	8.40	192.4?
July Taheiho	61,497	644.0?	48,189	839.67	27,521	217.64	3,850	305.47	7	0.75	36	0.18	628.07	2,635.7?
Aigun	3,52?	17.7?	?,417	20.4?	1,518	20.4?		2.70	2?	3.70	24	1.23	3.??	66.9?
Aug. Taheiho	69,983	659.23	68,804	1,214.58	8,54?	69.42	3,11?	245.94	7	0.76	...	...	503.62	2,693.5?
Aigun	1,61?	3.4?	5,49?	101.58					46	3.47			5.??	119.7?
Sept. Taheiho	64,283	663.0?	133,863	2,337.83	23,32?	201.16	2,75?	324.90	131	13.23	30	0.15	638.98	4,085.3?
Aigun	89?	6.2?	3,4??	117.?4					12?	5.79	30	0.35	9.38	179.6?
Oct. Taheiho	40,472	264.84	137,001	2,611.91	28,048	275.82	?,89?	255.92	2?	1.20	30	0.15	496.03	3,902.6?
Aigun	1,65?	21.?3	3,4??	46.??	6,873	47.?4			12?		30	0.2?	12.??	1??.4?
Total Taheiho	437,044	3,949.52	505,855	9,287.00	125,160	1,121.11	15,352	1,342.36	169	24.79	121	0.73	3,209.64	19,935.1?
Aigun	3?,36?	3?3.10	1?,4??	4??.?3	9,41?	??.31	1?	2.30	1?1	?.4?	390	1.?6	35.90	6?6.7?
Lahasusu														*14,837.5?
Grand Total:	4?5,?1?	6.?2	528,?32	9,??4.?3	133,?01	190.4?	15,36?	315.1?	3??.??	67.?0	511	2.?9	*3,245.54	2?,???.4?

*Collection on passenger tickets at Lahasusu- $ 3,202.47 - not included, i.e. grand total under this heading is $ 6,248.01.

*Including collection on passenger tickets, $ 3,202.47.

N.B. Figures for Lahasusu under different headings not available.

Certified Correct:

P. Lysnekoff
Technical Adviser.

Prepared by:

2nd Clerk, B.

Technical Adviser's Office,
H.B. Custom House,
Aigun/Taheiho, 3rd April, 1927.

Copy for Aigun Commissioner.

M E M O R A N D U M.

CUSTOM HOUSE,
HARBIN, 20th May, 1927.

28 MAY 1927

To
The Chief Secretary,
Inspectorate General of Customs
P E K I N G.

Harbin Commissioner's comments on Aigun
Despatch No.315/I.G. dated 3rd May, 1927,
docketed,

<u>Amur Aids to Navigation</u>: Renewal of
Agreement for 1927 notifying; estimates
and budget for Chinese Aids commission
for 1927 submitting; discussions between
the two Commissions of the question of
Aids on Argun and Ussuri, and dredging
on the Upper Amur, reporting on.

The old Russian Rules of Navigation are still
more or less functioning and followed by Chinese
shipping as " unwritten " law or tacidly accepted as
"rules of the road". If the Aigun Commissioner
succeeds in having them promulgated in toto or in part
as actual jointly recognised and accepted laws for
Chinese and Russian shipping on the frontier rivers,
I anticipate no difficulty in obtaining sanction for
their adoption on the purely Chinese rivers (Sungari
and Nonni) adjoining the former. I would not advocate
simultaneous negotiations of this question at Aigun
and Harbin/such would undoubtedly add to the difficulties
of reaching an agreement with the Chinese faction.

The control of shipping on the Sungari is at the
present time on a no more satisfactory basis than it is
on the

on the Amur. There are no legally accepted rules and
the Customs are not empowered - and would not be able -
to enforce the old Russian rules referred to above, their
tacid acceptance by shipping amounting to a purely
voluntary expedient.

If rules, new or old, be promulgated, the Customs
should and - I trust - would naturally be empowered with
their enforcement. To avoid or minimise disputes
such rules should be accompanied by a fixed scale of
penalties for contravention, graduated upwards to meet
cases of repetition and of habitual offence.

In Chinese lawsuits arising out of collision and
other accidents the Commissioner (or his Deputy, the
Harbour Master) and the Superintendent might be empowered
to sit as assessors or advisors in Chinese courts but
in international cases as advisors only.

Acting Commissioner.

Copy of these comments is being sent to the Aigun
Commissioner and the Coast Inspector.

呈海关总税务司署 315 号文　　　　　　　　　　　　瑷珲关 1927 年 5 月 3 日

尊敬的代理海关总税务司（北京）：

根据 1923 年 12 月 29 日瑷珲关第 144 号呈：

"兹汇报，为继续维护黑龙江航路标志，已签署《1923/1924 年黑龙江航路标志协议》。"

及瑷珲关第 230 号、263 号呈：

"基于《1923/1924 年黑龙江航路标志协议》的内容，协商 1925 年、1926 年《黑龙江航路标志协议》的续约事宜。"

兹报告，已于 1927 年 1 月 10 日签订《黑龙江航路标志协议》，有效期为 1926 年 12 月 1 日至 1927 年 11 月 30 日，为《1923/1924 黑龙江航路标志协议》的续约协议。

为获得协议抄件，耽搁良久，现兹附协议各版本抄件：

附件 1：中文版续约协议

附件 2：中文版续约协议的英文译本

附件 3：俄文版续约协议

附件 4：俄文版续约协议的英文译本

中文和俄文两版协议在形式和措辞上存在很大差异，且先前的续约协议中也存在同样问题。但本署告知道尹后，其依然希望尽可能沿用前例，继续保持旧版协议的形式，以便尽快取得省政府和北京政府的批准。俄方代表于协议上签字时亦未注意中文版协议的措辞。不过，中俄双方协商续约事宜时，使用的却是俄文版协议，且在拟订供签署之用的协议原始抄件之前，双方委员已在联合会议上口头肯定了该版本协议。

起初，俄方提交了一份全新的协议，在保留旧版协议大部分内容的基础之上，删除了一些过时的规定，同旧版协议相比更具条理。航务专门顾问和本署均更倾向于新版协议，但道尹还是希望尽可能沿用前例。俄国航政委员会在本次协商中一直秉持着互相谅解的原则，对道尹的立场给予了认可，因而撤销了拟订新协议之提议。

在协商《协议》续约一事时，华方面对的主要难题是削减预算。俄国航政委员会资金充足，故原定预算为 338000 金卢布；但该预算中含超出协议之项目，可以从中扣除：

黑龙江疏浚项目	120000 金卢布
乌苏里江航路标志项目	18000 金卢布
额尔古纳河建立航路标志与清理石块项目	20000 金卢布
总计	158000 金卢布

因中国航政委员会资金薄弱,剩下的 180000 金卢布预算额仍须削减。

航务专门顾问作为中国航政委员会的协商主力,曾于俄阿穆尔水道局工作多年,并参与中国航政委员会工作五年,与俄国航政委员会成员的关系亦十分融洽(他所提出的建议和意见,俄方委员大都会予以考虑并接受),最终成功地将预算削减至 60000 金卢布。兹附航务专门顾问编制的摘要报告,前两栏是 1926 年及 1927 年不同项目的协商预算,第三栏是俄国航政委员会所提议的 1927 年预算。如果海关总税务司署得知俄阿穆尔水道局 1927 年的初拟预算本为 1200000 卢布(后莫斯科政府将之减少至 780000 卢布),相信会更加理解俄国航政委员会所做出的巨大牺牲,从而接受中国将承担的 30000 卢布的预算额。航务专门顾问认为,全赖双方委员的友好态度和相互体谅,才能最终达成这一令华方十分满意的协议。但俄国今后是否会再次同意大幅削减预算,实难以确定。

华方已承诺支出 30000 卢布(即预算额的一半),用于 1927 年黑龙江航路标志的维护工程,因此必须核验所需资金的来源,以确保如约支付该笔款项以及中国航政委员会办事处的开支。拟定 1927 年预算如下。

预计支出

黑龙江航路标志维护工作华方摊款	30000 银圆
道尹公署办公经费	2000 银圆
航务专门顾问办事处办公经费	9000 银圆
江捐税收扣除 10% 海关征税佣金	4500 银圆
汇兑损失及意外开支	1200 银圆
总计	46700 银圆

预计收入:

1927 年江捐税收	45000 银圆
自松花江航路标志账户预支款账	5000 银圆
1926 年结余	3700 银圆
总 计	53700 银圆

　　附件 5 为 1926 年江捐税收分配图表。如表所示,1926 年大黑河口岸、瑷珲口岸与拉哈苏苏口岸的江捐税收总计 35469 银圆,与 1925 年的 28819 银圆相比,1926 年显然形势更佳。税收增长主要因为 1926 年末在拉哈苏苏口岸针对乌苏里江船运对乘客征收船票税,而且乌苏里江上的货运量也有大幅增长。根据瑷珲关第 311 号呈,可知随着关税的逐步提高,江捐也必会有所增加,预计 1927 年可达 45000 银圆。1926 年末自松花江航路标志账户所贷款项的可用余额为 20000 银圆,之后又从松花江航路标志账户预支了 5000 银圆(参见上述 1927 年收入预算),但随着税收收入增加,相信无须再支用此类贷款,甚至或可偿还自松花江航路标志预支的部分款项。

　　由上述预算可知,1927 年末的结余为 7000 银圆,如果一切正常,相信还会有更多的盈余。另外,双方航政委员会已开始讨论联合维护乌苏里江航路标志的相关事宜,很有可能会参考《黑龙江航路标志协议》的内容,签订有关乌苏里江航路标志的协议。若该协议得以签订,则第一年华方需承担约 5000 银圆(之后会陆续减少)的费用,盈余自然也会相应减少。鉴于 1926 年拉哈苏苏段乌苏里江的江捐税收只有 10272 银圆,兹认为确实有改善乌苏里江航路标志的必要,道尹对此亦表示支持。

　　据瑷珲关第 230 号和第 263 号呈所示,当中国航政委员会认识到改善乌苏里江航路标志的必要性之后,分别于 1925 年和 1926 年两次提出有关维护乌苏里江与嘎杂克维池(Kasakevich)水道航路标志的问题。但是中俄双方关于哈巴罗夫斯克(Habarovsk,即伯力)附近的边界问题一直存有争议,且乌苏里江航道与嘎杂克维池水道更因流经吉林省而导致情况愈加复杂,因而至今仍未能达成任何协议。

　　现任道尹张寿增先生对上述问题一直保持着高度的关注,并频频参与有关会议,希望能够达成一份让中俄双方都满意的协议。但其实张先生并不愿意参加此类会议,因为这就意味着他间接认同了中国轮船没有在黑龙江与哈巴罗夫斯克以及乌苏里江之间航行的权利。本署也认为达成协议的前提,是要制订出一个中俄双方都愿意接受的方案。兹建议，由中国航政委员会负责乌苏里江（虎林至饶河县段）上游部分（大约自虎林至哈巴罗夫斯克之间）的航路标志维护工作；而下游部分则交由俄方全权负责。如此，俄方可自行决定所负责部分内的所有事宜，从而避免任何的边境争端。至于嘎杂克维池水道航路标志的维护问题，则容后再议。

道尹同意本署的建议并已将之呈送至吉林省政府。然而在之后的一次会议上，当讨论到这一建议的时候，道尹却指出，如果俄方不肯承认中国轮船拥有在黑龙江与哈巴罗夫斯克以及乌苏里江之间航行的权利，则中国坚决不会签署任何的协议。于是，联合维护乌苏里江航路标志一事又再次陷入了僵局。在本署的建议下，双方同意该问题由莫斯科政府和吉林省政府在即将召开于北京的中俄会议上解决。1927 年 3 月 11 日，道尹正式发函通知俄国航政委员会，表示已收到吉林省政府的通知，该问题将正式提交中俄会议处理，在此期间，双方航政委员会均不得在乌苏里江上进行任何活动。俄国航政委员会提出抗议，认为他们有继续在乌苏里江上活动的权利，并可以自费在乌苏里江归属于俄国的一边（非争议区域）建设航路标志。本署认为俄方的说法并无违理之处。目前尚不确定道尹是否能暂且放下中国轮船航行权的问题，允许中国航政委员会只就联合维护乌苏里江航路标志一事与俄方签订纯粹技术性的协议。

1926 年末，俄国航政委员会提出申请，欲自费清理额尔古纳河中危害航运安全的石块。道尹将该申请转呈至齐齐哈尔后，该申请得到了批准。然而之后，当俄国航政委员会准备在额尔古纳河两侧建立航路标志时，道尹却拒绝给出在中国管辖一侧进行施工的许可。此举相当于废除了前令的效力，因为道尹曾同意俄国航政委员会自费在边境河道两侧开展工事。然而，额尔古纳河上并无中国的轮船往来，也几乎看不到有俄国的轮船。俄国航政委员会之所以希望开展额尔古纳河航路标志项目和石块清理工事，并提出 20000 银圆的预算，其实是为了向莫斯科方面夸大俄阿穆尔水道局 1927 年部分工程的重要性，以便于申请更多的资金。

1927 年，本已决定黑龙江上游的疏浚工事继续且长期由俄国航政委员会全权负责，不过后来又发生了变化。起初，道尹曾一度考虑过同俄方联合开展部分疏浚工事，但航务专门顾问却认为，仅仅为了方便华方的一艘小轮船和俄方的三艘轮船，而支出高达 120000 银圆的疏浚费用，实在是得不偿失，道尹遂放弃了这一想法。而最近，俄国航政委员会也产生了同航务专门顾问一样的看法，并提出了完全撤销疏浚工事的申请，希望将经费用在更重要的地方。

1926 年双方航政委员会之间的遗留问题，主要是关于边境河道上中俄轮船的管理一事。据1920年4月海关总税务司署致哈尔滨关第2248/78057号令指示,海关总税务司署已收到税务处的指令,大意是:鉴于目前难以同俄方代表展开"正式商讨",故决定通过黑龙江督军与西伯利亚阿穆尔省的俄国政府进行协商,以暂时安排中国轮船在黑龙江上的航运事宜;因此命令哈尔滨关税务司尽一切可能,协助督军安排有关事宜。由于税务处之指令的抄件尚未发送至本署,故具体内容还不甚清楚。

1922年4月5日,瑷珲关第11号机要文件报告,阿穆尔省政府已向道尹提交了《黑龙江航务与松花江航务暂行安排计划》,而瑷珲关署理税务司业已根据海关总税务司署致哈尔滨关第2248/78057号令,为道尹编写了一份回复给俄方的计划,力求更好地保护华方的利益。1922年5月24日,海关总税务司署回复瑷珲关第11号机要文件,黑龙江与松花江的航务问题已交由北京相关商会处理,计划草案将作为中俄双方相关政府的谈判基础;同时,地方不得采取任何行动影响谈判。此事除1926年2月15日瑷珲关第54号机要文件外,再无任何相关记录。据瑷珲关第54号机要文件称,俄国航政委员会急于采用《边界河道航务与船舶检查联合条例》,而道尹则以此举有损航政委员会利益为由表示拒绝。海关总税务司署1926年3月15日机要文件回复,同意道尹的观点,认为《海运法》确实与黑龙江航路标志无关,此为国家级事宜,不在地方的管辖范围之内。

该问题遂一直搁置,直到1926年10月30日,俄国航政委员会致信中国航政委员会委员长(道尹),指出在航运季期间,有部分中国轮船违反《航务条例》,而该条例理应由黑龙江上的所有轮船共同遵守。俄国航政委员会再次强调,此前之所以提出采用《联合条例》,就是为了保证中俄轮船的安全。

由于过去黑龙江与松花江上的航运工作均归俄国所有,所适用的《航务条例》《检查条例》等也均为俄国所制定,因此许多中国人都曾在俄国的轮船上工作并接受培训。后来俄国经济衰退,中国轮船遂开始在黑龙江和松花江上运营,但中国轮船上的船员仍是以俄籍职员和俄籍引水员为主,即使有华籍的水手,也大多是由俄国培训出来的,因此中国的新建船队仍然沿用先前俄国的航务条例及惯例。但是最近,由于各种原因,中国轮船上的俄籍职员与俄籍引水员不断减少,许多时候,空缺的职位不得不由一些训练不足、能力有限的华籍职员来顶替。然而中国政府却未能在黑龙江上很好地施行此前的俄国航务条例,这就导致中国轮船在黑龙江上航行时未能很好地遵守航务条例,且不会因此而受到任何惩罚,从而为船上的生命及财产带来了巨大的隐患。全凭运气好(而非航运技术好),才没有发生更多的事故。但是随着中国轮船上的职员与引水员素质的下降(海关并不要求他们出示任何的能力证明),事故的发生只不过是时间问题而已,并且会愈发频繁。

在收到俄国航政委员会于 1926 年 10 月 30 日发来的信件后，道尹遂于中国航政委员会会议上表示，建议采用《中俄边界河道联合航务条例》中的适用部分；本署业已向道尹说明，海关总税务司署的意思是，该问题应由两国政府进行协商。不过道尹和中国航政委员会考虑到两国政府先前关系的紧张，担心会妨碍协商的顺利进行，所以希望在两国政府正式签订常规协议之前，能够依俄国航政委员会的期望，暂时使用非争议性的简单条例。对于两国政府是否能够顺利地进行协商，本署暂不发表任何看法。

航务专门顾问易保罗（P. I. Ignatieff）先生于 1926 年 12 月 20 日收到道尹的来信（随呈附上信件抄件），信中委托易保罗先生与东北航务局经理为代表，负责《中俄边界河道联合航务条例》的草拟工作，俄国航政委员会也同样委派了两名代表，准备参与其中，此事航务专门顾问已汇报至省政府政府。

在易保罗先生将道尹的委托告知于本署后，本署立即拜访了道尹，向其解释说易保罗先生只是担任航务专门顾问一职，如果想对其另加委任，则必须先通过本署向海关总税务司署申请，这方面可参考前道尹申请委任航务专门顾问为奉天会议代表之先例。同时，本署还向道尹解释，海关总税务司署并不认为地方政府具有制定《航务条例》的权限，道尹对易保罗先生的委任，很可能会使易保罗先生遭到海关总税务司署的责难。道尹很快便意识到了自己的考虑不周，但令文已经发出且无法撤回；事实上，即使可以撤回，道尹也并没有真将之撤回的打算。于是，在经过长时间的讨论后，本署和道尹暂时决定，易保罗先生和东北行业公司经理二人与俄方代表所商定的初步结果，可先汇报至中国航政委员会，再由中国航政委员会通过道尹和省政府政府呈报税务处，请示批准。如此，既可以避免有关航务专门顾问职权范围的争议，更可以顺势将之后的协商事宜移交中国航政委员会负责，而不再由道尹插手。

本署已在第 69 号机要文件中向海关总税务司署汇报了道尹对此事的态度，而海关总税务司署亦于 1927 年 1 月 22 日回复本署，根据《国际航海避碰章程》第三十条，同意航务专门顾问协助草拟条例。相关章程内容如下：

港口及内陆航运继续遵照《航务条例》

第三十条：凡地方政府有正式制定与港口河道或内陆水道航运有关的特殊条例，则此章程中的任何条例不得影响该特殊条例的施行。

在收到海关总税务司署的指令后,航务专门顾问起草了《拟定航务条例》,抄件已随第72号机要文件呈送至海关总税务司署,并将两份抄件分别送至哈尔滨关税务司与巡工司。松花江上也可以适用该条例,并遵守同黑龙江上一样的规定。条例草案已送交至俄国航政委员会,俄国航政委员会对条例草案做了某些修改和补充,但并无重大改动,之后条例草案又送回至中国航政委员会,中国航政委员会对俄方所做改动表示无异议。本署可在收到海关总税务司署的指令以及哈尔滨关税务司和巡工司的意见后,再将条例付诸施行。

据本署分析,一旦中俄黑龙江水道委员会批准该《拟定航务条例》(海关总税务司署亦批准),则道尹在将该条例提交省政府政府以转呈税务处申请批准时,可能会请求税务处正式向海关总税务司署下达实施该条例的命令,以管理边境河道中的中国轮船。若违反条例的事件中同时涉及中俄双方的轮船,则地方政府应向海关总税务司署咨询处理办法。

中俄黑龙江水道委员会续签1926年协议之后的所有活动几乎都已在呈文中做了汇报,请连同瑷珲关第313号呈中的航务专门顾问年度报告一同查阅。

您忠诚的仆人

铎博赉(R. M. Talbot)

瑷珲关署理税务司

航务专门顾问办事处

1927年5月3日瑷珲关/大黑河

附录 1

1926 年及 1927 年黑龙江航路标志维护预算费用报表

及 1927 年俄阿穆尔水道局首次提交预算费用报表

明细	1926 年	1927 年	
	预算	预算	俄阿穆尔水道局首次提交预算
	金卢布	金卢布	金卢布
地区职员薪俸	13959	7020	15000
水深信号站职员薪俸	2730	4100	9000
交通站职员薪俸	386	427	1000
水深信号站的建立及运营	350	—	—
交通站的建立及运营	51	—	—
航路标志的建立、修理及维护	11836	11900	30000
安设灯桩	4565	5365	10000
房屋维修	500	500	1000
邮费、电报费、固定费用及杂费	750	750	2000
房屋供暖	350	350	500
电费	100	100	200
差旅费	350	350	4000
医疗护理费的 5%	2214	2000	7000
折旧费	2238	1748	2000
工作艇维护	8600	18500	60000
地区办事处维修费	9150	6000	36000
石头清理	400	600	1000
意外支出	1502	290	1300
总计	60031	60000	
1927 年黑龙江航路标志首次预算总计			180000

明细	1926 年	1927 年	
	预算	预算	俄阿穆尔水道局首次提交预算
黑龙江航路标志补充			
黑龙江疏浚工事			120000
乌苏里江航路标志的建立			18000
额尔古纳河清理石块			8000
额尔古纳河航路标志的建立			12000
1927 年首次预算总计			338000

兹证明,报表正确无误。

易保罗航务专门顾问

此抄件发送至巡工司与哈尔滨关税务司。

录事: 屠守鑫四等帮办后班

瑷珲关致海关总税务司署第 315 号呈附件 2

1923/1924 年黑龙江航路标志协议于 1926 年 12 月 1 日起续约一年，此为续约协议之中文版译本

　　中华民国黑龙江省黑河道尹兼瑷珲交涉员张寿增与苏维亚社会联邦共和国驻黑河领事默拉美德声明，中华民国十二年（1923）双方所订黑龙江等中俄两国交界河流航行地方临时协议暨附则，以及第一、第二号附件，兹再展期一年，即自中华民国十五年十二月一日（1926 年 12 月 1 日）起，至中华民国十六年十二月一日（1927 年 12 月 1 日）止，继续有效，仍照旧章办理。在此期间，如中苏会议国际航行订有办法，该项地方协议等件即行废止。又本年修理黑龙江一切经费，不得超过预算金（60000 金卢布）。除机器挖江及修理乌苏里江、额尔古纳河等三项另议外。

　　为此，双方协定声明书一件，计中、俄文各两份，互相签字盖印，各执中、俄文各一份，以恪信守。

　　中华民国十六年一月十日（1927 年 1 月 10 日）订于大黑河。

华方：

黑河道尹兼瑷珲交涉员	张寿增
黑河道署外交顾问	车席珍
黑河道署外交科长	沈廷荣
瑷珲关税务司	铎博贲
航务专门顾问	易保罗

俄方：

驻黑河苏俄领事	默拉美德
阿穆尔国家水道局局长	托阿诺夫
阿穆尔国家水道局副局长	且比索夫
阿穆尔国家水道局航路工程师	弥哈依洛夫（米海依罗夫）

该抄件内容真实有效，特此证明。

录事：屠守鑫四等帮办后班

瑷珲关致海关总税务司署第 315 号呈附件 4[①]

协议

1927 年 1 月 10 日于大黑河中俄黑龙江水道委员会会议纪要

参会代表：

黑河道尹兼瑷珲交涉员	张寿增先生
瑷珲关税务司	铎博赉先生
黑河道署外交顾问	车席珍先生
黑龙江航务专门顾问	易保罗先生
驻黑河苏俄领事	默拉美德先生
阿穆尔水道局局长	托阿诺夫先生
阿穆尔水道局副局长	且比索夫先生
阿穆尔水道局航路工程师	米海依罗夫先生

提案：

（一）关于展期 1923 年 10 月 28 日俄阿穆尔水道局与大中华民国黑河道尹签订之协议至 1927 年之问题。

议决：

（一）查 1923 年 10 月 28 日至 1926 年 12 月 1 日之临时协议现已期满不生效力，本署决定：

（甲）上述协议续约一年至 1927 年 12 月 1 日止；除附件 3 以外，其余附件均与协议一起继续有效；

（乙）倘于本年内，中俄会议对于共用边境河道事宜达成新协议，则本协议即行废止。

提案：

（二）预估中俄双方 1927 年对黑龙江边界河道（自波克罗夫卡（Pokrovka）至嘎杂克维池水道）的使用情况及所需费用。

议决：

---

① 注：附件 3 为协议俄文版，不予翻译。

（二）批准中俄双方对黑龙江边界河道的使用及费用预算，预计总额为 60000 金卢布，实际支出不得超出该预算额。

提案：

（三）1926 年阿穆尔水道局维护黑龙江边界河道（自波克罗夫卡至嘎杂克维池）航路标志的支出明细。

议决：

（三）批准总计为 59800 金卢布的支出，确定中国航政委员会最终应付款项。

提案：

（四）与河道使用相关的其他事项，比如石块的清理工事，额尔古纳河航路标志的建立工事，黑龙江航道的疏浚工事，以及乌苏里江航路标志的建立工事等。

议决：

（四）上述计划将在两国特殊联合会议上分别讨论和审议。

提案：

（五）会议纪要之要求。

议决：

（五）会议纪要须分别以中文和俄文书写，双方各保存中、俄文协议副本各一份。

（签字）

俄方航政委员会委员长	默拉美德
俄方航政委员会委员	托阿诺夫
	且比索夫
	米海依罗夫
华方航政委员会委员长兼黑河道尹	张寿增
华方航政委员会委员	车席珍
	铎博赉易保罗

该抄件内容真实有效，特此证明。

录事：王德懋二等同文供事中班

瑷珲关致海关总税务司署第 315 号呈附件 5

1926 年江捐税收分配图表（口岸及关税种类）

月	口岸	类别 I 普特	类别 I 银圆	类别 II 普特	类别 II 银圆	杂项类 木料 单位	杂项类 木料 银圆	杂项类 木桻 俄丈	杂项类 木桻 银圆	杂项类 牲畜 头	杂项类 牲畜 银圆	杂项类 家禽 数量	杂项类 家禽 银圆	杂项类 乘客船票 银圆	总计 银圆
5 月	大黑河口岸	73682	875.73	59483	1085.15	17772	127.43	1034	80.26	6	0.90	—	—	336.33	2505.80
	瑷珲口岸	5629	28.20	1495	23.97	—	—	—	—	—	—	—	—	—	52.17
6 月	大黑河口岸	127127	1842.66	68515	1197.86	19952	232.84	2698	229.87	14	1.95	25	0.25	606.61	4112.04
	瑷珲口岸	2944	134.12	3027	46.40	250	0.63	14	2.80	—	—	20	0.10	8.40	192.45
7 月	大黑河口岸	61497	644.00	48189	839.67	27521	217.64	3850	305.47	7	0.75	36	0.18	628.07	2635.78
	瑷珲口岸	3525	17.72	1417	20.49	1518	20.74	—	—	36	2.70	245	1.23	3.92	66.80
8 月	大黑河口岸	69983	659.23	68804	1214.58	8543	69.42	3117	245.94	7	0.76	—	—	503.62	2693.55
	瑷珲口岸	1616	9.48	5488	101.58	—	—	—	—	46	3.47	—	—	5.22	119.75
9 月	大黑河口岸	64283	663.06	123863	2337.83	23324	201.16	2756	224.90	131	19.23	30	0.15	638.98	4085.31
	瑷珲口岸	899	6.25	7477	117.84	—	—	—	—	77	5.79	70	0.35	9.38	139.61
10 月	大黑河口岸	40472	264.84	137001	2611.91	28048	272.62	1897	255.92	4	1.20	30	0.15	496.03	3902.67
	瑷珲口岸	1656	11.33	3473	56.95	6873	47.94	—	—	6	0.45	55	0.28	8.98	125.93
1926 年总计	大黑河口岸	437044	4949.52	505855	9287.00	125160	1121.11	15352	1342.36	169	24.79	121	0.73	3209.64	19935.15
	瑷珲口岸	38269	207.10	22377	367.23	8641	69.31	14	2.80	165	12.41	390	1.96	35.90	696.71
	拉哈苏苏口岸	—	—	—	—	—	—	—	—	—	—	—	—	—	*14837.56
	1926 年总计	475313	5156.62	528232	9654.23	133801	1190.42	15366	1345.16	334	37.20	511	2.69	+3245.54	35469.42

+ 拉哈苏苏的船票税收为 3202.47 银圆。

* 拉哈苏苏的船票税收 3202.47 银圆（未列入表中），因此，乘客船票条目下的累计总额应为 6428.01 银圆。

注：拉哈苏苏口岸无各项数据。

* 包括船票税收 3202.47 银圆。

制表：王德穗　二等同文供事中班

抄送：瑷珲关税务司

通函

由：	致：
哈尔滨关	海关总税务司署（北京）总务科税务司
1927 年 5 月 20 日	

1927 年 5 月 3 日瑷珲关致海关总税务司署第 315 号呈收悉：

"黑龙江航务：汇报 1927 年《黑龙江航路标志协议》续约事宜；呈送中国航政委员会 1927 年预算；汇报中俄黑龙江水道委员会就额尔古纳河航路标志与乌苏里江航路标志问题，以及黑龙江上游疏浚工事的协商情况。"

于中国船运而言，俄国旧《航务条例》仍具有一定效力，不仅被视为"不成文"之规章，甚至当作"道路条例"之用。若瑷珲关税务司能够将俄国旧《航务条例》的全部或部分内容重新发布，成为边界河道上的中俄船运共同承认之条例，相信此新条例定会获得批准于与俄相连之中国境内河道（松花江和嫩江）上施行。但本署并不建议瑷珲关与哈尔滨同时协商此项事宜，因如此会为中国内部协议之达成徒增困难。

目前，松花江与黑龙江上的航运管理皆有不尽如人意之处。鉴于没有合法的条例，海关无权也无法实施俄国旧《航务条例》，所以中国船运对该条例的默认仅为自愿之行为。

无论新旧条例，一经发布，相信海关定会获得实施条例之授权。为了避免或减少争议，发布条例的同时，应制定相应的违规处罚措施，以应对反复违规之行为。

关于因碰撞或其他事故而引起的诉讼，税务司（或者副税务司、理船厅）及海关监督在中国法庭之上或有权担任陪审员或者顾问，但若为国际诉讼，则只能担任顾问。

巴闰森（P. G. S. Barentzen）

哈尔滨关署理税务司

此抄件发送至瑷珲关税务司及巡工司。

22. 1927 年《联合维护乌苏里江航路标志临时协议》

USSURI AIDS: Signing of provisional Agreement for
joint upkeep of, by Amur Aids Commission for remainder
of year 1927, reporting. Russian and Chinese versions
322. of Agreement, together with summary of correspondence
in re. estimate and charts, forwarding.

I.G.

322.
I.G.

Aigun   12th   July, 1927.

Sir,

1.   I have the honour to inform you that
a provisional Agreement for the joint upkeep of
Aids on the Ussuri from Hulin to Kasakevich was
signed at a meeting of the Sino-Russian Amur
Aids Commission at the Taoyin's yamen on the
17th ultimo.

2.   Copies and translations of documents in
this connection are enclosed as follows:

Enclosure No.1.   The Chinese version of the Agreement.

Enclosure No.2.   The English translation of same.

Enclosure No.3.   The Russian version of the Agreement.

Enclosure No.4.   The English translation of same.

3.   As in the case of the recent renewal
of the Amur Aids Agreement, reported in Aigun
despatch No. 315, it will be noticed that there
are certain discrepancies between the two versions

The

The Officiating Inspector General of Customs,
Peking.

The question of which one should be followed
in case of a dispute was not brought up though,
in the present instance, the two versions were
exchanged and approved by the different sides
before the day of their signing.

4.   The question of the joint establishment
of Aids on the Ussuri has been the subject of
long and complicated negotiations due to the
dispute between the authorities of the two
countries as to (1.) the exact location of the
boundary in the vicinity of Harbarovsk, and (2.)
the consequent right of the Chinese to navigate
the Amur from Irga to Harbarovsk (and the sea)
and the Ussuri from Harbarovsk to Kasakevich
village.

5.   In order to facilitate reference to
correspondence that has passed between the
Inspectorate and the Aigun Customs regarding the
joint establishment of Aids on the Ussuri (and
Append No.1.   Kasakevich Waterway) I append a summary of the
most important communications. At the same time

I

I should like to record a few observations on the political and technical points of the question.

6.　　First, as to some of the political issues involved. With the best will in the world it would be impossible to disassociate the Commission from politics. Given the Taoyin and the Soviet Consul as respective heads of the two sides of the Commission it could not well be otherwise. The time of every meeting of the joint Commission was taken up almost entirely in trying to come to an understanding as to the wording of an agreement that would not prejudice the interests of either country in any future negotiations over the reallocation of frontier lines. At these meetings I remained a passive auditor unless my opinion was requested. I was actively interested, however, in seeing that an agreement was drawn up so that something could be done for the improvement of Ussuri Aids in exchange for the dues we were collecting on traffic on that river. Both the Technical Adviser and myself often had

occasion

occasion to suggest to the Taoyin possible solutions of some *impasse* that had arisen, to advise him on the international aspects of a question and to act as go-betweens to the two sides in an endeavour to create in advance as friendly an atmosphere as possible for the meetings of the Commission. There seems little doubt but that the Kasakevich Waterway has been the commonly accepted boundary up until recently. On the other hand it would seem quite clear that according to international practice the boundary should follow the main channel of the Amur (and Ussuri) and that the island in dispute, at the junction of the Amur and Ussuri, should belong entirely to China together with the Kasakevich Waterway. During the negotiations the Russians several times raised the question of the status of this Waterway but the Taoyin cleverly kept it from being mentioned in the Agreement. He did not definitely assume the position during the discussions (though he did with me privately) that it was a Chinese inland

waterway

waterway but the mere fact that agreements have now been made regarding all contiguous waters and not the Kasakevich Waterway would rather indicate that the question of establishment of joint aids on that branch of the Amur was not open to negotiation. An interesting point raised by the Taoyin but left unsettled was as to whether or not Chinese vessels, if the water became insufficient in the Kasakevich Waterway, could proceed via Harbarovsk. The negotiations, for the most part, were conducted in a friendly spirit the Amur Navigation Bureau officials meeting the Taoyin's wishes whenever possible. The Soviet Consul, however, showed the "cloven hoof" at the final meeting talking in a very dictatorial and often impolite manner. It was only the conciliatoriness of the Taoyin on this occasion that carried the matter to a successful conclusion.

7.   To turn now to the technical aspects of the Agreement; there was no difficulty in reaching an understanding as to the points involved. The

estimate

Enclosure No.5.

estimate prepared by the Technical Adviser (for the remainder of the year) was for G.Rbls.8,200. This was raised Rbls.400 by the Amur Navigation Bureau, the sum of G.Rbls.8,600 being eventually agreed to - one half to be paid by the Chinese Commission. A copy of the estimate as approved is enclosed. With the recent increase in the River Dues Tariff and with greater activity amongst Chinese shipping on the Ussuri, the River Dues Collection at Lahasusu on Ussuri traffic has shown a marked advance and has now reached proportions where the question of improvement of Ussuri aids can no longer be ignored. I took every occasion to point this out to the Taoyin and it was a strong factor in determining him to arrange for aids on the Ussuri. The Technical Adviser reports that there have been practically no repairs to Aids on the stretch Kasakevich to Hulin since 1916. A rough estimate of the work to be done is as follows:

New Signals Required.
River type: poles   150
River type: shields 200

Repairs

Repairs to Signals.

River type:	poles	60
River type:	shields	100
Sea type:	pyramids (poles)	10
Sea type:	pyramids (shields)	14

8.   In my despatch No. 315 to I.G. I drew up a budget for the coming year in which I estimated that, if normal conditions continued and with the increased tariff, the River Dues Collection would be some $45,000 and the surplus at the end of the year some $7,000 out of which the cost of Aids on the Ussuri might have to be paid. The collection for 1926 was $35,500. Up to the 1st July of this year, from the opening of navigation in May, the River Dues Collection has amounted to $21,500 as compared with $11,300 for the same period last year; almost double. At the present rate of increase my estimated surplus will be greatly exceeded and the additional cost of Ussuri Aids (G.Rbls.4,300) will easily be taken care of.

9.   Under separate cover I am forwarding two charts prepared by the Technical Adviser, Mr. Ignatieff,

which will be found useful in studying the technical and political issues involved in the question of joint maintenance of Aids on the waterways in the region of Harbarovsk. The charts are as follows:-

Enclosure No.6.
Under separate cover.

Enclosure No.6.
    Chart of Island bounded by Rivers Amur, Ussuri and Kasakevich Waterway.

Enclosure No.7.
Under separate cover.

Enclosure No.7.
    Chart of Northern Section of Kirin Province bounded by Rivers Amur, Sungari and Ussuri.

10.   In concluding this despatch I should like to mention, as I did in my despatch No. 315 informing you of the renewal of the Amur Aids Agreement, the valuable assistance of the Technical Adviser to both myself and the Taoyin during the negotiations preliminary to the signing of this Agreement.

      I have the honour to be,

          Sir,

          Your obedient Servant,

          Acting Commissioner.

          Appendix.

Appendix No.1.

Aigun despatch No. 322 to I. G.

Summary of correspondence between the
Inspectorate and the Aigun Commissioner regarding
upkeep of Aids on the Ussuri River.

Aigun despatch No. 44 of 23rd April, 1922,
tentatively suggests the idea of Aids on the Ussuri.
Harbin despatch No. 2634 to I. G., commenting on this
despatch, says that Aids on the Ussuri more directly
concerns the Harbin Office but that the question should
be left in abeyance until conditions are more settled.

Aigun despatch No. 144 of 29th December, 1923,
forwards a copy of the Agreement for upkeep of Aids
on the Amur for 1923/24. In that document (Article X)
the Chinese place on record their claim to the right
to navigate the Ussuri from Kasakevich to Harbarovsk.
At the same time it is stated that this is a
political question for settlement by the Sino-Russian
conference at Peking and the Russian members of the
Aids Commission have no authority to discuss it.

Aigun despatch No. 155 of 27th March, 1924,
§ 30 of the Technical Adviser's Annual Report, forming
an enclosure to this despatch, states that with the
outbreak of the Revolution in Russia some 40% of the
Russian owned shipping in this region was transferred to
Chinese hands and steamers flying the Chinese flag had
begun to operate on the Amur as far as Harbarovsk
(and from there up the Ussuri). At the end of the
Kolchak regime, however, and the occupation of that
city by the Bolsheviks, troubles were experienced and
                                                    in

in the winter of 1922/23 the Soviet authorities
decided to resume the "fiction" that that part of the
Amur from Irga to Harbarovsk and of the Ussuri from
Kasakevich to the same place were inland waters and
that Chinese steamers desiring to pass from the Amur
to the Ussuri must use the Kasakevich Waterway which
(the Russians contended) forms the boundary at that
point.

Aigun despatch No. 218, § 10, of 24th April,
1925, reports that the Amur Navigation Office, under
instructions from Moscow, was pressing for the inclusion
of a sum of $5,000 in the estimates for 1925 for
upkeep of Aids on the Ussuri, and that the Taoyin
had taken the stand that as the Ussuri was in another
Province he could not deal with question and that,
moreover, it was not one for hasty settlement.

Aigun despatch No.230 of 4th August, 1925,
§ 2, reports that the Amur Navigation Bureau submitted
an item of Roubls 5,732 in its estimate for 1925 for
Aids on the Ussuri but the Taoyin declined to sanction
it. § 5 goes on to say that the proposal to erect
Aids on the Ussuri is a new one and requires close
investigation before the agreement is drawn up.

In Mr. Hedgeland's Handing-Over-Memo forming an
enclosure to Aigun despatch No.240 of 16th October,
1925, 7. AMUR AIDS TO NAVIGATION, the situation with
regard to the joint upkeep of Aids on the Ussuri is
commented on to the following effect: the proposal of
the Amur Navigation Bureau that such work be carried
out had not been approved by The Taoyin as he did
                                                    not

not wish to be rushed and the matter really concerned Kirin Province. An attempt on the part of the Soviet to open direct negotiations with the Kirin authorities had failed. The Commissioner was of the opinion that the Amur Aids Commission should take over the Ussuri as being a frontier river and had pointed out to the Taoyin that the Commission had already assumed control of that stretch of the Amur from the Sungari to Irga which was in Kirin Province. The Taoyin had agreed to report to the effect that the Amur Aids Commission should take over the Ussuri with a view to the erection of Aids thereon.

Aigun despatch No.262 of 1st May, 1926, forwards the Technical Adviser's Annual Report for 1925. Under 1. General: of this report it is stated that as the Sino-Russian Conference had failed to come to an agreement about Aids on the frontier rivers the matter had been taken up locally. Owing, however, to the lack of receipt of definite authorization on the part of the Kirin authorities for the Taoyin to represent that province in the negotiations nothing could be done. This Report goes on to outline under 2. Inspection Tour, (a) Aids on the Kasakevich Waterway, and, (b) Aids on the Ussuri as far as Hulin, the need for Aids on those waterways, and what will be required to restore them to their former state of efficiency.

Aigun despatch No. 263 of 8th May, 1926, following and referring to the above despatch, reports that despite the low financial resources of the Chinese Commission it had been decided to favourably consider the

the project of Aids on the Kasakevich Waterway and the Ussuri. The Kirin authorities on their part had recognized the necessity for Aids on the Ussuri and had agreed to send a representative to Taheiho to represent that Province. This delegate did not materialize and with the transfer of the Taoyin and the Commissioner the drawing up of the proposed agreement was again postponed.

At this point interest shifts to the Summary of Non-Urgent Correspondence.

Taoyin's Letter No. 221 of 17th November, 1925, informs the Commissioner that under instructions from Moukden the Kirin and Heilungchiang authorities were arranging to place "supervision" of the Ussuri Aids in the Heiho Taoyin's hands and that a representative from Kirin would shortly arrive.

Commissioner's Letter No. 167 of 27th November, 1925, in reply forwards the report on a recent tour of the Technical Adviser of the Kasakevich Waterway and the Ussuri and details the work that will be necessary for the improvement of Aids on those two waterways.

Taoyin's Letter No.240 of 24th April, 1926, is to the effect that he is in receipt of telegraphic instructions from the Kirin authorities that as Kasakevich Waterway belongs solely to China, Aids thereon will be taken care of by the Suiyuan Hsien.

Letter No. 242 from Taoyin of 27th April, 1926, reports the receipt of confirmatory instructions from the Kirin Governor, transmitted through the Heilungchiang Governor, to the effect that according to international practice river boundaries between two countries follow the main channel and therefore Kasakevich Waterway (which is a

a minor channel of the Amur on the Chinese side) should
be considered as an inland waterway of China. The
Suiyuan Hsien was being instructed to begin Aids work
at once and the Kasakevich Waterway should not form a
subject of discussion between the Chinese and Russian
river authorities. Note: the Suiyuan Hsien did nothing.

Commissioner's Letter No.178 of 8th May, 1926,
to Taoyin in reply is to the effect that the Aids
Commission and the Customs should not concern themselves
with boundary questions but only with technical matters
and requesting that the Taoyin send a telegram urging
the Kirin authorities to send their delegate at once.

Taoyin's letter No.245 of the 11th May, 1926,
in reply said that the required telegram is being sent.

Aigun S/O No.34 of 15th February, 1926, comments
at length on the status of the Ussuri Aids question,
quoting from Aigun despatch No.230 (mentioned above) that
it was still the opinion of the Amur Navigation Bureau
"that refusal on China's part to be responsible for her
"share of joint ownership of the Ussuri would be in the
"nature of wilful discouragement." The proposal on the
Russian part to maintain Aids above Hulin and on Lake
Hanka could not be entertained as there was neither
Russian nor Chinese trade in those regions. The history
of the boundary question in the vicinity of Harbarovsk
is also gone into in an informative manner. The
possibilty of the Sungari Aids taking over the Kasakevich
Waterway Aids is further suggested. The Harbin Commissioner
in his comments on this S/O (his S/O No.656 to I.G.),
does not favour the idea of the Sungari Aids taking over
additional responsibilities and consequent obligations.

S/O

S/O from I.G. of 15th March, 1926, says, inter
alia, that the attitude adopted that boundary questions
have nothing to do with the Aids Commission is quite
right.

Mr. Petterson's Handing-over-charge Memorandum,
forming an enclosure to Aigun despatch No. 264 to I. G.
of 15th May, 1926, summarises the situation as outlined
above.

There were no further developments until my
arrival in October, 1926.

In my S/O No.66 of 9th November, 1926, I
report the departure of the Taoyin for Tsitsihar and
Kirin for the purpose of discussing Aids questions on
the Amur and the Ussuri with the authorities of the
two Provinces.

My S/O No. 67 of 17th December, 1926, reports
the return of the Taoyin from his trip and his apparent
lack of instructions. At a meeting of the Chinese
members of the Aids Commission the question of an
Agreement re Aids on the Ussuri was discussed and in
lieu of an understanding that would require mention of
the boundary question in the vicinity of Harbarovsk the
Taoyin approved my suggestion that an agreement be
proposed dividing the Ussuri into two sections, the
Chinese to keep up the Aids on both sides of the upper
section from Jaohaohsien to Hulin leaving the Russians
to do as they pleased on both sides of the lower section
to Harbarovsk. The Kasakevich Waterway could continue for
the present without improvement thus avoiding the raising
of further boundary questions.

My S/O No. 71 of the 2nd February, 1927, reports

a joint meeting of the Aids Commissions and the
impossibility of arriving at an understanding regarding
Aids on the Ussuri owing to the troublesome boundary
questions. The matter was being referred to the Sino-
Russian Conference by both sides and the further
discussion of it locally would be dropped for the time
being.

My S/O No.74 of 3rd May, 1927: The Taoyin,
acting on the instructions of the Kirin authorities,
informed the Amur Navigation Bureau that the question of
joint Aids on the Ussuri having been mutually referred
to the Sino-Russian Conference neither Commission should
do any work on that river pending a decision. On my
pointing out to the Taoyin that this position was not
a very strong one (as there was no dispute about the
Russian aids of the Ussuri), and that to await a
decision of the Conference might take years, he decided
to reopen the subject and at his request the Amur
Navigation Bureau replied to his letter in a way that
permitted of this.

My S/O No. 75 of 24th May, 1927: the Taoyin is
reported as having verbally informed the Russian Commission
that if they are willing to put in the form of a
despatch or in an agreement that the Harbarovsk boundary
question will be referred to the Sino-Russian Conference
that he will enter into an arrangement for the immediate
erection of joint Aids on the Ussuri. It is believed
that this request can be acceded to.

My S/O No. 76 of 15th June, 1927: reports the
satisfactory progress of negotiations and says the agreement
will be signed the next day, and

My S/O No. 77 of 24th June, 1927, reporting the
actual

actual signing of the Agreement. It follows the lines
of the 1923/24 Amur Aids Agreement and contains the
reservation by the Chinese that as the boundary from
Kasakevich to Harbarovsk is in dispute the question of
Aids on that section will be settled by the Sino-Russian
Conference and does not concern the local Commission. In
the meantime Aids will jointly be erected from Kasakevich
to Hulin.

Enclosure No.1.
to
Aigun despatch No. 322 to I. G.

聲明書

聲明書

大中華民國黑龍江省黑河道尹兼琿琿交涉員張壽增與

大蘇維埃社會聯邦共和國駐黑河領事默拉美德對於會修為蘇里江事共同

聲明如左

（一）中蘇雙方議定為蘇里江由邊雅克維池嶺屯至虎林縣一段應行修理江道安設

燈照事宜按照中華民國十二年即西歷一九二三年十月二十八日所訂黑龍

江協議之辦法辦理除第三附件方議外其餘所有附件均曾有效

庄此期間加中央中蘇會議國際航行訂有辦法此項地方協議即行廢止

（二）華方要求安設燈照內嗄雜先維池伐危到俏利之問題因具有牽涉及於中

蘇界務之關係非地方委員會所能解決該項問題應候北京中蘇會

議決足之

（三）自本年六月一日起至十二月一日止所有由慢雅克維池俄屯至虎林縣一
叚共同修理江道安設燈照之工程經費議定金洋八十六百元不得超
過議定預算數目

（四）此項聲明書計華俄文各兩份由雙方簽字蓋印彼此各執華俄文各
一份以昭信守

中國方面黑河道尹兼交涉員張壽增

黑河道署外交顧問章聘珊

黑河道署外交科長沈廷榮

瑷琿關稅務司鐸博賚

大中華民國十六年六月　十七　日

西歷一千九百二十七年六月　十七　日　訂於黑河

航務專門顧問易休羅

蘇俄方面駐黑蘇俄領事嘿拉美德

阿穆爾國家水道局局長紀阿諾夫

阿穆爾國家水道局副局長哀彼索夫

阿穆爾國家水道航路工程師補寃依洛夫

Enclosure No.2.

to

Aigun despatch No. 322 to I. G.

Translation of the Chinese version of the Protocol
extending the 1923/24 Amur Aids Agreement to the joint upkeep
of Aids on the Ussuri River from Kasakevich to Hulin.

The Heiho Taoyin of Heilungkiang Province and
concurrently Commissioner of Foreign Affairs for the Aigun
District, of the Great Republic of China, Chang Shou-tsen,
and the Consul of the Great United Socialistic Soviet
Republic at Tahsiho, Melamed, hereby jointly declare that,
with a view to the joint upkeep of Aids on the Ussuri
river:

(1) the Agreement for the repairing of the
channel and the establishment of beacons on the Ussuri
river for the section Kasakevich village to Hulin Hsien
now drawn up by the two parties, Chinese and Russian,
is to follow the lines of the Amur Agreement made on
the 28th day 10th month of the 12th year of the Republic
of China (i. e. 1923). With the exception of Annex III.
which shall be discussed later; all the other annexes are
to be put into effect.

If during this (sic) period an agreement be
reached by the Central Sino-Russian Conference concerning
frontier navigation, the present local Agreement is to
be cancelled.

(2) At the request of the Chinese side, the
question of the establishment of beacons on the section
from Kasakevich village to Harbarovsk, which involves the
boundary relations between China and Russia, being outside
the scope and competence of the local Commission, is to
be settled by the Sino-Russian Conference, Peking.

(3)

(3) The total expenditure for the joint
repairing of the channel and the establishment of
beacons on the section from Kasakevich village to
Hulin Hsien for the period from 1st June to 1st
December of this year shall not exceed the agreed
estimate of Gold Roubles 8,600, and

(4) to confirm this Agreement, this
declaration is made out in the Chinese and Russian
languages, in duplicate, and is signed and sealed
by both parties, each party keeping one copy in
Chinese and one in Russian.

Done at Tahsiho on the 17th day of the
6th month of the 16th year of the Great Republic
of China corresponding to the 17th day of June,
in the year one thousand nine hundred and twenty
seven.

Chinese side:

Chang Shou-tsen, Heiho Taoyin and Commissioner
for Foreign Affairs.

Ch'e P'ing-shan, Diplomatic Adviser to the
Heiho Taoyin's yamen.

Shen Ting-jun, Head of the Diplomatic Department
of the Heiho Taoyin's yamen.

R. M. Talbot, Commissioner of Aigun Customs.

P. I. Ignatieff, Technical Adviser to the
Amur Aids Commission.

Soviet Russian side:

Melamed, Soviet Russian Consul at Tahsiho.

Dianoff, Director of the Amur Government
Navigation Office.

Chebisheff, Assistant Director of the Amur
Government

Government Navigation Office.

Mihailoff, Engineer of Way Department of the
Amur Government Navigation
Office.

True translation:

Tseh hou Chin
4th Assistant B.

Enclosure No.3.
to
Aigun despatch No. 322 to I. G.

ПРОТОКОЛ

заседания Временной Местной Технической Комиссии в городе Сахаляне
" 17 " Июня 1927 года.

ПРИСУТСТВОВАЛИ : Хэйхэсский Дао-Инь и дипломатичес-

кий Чиновник в Айгуне .... Г.ЧПАН-ШОУ-ДЗЕН

Комиссар Айгунской Таможни .... Г.ТАЛБОТ.

Старший Советник по дипломатичес-

кой Части .... Г.ЧЕ-ПИН-ШАН.

Технический Советник .... Г.ИГНАТЬЕВ.

Консул СССР в Сахаляне .... Г.МЕЛАМЕД.

Начальник Управления Водных Путей

Амурского бассейна .... Г.ИВАНОВ.

Помощник Начальника Управления

Водных Путей, Инженер .... Г.ЧЕЛЫШЕВ.

Начальник Отдела Пути АВУ, Инженер .....Г.МИХА ЛОВ.

СЛУШАЛИ	ПОСТАНОВИЛИ
I/ Вопрос о совместном об- служивании обстановкой водного пути по р.Уссури	I/ а/ Произвести совместную обстановку от Русской деревни Казакевичево до города Хулина, распространив на этот участок р.Уссури соглашение по р.Амуру, состо- явшееся 28 Октября 1923 г., со всеми к нему приложениями,кроме приложения № 3, которое согласуется особо. б/ Если в течении срока настоящего согла- шения состоится постановление Советско- Китайской Конференции в части ее,каса- щейся совместного пользования погранич- ными путями, настоящее соглашение теря- ет силу.

2/ Предложение Китайской стороны совместной обстановки от Русской деревни Казакевичево до города Хабаровска.

3/ Смета на 1927 год по водному пути реки Уссури от Русской деревни Казакевичево до города Хулин.

4/ О составлении протокола.

Председатель Временной Местной Технической Комиссии со стороны СССР, Консул СССР в Сахаляне
/ Меламед /

Члены Комиссии: Начальник Амурского Водного Управления
/ Дианов /

Помощник Начальника Водного Управления
/ Чебышев /

Начальник Отдела Пути Водного Управления
/ Михайлов /

С подлинным верно
Технический Советник

2/ Так как вопрос о совместном устройстве обстановки от Русской деревни Казакевичево до города Хабаровска связан с влиянием на положение существующих между Китаем и СССР водных границ, рассмотрение какового вопроса не входит в компетенцию Местной Технической Комиссии,- указанный вопрос оставить открытым до решения Советско-Китайской Конференции.

3/ Смету на время от 1-го Июня до 1-го Декабря 1927 г., на совместное обслуживание пути от Русской деревни Казакевичево до города Хулин, утвердить в сумме 8.600 рублей. Сумма расхода не должна превышать исчисленную в смете сумму.

4/ Протокол должен быть составлен на Русском и Китайском языках, по 2 экземпляра из которых по одному экземпляру Русского и Китайского текста получает Комиссия с Китайской стороны и по одному экземпляру Комиссия со стороны СССР.

Председатель Комиссии с Китайской стороны Хэйхэский Дао-инь и Айгунский дипломатический Чиновник
/ Чжан-Шоу-Джен /

За Че-Пин-Шан'а / Шен /

/ Игнатьев /

Enclosure No.4.
to
Aigun despatch No. 322 to I.G.

Free translation of the Russian version of the Protocol extending the 1923/24 Amur Aids Agreement to the joint upkeep of Aids on the Ussuri River from Kasakevich to Hulin.

PROTOCOL.

MINUTES OF A MEETING OF THE RUSSO-CHINESE AMUR AIDS COMMISSION AT TAHEIHO THE 17TH JUNE, 1927.

Representatives:

The Heiho Taoyin and concurrently Commissioner of Foreign Affairs, Aigun. Chang Shou-tsen.
Commissioner of Customs, Aigun. Mr. Talbot.
Diplomatic Adviser to Taoyin. Ch'e P'ing-shan.
Technical Adviser on Amur Aids. Mr. Ignatieff.
Consul of U.S.S.R., Taheiho. Mr. Melamed.
Director of Amur Navigation Office. Mr. Dianoff.
Assistant Director of Amur Navigation Office. Mr. Chebisheff.
Manager of Way Department, Amur Navigation Office. Mr. Mihailoff.

Subject Discussed:	Decision:
The question of joint upkeep of Aids on the Ussuri River.	1. (a) To establish joint Aids to Navigation on the stretch from the Russian village of Kasakevich to the town Hulin by extending to the Ussuri the Agreement concluded for the Amur River on the 28th October, 1923, with all its annexes, with the exception of Annex No.3 which will be considered separately.
	(b) If during the period of the present

present Agreement the Sino-Russian Conference reaches a decision with reference to the mutual use of frontier rivers, this Agreement loses its force.

2. A proposal made by the Chinese side of the Aids Commission for joint Aids work on the stretch of the Ussuri from the Russian village Kasakevich to Harbarovsk.

2. As the question of joint Aids work on that stretch of the Ussuri from the Russian village Kasakevich to Harbarovsk, if provided for in this Agreement, might prejudice the negotiations now pending for the settlement of the boundary question in that vicinity and, moreover, as the discussion of the boundary question is outside the scope of this Commission, the matter of the erection of Aids on this section of the Ussuri shall be left to the decision of the Sino-Russian Conference.

3. The estimate for the balance of the year 1927 for the upkeep of Aids on the Ussuri River between the Russian village Kasakevich and the town Hulin.

3. To sanction an estimate amounting to Gold Rouble 8,600 for the period 1st June to 1st December, 1927, for Aids work on the Ussuri between the Russian village Kasakevich and the town Hulin. The amount expended shall not exceed the above amount.

4. Records to be made.

4. Records shall be made out in the Russian and Chinese languages, in duplicate, each party retaining one copy in Chinese and one in Russian.

Signed:

Melamed, President of the Russian side of the Amur Aids Commission and, concurrently, Consul for the U.S.S.R. at Taheiho.
Dianoff, Director of the Amur Navigation Office.

Members of the Commission:
Chebisheff, Asst.-Director of the Amur Navigation Office.
Mihailoff, Manager of Waterways Department, Amur Navigation Office.

Signed:

Chang Shou-tsen, President of the Chinese side of the Amur Aids Commission, and concurrently, Heiho Taoyin and Commissioner of Foreign Affairs, Aigun.
Talbot.
Shen Ting-jun, for Ch'e P'ing-shan.
Ignatieff.

True translation:

P. Ignatieff

Technical Adviser on Amur Aids to Navigation.

Summary of the estimated expenditure of the Amur
Navigation Office on behalf of the joint upkeep of
Ussuri Aids (from the town Hulin to the Russian
village Kasakevich) for the period from the 1st of
June to the 1st of December, 1927.

No.	Items	Gold Roubles
1.	Salaries to District employees	756.60
2.	Re-erecting, repairing and maintenance of beacons	3,640.60
3.	Repairs to buildings	40.00
4.	Postage, telegraph, stationery, sundries	50.00
5.	Travelling expenses and allowances	100.00
6.	5% of Medical Attendance	200.00
7.	Depreciation	60.00
8.	Maintenance of District Office	1,500.00
9.	Unforeseen	102.80
10.	Upkeep of steam-launch	2,150.00
	TOTAL:	8,600.00

Signed:
Mr. Mihailoff, Manager of
Waterways Department of the
Amur Navigation Office.

Mr. Ignatieff, Technical
Adviser on Amur Aids to
Navigation.

Checked with detailed Accounts
and Statements on record in
this Office and certified correct

P. Ignatieff

Technical Adviser on Amur
Aids to Navigation.

Technical Adviser's Office.

Custom House,

Aigun/Taheiho, 17th June, 1927.

呈海关总税务司署 <u>322</u> 号文　　　　　　　瑷珲关 1927 年 7 月 12 日

尊敬的代理海关总税务司（北京）：

1. 兹报告,中俄黑龙江航政委员会会议于 6 月 17 日在道尹公署召开,双方就联合维护乌苏里江自虎林至嘎杂克维池（Kasakevich）河段的航路标志事宜签署了临时协议。

2. 兹附协议抄件和译文：

附件 1：中文版协议

附件 2：中文版协议的英文译本

附件 3：俄文版协议

附件 4：俄文版协议的英文译本

3. 与瑷珲关第 315 号呈中汇报的《黑龙江航路标志协议》续约一事情况相同,该呈所附之中文、俄文两版本协议亦存在一些差别,但双方尚未约定,当产生争议之时,应以哪一版本的协议为准。双方于签署协议的前一天,交换了两个版本的协议并互相予以通过。

4. 由于两国当局之间的争端,对于在乌苏里江建立航路标志的协商一直是艰难而曲折的,所争论的内容主要包括：（1）哈巴罗夫斯克（Habarovsk,即伯力）附近边界线的划定；（2）中国轮船在黑龙江自伊力嘎（Irga）至哈巴罗夫斯克（及入海口）河段以及乌苏里江自哈巴罗夫斯克至嘎杂克维池村河段的航运权。

5. 兹附海关总税务司署与瑷珲关之间关于在乌苏里江（及嘎杂克维池水道）建立联合航路标志一事的往来信函摘要,以供参阅；同时,随附本署对该问题在政治和技术方面的一些意见。

6. 首先是政治方面。即使中俄黑龙江水道委员会的双方委员长是由道尹与苏维埃领事所担任,双方委员会之间的协商也不可能脱离政治大环境。中俄黑龙江水道委员会在每一次关于重新划定边界线问题的协商中,都尽可能地相互谅解,力求协议不会因措辞的失当而损害到任何一方的利益。但若无要求,本署一般不会主动在会议上发表意见；不过该协议达成后必将大大促进乌苏里江航路标志的建设进程。本署和航务专门顾问经常就当下的僵局为道尹提供一些可行的解决方案,我们建议道尹在国际政治问题上扮演双方中间人的角色,尽可能为中俄黑龙江水道委员会会议营造友好的氛围。关于嘎杂克维池水道被视为边界线一事,亦是到近期方被普遍接受。然而,根据国际惯例,两国边界线必须遵照黑龙江（乌苏里江）主航道确定,因此位于黑龙江与乌苏里交叉处备受争议的岛屿以及嘎杂克维池水道应完全属于中国。俄方在协商过程中多次提及嘎杂克维池水道的归属权问题,而道尹则明智地表示,该问题不应出现在协议之中。虽然在协商过程中,道尹从未明确表示嘎杂克维池水道为中国的内河水道(私下里已向本署表明立场),但目前所有协议皆是针对两国连续水域而定,并非嘎杂克维池水道,如此更加表明在黑龙江支流河道联合建立航路标志一事不容商议。道尹提出,若嘎杂克维池水道的水量不足,中国轮船是否可改经哈巴罗夫斯克,但最终并未得到明确的答案。大部分时间里,双方的协商都是在友好的氛围下进行的,对于道尹提出的要求,俄阿穆尔水道局官员也总是认真考虑并尽量予以满足。然而,在最后的会议上,苏维埃领事"原形毕露",独断专横并出言不逊。在这种情况下,全赖道尹的努力调和,会议才得以圆满结束。

7. 再者是技术方面。航务专门顾问最初提出的预算(本年度剩余时间)为8200卢布,俄阿穆尔水道局又将之增加了400卢布,最终预算被确定为8600卢布,由中国航政委员会承担一半。预算副本已随呈附上。随着最近江捐税率的提高和乌苏里江上中国航运活动的日渐频繁,乌苏里江拉哈苏苏段的江捐税收已有显著增加,修建乌苏里江航路标志一事也不应再迁延不决。据航务专门顾问报告,从1926年开始,自嘎杂克维池水道至虎林的延展段上从未有过修整。待办事宜大致如下。

新立标桩	
类型	数量
江式:杆状标桩	150
江式:盾形标桩	200
修复标桩	
江式:杆状标桩	60
江式:盾形标桩	100
海式:角锥形(杆状)标桩	10
海式:角锥形(盾形)标桩	14

8. 本署在瑷珲关致海关总税务司署第315号呈中提交了明年的预算,江捐税收在继续保持增长的情况下,明年应该可以达到45000银圆,如此,则明年年底预计会有7000银圆左右的结余,应当足以支付乌苏里江航路标志的维护费用。1926年的江捐税收为35500银圆。而今年,自5月航运开通起至7月1日,江捐税收总计21500银圆,比去年同期的11300银圆几乎翻了一倍。据目前江捐税收的增长速度来看,本署预计结余情况必会大胜

从前,当足以支付乌苏里江航路标志的维护费用(4300金卢布)。

9. 另函附寄航务专门顾问易保罗(P. I. Ignatieff)先生所拟的两份图表。这两份图表对于解决联合维护哈巴罗夫斯克区域内航路标志所涉及的政治和技术问题大有裨益。图表如下:

10. 最后,与瑷珲关致海关总税务司署第315号呈(关于《黑龙江航路标志协议》续约一事)一样,本署望提及航务专门顾问在协议谈判过程中对本署与道尹的大力帮助。

您忠诚的仆人

铎博赉(R. M. Talbot)

瑷珲关署理税务司

附录 1

瑷珲关致海关总税务司署第 322 号呈

海关总税务司与瑷珲关税务司就共同维护乌苏里江航路标志的通信摘要

1922 年 4 月 23 日瑷珲关第 44 号呈试探性地提出了关于维护乌苏里江航路标志的建议。哈尔滨关致海关总税务司署第 2643 号呈对此发表了意见,认为哈尔滨关更应该对乌苏里江航路标志负责,而目前应该搁置这一问题,直至情况更加稳定时再议。

1923 年 12 月 29 日瑷珲关第 144 号呈提交了《1923/1924 年联合维护黑龙江航路标志协议》的副本。华方于该协议中公开声明有权于乌苏里江航道(自嘎杂克维池至哈巴罗夫斯克河段)上航行,并说明此为政治问题,中俄双方将于北京召开会议予以解决,因此航政委员会的俄方成员对此无权讨论。

1924 年 3 月 27 日瑷珲关第 155 号呈附件航务专门顾问的年度报告第 30 章写明,随着俄国革命的爆发,该区域内 40% 的俄方航运产业都转移到了华人手中,黑龙江航道至哈巴罗夫斯克(上至乌苏里江)一段的轮船都飘扬着中国旗帜。然而,高尔察克政权末期,布尔什维克占领了哈巴罗夫斯克(伯力),问题便接踵而至。1922/1923 年冬天,苏维埃政府欲将黑龙江自伊力嘎至哈巴罗夫斯克河段以及乌苏里江自嘎杂克维池至哈巴罗夫斯克河段重新规划为俄国内江,且凡欲从黑龙江驶入乌苏里江之轮船,均需经由嘎杂克维池水道。俄方认为嘎杂克维池水道应为该处中俄边界线。

1925 年 4 月 24 日瑷珲关第 218 号呈(第 10 章)汇报,阿穆尔水道局奉莫斯科指示,欲将乌苏里江航路标志维护费用 5000 银圆纳入 1925 年预算中;道尹认为乌苏里江由别省管辖,非其能解决之问题,且不可仓促决断。

1925 年 8 月 4 日瑷珲关第 230 号呈(第 2 章)汇报,阿穆尔水道局提交的 1925 年预算中包括了乌苏里江航路标志维护费用 5732 卢布,但道尹未予批准。瑷珲关第 230 号呈(第 5 章)再次强调在乌苏里江竖立航路标志一事乃新生成的决议,因此在起草协议前一定要做详细的调查。

1925 年 10 月 16 日瑷珲关致海关总税务司署第 240 号呈附件——瑷珲关税务司贺智兰(R. F. C. Hedgeland)先生的工作移交书中,就联合维护乌苏里江航路标志一事发表了意见:鉴于乌苏里江属吉林省管辖,道尹不希望草率行事,遂尚未批准阿穆尔水道局开展该项工作。苏维埃政府试图与吉林省政府直接协商,但未能达成。瑷珲关税务司贺智兰先生认为，乌苏里江为边界河道，应由黑龙江航政委员会接管，并向道尹指出黑龙江自松花江至伊力嘎（吉林省）河段一直由黑龙江航政委员会管辖。道尹表示认同——为了之后的航路标志建立工作，黑龙江航政委员会确有接管乌苏里江的必要，并愿意将此事向有关部门上报。

1926 年 5 月 1 日瑷珲关第 262 号呈附寄航务专门顾问编制的《1925 年航务年度报告》。报告包括：1. 通则：中俄会议未能达成关于边界河道航路标志的协议，所以此事移交地方接管。然而，由于缺少吉林省政府出具的明确授权，在协商中道尹无法代表该省有所作为。2. 巡查：（1）嘎杂克维池水道的航路标志；（2）乌苏里江航道（至虎林）的航路标志，以及两段航道上需要修建及修复的航路标志。

根据瑷珲关第 262 号呈文，1926 年 5 月 8 日瑷珲关第 263 号呈汇报，中国航政委员会虽缺乏资金来源，但仍然愿意对嘎杂克维池水道与乌苏里江的航路标志工程予以考虑。吉林省政府已意识到于乌苏里江航道修建航路标志的必要性，并同意派遣代表前往大黑河，然而最终未能成行，且道尹及瑷珲关税务司的调任也使得已经起草的协议再次被搁置了。

1925 年 11 月 17 日道尹第 221 号信函告知瑷珲关税务司贺智兰先生，奉奉天政府之指示，吉林省和黑龙江省政府已安排由黑河道尹来"监理"乌苏里江航道的航路标志工作，且吉林省代表不日即可抵达。

1925 年 11 月 27 日瑷珲关税务司第 167 号信函回复道尹第 221 号信函，转呈航务专门顾问近期在嘎杂克维池水道及乌苏里江航道巡查的报告，并对两条航道所需的航路标志改建工作进行了详述。

1926 年 4 月 24 日道尹第 240 号信函说明：道尹已收到吉林省政府的电令——鉴于嘎杂克维池水道只属于中国，因此该段航道之航路标志工作将由绥远县负责。

1926 年 4 月 27 日道尹第 242 号信函汇报：已收悉吉林省省长的确认指令（由黑龙江省省长传达）——根据国际惯例，两国边界线必须遵照主航道确定，嘎杂克维池水道是中国境内的黑龙江支流航道，因此应视为中国内河。绥远县已收到指示——即刻开始该段航道航路标志的相关工作。中俄航务当局不应再讨论嘎杂克维池水道的相关问题。备注：绥远县尚未行动。

1926 年 5 月 8 日瑷珲关税务司致道尹的第 178 号信函回复：黑龙江航政委员会及海关应将重心放在技术问题而非边界线问题上，请道尹致电吉林省当局，请求其尽快派遣代表。

1926 年 5 月 11 日道尹第 246 号信函回复：电报已发送。

　　1926年2月15日瑷珲关第54号机要文件详细评述了乌苏里江航路标志问题（引自瑷珲关第230号呈）：阿穆尔水道局认为华方"拒绝承担"联合维护乌苏里江之责任乃"蓄意阻挠"之意。俄方关于维护虎林及兴凯湖上航路标志的提议，落实机会渺茫，因为这些区域并没有俄方贸易或者华方贸易。哈巴罗夫斯克区域边界线的历史问题也经过详细调查。松花江航路标志机构接管嘎杂克维池水道航路标志的可能性被进一步提出。哈尔滨关税务司对瑷珲关第54号机要文件发表意见（参阅哈尔滨关致海关总税务司署第656号机要文件），表示并不赞成松花江航路标志机构再承担额外的职责和后续的工作。

　　1926年3月15日海关税务司公署机要文件特别表明，支持航政委员会与边界线问题无关这一立场。

　　1926年5月15日瑷珲关致海关总税务司署第264号呈所附的裴德生（Mr. Petterson）先生的工作移交书，对上述情况作了总结。

　　直至1926年10月本人抵达后事情才有所进展。

　　本署于1926年11月9日瑷珲关第66号机要文件中汇报，道尹前往齐齐哈尔和吉林省，与两省政府讨论黑龙江及乌苏里江航路标志事宜。

　　1926年12月17日瑷珲关第67号机要文件报告，道尹已归来，但尚未作出任何指示。黑龙江航政委员会华方委员召开会议讨论乌苏里江航路标志协议事宜，为避免牵涉哈巴罗夫斯克区域的边界线问题，道尹同意本署提议——将乌苏里江划分为两部分，华方负责乌苏里江上游（自虎林至饶河县）航路标志维护工作，俄方则负责乌苏里江下游（至哈巴罗夫斯克）航路标志维护工作。嘎杂克维池水道可以维持现状，无须改建，如此可以避免产生新的边界线问题。

　　1927年2月2日瑷珲关第71号机要文件就黑龙江航政委员会的联合会议进行了汇报，说明由于棘手的边界线问题，双方无法就乌苏里江航路标志问题取得一致意见，并已将该问题提交给中俄会议，地方将暂停讨论该问题。

　　1927年5月3日瑷珲关第74号机要文件说明，道尹已按照吉林省政府之指示，向阿穆尔水道局说明，乌苏里江联合航路标志问题已经由双方提交至中俄会议，而黑龙江航政委员会是否应对此有所作为仍有待商榷。本署向道尹指出该解决办法成功之可能性甚微（因并未对乌苏里江的俄方部分提出异议），且等待会议决议也许会耗费数年。因此，道尹决定重新处理这一问题，阿穆尔水道局应道尹之要求回复信函表示同意重新讨论乌苏里江联合航路标志事宜。

　　1927年5月24日瑷珲关第75号机要文件报告，道尹已向俄方委员口头说明，若其愿意以呈文或协议之形式将哈巴罗夫斯克的边界线问题提交至中俄会议,道尹便会迅速安排于乌苏里江竖立航路标志的相关事宜。兹认为,此请求可以得到批准。

1927年6月15日瑷珲关第76号机要文件报告,协商顺利,次日将签署协议。

1927年6月24日瑷珲关第77号机要文件汇报已签署协议。协议遵循《1923/1924年黑龙江航路标志协议》的方针,但华方于协议中说明,鉴于嘎杂克维池至哈巴罗夫斯克河段的边界线问题仍在讨论之中,该河段的航路标志问题将由中俄会议会解决,因此黑龙江航政委员会无须牵涉其中,但自嘎杂克维池至虎林河段的航路标志将由双方联合建立。

璦珲关致海关总税务司署第 322 号呈附件 2

1923/1924 年黑龙江航路标志协议就联合维护乌苏里江自嘎杂克维池至虎林一段航路标志事宜续约,此为续约协议之中文版译本

中华民国黑龙江省黑河道尹兼璦珲交涉员张寿增与苏维亚社会联邦共和国驻黑河领事默拉美德就维护乌苏里江航路标志一事发表联合声明。

（1）中俄双方在乌苏里江自嘎杂克维池村至虎林县一段所开展的修理河道与安设航路标志等工事,皆依照中华民国十二年（1923）十月二十八日所签订的《黑龙江航路标志协议》内容办理,除附件三需要另议外,其他所有附件均继续生效。

在此期间,如中俄会议就边界航运问题达成协议,则现行地方协议即行废止。

（2）按照华方的要求,由于在乌苏里江自嘎杂克维池村至虎林县一段安设航路标志一事,牵涉到中俄边界线问题,已超出地方航政委员会的职权范围,故应将之提交即将于北京召开的中俄会议裁定。

（3）针对今年 6 月 1 日至 12 月 1 日期间,于乌苏里江自嘎杂克维池村至虎林县一段联合修理河道与安设航路标志等工事,双方议定预算为 8600 金卢布; 实际支出不得超出该预算金额。

（4）该协议计中、俄文本各两份,双方签字盖印后,各执中、俄文本各一份,以恪信守。

中华民国十六年六月十七日（1927 年 6 月 17 日）订于大黑河。

华方：

黑河道尹兼璦珲交涉员	张寿增
黑河道署外交顾问	车聘珊
黑河道署外交科长	沈廷荣
璦珲关税务司	铎博赍
航务专门顾问	易保罗

俄方：

驻黑河苏俄领事	默拉美德

阿穆尔国家水道局局长　　　　　托阿诺夫

阿穆尔国家水道局副局长　　　　且比索夫

阿穆尔国家水道局航路工程师　　弥哈依洛夫（米海依罗夫）

该抄件内容真实有效，特此证明。

录事：屠守鑫　四等帮办后班

瑷珲关致海关总税务司署第 322 号呈附件 4[①]

1923/1924 年黑龙江航路标志协议就联合维护乌苏里江自嘎杂克维池至虎林一段航路标志事宜续约，此为续约协议之俄文版译本

协议

中俄黑龙江航政委员会会议纪要

（1927 年 6 月 17 日于大黑河）

参会代表

大黑河道尹兼瑷珲交涉员	张寿增先生
瑷珲关税务司	铎博赉先生
黑河道署外交顾问	车聘珊先生
黑龙江航务专门顾问	易保罗先生
驻大黑河苏俄领事	默拉美德先生
阿穆尔国家水道局局长	托阿诺夫先生
阿穆尔国家水道局副局长	且比索夫先生
阿穆尔国家水道局航路工程师	米海依罗夫先生

---

① 注：附件 3 为协议俄文版，不予翻译。

提案	议决
1.联合维护乌苏里江航路标志事宜。	1.(a)修改签订于1923年10月28日的协议,将协议中的黑龙江河段延展至乌苏里江河段,在嘎杂克维池村至虎林县之间的延展段上联合建立航路标志；除附件三需要另议外,其余所有附件均继续生效。 (b)在此期间,如中俄会议就边界河道问题达成协议,则现行地方协议即行废止。
2.中俄黑龙江航政委员会华方委员提出在乌苏里江自嘎杂克维池村至哈巴罗夫斯克一段的延展段上联合建立航路标志。	2.由于在乌苏里江自嘎杂克维池村至哈巴罗夫斯克一段的延展段上联合建立航路标志事宜,可能会为附近边界线问题的协商带来不利影响,且边界线问题超出了地方航政委员会的职权范围,故此项问题应由中俄会议解决。
3.1927年乌苏里江自嘎杂克维池村至虎林县一段航路标维护费用之预算。	3.批准8600金卢布的预算,用于1927年6月1日至12月1日期间,乌苏里江自嘎杂克维池村至虎林县一段航路标志维护工事；实际支出不得超过该预算金额。
4.会议纪要之要求。	4.会议纪要须分别以中、俄文撰写,各一式两份,双方各执中、俄文版本各一份,以恪信守。

签字	签字
中俄黑龙江航政委员会俄方委员长兼驻大黑河苏俄领事 默拉美德 委员： 阿穆尔国家水道局局长 托阿诺夫 阿穆尔国家水道局副局长 且比索夫 阿穆尔国家水道局航路工程师 米海依罗夫	中俄黑龙江航政委员会华方委员长兼黑河道尹兼瑷珲交涉员 张寿增 委员： 黑河道署外交顾问　车聘珊 黑河道署外交科长　沈廷荣 瑷珲关税务司　铎博赉 航务专门顾问　易保罗

该抄件内容真实有效,特此证明。

录事：易保罗　航务专门顾问

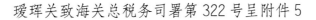

瑷珲关致海关总税务司署第 322 号呈附件 5

1927 年 6 月 1 日至 12 月 1 日俄阿穆尔水道局维护乌苏里江航路标志支出报表

（自嘎杂克维池村至虎林县）

支出	金卢布
1. 地区职员薪俸	756.60
2. 标桩的重建、维修与维护	3640.60
3. 房屋维修	40.00
4. 邮费、电报费、信纸费及杂物费	50.00
5. 差旅费	100.00
6. 5% 的医疗护理费	200.00
7. 折旧费	60.00
8. 地方办事处维修费	1500.00
9. 意外支出	102.80
10. 汽艇维护	2150.00
总计	8600.00

签字：

俄阿穆尔水道局航务部经理　米海依罗夫（Mihailoff）

黑龙江航务专门顾问　易保罗

兹证明，报表正确无误。

易保罗黑龙江航务专门顾问

航务专门顾问办事处

1927 年 6 月 17 日　瑷珲关 / 大黑河

23. 1927年《外洋官商报运禁品领用军事部护照办法》

382
I.G.

382   COMMRS.   INSPECTORATE GENERAL OF CUSTOMS.

PEKING,   16th December 1927.

gun   No. 115,363

Sir,

1.   With reference to previous instructions :

regarding the mode of procedure to be
followed and the kind of huchao required
for the importation by foreigners of arms,
ammunition and other prohibited articles
for self-defence, sport, industrial purposes,
etc., etc. :

I append, for your information and guidance, copy
of Shui-wu Ch'u despatch No. 927, from which you will
see that, commencing from 20th December 1927, the
Superintendents of Customs are no longer to be
permitted to issue huchao for arms, ammunition and
other prohibited articles imported by foreigners and
that, in future, in all cases where, according to
present procedure, Superintendent's huchao would suffice,
huchao issued by the Chūn Shih Pu (軍事部), is
required instead.   A copy of seven rules

detailing

Commissioner of Customs,
A I G U N.

detailing the procedure governing the issue of the
latter, together with a pro forma of the huchao
itself is enclosed in the Ch'u despatch.

As in such cases it rests with the importer
to obtain, through his National Authorities, the
huchao required, and seeing that the Superintendents
have been given the necessary instructions regarding
the new procedure, you will be called upon to make
no change in your actual practice in this connection
except that whereas certain prohibited articles
imported by foreigners have hitherto been passed under
Superintendent's huchao, such articles will in future
be covered by huchao issued by the Chūn Shih Pu.
The new procedure does not call for specific authority
to be transmitted through the Officiating Inspector
General to the ports concerned for each importation by
foreigners of arms, ammunition and other prohibited
articles, when such authority has not been required
heretofore.

Should huchao other than Chūn Shih Pu huchao

be

be presented to cover articles, which, according to present practice, may be passed under Superintendent's huchao, you are to refer the question to the Superintendent before effecting release.

In the event of foreigners addressing enquiries regarding the new procedure for issue of huchao to you, you should refer them to their National Authorities with whom it rests to take up the matter with the Superintendent or Higher Chinese Authority.

I am,

Sir,

Your obedient Servant,

Officiating Inspector General.

Appendix.

役務廳令第九二七號中華民國十六年十二月十二日

案查前准軍事部咨開宣佈前洋商搬運貨品有沿用海關監督護照者現本部為劃一護照發行起見凑將各省區及各軍事機關護照一律取消海關監督護照目應停止發給嗣後洋商運輸貨品應令一律用本部護照又准咨稱本部前咨所指裝品卸包括防身攜用審椒子彈在內嗣一律嗣用部照至軍用之審椒子彈目更在嗣用部之列各等因嗣經本廳於本年八月二十三日及九月三十等日先後令行津海等嗣監督遵照在案嗣經軍事部咨訂辦法七條咨嗣復值本廳富以此項嗣嗣辦法既經軍事部議並無異議備訂水廳查事軍事部咨嗣復本部嗣訂外洋官商嗣運貨品嗣用軍事部護嗣辦法亦在案茲復值軍事部咨嗣査廳及外交部嗣行建京各國公使在案茲本部議定於十六年十月十八日實行嗣分行外交部嗣査嗣分別令行各國宣佈第一俟本部嗣發空白護嗣嗣嗣署時即通嗣辦理等因並復嗣護嗣式樣及訂定辦法一併咨請前二月二十日貴行廳及外交部外來咨嗣分別令行各國

月十八日實行廳及外交部嗣行建京各國公使在案茲本

外洋官商報運禁品領用軍事部護照辦法

第一條　本部爲同不靖需重禁品運輸便利外洋官商報運起見應依照本部
法領用本照

第二條　外洋官商報運禁品聲明數目用通諦該官公使證明照會外交部行
本部後辦或該官領事照會海關監督呈請稅務處施行本部後將在各
公使或領事照含外交部或海關監督時可同照本部一經本部後
准即電詢外交部或稅務處查封無訛即由本部電詢海關監督驗照本
護照放行

第三條　本部爲便利外洋官商報運禁品起見應由本部直接發護照外并發
空白護照存放海關監督公著以便監督奉到稅務處達本部核准
公文或本部核准之電即可由本部遵行填發本部空白護照

第四條　此項空白護照上方加蓋"此照每逢外洋官商報運實業需用禁品之用"

第五條　外洋官商報運作槍枝子彈防身槍枝子彈待接槍彈
退口新章此調數目填用存倉空白護照但報運槍手細應依照本部
法第二三兩條辦理

字樣其正式軍火灰可以直接供給軍用之禁品仍照同章由本部自行
填發護照存倉空白護照不能通用

第六條　海關監督填發本照應查左列辦法辦理

(甲)硝　硝磺戡鉀(即鹽磺硝)　白硝　紫硝　以上各物每照各以
五千斤爲最大區(每照不得填收兩種物品)

硝磺水　以上各物每照各以二千斤爲最大

(乙)礦藥(物品)

取險沉濟便用之調火藥(即雷管)每照以二千枚爲最
大區　導火藥每照以二千斤爲最大區　火藥每照以二千斤爲最大

護照

照　發給護照事

軍事部　　字第　　號　　為

此照專備外洋官給護照仰沿途各關卡營汛勿得阻攔以利遠行須至護照者

報運實業需

团禁品之用

中華民國十　年　月　日由　　填發

所有詳細種數另表詳列照後為此發

右仰沿途各關卡營汛准此

此照限中華民國十　年　月　　日繳銷

照過期作廢

（丙）游藝用之無綫電收音機每照以五架為最大區　作模型用之無綫

電機每照以五架為最大區

但游藝用之無綫電收音機須有註在地辦事担保其不作營業之用

（丁）作模型用或作游藝用之飛艇（作游藝用者運輸莫訂之須不逾三英

尺每照以五艇為最大區

（戊）以上丙丁兩項所罸之艇其體積以十二立方尺為最大區（每照總

數不逾六十立方尺）

（己）填用空白護照每月月到應繳前一兩月填用護照存根繳銷

（庚）填發護照每照應收照費洋五元（貼印花一元五角）每月月到匯繳

照存根一併繳銷

（辛）自發照之日起最大有效期間以半年為限

第七條　本辦法自公布之日實行

致瑷珲关第 382/115363 号令　　　海关总税务司署（北京）1927 年 12 月 16 日

尊敬的瑷珲关税务司：

根据先前指示：

"关于为自卫、工业及体育运动等目的，洋商进口军火及其他禁品须遵守的办法及所需领用的护照类型。"

为了便于贵署顺利执行，兹附税务处第 927 号令，以供参考。据该令所示，自 1927 年 12 月 20 日起，海关监督不得再为洋商进口军火及其他禁品签发护照。根据现行办法，之前凡需要海关监督签发护照的情形，今后均须由军事部（Chün Shih Pu）签发的护照代替。该税务处令还随附了军事部发放护照的七条办法副本以及护照模板。

在上述形势下，由于禁品进口取决于进口商通过其所在国家的公使或领事取得规定的护照。鉴于海关监督已接到有关新护照办法的指示，贵署无须就此事改变实际做法，除了迄今为止洋商进口某些禁品使用海关监督签发的护照通过海关的情形，今后此类商品进口亦需军事部签发的护照。在外商每次进口军火及其他禁品时，新办法并不要求代理总税务司向相关口岸进行专门授权，迄今为止也未要求过此种授权。

根据当前惯例，可使用海关监督签发的护照通过海关的物品，现在是需要使用护照还是使用军事部护照，贵署可在办法生效前，将此问题提交至海关监督。

如果洋商向贵署咨询护照发放新办法事宜，贵署可让其询问各自国家的公使或领事，请他们呈请中国较高级别的海关监督处理。

您忠诚的仆人

易纨士（A. H. F. Edwardes）

代理海关总税务司

24. 1928 年《黑龙江航路标志协议》

AMUR AIDS TO NAVIGATION: renewal of Agreement for 1928
reporting; copies of Chinese and Russian version of
Agreement together with their English translations,
forwarding.

362.
362.
I. G.

I. G.   Aigun   10th March, 1928.

Sir,

With reference to Aigun despatch No. 315

reporting, <u>inter alia</u>, the renewal of the 1923

Agreement for the joint upkeep of Aids on the

Amur, I now have the honour to report that this

Agreement was again renewed on the 11th January

for the coming year.

On that date the joint Amur Aids

Commission met at the Soviet Consulate and affixed

their signatures to the documents concerned, i. e.

to the Russian and Chinese versions of the

4 Appendixes.   Agreement, copies of which are appended together

with English translations of both. It will be

noted that discrepancies between the two versions,

as pointed out on previous occasions, still

continue.

The Inspector General of Customs,

Peking.

continue. It should be mentioned, however, that

the two versions were exchanged and approved

by the different sides the day before they

were signed.

The Agreement now signed covers the

usual fiscal year of 1st December, 1927, to

1st December, 1928. The estimate calls for a

total expenditure of G.Rbls.60,000, the same

amount as last year, China's share continuing

to be half or G.Rbls.30,000. The Chinese

Commission took the stand early in the year

that the estimates should not exceed those of

1927 and the Technical Adviser, Mr. Ignatieff,

is to be complimented on the resourceful manner

in which he handled the matter.

The Commission had no preliminary

meetings prior to the signing of this Agreement.

Views were exchanged between the Taoyin and the

Soviet Commission through the medium of the

Technical Adviser and myself. Divergencies were

thus

thus reconciled, compromises arrived at and personal differences smoothed over, and when the Commission finally met to affix their signatures to the documents that had already been prepared the best of feeling prevailed.

A suggestion to combine the two Agreements concerning the maintenance of Aids on the Amur and Ussuri was brought forward but the Taoyin preferred separate Agreements as two different provinces, Heilungchiang and Kirin, were concerned. The renewal of the Agreement concerning the upkeep of Aids on the Ussuri is reported in the despatch following this.

The question of dredging the Upper Amur was again strongly pressed by the Amur Navigation Bureau during the year. The Taoyin, on the advice of the Technical Adviser, continued to maintain that expensive dredging operations were not warranted when only one Chinese and two or three Russian vessels would be

be benefitted; while it was true that three shallows might be difficult to navigate during short periods of low water the limited amount of shipping concerned could still carry on and a dredging campaign should be postponed. The Soviet authorities were not content with this attitude and gave indications of going over the heads of the Chinese Commission in an attempt to influence the Moukden Authorities to take independent action. At the same time they, however, began to display a more reasonable attitude toward the amount of dredging to be done and the cost thereof, finally proposing that not over G.Rbls.10,000 be expended, China to pay half. The Taoyin now agrees to this expenditure in principle and is laying the matter before the Higher Authorities, it being expected that this amount, if expended, should be raised from outside sources.

The question of the budget for 1928

will

will be taken up in the despatch forwarding the
Annual Statement of Aids Accounts now being
prepared. It seems sufficient to say at present
that, thanks to the increase in River Dues
Tariff, enforced from the beginning of 1927, the
income will meet the expenditure now being planned
for the coming year, given normal conditions,
without recourse to further borrowings from Sungari
Aids funds.

Appendix No.3.

  I am appending a summary, prepared by the
Technical Adviser, comparing the estimate for 1927
with that agreed to for 1928. The annual
statement showing the distribution and amount of
River Dues Collection for 1927 will be forwarded
with the Annual Statement of Accounts just
mentioned.

    I have the honour to be,

      Sir,

     Your obedient Servant,

      Acting Commissioner.

        Appendix

Appendix No. 1.

ПРОТОКОЛ

заседания Временной Местной Советско-Китайской Технической
Комиссии

    Января " II " дня 1928 года, г. Сахалян.

ПРИСУТСТВОВАЛИ:

 Хэйхэсский Дао-Инь и дипломатический
 Чиновник в Айгуне.................. Г. ЧЖАН-ШОУ-ГЗЕН.
 Комиссар Айгунской Таможни........... Г. ТАЛБОТ.
 Чиновник при Управлении Хэйхэсского
 Дао-Иня........................ Г. ШЕН-ТИН-ТУН.
 Технический Советник................ Г. ИГНАТЬЕВ.
 Консул СССР в гор. Сахаляне........ Г. МЕЛАМЕД.
 Начальник Управления Водных Путей
 Амурского бассейна.................. Г. ЛИАНОВ.
 Помощник Начальника Управления Вод-
 ных Путей, Инженер.............. Г. ЧЕПИНОВ.
 Начальник Отдела Пути АВУ, Инженер Г. МИХАЙЛОВ.

СЛУШАЛИ:	ПОСТАНОВИЛИ:
I/ Вопрос о продлении на 1928 год Соглашения между Правлением Амурского Государственного Водного Транспорта и Великой Китайской Республики Хэйхэсским Дао-Инем, заключенного 28 октября 1923 года, по р. Амуру от Покровки до Казакевичевой протоки	Принимая во внимание, что временное соглашение от 28 октября 1923 года, продленное до I-го декабря 1927 года, потеряло свою силу за окончанием срока, ПОСТАНОВИЛИ: I/ Продлить это соглашение еще на один год, т.е. до I-го декабря 1928 года, по Амуру от Покровки до Казакевичевой протоки, со всеми к нему приложениями, кроме приложение № 3, которое согласуется отдельно.

2/ Смета на 1928 год по водному пути Амура в пределах общего пользования от Покровки до Казакевичевой протоки.

3/ Отчет по расходам, произведенным АВУ по ремонту и обслуживанию обстановкой р. Амура от Покровки до Казакевичева в навигацию 1927 года.

4/ Производство других работ на реках общего пользования, как то: Камнеуборные и обстановочные работы на Аргуни и землечерпание на Амуре.

5/ О составлении протокола.

2/ Если в течение этого года состоится постановление работающей ныне Советско-Китайской Конференции в части его касающейся совместного пользования пограничными путями, настоящее соглашение теряет свою силу.

Смету на 1928 год по обслуживанию водных путей общего пользования УТВЕРДИТЬ: в сумме 60,000 рублей. Сумма расхода не должна превышать исчисленную по смете сумму.

Отчет за 1927 год в сумме 60,000 рублей УТВЕРДИТЬ и расчет по этому отчету закончить.

Прочие работы на путях общего пользования подлежат особому согласованию в заседаниях Местной Технической Комиссии по каждому роду работ отдельно

Протокол должен быть составлен на русском и китайском языках по 2 экземпляра, из которых по одному экземпляру русского и китайского текста получает Комиссия с Китайской стороны и по одному экземпляру- Комиссия со стороны СССР.

Председатель Временной Местной Технической Комиссии со стороны СССР, Консул СССР в Сахаляне

/Г.И.Меламед/

Начальник АВУ /Дианов/

Члены Комиссии: /Чебышов/ /Михайлов/

Председатель Комиссии с Китайской стороны, Хэйхэский Г а о - И н ь

/Чжан-Шоу-Цзэн/

Члены: /Талбот/ /Шен-Тин-Чун/ /Игнатьев/

True copy:

P. Ignatieff

Technical Adviser on
Amur Aids to Navigation

Appendix No. 2.

<u>Translation of the Russian version of the Declaration concerning Upkeep of Aids on the Amur for the year 1928.</u>

P R O T O C O L.

<u>Minutes of a meeting of the local Provisional Sino-Soviet Technical Commission, held at Taheiho on the 11th January, 1928.</u>

Representatives:-

Heiho Taoyin and concurrently Commissioner for Foreign Affairs:	Mr. Chang Shou-tsen
Commissioner of Customs, Aigun:	Mr. Talbot
Representative from the Heiho Taoyin's Office:	Mr. Shen Ting-jun
Technical Adviser:	Mr. Ignatieff
Consul of U.S.S.R. at Taheiho:	Mr. Melamed
Director of Amur Navigation Bureau:	Mr. Dianoff
Assistant Director of Amur Navigation Bureau:	Mr. Chebisheff
Manager of Way Department of Amur Navigation Bureau:	Mr. Mihailoff

Subject Discussed:	Decision:
1 The Agreement concluded on the 28th October, 1923, on Amur Aids from Pokrovka to Kasakevich Waterway between the Soviet Amur Government Water Transport and the Heiho Taoyin of the Great Chinese Republic, will continue to be in force for the year 1928.	1. Taking into consideration that the provisional Agreement of 28th October, 1923, renewed to the 1st December 1927, comes to an end on this latter date, the Commission decides: a) To continue the Agreement for one more year, i.e. to the last December, 1928, as applying to the Amur from Pokrovka to Kasakevich Waterway, with all Annexes, excepting Annex 3, which will be discussed separately. b) If during the present year, the Sino-Soviet Conference should conclude a new agreement regarding the mutual use of frontier waterways, the present Agreement ceases to be operative.
2. Estimate for the year 1928, for the frontier Amur Waterway, from Pokrovka to Kasakevich Waterway.	2. To sanction the estimate for the year 1928, for Aids on the frontier Amur Waterway, for the sum of Gold Roubles 60,000. The total amount of expenses must not exceed the sum estimated.
3. Statement of expenses incurred by the Amur Navigation Bureau on Amur Aids work from Pokrovka to Kasakevich Waterway for the past year.	3. To approve the Accounts for the 1927 year, to the amount of Gold Roubles 60,000, and to regard the last payment by the Chinese side as final.
4 Other operations on waterways of mutual use, such as removal of rocks and Aids work on the Argun, and dredging work on the Amur.	4. Such operations will be discussed and agreed to at a special meeting of the local Technical Commission, the work to be undertaken separately.
5. Records to be made.	5. Records of the meetings must be written in Chinese and Russian, and one copy each of the Chinese and the Russian version shall be handed to each party.

President

President of the local Provisional
Technical Commission Soviet Side,
Consul of U.S.S.R. at Taheiho,
/ G. I. Melamed /

President of the Chinese Aids
Commission, the Heiho Taoyin,
/ Chang Shou-tsen /

Members:

Director of Amur
Navigation Bureau,
/ Dianoff /

/ Chebisheff /

/ Mihailoff /

Members:

/ Talbot /

/ Shen Ting-jun /

/ Ignatieff /

Translated by:

P. Ignatieff

Technical Adviser on
Amur Aids to Navigation.

聲明書

華方委員長大中華民國黑河道尹兼瑷琿交涉員張壽增

華方委員瑷琿關稅務司鐸博賚黑河道尹公署外交科長

沈廷榮航路專門顧問易保羅

俄方委員長大蘇維亞社會聯邦共和國駐黑河領事

默拉美德俄方委員阿穆爾國家水道局局長吉阿

諾夫阿穆爾國家水道局副局長且彼索夫阿穆爾

國家水道局航路工程師耒哈依羅夫於民國十七年

（即西歷一千九百二十八年）二月十一日在大黑河地方臨時

協議工程委員會正式會議共同商定聲明如左

中華民國十二年卽西歷一千九百二十三年雙方所訂黑龍

少牛

江等中俄兩國交界河流航行地方臨時協議所有附則附
件等除第三附件另行規定外其餘仍照舊章辦理再
展期一年自中華民國十六年即西歷一千九百二十七年十
二月一日起至中華民國十七年即西歷一千九百二十八年
十二月一日止繼續有效在此期間如中蘇會議國際航
行訂有辦法該項地方協議等件即行廢止又本年
共同修理黑龍江一切經費議定金洋六萬元各支出
欵項不得超過議定預算數目除機器挖江及修理額
一爾古訥河等工程另議外為此雙方協訂聲明書一件
計中俄文各兩份互相簽字蓋印各執中俄文各一份
以昭信守

大中華民國十七年一月十一日
西歷一千九百二十八年一月十一日訂於黑河

中國方面黑河道尹兼交涉員張壽增

璦琿關稅務司鐸博費

黑河道署外交科長沈廷榮

航路專門顧問易保羅

蘇俄方面駐黑河代領事點拉美德

阿穆爾國家水道局局長阿諾夫

阿穆爾國家水道局副局長且叛棠夫

阿穆爾國家水道局航路工程師末令依洛夫

<u>Appendix No. 4.</u>

<u>Translation of the Chinese Version of the Declaration
concerning Upkeep of Aids on the Amur for the year 1928.</u>

The President of the Chinese Aids
Commission and Heiho Taoyin of the Great
Republic of China (concurrently Commissioner
for Foreign Affairs for the Aigun District),
<u>Chang Shou-tsen</u>, and members of the Chinese
Commission: Commissioner of Aigun Customs,
<u>R. M. Talbot</u>, Chief of the Diplomatic
Department of the Heiho Taoyin's yamen,
<u>Shen Ting-jun</u>, and the Technical Adviser to
the Chinese Aids Commission, <u>P. I. Ignatieff</u>;
and the President of the Russian Aids
Commission and the Consul of the Great
United Socialistic Soviet Republic at Taheiho,
<u>Melamed</u>, and the members of the Russian
Commission: Director of the Amur Government
Navigation Bureau, <u>Dianoff</u>, Assistant Director
of the Amur Government Navigation Bureau,
<u>Chebisheff</u>, and the Engineer of the Amur
Government Navigation Bureau, <u>Mihailoff</u>:
hereby jointly declare on the eleventh day of the first
month of the seventeenth year of the Republic (<u>i. e.</u> 1928),
at a formal meeting held at Taheiho by the Provisional
Aids Commission, that the Provisional Agreement concerning
navigation on the Sino-Russian Frontier Waters of the Amur
River, etc., drawn up by the two parties for the twelfth
year of the Chinese Republic (<u>i. e.</u> 1923), together with
the Annexes thereto, with the exception of Annex No. 3
which shall be decided separately, are to continue in force
as before for one more year, from the first day of the
twelfth

twelfth month of the sixteenth year of the Republic
of China (<u>i. e.</u> 1927) to the first day of the twelfth
month of the seventeenth year of the Republic of
China (<u>i. e.</u> 1928). If an agreement be reached
concerning Frontier Navigation by the Sino-Russian
Conference during the above mentioned period, the present
local Agreement together with its Annexes shall
automatically cease to operate. The total expenditure
for the joint upkeep of Aids to Navigation on the
Amur for the year 1928 is agreed upon as Gold
Roubles 60,000; all expenses in connection therewith
shall not exceed this amount. The dredging of the
channel of the Amur and upkeep of Aids on the Argun,
etc., are to be discussed separately.

To confirm this Agreement each side agrees to
make out two copies, to be signed and sealed by both
parties, each party keeping one Chinese and one
Russian version.

Done at Taheiho on the eleventh day of the
first month of the seventeenth year of the Great
Republic of China corresponding to the eleventh day
of January, in the year one Thousand nine Hundred and
twenty eight.

<u>Chinese side:</u>

(Signed) Chang Shou-tsen, Heiho Taoyin and
      Commissioner for Foreign Affairs.

" R. M. Talbot, Commissioner of Aigun
      Customs.

" Shen Ting-jun, Chief of the Diplomatic
      Department of the Heiho Taoyin's
      yamen.

" P. I. Ignatieff, Technical Adviser to
      the

the Chinese Aids Commission.

Soviet Russian side:

(Signed) Melamed, Consul of U.S.S.R. at Taheiho.

  " Dianoff, Director of the Amur Government
        Navigation Bureau.

  " Chebisheff, Assistant Director of the
        Amur Government Navigation Bureau.

  " Mihailoff, Engineer of the Amur
        Government Navigation Bureau.

Translated by:

4th Assistant B.

Appendix No. 5.

SUMMARY OF ESTIMATE AGREED TO FOR THE JOINT UPKEEP OF

AIDS ON THE AMUR FOR THE YEAR 1928 AS COMPARED WITH THAT OF 1927.

No.	Particulars	Amount agreed to for 1927.	Amount agreed to for 1928.
		Rbls.	Rbls.
1.	Salaries of District employees	7,020.00	7,020.00
2.	Salaries of Foremen	4,100.00	3,349.00
3.	Salaries of Traffice-station watchers	427.00	609.00
4.	Re-erection, repairs to, and upkeep of Aids	11,900.00	11,836.00
5.	Lighting of Beacons	5,365.00	7,000.00
6.	Repairs to buildings	500.00	400.00
7.	Post, telegraph and sundry	750.00	750.00
8.	Heating	350.00	350.00
9.	Lighting of Houses	100.00	100.00
10.	Travelling expenses and allowances	350.00	290.00
11.	5% Medical attendance	2,000.00	2,000.00
12.	Depreciation	1,748.00	1,796.00
13.	Upkeep of launch	18,500.00	18,500.00
14.	Office expenses	6,000.00	6,000.00
15.	Stone removal work	600.00	. ..
16.	Unforeseen	290.00	. ..
		60,000.00	60,000.00

(Signed) Manager of Way Department / Mr. Mihailoff /

(Signed) Technical Adviser on Amur Aids / Mr. Ignatieff /

Certified correct:

P. Ignatieff

Technical Adviser on Amur
Aids to Navigation.

呈海关总税务司署 362 号文　　　　　　　　瑷珲关 1928 年 3 月 10 日

尊敬的海关总税务司（北京）：

根据瑷珲关第 315 号呈：

"汇报 1927 年就联合维护黑龙江航路标志事宜续签 1923 年《黑龙江航路标志协议》事。"

兹报告，1928 年 1 月 11 日已再次续签该协议。

1928 年 1 月 11 日，黑龙江航路标志联合委员会于苏维埃领事馆中召开会议，签署中文版及俄文版续约协议，两版续约协议抄件各附一份英文译本。但中文及俄文两版新协议与此前情况相同仍然存在一定的差异。然而，双方确于签署协议的前一天，交换了两个版本的协议，并互相予以通过。

今年签署的《黑龙江航路标志协议》财政年度自 1927 年 12 月 1 日至 1928 年 12 月 1 日。协议规定支出预算为 60000 金卢布，与去年金额相同，华方摊款仍为预算总额之半数，即 30000 金卢布。华方委员会在年初就已表明预算不得超过 1927 年的预算额，此外，航务专门顾问易保罗先生（P. I. Ignatieff）亦会因其对此事处理得当而受到褒奖。

在签署该协议之前，黑龙江航路标志联合委员会并未组织先导会，道尹与俄方委员会的意见分别由本署和航务专门顾问相互传达。双方就彼此意见的分歧做出了协商与让步，最终，在最佳形势下，双方委员共同签署了该协议。

会上曾一度提出将《黑龙江航路标志协议》与《乌苏里江航路标志协议》合并，但是道尹却认为，鉴于该两份协议涉及黑龙江与吉林两个省份，因此更加希望这两份协议继续各自独立存在。本署随后将呈文汇报《乌苏里江航路标志协议》的续约事宜。

今年，俄阿穆尔水道局又一次极力敦促对黑龙江上游河道开展疏浚工事。然而在航务专门顾问的建议下，道尹依旧表示，鉴于从中受益的只有一艘中国轮船和两到三艘俄国轮船，且该项疏浚工事所需费用较高，因此确无开展此项工程之必要。道尹认为黑龙江上游每年水位较低的时间极短，而且即使是在这段时间内，确实有三处浅滩难以航行，但由于航运量十分有限，航运工作亦可以继续进行，故该项疏浚工事应予以推迟。苏维埃当局对道尹的这一态度十分不满，更一度表示要越过中国航政委员会，直接与奉天（沈阳）政府交涉，以期独立开展工事。但同时俄方对疏浚工事也提出了更为合理的方案，而且也将预算一再削减，最终提出了不超过 1000 金卢布的预算额，华方摊付一半。目前，道尹原则上同意了该项预算，并已将之呈报上级政府，同时指出，如确有支出该笔费用的需要，则最好可以从外部来筹集资金。

黑龙江航路标志账户的年度财务报表正在编制之中,当随呈提交报表时,亦将开始制订 1928 年预算。幸于 1927 年初提高了江捐税率,目前看来,江捐税收足以应对今年的支出预算,相信正常情况下无须再向松花江航路标志账户贷款。

兹附航务专门顾问编制的 1927 年与 1928 年预算对比报表(见附件 5)。1927 年江捐税收分配图表将与上段中提到的年度财务报表一起随呈附上。

您忠诚的仆人

铎博赉(R. M. Talbot)

瑷珲关署理税务司

附件 2[①]

1928 年黑龙江航路标志协议俄文版译本

中俄临时地方工程委员会会议纪要

（1928 年 1 月 11 日于大黑河）

参会代表

大黑河道尹兼瑷珲交涉员	张增寿先生
瑷珲关税务司	铎博赉先生
黑河道尹公署代表	沈廷荣先生
黑龙江航务专门顾问	易保罗先生
驻大黑河苏俄领事	默拉美德（Melamed）先生
阿穆尔水道局局长	托阿诺夫（Dianoff）先生
阿穆尔水道局副局长	且比索夫（Chebisheff）先生
阿穆尔水道局航路工程师	米海依罗夫（Mihailoff）先生

---

① 注：附件 1 为协议俄文版，不予翻译。

提案	议决
1.俄阿穆尔水道局与黑河道尹于1923年10月28日所签之关于维护黑龙江边界河道(自波克罗夫卡(Pokrovka)至嘎杂克维池(Kasakevich))航路标志的协议,于1928年续约一年。	1.鉴于1923年10月28日所签署的《黑龙江航路标志协议》仅续约至1927年12月1日,且即将到期,兹决定: (a)再次续约一年,至1928年12月1日止,除附件三需要另议外,其余附件均随协议一同继续生效; (b)在此期间,如中俄会议就边界河道问题达成协议,则现行地方协议即行废止。
2.1928年黑龙江边界河道(自波克罗夫卡至嘎杂克维池)航路标志预算。	2.批准1928年用于黑龙江边界河道(自波克罗夫卡至嘎杂克维池)航路标志的60000金卢布预算,实际支出不得超出该预算额。
3.俄阿穆尔水道局去年关于黑龙江边界河道(自波克罗夫卡至嘎杂克维池)航路标志的预算报表。	3.批准1927年总计60000金卢布的预算,并由华方支付最后尾款。
4.黑龙江边界河道(自波克罗夫卡至嘎杂克维池)的其他相关事项,如石块清理工作、额尔古纳河航路标志项目、黑龙江疏浚工程等。	4.中俄临时地方工程委员会特别会议将对此类事项予以讨论、批复,并独立执行。
5.会议纪要之要求。	5.会议纪要须分别以中、俄文撰写,各一式两份,双方各执中、俄文本各一份,以恪信守。

签字	签字
中俄临时地方工程委员会俄方委员长兼驻大黑河苏俄领事 默拉美德 委员: 阿穆尔水道局局长 托阿诺夫 阿穆尔水道局副局长 且比索夫 阿穆尔水道局航路工程师 米海依罗夫	中俄临时地方工程委员会华方委员长兼黑河道尹 张寿增 委员: 瑷珲关税务司 铎博赍 黑河道尹公署代表 沈廷荣 黑龙江航务专门顾问 易保罗

翻译:易保罗黑龙江航务专门顾问

附件 4[①]

1928 年黑龙江航路标志协议中文版译本

中俄黑龙江水道委员会华方委员长兼黑河道尹兼瑷珲交涉员张寿增，华方委员瑷珲关税务司铎博赉、黑河道尹公署外交科长沈廷荣、航务专门顾问易保罗；俄方委员长兼驻黑河苏俄领事默拉美德，俄方委员阿穆尔水道局局长托阿诺夫、阿穆尔水道局副局长且比索夫、阿穆尔水道局航路工程师米海依罗夫，共同于民国十七年元月十一日（1928 年 1 月11 日），在中俄临时地方工程委员会召开于大黑河的正式会议上发表联合声明，内容如下。

中华民国十二年（1923）双方所订黑龙江等中俄两国交界河流航行地方临时协议所有附则附件等，除第三附件另行规定外，其余仍照旧章办理，再展期一年，自民国十六年十二月一日（1927 年 12 月 1 日）起，至民国十七年十二月一日（1928 年 12 月 1 日）止，继续有效。在此期间，如中俄会议就国际航行订有办法，该项地方协议等件即行废止。又本年共同修理黑龙江一切经费议定为 60000 金卢布，各项支出款项不得超过议定预算数目；机器挖江及修理额尔古纳河等工程另议。

为此双方协定此协议，计中、俄文本各两份，互相签字盖印，各执中、俄文本各一份，以恪信守。

中华民国十七年一月十一日（1928 年 1 月 11 日）于大黑河签订。

华方：

黑河道尹兼瑷珲交涉员	张寿增
瑷珲关税务司	铎博赉
黑河道尹公署外交科长	沈廷荣
航务专门顾问	易保罗

俄方：

驻大黑河苏俄领事	默拉美德
阿穆尔水道局局长	托阿诺夫
阿穆尔水道局副局长	且比索夫
阿穆尔水道局航路工程师	米海依罗夫

---

① 注：附件 3 为协议俄文版，不予翻译。

翻译：屠守鑫　四等帮办后班

附件 5

1927 年与 1928 年联合维护黑龙江航路标志预算对比报表

支出	1927 年预算 （卢布）	1928 年预算 （卢布）
1. 地区职员薪俸	7020.00	7020.00
2. 监工员薪俸	4400.00	3349.00
3. 交通站观察员薪俸	427.00	609.00
4. 航路标志的重建、维修与维护	11900.00	11836.00
5. 灯塔照明费	5365.00	7000.00
6. 建筑维修费	500.00	400.00
7. 邮费、电报费及杂物费	750.00	750.00
8. 供暖费	350.00	350.00
9. 宿舍照明费	100.00	100.00
10. 差旅费及津贴	350.00	290.00
11. 5% 的医疗护理费	2000.00	2000.00
12. 折旧费	1748.00	1796.00
13. 汽艇维护	18500.00	18500.00
14. 办公经费	6000.00	6000.00
15. 石块清理费	600.00	——
16. 意外支出	290.00	——
总计	60000.00	60000.00

（签字）阿穆尔水道局航路工程师　米海依罗夫

（签字）黑龙江航务专门顾问　易保罗

兹证明，报表正确无误。

易保罗　黑龙江航务专门顾问

此抄件发送至哈尔滨关税务司及巡工司。

录事：屠守鑫　四等帮办后班

25. 1928 年《乌苏里江航路标志协议》

USSURI AIDS TO NAVIGATION: renewal of Agreement for
1928 reporting; copies of Chinese and Russian version
of Agreement together with their English translations,
forwarding.

363.

I.G.   Aigun   10th March, 1928.

Sir,

With reference to my despatch No. 322:

reporting the signing of
an Agreement on the 17th
June, 1927 for the
rehabilitation of Aids on
the Ussuri:

and to my despatch No. 362:

informing you of the
renewal of the Amur Aids
Agreement on the 11th
January, 1928, for a
further period of one year:

I now have the honour to report that the Ussuri
Aids Agreement was renewed for 1928 at the same
time as the Amur Aids Agreement. The negotiation
in connection therewith were conducted jointly with
those of the latter Agreement which have already

been

The Inspector General of Customs,

Peking.

been reported in my preceeding despatch.

The Agreement now concluded is in the
form of a renewal of that of June, 1927, and
is for one year from 1st December, 1927, in
conformity with the term of the Amur Aids
Agreement. Copies of the documents concerned are
appended as follows:

Appendix No.1.   Russian version of the renewed Agreement.
Appendix No.2.   English version of same.
Appendix No.3.   Chinese version of the renewed Agreement.
Appendix No.4.   English version of same.

The estimate for the coming year, as
approved, is G.Rbls.8,600 of which China is to
pay half. This estimate is the same as that of
the last Agreement but is for a period of one
year instead of six months, the life of the 1927
Agreement. There would seem to be an anomaly in
that the estimates are the same for the two
Agreements. It should be explained, therefore,
that whereas the Aids had to be wholly renewed
in 1927 there were only six months of overhead

expenses

expenses while in 1928, though there will only be the expense of keeping the renewed Aids in order, there will be overhead expenses for one year. A summary of the estimates for 1927 and 1928 is appended, as prepared by the Technical Adviser, comparing the amounts under the different headings for the two years.

Appendix No.5.

As in the case of the Amur Aids Agreement, the budget for the maintenance of Ussuri Aids will be dealt with in the despatch now being prepared submitting the Annual Statement of Aids (Amur and Ussuri) Accounts.

Although the Agreement for the reerection and maintenance of Aids on the Ussuri from Kasakevich village to Hulin was signed on 17th June, 1927, the work in connection therewith was not commenced until a month later owing to trouble with the Soviet Frontier Guard Authorities. The channel was surveyed and all beacons placed in position before the end of the year but only

one

one coat of paint was applied to the latter. They will be given a second coat and numbered at the opening of navigation this year.

The members of the Chinese side of the Aids Commission, consisting of the Heiho Taoyin, the Technical Adviser and myself, left for a trip of inspection of Aids on the Lower Amur and the Ussuri on the 2nd August last year. We were joined at Lahasusu by the Ilan Taoyin detailed by the Kirin Governor as his representative. The party proceeded as far as Hulin, to which point Aids are to be maintained, the trip being without incident. At that time the erection of Aids had not quite been completed. We found trade flourishing on the Ussuri and met more steamers on it than on the Amur. The erection of Aids was a great necessity and shipping interests were very appreciative of what was being done. It should be recorded that only one Russian steamer plies

the

the Ussuri. and that without passengers and cargo
worth mentioning, so that the joint erection of
Aids on that river is almost solely in the
interests of Chinese shipping. Within a day or
so after our party left the Ussuri on the
return trip an unprecedented flood occurred doing
great damage to the towns and fields on the
low lying Chinese side of the river. Fortunately
the beacons withstood the rush of the water.
Trade for the rest of the year was at a
standstill and River Dues Collection suffered
accordingly. It remains to be seen whether
trade will resume its former proportions the
coming year. The Technical Adviser will touch
on the trips of inspection made on the Ussuri
in his Annual Report for 1927, to be forwarded
shortly.

There has been some agitation by the
Tungpei Steamship Company for dredging on the
Ussuri but it is the considered opinion of the
                                        Technical

Technical Adviser that such work would not be
practical owing to the sandy nature of the
river bed and the consequent difficulty of
confining the channel for long to any particular
course.

A statement showing the collection of
River Dues on Ussuri traffic will be forwarded
in the despatch submitting the Annual Statement
of Aids Accounts mentioned above.

I have the honour to be,

Sir,

Your obedient Servant,

Acting Commissioner.

Appendix

Appendix No. 1.

ПРОТОКОЛ

заседания Временной Местной Советско-Китайской Комиссии

Января " II " дня 1928 года, гор. Сахалян.

ПРИСУТСТВОВАЛИ:

Хэйхэсский Дао-Инь и дипломатический

Чиновник в Айгуне.................. Г. ЧЖАН-ШОУ-ДЗЕН.

Комиссар Айгунской Таможни.......... Г. ТАЛБОТ.

Чиновник при Управлении Иланскаго

Дао-Иня........................ Г. ЧЖЕН-ПУ-ЧАН.

Техническй Советник.............. Г. ИГНАТЬЕВ.

Консул СССР в гор. Сахаляне....... Г. МЕЛАМЕД.

Начальник Управления Водных Путей

Амурскаго бассейна................. Г. ДМАНОВ.

Помощник Начальника Управления Вод-

ных Путей, Инженер............... Г. ЧЕНЫШОВ.

Начальник Отдела Пути АВУ, Инженер Г. МИХАЙЛОВ.

СЛУШАЛИ:	ПОСТАНОВИЛИ:
1/ Вопрос о продлении на 1928 год Соглашения о совместном обслуживании обстановкой водного пути общего пользования по р. Уссури от русской деревни Казакевичево до гор. Ху-лин.	Принимая во внимание, что временное соглашение от 28 октября 1923 года, распространенное до 1-го декабря 1927 года на Уссури от русской деревни Казакевичево до гор. Ху-лини, потеряло свою силу за окончанием срока. ПОСТАНОВИЛИ: 1/ Продлить это соглашение еще еще на один год, т.е. до 1-го декабря 1928 года по Уссури от русской деревни Казакевичево до города Ху-лина, со всеми к нему приложениями, кроме приложения № 3, которое согласуется отдельно. 2/ Если в течение этого года состоится постановление работающей ныне Советско-Китайской Конференции, в части его касающейся совместного пользования пограничными путями, настоящее соглашение теряет свою силу.
2/ Предложение Китайской стороны о совместной обстановке от русской деревни Казакевичевой до города Хабаровска.	Так как вопрос о совместном устройстве обстановки от русской деревни Казакевичево до города Хабаровска связан с влиянием на положение существующих между Китаем и СССР водных границ, рассмотрение какового вопроса не входит в компетенцию Местной Технической Комиссии, - указанный вопрос оставить открытым до решения Советско-Китайской Конференции.
3/ Смета на 1928 год по водному пути р. Уссури в пределах общего пользования от русской деревни Казакевичево до города Ху-лина.	Смету на 1928 год по обслуживанию водных путей общего пользования по р. Уссури в сумме 8,600 рублей - УТВЕРДИТЬ. Сумма расхода не должна превышать исчисленную по смете сумму.

4/ Отчот по расходам, произведенным АВУ по ремонту и обслуживанию обстановки р. Уссури от
русской деревни Казакевичево до
гор. Ху-лина в навигацию 1927
года.

Отчет за 1927 год в сумме
8,600 рублей УТВЕРДИТЬ и
расчет по этому отчету
закончить.

5/ О составлении протокола.

Протокол должен быть составлен
на русском и китайском языках
по 2 экземпляра, из которых
по одному экземпляру русскаго
и китайского текста получает
Комиссия с Китайской стороны
и по одному экземпляру -
Комиссия со стороны СССР.

Председатель Временной Местной
Советско- Китайской Технический
Комиссии со стороны СССР, Кон-
сул СССР в городе Сахаляне

/Г.И. Мелямед/

Начальник АВУ / Лианов/

Члены Комиссии /Чебышов/
/Михайлов/

Председатель Комиссии с Китайской стороны, Хэйхэсский
Д а о - И н ь

/Чжан-Шоу-Дзэн/

Члены:

/Талйот/
/Чэзн-Гу-Чан/
/Игнатьев/

True copy:

P. Ignatieff

Technical Adviser on
Amur Aids to Navigation.

Appendix No. 2.

Translation of the Russian version of the Protocol extending
the 1923/24 Amur Aids Agreement to the joint upkeep of Aids on the
Ussuri River from Kasakevich village to Hulin Hsien for the year 1928.

P R O T O C O L.

Minutes of a meeting of the local Provisional Sino-Soviet
Technical Commission, held at Taheiho on the 11th January, 1928.

Representatives:-

Heiho Taoyin and concurrently Commissioner for Foreign Affairs, Aigun:	Mr. Chang Shou-tsen
Commissioner of Customs, Aigun:	Mr. Talbot
Representative from the Ilan Taoyin's Office:	Mr. Cheng Fu-chan
Technical Adviser on Amur Aids:	Mr. Ignatieff
Consul of U.S.S.R. at Taheiho:	Mr. Melamed
Director of Amur Navigation Bureau:	Mr. Dianoff:
Assistant Director of Amur Navigation Bureau:	Mr. Chebisheff
Manager of Way Department of Amur Navigation Bureau:	Mr. Mihailoff

Subject Discussed:	Decision：
1. The continuation during 1928 of the Agreement for the joint Upkeep of Aids on the frontier river Ussuri from the Russian village Kasakevich to the town Hulin.	1. In view of the fact that the Provisional Aids Agreement of 28th October, 1923, extended to the Ussuri to the 1st December, 1927, for the section from the Russian village Kasakevich to the town Hulin has expired, the Commission decides: a) to continue the Agreement for the Ussuri

Ussuri for the stretch Russian village Kasakevich to Hulin for a period of one year, i.e. to 1st December, 1928, with all Annexes, excepting Annex 3 which will be agreed to separately.

b) If during the period of the present Agreement the Sino-Russian Conference reaches a decision with reference to the mutual use of frontier rivers, this Agreement loses its force.

2. A proposal made by the Chinese side of the Aids Commission for joint work on the stretch of the Ussuri from the Russian village Kasakevich to Harbarovsk.

2. As the question of joint Aids work on the stretch of the Ussuri from the Russian village Kasakevich to Harbarovsk, if provided for in this Agreement, might prejudice the negotiations now pending for the settlement of the boundary question in that vicinity and, moreover, as the discussion of the boundary question is outside the scope of this Commission, the matter of erecting Aids on this section of the Ussuri shall be left to the decision of the Sino-Russian Conference.

3. Estimate for the year 1928, for the upkeep of Aids on the Ussuri Waterway, from the Russian village Kasakevich to the town Hulin.

3. To sanction an estimate amounting to Gold Roubles 8,600 for the year 1928 for Aids work on the Ussuri between the Russian village Kasakevich and the town Hulin. The amount expended shall not exceed this sum.

4. Statement of expenses incurred by the Amur Navigation Bureau for Ussuri Aids work from the Russian village Kasakevich to the town Hulin for the year 1927.

4. To approve the accounts as presented for 1927, to the amount of Gold Roubles 8,600 and to regard the last payment made by the Chinese side as final.

5. Records to be made.

5. Records shall be made out in the Chinese and Russian language, in duplicate, each party retaining one copy in Chinese and one in Russian.

The President of the local Provisional Technical Commission for the Soviet side, the Consul of the U.S.S.R. at Taheiho.
/ G. I. Melamed /

The President of the Chinese Aids Commission, the Heiho Taoyin.
/ Chang Shou-tsen /

Members:
Director of Amur Navigation Bureau,
/ Dianoff /
/ Chebisheff /
/ Mihailoff /

Members:
/ Talbot /
/ Cheng Fu-ch'an /
/ Ignatieff /

Translated by :

P. Ignatieff

Technical Adviser on Amur Aids to Navigation.

Appendix No. 3.

聲明書

聲明書

華方委員長大中華民國黑河道尹秉瓊琿交涉員張壽增

華方委員瓊琿關稅務司鐸博費依蘭道署外交科長鄭

步蟾航路專門顧問易保羅

俄方委員長大蘇維亞社會聯邦共和國駐黑河領事默拉美德

俄方委員阿穆爾省國家水道局局長吉阿諾夫阿穆爾省國家

水道局副局長且彼索夫阿穆爾省國家水道局航路工程師米

哈依羅夫於中華民國十七年（即西歷一千九百二十八年）一月十日

在大黑河地方臨時協議工程委員會正式會議共同商定聲明

如左

（一）中華民國十二年（西歷一千九百二十三年）十月二十八日貨方所訂

中俄兩國交界河流航行地方臨時協議關於烏蘇里江由俄屯

嘎雜克維池至虎林一段至中華民國十六年（即西歷一千九百二七年）

十二月一日期滿現經雙方決定照此協議再展期一年至中華民

國十七年（即西歷一千九百二十八年）十二月一日止該協議以及所有

附件等除第三附件另行規定外其餘仍照舊章辦理繼續

（二）有效

在此期間如中俄會議國際航行訂有辦法此項地方協議即

行廢止華要求安設燈照由嘎雜克維池俄屯到伯力之間因

其有章涉及於中俄界務之關係非地方委員會所能解決

該項問題應候北京中俄會議決定之

（三）中華民國十七年份（即西歷一千九百二十八年）共同修理烏蘇里江

江道由俄屯嘎雜克維池至虎林縣一段安設燈照之工程全年

經費定為金洋八千六百元各項支出之款不得超過議定

預算數目

（四）中華民國十六年份（即西歷一千九百二七年）共同修理烏蘇里江

由俄屯嘎雜克維池至虎林縣一段共支出金洋八千六百元之

決算表應行核對完竣以便清結

（五）此項聲明書計華俄文各兩份由雙方簽字蓋印彼此各執華

俄文各一份以昭信守

大中華民國十七年一月十一日訂於黑河

西歷一千九百二十八年一月十一日

中國方面委員長黑河道尹兼辦理交涉員張壽增

璦琿關稅務司譯博贊

依蘭道署外交科　長鄭必蜡

航　路　顧　問　易保羅

俄國方面委員長駐黑蘇俄顧事默拉美德

阿穆爾省國家水道局局長吉阿諾夫

阿穆爾省國家水道局副局長且彼索夫

阿穆爾省國家水道局航路工程師米哈依羅夫

Appendix No. 4.

Translation of the Chinese version of the Protocol extending
the 1923/24 Amur Aids Agreement to the joint upkeep of Aids on the
Ussuri River from Kasakevich village to Hulin Hsien for the year 1928.

The President of the Chinese Aids
Commission and Heiho Taoyin of the Great Republic
of China (concurrently Commissioner of Foreign
Affairs for the Aigun District), Chang Shou-tsen,
and the members of the Chinese Commission:
Commissioner of Aigun Customs, N. M. Talbot,
Chief of the Diplomatic Department of the Ilan
Taoyin's yamen, Cheng Fu-ch'an, and the Technical
Adviser to the Chinese Aids Commission, P. I.
Ignatieff; and the President of Russian Aids
Commission and the Consul of the Great United
Socialistic Soviet Republic at Taheiho, Melamed,
and the members of the Russian Commission:
Director of the Amur Government Navigation Bureau,
Dianoff, Assistant Director of the Amur Government
Navigation Bureau, Chebisheff, and the Engineer
of the Amur Government Navigation Bureau,
Mihailoff:

hereby jointly declare on the eleventh day of the first month of the
seventeenth year of the Chinese Republic (i.e. 1928) at a formal
meeting held by the local Provisional Aids Commission at Taheiho, that

(1) As the local Provisional Agreement of the Sino-Russian Frontier River
Navigation Commission concerning the Ussuri River for the section from
the Russian village Kasakevich to Hulin, drawn up by the two parties
on the 28th day of the 10th month of the twelfth year of the Republic
of China (i.e. 1923), is to expire on the 1st day of the 12th month
of the 16th year of the Republic of China (i.e. 1927), it is now
agreed by both parties that this Agreement is to be extended for a
further

further period of one year to the 1st day of the 12th month
of the 17th year of the Republic of China (i.e. 1928) together
with the Annexes thereto, with the exception of Annex No. 3
which shall be settled separately.

(2) If during this period, an agreement be reached concerning
frontier navigation by the Sino-Russian Conference, the
present local Agreement is to be cancelled. At the request
of the Chinese side, the question of the establishment of
beacons on the section from the Russian village Kasakevich
to Harbarovsk, which involves Sino-Russian boundary relations
and therefore cannot be discussed by the local Commission, is
to be settled by the Sino-Russian Conference, Peking.

(3) The total expenditure for the joint upkeep of the Ussuri
channel and the establishment of beacons for the section from
Russian village Kasakevich to Hulin Hsien for the 17th year
of the Republic of China (i.e. 1928) is fixed at Gold Roubles
8,600; all expenses in connection therewith shall not exceed
this estimate.

(4) The Accounts for the 16th year of the Republic of China (i.e.
1927), involving the expenditure of Gold Roubles 8,600, for
the joint upkeep of Aids on the Ussuri for the section from
the Russian village Kasakevich to Hulin Hsien, are to be
audited and passed if found correct.

(5) To confirm this Agreement, this Declaration is made out, in
the Chinese and Russian languages, in duplicate, and is signed
and sealed by both parties, each party keeping one copy in
Chinese and one in Russian.

Done at Taheiho on the 11th day of the 1st month of
the 17th year of the Great Republic of China corresponding to
the 11th day of January, in the year one Thousand nine Hundred
and

and twenty eight.

    <u>Chinese side:</u>

    (Signed) Chang Shou-tsen, President and Heiho
                   Taoyin and concurrently
                   Commissioner for Foreign Affairs.

       "   R. M. Talbot, Commissioner of Aigun
                   Customs.

       "   Chêng Pu-ch'an, Chief of the Diplomatic
                   Department of the Ilan Taoyin's
                   yamen.

       "   P. I. Ignatieff, Technical Adviser to
                   the Chinese Aids Commission.

<u>Soviet Russian side:</u>

    (Signed) Melamed, President and Consul of U.S.S.R.
                   at Taheiho.

       "   Dianoff, Director of the Amur Navigation
                   Bureau.

       "   Chebisheff, Assistant Director of the
                   Amur Navigation Bureau.

       "   Mihailoff, Engineer of the Amur
                   Navigation Bureau.

Translated by:

    4th Assistant B.

Appendix No. 5.

SUMMARY OF ESTIMATE AGREED TO FOR THE JOINT UPKEEP OF AIDS ON THE USSURI FOR THE YEAR 1928 AS COMPARED WITH THAT OF 1927.

No.	Particulars.	Amount agreed to for 1927. Rbls.	Amount agreed to for 1928. Rbls.
1.	Salaries of employees	756.60	1,404.00
2.	Erection of new beacons	1,694.00	78.00
3.	Repairs to beacons	1,830.60	2,070.00
4.	Repairs to small boats	86.00	90.00
5.	Repairs to equipment	30.00	33.00
6.	Repairs to houses and stores	40.00	40.00
7.	Post and telegraph	50.00	50.00
8.	Travelling expenses and allowances	100.00	100.00
9.	5% Medical attendance	200.00	275.00
10.	Depreciation	60.00	60.00
11.	District Office expenses	1,500.00	3,000.00
12.	Upkeep of launch	2,150.00	1,400.00
13.	Unforeseen	102.80	...
		8,600.00	8,600.00

(Signed) Manager of Way Department / Mr. Mihailoff /

(Signed) Technical Adviser on Amur Aids / Mr. Ignatieff /

Certified correct:

P. Ignatieff.

Technical Adviser on Amur
Aids to Navigation.

呈海关总税务司署 363 号文　　　　　　　　瑷珲关 1928 年 3 月 10 日

尊敬的海关总税务司（北京）：

根据瑷珲关第 322 号呈：

"汇报于 1927 年 6 月 17 日签订《乌苏里江航路标志协议》一事。"

及瑷珲关第 362 号呈：

"汇报自 1928 年 1 月 11 日起再次续签《黑龙江航路标志协议》一年。"

兹报告，《乌苏里江航路标志协议》和《黑龙江航路标志协议》于 1928 年同时续约。两份协议的相关协商事宜亦是同时进行的。本署已于之前的呈文中汇报了协商过程。

同《黑龙江航路标志协议》一样，《乌苏里江航路标志协议》亦在 1927 年 6 月协议的基础上续签一年，有效期自 1927 年 12 月 1 日始。兹附相关文件的抄件：

附件 1：俄文版续约协议

附件 2：俄文版续约协议的英文译本

附件 3：中文版续约协议

附件 4：中文版续约协议的英文译本

协议规定支出预算为 8600 金卢布，与 1927 年预算相同，华方摊款仍为预算总额之半数。两年的预算虽相同，但 1927 年协议规定之期限仅为六个月，而今年则为一整年，原因在于 1927 年航路标志需要全部翻新，而 1928 年只需要对航路标志予以适当维护。随函附上航务专门顾问编制的 1927 年与 1928 年预算对比报表，航务专门顾问在报表中对这两年的各项支出情况做了详细的对比。

乌苏里江航路标志维护工作预算将与黑龙江及乌苏里江航路标志年度财务报表遂同一呈文（编制中）附上。

1927 年 6 月 17 日签订的《乌苏里江航路标志协议》，就重建乌苏里江自嘎杂克维池（Kasakevich）村至虎林河段的航路标志及相关维护事宜做出了明确规定，但由于苏维埃边境警卫局的阻挠，一应工作直至一个月后才得以开展。至 1927 年底，河道测量工作已顺利完成，所有标桩业已安设完毕，不过只来得及为标桩外层刷上一层的保护漆。在今年航运季开始之前，还须为标桩刷上第二层保护漆，并为标桩加上编号。

作为中俄黑龙江水道委员会华方委员，黑河道尹、航务专门顾问和本署于去年八月二日开始对黑龙江下游和乌苏里江上的航路标志进行巡查。吉林省省长委派依兰道尹担任吉林省代表，于拉哈苏苏河段加入了我们的巡查队伍。此次巡查远至虎林（航路标志亟待维护河段之终点）。巡查进行得非常顺利，但当时航路标志的安设工作还尚未全部完成。鉴于乌苏里江上的贸易呈现出一派欣欣向荣的景象，航运量更是远远超过了黑龙江，因此在乌苏里江上建立航路标志就变得十分必要，这对航运业的发展可以说是大有裨益的。而且，目前往返于乌苏里江上的俄国轮船仅有一艘，更遑论客运与货运的情况了，所以在乌苏里江上建立航路标志，实际上完全是在为中国航运业创造便利。当天，大约在我们自乌苏里江返城后，一场突如其来的洪水几乎冲毁了乌苏里江下游华岸所有村庄及农田。所幸标桩的损毁情况并不严重。接下来的时间里，贸易发展停滞，江捐征收也受到了影响。今年贸易情况是否能够恢复正常仍有待考察。在1927年航务年度报告（即将呈送）中，航务专门顾问对巡查乌苏里江一事亦有所叙述。

戊通航业公司曾一度提议于乌苏里江上开展疏浚工事，不过航务专门顾问则认为乌苏里江的河床属沙质，时间一长，便难于固定航道路线，因此疏浚乌苏里江的想法不切实际。

乌苏里江江捐税收分配图表将与上段中提到的航务年度报告一并随呈附上。

您忠诚的仆人

铎博赉（R. M. Talbot）

瑷珲关署理税务司

附件 2[①]

1923/1924 年黑龙江航路标志协议就联合维护乌苏里江（自嘎杂克维池村至虎林）航

路标志事宜再次续约一年，此为 1928 年续约协议俄文版译本

协议

中俄临时地方工程委员会会议纪要

（1928 年 1 月 11 日于大黑河）

参会代表

大黑河道尹兼瑷珲交涉员	张寿增先生
瑷珲关税务司	铎博赉先生
依兰道尹公署代表	郑步蟾先生
黑龙江航务专门顾问	易保罗（P. I. Ignatieff）先生
驻大黑河苏俄领事	默拉美德（Melamed）先生
阿穆尔水道局局长	托阿诺夫（Dianoff）先生
阿穆尔水道局副局长	且比索夫（Chebisheff）先生
阿穆尔水道局航路工程师	米海依罗夫（Mihailoff）先生

---

① 注：附件 1 为协议俄文版，不予翻译。

提案	议决
1.《1923/1924 年黑龙江航路标志协议》就联合维护乌苏里江（自嘎杂克维池村至虎林）航路标志事宜于 1928 年再次续约一年。	1. 鉴于《1923/1924 年黑龙江航路标志协议》的续约协议至 1927 年 12 月 1 日已到期，且该协议包括了联合维护乌苏里江（自嘎杂克维池村至虎林）航路标志事宜，兹决定： （a）1928 年再次续约一年，除附件三需要另议外，其余所有附件均随协议一并继续生效； （b）在此期间，如中俄会议就边界河道问题达成协议，则现行地方协议即行废止。
2. 中俄黑龙江水道委员会华方委员会提出在乌苏里江的延展段［自嘎杂克维池村至（哈巴罗夫斯克 Habarovsk，即伯力）］上联合建立航路标志。	2. 考虑到如果在协议中提及于乌苏里江延展段（自嘎杂克维池村至哈巴罗夫斯克）上联合建立航路标志一事，很可能会为当下的关于附近边界线问题的谈判事宜带来不利影响；而且边界线问题并不在中俄黑龙江水道委员会的职能范围之内，因此，该事项应交由中俄会议决定。
3. 1928 年乌苏里江（自嘎杂克维池村至虎林）航路标志预算。	3. 批准 1928 年用于乌苏里江（自嘎杂克维池村至虎林）航路标志的 8600 金卢布预算，实际支出不得超出该预算额。
4. 俄阿穆尔水道局 1927 年乌苏里江（自嘎杂克维池村至虎林）航路标志支出报表。	4. 批准 1927 年总计 8600 金卢布的预算，并由华方支付最后尾款。
5. 会议纪要之要求。	5. 会议记录须分别以中、俄文撰写，各一式两份，双方各执中、俄文本各一份，以恪信守。

签字	签字
中俄临时地方工程委员会俄方委员长兼驻大黑河苏俄领事 默拉美德 委员： 阿穆尔水道局局长 托阿诺夫 阿穆尔水道局副局长 且比索夫 阿穆尔水道局航路工程师 米海依罗夫	中俄临时地方工程委员会华方委员长兼黑河道尹 张寿增 委员： 瑷珲关税务司 铎博赉 依兰道尹公署代表 郑步蟾 黑龙江航务专门顾问 易保罗

翻译：易保罗黑龙江航务专门顾问

附件 4

1923/1924 年黑龙江航路标志协议就联合维护乌苏里江（自嘎杂克维池村至虎林）航路标志事宜再次续约一年，此为 1928 年续约协议中文版译本

　　中俄黑龙江水道委员会华方委员长兼黑河道尹兼瑷珲交涉员张寿增，华方委员瑷珲关税务司铎博赉、依兰道尹公署外交科长郑步蟾、航务专门顾问易保罗；俄方委员长兼驻黑河苏俄领事默拉美德，俄方委员阿穆尔水道局局长托阿诺夫、阿穆尔水道局副局长且比索夫、阿穆尔水道局航路工程师米海依罗夫，共同于民国十七年元月十一日（1928 年 1 月 11 日），在中俄临时地方工程委员会召开于大黑河的正式会议上发表联合声明，内容如下。

　　中华民国十二年十月二十八日（1923 年 10 月 28 日），双方所订中俄两国交界河流航行地方临时协议（关于乌苏里江自嘎杂克维池村至虎林一段），至中华民国十六年十二月一日（1927 年 12 月 1 日）期满。现经双方决定，照此协议，再展期一年，至中华民国十七年十二月一日（1928 年 12 月 1 日）为止。除第三附件另行规定外，其余仍照旧章办理，继续有效。

　　在此期间，如中俄会议就国际航行订有办法，该项地方协议即行废止。华方所提出的在嘎杂克维池村至哈巴罗夫斯克之间安设标桩的要求，因牵涉到边界线问题，非地方委员会所能解决，故须提交北京中俄会议决定。

　　中华民国十七年（1928）共同修理乌苏里江河道，以及在嘎杂克维池村至虎林之间安设标桩，两项工程的预算共计 8600 金卢布，实际支出不得超过议定预算金额。

　　中华民国十六年（1927）共同修理乌苏里江自嘎杂克维池村至虎林一段的工程，共计支出 8600 金卢布，现应对该账目予以核对，以便清结。

　　此项声明书计中、俄文本各两份，由双方签字盖印，彼此各执中、俄文本各一份，以昭信守。

　　中华民国十七年一月十一日（1928 年 1 月 11 日）于大黑河签订。

华方：

黑河道尹兼瑷珲交涉员	张寿增
瑷珲关税务司	铎博赉
依兰道尹公署外交科长	郑步蟾
黑龙江航务专门顾问	易保罗

俄方：

驻大黑河苏俄领事	默拉美德
阿穆尔水道局局长	托阿诺夫
阿穆尔水道局副局长	且比索夫
阿穆尔水道局航路工程师	米海依罗夫

录事：屠守鑫　四等帮办后班

附件 5

1927 年与 1928 年联合维护乌苏里江航路标志预算对比报表

支出	1927 年预算（卢布）	1928 年预算（卢布）
1. 地区职员薪俸	756.60	1404.00
2. 新建灯塔	1694.00	78.00
3. 维修灯塔	1830.60	2070.00
4. 维修小船	86.00	90.00
5. 维修设备	30.00	33.00
6. 修缮宿舍及商铺	40.00	40.00
7. 邮费和电报费	50.00	50.00
8. 差旅费	100.00	100.00
9. 5% 的医疗护理费	200.00	275.00
10. 折旧费	60.00	60.00
11. 地区办公经费	1500.00	3000.00
12. 汽艇维护	2150.00	1400.00
13. 机动费	102.80	——
总计	8600.00	8600.00

（签字）阿穆尔水道局航路工程师　米海依罗夫

（签字）黑龙江航务专门顾问　易保罗

兹证明,报表正确无误。

易保罗　黑龙江航务专门顾问

此抄件发送至哈尔滨关税务司及巡工司。

录事：屠守鑫　四等帮办后班

26. 1928 年《稽核智利硝进口后预防危险暂行办法》

No. 407   COMMRS.   INSPECTORATE GENERAL OF CUSTOMS.

Aigun   No. 117,089   PEKING, 17th May 1928.

Sir,

1.   With reference to Circular No. 3385 :

Chile Saltpetre (sodium nitrate) to be removed from prohibited list: saltpetre (potassium nitrate) to remain on prohibited list :

and to Circular No. 3723 :

Chile Saltpetre (sodium nitrate) not a prohibited or restricted article: particulars of each importation to be supplied to the Superintendent :

I append, for your information and guidance, copy of Shui-wu Ch'u despatches Nos. 973 of 1927 and 112 and 403 (enclosure not sent) of the current year, from which you will see that, with a view to exercising stricter control over movements of Chile Saltpetre and preventing it from being used for the manufacture of munitions of war, provisional rules to govern the movement of this article have been drawn up by the Chün-shih Pu and approved by the Cabinet, and that the Shui-wu Ch'u instructs that these rules are to be put into force and in the event of difficulties or disputes arising owing to their enforcement full particulars of such difficulties or disputes are to be reported to the Ch'u for transmission to the authorities concerned for settlement.

2.

The Commissioner of Customs,
     AIGUN.

2.   An English translation of the rules is appended, for your reference, and as you will observe the rules which concern the Customs are Nos. 1, 4 and 5. Rule No. 1 calls for full details regarding importations and transhipments to be reported by the Customs to the Shui-wu Ch'u for transmission to the Chün-shih Pu; Rule No. 4 limits the transport of Chile Saltpetre by foreigners to importations into Treaty Ports, and to inter-Treaty Port movements; and Rule No. 5 lays down that at the time of importation the applicant must produce a Chün-shih Pu P'ingchao, the fee for which is $0.50 for every 10 piculs of Chile Saltpetre imported, before release can be allowed.

3.   I have to request you, therefore, to consult with the Superintendent and issue a joint notification stating that in future Chile Saltpetre (sodium nitrate) can only be imported if covered by a Chün-shih Pu P'ingchao, which can be obtained from the Superintendent of Customs, and that transit into the interior, of this article, requires the special permission of the Chün-shih Pu.

4.   In view of the fact that it will now be necessary for particulars of each consignment of Chile Saltpetre to be supplied to the Superintendent at the time when application for P'ingchao is made, it would seem that the reports hitherto made to him in accordance with the instructions of Circular No. 3723, quoted above, will be redundant; at the time when the first application for Chile Saltpetre is made after receipt of these instructions therefore you should inform the

the Superintendent that in future you are leaving it to
him to collect the necessary information for report
to the Shui-wu Ch'u.

5.   Finally, in the event of complaints being
received or disputes arising regarding the new procedure,
the nature of such complaints or disputes should be
referred to the Superintendent, and at the same time you
should submit a report to me with Chinese version in
duplicate, giving full details thereof for transmission to
the Shui-wu Ch'u.

                        I am,
                          Sir,
                  Your obedient Servant,

                  Officiating Inspector General.

                                    Appendix.

税務處令第九七三號　中華民國十六年十二月二十八日

查關於智利硝卸硝廢鈞一項准作爲非禁品一事上年十月間本處接准國務院來
函並附鈔外交等部會咨當經照錄原咨於上年第九七九號令文行知代理總稅務
司轉令各關稅務司遵照並於令文內聲明陸軍部所擬酌訂稽核辦法俟擬定行知
本處後再行分文辦理等因在案近准軍事部來咨以稽核智利硝進口後預防危險
辦法業經本部與各關係部處派員會議本部爲便利施行起見分別將條文酌量修
改並定爲暫行辦法除分行外應檢同原咨送交關監督等因並附稽核辦法各關遵照辦理主應
發存關備用之戀照由本部直接送交關監督等因並附稽核智利硝進口後預防危險
照除分行外相應檢同原送稽核辦法一分令行代理總稅務司宣照轉令各海關稅
宣前項稽核智利硝進口後預防危險暫行辦法飭經軍事部核訂定目應由關遵

務司一體遵辦可也此令附件

第一條　稽核智利硝進口後預防危險暫行辦法

智利硝進口時報運着應將總數及運硝人姓名住址並存放地點報關由
關呈報稅務處轉行軍事部查核及農工部備案並由軍事部行知存放地
長官查照如該硝運往他關轉運時亦照上項辦法辦理偷報運着違反此
種規定即將硝斤扣留須令完備報運手續方准起運

第二條　內地商店購運智利硝運數目並備具專作農田肥料不移作火
藥或他項使用之保證書呈請軍事部發給准運護照方可販運農民向地
方商店購智利硝可依照地方習慣運硝辦法辦理偷農民直接向口岸洋
商購運時應照內地商店購運辦法辦理偷運着如不照本條逕行應按第

四條處理

第三條　洋商報運智利硝進口及內地商店販運或農民購用地方官廳應切實稽
核其鈴境內之進口販運購用各數目及應用情形每半年由該管地方長

第四條

官容報軍事部查核及農工部備案

　洋商輸入智利硝只以運至通商之口岸為止內地商店或農民向口岸洋

商購運之智利硝如發覺有供給不正當用途或用途不確時一經查明卽

由軍事部會商地方官躪沒收其硝斤並分別科以貨價兩倍至五倍之罰

金如舉發人有藉端詐陷情事亦應依法反坐

第五條

　智利硝進口時應由海關塡用軍事部憑照予報運者每硝十擔由報運

省徵憑照費五角每月月初海關應將前一個月所塡用之憑照存根及憑

照費一併繳送軍事部

稅務處令第一一二號 中華民國十七年二月十四日

　案查關於稽核智利硝進口後預防危險辦法應通行各關遵照一事前據代理總稅

務司露字第一號來呈以此項預防危險暫行辦法核與外交團有關應請鈞處於政

府徵得外交團同意時遵行示知以便通令各關遵照施行等因當經本處容請軍事

部與外交部商辦去後茲准軍事部容復稱此案經部轉商外交部查核准復以此項

智利硝係由禁品改作非禁品與其他原屬非禁物品性質不同自應仍需稽核防免

危險是以弛禁之初卽經政府定有購運辦法此次所訂不過詳加規定以期稽核周

密本部意見正與貴部相同代理總稅務司以為政府對外倘應徵得使團同意不知

何所依擴旣經稅務處擴以容轉商酌自保爲期於周妥起見應如何的爲解釋俾無

誤會之處應容復查照核辦等因本部查前訂稽核智利硝進口後預防危險辦法並

無徵求外交團同意之必要應容復查照轉令總稅務司仍遵照原案辦理並希見復

等因前來本處復准軍事部容復前因所有關於稽核智利硝進口後預防

危險各手續應卽按照軍事部所訂辦法辦理相應令代理總稅務司查照迅卽轉

令各關稅務司遵辦可也此令

稅務處令第四○三號 中華民國十七年五月七日

　案查關於智利硝進口後預防危險辦法應通行各關遵照一事前擄露字第五五

來呈以智利硝一項按外交團意見並未認作禁品以為實係一種普通貨物應依照
關係各國所訂約章辦理即凡關洋貨於進口後如轉運內地不應加以何等剽征
照征子口稅壞發子口惡軍或對於未領子口惡軍者沿途征收稅靈而詳核軍事部
所訂稽核智利硝進口後預防危險暫行辦法第四條內開洋商輸入智利硝只以運
至通商之口岸為止等語核與條約之規定有所不符是以必須先行徵求外交團同
意然後海關方可施行又該辦法第五條載有智利硝用軍事部
惡照給予報運者每硝十担由報運者繳惡照費五角等語查此項惡照係為限制智
利硝進口之一種手續惟外交團既未承認智利硝進口之惡制故惡先行徵得同意
後海關始可對於中國商人及外國商人准按此辦理實非公允辦法緣
稅司施行於中國商人及中國法權所及之各國商人為不利惟之此案以代理總稅務司之
此等商人比較亨有治外法權之各國商人此辦法迪令各關
意應仍照約處容行外交團同意後行知迪署以惡迪令各關遵照等因

當經本處據以咨請軍事部與外交部妥商定奪見復去後尚未准復茲准國務院函
稱准軍事部提議擬將智利硝仍改為禁品嚴加限制否則亦應實成稅務處將本部
合訂稽核智利硝進口後預防危險暫行辦法速轉行各海關切實遵行等因現經
國務會議決行知稅務處將稽核辦法行令代理總稅務司遵照辦理除分行外應
抄錄原案暨附件函達查照提前案前來本處查此案既經國
務會議亦以為前項稽核辦法令各關遵行自應照抄錄原提案再令代
理總稅務司飭前案迅速迪令各關於應按該稽核辦法一律切實施行倘或
其為中外商人以及外商之籍隸何國者均應照該稽核辦法一律切實施行倘或
因此發生問題再報由本處轉商與有關係之各機關設法解決可也此令附件

文
建學謙
桂同校

PROVISIONAL RULES FOR CONTROL OF CHILE SALTPETRE IN
ORDER TO PREVENT IT BEING PUT TO DANGEROUS USES.

RULE I.   On the importation of Chile Saltpetre, the total
quantity imported, the name and address of the
applicant and the place of storage are to be reported
to the Customs and by the latter to the Shui-wu Ch'u
for transmission to the Chün Shih Pu and the Nung
Kung Pu.   The Chün Shih Pu will inform the
authorities at the place of storage accordingly.   The
same procedure is to be followed when such saltpetre
is transhipped to other ports.   Should any intention
of evading this rule be detected the saltpetre will
be detained and will not be released until the
provisions of the above rule have been complied with.

RULE II.   Dealers in the interior who wish to purchase and
transport Chile Saltpetre are to state the quantity
required, and give a bond guaranteeing that the Chile
Saltpetre is to be used solely for fertilising
purposes and not in the manufacture of explosives or
for other uses.   A huchao must first be obtained from
the Chün Shih Pu allowing transportation.   If farmers
wish to purchase Saltpetre from local dealers they
must comply with the local practice concerning the
transportation of Saltpetre, and if they wish to
purchase it from foreign firms at the Treaty Ports
the same procedure as that governing dealers in the
interior is to be followed.   Should the purchaser
ignore this rule he will be dealt with in accordance
with Rule 4.
                                                    RULE III.

RULE III.   The local authorities will exercise strict control of
the districts under their jurisdiction, and check the
amounts of Chile Saltpetre, either imported by foreign
merchants, transported by dealers in the interior or
bought by farmers, and verify the use to which it
is put.   They are to render half yearly reports in
this connection to the Chün Shih Pu and Nung Kung
Pu respectively.

RULE IV.   Chile Saltpetre imported by foreign merchants is not
allowed to be transported by them to places other
than Treaty Ports.   If dealers from the interior or
farmers purchase Chile Saltpetre from foreign merchants
at the Treaty Ports, and it is discovered that the
supply is meant for illegal or unknown purposes, the
Chün Shih Pu will, in consultation with the local
authorities, order the Saltpetre to be confiscated and
will in addition impose on the delinquent a fine
varying from 2 to 5 times the value of the Saltpetre
confiscated.   Should an informant produce false
evidence leading to wrong accusation he will be dealt
with in accordance with the law.

RULE V.   At the time of importation of Chile Saltpetre a Chün
Shih Pu P'ingchao is to be filled in by the Customs
(Superintendent) and issued to the applicant against
payment by the latter of $0.50 per 10 piculs of
Saltpetre applied for.   The fees collected and the
butts of the P'ingchao issued during each month are
to be forwarded by the Customs to the Chün Shih Pu
at the beginning of the following month.

致瑷珲关第 <u>407/117089</u> 号令　　　　海关总税务司署（北京）1928 年 5 月 17 日

尊敬的瑷珲关税务司：

根据第 3385 号通令：

"从禁品清单中移除智利硝石（硝酸钠）；硝酸钾仍为禁品。"

第 3723 号通令：

"智利硝石（硝酸钠）并非禁品；每次进口细节需呈报海关监督。"

为了便于贵署顺利执行，兹附税务处 1927 年第 973 号令，1928 年第 112 号及第 403 号令（未发送附件），以供参考。据该令所示，为严格管理智利硝石，防止其被用于制造军火，军事部已拟定智利硝石暂行管理条例，此条例已通过内阁审核。税务处命令实施此条例，如因实施条例而引起任何问题或争议，请将问题细节报告至税务处，转呈相关当局予以解决。

随函附上此条例英文译版，以供参考，瑷珲关须遵守条例中相关部分，包括第一条、第四条及第五条。第一条要求瑷珲关将进口及转运相关详情呈报税务处，并转呈军事部；第四条外商进口智利硝石，运输硝石需限制在通商口岸或转口通商口岸范围内；第五条规定，进口硝石时，须申请办理军事部凭照（P'ingchao），进口每十担智利硝石须缴纳 0.50 银圆，然后方可通行。

因此，请瑷珲关咨询海关监督，发布联合通知，今后仅持有军事部凭照者可进口智利硝石（硝酸钠），可向海关监督申请办理凭照，且仅在军事部特别准许时，才可运进内地。

鉴于申请办理凭照时需向海关监督提供智利硝石运输的详情，根据上述引用的第 3723 号通令，需向海关监督提交大量重复的报告；在收到第 3723 号通令，成功办理第一份智利硝石申请后，瑷珲关须告知海关监督，今后将由海关监督独自收集相关信息，向税务处报告。

最后，因办理申请引起的任何投诉或争议须提交至海关监督，同时，瑷珲关须向本署呈报详情，报告需用中文，一式两份，并抄送至税务处。

您忠诚的仆人

易纨士（A. H. F. Edwardes）

代理总税务司

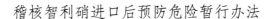

稽核智利硝进口后预防危险暂行办法

第一条　智利硝石进口时,报运者应将总数及运销人姓名、住址及存放地点呈报海关,由海关呈报税务处,税务部转呈军事部查核及农工部备案。军事部通知存放地长官查核。如该硝石向他关转运,亦照上项办法办理。倘若报运者违反此规定,应立即将该硝石扣留,直至其完全遵照上述条例规定,方准起运。

第二条　内地商店购运智利硝石须声明购运数目,并签订保证书,保证只将智利硝石用作农田肥料,不移作火药或他项使用。呈请军事部发给准运护照后,方可贩运。农民直接向地方商店购买智利硝石时,可依照地方习惯运硝办法办理。倘若农民直接向口岸洋商购运时,应照内地商店购运办法办理。购运者如不照本条遵行,应按第四条处理。

第三条　洋商报运智利硝石进口及内地商店贩运或农民购用,地方长官应切实稽核下境内的贩运购用数目及应用情形。每半年由地方长官呈报军事部查核及农工部备案。

第四条　外商只能将智利硝石运至通商口岸为止。内地商店或农民向口岸外商购运智利硝石,如发觉有供给不正当用途或用途未知时,一经查明即由军事部同地方长官协商,没收其硝石,并分别以货价两倍至五倍进行罚款。如告发人诬陷,则依法处置此人。

第五条　智利硝石进口时应由海关(监督)填报军事部,向报运者发放凭照,每十担智利硝石报运者需缴纳凭照费0.50银圆。每月月初海关应将前一个月所填用之凭照存根及凭照费用一并缴送军事部。

27. 1928 年《中俄边界河道临时航务条例》

377.

I.G.

Aigun   12th June, 1928.

Sir,

1.   I have the honour to inform you that at a meeting of the Sino-Soviet Amur Aids Commission held at the Heiho Taoyin's office the 11th January, 1928, Provisional Rules for the Joint Navigation of the Amur, Argun and Ussuri Rivers were agreed to.

2.   The reporting of the adoption of these Rules has been delayed pending their publication in permanent form. The Harbin Commissioner kindly consented to see them through the press and the bound copies have just been received.

3.   Two copies of the printed Rules are being forwarded under separate cover and an English version is enclosed. At the same time I append Chinese and Russian versions of the Protocol adopting the Rules together with translations into English. The English translation of the Rules is only roughly done. The Russian and Chinese are the authoritative (and printed) versions, the latter being translated from the Russian by Mr. Wang Te-mao, 2nd Clerk A., of the Aigun Customs. He received the special

          thanks

Enclosure No.1.
Appendix No.1.
Appendix No.2.
Appendix No.3.
Appendix No.4.

The Inspector General of Customs,
    Peking.

thanks of the Aids Commission for the work involved. It will be seen that there are many needless repetitions and useless paragraphs in the Rules themselves but it was thought best in drawing up the present Rules to follow the old Russian Regulations as literally as possible in order to make a minimum of change in the present order of things.

4.   I understand that the Taoyin has already reported the Agreement to the Wai-chiao Pu, Chiao-t'ung Pu and the Shui-wu Ch'u through the Tsitsihar Authorities but that he is only now requesting the latter to send the Rules themselves to these Boards.

5.   Copies of the Rules have been sent to the Lahasusu Customs with the request that they be distributed to all steamers touching there which ply on the Amur and Ussuri. I have explained that it is not the intention of the Aids Commission, as I understand it, to interfere in any way with the present control by the Customs over steamers plying on these rivers but as the Soviet Authorities have concurrently put the Rules in force as affecting their shipping on the Sino-Soviet frontier rivers I would be obliged if full reports would be made of any breaches of the Rules by either Chinese or Russian vessels that might come to the notice of the Lahasusu Customs. I further stated that no

          instructions

instructions had as yet been received by the
Customs from a Central Authority for the
enforcement of the Rules. The Harbin Customs
was also addressed to the same effect.

6.   No notification has been issued by the
Taoyin to Chinese shipping regarding the
introduction of these Rules. It will be noted
that they are signed by both the Chinese and
Russian members of the Aids Commission and it
is stated that all Chinese and Russian vessels
must obey them.

7.   Extracts of the Rules in abbreviated form
have been printed for free distribution to junks
and rafts. One copy each of the complete Rules
is being issued _gratis_ to all steamers plying
the Amur and Ussuri. Additional copies will be
sold at a nominal charge of $0.75.

8.   It might be well to give a brief
historical background to the adoption of the
present Rules for your information in event the
Shui-wu Ch'u refers the question of their
enforcement to you. It is probable that the
Harbin Commissioner may be able to supplement
what follows from correspondence on file in his
office before Aigun was separated from Harbin
in 1922.

9.   I. G. despatch No. 2111/74,776 to Harbin
of the 29th August, 1919, places on record the
circumstances leading up to the commencement of
                                    the

the navigating of the Amur by Chinese shipping
with the consequent need of joint Rules of
Navigation. Paragraph 2 of this despatch refers
to copies of correspondence with the Ch'u, which
are enclosed, instructing that the Harbin
Commissioner is to associate himself with the
Heiho Taoyin in the negotiations with the Russian
side for a temporary procedure for Chinese
navigation on the Amur and that he had recommended
the appointment of Mr. W. F. Tyler as an additional
delegate on the Chinese side. In the summary in
English of the Chinese correspondence enclosed the
following is of interest as bearing on the
question of provisional Rules for Chinese
navigation on the Amur:

| D.No.1058 from Ch'u of 1st July, 1919. | The Russian Minister refuses to enter into negotiations as regards China's rights to navigation on the Amur pending establishment of a formal government. In the meantime it is decided that General Howarth and Minister Liu of Vladivostock shall carry on negotiations and the Wai-chiao Pu desires that the Harbin Commissioner should assist the Heiho Taoyin in the matter of negotiating this temporary procedure. |
| D.No.1081 from Ch'u of 7th July, 1919. | The Chiao-t'ang Pu has received a report from Minister Liu stating that General Howarth proposes that until China is able to establish her own Aids to Navigation, Chinese shipping had better run under the Russian Regulations and requesting the I. G. to instruct the Harbin Commissioner and Mr. Garden to assist the Heiho Taoyin in negotiating |

negotiating such procedure.

D.No.1205 from Ch'u of 2nd August, 1919.

The Wai-chiao Pu is in receipt of a letter from the Russian Minister that General Howarth has appointed delegates to the coming conference. The Harbin Commissioner is to be informed accordingly.

D.No.191 to Ch'u of 4th August, 1919. In reply to No.1205.

As Mr. Garden is ill from typhoid it is suggested that Mr. Tyler be made a member of the Chinese side of the Commission to advise on technical questions.

10.   I. G. despatch No.2248/78,057 of the 27th April, 1920, informed the Harbin Commissioner that on account of the political changes which had taken place in Siberia the Shui-wu Ch'u in its despatch No. 523 had notified the I. G. that it had been decided that a temporary arrangement for the navigation of the Amur by Chinese vessels should be negotiated between the Heilungchiang Tuchün and the Authorities of the Amur Province, Siberia, and that the Harbin Commissioner was to render all possible assistance to the Tuchün in the matter.

11.   Nothing further is on record until Aigun S/O No. 11 of the 5th April, 1922, when it is reported that the Emissar (of Blagovestchensk) had submitted to the local Taoyin a draft of Rules of Navigation for the Amur and Sungari rivers, that the Commissioner had found much to criticise in it and that he had drafted an amended set of rules at the Taoyin's request. Copies of

neither

neither draft can be found in the archives of this port.

12.   The Inspector General in his S/O of 24th May, 1922, in reply to Aigun S/O No. 11, informs the Aigun Commissioner that "at a conference of "representatives of various Boards held in Peking, "a draft set of Rules for the navigation by "Chinese and Russian vessels of the Amur and "Sungari rivers had been drawn up to form a "basis of discussion between the Chinese Government "and the Russian Authorities concerned", and that the Taoyin should be advised not to commit himself by coming to local arrangements about anything.

13.   Political disturbances both in Russia and China now appear to have driven the negotiations into the background and no mention of them can be found until the convening of the Sino-Soviet Conference in Moukden in the Spring of 1925. The discussion of the proposed Rules was apparently on the addenda of the Conference and it is on record that the Technical Adviser, Mr. Ignatieff, who was a delegate to that Conference, left with Admiral Shen Hung Lieh (沈鸿烈) a draft of Rules he proposed should be adopted. Mr. Ignatieff is absent on a tour of inspection and, as no report of the deliberations of the Conference are on file, it is not known if the question was discussed. In as much as the Conference proved abortive, however, the negotiations with reference

to

to the Rules were not advanced any.

14.   From this point onward the history of the negotiations in question is continued in Aigun despatch No. 315, last paragraph of the thirteenth page. In your reply to this despatch, I. G. despatch No. 358/113,628, you state that "Rules of "Navigation is not a Customs question proper; also that "there is no objection, however, to yourself "and Mr. Ignatieff signing the forthcoming Agreement "as members of the Aids Commission, but the "Customs cannot enforce the Rules until they have "been approved by the Ch'u and instructions sent "by the Ch'u to me that you are to enforce "them. Until this happens you must leave the "question of enforcement in abeyance". In pursuance with these instructions I have carefully refrained from associating the Customs in any way with the question of enforcement of the Rules as such.

    I have the honour to be,
    Sir,
    Your obedient Servant,

Acting Commissioner.

Appendix

Aigun despatch No. 377 to I. G.

Appendix No.1.

聲明書

聲明書

華方委員長大中華民國黑河道尹兼瓈理交涉員張壽增

副委員長發琿關稅務司鐸博費華方委員東北航務

局長陳廣赳航務專門顧問易保羅

俄方委員長大蘇維亞社會聯邦共和國駐黑河領事然控美德

蘇俄方面代理委員長阿穆爾省國家水道局局長吉阿諾夫

俄方委員阿穆爾省國家水道局副局長且彼索夫阿穆爾省

國家水道局航路工程師米哈依羅夫於中華民國十七年（即西

歷一千九百二十八年）二月十一日在黑河中俄委員會正式會議共

同商定聲明如左

（一）雙方議決規定一中俄兩國各式船隻及木排箕航行交界

河流之章程如左

（甲）核定暫行試辦航行章程共九十六條

（乙）暫行試辦航行章程由中華民國十七年（即西曆一千九百二十八年）航行期起施行於中俄兩國各式船隻及木排等航行於交界河流者

（丙）如中俄會議國際航行訂有辦法時此項暫行試辦航行章程即行廢止

（丁）該章程如有添改之處可以脩正但須經工程委員會議商

（二）此項聲明書附帶暫行試辦航行交界河流章程計華俄文各兩份由雙方簽字蓋印彼此各執華俄文各一份以昭信守

中華民國十七年一月十日
西曆二千九百二十八年月十日訂於黑河

中國方面委員長黑河道尹兼璦琿交涉員張壽增

副委員長（印章）鐸博賚

委員東北航務局局長陳廣起

航路專門顧問易保羅

蘇俄方面委員長駐黑蘇俄領事黙拉美德

代理委員長阿穆爾省國家水道局吉阿諾夫

委員阿穆爾省國家水道局副局長且彼索夫

阿穆爾省國家水道局航路程工師末哈依羅夫

Aigun despatch No. 377 to I. G.

Appendix No.2.

Translation of the Chinese version of the Protocol concerning
Provisional Joint Rules of Navigation for Sino-Soviet Frontier Rivers.

The President of the Chinese Aids
Commission and Heiho Taoyin of the Great Republic
of China (concurrently Commissioner of Foreign
Affairs for the Aigun District) Chang Shou-tsen;
Vice-President of the Chinese Aids Commission,
R. M. Talbot; and the members of the Chinese Aids
Commission - Manager of the Tungpei Navigation
Bureau, Ch'en Kuang Ch'i, and Technical Adviser
on Amur Aids to Navigation, P. I. Ignatieff; and
the President of the Russian Aids Commission and
the Consul of the Great United Socialistic Soviet
Republic at Taheiho, Melamed; Acting President
(Sic.) of the Soviet Russian side and Director of
the Amur Navigation Bureau, Dianoff; and the
members of the Russian Aids Commission - Assistant
Director of the Amur Navigation Bureau, Chebisheff
and the Engineer of Way Department of the Amur
Navigation Bureau, Mihailoff:

hereby jointly declare on the 11th day of the 1st month of the 17th
year of the Republic of China (i.e. 1928) at a formal meeting held
by the Sino-Soviet Aids Commission at Taheiho, that

(1)   It is agreed by the two parties that Provisional Joint Rules
of Navigation governing the navigation of Chinese and Russian
vessels and rafts on Sino-Soviet frontier rivers shall be drawn
up as follows:

> (a)   The Provisional Joint Rules of
> Navigation shall consist of 96 articles.
>
> (b)   The said Provisional Joint Rules of
> Navigation shall apply to all Chinese and
> Russian

Russian vessels and rafts plying on Sino-
Soviet frontier rivers from the beginning
of the navigation season of the 17th year
of the Republic of China, i.e. 1928.

> (c)   Should an agreement be reached by the
> Sino-Soviet Conference the present
> Provisional Joint Rules of Navigation shall
> cease to be operative.
>
> (d)   Any alterations or additions to these
> Rules shall first be jointly decided on
> by the Commission.

(2)   To confirm this Agreement this Protocol together with a
copy of the Provisional Joint Rules of Navigation are made out
in the Chinese and Russian languages, in duplicate, and are
signed and sealed by both Parties, each Party keeping one copy
in Chinese and one in Russian.

Done at Taheiho on the 11th Day of the 1st month of the
17th year of the Republic of China corresponding to the 11th
day of January in the year one thousand nine hundred and twenty
eight.

Chinese side:

> (Signed) Chang Shou-tsen, President and Heiho
>   Taoyin and concurrently
>   Commissioner of Foreign Affairs
>   for Aigun District.
>
> "   R. M. Talbot, Vice-President.
>
> "   Ch'en Kuang Ch'i, Manager of Tungpei
>   Navigation Bureau.
>
> "   P. I. Ignatieff, Technical Adviser on
>   Amur Aids to Navigation.

Soviet Russian side:

> (Signed) Melamed, President and Consul of
>   U.S.S.R. at Taheiho.
>
> "   Dianoff, Acting President (Sic) and
>   Director

Director of Amur Navigation Bureau.

(Signed) Chebisheff, Assistant Director of Amur
Navigation Bureau.

" Mihailoff, Engineer of Way Department
of Amur Navigation Bureau.

Translated by:

4th Assistant B.

Aigun despatch No. 377 to I. G.

Appendix No.3.

ПРОТОКОЛ

заседания Временной Местной Советско-Китайской Технической

Комиссии Января "II" дня 1928 года, г. Сахалян.

ПРИСУТСТВОВАЛИ:

Председатель Комиссии с Китайской
стороны, Хэйхэсский Дао-Инь и Дипломатический Чиновник в Айгуне....Г. ЧЖАН-ШОУ-ДЗЕН.

Вице-Председатель Комиссии с Китайской стороны.....................Г. ТАЛБОТ.

Члены Комиссии с Китайской стороны:

Вр. Член Комиссии, директор Саха-
линского Отделения Северо-Восточ-
ного Государственного Пароходст-
ва..................................Г. ЧЕН-ГУАН-ЧИ.

Технический Советник............Г. ИГНАТЬЕВ.

Председатель Комиссии со стороны
СССР, Консул СССР в гор. Сахаляне..Г. МЕЛАМЕД.

Заместитель Председателя со стороны СССР, Начальник Управления Водных Путей Амурского бассейна.......Г. ДИАНОВ.

Члены Комиссии со стороны СССР:

Помощник Начальника Управления
Водных Путей, Инженер..........Г. ЧЕБНШОВ.

Начальник Отдела Пути АВУ,
Инженер..................Г. МИХАЙЛОВ.

СЛУШАЛИ:	ПОСТАНОВИЛИ:
I/ Вопрос о правилах плавания для советских и китайских судов и плотов по пограничным рекам.	Признавая необходимым установление однообразного порядка для Советского и Китайского флота при плавании по пограничным рекам, ПОСТАНОВИЛИ: а/ Временные правила плавания в об"еме 96 параграфов УТВЕРДИТЬ.

б/ ввести в действие временные
правила с навигации 1928 года, как
обязательные для всех Советских и
Китайских судов и плотов, плавающих
по пограничным рекам.

в/ если последует постановление
Советско-Китайской Конференции в части
касающейся совместного пользования
пограничными путями настоящее постановление теряет свою силу.

г/ всякие добавления и изменения
Правила плавания могут быть вносимы
не иначе как по постановлению Местной
Технической Комиссии.

2/ О составлении протокола.

Протокол, с приложениями к нему
временных правил плавания, должен быть
составлен на русском и китайском языках по 2 экземпляра, из которых по одному экземпляру русского и китайского
текста получает Комиссия с Китайской
стороны и по одному экземпляру Комиссия
со стороны СССР.

Председатель Временной Местной Технической Комиссии со стороны СССР, Консул СССР в Сахалине / Г.И. Меламед/	Председатель Комиссии с Китайской стороны, Хэйхэсский Дао-Инь / Чжан-Шоу-Цзен /
Заместитель Председателя, Начальник АВУ / Дианов/	Вице-Председатель / Талбот /
Члены Комиссии: / Чебышов / / Михайлов /	Члены Комиссии: / Чен-Гуан-Чи / / Игнатьев /

True Copy:

2nd Clerk, A.

Aigun despatch No. 377 to I. G.

Appendix No.4.

Translation of the Russian version of the Protocol concerning
Provisional Joint Rules of Navigation for Sino-Soviet Frontier Rivers.

P R O T O C O L.

Minutes of a meeting of the local Provisional Sino-Soviet
Technical Commission, held at Taheiho on the 11th January, 1928.

Representatives:-

The President of the Chinese Commission the Heiho Taoyin, and concurrently Commissioner of Foreign Affairs:	Chang Shou-tsen
The Vice-President of the Chinese Commission:	R. M. Talbot
Members of the Chinese Commission:	
Manager of Tungpei Navigation Bureau:	Ch'en Kuang Ch'i
Technical Adviser on Amur Aids to Navigation:	P. I. Ignatieff
The President of the Soviet Commission and Consul of U.S.S.R. at Taheiho:	Melamed
Acting President of the Soviet Commission (Sic) and Director of Amur Navigation Bureau:	Dianoff
Members of the Soviet Commission:	
Assistant Director of Amur Navigation Bureau:	Chebisheff
Engineer of Way Department of Amur Navigation Bureau:	Mihailoff

Subject Discussed:	Decision:
Rules of Navigation for vessels and rafts, both Chinese and Russian, plying on frontier rivers.	Wishing to establish Rules to be jointly observed by Chinese and Soviet shipping plying on frontier rivers the Commission decided: a) To adopt the Provisional Rules consisting of 96 articles which have

have been drawn up.

b) These Provisional Rules to be in force from the beginning of the navigation season of 1928 and to apply to all Chinese and Soviet vessels and rafts navigating the frontier rivers.

c) If a new agreement should be adopted by the Sino-Soviet Conference regarding the control of shipping on frontier rivers this present Agreement ceases to be operative.

d) Alterations or additions to these Rules can only be made with the approval of this Commission.

Records to be made.

The record of this meeting together with the Provisional Rules of Navigation, herewith attached, shall be drawn up in Russian and Chinese in duplicate and after being signed two copies, one Chinese and one Russian, shall be handed to each party.

The President of the local Provisional Technical Soviet Commission, the Consul of U.S.S.R. at Taheiho. / G. I. Melamed /	The President of the Chinese Aids Commission, the Heiho Taoyin. / Chang Shou-tsen /
Acting President (Sic), the Director of Amur Navigation Bureau. / Dianoff /	Vice-President / Talbot /
Members: / Chebisheff / / Mihailoff /	Members: / Ch'en Kuang Ch'i / / Ignatieff /
	Translated by:
	2nd Clerk A.

Enclosure to Aigun No.377 to I. G.

Translation of the Introduction to the Printed
Provisional Rules of Navigation for Sino-Soviet Frontier Rivers.

In order to introduce rules of navigation to be observed by Chinese and Russian vessels and rafts plying on frontier rivers the Provisional Local Sino-Russian Technical Commission adopted, in an Agreement signed on the 11th January, 1928, Provisional Joint Rules of Navigation, consisting of 96 paragraphs, to come into effect from the beginning of the navigation season of 1928.

Signed:

Chang Shou-tsen	Melamed
President of the Commission of the Chinese side, and Heiho Taoyin (concurrently Commissioner for Foreign Affairs).	President of the Commission of the Russian side and Consul of U.S.S.R. at Taheiho.
R. M. Talbot	Dianoff
Vice-President of the Commission of the Chinese side.	Acting President (Sic) of the Commission of the Russian side and Director of Amur Navigation Bureau.
Members of the Commission of the Chinese side:	Members of the Commission of the Russian side:
Ch'en Kuang Ch'i	Chebisheff
Manager of Tungpei Navigation Bureau.	Assistant Director of Amur Navigation Bureau.
P. I. Ignatieff	Mihailoff
Technical Adviser on Amur Aids to Navigation.	Engineer of Way Department of Amur Navigation Bureau.

Note: The original drafts of the Rules in Russian and Chinese were signed by the Commission. In the case of the printed Rules, signatures are shown affixed to both versions of the introduction (as above) but not attached to the Chinese version of the Rules themselves.

PROVISIONAL RULES OF NAVIGATION.

In order to promote the safety of navigation on the frontier rivers Amur, Ussuri and Argun all Chinese and Russian vessels and rafts plying these waters, and crews and persons thereon, are required to follow the rules herein laid down.

PART I.

ARTICLE I.

GENERAL RULES:

1.   A copy of these Rules must be kept in an available place on board all vessels and rafts navigating the above named frontier rivers.

2.   All Chinese and Russian vessels are required to fly their national flag in a manner laid down by the respective laws of the two countries, but it is permitted that vessels may fly in addition a distinctive house flag at the foremast to show the ownership of, or the company chartering, the vessel in question. Every vessel should have its name painted plainly on both sides.

ARTICLE II.

AIDS TO NAVIGATION ALONG THE CHANNEL:

3.   The channel of the river concerned shall be marked by signal beacons (showing the course to be followed), bearing-line beacons, floating beacons and way-marks. On the right bank of the river these signals shall be red, on the left, white.

4.   Dangerous rocks or shoals are indicated by either floating beacons or way-marks, red or white, depending on whether they are to be passed on the right or left side. Dangerous places which may be passed on either side are indicated during the day by beacons or way-marks with alternating horizontal red and white stripes. The above beacons are lighted during the night time by lanterns either red

red or white, or white over red (vertical), as the case may require.

5.   At shoals and narrow places dangerous to vessels and rafts depth signal and traffic stations are erected.

6.   The Foremen stationed at such points, after a careful sounding of the channel, shall hoist on masts signals indicating the depth in centimetres, as follows: a horizontal cylinder means a depth of 100 cm. while each additional large or small ball represents an additional depth of 20 cm. and 5 cm. respectively.

7.   At traffic stations, signals shall be hoisted directing the passage of vessels or rafts as follows:

    (a) a ball by day or a red light by night shows that passage is forbidden to vessels proceeding up river.

    (b) a cone by day, and by night vertical lights, red over white, indicates that passage is closed to vessels or rafts proceeding down river.

    (c) a ball and cone by day or two vertical red lights by night show that passage is forbidden to vessels and rafts either proceeding up or down river.

    (d) no signals on the mast indicates that traffic may proceed in either direction and that no vessels or rafts are visible.

PART

PART II.
Equipment of Vessels and Rafts.
ARTICLE I.

FOR SIGNALLING PURPOSES:

8. For purposes of signalling, every vessel or raft must be equipped with the following: (a) signalling lanterns, (b) a bell weighing not less than 4 kilogrammes, or a metallic gong or horn (trumpet) (to be known hereafter as sound signals) (c) a white flag 70 cm. square, (d) a lantern with one glass only showing a white light, (e) on steam vessels two steam whistles (in good order), and on motor boats a siren.

> N. B. In the wheel house lanterns, lamps, candles and matches should be kept for the purpose of at once lighting signal lamps, should the electric light fail.

9. All steam vessels (or motor boats) of more than 60 horsepower, as well as barges and junks capable of carrying more than 50 tons of cargo, must be equipped with a suitable number of small boats.

10. All anchors and sounding leads must be marked with their weight and with the names of the vessels or rafts to which they belong as well as with the names of the owner of the vessels or rafts of which they form part of the equipment.

11. Every anchor must have a buoy attached to it, painted with alternating white and red stripes and of such a size as to be visible when floating. If the anchor is cast in a navigable part of the river a small boat must be moored over it, with a lantern as a warning signal by night. The length of cable paid out in casting anchor must correspond to the depth

depth where the anchor is cast.

12. Rafts must have a board erected on a pole at their centers and on this board there shall be painted the name of the owner, the place of origin of the raft, as well as the number of the raft.

PART III.
Lighting of Vessels.
ARTICLE I.

GENERAL RULES:

13. In the lighting of vessels or rafts it is permissible to use electric light, vegetable oils, pyronaphta, stearin candles and , in extraordinary cases only, petroleum - the latter to be used with great care.

14. Every vessel illuminated by electric light must have the necessary number of lamps and lanterns to carry on with in case the electricity fails (Vide also §8)

ARTICLE II.

USE OF THE SEARCH LIGHT:

15. The use of the search light is permissible on vessels and dredges in the following cases:

> (a) When under weigh only; to pick up the channel, shore or aids to navigation.
> (b) When wishing to tie up to shore and hindered from doing so by vessels already anchored.

> N.B. The search light must be extinguished when meeting other vessels.

PART IV.
Navigation of Vessels, Rafts and Dredges.
ARTICLE I.

GENERAL

GENERAL RULES:

16.   Masters of vessels and raftsmen must take every
precaution for the safety of their craft, passengers and cargo;
and, also, not to impede navigation or cause damage to other
vessels or rafts, landing places, tow paths or aids to
navigation afloat and ashore.

17.   Vessels and rafts are not allowed to ply when they are
not equipped with (a) sufficient anchors and tackle used in
connection therewith (b) means of signalling by night or day
(c) sufficient crew (d) a sufficient number of small boats in
good order (§9).

18.   When under weigh or anchored vessels and rafts are
forbidden to scratch the foreshore or slant.

19.   The Master is solely responsible for the management of
his vessel or raft, for its navigation and for the discipline
of the crew. He may delegate his authority to his assistants
when off watch but he is to be held responsible for all
accidents or infringements of these Rules. The crews of rafts
or barges in tow must also obey all his orders.

20.   A number of steamers plying in the same direction and
keeping the same line must maintain distances from each other
sufficient to ensure safe navigation.

21.   Masters of steamers are forbidden to make any evolutions
when under weigh, or at a landing place, which may stop or
retard the speed of other vessels or tend to cause an accident
(vide §29).

22.   Steamers without tow, on passing close to landing
places, dredges, several steamers close together, or a steamer
loading, must slow down in order that the waves produced shall
not

not endanger such craft or landing places.

ARTICLE II.

NAVIGATION IN FOG, SNOW AND RAIN:

23.   When fog, rain or snow is very dense and screens even
the nearest objects only steamers plying up-stream without
tow are allowed to proceed. All other vessels and rafts
must cast anchor out of the channel or tie up alongside the
shore. Those so tied up must ring a bell, strike a gong or
blow a trumpet at frequent intervals. Those under weigh
must give prolonged whistles every minute.

24.   When fog, rain or falling snow is less dense but
visibility is poor vessels and rafts, when under weigh, must
proceed slowly and with caution and give the necessary sound
signal at intervals of a minute.

25.   Floating vessels and rafts other than passenger
steamers are forbidden to ply in dense fog, rain or snow.
They must tie up to shore and give warning sound signals
every minute.

ARTICLE III.

RULES CONCERNING THE MEETING OR OVERTAKING OF VESSELS,
RAFTS OR DREDGES:

26.   When vessels are approaching each other the right of
choosing the course belongs to the vessel proceeding down
stream.

27.   Steamers either proceeding up or down stream, on
meeting junks or rafts, have the right to choose their
course (Vide §69). Junks, rafts and small craft must assume
the course indicated by the steamer (Vide Part VII, Article I).

28.   If several vessels are plying in the same direction one
after

after the other and meet other vessels in line they must all
exchange signals, the foremost vessel setting the course.
If it becomes necessary for the down coming line to cross the
course of the up coming steamers, in following the bearing
lines, the latter must slow down and give them the right of
way.

29.   To avoid collisions a steamer can only turn behind
other steamers, and not in front of them (Vide §21).

30.   If a steamer is overtaken by another steamer she must
not prevent the latter passing but must slow down and give the
passing steamer the right of way.

    Places where, in the opinion of the River Authorities,
it is dangerous for one vessel to overtake another may be
notified to the shipping and overtaking at such places may be
forbidden.

31.   Small craft must not impede the movements of steam
vessels by crossing their course, plying near their course
in the same direction or towards them.

ARTICLE IV.

NAVIGATION OF VESSELS AND RAFTS THROUGH SHALLOWS:

32.   All vessels and rafts when crossing shallows must have
a draft less than the depth of the channel as follows:

        (a) On the Upper Amur 6" (15 cm.)

        (b) On the Middle Amur 8" (20 cm.)

If vessels are loaded with explosives they must have a
draft less than the depth of the channel, as follows:

        (a) On the Upper Amur 10" (25 cm.)

        (b) On the Middle Amur 12" (30 cm.)

33.   All vessels must have distinctly visible depth-line
marks

marks on both sides of their bow, middle and stern, in order
that the officials of the River Inspector Staff may have no
difficulty in supervising the vessels. These marks must show
the draft of the vessel in either English feet or centimetres.

34.   All vessels and rafts approaching shallows must note
the depth of the channel on the signal mast. If it is not
sufficient they must stop and be lightered, if they wish to
proceed.

PART V.

Anchorage of Vessels and Rafts.

ARTICLE I.

GENERAL RULES:

35.   All vessels and rafts of any type must anchor out of
the channel.

36.   Vessels and rafts are forbidden to cast anchor where
marks on shore indicate cable crossings, or to moor to
telegraph posts, signal masts or signal beacons, unless intended
for that purpose.

37.   On shallows, in gorges and at points where the current
sets in close to the shore the anchoring of vessels and rafts
is absolutely forbidden.

38.   The moorings of vessels to the shore or other places of
landing must be strong and secure.

PART VI.

Concerning the Use of Lights.

ARTICLE I.

GENERAL RULES:

39.   The Rules concerning lights shall be complied with in
all weathers from sunset to sunrise, and during such time no
other lights which may be mistaken for the prescribed lights
shall

shall be exhibited.

        N.B. Ordinary lanterns used for soundings must
not be mistaken for signal lights.

40.   In carrying cargo which is easily ignited, vessels must
exhibit in the daytime special flag signals and at night
additional lights (Vide §53, 54).

ARTICLE II.

LIGHTS ON ANCHORED VESSELS AND RAFTS:

41.   All vessels and rafts, when anchored, shall exhibit in
a conspicuous position metallic lanterns capable of throwing
a bright and steady white light visible all around the horizon
for a distance of not less than 1½ kilo. (1½ versts).

42.   When a vessel or raft has gone aground and is not
refloated before night, besides showing the usual anchor
lights, it must show an additional light on the outboard
side where the channel is free.

ARTICLE III.

LIGHTS OF VESSELS AND RAFTS UNDER WEIGH:

43.   When under weigh:

    (a) every steamer must exhibit one bright white
light at the top of the foremast, or at the
bow capable of throwing an even steady light
in a semicircle of 220°. This light must be
visible on dark nights with clear atmosphere
for a distance of not less than 8 kilo(about
8 versts or 4½ nautical miles).

    (b) every junk or raft must exhibit one white
light at the top of the mast, throwing a
steady light in a circle of 360°, visible
at a distance of not less than 1½ kilos.

    (c) sidelights for steamers - green on the right
and red on the left side, each of which must
throw a steady bright light in a semicircle
with a range from the bow of 20° behind the
traverse and in a semicircle of 110° from
each side. These lights must be visible on
dark

dark nights with clear atmosphere at a
distance of not less than 4 kilos (about
4 versts). The said green and red side
lights shall be fitted with inboard screens
projecting at least 3 feet forward from the
light, so as to prevent these lights being
seen across the bow.

    (d) one white light on the stern not visible
forward of the beam.

44.   In order to indicate the course to an approaching vessel
or raft a waving signal shall be used. The lantern employed to
give such signals must have the glass on one side only. The
other three sides must be blind in order that during the reverse
movement of the lantern from outboard to middle the light shall
not be visible. The light of this lantern must be visible on
steam vessels the same distance as the mast lights, i.e. 4 km.
(about 4 versts); on junks and rafts the same distance as bow
lights, i.e. 1½ km.

ARTICLE IV.

**Installation and Use of Lights on Different
Types of Vessels, and on Rafts.**

A: LIGHTS ON STEAMERS:

45.   Steamers must show lights as follows:

    (a) when anchored, one white light (§41) showing
at the mast or bow, not less than 6 metres
(about 20 ft.) above the deck.

    (b) when under weigh and without a tow, one white
light at the foremast not less than 6 metres
(about 20 ft.) above the deck, and the two
side lights, green and red (§43).

    (c) when under weigh with a tow, besides the red
and green side lights, two white lights at
the foremast in a vertical position not less
than 6 metres (about 20ft.) above the deck,
and separated by not less than 1 metre (about
3 ft.). The vessels in tow must each have
one white light (§43b) not less than 6 metres
(about 20 ft.) above the deck.

46.   In the case of two steamers both towing the same barges,

both

both steamers must carry the prescribed lights (§45) and must both give the same waving and/or sound signals in passing other craft.

47. **B. LIGHTS ON BARGES:**

Barges must show lights as follows:

    (a) when anchored, one white light (§41) exhibited not less than 6 metres (about 20 ft.) above the deck.

        N.B. Barges less than 30 metres (15 sajens) long shall exhibit this light not lower than 2 metres (about 7 ft.) above the deck.

    (b) when under weigh:

        (1) if towed the light exhibited shall be as in (a) of the present paragraph.

        (2) when proceeding down stream and not under tow, two white lights must be exhibited one at the bow and one at the stern at heights specified under (a) of the present paragraph.

48. **C. LIGHTS ON SAILING VESSELS:**

Sailing vessels must exhibit the following lights:

    (a) when anchored, one white light (§41) as follows:

        (1) on vessels 30 metres (15 sajens) or more in length, not less than 6 metres (about 20 ft.) above the deck.

        (2) on vessels less than the above mentioned length, 2 metres (about 7 ft.) above the deck.

    (b) when sailing, two white lights (§43-b) at the top of the mast in a vertical position not less than 6 metres (about 20 ft.) above the deck and separated by not less than one metre.

49. **D. LIGHTS ON FISHING VESSELS AND SMALL BOATS:**

All fishing vessels or small boats, whether anchored or under weigh, must exhibit one white light at the top of the mast (§ 41)

(§41 and 43b) not less than 2 metres (about 7 ft.) above the deck.

50. **E. LIGHTS ON RAFTS ANCHORED OR UNDER WEIGH:**

    (a) All rafts of 50 metres (25 sajens) or less in length must exhibit one white light in the middle; (b) rafts more than 50 metres and less than 100 metres (50 sajens) shall show two white lights, one at the bow and one at the stern; (c) rafts more than 100 metres must have an additional white light in the middle of the raft (§41 and 43b).

51. **F. LIGHTS ON SMALL CRAFT:**

Small craft when plying in the channel or crossing the river must carry one visible white light in the bow.

52. **G. LIGHTS ON DREDGES:**

    (a) Anchored and under weigh: dredges of all kinds, barges and guardships, whether close together and anchored at a landing place, as well as those in tow, must exhibit one white light on the mast of each not less than 6 metres (about 20 ft.) above the deck.

    (b) When working: must exhibit one green light on the mast not less than 6 metres above the deck.

        N. B. When dredges are anchored in or near the channel, whether working or not, vessels in passing them must use caution and moderate their speed when necessary (§22).

53. **H. LIGHTS ON VESSELS CARRYING EXPLOSIVES, PETROLEUM OR OTHER DANGEROUS CARGO:**

    (a) All vessels loaded with kerosene or petrol or their products, which may explode when their temperature is above 28°C., are required to exhibit, besides the usual lights, one red light at night and one red flag by day at the foremast not less than 6 metres (about 20 ft.) above the deck.

    (b) All vessels loaded with explosives or other dangerous cargo

cargo must exhibit at the foremast two red lights
at night and two red flags by day in a vertical
position separated by not less than 1 metre and at
the same height above deck as laid down under (a)
of this paragraph.

54.   Steamers carrying such explosive cargo and having in tow
barges with similar cargo must carry three mast lights - two
white and one red.

ARTICLE V.

SPECIAL LIGHTS ON VESSELS:

55   Vessels in tow alongside a steamer, besides the lights
specified above (§47 (b) (1)) must exhibit one bright white
light on its outboard side.

56.   Vessels with cases of dangerous communicable disease on
board must display by day a square yellow flag at the foremast
and by night one green and one red light at the foremast at
least 75 cm. above the usual white light.

PART VII.

Signals between Vessels before Passing.

ARTICLE I.

GENERAL RULES:

57.   All vessels or rafts when meeting, overtaking or being
overtaken, whether in the day time or at night, must exchange
signals in good time; these signals are to be given on all
occasions even when it is to be seen by the course of a vessel
or a raft that a collision is unlikely.

        N. B. (1) Signals to be used on meeting and
              overtaking are to be as follows:

              (a) All kinds of vessels and rafts
                  must make waving signals by flag
                  in day time and by lantern at night.

              (b) Steamers must also blow the whistle,
                  all

                  all other vessels and rafts must
                  give a sound signal.

        (2) A signal by whistle shall be defined
            according to its duration, namely:
            a "prolonged whistle" means an
            uninterrupted blast of 6 or 8 seconds
            in length. A "short whistle" is one
            lasting ½ second and repeated, if
            necessary, at intervals.

58.   Means of signalling must be always ready.

59.   Waving signals are to be given from that side of a vessel
or raft which the vessel being met or overhauled will pass.

        N.B. On steam vessels the waving signals
             must be given above the side lights.

60.   Steamers before making signals must give one prolonged
blast. Other vessels or rafts may give the usual sound signal.
The waving signal will then be given immediately, from the side
of the vessel or from the edge of the raft but never from the
wheelhouse or from any other place in the middle of the vessel
or raft.

61.   In the day time signals for passing shall be given by a
white flag and by a lantern at night (§44); the flag or lantern
is to be left at the place where the signals are made until the
signals from the other vessel are given in exchange.

62.   Acknowledgement of any given signal is announced by a
prolonged blast or other sound signal and by the waving of a
flag or lantern from the side indicated by the approaching
vessel or raft.

        N. B. Signals to be given when a steamer is
              not able to assume the course indicated
              are laid down in §66 and §67.

63.   The whistle of a steamer is only to be used for the purpose
of making navigation signals; the using of such for salutation
when two steamers meet or for giving orders to the vessel's staff

                                                    or

or crew is forbidden.

ARTICLE II.

SIGNALS BY VESSELS AND RAFTS APPROACHING FROM OPPOSITE DIRECTIONS:

64.   A vessel or raft plying down stream, on meeting another, must give a blast or other sound signal at a distance of not less than 1 kilo followed by waving signals to indicate the side on which the vessel or raft proceeding up stream shall pass. The latter must return these signals. Steamers proceeding stern ahead must give two prolonged whistles instead of one, before making waving signals.

65.   If the vessel or raft plying up stream notices any danger menacing the vessel or raft plying down stream which the latter may not see, the vessel or raft proceeding up stream must give several (more than three) short blasts or other sound signals as warning of danger.

66.   In case the vessel or raft plying up stream cannot obey the waving signal given by the downward bound vessel or raft without danger to herself or the approaching raft or vessel she must immediately give two short blasts and indicate the desirable side to pass by waving signals.
If the upward bound vessel has a tow she must then slow down. If she has no tow she must slow down or go astern as is required.

67.   The vessel or raft plying down stream, after having received such a signal (of inability to obey a signal) is obliged:

> (a) to give a prolonged blast, or other sound signal, indicating that she is able to assume

assume a different course.

> (b) in case she is not able to assume a different course as indicated and has no tow she must give a short blast or other sound signal and go astern. In case a steamer has a tow, or in the case of rafts or other vessels, they must be anchored, from the stern if possible.

68.   If signals have not been given by either one or both of the approaching vessels or rafts, or have not been answered, or have not been well understood, the vessel or raft plying up stream must stop and wait until she receives satisfactory signals from the one proceeding down stream. Only after all signals are satisfactorily exchanged may vessels or rafts proceed on their way.

69.   A steamer meeting other vessels or rafts has the right to choose the course, and such vessels or rafts must assume the course indicated by the steamer (vide §27).

ARTICLE III.

SIGNALS BY OVERTAKING VESSELS OR RAFTS:

70.   If a vessel, whether with tow or not, is overtaking another vessel or raft she must give 3 short blasts or other sound signals at a distance of not less than 400 metres, followed by the waving signal indicating which side the vessel or raft being overtaken must assume its course.

The vessel or raft being overtaken, on receiving such a signal, is obliged:

> (a) if able to assume the indicated course, to give one long whistle or other sound signal and make a waving signal from the side to be passed.
> (b) if unable to assume the course indicated by the overtaking

overtaking vessel she must give two short blasts
or other sound signals and make a waving signal
indicating the side on which passing is possible.

71.   If the vessel or raft being overtaken is prevented by
some circumstance from assuming the indicated course, it is
obliged to give immediately several warning whistles or other
sound signals; in such cases the overtaking vessel must wait
for a more convenient place and moment to pass.

ARTICLE IV.

SIGNALS ON PASSING NARROW GORGES:

72.   Steamers approaching a bend in the river, a narrow place,
or a place where an approaching vessel cannot be seen in good
time, must give a prolonged blast; in case an acknowledgement
is not received she must again give two long blasts before
entering the place in question. Junks and rafts must signal
their approach to, and entrance of, such places by sound signals
in the same manner.

73.   In case a steamer plying up stream receives the same
response to her signals as those given, she must:

(a) if not having rounded the bend or entered
the gorge, stop and let the down coming
steamer pass, or

(b) if she has already rounded the bend or
entered the gorge she must slow down and
wait for a further signal from the steamer
coming down stream; the latter must also
slow down sufficiently to make it possible
for her to be steered in any direction and
must proceed as slowly as possible.

ARTICLE V.

SIGNALS ON PASSING DREDGES IN OPERATION (§15):

74.   All vessels and rafts on approaching a dredge operating
in the channel shall give a blast or sound signal at a distance
of not less than 400 metres.

75.   If the channel is clear, the dredge, after receiving a
warning

warning signal from an approaching vessel or raft must give a
prolonged blast in reply. In case the whistle is out of order
she may use another suitable sound signal. The dredge must
also give waving signals by day, and at night by lantern, to
indicate on which side the approaching vessel or raft must pass.

76.   If the passage is blocked by a dredge operating in the
channel, the latter must give several brief alarm signals by
whistles or other instruments after which the raft or vessel
must stop. They may proceed again only after the dredge gives
a prolonged whistle or other sound signal accompanied by waving
signals.

ARTICLE VI.

SIGNALS FOR ASSISTANCE:

77.   In case of fire, wreck or other accidents the following
signals must be given:

(a) Steamers: long continuous blasts and the
flag lowered to the middle of the mast in
the day time; long continuous blasts at
night and the mast light alternately raised
and lowered.

(b) Junks and rafts must frequently give a sound
signal as an alarm.

(c) All vessels which are near the one in distress
must also give signals of alarm.

ARTICLE VII.

SIGNALS FOR CALLING OUT A BOAT:

78.   In order to call out a boat from the shore two long and
one short blast shall be given.

79.   If a boat is to be called out from the depth-signal
station, one long and one short blast is to be given.

ARTICLE VIII.

SIGNALS AT A LANDING PLACE:

80.   On approaching a landing place steamers must give a
prolonged

prolonged whistle.

81. Before leaving a landing place steamers must give at intervals, as a warning, one long and one short, one long and two short, one long and three short blasts, after which she may leave.

PART VIII.

Obstructions to Navigation.

ARTICLE I.

OBSTACLES IN CHANNEL OR LACK OF DEPTH:

82. It is forbidden to throw from vessels into the water or, in the winter, on to the ice, stones, ashes, sand, coal, or any kind of rubbish that might obstruct the waterway.

83. If a vessel or raft accidently loses in the water an anchor or some other object which can endanger navigation the master, bargeman or raftsman concerned must take all possible measures to find and remove it at once. If they are unable to do this, they must mark the place with a buoy or some other signal afloat or ashore - if ashore, then opposite the place where the object was dropped. The nearest Shallows Watcher must then be informed and afterwards the first River Authority concerned.

84. The place where a vessel has been sunk or where cargo has been lost must be marked by waving signals (Vide §4), and the master, bargeman or raftsman concerned must immediately inform the nearest Shallow Watcher, and the River Authority of the country under whose flag the vessel is plying.

85. Vessels, rafts, cargo or such objects as referred to in §83, which have been sunk must be raised by their owners. If they fail to do this within the time fixed by the River Authority of the country of the flag concerned, the latter will undertake the

the work at the expense of the owner.

86. When a Captain or bargeman or raftsman finds it necessary to stop and go alongside the bank, because of an accident to his craft, or for lightering because of shallow water, he shall be allowed to unload the cargo on shore as required. In case he is compelled to unload cargo by force majeur, the master, bargeman or raftsman concerned shall inform at once the nearest local and River Authority in order that measures may be taken to meet the situation. During the time which the cargo remains on shore those responsible must conform to all legal regulations in accordance with the orders of the local officials.

87. If a master, bargeman or raftsman finds an obstruction in the channel or an error in, or absence of, marks or beacons, he must inform the nearest Shallows Watcher and River Authority.

PART IX.

Regulations in Connection with Accidents.

ARTICLE I.

GENERAL RULES:

88. Those in charge of vessels or rafts must inform the nearest authority concerned of any accidents to his vessel, raft, cargo or passengers, without exception.

89. In every case where a vessel, raft, cargo or passengers are menaced by danger, or the free passage of the channel is in danger of being interrupted, all vessels passing or in the vicinity, regardless of nationality, are required to give immediate help.

90. The master of a steamer, barge or raft to which some accident has happened must first take all possible measures to save

save life, the saving of cargo coming afterwards.

91.　　After an accident has happened to a vessel and after having taken all necessary steps called for in the emergency, the man in charge of the cargo, shall make out a detailed report giving the actual causes and consequences of the accident regardless of its importance. This report is to be signed by himself and other responsible witnesses. Should the accident be to the vessel itself, the master shall make out a similar report, to be signed by himself and two responsible boatmen as well as other witnesses. If the report is not made out in sufficient detail or what is related therein is not in agreement with the actual facts, the witnesses can express their own opinion for reference. A report should be at once submitted to the staff of the nearest River Authority of the country concerned.

92.　　All witnesses signing the statement must add their professions and full names and addresses.

> N. B. If it is impossible for the principals and/or witnesses concerned to make out a statement owing to the difference in languages spoken on the two vessels, the masters, bargemen or raftsmen concerned shall be obliged to inform the nearest River Authority of the nationality of the vessel concerned who, after due investigation, will make out the required statement.

93.　　The statement must contain:

(a) the time of the accident.

(b) detailed description of where and how it took place.

(c) all relevant orders given by the master (or officer in charge) before, at the time of, and subsequent to the accident.

(d) detailed description of damaged and/or lost cargo, also apparent and/or supposed damage done the vessel or raft concerned.

(e) What measures were taken to avoid the accident and whether the Rules of Navigation were followed.

(f)

(f) what fatalities and injuries occurred amongst passengers.

(g) sketch map showing how and where the accident took place and the subsequent movements of the vessel or raft.

(h) full name and address of the person who made the statement.

94.　　In the case of a criminal act on board the master of the vessel or raft concerned must immediately inform the nearest Police official as well as River Authority of the nationality of the vessel or raft concerned.

95.　　In event of a collision the master, bargemen or raftsmen of the vessels involved in the collision must immediately stop their vessels or rafts and lend assistance as required, and make out a mutual statement (Vide §93) which each must sign with witnesses. In case of a disagreement as to the causes of the accident, each must make out a separate statement and after having signed it with witnesses, exchange copies in return for receipts.

96.　　Nothing in these rules shall exonerate any vessel or the owner or master or crew thereof from the consequence of any neglect to keep a proper lookout, or of the neglect of any precaution which may be required by the ordinary practices of navigation.

Acting Commissioner.

CUSTOM HOUSE,
Aigun. 9th June. 1928.

呈海关总税务司署 <u>377</u> 号文　　　　　　　　瑷珲关 1928 年 6 月 12 日

尊敬的海关总税务司（北京）：

1. 兹汇报，中俄黑龙江水道委员会于 1928 年 1 月 11 日在黑河道尹公署召开会议，就联合维护边界河道黑龙江、乌苏里江及额尔古纳河航路标志一事通过了《中俄边界河道临时航务条例》。

2. 但鉴于该《中俄边界河道临时航务条例》之最终版本至今日方得以敲定，并在哈尔滨关税务司的支持下由出版社刊行，本署亦是刚刚收到装订成册的《航务条例》抄件，故该临时《航务条例》之相关汇报延误至今，望贵署谅解。

3. 另函附寄该《航务条例》中文及俄文两版之印刷本及其英文译本（附件 1）。兹附决定通过该《航务条例》的协议书之华方及俄方各一份，以及英文译本。《航务条例》的英文译本仍为初稿，但《航务条例》之中文版与俄文版均为官方权威（印刷）版本，中文版《航务条例》译自俄文版，乃由瑷珲关二等一级税务员王德懋先生所翻译，对此，中俄黑龙江水道委员会特向王德懋先生致以衷心的感谢。尽管旧版俄国航务条例中有很多重复甚至无用之段落，但在草拟新条例之时，双方均一致主张尽可能按照旧版俄国航务条例逐字逐句地翻译，以减少对现行规定之改动。

4. 道尹日前已通过齐齐哈尔当局向外交部、交通部及税务处汇报中俄双方就新《航务条例》的实施签署协议书一事，并于近日向齐齐哈尔当局提出将《航务条例》呈送至外交部和交通部之要求。

5. 拉哈苏苏海关已收到该临时《航务条例》的抄件，并按要求分发给了所有往来于黑龙江及乌苏里江上的轮船。需要说明的是，中俄黑龙江水道委员会并未打算以任何方式介入海关对边界河道上往来轮船的管理，但鉴于苏维埃当局为管理其航运事宜已开始于中俄边界河道施行《航务条例》，因此若拉哈苏苏分关可以对其辖区以内中俄轮船违反《航务条例》之行为做出全面的汇报，本署将不胜感激。此外，瑷珲关并未收到中央政府任何关于执行该临时《航务条例》的指示，哈尔滨关也是如此。

6. 关于该临时《航务条例》的施行，道尹尚未向中国轮船下达任何通知。不过，中俄黑龙江水道委员会的双方委员都已签署了同意实施该临时《航务条例》的协议，并声明中俄双方的所有轮船都必须遵守该临时《航务条例》。

7. 该临时《航务条例》之简略版本已印制完成并免费发放给民船和木筏，完整版《航务条例》之印刷本业已免费分发至所有往来于黑龙江及乌苏里江上的轮船。剩下的印刷本将以每份 0.75 银圆的价格进行售卖。

8. 鉴于税务处或许会就该临时《航务条例》的施行问题向海关总税务司署征询意见，兹简要汇报该临时《航务条例》之历史背景资料，以供贵署参考。此外，鉴于在瑷珲关于1922 年从哈尔滨关独立出来以前，哈尔滨关之档案中或存有与该条例相关之信函，因此哈尔滨关税务司对下文所述之情况或有补充之处。

9. 1919 年 8 月 29 日海关总税务司署致哈尔滨关第 2111/74778 号令记载了中国轮船开始在黑龙江上航行的契机以及随后对《中俄边界河道联合航务条例》之需要，该令文第二段提及与税务处往来之信件（兹附信件抄件），指示哈尔滨关税务司应与道尹一同就中国轮船在黑龙江上的航运问题与俄方商定临时协议，并推荐戴理尔（W. F. Tyler）先生加入华方代表之列。根据所附中文信件之英译摘要，兹列举其中与中国轮船于黑龙江上航行时所遵循之临时航务条例的相关内容。

1. 1919 年 7 月 1 日税务处第 1058 号文。	1. 因俄国政府尚未正式成立，故俄国公使拒绝就中国轮船在黑龙江上的航运权问题进行协商。不过郝沃斯（Howarth）将军将继续与驻符拉迪沃斯托克（Vladivostok，即海参崴）公使刘先生进行协商，外交部希望哈尔滨关税务司继续协助黑河道尹协商临时航务条例事宜。
2. 1919 年 7 月 7 日税务处第 1081 号文。	2. 公使刘先生已向交通部汇报称郝沃斯将军提议，在中国有能力建立自己的航路标志以前，中国航运还是遵循俄国有关条例的规定为好，并要求海关总税务司署下令，指示哈尔滨关税务司及贾登（H. G. Garden）先生一同协助黑河道尹协商临时航务条例事宜。
3. 1919 年 8 月 2 日税务处第 1205 号文。	3. 外交部已收到俄国公使来信，称郝沃斯将军已派道代表参加即将召开的会议。哈尔滨关税务司也已收到了通知。
4. 1919 年 8 月 4 日海关总税务司署第 191 号文对税务处第 1205 号文的回复。	4. 由于贾登先生身患伤寒，将由戴理尔先生代表华方委员会来解答技术问题。

10. 根据 1920 年 4 月 27 日海关总税务司署致哈尔滨关第 2248/78057 号令，由于西伯利亚发生政变，税务处已在致总税务司署第 523 号文中指示，有关中国轮船在黑龙江上的航行事宜应由黑龙江督军与阿穆尔省西伯利亚当局共同协商决定，哈尔滨关税务司应倾力协助。

11.1922 年 4 月 5 日瑷珲关第 11 号机要文件汇报，布拉戈维申斯克（Blagovestchensk，即海兰泡）密使向大黑河道尹呈送了一份适用于黑龙江及松花江的《航务条例》草案，当时的税务司发现其中存在许多问题，并按照道尹之要求做出了相应地修改。但瑷珲关档案处并无该两份《航务条例》草案之抄件。

12.1922 年 5 月 24 日，海关总税务司署在回复瑷珲关第 11 号机要文件时告知瑷珲关税务司，"黑龙江与松花江上的航务问题已交由北京相关委员会处理，已经起草的条例将作为中俄有关当局谈判的基础"，并建议道尹不要对地方工作做出任何安排。

13. 而后中俄两国内部均发生政治动乱，以致与条例相关的协商之事被暂时搁置，直到 1925 年春于奉天召开中俄会议，条例之事才再次被提及。会议的补充材料中明确记载会议已就拟议的《航务条例》进行了讨论，且与会代表航务专门顾问易保罗（P. I. Ignatieff）先生将其拟议的《航务条例》草案留给了海军上将沈鸿烈先生。不过，因易保罗先生并未参与巡查活动，且档案中亦无会议审议结果之报告，故易保罗先生所拟之《航务条例》草案有否讨论并不明确。但因本次会议以失败告终，故关于临时《航务条例》的协商事实上并未取得任何进展。

14. 瑷珲关第 315 号呈第 13 页的最后一段，进一步汇报了与条例协商事宜相关的历史背景资料。海关总税务司致瑷珲关第 358/113628 号令回复道："《航务条例》非海关需要处理之问题，但鉴于瑷珲关税务司和易保罗先生均为黑龙江航政委员会之委员，遂本署并不反对二人参与协议之签署。然临时《航务条例》只有得到税务处之批准，并由税务处向海关总税务司署下达实施指令后，瑷珲关方可施行该临时《航务条例》。"因此，本署已尽可能地避免海关牵涉到《航务条例》的实施事宜之中。

您忠诚的仆人

铎博赉（R. M. Talbot）

瑷珲关署理税务司

瑷珲关致海关总税务司署第 377 号呈附件 2

《中俄边界河道临时航务条例》相关协议（华方）之译本

　　中俄临时地方工程委员会华方委员长兼黑河道尹兼瑷珲交涉员张寿增，副委员长铎博赉，以及华方委员东北航务局局长陈广起、黑龙江航务专门顾问易保罗；俄方委员长兼驻大黑河苏俄领事默拉美德，代理委员长兼俄阿穆尔水道局局长托阿诺夫，以及俄方委员俄阿穆尔水道局副局长且比索夫、俄阿穆尔水道局航路工程师米海依罗夫，共同于中华民国十七年元月十一日（1928 年 1 月 11 日），在中俄临时地方工程委员会召开于大黑河的正式会议上发表联合声明，内容如下。

　　（一）双方议决，规定中俄两国轮船及木筏等航行边界河道之《中俄边界河道临时航务条例》如下：

　　（甲）核定《中俄边界河道临时航务条例》共计九十六条；

　　（乙）《中俄边界河道临时航务条例》由中华民国十七年（1928）之航运季开始施行，适用于所有航行于中俄边界河道上的中俄轮船及木筏；

　　（丙）如果中俄会议就边界河道上的航运问题达成新协议，则《中俄边界河道临时航务条例》即行废止；

　　（丁）对于《中俄边界河道临时航务条例》的任何修改或补充，都应提交中俄黑龙江水道委员会裁定。

　　（二）此项声明书及《中俄边界河道临时航务条例》，计中、俄文本各两份，由双方签字盖印，彼此各执中、俄文本各一份，以昭信守。

　　中华民国十七年一月十一日（1928 年 1 月 11 日）订于大黑河。

华方：

华方委员长兼黑河道尹兼瑷珲交涉员　　　张寿增

副委员长　　　　　　　　　　　　　　　铎博赉

东北航务局局长　　　　　　　　　　　　陈广起

黑龙江航务专门顾问　　　　　　　　　　易保罗

俄方：

俄方委员长兼驻大黑河苏俄领事　　　　　默拉美德

代理委员长兼俄阿穆尔水道局局长　　　托阿诺夫

俄阿穆尔水道局副局长　　　且比索夫

俄阿穆尔水道局航路部工程师　　　米海依罗夫

录事：屠守鑫　四等二级帮办

瑷珲关致海关总税务司署第 377 号呈附件 4

《中俄边界河道临时航务条例》相关协议（俄方）之译本

中俄临时地方工程委员会会议纪要

（1928 年 1 月 11 日于大黑河）

参会代表

中俄黑龙江水道委员会华方委员长兼黑河道尹兼瑷珲交涉员	张寿增先生
华方副委员长	铎博赉先生
东北航务局局长	陈广起先生
黑龙江航务专门顾问	易保罗先生
俄方委员长兼驻大黑河苏俄领事	默拉美德（Melamed）先生
俄方代理委员长兼俄阿穆尔水道局局长	托阿诺夫（Dianoff）先生
俄阿穆尔水道局副局长	且比索夫（Chebisheff）先生
俄阿穆尔水道局航路部工程师	米海依罗夫（Mihailoff）先生

提案	议决
1.《中俄边界河道临时航务条例》适用于所有在边界河道上航行的中俄轮船。	1. 鉴于该航务条例须适用于所有在边界河道上航行的中俄两国轮船，兹决定： a）通过拟订的《中俄边界河道临时航务条例》（含 96 项条款）； b）该《航务条例》自 1928 年航运季开始生效，适用于边界河道上的一切中俄轮船及木筏； c）如果中俄会议就边境河道的航运问题达成新协议，则该《航务条例》即行废止； d）对于该《航务条例》的任何修改或补充，均须提交中俄黑龙江水道委员会决定。
2. 会议纪要之要求。	2. 会议纪要及所附《中俄边界河道临时航务条例》应分别用中、俄文撰写，俱一式两份，双方互相签字盖印，各执中、俄文本各一份。

签字	签字
中俄临时地方工程委员会俄方委员长兼驻大黑河苏俄领事 默拉美德（G. I. Melamed） 代理委员长兼俄阿穆尔水道局局长 托阿诺夫 委员： 俄阿穆尔水道局副局长 且比索夫 俄阿穆尔水道局航路部工程师 米海依罗夫	中俄临时地方工程委员会华方委员长兼黑河道尹 张寿增 副委员长 铎博赉 委员： 东北航务局局长 陈广起 黑龙江航务专门顾问 易保罗

翻译：王德懋　二等一级税务员

瑷珲关致海关总税务司署第 377 号呈附件

《中俄边界河道临时航务条例》印刷本译本

　　为保证中俄双方在边界河道上的所有往来轮船及木筏都能恪守航务条例，中俄临时地方工程委员会于 1928 年 1 月 11 日签署协议，协定《中俄边界河道临时航务条例》（含 96 项条款）自 1928 年航运季伊始开始生效。

签字	签字
中俄黑龙江水道委员会华方委员长兼黑河道尹兼瑷珲交涉员张寿增	中俄黑龙江水道委员会俄方委员长兼驻大黑河苏俄领事默拉美德
华方副委员长 铎博赉	俄方代理委员长兼阿穆尔水道局局长 托阿诺夫
华方委员 东北航务局局长 陈广起 黑龙江航务专门顾问 易保罗	俄方委员 阿穆尔水道局副局长 且比索夫 阿穆尔水道局航路部工程师 米海依罗夫

　　注：条例初稿已由中俄黑龙江水道委员会签署。在印刷版条例中，中文、俄文两个版本的介绍部分均附有签名，但条例的中文版本未附签名。

中俄边界河道临时航务条例

为保证中俄两国轮船、木筏以及船员和乘客能够安全往来于边界河道黑龙江、乌苏里江及额尔古纳河,特制定如下条例。

第一部分

第一条

通则

1. 凡航行于中俄边界河道黑龙江、乌苏里江及额尔古纳河之轮船及木筏必须随船携带《航务条例》之抄件,以供随时翻阅。

2. 中俄两国轮船必须按照两国相关法律之规定悬挂国旗。此外,轮船还可于前桅上悬挂商号旗,以明示轮船之所属或受雇公司。所有轮船均须于船身两侧清楚地印上船名。

第二条

航道沿线的航路标志

3. 边界河道沿线均应安设信号标桩(标示航道方向)、直行标桩、浮桩及旗式标桩。凡立于河道右岸之航路标志均漆红色,凡立于河道左岸之航路标志均漆白色。

4. 若有礁石或浅滩之危险,则立以浮标或者旗式标桩警之,而标桩之颜色(红色或白色)则依照河道左右两岸而区分。若航道有危险地带,则于河道两侧立以标桩或者旗式标桩警之,标桩漆红白相间横纹以供于日间做警示之用;标桩于夜间按照实际情况发红光或者白光,抑或发上白下红(纵向)光。

5. 若有易对轮船和木筏造成危险之浅滩或狭窄航道,则立以狭窄处管理站与通行信号站标杆警之。

6. 狭窄处管理站与通行信号站的驻守人员,应在详细探测水位深度之后,于标杆上悬挂横式板和球形标志以明示水位深度(以厘米为单位):横式板每个表示水深100厘米,每增加一个大球表示水深增加20厘米,每增加一个小球表示水深增加5厘米。

7. 按照以下方式于通行信号站标杆上悬挂信号标志,以向轮船及木筏明示通行情况:

（1）于日间悬挂一个球形标志,于夜间发红光,以标示该河段上游禁止轮船通行;

（2）于日间悬挂一个锥形标志,于夜间发上红下白（纵向）光,以标示该河段下游禁止轮船及木筏通行;

（3）于日间悬挂一个球形标志和一个锥形标志,于夜间发两道（纵向）红光,以标示该河段上游及下游均禁止轮船及木筏通行;

（4）若通行信号站标杆上未悬挂信号标志,则标示该河段上游及下游均可通行,目及之处未见轮船及木筏。

第二部分

轮船和木筏上的装备

第一条

以发送信号之用

8. 为发送信号,轮船和木筏上均应配有如下装备:（1）信号灯;（2）重达 4 公斤以上的号钟,或者金属铜锣,或者号角（喇叭）（以下简称为"声响信号"）;（3）70 平方厘米的白色号旗;（4）带玻璃罩的信号灯,仅发白光;（5）汽船上须配备两个汽笛;摩托艇上须配备一个汽笛。

注：驾驶室须备有灯笼、灯、蜡烛及火柴,以确保电灯发生故障时,可以立即点燃信号灯。

9. 凡轮船（或者汽船）达 60 马力以上,驳船和民船承载量达 50 吨以上者,必须配备一定数量的小船。

10. 船锚和测深锤上均须标注重量、所属轮船或木筏的名称以及所属轮船或木筏船主之名号。

11. 船锚均须悬挂浮标,浮标应漆红白相间的条纹,漂浮时须清晰可见。若船锚抛于航道通行之处,则须在其旁停靠一艘小船,并于夜间点亮信号灯以警示其他船只。抛锚时,锚链的长度必须与抛锚点的水深一致。

12. 木筏均须于船中心立一桅杆,并悬挂一块牌子,标明船主姓名、木筏出发地及木筏编号。

第三部分

轮船照明

第一条

通则

13. 轮船及木筏在照明时可使用电灯、植物油、吡喃酮、硬脂蜡等,在特殊情况下还可使用汽油,但须谨慎使用。

14. 凡使用电灯照明之轮船,必须携带一定数量的灯笼,以备不时之需(参阅第8条)。

第二条

探照灯的使用

15. 凡轮船和挖泥船遇到下述情形者,可于船上使用探照灯。

(1)仅于行驶中:寻找航道、浅滩或航路标志时使用;

(2)当轮船准备靠岸时,或因停泊处已有轮船停靠而无法靠岸时使用。

注:当遇上其他轮船时,必须熄灭探照灯。

第四部分

轮船、木筏和挖泥船的航运工作

第一条

通则

16. 船主和撑筏者必须为轮船、乘客及货物的安全负责;不得阻碍航行或者损坏其他轮船、木筏、码头、拖船路线以及航路浮标和堤岸标志。

17. 凡轮船及木筏未具备如下条件者,不得航行:(1)配备之船锚及滑车数量充足;(2)配备夜晚或白天使用的信号工具;(3)船员人数充足;(4)配备之小船状态良好且数量充足(参阅第6条)。

18. 轮船与木筏无论于行驶或停泊时，均不得破坏前滩，亦不得倾斜。

19. 轮船或木筏的船长仅对航行以及船员纪律负责，若有无暇监管之时，可以将权利下放给副手，但必须对所有事故或违反相关条例的事件负责。所有牵引木筏或驳船的船员也必须服从船长的命令。

20. 为确保安全航行，所有往来于同一方向同一航线上的船只，相互之间必须保持一定的距离。

21. 航行或停泊时，船长不得骤然改变轮船状态，以免阻碍其他轮船航行或影响其他轮船航行之速度，从而造成事故（参阅第 29 条）。

22. 凡无拖船之轮船靠近码头时，或挖泥船及许多轮船聚集在一起时，又或轮船进行装载时，均须减速，以免行驶产生的水波过人对轮船或者码头造成损坏。

第二条

雾天、雪天和雨天的航运工作

23. 在浓雾、暴雨、大雪天气时，即使最近的物体都难以看清，因此只允许无拖船之轮船驶入航道。其他一切轮船与木筏都必须停泊于航道之外或者岸边。停泊于岸边之轮船必须每隔一段时间便鸣钟、敲锣或者吹号以警示其他船只。航行中之轮船必须每分钟鸣响长笛一次。

24. 鉴于浓雾渐散、大雨转小、暴雪渐停之时，能见度依然很低，故航行中之轮船和木筏必须减速，谨慎行驶，每隔几分钟便要发出的声响信号以警示其他船只。

25. 若遇浓雾、暴雨、大雪等天气，除客船以外，浮船及木筏均禁止出航，必须停泊靠岸，并每分钟发出一次声响信号以警示其他船只。

第三条

轮船、木筏或挖泥船相遇、超船相关条例

26. 当轮船相向行驶时，由向下游行驶之轮船首先选择航道。

27. 当轮船与民船或木筏相向行驶时，则无论轮船是向上游或是向下游行驶，均有优先选择航道之权利（参阅第 69 条）。民船、木筏及小船均须根据轮船的指示选择航道（参阅第七部分第一条）。

28. 当数艘轮船井然有序地向同一方向行驶时,迎面遇到了另外数艘按同一航线行驶之轮船,则两边的轮船应交换信号,由领头的轮船决定航道。若自下游而来之轮船因直行而需要穿过自上游而来之轮船行进的航道,则自上游而来之轮船须减速慢行,为自下游而来之轮船让路。

29. 为避免发生碰撞,轮船只可尾随其他轮船,而不可超越其他轮船(参阅第 21 条)。

30. 当轮船发现其他轮船有超船之举时,不得阻碍,须减速慢行,为后者让路。

航路厅认为,航道上若有易因超船而发生危险之处,应通告所有轮船,甚至明令禁止于此类地方超船。

31. 小船行驶时,若遇到轮船欲穿过其行进之航道,或在其行进之航道旁边与其同向或相向而行,则不得有妨碍之行为。

第四条

轮船和木筏穿越浅滩的航运工作

32. 凡穿越浅滩之轮船和木筏,吃水量须低于航道水深:

(1)黑龙江上游 6 英寸(15 厘米)

(2)黑龙江中游 8 英寸(20 厘米)

凡轮船和木筏穿越浅滩时装载炸药者,吃水量须低于航道水深:

(1)黑龙江上游 10 英寸(25 厘米)

(2)黑龙江中游 12 英寸(30 厘米)

33. 轮船均需于船头、船身及船尾两侧标记明显可见的深水线标志,以便巡江事务长检查。这些标志必须标明单位为英尺或厘米。

34. 凡靠近浅滩之轮船和木筏,均须查看灯照管理站标识所示的河道深度。如若所示深度不足,则须停船;若欲通过浅谈,则只能用驳船渡过。

第五部分

轮船和木筏的停泊所

第一条

通则

35. 各式轮船和木筏均须停泊于航道之外。

36. 轮船和木筏禁止停泊于岸上有绳索标记之处，若无特殊目的，不得系泊于电线杆、灯照管理站标杆或信号标桩上。

37. 轮船和木筏严禁停泊于浅滩、峡谷及近岸的水流中。

38. 凡轮船系泊于岸边或其他停泊之所者，所用之系泊绳索必须坚固且安全。

第六部分

信号灯的使用

第一条

通则

39. 与信号灯相关之条例规定自日落到日出期间，无论何种天气下，均应当遵守；凡可能误认为指定信号灯之其他灯光均不得于此期间使用。

注：切勿将用于测量水深的普通灯被误认为信号灯。

40. 凡携带易燃货物之轮船，均须于日间悬挂特殊号旗，并于夜间点亮额外的信号灯（参阅第 53、54 条）。

第二条

轮船和木筏停泊时的信号灯

41. 凡轮船和木筏停泊时，均须于明显位置安装金属灯，能够发出亮度稳定之白光，光亮能见里程至少为地平线上 1.5 公里（1.5 俄丈）范围以内。

42. 凡轮船或木筏搁浅后未能于夜晚来临之前重新漂浮起来者，除须点亮平常的锚泊灯以外,还须在暴露于通行航道一侧的船舷外部点亮额外的信号灯。

第三条

<u>轮船和木筏行进时的信号灯</u>

43. 行进时:

（1）轮船均须于前桅顶部或船艄安装一盏明亮的白灯,能够稳定地发出呈 220° 半圆形的灯光,该灯光必须在暗夜里清晰可见,光亮能见里程至少为 8 公里（约 8 俄丈或 4.5 海里）;

（2）民船和木筏均须于前桅顶部安装一盏明亮的白灯,能够稳定地发出呈 360° 圆弧形的灯光,光亮能见里程至少为 1.5 公里;

（3）轮船舷灯,右侧为绿灯,左侧为红灯,每盏舷灯必须能够投射出半圆形的灯光,且灯光能够稳定地照射到横梁后方自船艄出发的 20° 范围以及每侧 110° 的半圆形范围之内;该灯光必须在暗夜里清晰可见,光亮能见里程至少为 4 公里（约 4 俄丈）;应于船舱内为绿色和红色舷灯配置挡板,以保证灯光可直射 3 英尺,避免于船头看见灯光;

（4）面向轮船的横梁前方不可看见船尾发射的白光。

44. 轮船须挥动信号以向靠近的轮船和木筏指示航道。挥动的信号灯仅可在一侧装有玻璃罩,另外三面必须遮蔽起来,以便于舷外灯反向转到中部时,发射出的灯光不可见。但该信号灯向外发出的必须清晰可见,其光亮能见里程与桅杆上悬挂的信号灯一样均为 4 公里（约为 4 俄丈）;民船与木筏的信号灯光亮能见里程须与船尾灯一致,为 5 公里。

第四条

<u>各式轮船和木筏上信号灯的安装使用</u>

<u>1. 轮船上的信号灯</u>

45. 轮船上的信号灯要求如下。

（1）轮船停泊时,须在高于甲板至少 6 米（约 20 英尺）的桅杆上或船头安装一盏白灯（参阅第 41 条）;

（2）若轮船行进时未拖带船只,则须在高于甲板至少 6 米（约 20 英尺）的前桅杆上安

437

装一盏白灯,并于两侧安装绿色和红色舷灯(参阅第43条);

（3）若轮船行进时拖带船只,则须于两侧安装绿色和红色舷灯的同时,在高于甲板至少6米(约20英尺)的前桅杆上安装两盏白灯,两盏白灯垂直排列,间距不超过1米(约3英尺);被拖带之船只均须在高于甲板至少6米(约20英尺)处安装一盏白灯[参阅第43条(2)]。

46.若两艘轮船共同拖带驳船,则每艘轮船均须配备指定的信号灯(参阅第45条),并向过往的轮船挥动信号或发送声响信号。

2. 驳船上的信号灯

47.驳船上的信号灯要求如下。

（1）驳船停泊时,须在高于甲板至少6米(约20英尺)处安装一盏白灯(参阅第41条);

注：若驳船长度低于30米(15俄丈),则须在高于甲板至少2米(约7英尺)处安装信号灯。

（2）驳船行进时：

① 若被其他轮船拖带,则须在高于甲板至少6米(约20英尺)处安装信号灯;

② 若未被其他轮船拖带且向下游行驶时,则须在高于甲板至少6米(约20英尺)处,分别于船头和船尾各安装一盏白灯。

3. 帆船上的信号灯

48.帆船上的信号灯要求如下。

（1）帆船停泊时,须按如下要求安装一盏白灯(参阅第41条):

① 若帆船长度为30米(15俄丈)及以上,则须在高于甲板至少6米(约20英尺)处安装信号灯;

② 若帆船长度低于30米(15俄丈),则须在高于甲板至少2米(约7英尺)处安装信号灯;

（2）帆船行进时,须在高于甲板至少6米(约20英尺)的前桅顶部安装两盏白灯[参阅第43条(2)],两盏白灯间距不超过1米。

4. 渔船及小船上的信号灯

49.凡渔船及小船停泊或行进之时,均须在高于甲板至少2米(约7英尺)的前桅顶部[参阅第41条及第43条(2)]安装一盏白灯。

5. 木筏上的信号灯

50. 木筏上的信号灯要求如下。

（1）若木筏长度为 50 米（25 俄丈）及以下，则须在木筏中间安装一盏白灯；

（2）若木筏长度超过 50 米但低于 100 米（50 俄丈），则须分别于船头和船尾各安装一盏白灯；

（3）若木筏长度超过 100 米，则须在木筏中间再安装一盏白灯［参阅第 41 条及第 43 条（2）］。

6. 小船上的信号灯

51. 小船于航道上行驶或穿过航道时，须在船头安装一盏白灯，灯光须清晰可见。

7. 挖泥船上的信号灯

52. 挖泥船上的信号灯要求如下。

（1）停泊或行进中的挖泥船：各式挖泥船、驳船和守卫船，无论是聚集在一起航行还是停泊在码头，或是被轮船拖带，均须在高于甲板至少 6 米（约 20 英尺）的桅杆上安装一盏白灯；

（2）工作中的挖泥船：须在高于甲板至少 6 米（约 20 英尺）的桅杆上安装一盏绿灯。

注：当挖泥船停泊或者靠近河道时，无论是否正在工作，过往轮船都必须发出警报信号，必要时还需要调整航速（参阅第 22 条）。

H. 携带炸药、石油及其他危险品的轮船上的信号灯

53. 携带炸药、石油及其他危险品的轮船上的信号灯要求如下。

（1）凡装载有煤油、石油或 28℃ 以上易燃易爆品之轮船，除常用信号灯之外，还须在高于甲板至少 6 米（约 20 英尺）的前桅上安装一盏红灯（夜间使用）或悬挂一面红旗（日间使用）；

（2）凡装载有炸药及其他危险品之轮船，均须在高于甲板至少 6 米（约 20 英尺）的前桅杆上安装两盏红灯，两盏红灯垂直排列，间距不超过一米（夜间使用），或悬挂两面红旗，两面红旗垂直排列，间距不超过一米（日间使用）。

54. 凡轮船及其拖带之驳船均携带易爆货物者，须在桅杆上安装三盏信号灯，包括两盏白灯和一盏红灯。

第五条

<u>轮船上的特殊信号灯</u>

55. 轮船被拖带时,除按上述[第47条(b)(1)]规定要求安装信号灯以外,还须在船舷外部安装一盏明亮的白灯。

56. 凡携带危险传染病病源之轮船,须于日间在前桅杆上悬挂一面黄色方形旗,并于夜间在前桅杆上高于日常白灯至少75厘米处安装一盏绿灯和一盏红灯。

第七部分

轮船在超船前应发出的信号

第一条

<u>通则</u>

57. 凡轮船和木筏与其他船只相遇或超船时,无论是在日间或夜间,均须适时交换信号;无论在何种情况之下,即使轮船或木筏所行驶之航道几乎无发生碰撞事故之可能,亦须适时交换信号。

注:(1)两船相遇或超船信号如下。

① 所有轮船和木筏均须于日间挥动号旗发送信号,并于夜间点亮信号灯;

② 轮船亦须鸣笛,其他船只和木筏亦须发出声响信号;

(2)汽笛信号以鸣笛时间长短而区分:"长笛"鸣笛时间为6—8秒,不可间断;"短笛"鸣笛时间为0.5秒,须重复,如有需要,则间隔重复鸣笛。

58. 须时刻准备发送信号。

59. 当轮船或木筏与另一艘轮船相遇或经过正在检修之轮船时,应于会船一侧挥动信号。

注:须在舷灯上方挥动信号。

60. 在发送信号之前,轮船须先鸣一声长笛;其他船只或木筏则须发送日常声响信号。声响信号发送完毕后,轮船或木筏须立即于其船身一侧挥动信号,但不得于驾驶室或轮船及木筏的中间位置挥动信号。

61. 当轮船准备超船时,须于日间须悬挂白色号旗,于夜间点亮信号灯(参阅第44条);

在收到对方船只回应信号之前,号旗或信号灯须于原地保持发送状态。

62. 轮船或木筏回应信号时,须鸣长笛或发出其他声响信号,随后在靠近发送信号的轮船或木筏一侧挥动号旗或信号灯以作回应。

注: 若轮船无法按照对方船只所指示之航道行驶,则按照第66条和第67条之规定发送信号。

63. 轮船仅可将号笛作航行信号之用; 不得将之作会船致意或者向船员发号施令之用。

第二条

轮船和木筏从相反方向驶入时应发出的信号

64. 当轮船或木筏向下游行驶时,若遇到其他船只,则须在至少一公里以外鸣笛或发送其他声响信号,随后挥动信号,以告知向上游行驶之轮船或木筏应从航道哪一侧通过。 对向轮船或木筏则须予以回应。 先行的轮船须于挥动信号之前鸣长笛两次(而非一次)。

65. 若向上游行驶的轮船或木筏注意到航道上存在向下游行驶的轮船或木筏可能忽视之危险,则须鸣数次(不得少于三次)短笛或发送其他声响信号以作警示之用。

66. 在对双方轮船均不会造成危险的情况之下,若向上游行驶的轮船或木筏无法按照向下游行驶的轮船或木筏所指示之航道行驶,则须立即鸣短笛两次,并通过挥动信号明示自己想要选择的航路。 若向上游行驶的轮船拖带船只,则须减速; 若未拖带船只,亦须减速或者按要求后退。

67. 当向下游行驶的轮船或木筏收到对向船只此类信号(无法按照其指示之航道行驶)时:

(1)若能够选择另外一侧航道,则鸣长笛或者发送其他声响信号;

(2)若无法按照对方指示之航道行驶,在未拖带船只的情况下,则鸣短笛或发送其他声响信号并后退; 若该船拖带船只或为木筏或其他船只,若情况允许,须船尾相依地停泊在一起。

68. 若相遇的轮船或木筏有一方未发送信号,或者双方均未发送信号,或者未收到对方的回复信号,又或者未能充分理解对方信号之意义,则向上游行驶的轮船或木筏须停船,等待向上游行驶的轮船或木筏发出可行之信号。 只有相遇的双方收到的信号一致,轮船或木筏方可继续前行。

69. 当轮船与民船或木筏相向行驶时,均由轮船优先选择航道,民船或木筏均须根据轮船的指示选择航路(参阅第 27 条)。

第三条

轮船和木筏超越其他船只时应发出的信号

70. 凡意图超越其他轮船或木筏之船只,无论是否有拖船,均须在至少 400 米以外鸣三声短笛或发送其他声响信号,随后挥动信号,以向欲赶超之轮船或木筏告知其欲从哪一侧航道超船。

当被赶超的轮船或木筏接收到这一信号时:

(1)若能够按照指示之航道行驶,则鸣长笛或者发送其他声响信号,同时在被赶超的一侧挥动信号以告知欲超船之轮船可以通过;

(2)若无法按照指示之航道行驶,则鸣短笛两次或者发送其他声响信号,同时在被赶超的一侧挥动信号以告知欲超船之轮船可以从哪一侧航道通过。

71. 若被赶超的轮船或木筏受某些情况阻止而无法按照指示之航道行驶,则必须立即鸣笛数次或发送其他声响信号; 在这种情况下,后面的轮船必须等待更合适的航道和时机再行超船。

第四条

轮船和木筏穿越狭窄峡谷时应发出的信号

72. 当轮船即将驶入河道的弯曲处、狭窄处或者难以及时观测到其他轮船靠近之处,必须鸣响长笛一次; 若未收到回应信号,则须在驶入该地点前再次鸣响长笛两次。民船和木筏在驶入此类地点之前,亦须以同样的方式发送声响信号。

73. 当向上游行驶的轮船收到的回应信号与自己所发信号相同时:

(1)若还未在河道弯曲处转弯或尚未进入峡谷,则须暂停前进,以待向下游行驶的轮船通过;

(2)若已在河道弯曲处转弯或者已进入峡谷,则必须减速,以等待向下游行驶的轮船再次发送信号; 同时,向下游行驶的轮船亦须尽可能地减速,以确保可以向任何方向转弯,并且要尽可能地慢速行驶。

第五条

轮船和木筏经过正在施工的挖泥船时应发出的信号

74. 凡轮船和木筏靠近正在施工的挖泥船时,须在至少 400 米的距离外鸣笛或发送声响信号。

75. 若河道畅通,挖泥船须在接收到靠近的轮船或木筏发送的警示信号后,鸣响长笛以作回应。若长笛发生故障,挖泥船可发送其他合适的声响信号代之。挖泥船须于日间挥动信号,夜间点亮信号灯,以告知靠近的轮船或木筏应从哪一侧航道通过。

76. 若河道被正在施工的挖泥船堵塞,挖泥船则须通过号笛或其他工具发送短促的警报信号,轮船或木筏收到信号后必须停止前进。轮船或木筏只有在听到挖泥船鸣长笛或发送其他声响信号,并见到挖泥船挥动信号后,方可继续前进。

第六条

求助信号

77. 轮船或木筏若遇火灾、失事或其他事故,则应按如下要求发送信号。

（1）轮船须于日间持续鸣长笛并降半旗,于夜间持续鸣长笛并将桅杆信号灯交替升降；

（2）民船和木筏须持续发送声响信号作为警报；

（3）所有处于失事轮船附近的轮船也必须发送求助信号。

第七条

召唤轮船的信号

78. 从岸边召唤轮船时,应发送两长一短鸣笛信号。

79. 从狭窄处管理站召唤轮船时,应发送一长一短鸣笛信号。

第八条

码头信号

80. 当轮船即将靠近码头时,须鸣响长笛。

81. 轮船离岸时必须发送数组信号,即一长一短鸣笛信号、一长两短鸣笛信号、一长三短鸣笛信号,然后方可离岸。

第八部分

航道障碍物

第一条

<u>航道存在障碍物或航道水深不足</u>

82. 严禁船只向河中或者冰面上(冬季)倾倒石块、烟灰、沙砾、煤炭及一切有可能阻塞河道的垃圾。

83. 若轮船或木筏意外于航道上丢失了锚或其他有可能影响航运安全的物品,船长、驳船船员或撑筏者必须尽可能地采取一切措施找到并立即处理此类物品。若无法寻得丢失的物品,则必须于丢失出处立以浮标或者其他可漂浮的信号标识警之;若在岸上做标记,则应在物体掉落的对应位置做上标记,并告知最近的浅滩巡役,然后再向相关航路厅汇报。

84. 沉船或丢失货物之处必须立以旗式标识警之(参阅第4条),相关船长、驳船船员或撑筏者必须立即告知最近的浅滩巡役以及负责该船航运事宜的航路厅。

85. 轮船、木筏、货物或船锚及其他可能影响航运安全之物品(如第83条所述),一旦沉入水中,均须由船主负责打捞。若未能于规定时间内打捞起沉没的物品,则移交相关国家的航路厅负责,并由船主出资以支持相关工作。

86. 当发生航运事故或在浅滩进行驳运工作时,若船长、驳船船员或撑筏者认为有必要在岸边停泊,可以按规定在岸边卸载货物。若轮船或木筏由于不可抗力因素而被迫卸货,相关船长、驳船船员或撑筏者则须立即通知最近的地方政府和航路厅,以便采取相应措施来应对突发状况。货物停放在岸上期间,必须服从地方官员指令,遵循地方的法律法规。

87. 若船长、驳船船员或者撑筏者发现航道上有障碍物或者航路标志有问题或缺失,则必须告知最近的浅滩巡役和航路厅。

第九部分

事故相关条例

_通则_

88. 凡轮船或木筏发事故,或者船上乘客或货物发生事故者,轮船或木筏的负责人员均须向距其最近的有关当局汇报,无一例外。

89. 凡遇到轮船、木筏、货物或乘客遇到危险者,或者发现通行航道有受到阻断风险者,无论是行船经过还是在事故地点附近,不论国籍,均须立即施以援手。

90. 如有意外发生,轮船、驳船或木筏的船长必须尽一切可能先救人,然后再抢救货物。

91. 当轮船发生意外事故,在采取了所有必要的紧急救援措施后,无论损失大小,货物负责人均须出具一份详细报告,汇报事故发生的真实原因及结果。汇报人及其他责任见证人均须于报告上签名。如果是轮船本身发生了意外事故,船长则应出具一份类似的报告,由船长本人、两名责任船员以及其他见证人共同签署。若报告内容不够详尽,或者存在与事实不符之陈述,见证人有权提出异议并出具佐证。报告应立即呈送至相关国家距离最近的航路厅。

92. 所有签署姓名的见证人均须附上自己的职业、完整姓名及地址。

  注: 如果两艘轮船上的船长或见证人由于语言不通而无法做出有关声明时,相关船长、驳船船员或者撑筏者务必通知发生事故轮船所属国家的最近航路厅,由航路厅做出详尽调查并出具必要声明。

93. 上述声明必须包括:

(1)事故发生的时间;

(2)对事故发生地点及原因的详细陈述;

(3)船长(或负责人)在事故发生前、事故中及发生事故后下达的所有指示;

(4)对于受损或丢失货物的详细陈述,以及对于轮船或木筏所遭受的显性或隐性之损坏的详细陈述;

(5)曾采取何种措施以避免事故发生,是否有遵循《航务条例》的指引;

(6)乘客的伤亡情况;

(7)包含事故发生原因、地点及轮船或木筏的后续行动的草图;

(8)负责起草声明人员的完整姓名以及地址。

94. 若船上发生犯罪行为,船长须立即向距离最近的巡警和该船所属国家的航路厅报告。

95. 在撞船事故中,行船经过的船长、驳船船员或撑筏者必须立即停船,提供必要的援助,并出具以见证人身份签署的共同声明(参阅第93条)。如果对事故发生原因未能达成一致认识,则各方须出具独立的声明,并由见证人签署后,互相交换抄件,以示收悉。

96. 凡船只或者其船主、船长或船员因未按照航运惯例之要求进行瞭望或采取预防措施而造成事故者,按照本条例,均无免除责任之可能。

铎博赉

瑷珲关署理税务司

1928 年 6 月 9 日

28. 1928 年《黑龙江上游联合疏浚协议》

AMUR AIDS TO NAVIGATION:
dredging of Upper Amur: signing of Agreement by
Sino-Soviet Amur Aids Commission adopting limited
program for, notifying.

379.

I.G.

Registered   Aigun   28th June, 1928.
INDEX

379
I.G.

Sir,

I have the honour to report that at a meeting of the Sino-Soviet Amur Aids Commission on the 19th instant, convened at the local Soviet Consulate for the purpose, an Agreement was signed for the carrying out of a limited dredging program on the Upper Amur.

I am appending copies of the Agreement in Russian and Chinese together with English versions of the same; also a translation from the Russian of the estimate of expenditure agreed to.

The Agreement is for the year 1928 only and involves the dredging of certain shallows between the Soviet villages Cherniayevo and Djalinda corresponding to the villages Wo Hsi Men (倭西們) and Lien Yin (連崟) respectively on the Chinese side of the Amur. It will be seen that the estimated cost of the dredging required is G. Rbls. 6,000. Of this amount China will pay half. The work will be done by the Amur Navigation Bureau who will employ their own dredges.

The Soviet Authorities have been urging the

Appendix No.1.
Appendix No.2.
Appendix No.3.
Appendix No.4.
Appendix No.5.

The Inspector General of Customs,
      Peking.

the necessity for dredging the Upper Amur for the last two years but their arguments have not been convincing - especially in view of the amount of the original estimate (some G. Rbls. 120,000) and the very limited number of steamers that would be benefitted. The Taoyin, as President of the Chinese side of the Aids Commission, has felt of late, however, that some concession should be made to the demands of the Soviet Authorities as a gesture of admission in general to the principle of the necessity of joint dredging and when the Amur Navigation Bureau reduced the estimate to G. Rbls. 6,000 he received the instructions of the Tsitsihar Government to conclude the Agreement now reported.

With regard to the payment of China's share of the estimate, G. Rbls. 3,000, which at the present rate of exchange would equal Harbin $1,800, the Taoyin is undertaking to raise the required amount from outside sources.

I have the honour to be,
                Sir,
        Your obedient Servant,

Acting Commissioner.

Appendix

Aigun No. 379 to I. G.

Appendix No.1.

ПРОТОКОЛ

заседания Временной Местной Советско-Китайской Технической Комиссии
"19" июня 1928 года, гор. Сахалян.

ПРИСУТСТВОВАЛИ:

Хэйхэсский Даоинъ и Дипломатический Чиновник
в Айгуне....................................Г. ЧЖАН-ШОУ-ДЗЕН.

Комиссар Айгунской Таможни...................Г. ТАЛБОТ.

Чиновник при Управлении Хэйхэсского Даоина...Г. ШЕН-ТИН-КУН.

Технический Советник.........................Г. ИГНАТЬЕВ.

Консул СССР в Сахаляне.......................Г. МЕЛАМЕД.

Начальник Управления Водных Путей Амурского
бассейна....................................Г. ДИАНОВ.

Помощник Начальника Управления Водных Путей,
Инженер.....................................Г. ЧЕБЫШОВ.

СЛУШАЛИ:	ПОСТАНОВИЛИ:
I. Вопрос о землечерпательных работах на Верхнем Амуре в районе от деревни ЧЕРНЯЕВО до деревни ДЖАЛИНДА.	I. Принимая во внимание наблюдающиеся затруднения при плавании на Верхнем Амуре, вследствие недостаточной глубины и ширины хода на перекатах в мелкую воду, в районе от деревни ЧЕРНЯЕВО до деревни ДЖАЛИНДА произвести совместно землечерпательные работы снарядом Амурского Водного Управления, применив Соглашение от 28 октября 1923 года со всеми к нему приложениями, кроме приложения № 3, которое согласуется отдельно.
2. Смета по совместному землечерпанию в пределах от деревни ЧЕРНЯЕВО до деревни ДЖАЛИНДА.	2. Смету по землечерпанию УТВЕРДИТЬ в сумме ШЕСТИ ТЫСЯЧ РУБЛЕЙ сумма расхода не должна превышать исчисленную по смете сумму.
3. Сроки платежей.	3. Китайская сторона вносит причитающуюся на ее долю сумму в 3000 рублей в 2 срока: I/ после исполнения половины работ, около 15-го июля в сумме 1500 рублей и 2/ по окончании работ и по представлении и рассмотрении отчета в сумме 1500 рублей.
4. О составлении протокола.	4. Протокол должен быть составлен на русском и китайском языках по 2 экземпляра, из которых по одному экземпляру русского и китайского текста получает Комиссия с Китайской стороны и по одному экземпляру- Комиссия со стороны СССР.

Председатель Временной Местной
Советско-Китайской Технической
Комиссии со стороны СССР,
Консул СССР в Сахаляне
/Г.И. Меламед/

Начальник Амурского Водного
Управления
/Дианов/

Члены Ко-
миссии: /Чебышов/

Председатель Временной Местной
Советско-Китайской Технической
Комиссии с Китайской стороны,
Хэйхэсский Даоинъ и Дипломатический
Чиновник в Айгуне
/Чжан-Шоу-Дзен/

/Талбот/

Члены Ко-
миссии: /Шен-Тин-Кун/
               /Игнатьев/

True copy:

2nd Clerk A.

448

章程协议

Aigun No. 379 to I. G.

Appendix No.2.

Translation of the Russian version of the Protocol concerning
the joint Dredging of the Upper Amur.

P R O T O C O L.

Minutes of a meeting of the local Provisional Sino-Soviet
Technical Commission, held at Taheiho on the 19th June,1928.

Representatives:-

Heiho Taoyin (and concurrently Commissioner for Foreign Affairs, Aigun):	Mr. Chang Shou-tsen.
Commissioner of the Aigun Customs:	Mr. Talbot.
Official from the Heiho Taoyin's Office:	Mr. Shen Ting-jun.
Technical Adviser:	Mr. Ignatieff.
Consul of U.S.S.R. at Taheihô:	Mr. Melamed.
Director of the Amur Navigation Bureau:	Mr. Dianoff.
Assistant Director of the Amur Navigation Bureau:	Mr. Chebisheff.

Subject discussed:	Decision:
1. The question of dredge work on the Upper Amur from the village CHERNIAYEVO to the village DJALINDA.	1. Taking into consideration the difficulties incurred in navigating the Upper Amur, owing to insufficient depth and breadth of channel on the shallows, during the lower water season, in the reach from the village CHERNIAYEVO to the village DJALINDA, joint dredge work is to be carried out by a dredge of the Amur Navigation Bureau, in accordance with the Agreement of 28th October, 1923, with the exception of Annex No.3, which will be considered separately.
2. Estimate for joint dredge work on the Upper Amur in the reach extending from the village CHERNIAYEVO to the village DJALINDA.	2. To sanction the estimate for dredge work to the amount of G.Rbls.6,000. The total expenditure must not exceed the sum estimated.
3. The time of payments.	3. The Chinese share of the estimate, amounting to G.Rbls.3,000, shall be paid in two instalments - 1) the first instalment, amounting to G.Rbls.1,500, shall be paid after the work is half done, about the 15th July, and 2) the second instalment, amounting to G.Rbls.1,500, shall be paid after the completion of the work and on presentation and passing of the accounts.
4. Protocol to be made.	4. This Protocol must be written in the Russian and Chinese languages, and in duplicate, each party keeping one copy in Chinese and one in Russian.

The President of the Local Provisional Technical Commission for the U.S.S.R. Side, the Consul of U.S.S.R. at Taheiho /G. I. Melamed/

Members of the Commission:
Director of the Amur Navigation Bureau /Dianoff/
/Chebisheff/

The President of the Local Provisional Sino-Russian Technical Commission for the Chinese side, Heiho Taoyin (and concurrently Commissioner for Foreign Affairs, Aigun) /Chang Shou-tsen/

Members of the Commission:
/Talbot/
/Shen Ting-jun/
/Ignatieff/

Translated by:

2nd Clerk A.

Aigun No. 379 to I. G.
Appendix No.3.

聲明書

聲明書

華方委員長大中華民國黑河道尹兼瑷琿交涉員張壽增華方委
員瑷琿關稅務司鐸博睿黑河道署外交科長沈廷榮舤務專門
顧問易保羅

俄方委員長大蘇維亞社會聯邦共和國駐黑河領事默拉美德俄
方委員阿穆爾國家水道局局長吉阿諾夫阿穆爾國家水道局副
局長且彼索夫於中華民國十七年（即西應一千九百二十八年六月十九日

在大黑河中俄地方臨時協議工程委員會正式會議共同定聲明如左

（一）根據中華民國十二年（即西應一千九百二十三年十月二十八日中俄
地方所訂黑龍江修江協議各條欵為原則除第三班件關於預
算呂議外兹因黑龍江上游江道水量較淺及各戈灘中之航路

狹窄致發生航行之□難逕經中俄雙方議定使□阿穆爾兩水道

局之挖江機船共同濬深由俄屯且爾年也夫起至札林達止一段

之江道

（二）挖江工作由且爾年也夫起至札林達止此項經費預算估定共六千盧

布各項間支之欵不得超過（議定預算數目

（三）該項預算中國方面應攤三千盧布按兩期交付第一期須工

程做之一半交付約七月十五日期間）為數一千五百盧布第二

期俟工竣後決算送到再行交付為數一千五百盧布

（四）此項聲明書計華俄文各兩份由雙方簽字蓋即彼此各執華

俄文各一分以照信守

大中華民國十七年六月十九日訂於黑河

即西曆一千八百二十八年六月十九日訂於黑河

中國方面委員長黑河道尹兼璦琿交涉員張壽增

委員璦琿關稅務司鐸博賚

黑河道署外交科長沈廷榮

航務專門顧問易保羅

蘇俄方面委員長駐黑俄領事黙拉美德

委員阿穆爾國家水道局局長吉阿諾夫

阿穆爾國家水道局副局長貝彼索夫

Aigun No. 379 to I. G.

Appendix No.4.

Translation of the Chinese version of the Protocol concerning
the Joint Dredging of the Upper Amur.

The President of the Chinese Aids
Commission and Heiho Taoyin of the Great
Republic of China (concurrently Commissioner
of Foreign Affairs for the Aigun District)
Chang Shou-tsen, and members of the Chinese
Commission: Commissioner of Aigun Customs,
R. M. Talbot; Chief of the Diplomatic Department
of the Taoyin's Office: Shen Ting-jun and
Technical Adviser on Amur Aids to Navigation,
P. I. Ignatieff; and the President of the
Russian Aids Commission and the Consul of the
Great United Socialistic Soviet Republic at
Taheiho, Melamed, and members of the Russian
Commission: Director of the Amur Navigation
Bureau, Dianoff, and the Assistant Director
of the Amur Navigation Bureau, Chebisheff:
hereby jointly declare on the 19th day of the 6th month of
the 17th year of the Republic of China (i.e. 1928) at a
formal meeting held by the local Provisional Sino-Soviet
Aids Commission at Taheiho, that

(1)   Owing to the comparatively low depth of water and the
winding channel through the shallows of the Upper Amur,
with the consequent hindrance to navigation, it is hereby
agreed that joint dredging shall be carried out with the Amur
Navigation Bureau's dredge on that section of the channel
between the Russian villages Cherniayevo and Djalinda in
accordance with the Annexes of the Amur Aids Agreement drawn
                                                            up

up by the local Sino-Soviet Amur Aids Commission on the 28th
day of the 10th month of the 12th year of the Republic of
China, i.e. 1923, with the exception of Annex 3 which concerns
the question of the budget and which will be discussed
separately.

(2)   The dredging work will be carried out on the section from
the Russian village Cherniayevo to the Russian village Djalinda
at an estimated cost of Roubles 6,000.   The total expenses in
connection therewith shall not exceed this amount.

(3)   The Chinese share of the estimated expenses amounting to
Rbls.3,000 shall be paid in two instalments - the first
instalment amounting to Rbls.1,500 shall be paid as soon as
the work is half done (about the 15th July) whereas the second
instalment to the amount of Rbls.1,500 shall be paid after the
completion of the work and on receipt of the accounts statement.

(4)   To confirm this Agreement this Protocol is made out in the
Chinese and Russian languages, in duplicate, and is signed and
sealed by both parties, each party keeping one copy in Chinese
and one in Russian.

Done at Taheiho on the 19th day of the 6th month of the
17th year of the Great Republic of China corresponding to the
19th day of June in the year one thousand nine hundred and
twenty eight.

Chinese side:

(Signed) Chang Shou-tsen, President and Heiho
          Taoyin and concurrently
          Commissioner of Foreign Affairs
          for Aigun District.

   "   R. M. Talbot, Commissioner of Aigun
          Customs.

   "   Shen Ting-jun, Chief of Diplomatic
          Department

452

Department of the Heiho Taoyin's
Office.

(Signed) P. I. Ignatieff, Technical Adviser on
Amur Aids to Navigation.

Soviet Russian side:

(Signed) Melamed, President and Russian Consul
at Taheiho.

" Dianoff, Director of Amur Navigation
Bureau.

" Chebisheff, Assistant Director of Amur

Navigation Bureau.

Translated by:

4th Assistant B.

Aigun No. 379 to I. G.
Appendix No.5.

Summary of Estimate agreed to for Dredge Work.
Dredger "Amurskaya No.5".

No.	Particulars.	G. Roubles.
1.	Salaries for Staff	3,946.00
2.	Heating	1,241.00
3.	Lubricating oil and cotton waste for cleaning machinery	257.00
4.	Oil for light	88.00
5.	Stationary, Postal and Telegraph fees	54.00
(	Navigation repairs and miscellaneous expenses	389.00
7.	Materials for working	25.00
	Total:	6,000.00

(Signed) Shen Ting-jun   Chebisheff
For Technical Adviser.   Assistant Director of Amur
Navigation Bureau.

Certified correct:

2nd Clerk A.

呈海关总税务司署 <u>379</u> 号文　　　　　　　　瑷珲关 1928 年 6 月 28 日

尊敬的海关总税务司（北京）：

　　兹汇报，中俄黑龙江水道委员会于 6 月 19 日在大黑河苏维埃领事馆内召开会议，就在黑龙江上游河段开展疏浚工程一事签署了协议。

　　兹附华方及俄方协议及两方协议的英文译本，以及协定之预算报表（俄文）译本。

　　该协议仅适用于 1928 年，在黑龙江上游浅滩开展疏浚工程，疏浚范围限于俄岸自俄村切尔纳耶瓦（Chernayeva）起至加林达（Jalinda）止，华岸相应自中国村庄倭西们起至连鋈止。该项疏浚工程的预算为 6000 金卢布，华方摊款为预算总额之半数。此外，该项工程将由俄阿穆尔水道局使用自己的挖泥船来完成。

　　在过去两年中，俄方当局一直反复强调疏浚黑龙江上游之重要性，但却始终未能给出令人信服的依据；且因该项工程最初拟订的预算（约 120000 金卢布）较高，而只有少数轮船能够从中获益，故中国对该项工程之开展一直未曾表示支持。不过兼任黑龙江航政委员会华方委员长的道尹认为，对于俄方当局的要求应该做出适当的让步，以彰显联合疏浚工程的必要性。因此当俄阿穆尔水道局将预算削减至 6000 金卢布后，道尹按照齐齐哈尔政府之指示签署了就黑龙江上游疏浚工程所拟订的协议。

　　华方摊款约 3000 金卢布，按现行汇率兑换，约合哈大洋 1800 元，由道尹负责从外部渠道筹集所需资金。

您忠诚的仆人

铎博赉（R. M. Talbot）

瑷珲关署理税务司

瑷珲关致海关总税务司署第 379 号呈附件 2^①

黑龙江上游联合疏浚协议（俄方）

协议

中俄临时地方工程委员会会议纪要

（1928 年 6 月 19 日于大黑河）

参会代表

黑河道尹兼瑷珲交涉员	张寿增先生
瑷珲关税务司	铎博赉先生
黑河道尹公署代表	沈廷荣先生
黑龙江航务专门顾问	易保罗（P. I. Ignatieff）先生
驻黑河苏俄领事	默拉美德（Melamed）先生
俄阿穆尔水道局局长	托阿诺夫（Dianoff）先生
俄阿穆尔水道局副局长	且比索夫（Chebisheff）先生

---

① 注：附件 1 为协议俄文版，不予翻译。

提案	议决
1.联合疏浚黑龙江上游自俄村切尔纳耶瓦至加林达之间的浅滩河段。	1.考虑到在航运季水位较低期间,浅滩处航道的深度与宽度均不足,以致在黑龙江上游航行十分困难,兹决定参照1923年10月28日所签署之协议,由俄阿穆尔水道局派遣挖泥船在黑龙江上游自俄村切尔纳耶瓦至加林达之间的浅滩河段开展联合疏浚工程;除附件三需另议外,其余附件皆随协议一同继续生效。
2.联合疏浚黑龙江上游自俄村切尔纳耶瓦至加林达之间浅滩河段的预算。	2.批准6000金卢布的预算,实际支出不得超过该预算金额。
3.付款时间。	3.华方摊款为3000金卢布,按两期支付。第一期支付1500金卢布,应于工程完成过半(约7月15日)后支付;第二期支付1500金卢布,应于工程结束并收到对账单后支付。
4.会议纪要之要求。	4.会议纪要须分别以中、俄文撰写,各一式两份,双方各执中、俄文本各一份,以昭信守。

签字	签字
中俄临时地方工程委员会俄方委员长兼驻大黑河苏俄领事 默拉美德 委员: 俄阿穆尔水道局局长 托阿诺夫 俄阿穆尔水道局副局长 且比索夫	中俄临时地方工程委员会华方委员长兼黑河道尹兼瑷珲交涉员 张寿增 委员: 瑷珲关税务司 铎博赉 黑河道尹公署代表 沈廷荣 黑龙江航务专门顾问 易保罗

翻译：王德懋　二等一级税务员

瑷珲关致海关总税务司署第 379 号呈附件 4

黑龙江上游联合疏浚协议（华方）

中俄临时地方工程委员会华方委员长兼黑河道尹兼瑷珲交涉员张寿增，华方委员瑷珲关税务司铎博赉、黑河道尹公署外交科长沈廷荣、黑龙江航务专门顾问易保罗；俄方委员长兼驻大黑河苏俄领事默拉美德，俄方委员俄阿穆尔水道局局长托阿诺夫、俄阿穆尔水道局副局长且比索夫，共同于民国十七年六月十九日（1928 年 6 月 19 日），在中俄临时地方工程委员会召开于大黑河的正式会议上发表联合声明，内容如下。

（一）鉴于黑龙江上游河道水位较浅，且各浅滩中之航路过于狭窄，易对航运造成危险，兹协定由俄阿穆尔水道局派遣挖泥船对黑龙江上游自俄村切尔纳耶瓦至加林达之间的浅滩河段开展疏浚工程，一应事宜均依照民国十二年十月二十八日（1923 年 10 月 28 日）签订的《黑龙江航路标志协议》进行，该协议中，除附件三须另议外，其余附件均随协议一并继续生效。

（二）批准用于黑龙江上游疏浚工程的 6000 金卢布预算，实际支出不得超出该预算金额。

（三）华方摊款为 3000 金卢布，按两期支付。第一期支付 1500 金卢布，应于工程完成过半（约 7 月 15 日）后支付；第二期支付 1500 金卢布，应于工程结束并收到对账单后支付。

（四）此协议计中、俄文本各两份，互相签字盖印，双方各执中、俄文本各一份，以昭信守。

中华民国十七年六月十九（1928 年 6 月 19 日）于大黑河签订。

华方：

黑河道尹兼瑷珲交涉员	张寿增
瑷珲关税务司	铎博赉
黑河道尹公署外交科长	沈廷荣
黑龙江航务专门顾问	易保罗

俄方：

驻大黑河苏俄领事 　　　　默拉美德

俄阿穆尔水道局局长 　　　　托阿诺夫

俄阿穆尔水道局副局长 　　　且比索夫

翻译：屠守鑫　四等二级帮办

瑷珲关致海关总税务司署第 379 号呈附件 5

1928 年黑龙江上游联合疏浚工事预算报表

（"阿穆尔斯卡亚（Amurskaya）5 号"挖泥船）

支出	1928 年预算 （卢布）
1. 地区职员薪俸	3946.00
2. 供暖费	1241.00
3. 清洁机器所需润滑油及废棉费用	257.00
4. 照明费	54.00
5. 信纸费、邮费及电报费	88.00
6. 航运维修费及杂费	389.00
7. 物料费	25.00
总计	6000.00

（签字）黑河道尹公署代表沈廷荣（代航务专门顾问）

（签字）俄阿穆尔水道局副局长　且比索夫

兹证明，报表正确无误。

王德懋　二等一级税务员

29. 1929 年《联合维护边界河道航路标志协议》

AIDS TO NAVIGATION ON THE AMUR, USSURI AND ARGUN
RIVERS: renewal of Agreements by Sino-Soviet Amur
Aids Commission for joint upkeep of, reporting;
copies of Russian and Chinese versions of the
Agreement, together with translations, forwarding.

436.

I. G.   Aigun   17th July, 1929.

Rosenberg

Sir,

1.   With reference to Aigun despatches Nos.
362, 363 and 364 of 1928 reporting, respectively,
the renewal of the Agreement for the upkeep of
Aids on the Amur, the continuation of the
Agreement for the maintenance of Aids on the
Ussuri, and the signing of an Agreement for the
establishment of simplified Aids on the Argun.
I now have the honour to report that on the
9th February, 1929, the Joint Amur Aids Commission
met at the Taoyin's yamen in Taheiho and renewed
the above Agreements for 1929. Long and difficult
negotiations preceded the signing of the Agreement
this year and certain details as to estimates and
specifications were only settled recently which,
with the long absence of the Technical Adviser on
inspection trips down-river, has delayed the
reporting of the matter officially.

2.   For 1929 the three 1928 Agreements,
mentioned above, for the maintenance of Aids on
the Amur, Ussuri and Argun rivers, were combined
in one document. The Soviet side wished this to
be done last year but the Taoyin had objections
                                            then

THE INSPECTOR GENERAL OF CUSTOMS,
     SHANGHAI.

then which he now waives - that since the Ussuri
concerned Kirin Province alone a separate Agreement
should be made for it. The Agreement now being
reported makes no changes in last year's projects
for Aids on the Amur and Argun but on the
Ussuri the aids are to be extended from Gulin
to the mouth of the river Sungacha which connects
Lake Hanka and the Ussuri - a distance of 84
versts.

3.   Copies of the Russian and Chinese versions
of the new Agreement are appended together with
translations into English of both documents. I
further append copies of the statements of the
work required to be done on the Amur, Ussuri
and Argun rivers for 1929, as mentioned in the
Agreement. As they are practically the same as
those of last year, with the exception of the
new Aids on the Ussuri above Gulin, a comparison
for the two years is not shown. The Agreement
as signed covers the fiscal year 1st December,
1928, to 1st December, 1929.

4.   Contrary to the friendly atmosphere
prevailing during most of the negotiations leading
up to the signing of the 1928 Agreements, the
discussions preliminary to the 1929 Agreement were
conducted in anything but an amicable spirit, an
impasse being reached on several occasions. The
principle bone of contention was the demand of
the Soviet side that payments hereafter should
be made in Dollars instead of Roubles and that
                                            the

Appendices Nos.1 to 4.

Appendices Nos.5 to 7.

the estimates should no longer be made in the latter currency. Their reason for such a request was that Soviet regulations now forbid Roubles being taken into that country and were we to continue our payments in that currency they could do nothing with the money received.

5.   As a solution of this question I suggested that the Agreements be made as heretofore but that there be a subsequent exchange of letters between the Taoyin and Soviet Consul in which the Taoyin would agree to pay $21,679.50 as the Chinese share of Aids upkeep (being the amount paid by the Chinese side for the Roubles purchased for payment to the Soviet side in 1928) for 1929. This was agreed to verbally by both sides. After the lapse of a month, however, the Consul informed us that he could not carry out such an arrangement and that if there was to be an exchange of letters he would have to stipulate the official Soviet rate of exchange or the Chinese Eastern Railway rate. In-as-much as these two rates, respectively, were $167 = Roubles 100 and $156 = Roubles 100 while the market rate of the day was $45 = Roubles 100 the Chinese Commission, naturally, could not agree to such conditions. The Chinese share of Aids expenditure last year was Roubles 35,800 which, at the various rates of exchange at which we purchased these Roubles, worked out at $21,679.50. At the official rates just quoted Roubles 35,800 at 167 would equal $60,786 and at

156 to $48,688.

6.   As an alternative the Consul proposed an Agreement leaving out all mention of work done before, an estimate not being required from the Soviet side, and no accounts to be rendered at the end of the year, it being merely stipulated where Aids should be maintained on the frontier rivers and that the Chinese share for their upkeep should be $22,000. This proposal was also not agreeable to the Chinese side which maintained that estimates and accounts should continue to be rendered in Roubles as that was the currency in which expenditure for Aids upkeep was made.

7.   At this point, early in December, 1928, the Taoyin declared himself tired of trying to meet the evasive offers of the Consul and withdrew from the negotiations requesting the Technical Adviser and myself to carry on until more reasonable proposals were made by the Soviet side. For some time we had daily interviews with the Taoyin and Consul and though many ways of settling the currency question were suggested by us it finally became evident that we were getting no nearer to a solution of the difficulty. The Taoyin thereupon ordered us to drop the negotiations.

8.   Shortly after this the Consul called on the Taoyin and after a stormy interview the former was requested to put what he wanted in writing which he did a little later. It was stated in this letter that as it was now forbidden to take Roubles

136

Roubles into Soviet Russia estimates might be
made in Roubles but payments by the Chinese
side in future would have to be in Dollars at
either the Chinese Eastern Railway rate or the
Soviet official rate of exchange. This made the
position even more difficult as the Consul now
recorded in writing what he had only stated
verbally before. As the Chinese Commission could
not alter its objections to such proposals it
was agreed that the Taoyin should reply that such
rates of exchange were not acceptable but that
we were prepared to request the Chinese Consul
at Blagoveatchensk to pay there the Rouble amounts
required during the year thus doing away with the
necessity of taking Roubles into Soviet Russia
(the Consul could pay from the routine fees he
collected in Roubles and we would reimburse him
in Dollars, at the market rate of the day, in
Taheiho). It was felt that this offer would not
be acceptable to the Soviet Consul who had his
instructions to make the Agreement in Dollars -
foreign currency is in great demand by the Soviet -
and we were not surprised when no reply was
received to this proposal.

9.   As there now appeared to be no chance of
renewing last year's Agreements on terms which we
could accept, the Technical Adviser was instructed
to begin the preparation of independent plans for
the upkeep of Aids on the Chinese side only of
the three rivers concerned. At the end of December
                                        the

the Taoyin left for Tsitsihar and Moukden and
reported to the Authorities there the negative
result of our negotiations todate, and the
preparations we were making to go ahead, under
the experienced direction of the Technical Adviser,
with the upkeep of Aids on the Chinese side of
the three frontier rivers from our own funds. The
Taoyin returned from this trip in the middle of
January and reported that he had had a long
interview with Admiral Shen Hung-lieh (沈鸿烈)
at Moukden regarding Aids matters and that the
latter had expressed his thanks for, and approval
of, the manner in which the affairs of the Aids
Commission had been conducted in the past and said
that he did not wish to interfere or advise
regarding the present negotiations as he felt he
could leave everything to the Taoyin with perfect
confidence and would approve any reasonable agreement
we were able to conclude.

10.   Returning thus with a free hand to carry
on further negotiations the Taoyin requested me to
call on the Consul and tell him that we were
prepared to reopen the discussion and to express
our willingness to an agreement from which all
mention of Roubles would be omitted though an
estimate should be drawn up showing the amount of
work to be done, omitting the cost, which was not
to be less than last year, and the amount of
$22.000 was to be fixed as the Chinese share of
the joint expenditure for 1929. The Consul was
                                        surprised

surprised to receive these conciliatory proposals
as the Soviet Commission considered that there
had been a final rupture of negotiations and
were likewise drawing up plans for maintaining
Aids on their side only of the Amur, Ussuri and
Argun. After several days of further discussion
a draft Agreement was finally drawn up by the
Technical Adviser and myself which was initialled
by the Consul and Taoyin at a final meeting when
great tact was required to keep personal feelings
from undoing all that we had accomplished. As
stated above the Agreement was formally signed on
the 9th February.

11.   It might be recorded here that had the
Soviet and Chinese sides undertaken to maintain
Aids separately, each on their own side of the
three rivers, the cost to each would have been
nearly doubled. For our part we would have had
to look for financial assistance from the
Heilungchiang and Kirin Governments to supplement our
River Dues collection. With reference to the fact
that under the new Agreement no figures are required
from the Soviet side in the way of estimated cost
of work to be done, etc., it should be explained
that it is known to ourselves that the Soviet
estimates supplied to the Chinese side in the past
have been lower than the amounts actually to be
expended. Under these circumstances we feel that
we should not quibble over the manner in which our
share was to be spent as long as the Aids were
                                              kept

kept up to their former standard of efficiency.

12.   The extension of Aids on the Ussuri from
Mulin to the point where the Sungacha river flows
into it from Lake Hanka was at the request of
the Soviet side. The estimated cost of the new
Aids is $600 of which China's share is $300 and
is included in the $22,000 of the Agreement. The
erection of Aids on this upper section of the
Ussuri will facilitate the navigation of Chinese
junks and may lead to the introduction of Chinese
steamers on that run.

13.   A statement of the Annual Accounts, a
summary of which was included with March quarter's
accounts, together with a budget for the coming
year, and a table showing distribution of the
River Dues collection between Taheiho, Aigun and
Lahasusu, has been prepared and will be forwarded
in the despatch following this.

                    I have the honour to be,
                              Sir,
                    Your obedient Servant,

                    Acting Commissioner.

                                   Appendix

Appendix No.1.   КОПИЯ.

ПРОТОКОЛ

заседания Временной Местной Советско-Китайской Технической Комиссии
состоял " 9 " дня 1929 года Гор. Сахалян.

ПРИСУТСТВОВАЛИ:

Хэйхэйский даинь и Дипломатический Чиновник в Айгуне
....Г. ЧЖИ-ГОУ-ДЖИН

Комиссар Айгунской Таможни.................Г. ТАЛБОТ

Чиновник при Управлении Итинского Даоина.....Г. ЧЖИ-БУ-ЧЖИ
/по Уссури /

Чиновник при Управлении Хэйхэского даоина.....Г. ЖИ-ТЮЙ-ЧЖИ
/по Амуру и Аргуни/

Технический Советник Айгунской Таможни.......Г. ИГНАТЬЕВ

Консул Союза Советских Социалистических
Республик в Сахаляне......................Г. МОЛЛЕД

Исполняющий обязанности Начальника Амурского Водного Управления, Инженер...........Г. ЧЕНГОВ

Секретарь Консульства Союза Советских
Социалистических Республик в Сахаляне........Г. ТАТАРИНОВ

Начальник Отдела Пути Амурского Водного
Управления, Инженер.......................Г. МОЛАЙЛОВ

СЛУШАЛИ:	ПОСТАНОВИЛИ:
1/ Вопрос о продлении на 1929 год Соглашения между Правлением Амурского Государственного Водного Транспорта и Вали 2 Китайской Республики Хэйхэского Даоина, заключенного 23 Октября 1928 года:	1/ Принимая во внимание, что временное Соглашение от 23 Октября 1928 года, продленное до 1 Декабря 1928 года потеряло силу за окончанием срока ПОСТАНОВИЛИ:
По Амуру: от поселка Покровского до Казакевичевой протоки.	а/ Продлить это соглашение еще на один год, т.е. до 1 Декабря 1929 года по Амуру: от поселка Покровского до Казакевичевой протоки;
По Уссури: от деревни Казакевичевой до устья реки Сунгачи.	По Уссури: от деревни Казакевич до устья реки Сунгачи;
По Аргуни: от поселка Покровского до деревни Олочи.	По Аргуни: от поселка Покровского до деревни Олочи.
С 1 Декабря 1928 года по 30 Ноября 1929 года.	б/ Если в течении этого года состоится постановление Советско-Китайской Конференции в части его каса...

2/ О перемычных работ по совместному обслуживанию обстановки на реках общего пользования и о расходах по этим работам.

Заявление Китайской стороны Комиссии, что ввиду падения судоходства и грузооборота на реках общего пользования, она согласна возможное уменьшение в совместных расходах по устройству и обслуживанию обстановки лишь в размере 22,000 Харбинских Китайских долларов.

3/ При заявлении Китайской стороны о совместной обстановке по реке Уссури от русской деревни Казакевичевой до города Хабаровска.

...рийми совместного пользования пограничные путями, настоящее Соглашение теряет свою силу.

2/ а/ Наименование и количество работ на реках общего пользования: Амуру, Уссури и Аргуни, с добавлением устройства новой обстановки по реке Уссури от гор. Луаня до реки Сунгачи с 1 Декабря 1928 года по 30 Ноября 1929 года, по прилагаемым при сем ведомостям работ УТВЕРДИТЬ.

б/ За все произведенные работы Китайская сторона уплачивает 22,000 Харбинских Китайских долларов каковая сумма вносится на текущий счет Советского Консульства в Сахаляне отделение Китайского банка: в Июле - 4,000 дол., в Июле - 4,000 дол., в Августе - 4,000 дол., в Сентябре - 4,000 долл. и остальные 6,000 долл. по окончании работ и приема их Китайской стороной.

в/ Так как вопрос о совместной устройстве обстановки от русской деревни Казакевичевой до города Хабаровска связан с изменением на полосатом сопротивляющихся между Китаем и Союзом Советских Социалистических Республик водных границ, рассмотрению какового вопроса не входит в компетенцию Местной Технической Комиссии, указанный вопрос оставить открытым до решения Советско-Китайской Конференции.

4/ О составлении протокола.

4/ Протокол должен быть составлен на Русском и Китайском языках по 2 экземпляра из которых по одному экземпляру русского и китайского текста получает Комиссия с Китайской стороны и по одному экземпляру Комиссия со стороны Союза Советских Социалистических Республик.

Подписали:
Председатель Временной Местной Технической Комиссии со стороны Союза Советских Социалистических Республик, Консул Союза Советских Социалистических Республик в Сахаляне /Т.И.Меламед/

/Чебышов/

Члены: /Тотаринов/

/Михайлов/

Подписали:
Председатель Комиссии с Китайской стороны, Хэйхэйский Даоинь и Дипломатический Чиновник в Айгуне /Чжан-Шоу-Дзэн/

/Талбот /

Члены: /Чжен-Бу-Чан/

/Шен-Тин-Кун/

/Игнатьев/

True copy:

S Ignatieff

Technical Adviser on
Amur Aids to Navigation.

Appendix No. 2.

Translation of the Russian version of the Protocol extending the 1923/24 Amur Aids Agreement to the joint upkeep of Aids on the Amur, Ussuri (including additional Aids from Fulin to Sungacha) and Argun for the year 1929.

P R O T O C O L.

Minutes of a Meeting of the local Provisional Sino-Soviet Technical Commission, held at Taheiho on the 9th February,1929.

Representatives:-

Heiho Taoyin and concurrently Commissioner of foreign Affairs, Aigun:	Mr. Chang Shou-tseng.
Commissioner of Customs,Aigun	Mr. Talbot.
Representative from Ilan Taoyin's Office:	Mr. Chong Fu-ch'an.
Representative from Heiho Taoyin's Office:	Mr. Shen Ting-jun.
Technical Adviser on Amur Aids	Mr. Ignatieff.
Consul of U.S.S.R. at Taehiho	Mr. Melamed.
Director of Amur Navigation Bureau	Mr. Chebisheff.
Secretary of U.S.S.R. Consulate, Taeiho	Mr. Tatarinoff.
Manager of Way Department of Amur Navigation Bureau	Mr. Mikailoff.

Subject discussed:	Decision:
1. The Agreement concluded on the 28th October, 1923, between the Amur Government water Transportation Bureau and the Heiho Taoyin of the Great Chinese Republic,	1. Taking into consideration that the provisional Agreement of the 28th October, 1923, extended to the 1st December,1928, terminated on this latter date, the

will continue to be in force for the next year 1929;

on the Amur, on the stretch from the village Pokrovka to the Kasakevich Waterway;

on the Ussuri, from the village Kasakevich to the mouth of the River Sungacha;

on the Argun, from the village Pokrovka to the village Olochi; for the term from the 1st December, 1928 to the 30th November, 1929.

2. The Statement of joint work to be done on the rivers of mutual use, and the Estimate of expenditure for this work.

The Chinese Commission place on record that in view of the reduced traffic on the rivers of mutual use, they consider that their share of expenses for the coming year should be only Harbin Dollars 22,000.00

the Commission decides;

a. To continue the Agreement for one year, to the 1st December, 1929, to apply as follows:

on the Amur, from the village of Pokrovka to the Kasakevich Waterway;

on the Ussuri, from the village of Kasakevich to the mouth of the Sungacha River;

on the Argun, from the village of Pokrovka to the village of Olochi.

b. If during the present year the Sino-Soviet Conference shall conclude a new Agreement regarding the mutual use of frontier waterways, the present Agreement ceases to be operative.

2.a.To sanction the statement, enclosed herewith, of Aids work necessary to be carried out on the rivers of mutual use, i.e., Amur, Ussuri, and Argun, including new Aids work on the Ussuri, from Hulin to Sungacha, for the term 1st December, 1928, to the 30th November, 1929.

b. The Chinese Commission will pay as its share of the work done Harbin Chinese Dollars 22,000.00, which sum will be deposited in the Bank of China at Tahesiho, to the current account of the Soviet Consulate as follows;

in

in June - $4,000; in July - $4,000; in August - $4,000; in September - $4,000; and the last $6,000 after the Aids work done during the year is inspected and approved by the Chinese Commission.

3. The proposal of the Chinese Commission for joint Aids work on the Ussuri from the village Kasakevich to Habarovsk.

3. As the question of joint Aids work on the stretch of the Ussuri from the Russian village Kasakevich to Habarovsk, if provided for in this Agreement, might prejudice the negotiations now pending for the settlement of the boundary question in that vicinity and, moreover, as the discussion of the boundary question is outside the scope of this Commission, the matter of erecting Aids on this section of the Ussuri shall be left to the decision of the Sino-Russian Conference.

4. Records to be made.

4. Records of this meeting shall be made out in the Chinese and Russian languages, in duplicate, each party retaining one copy in Chinese and one in Russian.

The President of the local Provisional Technical Commission for the Soviet side, the Consul of the U.S.S.R. at Tahsiho.
/G.I. Melamed/

Members:

/ Chebisheff/

The President of the Chinese Aids Commission, the Heiho Taoyin.
/ Cheng Shou-tseng /

Members:

/ Talbot /

/ Cheng

/ Tatarinoff /   /Cheng Fu-ch'an /

/ Mihailoff /   / Shen Ting-jun. /

                          / Ignatieff /

Translated by:

   P. Ignatieff

Technical Adviser on
River Aids to Navigation.

Appendix No. 4.

Translation of the Chinese Version of the Declaration
concerning the Joint Upkeep of Aids on the Amur, Ussuri
and Argun rivers for the year 1929.

The President of the Chinese Aids
Commission and Heiho Taoyin of the Great
Republic of China (concurrently Commissioner for
Foreign Affairs for the Aigun District), Chang
Shou-tsen, and members of the Chinese Commission:
Commissioner of Aigun Customs, E. M. Talbot, Chief
of the Diplomatic Department of the Ilan Taoyin's
Yamen, Cheng Fu-chan, Chief of the Diplomatic
Department of the Heiho Taoyin's yamen, Shen Ting-
jun, and the Technical Adviser to the Chinese Aids
Commission, P. I. Ignatieff; and the President of
the Russian Aids Commission and the Consul of the
Great United Socialistic Soviet Republic at Taheiho
Melamed, and the members of the Russian Commission:
Acting Director of the Amur Government Navigation
Bureau, Chabisheff, the Secretary of the Consulate
of the Great United Socialistic Soviet Republic at
Taheiho, Tatarinoff, and the Engineer of the Amur
Government Navigation Bureau, Mihailoff; at a
formal meeting held at Taheiho on the 9th Day of
the 2nd month of the 18th year of the Republic of
China (i.e. 1929) jointly agree to the following:

Proposal:

(1) Concerning the question of continuing the Agreement concluded
on the 28th October, 1923, between the Amur Government Navigation
Bureau and the Heiho Taoyin of the Great Chinese Republic for the
year of 1929, providing for the upkeep of Aids and erection of
beacons

beacons and signals as follows:- on the Amur from village
Pokrovka to the Kazakevich Waterway; on the Ussuri, from the
village Kazakevich to the mouth of the river Sungacha; and on
the Argun from the village Pokrovka to the village Clochi.

Decision:

(1) Taking into consideration that the Provisional Agreement of
the 28th October, 1923, which was extended to the 1st December,
1926, has expired, the Commission decides:

(a) To continue the above agreement to be in force for another
year i.e. to the 1st December, 1929; the upkeep of Aids and
erection of beacons and signals to be provided for as follows:
on the Amur, from the village of Pokrovka to the Kazakevich
Waterway; on the Ussuri, from the Kazakevich Waterway to the
mouth of the river Sungacha; and on the Argun, from the village
of Pokrovka to the village Clochi.

(b) If during this year, a new agreement be reached concerning
the mutual use of the frontier rivers by the Sino-Soviet
Conference the present local Agreement is to be cancelled.

Proposal:

(2) The statement of joint work to be done on the frontier
rivers, and the estimate of expenditure for this work. The
Chinese Commission suggested that, in view of the depressed
state of shipping and trade on the frontier rivers, the Chinese
Commission should share the expenditure for the upkeep of Aids
to the amount of Harbin Dollars 22,000 only.

Decision:

(2)

(a) To approve the statement enclosed herewith of various
works for the upkeep of Aids to be carried out on the frontier
rivers Amur, Ussuri, Argun, and including establishment of new
beacons and signals on the river Ussuri for the section

from

from Hu-Lin-Hsien to the river Sungacha, for the period
from the 1st December, 1928, to the 30th November, 1929.

(b) The Chinese Commission will pay as its share of the
above works Harbin Dollars 22,000, these moneys to be
deposited in the Bank of China at Taheiho to the credit
of the Soviet Consulate's Current Account as follows:
in June - $4,000; in July - $4,000; in August - $4,000;
in September - $4,000; and the balance, $6,000, to be paid
by the Chinese Commission after the work done during the
year has been inspected and approved by the Chinese Commission.

Proposal:

(3) The request of the Chinese Commission for joint Aids work
on the river Ussuri from the village of Kazakevich to Habarovsk.

Decision:

(3) As the upkeep of Aids and establishment of beacons on the
Ussuri river from the Russian village of Kazakevich to Habarovsk
involve the Sino-Soviet boundary relations and cannot be
discussed by the local Commission, this question is to be settled
by the Sino-Soviet Conference.

Proposal:

(4) Records to be kept of this meeting.

Decision:

(4) This declaration shall be made out in the Chinese and Russian
languages, in duplicate, each party retaining one copy in Chinese
and one copy in Russian.

Done at Taheiho on the 9th day of the second month of the
eighteenth year of the Republic of China corresponding to the
nineth day of February, in the year one thousand nine hundred
and twenty nine.

Chinese

Chinese side:

President of the Chinese Commission and
Taoyin of Heiho District (concurrently
Commissioner for Foreign Affairs, Aigun).
(signed) Chang Shou-tsen.

Vice-President of the Chinese Commission
and Commissioner of Customs, Aigun.
(signed) R. M. Talbot.

Chief of Diplomatic Department of the
Ilan Taoyin's yamen.
(signed) Cheng Fu-chan

Chief of Diplomatic Department of the
Heiho Taoyin's yamen.
(signed) Shen Ting-jun.

Technical Adviser on Amur Aids to Navigation.
(signed) P. I. Ignatieff.

Soviet Russian side:

President of the Soviet Commission and Consul
of U.S.S.R. at Taheiho.
(signed) Melamed.

Acting Director of the Amur Government
Navigation Bureau.
(signed) Chebisheff

Secretary of the Consulate of U.S.S.R. at
Taheiho.
(signed) Tatarinoff.

Engineer of the Amur Government Navigation
Bureau.
(signed) Mihailoff.

Translated by:
signature
2nd Clerk I.

Appendix No. 5.

Statement of work needed for the joint upkeep of Aids
on the frontier river Amur during 1929 from the village
Pokrovka to the Kasskevich Waterway (1,841 kilometre).

No.	Items	Number	Remarks
1.	Beacons in position on the 1st November, 1928.		
	River Type beacons: posts	1,315	
	" " shields	1,771	
	Sea " pyramids	182	
	" " shields	218	
2.	Beacons to be erected.		
	River type: posts	90	
	" " shields	110	
	Sea " pyramids	20	
	" " shields	27	
3.	Beacons to be repaired.		
	River type: posts	1,100	
	" " shields	1,414	
	Sea " pyramids	90	
	" " shields	56	
	Masts for signals	13	
4.	Repairs to rowing boats and aids equipment.		
	Number of Aids districts	5	
	Kept up by steam launches; (a) "Juney Pioneer"	1	
	(b) "Bijan"	1	
	Long boats	5	
	Yawls	5	
	Boats used for surveys	14	
	Watchers' boats	40	
	Boats "golovka"	6	
	Water Gauge stations	7	
	Traffic	1	
	Watchers'	41	
	Dwelling quarters	5	
	Stores	5	
	Summer quarters (during navigation season)	52	
	Workers' parties	5	
	Lighted Beacons	213	

Manager of ways department: (signed) Mihailoff

Technical Adviser: " Ignatieff

Certified correct:
signature
Technical Adviser on
Amur Aids to Navigation.

Appendix No. 6.

Statement of work needed for Aids upkeep (joint) during
1929 on the river Ussuri from the Russian village Kasakevich
to the town Hulin (336 versts), and for erection of new Aids
from the town Hulin to the river Sungacha (64 versts).

No.	Items	Number	Remarks
1.	Beacons in position on the 1st November,1928 on the Ussuri from Hulin to the village Kasakevich.		
	River type: posts............................	248	
	" " shields.............................	398	
	Sea " pyramids...........................	8	
	" " shields............................	9	
	Beacons to be erected.		
	River type: posts............................	17	
	" " shields............................	28	
	Sea " pyramids...........................	1	
	" " shields............................	1	
3.	Beacons to be repaired.		
	River type: posts............................	88	
	" " shields............................	133	
	Sea " pyramids...........................	2	
	" " shields............................	3	
4.	Repairs to rowing boats and aids equipment.		
	Aids are kept up by:		
	Steam launches............................	1	
	Long boats................................	1	
	Yawls.....................................	1	
	Boats used for surveys....................	1	
	" for watchers......................	1	
	Workers parties...........................	1	
	Water Gauge stations (one conditionally)	2	
5.	New Aids from Hulin to the river Sungacha.		
	River type (reduced size) posts...........	60	
	" shields............	110	

Manager of Ways Department: (signed) Mihailoff.

Technical Adviser: "   Ignatieff.

Certified correct:

P. Ignatieff

Technical Adviser on
Amur Aids to Navigation.

Appendix No. 7.

Statement of work needed for Aids upkeep (joint) during
1929 on the river Argun from the village of Pokrovka
to Olochi.

No.	Items	Number	Remarks
1.	Beacons in position on the 1st November, 1928.		
	River type: posts............................	379	
	" " shields...........................	668	
2.	Beacons to be erected.		
	River type: posts............................	186	
	" " shields...........................	337	
3.	Beacons to be repaired.		
	River type: posts............................	170	
	" " shields...........................	230	
4.	Repairs to rowing boats and aids equipment.		
	Aids are kept up by:		
	Steam launch "Sungacha"....................	1	
	Long boats.................................	1	
	Yawls......................................	1	
	Boats for surveys..........................	1	
	Watchers' boats............................	2	
	Workers' parties...........................	1	

Manager of Ways Department: (signed) Mihailoff.

Technical Adviser: "   Ignatieff.

Certified correct:

P. Ignatieff

Technical Adviser on
Amur Aids to Navigation.

呈海关总税务司署 <u>436</u> 号文　　　　　　　　　　　　　瑷珲关 1929 年 7 月 17 日

尊敬的海关总税务司（上海）：

根据 1928 年瑷珲关第 362 号呈、363 号呈和 364 呈依次汇报：

"续签《联合维护黑龙江航路标志协议》；续签《联合维护乌苏里江航路标志协议》；签订《额尔古纳河建立简易航路标志协议》。"

兹汇报，1929 年 2 月 9 日黑龙江航路标志联合委员会在大黑河道尹公署会晤，完成上述协议的续约事宜。今年前期谈判工作漫长而又艰难，具体预算和规划到近期才敲定，又因航务专门顾问巡查下游而长期缺席，该报告故此延误。

1929 年，上述 1928 年关于维护黑龙江、乌苏里江和额尔古纳河航路标志的三份协议合为一份。去年俄方欲将其合一，但道尹认为乌苏里江只与吉林省相关，应单独签订协议，今年道尹不再反对合一之事。续约协议中，黑龙江及额尔古纳河航路标志维护项目与去年无异，但是乌苏里江航路标志的维护工作自虎林延伸至松阿察河河口（连接兴凯湖与乌苏里江），距离 84 俄里。

兹附新协议的俄文版及中文版副本，以及两份文件的英文译本（附录 1 至附录 4）。另附协议所涉 1929 年黑龙江、乌苏里江、额尔古纳河应完成工作的文件副本（附录 5 至附录 7）。除虎林上游的乌苏里江需要新建航路标志以外，工作内容与去年几乎相同，因此未呈两年工作对比报告。协议自 1928 年 12 月 1 日起至 1929 年 12 月 1 日止。

1928 年前期谈判氛围相对友好，但 1929 年前期谈判数次陷入僵局，未能体现友好精神。谈判期间的争论主要在于俄方要求付款使用银圆而非卢布，也不再使用卢布制定预算，因为苏维埃政府规定禁止卢布流入，若继续使用卢布付款，俄方收到付款亦无所用。

为解决问题，本署建议按以往惯例签订协议，但之后道尹与苏维埃领事通信说明关于 1929 年联合维护航路标志共摊之经费，道尹同意支付华方之摊款 21679.50 银圆（即 1928 年华方为向俄方付款所购卢布之金额）。双方口头同意。然时隔一月，苏维埃领事告知本署此法不可行，且协议中应规定使用苏维埃官方汇率或中东铁路汇率。但因两种汇率分别为 167 银圆 =100 卢布，136 银圆 =100 卢布，而当天市场汇率为 45 银圆 =100 卢布，华方委员会自然无法同意该条件。1928 年联合维护航路标志华方之摊款为 35800 卢布，本署按市场汇率购买卢布，最终金额为 21679.50 银圆。若按 167 银圆 =100 卢布的汇率兑换，35800 卢布 =59786 银圆，若按 136 银圆 =100 卢布的汇率兑换，35800 卢布 =48688 银圆。

苏维埃领事提出另外一种解决办法，即协议中不再提及已完成之工作，只规定边界河道需要维护的航路标志地点，以及联合维护航路标志华方之摊款 22000 银圆，俄方不需要出预算，年末也不用提交账簿。华方不同意此提议，表示已使用卢布计算联合维护航路标志之支出，故亦应继续使用卢布提交预算和账簿。

1928 年 12 月初，道尹宣称不想再应付苏维埃领事的推诿，退出谈判，同时要求航务专门顾问及本署继续谈判，直至俄方提出更为合理的提议。本署与航务专门顾问曾一度日日与道尹和苏维埃领事会面，并提出诸多货币问题的解决方案，但显然都无疾而终。道尹遂命本署停止谈判。

不久苏维埃领事拜访道尹，双方激烈争辩后，道尹请苏维埃领事将其要求写入函中。苏维埃领事随后寄函说明由于俄国禁止卢布流入，可以使用卢布做出预算，但后期华方使用银圆付款，依照中东铁路汇率或苏维埃官方汇率。然而苏维埃领事写的只是之前的口头要求，形势更加艰难。华方委员会仍持反对意见，商定由道尹回复无法接受此汇率，但同意由中国驻布拉戈维申斯克领事在当地支付年需卢布金额，由此则无须卢布流入俄国（中国领事可用其日常所收卢布支付，本署将用银圆偿还，依照大黑河当天市场汇率）。苏维埃领事已下令使用银圆拟定协议，应该不会接受该提议，且俄国外币需求量很大，因此未收到回复也不足为奇。

如今看似已不可能按照我们可以接受的条件续约去年的协议，航务专门顾问已奉命开始准备三条边界河道（中国境内）的航路标志维护计划。12 月底，道尹前往齐齐哈尔及奉天，向当地政府报告谈判失败，并汇报瑷珲关下一步筹备工作，即在航务专门顾问的经验指导下，进行三条边界河道（中国境内）的航路标志维护工作，由华方支付资金。道尹于 1 月中旬返回，称其在奉天与沈鸿烈上将针对航路标志事宜进行了一次长谈。沈鸿烈上将对黑龙江航政委员会此前的外事处理方式表示感谢与支持，并表示不愿干扰当前谈判，亦不愿提出任何建议，完全相信道尹可以处理一切事宜，只要双方能够达成合理协议，其便会予以支持。

由此道尹便可全权处理后续谈判工作，遂命本署拜访苏维埃领事，提出愿意重新谈判，表示协议中可以不再使用卢布，但应拟订预算以估计预期工作量，预算中扣除成本（不会低于去年）后，确定 1929 年华方为联合维护航路标志承担之费用为 22000 银圆。苏维埃领事收悉和解提议后，很是意外，俄方委员会原以为最终谈判已经破裂，亦开始草拟黑龙江、乌苏里江以及额尔古纳河俄国侧的航路标志维护计划。数日后，航务专门顾问及本署终于草拟了一份协议，苏维埃领事及道尹在最后一次会议中同意该协议。如上所述，2 月 9 日双方正式签署协议。

若中俄双方分别维护三条河流各自境内的航路标志,双方成本几乎都要加倍。而本署则需向黑龙江及吉林政府寻求财务援助,补助本署江捐税收。根据新协议,俄方无须提供工事成本预算等。需要解释的是,本署知道俄方过去提供给华方的预算一直低于实际开支。基于此,本署认为只要航路标志工作与之前效率标准一致,不应再纠结于华方所承担费用的支付方式。

俄方要求乌苏里江上的航路标志自虎林延长至松阿察河从兴凯湖流入乌苏里江处。新建航路标志成本预算600银圆,华方摊款300银圆,包含在协议所定的22000银圆预算之中。乌苏里江上游该河段建立航路标志后,中国民船和轮船都将受益。

下呈呈送年度财务报表,包括第一季度账簿,下一年预算,以及大黑河、瑷珲关和拉哈苏苏之间的江捐税收分配图表。

您忠诚的仆人

铎博赉(R. M. Talbot)

瑷珲关署理税务司

附录 2①

1923/1924 年黑龙江航路标志协议就联合维护黑龙江、乌苏里江（包括虎林至松阿察河段新增的航路标志）以及额尔古纳河航路标志事宜延至 1929 年，此为续约协议之俄文版译本

协议

1929 年 2 月 9 日于黑河中俄临时地方工程委员会会议纪要

黑河道尹兼瑷珲关交涉员	张寿增先生
瑷珲关税务司	铎博赉先生
依兰道尹公署代表	郑步蟾先生
黑河道尹公署代表	沈廷荣先生
黑龙江航务专门顾问	易保罗（P. I. Ignatieff）先生
苏联驻大黑河领事	默拉美德（Melamed）先生
阿穆尔国家水道局局长	且比索夫（Chebisheff）先生
苏联驻大黑河领事馆文案	达达林瑙夫（Tatarinoff）先生
阿穆尔国家水道局航路部经理	米海依罗夫（Mihailoff）先生

---

① 注：附录 1 为协议俄文版，不予翻译。

提案	议决
1. 1923 年 10 月 28 日阿穆尔国家水道局董事会与中华民国黑河道尹签订之协议延续至 1929 年。 黑龙江航道：自波克罗夫卡（Pokrovka）村起至嘎杂克维池（Kasakevich）水道止； 乌苏里江航道：自嘎杂克维池村起至松阿察河河口止； 额尔古纳河航道：自波克罗夫卡村起至奥罗赤（Olochi）村止。 合约期自 1926 年 12 月 1 日起至 1929 年 11 月 30 日止。	1. 查 1923 年 10 月 28 日至 1928 年 12 月 1 日之临时协议现已满期不生效力，委员会决定： a. 上述协议续约一年至 1929 年 12 月 1 日止，适用于： 黑龙江航道：自波克罗夫卡村起至嘎杂克维池水道止； 乌苏里江航道：自嘎杂克维池村起至松阿察河河口止； 额尔古纳河航道：自波克罗夫卡村起至奥罗赤村止。 b. 倘于本年内，中俄会议对于共用边界河道事宜达成新协议，则本协议即行废止。
2. 联合维护边界河道航路标志工作声明书及开支数目。 华方委员会提议：鉴于边界河道航业不振，华方下一年摊款应为 22000.00 哈尔滨关银圆。	2. a. 批准所附联合维护边界河道航路标志工作声明书，即共用航道（黑龙江、乌苏里江和额尔古纳河）的各项航路标志工作，包括乌苏里江自虎林县至松阿察河段添设新灯桩及标杆，期限自 1928 年 12 月 1 日起至 1929 年 11 月 30 日止。 b. 华方委员会摊款 22000.00 哈尔滨关银圆，该款交由黑河中国银行存付苏联领事馆往来账内，明细如下： 6 月内付 4000 银圆；7 月内付 4000 银圆；8 月内付 4000 银圆；9 月内付 4000 银圆；其余 6000 银圆于工程告竣后由华方查验后交付。
3. 华方委员会对乌苏里江航道[嘎杂克维池村至（哈巴罗夫斯克）段]联合航路标志工作之提议。	3. 因于乌苏里江航道自俄村嘎杂克维池起至哈巴罗夫斯克段止维护及安设航路标志与中俄现有国界攸关，非地方工程委员会所能辨理，此项问题应由中俄会议解决。
4. 记录要求。	4. 此项声明书用中、俄文字拟成，缮写两份，每份内有中、俄原文各一纸由中俄双方收执各一式两份，以恪信守。

中俄临时地方工程委员会俄方委员长兼苏联驻大黑河领事 默拉美德（G. I. Melamed）	中俄临时地方工程委员会华方委员长兼黑河道尹 张寿增
委员： 且比索夫 达达林瑙夫 米海依罗夫	委员： 铎博赉 郑步蟾 沈廷荣 易保罗

翻译：易保罗

黑龙江航务专门顾问

附录 4

1929 年联合维护黑龙江、乌苏里江及额尔古纳河航道航路

标志工作声明书的中文版译本

华方委员长兼中华民国黑河道尹（兼瑷珲关交涉员）张寿增，及华方委员：瑷珲关税务司铎博赉，依兰道尹公署外交科科长郑步蟾，黑河道尹公署外交科科长沈廷荣，黑龙江航务专门顾问易保罗；俄方委员长兼苏联驻黑河领事默拉美德，及俄方委员：阿穆尔水道局代理局长且比索夫，苏联驻黑河领事馆秘书达达林瑙夫，阿穆尔国家水道局航路工程师米海依罗夫；于中华民国十八年二月九日（1929 年 2 月 9 日）在黑河召开正式会议，共同商定：

提案

（一）关于展期 1923 年 10 月 28 日阿穆尔国家水道局董事会与中华民国黑河道尹签订之协议至 1929 年之问题，联合维护航路标志及安设灯桩标杆规定如下：黑龙江航道自波克罗夫卡村起至嘎杂克维池水道止；乌苏里江航道自嘎杂克维池村起至松阿察河河口止；额尔古纳河航道自波克罗夫卡村起至奥罗赤村止。

议决

（一）查 1923 年 10 月 28 日至 1928 年 12 月 1 日之临时协议现已满期不生效力，委员会决定：

（甲）上述协议续约一年至 1929 年 12 月 1 日止；联合维护航路标志及安设灯桩标杆规定如下：黑龙江航道自波克罗夫卡村起至嘎杂克维池水道止；乌苏里江航道自嘎杂克维池村起至松阿察河河口止；额尔古纳河航道自波克罗夫卡村起至奥罗赤村止。

（乙）倘于本年内，中俄会议对于共用边界河道事宜达成新协议，则本协议即行废止。

提案：

（二）联合维护边界河道航路标志工作声明书及开支数目。华方委员会提议，鉴于边界河道航业不振、货物迟滞，关于联合维护航路标志共摊之经费，华方认为摊款应为 22000 哈尔滨关银圆。

议决

（二）（甲）批准所附联合维护边界河道航路标志工作声明书，即共用航道（黑龙江、乌苏里江和额尔古纳河）的各项航路标志工作，包括乌苏里江自虎林县至松阿察河段添设新

灯桩及标杆,期限自 1928 年 12 月 1 日起至 1929 年 11 月 30 日止。

（乙）按照上述各工程,华方摊款 22000 哈尔滨关银圆,该款交由黑河中国银行存付苏联领事馆往来账内,明细如下:

6 月内付 4000 银圆;7 月内付 4000 银圆;8 月内付 4000 银圆;9 月内付 4000 银圆;其余 6000 银圆于工程告竣后由华方查验后交付。

提案

（三）华方建议于乌苏里江航道自俄村嘎杂克维池起至哈巴罗夫斯克止安设航路标志。

议决

（三）因于乌苏里江航道自俄村嘎杂克维池起至哈巴罗夫斯克止维护及安设航路标志与中俄现有国界攸关,非地方工程委员会所能办理,此项问题应由中俄会议解决。

提案

（四）关于声明书之拟订。

议决:

（四）此项声明书用中俄文字拟成,缮写两份,每份内有中俄原文各一纸由中俄双方收执各一式两份,以恪信守。

中华民国十八年二月九日（1929 年 2 月 9 日）订于黑河。

华方

华方委员长兼黑河道尹（兼瑷珲关交涉员）

（签字）张寿增

华方副委员长兼瑷珲关税务司

（签字）铎博赉

依兰道尹公署外交科科长,

（签字）郑步蟾

黑河道尹公署外交科科长,

（签字）沈廷荣

黑龙江航务专门顾问,

（签字）易保罗

俄方

俄方委员长兼苏联驻大黑河领事，

（签字）默拉美德

阿穆尔国家水道局代理局长

（签字）且比索夫

苏联驻黑河领事馆秘书

（签字）达达林瑙夫

阿穆尔国家水道局航务工程师，

（签字）米海依罗夫

翻译：王德懋　二等一级税务员

附录5

1929 年联合维护黑龙江航道自波克罗夫卡村起至嘎杂克维池水道止（1841 千米）的
航路标志工作声明书

项目	数量	备注
1928 年 11 月 1 日标桩统计		
江式：杆状标桩	1315	
江式：盾形标桩	1771	
海式：角锥形标桩	182	
海式：盾形标桩	218	
预立标桩		
江式：杆状标桩	90	
江式：盾形标桩	110	
海式：角锥形标桩	20	
海式：盾形标桩	27	
预修标桩		
江式：杆状标桩	1100	
江式：盾形标桩	1414	
海式：角锥形标桩	90	
海式：盾形标桩	56	
标杆	13	
划艇及航路标志设备维修		
航路标志区域数量	5	
汽艇： （a）"朱尼先锋"（Juney Pioneer）号汽艇	1	
（b）"毕坚"（Bijian）号汽艇	1	
大艇	5	
船载小艇	5	
巡查艇	14	

项目	数量	备注
巡役艇	40	
"金伏加"（Goldovka）号艇	8	
水位观测站	7	
交通站	7	
巡役站	41	
宿舍	5	
仓库	5	
夏季宿舍（航运季）	32	
工人队	5	
灯桩	213	

阿穆尔国家水道局航路部经理：（签字）米海依罗夫

航务专门顾问：（签字）易保罗

兹证明，报表正确无误。

签字： 易保罗　黑龙江航务专门顾问

附录6

1929年联合维护乌苏里江航道自俄村嘎杂克维池起至虎林县止（336俄里）的航路标志工作以及自虎林县起至松阿察河止（84俄里）新建航路标志工作的声明书

项目	数量	备注
1928年11月1日标桩统计		
江式：杆状标桩	248	
江式：盾形标桩	398	
海式：角锥形标桩	8	
海式：盾形标桩	9	
预立标桩		
江式：杆状标桩	17	
江式：盾形标桩	28	
海式：角锥形标桩	1	
海式：盾形标桩	1	
预修标桩		
江式：杆状标桩	83	
江式：盾形标桩	133	
海式：角锥形标桩	2	
海式：盾形标桩	3	
划艇及航路标志设备维修		
维护航路标志之船只		
汽艇	1	
大艇	1	
船载小艇	1	
巡查艇	1	
巡役艇	1	
工人队	1	
水位观测站（其中一个受条件限制）	2	

项目	数量	备注
虎林至松阿察河段新建航路标志		
江式（小型）杆状标桩	60	
江式（小型）盾形标桩	110	

阿穆尔国家水道局航路部经理：（签字）米海依罗夫

航务专门顾问：（签字）易保罗

兹证明，报表正确无误。

易保罗　黑龙江航务专门顾问

附录 7

1929年联合维护额尔古纳河航道自波克罗夫卡村起至
奥罗赤村止的航路标志工作声明书

项目	数量	备注
1928年11月1日标桩统计		
江式：杆状标桩	379	
江式：盾形标桩	668	
预立标桩		
江式：杆状标桩	186	
江式：盾形标桩	337	
预修标桩		
江式：杆状标桩	170	
江式：盾形标桩	230	
划艇及航路标志设备维修		
维护航路标志之船只		
"松阿察"号汽艇	1	
大艇	1	
船载小艇	1	
巡查艇	1	
巡役艇	2	
工人队	1	

阿穆尔国家水道局航路部经理：(签字)米海依罗夫

航务专门顾问：(签字)易保罗

兹证明,报表正确无误。

易保罗　黑龙江航务专门顾问

此抄件发送至滨江关税务司及海务巡工司。

30. 1929 年《海港检疫章程》与《卫生章程》

QUARANTINE REGULATIONS AND EQUIPMENT AND SANITARY REGULATIONS:
Report on, and copies of Regulations concerned, as called
for by I.G. Circular No.3956, forwarding.

447.

I. G.   Registered   Aigun   18th October, 1929.

Sir,

  With reference to I. G. Circular No.
3956 :

    calling for two copies of the
    Sanitary Regulations in force
    at this port with a report,
    also in duplicate, on the
    Quarantine equipment in existance ;

  I have the honour to forward herewith copies of
the local Sanitary Regulations, one appended and
one enclosed, as furnished to me by the Chief
of Police.

  I further submit a report in duplicate,
one appended and the other as an enclosure, on
the quarantine facilities of the port. There
are no standing Quarantine Regulations but a
branch hospital of the Manchurian Plague Prevention
Service is located here under the charge of
a competent Chinese doctor who reports that it is
reasonably well equipped to cope with any
infection that may appear.

  The information now forwarded was not
sent sooner owing to the arrival of the Circular
         concerned

Appendix No.1

Enclosure No.1

Appendix No.2

Enclosure No.2.

concerned being delayed in the mails.

  I have the honour to be,

    Sir,

  Your obedient Servant,

  Acting Commissioner.

         Appendix

THE INSPECTOR GENERAL OF CUSTOMS,
  SHANGHAI.

大黑河市公安局衛生章程

污物掃除條例

第一條　本條例於城市及經地方長官指定之區村地方行之

第二條　土地房屋之所有者或占有者於其地域內負責掃除污物保持清潔之義務不屬前項之土地或房屋由管理市政機關負責掃除之

第三條　掃除之污物應集置於管理市政機關所指定之地點或容器內不准任意棄置

第四條　集置之污物由市政管理機關處分之處分之方法除依法令所定外得酌訂細則呈由監督機關核准施行(特別市所訂細則應報衛生部備案)

第五條　處分上所得之收入及應需費用由管理市政機關核實造報收入抵時得由地方稅內補充之

第六條　該管官吏為監查掃除之施行及實況得人私人之土地或房屋內查視

第七條　私人不履行掃除之義務時應由該管官吏切實勸告限期掃除屆時如仍不履行其義務得由該管官吏代為執行其費用向義務者徵收之

第八條　每年五月十五日十二月十五日各舉行大掃一次由衛生部及各有民政廳特別市縣市政府聯合各機關各團體及民眾行之

第九條　污物之種類及掃除之方法亦設備由衛生部另定之

第十條　本條例自公布日施行

True copy:

cting Commissioner.

Enclosure to Aigun despatch No.447 to I.G.

Quarantine Regulations and Equipment in Aigun.
(Report on, called for by I.G. Circular No.3956)

There are no standing Quarantine Regulations
for the port of Aigun/Taheiho.

At Taheiho there is a hospital which was
established in 1911 by the Manchurian Plague Prevention
Bureau. This is a substantial brick structure in
charge of Dr. Kwan Yen Min. He reports that the
hospital is equipped with 30 beds and in addition
there is a separate building used as an isolation
ward. There is a full equipment for disinfecting
and supplies are held in reserve for the treatment
of infectious diseases. Should it be necessary to
quarantine the port against the spread of contagion
from outside sources, Dr. Kwan reports that special
regulations will be drawn up in consultation with
the local authorities depending on the nature of the
malady to be dealt with.

It is presumed in this connection that the
functions and equipment of the above hospital are
much the same as other branches of the Manchurian
Plague Prevention Service located at Harbin, Manchouli,
Newchwang, Antung, etc.

Acting Commissioner.

CUSTOM HOUSE,
Aigun, 18th October, 1929.

呈海关总税务司署 <u>447</u> 号文　　　　　　　瑷珲关 1929 年 10 月 18 日

尊敬的海关总税务司（上海）：

　　根据海关总税务司署第 3956 号通令：

　　"要求呈送两份口岸现行《卫生章程》副本，及现有检疫设备报告，一式两份"

　　呈送由金事提供的地方《卫生章程》副本，附录及附件各一份（附录 1，附件 1）。

　　呈送口岸检疫设备报告，一式两份，附录及附件各一份（附录 2，附件 2）。口岸虽没有固定的《海港检疫章程》，但设有满洲防疫事务处分支医院，由一名很有能力的中国医生管理。医院负责人汇报称医院设备良好，能够应对可能出现的任何传染疾病。

　　通令因邮寄而延误，故该呈未能及时呈送。

您忠诚的仆人

铎博赉（R. M. Talbot）

瑷珲关署理税务司

附录 2

瑷珲关《海港检疫章程》及检疫设备

（依照海关总税务司署第 3956 号通令之要求）

瑷珲关 / 大黑河口岸无固定《海港检疫章程》。

满洲防疫局于 1911 年在大黑河设立了一家医院，用砖搭建，十分坚固。据负责人关任民医生汇报，医院配备 30 张床，有全套消毒设备及传染疾病医疗设备，还设有一处单独建筑作隔离区之用。关医生称若需将口岸与外界蔓延的传染源隔离，医院会与当地政府根据疾病类型商议起草特殊章程。

据此可知该医院之功能及设备与满洲防疫事务处在滨江关、满洲里分关（Manchouli）、牛庄关（Newchwang）、安东关等地所设分院基本相同。

铎博赉

瑷珲关署理税务司

录事：王德懋 二等一级税务员

31. 1930 年《危险物品关栈章程》

COMMRS. No. 127,443
Aigun No. 529
No.

SHANGHAI OFFICE OF THE
INSPECTORATE GENERAL OF CUSTOMS, 15th April, 1930.

SIR,

I append, for your information and guidance, copy of Kuan-wu Shu despatch No. 2,369, from which you will see that on my representations the Shu has approved temporary facilities for the bonding and shipment in bond of kerosene oil, naptha, benzine and fuel and lubricating oil, provided satisfactory arrangements can be made to insure safe storage.

You are, therefore, on receipt of this despatch to inform the Oil Companies that temporary bonding facilities have been granted to all kinds of petroleum oils.

In order to insure uniform procedure at ports, I also append copy of the regulations governing the bonding of petroleum oils which have been submitted to the Kuan-wu Shu for approval. As, however, these regulations have not yet received official sanction, they are to be regarded as purely provisional until receipt of further instructions.

I am,

Sir,

Your obedient Servant,

Commissioner of Customs,

AIGUN.

Inspector General.

Appendix.

APPENDIX. NO. A

財政部關務署指令第二五六九號

令總稅務司梅樂和

呈一件請准將火油一項撥入關棧辦法辦理由

呈悉據稱火油一項應於春汛戲洪蔣翰運在頒布危

險物品關棧章程以前實有准火油存棧之必要所請將

火油一項暫按關棧辦法辦理一節自可照行惟火油為

危險物品之一堆存貨棧應由該總稅務司妥籌安全

地點及辦法以備不虞仰即查明酌核辦理奧報此令

中華民國十九年四月五日

APPENDIX NO. 2

BONDING REGULATIONS

II - PETROLEUM OILS (Kerosene, Gasolene, Naptha, Benzine, Fuel and Lubricating).

Oil tanks at Open Ports may be established only on sites approved by the Chinese local territorial Authorities.

Tanks established with the approval and consent of the local authorities will, on application to the Customs, be licensed as bonded warehouses for Oil in bulk. Such bonding licences shall be renewable annually, and the Customs shall levy fees both for the licence and for superintendence of such bonded tanks.

Bonded warehouses for the storage of Oil in containers may also be established on sites approved by the Chinese local territorial Authorities.

The materials necessary for the making of tins, drums, barrels, cases and other approved containers may be imported in bond into warehouses bonded for Oil in containers, and the manufacture of such containers from these materials shall be permitted in these bonded warehouses under Customs supervision.

Bonded Oil in bulk may, under Customs supervision, be filled into containers manufactured in bond or entered in bond from abroad, which may then on special application be transferred to and stored in a bonded warehouse for Oil in containers pending local importation or shipment to another Open Port or abroad. Oil filled into such containers while in bond shall, on importation, pay duty as Oil in tins, cases, drums, etc., depending upon the type of container.

б. Bonded

Bonded Oil in bulk may, under Customs supervision, be filled into containers which have previously paid duty and have been returned empty to the bonded filling plant. Such oil may then, on special application, be transferred to, and stored in, a bonded warehouse for oil in containers pending local importation or shipment to another Open Port or abroad. Oil filled into duty-paid containers while in bond shall, on importation, pay duty as bulk oil.

Duty-paid containers returned to be re-filled with bonded bulk oil must be separately declared to, and examined by, the Customs before entering the bonded filling plant; and must, both before and after re-filling, be stored separately from non-duty-paid containers.

The filling and storage of oil in bond will not be permitted unless the Proprietors have a complete and detailed stock-accounting system; and failure to maintain such a system will entail cancellation of bonding privileges. The Customs Officer supervising tanks, filling plants and warehouses shall have access at all times to all records and inventories of stock kept by the Proprietors.

Oil removed from bond, whether in bulk or in containers, if going into local consumption, is to pay Import duty before removal from the Proprietor's premises. If going to another Open Port, it may either pay duty and be shipped under Exemption Certificate, or be shipped in bond. If shipped in bond to another Open Port, it may, on arrival, either pay duty or be re-entered in bond (if bonding

facilities

facilities exist) for the remainder of the twelve
months' period from date of original entry into bond
from abroad. If shipped abroad or to Dairen, such
oil shall be free of duty.

The manufacture and filling of containers in bond
shall be permitted only during Customs examination hours.
No work shall be permitted on Customs Holidays and
Sundays.

A special form of Bond will be required to cover
the manufacture and filling of oil containers in bond.

SCALE OF FEES TO BE CHARGED FOR BONDED WAREHOUSES
AND OIL TANKS.

	Hk. Tls.
Licence for bonded Oil Tank, Filling Plant, and/or Warehouse for Oil in containers:	250.00
Annual renewal of such licence:	50.00
Supervision Fee for bonded Oil Tank, per mensem:	100.00
Supervision Fee for bonded Warehouse for oil in containers, per mensem:	100.00

      N.B. The above Supervision Fees shall
not be leviable if the
proprietors provide furnished
quarters for the supervising
Customs Officer - or Officers
and pay to the Customs a
monthly sum of Hk. Tls. 300.00
in respect of each officer
required.

Supervision Fee for combined Bonded Oil Tanks, Filling Plant and Warehouses, requiring full-time services of Customs Officer; per mensem for each officer required (Furnished quarters for officer - or Officers - to be provided).	300.00

致瑷珲关第 <u>529/127443</u> 号令　　　　海关总税务司署（上海），1930 年 4 月 15 日

尊敬的瑷珲关税务司：

　　为了便于贵署顺利执行，兹附关务署第 2369 号令副本，以供参考。据该令所示，关务署已同意建立石油、轻石油、轻汽油、燃油以及润滑油的临时关栈（保税仓库），确保安全储存。

　　因此，贵署收悉此令后，应告知石油公司，已批准建立存放各类石油的临时关栈。

　　为确保各口岸程序统一，现附《危险物品关栈章程》，已呈关务署，申请批准。然而，章程尚未获得正式批准，在得到进一步指示之前，仅作临时条款使用。

您忠诚的仆人

梅乐和（F. W. Maze）

总务科税务司

附录 2

危险物品关栈章程

II. 石油（煤油、汽油、轻石油、轻汽油、燃油以及润滑油）

1. 通商口岸的油罐设立场所须经中国地方当局批准。

2. 经地方当局批准设立的油罐，向海关申请，经许可可以作为保存散装油的货仓。保税执照须每年更换，以对此类保税油罐进行监管。

3. 建立保税货仓，储存装油的集装箱，也须经过中国地方当局批准。

4. 允许进口制造罐、桶、筒、箱以及其他获得许可的容器所需的材料，其可运送到保税货仓；应在海关的监督下，经许可，于保税货仓中使用上述材料制造此类容器。

5. 在海关监督下，保税散装油可灌装到在保税仓内制造的容器中，或从国外进口的保税容器中；此类灌装油，可储存在保税货仓里，等待决定用于本地进口或运到其他通商口岸，也可出口。散装油灌装到这些容器中，若要进口，须按罐、桶、筒、箱装油缴税，税款取决于容器的种类。

6. 在海关监督下，保税散装油可在保税灌装厂灌装进已完税的空容器中。此类灌装油可以储存在保税货仓里，等待决定用于本地进口或运到其他通商口岸，也可出口。灌装到完税容器的油，若进口，则按散装油缴税。

7. 准备重新灌装散装油的已完税容器在进入保税灌装厂之前须与油分开向海关申报，并经过海关检验；并且在重新灌装前后，都要与未完税容器分别存放。

8. 保税货仓中油的灌装与储存，必须由货物所有人提供一个完整详细的存货账目，否则不予批准；若货物所有人无法维系此账目，则取消其资格。

9. 油从保税货仓中运出，无论散装或罐装，若在本地市场消费，则从业主的经营场所运出之前，须缴纳进口税。若运到另一通商口岸，可缴纳税款，凭免税执照进行船运，也可保税进行船运。若保税进行船运至另一通商口岸，在抵达时可缴纳税款，或重新保税进入（若有关栈），期限为从国外首次保税进入起 12 个月。若通过船运复出口或运至大连关，可免税。

10. 在保税货仓里制造容器和进行灌装只能在海关监督下内进行。海关假期及周日不可开工。

11. 制造装油容器与灌装容器须提供保税专用报单。

保税货仓与油罐
收费标准

	（海关两）
许可使用保税油罐、装灌厂与／或装油的集装箱货仓的费用	250.00
此许可年度续期费用	50.00
监管保税油罐费用（每月）	100.00
监管保税货仓中的装油集装箱费用（每月）	100.00
注意：若货物所有人为监管的海关关员提供有家具的住所，并每月付给海关关员每人 300 海关两的费用，则上述监管费可免交。	
保税油罐、灌装厂及保税货仓监管费中包含海关关员全天服务；每月每名关员所需监管费 （提供有家具的住所）	300.00

32. 1930—1931 年《联合维护黑龙江、乌苏里江及额尔古纳河航路标志协议》

504

AIDS TO NAVIGATION ON THE AMUR, USSURI, & ARGUN
RIVERS: renewal of Agreement by Sino-Soviet Amur Aids
Commission for joint upkeep of, reporting; copies of
Russian and Chinese versions of Agreement, together
with translation of latter, forwarding.

I.G.

A I G U N   3rd September 1930.

504
IG

Sir,

1.   With reference to Aigun despatch No. 436 :
Reporting the renewal for 1929 by the Sino-
Soviet Amur Aids Commission of the Amur,
Ussuri and Argun Agreements for the
maintenance of Aids on those rivers, the
three Agreements being for the first time
combined into one document :

I have the honour to report that, on the 16th August
1930, the Joint Aids Commission met at the Taoyin's
Office in Taheiho and renewed the Agreement for the
maintenance of Aids on the Amur, Ussuri, and Argun
rivers for the years 1930 and 1931.

2.   Copies of the Russian and Chinese versions of
the new Agreement are appended, together with an
English translation of the latter.   It is to be noted
that whereas former Agreements have covered a fiscal
year beginning on 1st December, this one commences on
1st January 1930 (not 1st December, 1929).

3.   From the bare statement that the Joint Aids
Commission met and renewed the Agreement it must not
be inferred that no difficulties were encountered.
That formal meeting was merely the culminating one of
very many others which had dragged their weary length
to several hours each and at which the manifested
wishes

The Inspector General of Customs,

S H A N G H A I .

wishes of both sides were so divergent as to appear
utterly irreconcilable.   The Taoyin had taken no
pains to avoid letting it be known that he was
anxious to renew the Agreement and would not engage
on any other mutual enterprises till that was settled;
the Russians naturally seized on such a declaration as
a suitable lever wherewith to extract extremely onerous
terms, stating that there were no other mutual
enterprises that interested them to such an extent as
to cause them to change their terms.   However, both
sides eventually made concessions up to a point where
common ground was reached, though Russia was beaten
down much more than China advanced owing to the
invaluable services of the Technical Adviser, Mr. P. I.
Ignatieff, who fought a stern battle with his
countrymen and, as usual, saved China an amount of
money that may conservatively be estimated at many
thousands of dollars.

(4)   It will be seen that China's annual
contribution has been raised from H.$22,000 per annum
to H.$34,200 per annum, that she is to pay an
additional H.$4,000 per annum for dredging operations,
a single payment of H.$1,500 towards the dredging of
1928, and a single payment of H.$7,000 for the
restoring to normality of lights and beacons on the
three frontier rivers.

The annual item of H.$34,200 represents a
55.5% increase on the H.$22,000 of last year, local
dollars having fallen by 57% from H.$1.40 = ¥1.00 in
February 1929 (when the 1929 Agreement was signed) to
H.$2.20 = ¥1.00 in August 1930 (when the 1930
conversations took place).   The equivalent 1931 figure
will

will depend on future fluctuation in exchange, but
will be based on H.\$34,200 @ H.\$2.20 = ¥1.00.

The single payment of H.\$1,500 for dredging
in 1928 is due to Russia in accordance with a
special Joint Amur Aids Commission's Agreement (vide
Aigun despatch No.452, Enclosure No.2, §22) in which,
however, no definite sum was fixed.

The single payment of H.\$7,000 is nominally
for restoring to normality the lights and beacons on
the three frontier rivers (some of which aids are
known to have been purposely destroyed by China at
the time of last year's conflict). It is recognised
verbally that this sum is more than necessary for its
defined purpose. The explanation of the figure is
that China last year only paid H.\$4,000 out of her
annual contribution of H.\$22,000, Russia having seized
her steamers and closed the frontier rivers, her
source of River Dues income, in July 1929, i.e., before
the middle of the navigation season. Russia claimed
the difference but China refused officially to
recognise her liability: it was, however, agreed to
raise to an extravagant figure the amount payable for
the reparation of the destroyed beacons, thereby
enabling last year's account to be considered closed.

(5) It is recognised that the River Dues Account
will be by no means able to meet all these, and
other, obligations and the Mayor has, I understand, been
promised the required help by the Provincial Authorities

I have the honour to be, Sir,

Your obedient Servant,

(H. G. Fletcher)   APPENDIX N°1.

КОПИЯ.

ПРОТОКОЛ

Заседания Временной Местной Советско-Китайской Технической Комиссии Августа " I " дня 1930 года, город Сахалян.

ПРИСУТСТВОВАЛИ:

Председатель Подготовительного Комитета Айгунского Муниципального Управления	Г. ЧЖАН-ШОУ-ДЗЫН.
Комиссар Айгунской Таможни	Г. ФЛЕТЧЕР.
Технический Советник Айгунской Таможни	Г. ИГНАТЬЕВ.
Консул Союза Советских Социалистических Республик в Сахаляне	Г. КОНЕЕВ.
Управляющий Амурским Государственным Речным Флотом	Г. МЕТКИШЦА.
Секретарь Консульства С.С.С.Р. в Сахаляне	Г. КОССОВ.

СЛУШАЛИ:	ПОСТАНОВИЛИ:
I. Вопрос о продлении на 1930 и 1931 год Временного Соглашения между Амурским Государственным Речным Транспортом и Великой Китайской Республики Хэйхэским Даоинем, заключенного 28-го Октября 1923 года, о совместном обслуживании фарватера по Амуру: от поселки Покровского до Казакевичевой протоки, по Уссури: от деревни Казакевичевой до устья реки Сунгача,	I. Принимая во внимание, что Временное Соглашение от 28 октября 1923 года, продленное до I декабря 1929 года потеряло силу с удовлетворением взаимных обязательств и за окончанием срок. ПОСТАНОВИЛИ: а/ Продлить это соглашение еще на два года, т.е. с I-го Января 1930 года по I января 1932 года." б/ Если в течение этих двух лет состоятся постановление Советско-Китайской Конференции

по Аргуни: от поселки Покровсто[го]
до деревни Олочи.-

2.0 ведомостях работ по совместному обслуживанию обстановки на реках общего пользования и о расходах по этим работам.
Заявление Китайской стороны что хотя предоставленных ведомостей А.Г.Р.Ф. расходы по пограничным рекам в навигацию 1930 года и выразятся в 300000 рублей, но ввиду падения Китайского судоходства и грузооборота на реках общего пользования, и принимая во внимание удорожание жизни и материалов против 1929 года, она считает возможным участвовать в совместных расходах по устройству и обслуживанию обстановки в размере 34200 Харб. Кит. Долларов ежегодно.-
На поддержание в порядке двухсторонней обстановке по пограничным рекам: Амуру, Уссури и Аргуни Китайская сторона единовременно уплачивает 7000 Харб. Китайских долларов.-

Конференции в части касающейся совместного пользования и обслуживании указанных в п. I-м водных линий, настоящее соглашение теряет свою силу.
2. а/ Наименование и количество работ на реках общего пользования: Амуру, Уссури и Аргуни, с добавлением устройства новой обстановки по реке Уссури от гор. Хулина до реки Сунгача с 1-го Января 1930 года по 1-января 1932 года по прилагаемым при сем ведомостей работ утвердить.
б/ За все произведенные работы Китайская сторона уплачивает ежегодно по 34200 Харбинских Китайских долларов, и единовременно 7000 Харб. Кит. долларов, каковая сумма вносится на текущий счет Советского Консульства в г. Сахаляне один из Китайских банков или уплачивается Консулу СССР в г. Сахаляне: 1930 60% суммы в Августе: 25% в октябре, и 25% по окончании работ и приемке их Китайской

3. О выплате Китайской стороной за землечерпательные работы 1928 года в размере 3000 рублей, согласно протокола Комиссии от 19-го июня 1928 года.-
4. Вопрос о землечерпательных работах на реках общего пользования заявление Китайской стороны, что ввиду падения судоходства и грузооборота она находит возможным участвовать ежегодно в совместных расходах по землечерпанию на пограничных реках лишь в размере 4000 Харб. Кит. долл.

Китайской стороной. В 1931 году: 20% в Июне, 20% в Июле, 20% в Августе, 20% в Сентябре и 20% по окончании работ и приемке их Китайской стороной. В виду возможных колебаний Харбинского Китайского доллар[а] уплата причитающихся сумм за работы 1931 года должна исчисляться в твердой валюте /ИЕНЫ/ и уплачиваться в Харбинских Китайских долларах по Харбинскому курсу дня платежа, при чем основной курс фиксируется на день подписания протокола в 2.20 доллара за Японскую Иену.-
3. За землечерпательные работы 1928 года Китайская сторона уплачивается 1500 Харб. Кит. долларов после подписания договора.-
4. Принимая во внимание наблюдающиеся иногда затруднения при плавании на пограничных реках вследствии недостаточной глубины и лишним хода на перекатах, в малкую воду, произвести совместные землечерпательные работы, с тем, что Китайская сторона участвует только

только в 4000 Харб. Кит. дол.
ежегодно, каковые уплачивается в два срока: 2000 долл.
в июле и 2000 долл. по
окончанию работ и приемке
их Китайской стороной.-

5. Об обслуживании обстановки и производстве работ по диоуглуб-
лению и диоочищению.

5. Для устройства и обслужива-
ния обстановки, а также
производства работ по дио-
углублению и диоочищению
Китайская сторона выдает
пропуски и оказывает необходимое содействие, личному
персоналу этим работами на
Китайской стороне. Советская
сторона выдает пропуски,
принимающим работы лицам
оказывает им необходимое
содействие, для осмотра
произведенных работ.-

6. Об устаревших пунктах соглашения 1923 года.

6. Устаревшие свое значение §§
3, 4, 5, и 6 части 2-ой и § 9
части 3-ей временного
соглашения 1923 года. Комиссия
постановляет считать недей-
ствующими.-

7. О составлении протокола.

7. Протокол должен быть
составлен на Русском и
Китайском языках по два
экземпляра

экземпляра из которых по одному
экземпляру Русского и Китайского
текста получает Комиссия с
Китайской стороны и по одному
экземпляру Комиссия со стороны
Союза Советских Социалистических
Республик.

Председатель Комиссии Китайской
стороны, Председатель Подгото-
вительного Комитета Лэйхэского
Муниципального Управления
/подписал/ Г. ЧЖАН ЛОУ ДЗН.

Комиссар Айгунской
Таможни
/подписал/ Г. ФЛЕТЧЕР.

Члены:
Технический Советник
Айгунской Таможни
/подписал/ Г. ИГНАТЬЕВ.

Председатель со стороны Союза
Советских Социалистических
Республик Консул СССР в г.
Сахаляне
/подписал/ Г. КОНКЕВ.

Управляющий Амурским Госу-
дарственным Речным Флотом
/подписал/ Г. МЕТЕЛИЦА.

Члены:
Секретарь Консульства
СССР в г. Сахаляне
/подписал/ Г. КОССОВ.

True Copy:

1st Clerk B.

照錄會議協訂書

茲於中華民國十九年即西歷一千九百三十年八月十六日在大黑河地方臨時中俄工程委員會正式會議共計提議案七條及商定確定條款七條分晰開列於下商議列席者列下

華方委員長大中華民國黑河市政籌備處處長兼愛琿交涉員張壽增

華方委員愛琿關稅務司富樂嘉

華方委員航路工程顧問易保羅

(三)俄方委員長大蘇聯駐黑河領事瀾爾轟耶夫

(二)俄方委員阿穆爾國家水道航路局局長米切利次

(三)俄方委員駐黑河領事館秘書瀾索夫

提議案七條列下

(一)關於一千九百二十三年十月二十八日由黑河道尹及阿穆爾國家水道局所訂

協議仍延長二年有效即中華民國十九年及中華民國二十年即一千九百三十年及一千九百三十一年維持公共水道工程至於地點在阿穆爾即黑龍江由巴各羅夫四克屯至喀雜克維持江於起點止在烏蘇里江內由喀雜克維持起起至烏蘇里江源松格察止在顱爾古納河內由巴各羅夫四克屯至阿羅陳七止

(二)討論國際河流內公共燈罩標杆各項工程計劃書及討論以上工程欵項華方聲明雖照據俄方國家航務局擱關於一千九百三十年國際河流工程計劃書欵項應需用在三十萬盧布之數然而因在公共國際河流內中國航業蕭條並因比較一千九百二十九年人工料件均加昂貴所以華方認為公共化貴按照雙方商定工程計劃書關於工程水道一切技術每年出給哈大洋三萬四千二百元關於修復公共河流如阿穆爾烏蘇里額爾古納河兩岸燈罩標杆華方出給一次貴哈大洋七千元

(三)討論按照一千九百二十八年六月十九日所定議案華方應給一千九百二十八年挖

江費三千盧布

（四）討論公共河流內挖江工程擴華方聲明現因航業蕭條中國方面每年出給
公共化錨挖江費支給哈大洋四千元

（五）討論挖江及打江石之辦法

（六）討論一千九百二十三年協訂內不適用之各條

（七）訂立會議協訂書

商定確定條款之條列下

（一）關於一千九百二十三年十月二十八日所訂之臨時協議至一千九百二十九年十二月一日失去效力並對於雙方義務業已實行盡到已經期滿現在商定

（甲）對於以上協議再延長限兩年即由民國十九年即一千九百三十年一月一號至民國二十一年即一千九百三十二年一月一號止

（乙）如在此兩年內中俄會議對於以上所載公共河流所指地方關於公共航行各

（二）（甲）所有阿檬爾烏蘇里及額爾古納河並添烏蘇里江內由虎林至松怡察由民國十九年即西歷一千九百三十年一月一號至民國二十一年即西歷一千九百三十二年一月一號止以上公共河流工程名目及數目均載明隨附該會議協訂書之工程計劃書該書內之工程均由雙方簽定

（乙）對於以上工程中國方面每年出給哈大洋三萬四千二百元並給一次費哈大洋七千元以上款項由指定銀行交給駐黑河俄領事館賑上或逕交給駐黑河領事民國十九年即一千九百三十年在八月內交給百分之五十在十月內交給百分之二十五下餘百分之二十五在工程完竣由中國方面接收工程全行付給至於民國二十年即一千九百三十一年應給之款在六月內給二十分之七月內給二十分八月內給二十分九月內給二十分下餘二十分在工程完竣由中國方面接收工程時全行支給因中國大洋行情長落不定關於

（三）如有規定辦法該臨時協議即當失其效力
事如有規定辦法該臨時協議即當失其效力

民國二十年即一千九百三十一年應給之款按照金票寶在行情核算並以簽字日支

付款項仍給中國哈大洋按照給款日之哈爾濱金票行情核算並且以簽字日

之金票行情之數為根據標準簽字日金票與哈大洋行情係哈大洋兩元

二角核金票一元

（三）在該會議協訂書簽字以後關於一千九百二十八年挖江費中國方面支給

哈大洋一千五百元

（四）因公共河流有時河底深或寬不足應用有碍航行因此對於公共工程挖江費

中國方面每年有攤給哈大洋四千元該款分兩期支給其第一期哈大洋二千

元在乂月內支給其餘二千元在工程完竣南中國方面接收工程時支給

（五）因燈罩標杆或因挖江及打石頭該項工程人員應遇華岸時中國方面應

給必須之帮助以為放行因察縣工程時之人員應遇俄岸時俄國方面應給

必須之帮助以為放行

（六）關於二十九百二十三年協議內第二條內第三款第四款第五款第六款及第

三條內第九款以上各款因不適用作為無效

（七）該會議協訂書應繕華俄文各兩份簽字後雙方各執華俄文各一份以

昭信守

華方委員長黑河市政籌備處處長兼愛琿交涉員張壽增

華方委員愛琿關稅務司富樂嘉

華方委員航路工程顧問易保羅

俄方委員長大蘇群駐黑河領事潤爾耳耶夫

俄方委員阿穆爾國家水通航路局長采卻利次

俄方委員駐黑河領事館秘書潤索夫

大中華民國十九年八月十六日　訂於大黑河

西歷一千九百三十年八月十六日

True copy:

Acting Commissioner.

APPENDIX NO. 3

Translation of the Agreement extending the 1923/4 Amur Aids Agreement to the joint upkeep of Aids on the Amur, Ussuri (including additional Aids from Hulin to Sungacha) and Argun for the years 1930 - 1931.

On the sixteenth day of August in the year nineteen hundred and thirty at Taheiho, China, at the meeting of the Sino-Soviet Local Provisional Technical Aids Commission THIS AGREEMENT was made between :

The Chinese Aids Commission consisting of :

Heiho Provisional Mayor and Delegate of
    Foreign Affairs and concurrently the
    President of the Chinese Commission:
                Mr. Chang Shou-tseng,

Commissioner of Customs, Aigun:
                Mr. H. G. Fletcher,

Technical Adviser on Amur Aids
    to Navigation: Mr. P. I. Ignatieff, and

The Russian Aids Commission consisting of :

Consul of U.S.S.R., Taheiho and
    concurrently the President of the
    Russian Commission: Mr. N. V. Kornieff,

Director of the Soviet Government Water
    Transport Bureau of Amur:Mr. A. J. Metelitza.

Secretary of the U.S.S.R.Consulate,
    Taheiho: Mr. V. A. Kossoff.

This Agreement contains the discussion of seven subjects together with the resolutions therefor.

(1) SUBJECT:

(1) SUBJECT: To extend for a further period of two years, for the years 1930 - 1931, the Agreement concluded on the 28th October 1923 between the Heiho Taoyin and the Soviet Government Water Transport Bureau of Amur for the joint upkeep of the Aids to Navigation on the frontier Rivers: on the Amur, from the villiage Pokrovka to the Kasakevich Waterway; on the Ussuri, from the villiage Kasakevich to the mouth of the River Sungacha; and on the Argun, from the villiage Pokrovka to the villiage Olochi.

RESOLUTION: Whereas the Agreement of the 28th October 1923 ceased to be operative as from the 1st December 1929, both contracting parties having fulfilled their respective obligations and the said Agreement having thus expired, it is now decided that :

(a) The said Agreement be extended for a further period of two years, from the 1st January 1930 to the 1st January 1932;

(b) In the event that within the period of two years, there be any definite instrument negotiated and proclaimed by the Sino-Soviet Conference with respect to Aids to Navigation, etc. within the prescribed limits on the frontier Rivers as above set forth, the said Agreement shall be then considered null and void.

(2) SUBJECT: With regard to the joint work, such as the installation of lights and beacons, etc., on the frontier Rivers and the cost thereof, the Chinese Commission declares that despite the statement of the Russian Government Navigation Office that the cost of the works to be done this year on the frontier Rivers would be some Rs.300,000, yet, taking into consideration the desolated state of China's navigation, whilst

whilst allowing for the high cost of labour and
materials, the Chinese Commission considers that the
cost of joint aids should be on the lines of a
specification to which both contracting parties express
mutual consent, and that it is prepared to contribute
for the upkeep of joint aids a yearly sum of
H.$34,200.   As for the repairs to the lights and
beacons on the frontier Rivers, China will make a
single payment of H.$7,000 only.

RESOLUTION: (a) The items and number of aids work on
the frontier Rivers and, in addition, on that part of
the Ussuri from Hulin to Sungacha, for the period
from the 1st January 1930 to the 1st January 1932 are
clearly stated on the appended specification which has
been generally agreed to by both contracting parties.
(b) For the above work China shall contribute a yearly
sum of H.$34,200 and a single payment of H.$7,000 to
be paid by instalment either by a specified Chinese
Bank to the Accounts of the Consul of U. S. S. R.,
Taheiho, or direct to the Consul himself thus :

For the 1930 payments :

    50 %   in   August,

    25 %   in   October, and

    25% on the completion, and taking over by
the Chinese Commission, of the Aids work;

For the 1931 payments :

    20 %   in   June,

    20 %   in   July,

    20 %   in   August,

    20 %   in   September, and

    20% on the completion, and taking over by
the Chinese Commission, of the Aids work.

                                       In

        In view of the possible fluctuation of the
Harbin Dollar, the 1931 payments shall be made in
Harbin dollars at the rate of the Harbin Dollar - Yen
exchange of the day taking the Harbin Dollar - Yen
exchange rate of the day of the signing of this
Agreement as the basis for comparison: the rate of
the day of the signing of this Agreement being
H.$2.20 = ¥1.00.

(3) SUBJECT: According to the terms of the Agreement of
the 19th June 1928, China has to pay towards dredging
work during 1928 a sum of Rs.3,000.

RESOLUTION: China shall pay, after the signing of this
Agreement, H.$1,500 for the dredging work done during
1928.

(4) SUBJECT: With regard to the dredging of the frontier
Rivers, the Chinese Commission declares that, in view
of the desolated state of China's navigation, China
will pay as its share in the expenses of dredging
work a yearly sum of H.$4,000.

RESOLUTION: Whereas the frontier Rivers are at times
not sufficiently deep and wide, making it difficult
for navigation, China shall share towards dredging work
a yearly sum of H.$4,000 to be paid by two
instalments :

First instalment: a sum of H.$2,000 in July, and
Second   "   : another H.$2,000 on the completion,
and taking over by the Chinese Commission, of the work.

(5) SUBJECT: Work of dredging and of breaking up rocks
with the purpose of deepening or widening the channel.

RESOLUTION: Those engaged in the Aids or dredging work,
etc. shall be afforded necessary assistance and given
passports by the Chinese Authorities when they come

                                       across

across to the Chinese side; similarly, those who come across to the Russian side on Inspection tours shall be afforded necessary assistance and given passports by the Russian Authorities.

(6) SUBJECT: The obsolete articles contained in the 1923 Agreement.

RESOLUTION: The sections (c), (d), (e) and (f) of Article II, and the section (i) of Article III, being now obsolete, shall be considered void.

(7) SUBJECT: Concluding this Agreement.

RESOLUTION: This Agreement shall be made in duplicate both in Chinese and Russian, each contracting party to keep a copy of each.

(Signed) Chang Shou-tseng

Heiho Provisional Mayor and Delegate of Foreign Affairs and concurrently the President of the Chinese Commission.

(Signed) H. G. Fletcher

Commissioner of Customs, Aigun.

(Signed) P. I. Ignatieff

Technical Adviser on Amur Aids to Navigation.

(Signed) N. V. Korneieff

Consul of U.S.S.R., Taheiho and concurrently the President of the Russian Commission.

(Signed) A. J. Metelitza

Director of the Soviet Government Water Transport Bureau of Amur.

(Signed) V. A. Kossoff

Secretary of the U. S. S. R. Consulate, Taheiho.

Taheiho, China, 16th August 1930.

Translated by:

3rd Clerk B.

呈海关总税务司署 <u>504</u> 号文　　　　　　　　　瑷珲关 1930 年 9 月 3 日

尊敬的海关总税务司：

　　1. 根据瑷珲关第 436 号呈：

　　　　"汇报中俄黑龙江航政委员会于 1929 年就维护边界河道航路标志一事续签《黑龙江航路标志协议》《乌苏里江航路标志协议》以及《额尔古纳河航路标志协议》，此乃首次将三份协议合为一份。"

　　兹汇报，中俄黑龙江水道委员会于 1930 年 8 月 16 日在大黑河道尹公署会面，并就于 1930 年及 1931 年联合维护黑龙江、乌苏里江及额尔古纳河航路标志一事续签协议。

　　2. 兹附华方及俄方续约协议抄件，以及华方续约协议之英文译本。但是需注意的是，此前所签协议之财政年度的起始日期为 12 月 1 日，但该续约协议之财政年度的起始日期为 1930 年 1 月 1 日（而非 1929 年 12 月 1 日）。

　　3. 虽然联合航政委员会经谈判后已续签协议，但谈判期间之困难亦无法估量。谈判中的每次会议皆耗时耗力，而最后一次的正式会议亦是如此。会议中，双方明示之意愿出现了严重的分歧，甚至一度无法调和。道尹于会议中一直未掩饰其迫切希望续签该协议之想法，且表示在协议签订之前不会与俄方共谋任何其他事项；而俄方则以道尹此言论为威胁之筹码，设法让华方答应其繁苛之条款，并声称除修改条款外，他们无意与华方共谋任何其他事项。然而，双方最终皆做出了让步，达成共识，且因航务专门顾问易保罗（P. I. Ignatieff）先生与俄方谈判之时，态度坚决，为谈判之事立下汗马功劳，以致俄方最终让步之尺度远大于华方，并一如往昔，为华方节省至少上万银圆之费用。

　　4. 如协议所示，华方年度摊款已从之前的哈大洋 22000 元增至哈大洋 34200 元，除此之外，每年亦须额外支付哈大洋 4000 元用于疏浚工事，支付哈大洋 1500 元用于 1928 年疏浚工事，一次性支付哈大洋 7000 元用于修复三条边界河道灯罩标杆之费用。

　　与上年相比，华方年度摊款从哈大洋 22000 元增至哈大洋 34200 元，涨幅高达 55.5%；1929 年 2 月（1929 年协议签订之时）哈大洋与金票之汇率为哈大洋 1.40 元核金票 1 元，而 1930 年 8 月（1930 年会谈发生之时）哈大洋与金票之汇率为哈大洋 2.20 元 = 金票 1 元，此间哈大洋之价值下跌了 57%。华方 1931 年应摊之款额将按照实际汇率核算，但核算依据标准仍为以哈大洋 2.20 元核金票 1 元之汇率兑换哈大洋 34200 元。

　　根据黑龙江航政委员会特殊协议（参阅瑷珲关第 452 号呈 2 号附件第 22 项），华方应向俄方一次性支付哈大洋 1500 元以作 1928 年疏浚河道之费用，然该协议中并未规定确切数额。

华方单笔支付的哈大洋 7000 元款额名义上是用来修复三条边界河道上的灯罩标杆（实际上部分航路标志是在去年发生冲突时由华方蓄意破坏的）。但俄方已口头承认，该数额已远超修复灯罩标杆所需之费用，对此俄方表示，索要该数额皆因华方去年仅支付其摊款哈大洋 22000 元中的哈大洋 4000 元，且俄方已因此于 1929 年 7 月（航运季节中期之前）扣押了华方轮船，封锁边界河道，切断了华方江捐税收之来源。俄方提出索要华方未支付的摊款，但华方已正式否认该笔欠款，尽管如此，双方最终依然协定为修复损坏之灯罩标杆拟此高额之费用，而双方去年之账目亦就此结清。

5.然而，江捐账户必不足以应对上述所有支出以及其他事项之费用，黑河市政筹备处处长已承诺如有需要可向省政府请求协助。

您忠实的仆人

富乐嘉（H. G. Fletcher）

瑷珲关署理税务司

附录 3[①]

1923/1924 年黑龙江航路标志协议就联合维护黑龙江、乌苏里江（含新增虎林至松阿察河段）及额尔古纳河航路标志事宜续约，此为华方 1930/1931 年续约协议之译本

　　于中华民国十九年（1930）八月十六日在大黑河中俄临时地方工程委员会正式会议共计提案七条，商定确定条款七条，会议列席者为：华方委员长中华民国黑河市政筹备处处长兼瑷珲交涉员张寿增，华方委员瑷珲关税务司富乐嘉，华方委员航务专门顾问易保罗；俄方委员长驻黑河苏联领事阔尔聂耶夫（N. V. Korneieff），俄方委员阿穆尔国家水运局局长密切利次（A. J. Metelitza）、俄方委员驻黑河领事馆秘书阔索夫（V. A. Kossoff）。提案七条列下。

　　提案

　　（一）关于 1923 年 10 月 28 日由黑河道尹及俄阿穆尔国家水运局就联合维护边界河道航路标志所订之协议仍延长两年，有效期至 1930/1931 年，联合维护范围：黑龙江航道自波克罗夫卡（Pokrovka）村起至嘎杂克维池（Kasakevich）水道止；乌苏里江航道自嘎杂克维池村起至松阿察河河口止，额尔古纳河航道自波克罗夫卡村起至奥罗赤（Olochi）村止。

　　决议

　　（一）查 1923 年 10 月 28 日双方所订之协议至 1929 年 12 月 1 日已满期不生效力，协议期间双方皆已履行各自应尽之义务，委员会决定：

　　（甲）上述协议将继续延期两年，自 1930 年 1 月 1 日起至 1932 年 1 月 1 日止。

　　（乙）倘于此两年之内，中俄会议对于上述边界河道之航路标志事宜达成新协议，则本协议即行废止。

　　提案

　　（二）关于中俄双方诸如于边界河道安装灯罩标杆等各项联合工程之计划书及讨论以上工程之款项，华方声明，虽然据俄阿穆尔国家水道局称，关于 1930 年边界河道工程计划书款项，应需三十万卢布，然而因在公共边界河道上，中国航运业萧条，并因与 1929 年相比较人工物料价格均上涨，所以华方认为华方之摊款应按照双方商定工程计划书中关于工程水道一切技术每年支付哈大洋三万四千二百元，关于修复公共边界河道黑龙江、乌苏里江以及额尔古纳河两岸灯罩标杆，华方将一次性支付哈大洋七千元。

---

　　① 注：附录 1 为协议俄文版，不予翻译。

决议

（二）（甲）所有黑龙江、乌苏里江及额尔古纳河并添乌苏里江自虎林至松阿察河段之航路标志工作由民国十九年（1930）一月一日起至民国二十一年（1932）一月一日止，以上公共边界河道工程名目及数目均载明随附工程计划书中，该计划书中所提之工程名目均由双方协定。

（乙）关于以上所提之工程名目，华方每年支付哈大洋三万四千二百元，此外，亦须额外一次性支付哈大洋七千元的灯罩标杆维护费用。以上费用或由指定银行交给驻黑河苏俄领事馆账上，或直接交给驻黑河苏俄领事，明细如下。

1930 年付款计划：

八月内付 50%，十月内付 25%，剩余 25% 于工程告竣后由华方查验之后全额付清。

1931 年付款计划：

六月内付 20%，七月内付 20%，八月内付 20%，九月内付 20%，剩余 20% 于工程告竣后由华方查验之后全额付清。

鉴于哈大洋之汇率波动不定，因此民国二十年（1931）应付之款项按照金票与哈大洋之实际汇率核算，但以签字日金票与哈大洋之汇率（哈大洋两元二角核金票一元）为根据标准。

提案

（三）根据 1928 年 6 月 19 日签署的协议条款，华方应为 1928 年联合疏浚工事支付三千卢布。

决议

（三）华方承诺在此协议签订之后将支付哈大洋一千五百元以作 1928 年联合疏浚河道之费用。

提案

（四）关于边界河道之疏浚工事，华方声明，现因航运业萧条，华方每年将为联合疏浚工事摊付哈大洋四千元。

决议

（四）因公共边界河道有时河底深或宽不足，有碍船只航行，所以华方每年支付哈大洋四千元用于疏浚河道，该款分两期支付。

第一期哈大洋二千元于七月内支付，剩余二千元于工程告竣后由华方查验之后交付。

提案

（五）进行河道疏浚及碎石工事以拓宽或加深河道。

决议

（五）关于为拓宽或加深河道而进行之河道疏浚及碎石工事，无论华方还是俄方皆应对跨境施工人员给予帮助并放行。

提案

（六）讨论1923年协议内不适用之各项条款。

决议

（六）关于1923年协议内第二条第三款、第四款、第五款、第六款及第三条内第九款，以上各款因不适用，于此无效。

提案

（七）订立协议。

决议

（七）该协议协定书应以中文和俄文拟成，缮写两份，签字后双方各执中文和俄文各一份，以昭信守。

中华民国十九年八月十六日（1930年8月16日）订于大黑河。

华方

华方委员长黑河市政筹备处处长兼瑷珲交涉员

（签字）张寿增

华方委员瑷珲关税务司

（签字）富乐嘉

华方委员航务专门顾问

（签字）易保罗

俄方

俄方委员长驻黑河苏联领事

（签字）阔尔聂耶夫

俄方委员阿穆尔国家水运局局长

（签字）米切利次

俄方委员驻黑河领事馆秘书

（签字）阔索夫

翻译：陈培因　三等二级税务员

33. 1931 年《中国海关船舶纪律维护章程》

No. 7.

Aigun.

THE MARITIME CUSTOMS,
MARINE DEPARTMENT,

SHANGHAI, 11th November 1931.

SIR,

I enclose herewith a copy of I.G. despatch No.
1,529/5,357, Cruisers:

REGULATIONS FOR THE MAINTENANCE OF DISCIPLINE
ON BOARD CUSTOMS VESSELS: copy of revised version drawn up by Kuan-wu Shu, with translation,
forwarding: now to be put into effect,
instructing;

and to enable you to comply with the Inspector General's
instructions I also forward copies of the Regulations in
Chinese and English.

I am,

Sir,

Your obedient Servant,

[signature]

Coast Inspector.

THE COMMISSIONER OF CUSTOMS,

AIGUN.

MARINE No.5,357

Cruisers No.1,529

SHANGHAI OFFICE OF THE

INSPECTORATE GENERAL OF CUSTOMS, 29th September, 1931.

SIR,

With reference to your despatch No.1,984:

inter alia, submitting a draft code of rules
to govern conduct on board revenue vessels,
cruising launches and light-tending vessels,
and to provide for strict enforcement of
discipline under all conditions of service;

and to I.G. despatch No.1,499/5,277:

approving the proposed regulations in
principle and stating that the draft was
being referred to the Kuan-wu Shu;

I have now to append, for your information and guidance,
copy of Kuan-wu Shu despatch No.6,240, together with its
enclosure, from which you will see that the above regulations
have been recast by the Shu with slight modifications, and
that the revised version is now issued for enforcement.

A translation of these regulations is also appended.
You are requested to act accordingly and to arrange that
copies, both in Chinese and English, are suitably mounted in
frames and fixed in a prominent place in the crews' quarters
in all Customs revenue vessels, cruising launches and light-
tending vessels.

I am,

Sir,

Your obedient Servant,

(Signed)   F. W. MAZE,

Inspector General.

THE COAST INSPECTOR,

SHANGHAI.

<u>Regulations for the maintenance of
good order and discipline on board Chinese
Maritime Customs Vessels.</u>

1.   Any member of the crews of the Chinese Maritime Customs vessels (Customs Steamers, Customs Preventive Steamers, Customs Launches and Customs Preventive Launches) found guilty of mutiny or neglect of duty shall be punished according to these regulations.

2.   The punishments laid down under these regulations are of the following four kinds:-
(1) Prosecution before the Court.
(2) Dismissal.
(3) Deduction from pay varying from a tenth to half a month's pay.
(4) Bad conduct marks, three marks for small offences equalling one mark for a large offence.

3.   In the event of any of the following offences, the controlling authority concerned shall send the offender to the Court for trial and punishment according to the law:-
(1) Mutiny attended with violence.
(2) Mutiny unattended with violence.
(3) Striking a superior officer.
(4) Theft of government or private property.

4.   Any of the following offences shall entail dismissal:-
(1) Refusal to obey a superior officer's lawful command.
(2) Insolence to a superior officer.
(3) Immoral conduct.

5.   In the event of any of the following offences, the offender shall be punished by bad conduct marks or by a deduction from his pay according to the gravity of the offence.
(1) Breaking out of the ship without first obtaining his superior officer's permission.

(2)

(2) Overstaying leave.
(3) Fighting on board ship.
(4) Slackness and bad behaviour.

6.   If a member of the crew has received bad conduct marks or had deductions from pay for three or more large offences, the controlling authority concerned shall consider dismissing him.

7.   These regulations are subject to revision from time to time whenever found necessary.

8.   These regulations shall come into force from the date of their promulgation.

海關輸隻水手管理規則

第一條　凡海關所屬巡船巡艇及燈塔運輸船隻之水手有違抗命令反抗
忽任務情事時均依本規則處理之

第二條　本規則所定處分分為左列四種
一　送交法院懲處
二　開除
三　扣薪自月新十分之一起至月新二分之一為止
四　記過記小過三次作大過一次

第三條　犯有左列情事之一者即由該管長官送交當地法院依法懲治
一　以武力抗拒長官命令者
二　抗拒長官合法命令者
三　毆辱長官者

第四條　犯有左列情事之一者即予開除
一　不服從長官合法命令者
二　侮慢長官者
三　有不道德之行為者
四　盜竊公有或私有財物者

第五條　犯有左列情事之一者按其情節輕重酌予記過或扣薪處分
一　未得長官之准許擅自離船者
二　請假期滿不回船銷假者
三　在船內互相鬥毆者
四　服務懈怠或行撿不修者

第六條　記大過或扣薪至三次以上者該管長官得斟酌情形予以開除

第七條　本規則有未盡事宜得隨時修正之

第八條　本規則自頒布之日起施行

致瑷珲关第 7 号函 　　　　　　　　江海关海务科 1931 年 11 月 11 日

尊敬的瑷珲关税务司：

根据海关总税务司署致海务科第 1529/5357 号令：

"发送关务署起草的《海关船舶纪律维护章程》（Regulations for the maintenance of discipline on board customs vessels）修订版抄件及译本；指示该章程即日起生效。"

兹发送上述章程汉文版及英文版抄件，请知照遵行。

您忠诚的仆人

（签名）奚理满（H. E. Hillman）

海务巡工司

附件

致江海关海务科第 <u>1529/5357</u> 号令　　　海关总税务司署（上海）1931 年 9 月 29 日

尊敬的江海关海务巡工司：

根据江海关海务科致海关总税务司署第 1984 号呈：

"呈送一份章程草案，用以管制海关所属巡船、巡艇及顶塔运输船只上水手之行为；规定严格遵守海关工作纪律。"

及海关总税务司署第 1499/5277 号令：

"批准施行所提议之章程，草案将提交至关务署修订。"

兹附关务署第 6240 号文及其附件之抄件，以供参考；从中可知，关务署已对上述章程进行修订，并将立即颁布施行。

随附章程译本，请知照遵行，并将该章程汉英版抄件裱入框架，固定于所有海关巡船、巡艇及顶塔运输船只船员宿舍显著之处。

您忠诚的仆人

（签名）梅乐和（F. W. Maze）

总税务司

附录

中国海关船舶纪律维护章程

第一条　凡中国海关所属船只（海关轮船、海关巡缉船、海关汽艇和海关缉私艇）船员有违抗命令及玩忽职守者，皆照本章程处置。

第二条　本章程规定之处分包括以下四种：

一、送交法院惩处

二、免职

三、扣除月薪十分之一至二分之一不等

四、记过，记小过三次作大过一次

第三条　凡有以下情节者，皆由相关监管部门送交法院依法惩治：

一、以武力反抗者

二、以非武力反抗者

三、殴打长官者

四、盗窃政府或私人财产者

第四条　凡有以下情节者，一律免职：

一、不服从长官合法命令者

二、辱骂长官者

三、行为不道德者

第五条　凡有以下情节者，一律视情节轻重酌予记过或扣薪处分：

一、未经上级长官准许擅自离船者

二、请假期满不回船销假者

三、在船上斗殴者

四、工作懈怠或行检不修者

第六条　凡记大过或扣薪三次以上者，相关监管部门应视情形予以免职。

第七条　本章程有未尽事宜得随时修订。

第八条　本章程自颁布之日起生效。